The Staging of Plays before Shakespeare

The Staging
of Plays before Shakespeare

RICHARD SOUTHERN

THEATRE ARTS BOOKS

New York

First published in 1973
in the United States
by Theatre Arts Books
333 Sixth Avenue
New York 10014
Printed in Great Britain by
Western Printing Services Ltd Bristol

ISBN 0-87830-130-5
Library of Congress Catalog No. 73-76707

Contents and Chronological Scheme

Part One: 1466–1527
THE DOORS OF ENTRANCE

The Earliest Surviving Interludes 1466–1508

Contemporary Court Staging 1511 onwards

Other Interludes to 1527

7

Part Three: 1553–1576
THE RISE OF THE STAGE

Contents

Part Four: 1576–1589
THE THEATRE BUILT

Final Plays and Footnotes

[The Theatre built 1576]

10

Illustrations

FIGURES

PLATES
(after page 262)

Acknowledgements

The author and publishers are grateful for permission to quote from the following:

The Elizabethan Stage by E. K. Chambers, published by The Clarendon Press, Oxford, in 1923.

Oxford English Dictionary published by The Clarendon Press.

Shakespeare Survey, Volume 12, address entitled 'Passing Over the Stage' by Professor Allardyce Nicol, published by Cambridge University Press in 1959.

The photographs in Plates 2 to 5 are of displays which were originally mounted in the Keio Department Store, Tokyo, during the British Week in 1969.

Foreword on the Subject of this Book

The title of this book is some guide to what it is about but it is a title chosen deliberately to give occasion for certain qualifications.

The first qualification concerns the word 'staging'. Today when we talk of 'staging a play' we mean (to use theatrical jargon) *putting a play on*. The *Oxford English Dictionary* gives the phrase 'to put on' in the sense of to stage (a play). It would seem that in modern parlance the words mean 'to put a play upon a stage', by which we understand the presenting of it before an audience. One of the chief points of this book, however, is to show that, formerly at any rate, to present a play before an audience did not necessarily imply putting it on a stage at all. A more exact phrase for presenting a play in early days would have been 'putting it on the floor', much as we talk now of putting a screen play or a television play 'on the floor'. One of the purposes of this book is to show how plays were presented before the use of a stage became common; and the technique involved, as I hope to show, was a very specialized and rather exciting one – and moreover a technique that is highly suggestive for companies of players today who may lack the sophistication of a 'proper theatre'.

Secondly, the word 'plays' in the title also needs qualification. Not *any* kind of play is here implied, but one particular kind of play created after the days of the Mystery Cycles and the great outdoor Morality Plays, but before the first regular dramas that marked the rise of the regular Elizabethan theatre. It is the kind of play generally called, if rather loosely, 'Interludes'.

Finally, the phrase 'before Shakespeare' needs a very slight qualification; I intend it to mean, before (or up to) the opening of what is sometimes called the Shakespearean playhouse. This would in fact limit my subject to plays presented before the building of The Theatre in 1576. However, I shall include three plays ascribed to years just after this date for reasons which the reader will see in due course.

The full intention then of the present title, *The Staging of Plays before Shakespeare*, is – the methods of presentation (whether on a

15

stage or not) of certain professional (or semi-professional) secular plays generally classified as 'Interludes', in the period between (about) 1450 and (about) 1576.

There is a particular purpose in dealing with the presentation methods of precisely these plays because the problems of the presentation of plays in the Elizabethan public playhouse where Shakespeare was acted is one of the most teasing and exacting problems in the whole study of drama and it is the thesis of this book that the methods used by the players whose work led to the foundation of the Elizabethan public playhouse may – in fact, must – contribute something to the understanding of the methods of that playhouse itself. And of course the man who built the first playhouse, James Burbage, had been the leader of a company of Interluders. It is my contention that he built The Theatre so as to exploit, and advance, the particular techniques of presentation which he and his predecessors had formulated in the three-quarters of a century immediately before 1576.

Thus, the technique of the Interluders should help to throw some light on the technique of Shakespeare.

Swanage 1971

Part One 1466–1527

The Doors of Entrance

The Earliest Surviving Interludes 1466–1508

House Entry ∽ *Mankind* ∽ The Tudor Great Hall ∽ *Nature* ∽
Fulgens and Lucrece ∽ *The World and the Child* ∽ Return to
Mankind

---

1 *House Entry*

In the last quarter of the fifteenth century, and particularly in
Henry VII's time, certain developments in theatrical presentation
were taking place. The performances of the great religious Mystery
cycles were just beginning to fall out of favour with the ideas of the
times. At court princely entertainments were leading towards the
birth of the masque. For the general people, the old Morality Play
had already taken that particular turn towards secularization that
produced what for want of a more precise term is called 'The Tudor
Interlude'. It is with the method of presenting a Tudor Interlude,
and with the developments in that method which led up to the
Elizabethan playhouse of the time of Shakespeare, that I am
especially concerned in this book.

The origin of the Interlude form is curiously obscure. The custom of many theatre histories is to trace the beginnings of theatre in
England to certain features of the Christian church service – especially to the famous *Quem quaeritis* Easter ceremony. This may be true
for the Mystery cycles, but it seems inadequate as suggesting a
source for the Interludes. For though in the earlier Interludes there
is much of a religious character there is also much that is distinctly
profane.

But apart from this there is, from the point of view of technical
presentation, one remarkable and indeed essential characteristic of
the Interludes that could not have sprung from any church ritual,
but which certainly has a remarkable parallel in another form of
theatre, quite independent of those three forms I mentioned at the
beginning. That fourth form is the Mummers' Play; and the essential

19

characteristic common to it and the Interludes is entry into a private house to perform.

This particular feature of the Mummers' Play is often overlooked, for the Mummers' Play is generally conceived – and with much justification – as taking place out of doors. But it is worth turning aside before taking up the Tudor Interlude, to look at some evidence about the special indoor performances by the Mummers.

Two references will serve to begin (and I italicize the significant words in either case). First, concerning the Oxfordshire St. George's Play as recorded in *Notes and Queries*, 5th series, II, 503–5, a correspondent says, 'I first saw it acted *in the Hall* of the old Vicarage House at Thame . . .'. (See also J. M. Manly, *Specimens of the Pre-Shakespearean Drama*, 1900.)

Second, in the Lutterworth (Leicestershire) Christmas Play, the first speech (with all its corruptions) is from Captain Slasher and begins,

> I beg your pardon for being so bold,
> I *enter your house*, the weather's so cold.
> For *in this house* we do resort
> Resort, resort for many a day.
> Step in, the King of England,
> And boldly clear the way. [. . .]

It is also relevant to any study of the presentation methods of the Interludes to notice another point made in a footnote by Manly. It concerns the fact that Mummers sometimes formed a circle in the midst of the spectators, in the centre of which they played their action. Manly's note is 'In such plays *enter* means "advance from the circle of players" ' – that is to say, advance from this ring into the centre. The entrance invitations in the play of the Mummers of Marshfield (Gloucestershire) are also relevant; each character ends his part with the formula: If Such-and-such – naming the next character – is in this room, let him step this way. The speaker then rejoins the ring and the new character takes his place in the centre. These words, with the reference to 'this room' are still used despite the fact that the Marshfield performances are now almost all in the open street. Precisely the same meaning attaches to the variant invitations, 'come in' and 'step in'.

As I hope to show, the existence of such traditions among the Mummers will explain some major features of Interlude performances that could not have sprung from any church ritual.

Now, bearing these preliminaries in mind, I want to turn and follow the Interludes themselves as they have survived to us.

It is difficult to say how far back we should go to find the first Interludes. There are tantalizing references in histories to a fragment commonly entitled *Interludium de Clerico et Puella* (c. 1300), but what the significance of the word *Interludium* in this title may be, I have not been able to find out. The fragment may conveniently be studied in Bruce Dickins and R. M. Wilson, *Early Middle English Texts* (1951 and 1956), p. 132; but whether it is or is not, as the editors claim, an example 'of secular drama', I can find nothing in it on which to base an opinion on how it was presented; and there is certainly no internal evidence that it was performed by any of those rising groups of professional, or semi-professional, players that were subsequently to be called 'Interluders'.

2 *Mankind*

The earliest surviving play which might possibly have been performed by a troupe of these players is *Mankind*. *Mankind* has special difficulties which make it hard to use at the beginning of an enquiry; it is in manuscript, it is not easy to decipher the handwriting, it has in several places lines which, even when deciphered, are still hard to interpret, from the one manuscript copy surviving there are certainly some pages missing, and finally the possibility obtains that even the pages we have may not be in their right order. The problem of how *Mankind* was originally presented from a technical point of view is, therefore, certain to be a complex one; and if it had to be considered on its own, apart from the suggestions obtainable from the study of later plays it would, I think, be an insoluble problem. It is for this reason that the plan of Part One of this book takes the form it does; that is to say, first to give a general summary of *Mankind*, but merely noting the production problems; next to make detailed studies of three later plays including *Nature* and *Fulgens and Lucrece*, where some possible explanations for these problems can be found; then to return to *Mankind* briefly and consider it again in the light of these suggestions. After that I shall be better able to go on to the later Interludes in the rest of the book.

I would add that this system, which I could call 'the juxtaposition of evidence', is essential to this study. I do not think that the presentation of any Interlude can be reconstructed on the evidence of that Interlude alone; it must be supplemented by evidence in other related Interludes, that is to say other plays which show signs of having been presented in the same method. It is the sum of all the fragments of information that helps to clarify each separately.

It is particularly noticeable how difficult it is to reconstruct the setting of a play which seems to be separate in some respect from the general run. There is then no chance of bringing together information from kindred examples and of making a more or less dependable picture from all the parts. This is one of the reasons that certain plays, such as *Gammer Gurton's Needle*, *Gorboduc* and *Supposes*, as we shall see later, offer difficulties which at present cannot, so far as I can see, be solved.

The three main plays treated in these opening pages will seve to illustrate something of the transition from the Morality Play to the earliest 'secular' plays. *Mankind* is a play still in the Morality idiom, though it is secularized about as far as a Morality could be. *Fulgens* on the other hand has good claim to be classed as 'the first secular comedy' so far known in our history. *Nature* falls pretty evenly between the two.

For *Mankind*, no authority has so far offered any certain claim to show how, or where, or by whom, it was performed; though there have been certain suggestions. For example, Pollard, in the introduction to the Early English Text Society's edition, says 'We must . . . regard the players as strollers . . . and almost certainly acting in the courtyards of inns, since in l. 725, when New-Guise wants a football, he calls to an ostler to lend him one.' Pollard also refers to one of the characters as leaving 'the stage'. In much the same vein J. Quincy Adams in *Chief Pre-Shakespearean Dramas* (1926), after relating the play with a locality near Cambridge, supposes it required six players 'who gave their performance in a public inn-yard (cf. ll. 29, 554, 722, 725) for gain'. The four lines he quotes as evidence for the inn-yard will be discussed in my review of the play as they come up.

One other statement is made by Adams about the method of presentation; in a footnote to his p. 305 he says, concerning certain lines in the script – '. . . Note also the familiar way in which the actors in coming in and going out address those standing about the stage.' These references to a stage are worth comment. Both Pollard and Adams refer to 'the stage'. The impression they give is that they have no doubt in their minds that *Mankind* was performed on a raised platform. I wish particularly not to be committed to this idea so early in the study; instead I would like to keep as open as possible the question of what sort of acting-area was really used, until after the play has been discussed. In any event the above opinions are not stated by the authors as certain conclusions.

A word about the script itself. The work is anonymous; it can be dated somewhere about 1466 (see 'The Date of *Mankind*' by Donald C. Baker in *Philological Quarterly*, XLII, 1, Jan. 1963). It is one of the group of 'Macro' plays. It is reprinted and discussed in the Early English Text Society's Extra Series No. XCI (1904 reprinted 1924), and the manuscript is reproduced in facsimile in the Tudor Facsimile Texts series.

All my quotations follow the text even when it is obscure. Abbreviations in the manuscript are expanded in the usual way by inserting italic letters. The punctuation is unaltered, or occasionally supplemented in square brackets. The use or non-use of capital letters is as in the original (save for speech ascriptions which I have put for clarity's sake in capitals to distinguish them from the speech lines). Modern type letters are used in place of the old yogh and thorn. A few words whose meaning only becomes clear after some searching are repeated in modern spelling in italics and between square brackets.

Some particular difficulty arises out of the spelling of proper names through the book. Here I must admit I have not been consistent. There are many names that read perfectly well in their old spelling, even if it is odd today; often indeed they are more vivid that way, and all these I have retained. But some read less happily; for instance Lucres, Vserie and Pite may not be so easily accepted as Lucrece, Usury and Pity, and it has seemed more natural when using names like these in the course of my own text, to adopt the modern spelling. When they occur in the text of a play script, however, I have of course kept them as in the original. I have also allowed myself some option about regularizing the spelling of play-titles when used apart from their immediate context.

Beyond these things there is one possible confusion that ought to be pointed out; especially in the early plays, where grammatical stops of any sort are nearly non-existent, has it seemed useful to insert a relevant question mark or exclamation mark when it helps to decide that an odd sentence is a question or an exclamation; for this I have always used square brackets. What I want to make clear is that such a sign does *not* indicate that the text itself is questionable, or contains something surprising. When any comment of that sort is needed it will be made separately and in the general text.

In looking through the play now to find what evidence it may offer to show how it was presented, there is one piece of information in particular that seems to me worth careful assessment, and this is intimately connected with the actions of a certain group of three 'knaves' in a particular sequence of events and speeches in the show as presented. To give this in proper perspective I must make a synopsis of the action of the whole play so far as it can be constructed from the script that has come down to us.

The opening speech in the script as it remains is delivered by a character called Mercy. It contains a direct address to the audience as 'sourence', or sovereigns, and at l. 29 as 'O ye sourens *that* sytt and ye brothern that stonde ryght wppe'. This line is the first of the four quoted by Quincy Adams as a proof that the show was given in a public inn-yard; but to me it seems in no way conclusive – all that is clear is that the author of the play foresaw a mixed audience among whom were certain spectators that might, with more or less justification, be addressed as 'sovereigns', and others that were apparently more hail-fellow with the players and could be addressed familiarly as 'brothers'; further, that the distinction in rank was recognized by the sovereigns having some sort of seats provided while the brothers stood.

It should be remarked at this point that one would scarcely be justified in recalling on this matter, that the Morality Play of *The Castle of Perseverance* (c. 1425) refers to the 'syrys semly' that 'syttyth on syde', and to the 'worthy wytis' that stand or squat in the Place, for there is no indication in *Mankind* that any arrangement resembling the Scaffolds and Hill of a performance in a Round was involved. It would seem better to do no more at present than remember merely that some spectators sat and some stood. (There is a study of the presentation-methods of *The Castle of Perseverance* in my book *The Medieval Theatre in the Round*, but in the present connexion I think we must abandon it and begin entirely afresh.)

At l. 45 Mercy's opening speech is interrupted by a second character called Myscheff who introduces some comic cross-talk, and incidentally refers to the time of year as winter. No entrance-direction is given for Myscheff; indeed it is interesting to note that, though several *exit* directions are found later in the play, not once throughout its whole length is any direction given for any character to *enter*. Entrances, and the place of entrance, seem to be taken for

24

granted. Should we see any significance in this? I reserve the question for later. To return to the action.

At l. 71 a gap occurs in the manuscript and a passage possibly some two pages in length is missing. When the script resumes, Myscheff has apparently gone out, and the three knaves to whom I have referred have already come in. They are called Newgyse, Nowadays and Nought. They make ribald fun of Mercy who finally cries,

143.   Out of this place I wolde ye went

The word 'place' might just possibly be thought to bear the specific meaning it had in some of the Moralities; namely that outdoor space in which spectators and players congregated for a performance. But what follows is unexpected; the three knaves pertly agree with Mercy's wish and prepare to leave. Their farewells now run as follows (I have marked the significant line with an asterisk) –

NEWGYSE   Goo we hens all three *with* on [*one*] assent [. . .]
NOWADAYS [. . .] Felouse go we hens tyght
NOUGHT   Go we hens a deull wey
          Here is the dore her ys the wey*
          Farwell jentyll Jaffrey
          I prey gode gyf yow goode nyght   Exi*ant* sil*entio*

So we learn that it is presumably night-time – unless the 'good night' was spoken merely as a comic gag. But if it is night-time the performance would seem unlikely to have been out of doors since some of the spectators are sitting, and the season of the year is winter.

But it is particularly the reference to a *door* that is remarkable. It would seem to prove that the author had in mind a performance in a room. Up to this point, four possible surroundings might have seemed plausible – a Round (on the basis of references to the 'Place'); an inn-yard (on the basis of the reference later to an 'ostler'); a raised stage in the open (as Adams suggests); or indoors. Now the Round and the booth stage would be ruled out by this reference to a door. The choice between an inn-yard and a room inside a house must depend on whether it is more likely that an actor would say, 'Here is the door' if he were indoors and about to go out, or if he were outdoors and about to go in. There is clearly not much to choose but the line is slightly more suggestive of going out of a room than in to a room and, taken with the fact of some of the audience (and the more dignified part) sitting, and the presumption of a night performance, and further a performance in winter, the evidence so far seems to indicate indoors.

At any rate, Mercy now sighs with relief –

> Thankyde be gode we haue a fayer dylyu*er*ance
> Of thes iij onthryfty gests

and he goes on to soliloquize about their 'unthriftiness' for twenty-four lines. Immediately he has finished the last line, a speech begins from a new character, Mankind himself; but there is no entrance-direction given for him. Editors commonly invent one in such cases, but I believe that it is of primary importance to keep the acting-directions exactly as in the original if we are to form any proper estimate of presentation-methods. This matter will come up for attention again later.

It is not until l. 200 that Mankind, who has then spoken for nine-teen lines telling the audience of his fleshly sinfulness, suddenly sees Mercy and says 'I xall go to yondyr man'. Thus the two characters would seem to have been in different parts of the room or Place. Mankind now goes, kneels, and says, 'All heyll semely father ye be welcome to this house'. Here then is a definite allusion to a house. Moreover it seems slightly to favour the interior of a house rather than the outside, and suggests Mankind as an actor playing the part of a welcoming member of the household within it.

This is Mankind's first appearance. Immediately before it, Mercy was speaking, yet Mankind on entering did not address himself to Mercy; he first spent nineteen lines announcing himself and address-ing the spectators – 'this holl co*n*grygacyon' and 'sou*er*ens'. Only after this does he turn to, and see, Mercy. We are thus introduced in simple terms to a convention that we shall find more marked later in the play – and one that is subsequently to become highly characteris-tic in the presentation of plays before Shakespeare. It is the conven-tion of 'separating' or 'differentiating' two players who are present at the same time, in such a way that one is not concerned with the other until it is convenient for the plot. My next reference illus-trates this more sharply still, and the situation needs introducing in careful detail.

After Mankind's speech, Mercy bids him rise from his knees and then introduces himself. Mankind is delighted; Mercy improves the occasion with an intimate little sermon of advice to Mankind on how to behave; he says:

229.   Dystempur*e* not yowur brayn wt goode ale nor wt wyn
         [. . .] be war*e* of excesse [. . .]
         Whe*n* natur*e* ys suffysyde a non th*a*t ye sese

and he concludes with a particular quatrain in which he points out by way of example that a horse which is kept 'to [*too*] hye', and 'fede ouer well', may 'in happe cast his mast*er* in the myre'. It is just at this point that there begins that particular sequence of events and speeches that I referred to above as of significance.

What follows is that immediately upon this line there comes a speech from the clown Newgyse in which he picks up what Mercy was saying. He begins (238), 'Ye sey trew s*er* . . . I haue fede my wyff so well / tyll sche ys my mast*er* . . .' and he goes on for an eight-line stanza. This stanza is a ribald one and so particularly full of meat that it was obviously meant for the audience's amusement, and to be delivered with full comic effect; yet (as the speech that immediately follows shows) all this time Newgyse *was apparently not visible*. Mankind in fact asks, 'Where spekys this felow wyll he not com*e* ner*e*'. Where then did Newgyse speak from?

It must be emphasized that what Newgyse said was not a brief comment which might be thrown in from round any corner; it is a definite extended speech. Yet Mercy's very next line confirms that Newgyse could not have entered to speak, for Mercy answers Mankind's question (Will he not come near?) with:

> All to[*o*] son*e* my brother I fer*e* me for yow
> he was her*e* ryght now by hym th*a*t bowte me der*e*
> Wt other of hys felouse thei kan moche sorow
> They wyll be her*e* ryght son*e* yf I owt dep*ar*te [. . .]

There is, I think, no avoiding that the meaning of this speech is: 'He was here just now and he will be here again with the others as soon as I go away', but the notable thing is that between the time when Newgyse '*was* here' and the time when he '*will be* here' – that is, during the period when he was *not present* – he has managed to ⸱ⱼⱼⱼ ⱼⱼⱼ ⱼⱼⱼⱼⱼⱼⱼⱼ ⱼⱼⱼⱼⱼ ⱼⱼⱼⱼⱼ.

There is not to be found so far, the slightest evidence about how the passage could have been presented. Yet very shortly afterwards, precisely the same sort of effect is repeated. The situation develops in this way: Mercy enjoins Mankind to learn his doctrine while he has the chance, and to set his heart on it because 'W*ith* in a schorte space I must ned*is* hens'. Then comes the second interruption; this time it is from Nowadays. He too has an eight-line stanza, in which he gibes at Mercy for taking so long to go away; he wants him hence and

> the sonner the leu*er* & yt be ewyn anon [. . .]
> yf ye wolde go hens we xall cu*m* eu*er*y chon

He is obviously implying that he and his fellows are not professedly present but are ready to come in if Mercy will only go. So much is this a repetition of the previous sequence that it would seem almost certain that it is an intentional device.

Then immediately after this, Nought also has a similar eight lines to much the same effect. Mercy affects not to hear, but he does warn Mankind that (271) – 'yow*ur* enmys wyll be her*e* a non thei made ther ava*u*nte'; the words 'your enemies *will be* here' again prove that the enemies were not there yet. Then Mercy's speech continues for another thirty-three lines; it includes a further warning against Newgyse, Nowadays and Nought, and particularly advises Mankind to beware of a fourth character, Titivillus, a major devil:

> 295. th*a*t goth invysybull & wyll not be sen
> he wyll ronde in yow*ur* er*e* & cast a nette befor yow*ur* eyn
> He ys worst of the*m* all [. . .]
> Kysse me now my der*e* darlynge gode sche[*l*]de yow from
> yow*ur* fon[. . .]
> The blyssynge of gode be wt yow & wt all thes worschypp[*f*]ull
> me*n*

and with this courteous gesture to the assembled audience and its dignity, Mercy presumably goes out of the action. But there is still no sign of the entrance of the knaves. Mankind, now alone, says,

> [. . .] my soull ys well sacyatt
> Wt ye mellyfluose doctryne of thys worschyppfull ma*n*

and he goes on to tell the audience that he will sit down and write on a piece of paper the 'gloryuse reme*m*brance' of his 'nobyll co*n*dy-cyon'. Where he sits we are not told, but he says that he writes to defend himself from all superstitious charms, and he concludes, 'lo I ber on my bryst the bagge of myn armys'; thus he may pin the paper on his bosom, and bear it much as the player in Breughel's print bears his (see Fig. 38 later). As he does so Newgyse, still absent, suddenly shudders with cold and loudly quotes a bunch of Latin

28

lines, slightly blasphemously. Mankind does now hear him, but all the same deliberately takes no notice – 'I her a felow speke wt hym I wyll not mell [*mix*]'. He then suddenly changes his occupation; still refusing to pay any attention to this voice of Newgyse, he decides, 'Thys erth wt my spade I xall assay to delffe'.

It is at this point, I feel, that several commentators have concluded that the performance of this play must have been out of doors. Against the vague evidence of sitting, and of doors, and of night, this essay at delving in the earth seems final; how could such an action *not* take place out of doors? But, on the other hand, what more amusing piece of business than to see Mankind (who anyway is treated in this script with more than a touch of humour) take his spade and begin to 'dig' industriously in the floor of the room where the play was performed! The fact that the Devil later slips a plank of wood over the 'earth' that Mankind was so industriously working, to stop his spade, is merely adding to the gag, not proving that there was any real earth.

Mankind proceeds with a muttered prayer to God to 'sende yt hys fusyon', and now – and now only – have we at last a clear sign that the three knaves come back into the action. There is a shout from Nowadays:

324.   Make rom sers for we haue be longe
        We wyll cum gyf yow a crystemes songe

and, wherever the three may have been up to this moment, they now push through the people ('make room, sirs!'), protest that they have been out of the action too long, announce a Christmas song, and summon the spectators to join in:

Now I prey all ye yemandry that ys here
To synge wt ws wt a mery chere

Before turning to the content of the song I recapitulate this puzzling sequence. Back at l. 156 there was the clear and specific acting-direction to the knaves to go out: 'Exiant silentio'. So they are not present. Mercy and Mankind then spoke together alone. At l. 238 Newgyse (without entering) spoke eight lines of comment on something Mercy said; Mankind heard the voice but did not know whence it came, and he asked if the speaker 'will come near' to which Mercy replied that he would be coming near all too soon. Then Nowadays in turn had an eight-line interjection (without entering). Then Nought followed with his similar eight-line interjection. But still none of them entered. Mercy then spoke on for another thirty-three lines and bade farewell and left at l. 302. Then Mankind had his writing business. During it Newgyse complained of the cold and quoted Latin but still without entering (l. 316). Mankind said that he heard some fellow speak but would not mix with him (l. 320). Then he began his digging business. And only then, at long last, have we the entry of Newgyse, Nowadays and Nought at l. 324. There is no doubt this really is their entrance for they precede it with the shout 'Make room sirs!', and there is no doubt that they all three of them come in together for all three have direct speeches and all three are to take part in the song.

It is clear from all this that, whatever theory one forms of the presentation technique of these early players, it must include a means for relatively long and pointed speeches to be delivered so that a character in the action may feign not to know where they come from, and also, so that at a given cue the 'concealed' speaker can break into the normal action where the other characters are.

The editors of the E.E.T.S. edition of *Mankind* have tackled the above difficulty by inserting a number of 'Exits' and 'Re-enters' for the knaves in the dialogue. But to allow these would be to make nonsense of all such lines as 'Where speaks this fellow?' and 'They *will be* here right soon', if the characters in question had been obviously present. Adams in *Chief Pre-Shakespearean Dramas* handles the matter a shade more consistently; he inserts at ll. 237, 253 and 261, directions that the relevant knave in each case '*speaks from behind*'. But of course this begs the question; Behind what? And it is a little too liable to suggest the modern phrase 'behind the scenes' as answer, whereas there is no evidence that there was any 'scene'. And so far in this present play there is not, I believe, any evidence at all upon which to base an adequate theory of how such things were managed; but I believe there is such evidence in later plays. For the present I am only concerned to show that this particular technical convention existed as early as the date of *Mankind*. To turn now to the song.

It is, I feel, pointless to state baldly that there now follows what must be one of the most ribald Christmas songs in our history, and then to omit it and leave the reader to imagine it. Besides, it makes a considerable contribution to the atmosphere of the performance. Here, then, it is:

328. NOUGHT
    [. . .] yt ys wretyn wt a coll yt ys wretyn wt a cole

NEWGYSE & NOWADAYS
  yt ys wretyn wt a colle yt ys wretyn etc.
NOUGHT
  He th*a*t schytyth wt hys hoyll he th*a*t schytyth wt hys hoyll
NEWGYSE NOWADAYS
  He th*a*t schytyth wt hys hoyll etc.
NOUGHT
  But he wyppe hys ars clen but he etc.
NEWGYSE NOWADAYS
  But he wype hys ars clen but he etc.
NOUGHT
  On hys breche yt xall be sen on hys breche etc.
NEWGYSE NOWADAYS
  On hys breche yt xall be sen on hys etc.
CANTANT OMNES
  Hoylyke holyke holyke holyke holyke holyke

From my own experience of the theatre, I have not a doubt that, given a certain kind of audience and a good trio, this song could meet with a rapturous reception. But our concern at the moment is, What was Mankind doing through the singing of this song? There is also a further question, What happened at Nowaday's call to 'Make room, sirs!' To whom was it addressed? And how and where did he and his two fellows come in to sing?

They called for a way to be cleared; they appealed to all the yeomanry ('Yeoman: which worde now signifieth among vs, a man well at ease and hauing honestlie to liue, and yet not a gentleman.' Sir Thomas Smith, *The Commonwealth of England*, 1584) to join them in the singing; they announced that they had come to give a Christmas song. It is perhaps not inappropriate that the image called up is of the waits – or even the Mummers – entering a house to perform in the Hall. Finally, the whole episode has taken place without the singers appearing to pay the slightest attention to Mankind and his efforts at digging.

Another question can be asked at this point. When and how did Mankind come by his spade? It is perhaps possible that his digging was mimed without any implement; but later, at l. 402, he says just before he leaves, 'Wt my spade I wyll dep*a*rte', addressing the audience directly, and this would rather imply that the spade was a real one which he took with him when he went. But there is little to suggest that he brought it in with him when he made his first entrance, and it would appear out of place in his opening speeches with Mercy, and more so still during his business of sitting and writing; but there seems to be no point in the dialogue up to the present where Mankind could have gone out and fetched his spade. And for want of more evidence we must suppose him carrying it in, as a normal labourer, at his first entrance and perhaps propping it against a bench till he needed it.

And now after the song the three knaves see Mankind at last. They advance upon him and bid God speed him with his digging. And there follows ribald chaffing till Mankind ups with his spade and beats them with it, so that they flee bellowing, with the clear direction 'Exi*a*nt'. Mankind turns to the audience and says (a little too trustingly),

394. I promytt yow thes felouse wyll no mor*e* cu*m* her*e*

and he shoulders his spade, farewells his 'worshipfull sovereigns' and concludes –

404. I xall go fett corn for my lande I prey yow of pacyence
       Ryght son*e* I xall reverte

There is no exit-direction.

Now presumably we have a moment's breathing space. Mankind has gone out; the bellowing of the beaten knaves has died away in the distance. It might occur to one to feel that if there were two possible ways out of the hall, it would be more suitable for Mankind to take another than the one the knaves had run out by. The audience could well be agog now to see what happens next.

What happens is in fact a speech from Myscheff, whom we have not seen since the break in the script, but who must now come in again. He bewails that he was born; since he was here, he says, he is utterly undone. 'I myscheff was her*e* at ye begynynge of ye game', but he says that while he was away Mercy has taught Mankind 'to fyght ma*n*ly ageyn hys fon'. He pities the poor beaten knaves (who must now be clamouring again outside), for he exclaims to the spectators 'Wyll ye lyst I her the*m* crye', and a direction in the margin reads 'clama*nt*'; so, wherever they are, they cry out once more. Myscheff shouts some comfort to them:

420. Pesse fayer babys ye xall haue a nappyll to morow
       Why grete ye so why

and there follow direct speeches from each of the three, together with comic business about curing their hurts. So the knaves must have come in again.

Now both the action and the lines seem to become confused. Nowadays proposes that, since Myscheff has come, they should all have an 'interleccyon' touching Mankind and try (apparently) to clear up the matter of his defection. Myscheff, somewhat unaccountably, answers by calling for a minstrel. Nought says he himself can 'pype in a walsyngh*a*m wystyll'. He is asked to blow apace and *thou* (unspecified) 'xall bryng*e* hym in wt a flewte'. Whether the phrase, 'bring him in' means 'accompany him' with a flute, or whether the whole passage is simply a build-up for the entrance of a new character who is to be brought into the action to the strains of a flute, is unclear. A remarkable point is that the next line is apparently ascribed to Titivillus (the Devil) who shouts 'I com wt my leggs vnd*e*r me'. But the ensuing lines show that in fact he does not come yet, for they clearly indicate that a collection of money has to be made from the audience 'ellys thei xall no ma*n* hym se'.

What is imminent is the introduction of the exciting and terrific spectacle of the Devil. The moment is seized to 'take round the hat' with the suggestion that until it is well filled, this fearful figure will not appear. So, Manly may be right in suggesting that that line of Titivillus's which seems to come before his entrance was, in fact, shouted from outside as an inducement to pay up and speed his appearance.

There may be another reason. If the company of players is a small one the part of Titivillus would have to be doubled by one of the other actors. A suitable candidate would be Mercy, who left the action (with a warning against Titivillus on his lips) some 150 lines plus a song and much comic business ago. If there now follows a further interval for the collection among the audience, with its accompanying twenty lines of opportunity for gagging, then there is quite reasonable time for the actor who played Mercy to don a possibly elaborate costume, including claws, tail and a mask, for the Devil. To have him call out a speech from some concealment while he was still changing would be an old actor's trick to help the effect and suggest his presence while still giving him further time to finish dressing.

But there is much interest in the lines before he comes on. Firstly, the verb 'to gather' is used of the money, reminding one of the term for the money-takers in an Elizabethan playhouse – the gatherers. Next, Newgyse makes their purpose quite clear by directly addressing the audience:

33

452.   Now [. . .] to ow*ur* p*ur*pos worschypfull soue*r*ence
We intende to gather mony yf yt plesse yow*ur* n*e*clygence
For a ma*n* wt a hede th*at* [*is*] of grett om*n*ipotens

perhaps the 'hede' is a reference to his mask. Nowadays next has a
remarkable line that may very well have got a laugh:

kepe yow*ur* tayll in goodness I prey yow goode brother

and immediately afterwards, to the audience:

He ys a worschypp[ʃ]ul ma*n* s*er*s sauyng yow*ur* reu*er*ens

He goes on to ask not just for pennies or twopences, but for red
royals (or gold coins) 'yf ye wyll se hys abhomynabull p*r*esens'.
Newgyse prudently tempers this with, if you can't pay the one, pay
the other. And then he has a line which seems to clinch the whole
matter of the place of the performance. He says:

At the goode ma*n* of this house fyrst we wyll assay
Gode blysse you mast*er* [. . .]

It would scarcely seem likely that an innkeeper could be so addressed in precedence over his guests; and so it follows that it is very
unlikely that the performance was visualized at an inn. If I am right
we can now eliminate the last alternative, and conclude that a private house is the answer to fit the evidence. We should then have
the normal picture of a group of strolling players performing of an
evening for the entertainment of a household and guests, in the hall
of a goodman's house with the goodman and his family seated at
their High Table, watching the feast. I say 'the normal picture'
because such an entry of players into a hall or houseplace is an event
of very ancient lineage, going back in principle to the minstrels and
the mummers.

The gathering or collection proceeds. Then the next line spoken
comes from Nought:

I sey Newgyse Nowadays est*is* vos pecuniat*us* [?]
I haue cryede a fayer wyll [. . .]

This would seem to be a prearranged signal that he does not expect
to collect any more. Was it said in Latin to suggest a private communication between the actors? Nowadays replies,

Ita vere magist*er* cum*me* forth now yow*ur* gatus

(the last probably loudly spoken as a cue to Titivillus); and then, to
the audience:

34

he ys a goodly ma*n* se*rs* make space & be ware

This could be as big a build-up as any actor could need for his entrance! Notice that there is again an appeal to certain of the spectators to clear the doorway so that the new character may come in. The suggestion obviously is that some of the standing watchers have moved together curiously around the action and now crowd before the door, so threatening to mask the entrance that has been so elaborately worked up. We suppose they compliantly fall back; and then, with all eyes presumably directed on his entrance, there suddenly appears Titivillus at last!

His opening speech contains a classic example of effective anti-climax as befits a comic devil. He begins in Latin:

468.   Ego su*m* domi*n*ancium domin*u*s & my name ys Titivillus
    ye th*at* haue goode hors to yow I sey caueat*is*
    he*re* ys an abyll felyschyppe to tryse hym out at yow*ur* gat*is*
    ego probo sic [—] se*r* Newgys lende me a peny

so, since Newgyse has just taken part in a collection Titivillus seizes the opportunity to break off and try to touch him for a loan.

The reference to those of the audience who have horses outside is not incomparable to announcements today that those with cars in the car park should see that they are safely locked. As we shall see later, it was a common gag for Vices in Interludes to pretend that there were thieves about the place.

The knaves all swear they have no money; in particular Nought (who seems the greatest knave of them all – possibly an early example of the Vice's character) asserts –

481.   The deull may dau*n*ce in my purse for ony peny
        yt ys as clen as a byrds ars.

There now follows the gag of Titivillus ordering the knaves to visit several actual local inhabitants (who are all mentioned by name) to try to get money from them; and off they go. We are reminded of Adam de la Halle's references, in *Le Jeu de la Feuillée* as far back as c. 1276, to several of the local inhabitants, with similar reflexions on their generosity. Titivillus, now left alone, tells the audience that he will wait invisible for Mankind to return to his digging, but will contrive that:

526.   Thys borde xall be hyde wndr ye erth preuely
        Hys spade xall entr I hope on [*?un*] redyly [. . .]
        Yondyr he com*m*yth [. . .]

thus Titivillus must have brought the board in with him under his invisible cloak.

Mankind therefore now comes in again, with his spade and his corn for sowing. He does not see Titivillus, since he is 'invisible', but walks to the spot where he had begun his digging:

> I haue brought seed her to sow wt my londe
> qwyll I our dylew yt [,] her yt xall stonde

Thus, while he takes up his digging again he puts the seed down beside him. When he begins to dig he of course finds that 'thys londe ys so harde', because of the board which the Devil has put in it. Then he lays down his spade, turns to pick up his corn and finds it is gone!

> Alasse my corn ys lost her ys a foull werke

(Titivillus has apparently snatched it up and hidden it under his invisible cloak.)

> Here I gyf wppe my spade for now & for euer
> to occupye my body I wyll not put me in deuer

and here there is no need for supposition, for a direction in the margin reads 'Here Titivillus goth out wt ye spade'. He must pick it up and flit quickly across the floor to the door. But Mankind decides to observe Evensong before breaking off and he proposes to make the place where he stands his 'kyrke'. He then kneels, begins in Latin his Paternoster – and then Titivillus comes darting back, saying to the spectators –

> I promes yow I haue no lede [*lead*] on my helys
> I am here a geyn [. . .]

and he quickly decides on the best way to interrupt Mankind's prayers. He leans over and calls into his ear that he is being taken short; he bids him

553.   A ryse & avent thee nature compellys

And Mankind accepts the suggestion, rises and gravely excuses himself to the spectators with a line (l. 554) that is the second line quoted by Adams as evidence that the play was presented in a public inn-yard (see above p. 22). But I believe it has rather the opposite implication. The line is

> I wyll in to ye yerde souerens & cum ageyn son

He explains that he goes for his health's sake:

> for drede of ye colyke, & eke of ye ston
> I wyll go do that nedis must be don

and, carefully putting down his rosary first, he rises to his feet and there follows a clear direction for him; 'Exiat'. Titivillus naturally gloats, asks the audience where they think he has gone, and proceeds to steal the beads that Mankind left behind. Thus we receive, as I see it, yet another hint to add to the rest that this performance is indoors and that to reach the yard one must *exit*, or go outside.

Titivillus promises the audience good sport if they 'wyll abyde', and then announces 'Mankynde cummyth a geyn'. He sees him coming and has three more lines after seeing him, which he speaks presumably while Mankind is walking from the door back across the room. Mankind protests that he is tired of both labour and prayer, and lays himself down to sleep. Titivillus enjoins the audience to silence – 'Not a worde I charge yow' – and proceeds to suggest a dream into Mankind's ear, to the effect that his benefactor, Mercy, is on the point of being hung for horse-stealing (this is a fate which, of course, is much more likely to have fallen upon Myscheff; and we shall find in the sequel that is what really has happened), and consequently he bids Mankind not to trust Mercy any more but, instead, to make it up with the three knaves. Then he turns to the audience with:

598.   For well euerychon for I haue don my game
      For I haue brought Mankynde to myscheff & to schame

and he then flits across the floor and out, to change back to Mercy for which he has the space of some 120 lines of text, just a little less than the time he had to dress up as the devil.

Mankind awakes confused, and resolves to haste him to an alehouse to speak there with the knaves and also to get himself 'a lemman wt a smattrynge face'. And at this point the action turns to a climax of confusion, and the knaves come back.

What the script gives in this: Newgyse (with a broken halter round his neck) is speaking suddenly, but neither has he any entrance-direction nor Mankind any exit-direction; he says:

> Make space for cokkesbody sakyrde make space
> A ha well on ron gode gyff hym ewyll grace [. . .]

and he goes on to say that he has just escaped hanging because the rope broke, and that Myscheff is in worse case. But he cries:

616. Do wey th*i*s halt*er*, What deull doth ma*n*kynde her*e* wt sorow [?]
      A lasse how my nek*e* ys sor*e* I mak*e* a vowe

I am open to correction here but my impression is that these obscure lines mean that just as Mankind is running out of one door to go to the inn, Newgyse runs in, shouting to clear the way, at another door. As he does so he catches sight of Mankind's flying heels and bids him an Irish 'God speed, bad cess to him' ('Run on! God give him evil grace!'); he then describes his own case and suddenly turns to find Mankind has stopped and come back, and is staring at him and his halter, having caught sight of him incidentally as he was fleeing. What Mankind now asks is '. . . Newgyse s*er* what cher*e* wt yow [?]' Now Newgyse covers up with:

    Well s*er* [.] I haue no cause to morn*e*

but he cannot get away with it; Mankind's eye is quick and he demands,

    What was th*er* abowte yowur neke

Newgyse puts him off with a fantastic tale of having had a 'runnynge rynge worme', and implies that he was trying to cure it with a muffler. Immediately upon this, his crony Nowadays calls:

624.   Stonde a rom I prey the*e* brother myn

and a few lines later Nought also calls similarly:

    A vante knawys lett me go by [. . .]

so these two return through the crowd at the doorway.

The next thing is that Myscheff (who seems to have been the one to be hanged, rather than Mercy) now enters on top of all the rest crying:

    Her cu*m*myth a ma*n* of armys why stonde ye so styll [. . .]

so, apparently, they are all standing aghast as at a ghost. Myscheff explains that he has escaped and incidentally that, as he went, he had the jailer's

637.   [. . .] fayer wyff halsyde in a corner*e*
        A how swetly I kyssyde yt swete mowth of hers [. . .]

Mankind now, somewhat inopportunely, breaks in and seizes the opportunity to offer an apology to the knaves in Myscheff's presence, and receives for his pains this demand from Newgyse:

> What a deull lykyth the*e* to be of this dysposycyon

but Mankind improves on the occasion, now quite repentant for his earlier aggression to them;

> I crye you mercy of all th*a*t I dyde amysse

and Nowadays suddenly jumps gleefully to the explanation of Mankind's change of front with:

> I sey newgys nought, Titivillus made all this –

and the quartet then decide to hold a mock trial to decide whether or not Mankind should be reinstated in their favour.

Now follows a particularly interesting piece of bye-play regarding Mankind's costume. Newgyse suddenly decides that the garment which Mankind is wearing is an old-fashioned, too-full gown, and calls out to Myscheff, alluding to it:

664. Maste*r* myscheff hys syde gown may be solde
 he may haue a jackett ther*of & mony tolde.

Mankind is caught by the idea:

> I wyll do for the best so I haue no colde
> Holde I prey yow & take yt wt yow
> Ande let me haue yt ageyn in ony wyse

Newgyse replies:

> I promytt yow a fresch jackett after the new gyse

and Mankind:

> Go & do that longyth to yowur offyce
> & spare that ye may—

and Newgyse presumably goes out with the gown. Meanwhile Nought (carrying on with the trial) has been busily writing according to a direction in the margin, and there is now comic business about his blots, to fill in while Newgyse is out with the gown.

But to go back for a moment to the business with the costume; what is involved is that the long, full gown had, about 1470, begun to be supplanted as a fashion by a much shorter garment, at any rate among the younger set. What Newgyse is claiming is that Mankind's long gown had enough material in it to allow a separate 'jacket' to be cut out of it, and still leave sufficient to sell for an acceptable sum of money. This resultant shorter jacket, he claims, would be 'after the new gyse', and what he is promising is to take the old gown away and turn it into something fashionable. He goes out with it. Then, after the interjection of the comic business about Nought's bad handwriting, Nowadays goes to the door and calls through it:

> What how neugyse thou makyst moche [*taryynge*]
> yt jackett **xall** not be worth a farthynge

(by the time you have done with it!). Thereupon Newgyse calls back, from outside the crowd of spectators, and with the cut garment now over his arm:

> Out of my wey sers for drede of fyghtynge
> lo here ys a feet tayll lyght to leppe a bowte

So he forces through the audience by the door, bringing a cut-off tail and waving it, and also (presumably) the resulting new garment; for now Nought complains of what he has done – he sneers:

> yt ys not schapyn worth a morsell of brede
> Ther ys too moche cloth yt weys as ony lede
> I xall goo & mende yt ellys I wyll lose my hede
> Make space sers lett me go owte.

So *he* proposes to take the new jacket himself now, and go out with it and cut it again because, as it is, it is still too heavy. As with all these passings in and out, he shouts at the spectators to make way for him as he goes.

To fill in the new interval there is next another piece of introduced bye-play; Myscheff puts Mankind through a catechism, making him promise to indulge in a list of specified sins; and then Nought bursts in again, exclaiming:

711.   Here ys a joly jakett how sey ye

and Newgyse is forced to admit that:

> yt ys a goode jake of fence for a mannys body

(J. M. Manly reads this term as 'iake[tt] of s[er]u[i]ce.') And then Newgyse is suddenly interrupted in a way that we shall see in a moment; but now to sum up the above comic business.

This business must have involved (a) the original gown which Mankind wore and which Newgyse took out, (b) a duplicate version of it with part of the skirts cut off and kept separate, but with the remaining garment still relatively long – say to just about the knee – and (c) a third version of the original gown from which still more of the skirt was lacking, so that the resulting little, short jacket showed out vividly as of ultra-fashionable brevity, with skirts probably no more than four inches below the waist-line – a typical jacket-of-fence, or body-defence jacket such as those used by fencers. All these variants of the original garment must each have been separately prepared and put ready in position just outside the door to await their brief appearance to give effect to this gag on contemporary fashions.

The interruption which I indicated above and which cuts short both the mock trial and the jape on the fashions, is that Myscheff suddenly calls out, like a ringleader of schoolboys at the approach of the master, that someone is coming! – Pick up your stuff and be gone! – And then Mercy enters who, so Titivillus said, had already been hanged for horse-stealing!

Mercy calls to Mankind to flee that fellowship; whereupon there is considerable confusion, and some lavatory humour round the door – and then some lines which offer one of the most considerable problems of the text. I quote the full passage beginning with Mankind's reply to Mercy at whom, apparently, he dare not even look; or, perhaps he looks with horror as at a ghost and flees with a trumped-up excuse:

720. I xall speke wt [*you*] a nother tym to morn or ye next day
    We xall goo forth to gether to kepe my faders yerday
    a tapster a tapster stow statt stow
 MYS. a myscheff go wt her I have a foull fall
    hens a wey from me or I xall be schyte yow all
 NEW. What how ostler hostler lende ws a foot ball
    Whoppe whow a now a now a now a now

These lines seem to need a great deal of reconstruction. Presuming that they are not hopelessly corrupt they suggest, I think, that Mankind thrusts past Mercy with a trumped-up excuse that he will speak with him tomorrow or the day after because at that particular moment he has to go off with the others to celebrate his father's birthday. And he then calls out (l. 722) for a 'tapster', in a line which is a sort of combination of excitement and fear. In this connexion a tapster may seem a not unlikely person to invoke when you are proposing to celebrate a birthday. (This line about the tapster is the

41

third piece of evidence which Adams offers for the performance being in an inn-yard; it seems no more conclusive than the others.)

Next Myscheff exploits his lavatory humour, presumably implying that he is ready to beray himself for fear on account of Mercy's sudden return.

Then, into this atmosphere of chaos and exclamation Newgyse flings a culminating bit of nonsense prompted by Mankind's call for the tapster, and shouts (l. 725) 'Hostler, lend us a foot ball!' with, I think, no more relevance or meaning than any clown today would have if he shouted 'Help! Murder! Fire! Man the lifeboat!' In other words, this is any nonsense that comes pat at the moment. That this line has a serious meaning in these particular circumstances, or that it can be, as Adams suggests, a fourth and final piece of evidence that the play is being performed in an inn-yard, I cannot personally believe. But the passage is admittedly a great problem.

To return to the action: All apparently now run out helter skelter, except Mercy who is left distracted and bewailing the day. He would not have believed that Mankind was so 'flexibull'. He mourns and sermonizes from l. 727 to l. 764, and at that point calls out aloud for Mankind. But it is Myscheff who replies (and thus presumably returns), and after him Nowadays and Nought with yet more lavatory humour. Then Newgyse produces some characteristic reasoning, saying to Myscheff with regard to Mankind:

784.   He wenyth Mercy were honge for stelynge of a mer [*mare*]
       Myscheff go sey to hym that Mercy sekyth euerywere
       He wyll honge hym selff I wndyrtake for fere

(because he will think he is summoned by a ghost); and Myscheff assents, and '[hic exit myscheff]'.

It is interesting to note that immediately after this definitely marked exit for Myscheff, the next line in the script is from Myscheff himself. He must then speak 'off', to use a modern term. He calls out –

How mankynde cum & speake wt mercy he is her[e] fast by

Mankind – presumably also 'off' – is devastated and moans –

A roppe A rope A rope I am not worthy

Myscheff's remarkable answer to this (which may partly account for his having gone 'off' to speak) is –

42

A non A non A non I haue yt her*e* redy
wt a tre also th*a*t I haue gett
holde ye tre nowadays nought take hede & be wyse

– so he apparently comes in again with Mankind, and brings with him a rope and a property gallows-tree as well, which he tells Nowadays to hold with Nought to help him. The climax is now reached. Into the ensuing confusion, with its opportunities for comic business, Mercy dashes to the rescue, laying about him. Mankind falls. The rest scatter – '[Exia*nt*'.

All that now remains after the dispersal of the knaves is ninety-two lines of religious dialogue between Mercy and repentant Mankind before Mankind goes out for the last time '[Hic exit Ma*n*kende', and leaves Mercy to address the 'Wyrschep[*f*]yll sofereyns' once again, saying 'I hawe do my pr*o*pirte', and to give a pious warning to them; and then the entertainment is over.

At this point there seem to be four essential points gained from the study of *Mankind*. The most obvious is the vision of the atmosphere that might obtain in an early pre-Shakespearean play. Besides this there are three practical points; first, that the performance seems to have taken place indoors in a room. Second, it appears that the presentation technique which was used permitted what I have called a 'differentiation' of the scene of action – that is to say a convention by which two players or groups of players could play separately without the one appearing to take notice of the other. Third, the means of entrance for the players was a *door* (or doors), that could be crowded by spectators, but through or from which the players might deliver lines at considerable length (possibly partly hiding themselves behind the adjacent spectators) before actually entering into the place of action. To these last three points I shall return in Section 7.

There is a further and more general reflexion that needs to be made here. One of the first questions a modern student asks about a play is: What is the scene of action? It is a question that presupposes that there must be a direct answer, such as: A Street in London, or A Wood near Athens, or the House of So-and-so. But I believe the fact of raising such a question at all indicates one of the biggest stumbling-blocks to understanding the Interludes. For instance, it might well be alleged by someone coming with such an approach to this play, that the scene of *Mankind* must represent a cornfield, or at least some stretch of arable ground, where Man works as a labourer, and to which there break in certain Temptations in the guise of rascals to corrupt him. But this would be to consider the play as having a 'narrative content' or as purporting to be a story with something in the nature of a plot. *Mankind* has no plot in this sense; it is admittedly a fiction, but fiction under another conception. It has meaning, but meaning conveyed not as in a story but rather as in a charade.

It is remarkable to see how difficult it is for us today to conceive of an action which conveys meaning through the interplay of characters only, and does not employ any tale or plot in the process. But in the early Interludes the vehicle of meaning is action rather than plot. For a simple example: to express the meaning, *Pride cometh before a fall*, the early Interlude might present a ribald character tripping a sumptuous character up, and simply embroider that situation. But it would not, primarily, borrow or invent a story whose plot should exemplify a certain proud man coming to grief because of this pride, and re-tell that story in dramatic form and against a representational setting.

As the Interlude form developed, no doubt the narrative element increased. But even in the highest achievement of Elizabethan drama the narrative element was never given the same importance as it attained in the late nineteenth and early twentieth centuries – in, for instance, the 'well-made play'. Always it was the action, not the story, that expressed the meaning.

If, then, an Interlude such as *Mankind* has no plot, it follows that it has no scene. For since it does not present a story it does not require a simulation of where the story took place. It does not even think in such terms. It has no need to.

It seemed to me important to emphasize this matter because some writers seem to take for granted that fifteenth- and sixteenth-century playwrights pictured theatre as we picture it today; that is, as a story acted on a stage before a background representing the surroundings of the story. In other words they assume a scenic setting for Interludes; I believe their assumption is proved wrong by this study of *Mankind*, and that the setting was in no way scenic.

But where exactly the early playwrights visualized their action as they wrote, or what they did see in their mind's eye as the background to the performers, and how far that eventually contributed to the planning of the Elizabethan playhouse, must be put aside for estimation later, in the light of the evidence from the next plays.

But first there is a point to be made about which these plays should be; for during the period when *Mankind* was still being per-formed there came about that epoch-making invention which brought a major revolution in the spread of ideas; namely, the first printing presses. So far as the study of plays goes it both helps and confuses; it produces something that is quite new – a considerable procession of printed, and thereby preserved, editions of plays. Many manuscripts are almost certain to have been lost, and what are left for study from now onwards are nearly all printed editions. In them are details that are of outstanding interest; the problem however is to date and order the *originals* (not the printed editions) with the intention of finding out what development comes after which; and in this matter there must be some measure of uncertainty.

The printed word has an air of authority and sometimes gives the impression that one is on firmer ground in the matter of dating than with handwritten copies. Unfortunately this is a wrong impression; not only are the early editions themselves often difficult to date precisely but, of course, the date of printing is no positive indication at all of the date of the original writing of a play. However, for convenience I take the very useful date-ordering of plays given by T. W. Craik in *The Tudor Interlude* (1958), where he himself makes it quite clear that almost every date in it is at present provisional. But this apparently grave disadvantage is not really as serious as it sounds because, however uncertain within a few years the dating may prove to be, yet the general picture as a whole is not likely to be greatly changed by some unexpected discovery that a play near the end of the period in fact belongs to half a century earlier, or anything as drastic as that.

Taking now this list as a guide, the next plays in date are *Nature* of about 1495, and *Fulgens and Lucrece* of about 1497, and these I next go on to consider.

3 The Tudor Great Hall

Of the two Interludes *Nature* and *Fulgens and Lucrece* we know the playwright's name for the first time in English dramatic history; it was Henry Medwall. With regard to Medwall himself almost the only date we have is that he was ordained 'acolyte' under Cardinal Morton, Archbishop of Canterbury, at Lambeth in 1490; but he does not seem to have advanced higher in orders. In a list of accounts, a Sir Henry Medwall is recorded in 1498–9 and again in 1501; he probably went abroad in that year. This information is drawn from the Introduction to Boas and Reed's edition of *Fulgens & Lucres* (1926).

Medwall's reputation as a dramatist has increased in recent estimation. For instance, the above-mentioned Introduction states that it sets out 'to clear away some of the traditional misconceptions that have done much to prevent the recognition of Medwall's merits as a dramatist, and especially of his remarkable anticipation of some points of Shakespearian technique'. This last remark is, of course, particularly relevant in the present consideration of the staging of plays before Shakespeare.

The 'traditional misconceptions' seem to be based on a certain 'document' quoted in Payne Collier's *The History of English Dramatic Poetry* (1831), which has, however, come under suspicion as a forgery. The relevant passage runs –

Inglyshe, and the oothers of the Kynges pleyers, after pleyed an Interluyt, whiche was wryten by Mayster Midwell, but yt was so long yt was not lykyd: yt was of the fyndyng of Troth, who was caryed away by ygnoraunce & ypocresy. The foolys part was the best; but the Kyng departyd befor the end to hys chambre.

[signed] Williame Cornysshe

We know nothing, apart from this mention, of any Interlude called *The Finding of Truth*. Whether the document itself was genuine or not, it is fair to say that Medwall was frequently given to long speeches; as well as that his fool's parts were well done. And the picture of the King's walking out before the end of a play may be worth keeping in mind. But there is not enough here to damn a writer's reputation.

One or two other passages from this Introduction of Boas and Reed's are especially relevant. First, 'Professional companies were already . . . competing for popular favour with the amateur actors of the Miracles and Moralities.'

Next, 'We get a remarkably vivid picture of their entry into the hall, pushing their way with difficulty among the silent and expectant throng . . .'

Especially would I like to note the following: 'There is nothing in the dialogue or directions that suggests a temporary stage.' I would note it because some confusion on this point seems to have been at the back of the editors' minds, for later they write: 'On a number of occasions . . . the audience is addressed or referred to as if it were itself on *the stage*, I 900–1, 1011–13. II 218–19, 590–1.' (The italics are mine.) This confusion particularly needs clearing up. Was there a stage, or not? I hope that the reviews of the plays which follow may offer some answer.

Before going into each play in detail it will be convenient to begin by examining two extracts separately, one from each play. First: In *Nature* there is an opening acting-direction before the dialogue begins which is unusual and particular in its details, and it implies at least one item about the presentation of an Interlude which is essential to any correct reconstruction. Second, in *Fulgens* one of the speeches contains a line which any reasonably close study of Interludes shows to be complementary to the above, and also essential to any correct reconstruction.

The opening direction to Nature is printed in two distinct paragraphs, suggesting two successive actions. It reads –

Fyrst cometh in Mundus and syttyth down [&] sayth nothynge and wyth hym Worldly affeccyon berynge a gown and cap and a gyrdyll for Man.

Than cometh in Nature / Man / Reason / and Innocencye / and Nature syttyth down and sayth . . .

To consider for the moment only the first of these paragraphs, relating to the entry of Mundus, the World; the important matter here is the clear implication that a seat must have been previously placed for the actor to sit on. Thus an atmosphere is suggested that seems already quite different from the robustious atmosphere in *Mankind*. Though in that play Mankind himself did in fact sit, it was apparently only briefly while he did his short piece of writing business; the rest of the time was pretty well filled with active movement. But in *Nature* there is a deliberation in this description of Mundus's entrance that suggests a particular intention after effect. The seat must have been brought into the Place and set before the play began; not only this but, as the second part of the direction shows, another seat must also have been set at the same time. Furthermore the action of the play to come is particularly hinged about these two seats. One, as we see, is World's seat, the other is Nature's. The action of the play is to show that Man is: 'a passenger That hast to do / a great and longe vyage' from Nature to the World, and quite early in the play Man in fact does take such a 'voyage' in actual action.

This fact has a certain influence on the placing of the two seats, in so far as it seems clear that they would have to be set fairly far apart – possibly at opposite ends of the Place – in order that Man could be effectively seen to undertake a significant journey.

At this point already, it is possible to form a somewhat clearer visualization of the performance of an Interlude; but first the term 'Place' needs elucidating. This is where the second piece of evidence, from Medwall's other play, becomes essential; it comes in a speech from a character called Publius Cornelius, who is one of Lucrece's two suitors. He has just had a talk with her father, Fulgens, which has decided him that he needs some sort of companion to act as friend and go-between if he is to proceed with his suit. What he then does is to turn – quite unexpectedly to our way of thinking – to the audience and address to them the following question:

> So many gode felowes as byn in this hall
> And is ther non syrs among you all
> That wyll enterprise this gere [. . .]

How this question is answered is explained in the next section; the essential point at this moment is that Cornelius frames his appeal to the good people that be in this *hall*. What did a hall mean in 1495?

The answer to this question should help to define the Place, and thus clarify the setting of the two chairs in *Nature*. But beyond that it will, I believe, offer a foundation on which to reconstruct the presentation-technique of nearly all these early plays before Shakespeare. And so, before enlarging on the placing of these seats and its significance, it is necessary to form a picture of the general surroundings in which they were placed.

For much of the information in the following account I am greatly indebted to the detailed study by Margaret E. Wood in *The English Mediaeval House* (1965).

A Great Hall was, and had been since the Middle Ages, the centre of the social and administrative life of an estate as well as serving for the common-room and the dining-room of the householder and his family and retainers – and even for the servants' bedroom. At one end, the 'upper end', the hall communicated with the family's private rooms; at the lower end, with the kitchens and storerooms. The Hall was thus the hub of the whole establishment. Across the upper end was a dais where the High Table stood; opposite this, at

the lower end, was a feature with a long history. This feature and
its function need describing in detail.

The main entrance into a Great Hall was in one of the side walls
down near the lower end. Often another door stood opposite in the
other side wall, leading out again into a private courtyard or
orchard. In this way, a visitor could pass straight from the outside
road through to the inner gardens, using the way across the lower
end of the hall as a sort of passage. One name for this passage was
'the entry'. Along one side of the Entry ran the end wall of the
hall with doors into the kitchen and buttery; on the other side was
the open hall. But not entirely open. For the body of the hall was
screened off from the Entry Passage.

Something of the history of this 'screening' device is diagrammatized in Fig. 1. Early medieval halls, when roof construction
was still primitive, were often divided down their length by two
rows of wooden columns or posts, reducing the roof-span and
making in effect a central nave and two side aisles; see Fig. 1, A.
As roof construction improved, these columns were dispensed with
and the floor-space thereby cleared; but two of the columns tended
to be retained – the pair at the lower end. They had an extra purpose – to help support a wooden 'spere' or small screen that shielded
the occupants of the hall from the adjacent outer doors; see Fig.
1, B. Sometimes the space between the two spere posts was partially
filled by a third screen, which might at first be removable; Fig. 1, C.
Later, this central screen became built in with the rest but in such
a way as still to leave two openings for the servants passing in and
out at mealtimes between hall and kitchen; Fig. 1, D. This trio of
screens with their two openings became, later still, a decorative
panelled unit, connected across the top with a beam or moulding;
Fig. 1, E. Later again, the screens passage, or entry, behind was
roofed over and a parapet added in front to form a 'minstrels'
gallery'; Fig. 1, F. In Renaissance times the whole unit became the
subject of richly decorative carving; Fig. 1, G and H.

Turning now to the more detailed arrangements in the body of
the hall itself (see Fig. 2, the High Table on the dais at the upper
end was occupied by the master of the house and his family and any
principal guests at meal times. A small door at the end of the dais
communicated with the family's private apartments.

On the floor down either side of the hall ran two other ranges of
tables, at which sat the remainder of the household according to
their degrees. At some point about the middle of each side was the

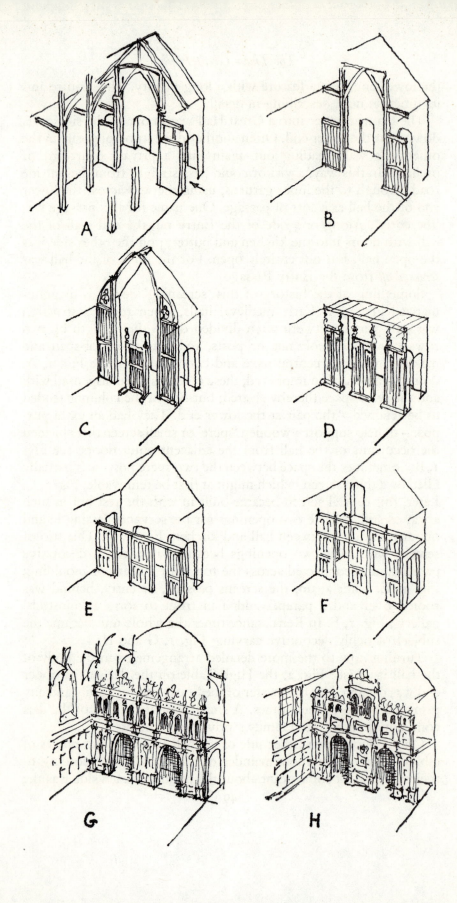

A

B

C

D

E

F

G

H

saler, or salt-bowl. Persons of higher distinction sat 'above the salt', or nearer the High Table, and others, 'below the salt' – whence our phrase today.

This makes a three-sided arrangement, High Table and two side tables, with the centre of the hall-floor free. On the fourth side, or lower end, were the 'screens'.

Fig. 2 shows this general scheme. In it there is no attempt at anything but a purely diagrammatic representation; the arrangement of screens shown at the far end of the hall is not based on any actual building, but simply assembles the various items referred to above. The High Table upon its dais is at the near end, marked HT. Of the entrances, C represents the main hall entrance at the far end of a side wall; the service doorways from hall to kitchens are in the end wall at D and E, only just visible beyond the screens (sometimes there were three of these doorways). The wooden partition in front with the openings for two-way service traffic – the screens – is represented at F and G and H. The possible 'back door' to the garden-court would be at J; this is the door that might have been involved at Mankind's exit into the yard to relieve himself in the previous play; it will be recalled again on at least two occasions later, when directions indicate that characters go out into an orchard.

FIG. 1. Theoretical origin and development of the Tudor Hall screens.
(The drawings are not exact records of specific screens)

A. illustrates an early style of aisled hall such as that at Amberley Court, Herefordshire

B. illustrates the removal of most of the posts but the retention of the 'spere truss' and the two screens at the sides; as at Sutton Courtenay, Berkshire (c. 1330)

C. illustrates the introduction of a central removable screen; as at Rufford Old Hall, Lancashire

D. illustrates the fixing permanently of the centre screen; as at Milton Abbas, Dorset (c. 1498) or Wortham Manor, Devonshire (early sixteenth century)

E. illustrates the unification of the three screens by a top beam; as at Great Chalfield, Wiltshire (c. 1450)

F. shows the introduction of a gallery above the entry passage; as at Penshurst, Kent (c. 1340) or at Haddon Hall, Derbyshire (later phase – c. 1475)

G. shows the considerable elaboration of the whole as one decorative unit; as at Trinity College, Cambridge

H. the height of decorative elaboration as at Leathersellers' Hall, London

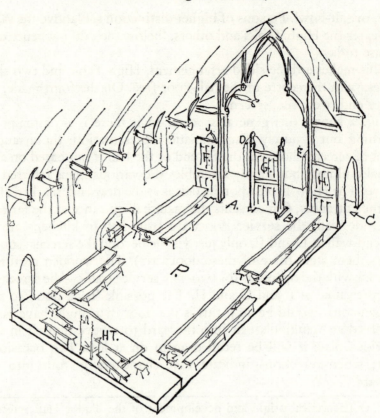

FIG. 2. General details of a typical Tudor hall arrangement

One can now feel in a better position to visualize a performance in a fifteenth-century hall. Already two things will be clear on considering Fig. 2; first, that any group of players coming from the Entry, through the Screens, and on to the hall floor would have a choice of two doorways, A and B. Thus the hints that I have already noted in *Mankind* which suggest the use of a second entrance may be quite justified. (That is, of course, always provided that there is justification in the first place for supposing that so early a play as *Mankind* was in fact presented, like *Fulgens*, in a Great Hall; so far this is my supposition, but it will be seen to grow more likely after consideration of later evidence.) It must also be remembered in connexion with these two doorways, that the description I have given of a Tudor Hall is nothing more than a general summary of a type; many houses had to be so sited and planned that a greater or lesser modification of the hall was enforced. A small Tudor house, for instance, might have a hall with a screen containing only one opening or, to put it another way, a hall so small that it needed nothing more than the two side speres. Indeed, a cottage might well need only one, at one side.

The second thing that becomes clear on considering Fig. 2 is that if a meal were served in the hall at some special feast, with many guests and their retainers present, then there might not be space for all to find seats, and so a lesser or greater number would have to stand, which was quite customary. But such people would be more likely to stand at the lower end than crowd round near the High Table; it is for this reason, then, that so many appeals are found in the plays for 'way' and 'room' to come in, since the players would have to thrust through the eagerly-watching throng to get from the passage behind the screens to their acting-area on the open floor.

Beside these two points a third may already, I think, claim to be obvious. This is that if there really was a fairly solid crowd of standing people across the lower end of the hall, then the performance would in effect become a performance 'in the round', or with audience on all four sides – however much the players might have tended to play towards the High Table. At any rate, and even on less crowded occasions, it will be pretty clear from the diagram that the acting-area (marked P) would continue down the middle of the hall floor, and not be restricted to one end. We see from Newgyse's speech in *Mankind* that a player might go right up to the dais where the High Table was, and address a direct appeal to the goodman of the house. The Interluders then must be thought of as having an oblong, central floor-space at their disposal, and as being fully prepared to make use of every inch of it – in complete contradistinction to the modern conception of a 'frontal' performance, isolated at the far end of a hall or theatre.

At this point it becomes clearly so important to reckon with the crowd of spectators in conceiving the effect made at a presentation that I need to remove the empty-classroom appearance of Fig. 2 and fill the hall with a combination of the throng of spectators and the movements of the actors in relation to that throng. Fig. 3 attempts this; but before looking at it in detail there must be some conception of the 'lighting effect' at this kind of performance.

The lighting must be imagined as something quite strikingly dim by modern standards. Admittedly some performances took place in daylight but many were at night, and we shall not form a true picture of evening shows in ordinary halls unless we visualize them in

G. 3. A Tudor hall at night, illustrating the preliminary moves in Medwall's *Nature* (see also Pl. 1)

what it is perhaps closest to the facts to call comparative darkness. At court a glittering profusion of candles might have been within the range of the Revels' expense account; in a normal country householder's home it was not. The lights would be few and flickering (compare Pl. 1). A very vivid picture of this is given a few years later by the Vice in Heywood's *The play of the wether* (despite the fact that this is possibly a boys' play presented at court). The Vice calls out as he comes in, pressing through the crowd of bystanders by the screens (see p. 236 below), 'Brother holde vp your torche a lytell hyer'. There were, therefore, torches held in hand by bearers in the crowd – whatever else there might or might not be in the way of other lights. Whether the Vice here was finding that the torch was in his way so that he couldn't get past it, or whether he wanted it held higher simply in order that more light should fall on himself, is not directly indicated. But it is pretty obvious that a playwright, however clearly he might visualize a future performance, could not be certain that a torchbearer would always be conveniently in the way to justify the Vice's line. What he might however very certainly foresee is the amusement to be got from the Vice's calling out to have the spotlight directed on to him – to use a modern wording – at his coming in. The torch becomes an authentic part of the picture even if it is a short distance away, and the Vice poses in it, with the shadows cast by it sharpening his features and outlining his action in light and dark on the floor round his feet. But in respect of lighting, my diagram has had to be deliberately over-simplified since it is intended to make clear other matters.

The first of these is the press of people round the screens entrances. Obviously, the laughter and sensations of the spectators would draw all those of the servants outside, who had a moment to spare, to step to the entry-doors so as to snatch a glimpse of what was going on, peering round the heads of the more fortunate spectators in front of them. This pressure would inevitably have to be taken into account and if possible turned to use by a player whose entrance had to be through these doorways; and the repetition in Interlude scripts of direct requests to the bystanders to get out of the way, was obviously aimed at making the most of this situation and turning it into an excuse for lifting the atmosphere and increasing the general effect, rather than treating it as a hindrance. The Interluders may have rather relished their licensed thrusting between the bystanders.

4 *Nature*

Returning now to the examination of *Nature*. In the following I have used the Tudor Facsimile Text Society's edition (1908) of a copy in the British Museum. The title in full reads:

Nature.
A goodly interlude of Nature compylyd by mayster
Henry Medwall chapleyn to the ryght re-
uerent father in god Johan Morton
somtyme Cardynall and arche
byshop of Can-
terbury.

Into such a scene as I have pictured above, of dimness, glitter and bustle, there have come two servants to set seats; probably they were scarcely distinguishable from the rest of the crowd through which they moved. The first seat would be set a little way inside the hall with its back to the screens and facing up to the the High Table. The other would, on the reasoning I have offered, be carried up the whole length of the hall and set with its back to the High Table. The servants would retire down the hall to the screens again, and pretty certainly, about this point, there would begin to be some attention focused on what was happening.

The atmosphere is being created – I think that even as far back as *Mankind* there is evidence that these early playwrights had some skill in making their effects – and into this picture there walks from one of the doors in the screens (let us say door A) a silent figure, the World. He will be dressed with some dignity in a long gown and will probably wear a headdress such as a chaperon. But this figure does not, on this occasion, issue any command to make way. He slips through the bystanders silently and inconspicuously, much as an ordinary person might, and once through the crowd he walks up the full length of the floor, quite deliberately and – as we are told – without a word. He is closely followed by a second figure, who sharpens attention and increases interest by the bundle he carries over his arm, of a gown, a cap and a girdle. The purpose of these is, of course, at present a mystery.

When they reach the upper end of the hall by the dais, the first figure turns and 'syttyth down'. He may smooth his skirts, arrange his sleeves and settle back; the audience wait for him to speak. And he still 'sayeth nothynge'. The second figure stations himself near the chair, still carrying the clothes. And still silence. (See the arrow leading to W and WA in Fig. 3.)

The next action draws attention again to the doors, for a new figure is coming in. Her movement is not so extended; she simply walks to the near chair in front of the centre screen 'and syttyth down'. The fact that in the acting-direction it is World who comes in first, and Lady Nature who follows after him, slightly increases the likelihood that World's seat would be the one near the dais, and Nature's seat the one near the screens. Immediately following Nature are four other figures. The direction reads, 'Than cometh in Nature / Man / Reason / and Innocencye / and Nature syttyth down . . .' Possibly these others wait for Nature to enter and seat herself and then they walk forward to her; first, Man 'naked' (that is, probably in a breechclout or a shift), conducted by Innocence his nurse, and then Reason, and lastly (though he is omitted from the direction) Sensuality (see at M, I, R, and S in the Fig. 3). Then the play proper begins.

Nature's opening speech is perhaps the first speech in English drama to give some account of natural science, and in this respect it must have been novel and 'modern' to its first hearers. It has some remarkable figures of expression; for instance, it observes that living things, without the help of Nature,

> [. . .] shuld neuer endure
> But sodenly peryshe / and wax all caytyfe[:]
> Atwyxt thelementys / that whylom were at stryfe
> I haue swaged / the old repugnaunce
> and knyt theym togeder / in maner of alyaunce [. . .]

It refers to the moon's effect on the tides, to meteors, and to Aristotle's works and Ovid's poetry. It contains some forceful poetic images as –

> Who taught the cok / hys watche howres to obserue
> And syng of corage / wyth shyrll [*shrill*] throte on hye
> who taught the pellycan / her tender hart to carue
> For she nolde suffer / her byrdys to dye
> Who taught the nyghtyngall / to recorde besyly
> Her strange entunys / in sylence of the nyght
> Certes I nature / and none other wyght

From the particular point of view of play presentation the speech contains a reference of prime importance about the appearance of the speaker, for we read,

> [. . .] god / of hys great largesse
> Hath [. . .] made me as who seyth / a wor[*l?*]dly goddesse

Thus we learn that this character is played as a woman.

After seventy-odd lines of introduction, she refers to the figure standing silently before her:

> [. . .] thow man / I speke to the alone
> Byfore all other / as chyef of hys creance [ ]
A.ii.*rev.*   [. . .] touchyng / the cause specyally
> wherfore I haue ordeyned the / thys nyght to appere
> It ys to put the / in knowlege and memorye
> To what entent / thow art ordeyned to be here
> I let the[*e*] wyt / thou arte a passanger

> That hast to do / a great and longe vyage
> and through the world / most be thy passage
> Addresse the selfe / now towardys thys iournay
> For as now thou shalt / nolenger here abyde
> Lo here Reason / to gouerne the[e] in thy way
> and sensualyte / vpon thyn other syde
> But reason I depute / to be thy chyef gyde
> wyth innocencye / that ys thy tender noryce
> Euermore to wene the[e] / from thappetyte of vyce

We have thus been provided by the playwright with a clear and neat outline of the plot to come (or at least the plot without the complications that we shall find intervene), and even some idea of the initial grouping of the figures before they make their first significant move in the action of the play. It is worth remarking that in the course of her speech Nature has specifically stated that the performance was taking place at night. We have therefore to visualize it (unlike the first part of *Fulgens and Lucrece* as we shall see) under the light of torches.

It should be noted that the picture given to us in the opening directions is incomplete since it makes no reference whatever to the entrance of Sensuality with the others; but the above text has made it quite clear that *two* figures stood one either side of Man while he was before Nature; the first was Reason and the second, 'vpon thyn other syde', was Sensuality. Innocence made the third, Man and Nature the fourth and fifth, and World and Worldly Affeccyon at the other seat the sixth and seventh. The number is emphasized here because some writers have claimed that *Nature* could be played by six players.

Man now replies in a speech of humble acquiescence, in which he details the gifts with which the 'lord god immortuall' has endowed him, but adds –

A.iii.
> yet for all that / haue I fre eleccyon
> Do what I wyll / be yt euyll or well
> And am put in the hande / of myne own counsell
> And in thys poynt / I am halfe angelyke
> Unto thy heuenly spyrytys / almost egall
> albeyt in some parte / I be to them vnlyke
> For they be ordeyned / to endure perpetuall
> And I wretched body / shall haue my funerall

At the end of this statement Nature replies that Man's prayers have been heard, and commands him –

> Now forth thy iournay / and loke well about [. . .]
> Let reason the gouerne / in euery condycyon [. . .]
> I wot well sensualyte / ys to the naturall

A.iii.*rev.*

> And graunted to the / in thy furst creacyon
> But not wythstandyng / yt ought to be ouerall
> Subdued to reason [. . .]

At this point Sensuality gives us the first sign that all is not to proceed on this smooth level; he protests very vigorously before Man can take any step on his fateful journey –

> What lady nature / haue I none intresse
> aswell as reason / or innocency [/]
> Thanke [*think*] ye thys [,] lady / a good processe
> That they are auaunced / and I let go by [. . .]
> Alas what coulde / the sely body do
> Or how sholde yt lyue / ne were the helpe of me [?]
> Certes yt could not well / crepe nor go
> At the lest wyse yt shuld / neyther fele [,] here nor se
> But be as other / incensate bodys be [. . .]
> And now ye put me out of hys seruyce
> And haue assygned / reason to be hys guyde
> Wyth innocencye hys noryse / thus am I set a syde
> ye clepe hym lorde / of all bestys lyuynge
> And nothyng worthy / as far as I can se
> For yf there be in hym / no maner of felynge
> Ne no lyuely quyknes / what lorde ys he
> A lorde made of clowts / or karued out of tre [/] [. . .]

(An additional illustration relevant to this passage may be seen in Pl. 2; it will be described later at p. 94.)

Sensuality goes on for forty-two lines of resentful and forceful reasoning. But this is lost on Nature, who replies at length simply restating her former decree that 'reason must be / preferred euermore', enjoining Man to bear that always in mind. If he does so she promises that she will never fail him. Then without permitting further argument she indicates the seat at the other end of the hall, saying:

> Lo yender the world / whyche thou must nedys to
> Now shape the thyder / there ys no more to say
> Thy lord and myne / guyde the in thy way

To clinch the matter (though somewhat arbitrarily), she rises, and we have the direction – 'Then Nature goeth out'. Nothing could be clearer than her last words as indication of what must follow. She says in effect: There is World, to him you must now take your way. She leaves Sensuality simmering with rage, and he calls after her departure –

> [. . .] By cryst yet / wyll I not hyde my face [. . .]

Meanwhile Reason listens with a tart smile and at length speaks with (it must be admitted) a provoking note –

A.iiii.*rev.*   Be not so passyonate / ne yt so furyouse
thou turmentyst thy selfe / [. . .]
thou takyst a selfe well / and wrong opynyon
Whyche shalbe thyn and others confusyon

This as might be expected provokes in Sensuality the most contemptuous response –

> ye Reason syr ye speke / lyke a noble man [. . .]
> I se yt well / that yf your lordshyp myght
> by meanes possyble / onys bryng yt about
> your selfe shuld be a ruler / and I but a cast owt

REA.   A rular? certes and so I owght to be
and a lord also / though ye say yt in scorne
SENS.   A lord? whose lord.   REA. Thy lord
SENS.   Nay so mote I the
thou lyest / yt may no lengar be forborne [. . .]

– and the wrangle goes on for over 100 lines with Innocence bringing in a voice on Reason's side, until in bitter impatience Sensuality jibes –

B.i.*rev.*   Well spoken and wysely / now haue ye all done?
Or haue ye ought ellys / to thys man to say

Reason immediately chips in, 'O syr ye.' but Sensuality instantly interrupts with –

> [. . .] pece no more of thys dysputacyon
> Here be many fantasyes / to dryue forth the day
> That one chatreth lyke a pye / that other lyke a iay
> And yet whan they both / haue done what they can
> Maugry theym teeth / I shall rule the man

There is an impetuosity and a personality in all this that steps beyond the reflections of a Morality, and looks forward to the humanities of secular comedy. The sharp, broken lines of the give-and-take dialogue add to the life of the incident; and it is all to the improvement of the effect that the whole scene is in the nature of an interruption coming unexpectedly at the moment of setting out on a grave journey. Man of course is bewildered at it all –

B.ii.   For I am wonderously / entryked in thys case
                   and almost brought / into perplexyte [. . .]

Reason, too, is reaching the end of patience and breaks in with:

        But now wyll ye call / to your remembraunce
        For what cause / ye be hyder sent
        I hold yt well done / and ryght expedyent
        that ye were brough[t] / vnto the worldys presence

And thus we have proof positive that the characters did not, at that point in the action, consider that they were yet in World's presence. But the action that will bring them to him is now imminent; Man agrees to the proposal with:

        Be yt so in goddys name / I pray you go we hens

Reason makes a final bid for supremacy:

        And wyll ye that I / shall for you declare
        Unto the world / the cause of your comyng
        What ys your intent / and what parson ye are [?]

Man implicitly agrees:

        ye I wold be glad / that euery thyng
        Be done euen / after your deuysyng

– and the group begins to break up and prepare to set forth up the hall, but Sensuality keeps his ground and cries,

        Shall I then stand / as I were tong tyde [/]

– and Man, pausing in his tracks while Reason presses on, replies to Sensuality,

        ye hardely / tyll reason haue sayd

Immediately after, Reason is saying to World, as Man and Innocence follow:

        Syr world / yt ys the mynde and also pleasure
        of lady nature / as she bad vs to you tell
        that ye accept / and receyue thys her creature
        Wyth you for a season / here to dwell
        Desyryng you hartely / to entreat hym well
        wyth all the fauour / that ye can deuyse
        Wherin ye shall do her / great pleasure and seruyce

And World says, silkily,

> Syrs ye be welcome [. . .]

The next passage of the play now opens, and we may pause here for a moment.

I cannot discover that there is any evidence that Interludes at this date were actually *produced*, in the sense that we in England give to the word today; that is, rehearsed under some individual who settled with the players beforehand exactly where they should go and when and how they should move. Whether rightly or wrongly, we incline to suppose some considerable degree of personal choice – even extemporization – left to Tudor actors in these matters. One reason perhaps why this is likely to have been so is that, as a matter of course, no performer then ever knew for certain that two consecutive presentations of a given show would be in similar surroundings – in particular, whether the entrances this time would be in the same place as last time or, if they were so, whether the acting-space available after he had passed through them and come into the Place would be the same, or alarmingly wider and loftier, or constrictingly less. His timing therefore *could not* be prearranged as an actor's can today who plays every night on the same stage; it would be inevitable that something would have to be left to his initiative of the moment, as he felt the surroundings of the occasion.

Therefore, in the above analysis of the opening passage of *Nature*, I did not intend to suggest that I was offering any final revelation of how exactly the play was paced and timed through all the years of its career – or even on any one given occasion. I would suppose that some degree of 'production' might have been put into the script, as the players learnt it together, by the man among them who led the team; but I would suppose the chief matter for such pre-arrangement might be the settling of effective agreement on the features of comic business, with the intention that two players might be saved from bungling each other's actions. But 'grouping' in the modern artistic sense would probably not be consciously thought of.

There is, however, a little more to be said here. In the dialogue one finds certain operative lines which, as one reads it through several times, assume a character or emphasis of their own – something that it would seem difficult for an actor to ignore. And moreover such lines would seem to have been deliberately incorporated so that he could not ignore them. For instance, one cannot possibly believe that Sensuality could deliver his most eloquent words, 'Shall I than stand / as I were tong tyed', and at the same time ruin half their point by moving. Without doubt, the line conveys that he is at issue with the other characters and, since they have just come to an agreement to 'go hens', they must move, or be on the point of moving, and he must in protest refuse to move. The lines are such that an actor would automatically take the action they suggest in order to make the point they embody.

There is thus some case to be made out for a belief that, given the smooth area of a hall floor, the Interluders performing their play upon it in free action would use its space variously and for deliberate effects – either sitting monumentally in inaction, their skirts gathered round them; or standing still while others moved past; or themselves swinging into movement and taking the floor with their gowns flowing behind them; or processing slowly in all solemnity – which ever was suitable. Any actor in these circumstances would do thus unless he were a dolt (and he wouldn't get very far with such lines if he were a dolt!). He would do it, essentially, because at this stage of history he would be beginning to be deeply concerned with the effect made by his show upon an audience. He no longer has available to shelter him from them, that pious awe which might be conventionally conceded to a great religious presentation of the Assumption of the Virgin Mary, or of the Passion of Jesus Christ. Those subjects (almost) created their own audience-reaction (which is not to say they couldn't be travestied in the hands of fools). But in a secular feast-hall, crowded with an assembly out for a treat, the Interluders were in much the same case as touring music-hall artistes on a Saturday night – possibly quite as open to jeers or cat-calls if they failed to hold their audience. (We know that even the King would get up and walk out of an Interlude if he couldn't stand it.) And the players were, on the other hand, probably quite as open as music-hallers to sensing the triumph of taking an audience with them, and turning an unruly heckle into an appreciative roar, when they had the ability to command it. In other words they were becoming *professional* actors, and thus combatants against failure.

In consideration of all this there is, I submit, good reason for seeing Medwall's *Nature* as making, and intended to make, some at least of the points and effects I have pictured above on the evidence of the lines.

The next passage in the play contains an effect of a different sort.

To resume; the action now contains three matters of considerable importance to the study of presentation, which must be reviewed in some detail. They are, the reception of Man by the World; the robing of Man; and the particular entrance of a significant new figure on the scene.

The first matter is an example once more of that convention which I have called the 'differentiation' of the acting-area. Despite the fact that throughout all the opening passages of this play there are two major groups of figures in equal evidence – that of Nature, Man, Innocence, Reason and Sensuality at one end of the Hall; and that of World and Worldly Affeccyon with the garments at the other – yet the action has proceded for the considerable length of 406 lines without any acknowledgement whatever by the former group of the presence of the latter. Reason's lines near the end of this long passage were –

> [. . .] now [. . .]
> I hold yt well done / and ryght expedyent
> that ye were brough[t] / vnto the worldys presence

This is as good as a downright statement that Man and his group did not consider themselves to be yet in World's presence – that Man had to be 'brought' away from where he was to reach that presence. And since the playwright has written this into his lines, it is to be presumed that he knew his audience would appreciate the intention.

But World himself has not only continued to sit saying nothing all this time but (what is so particularly to my point) has sat without being presumed to have heard anything either. He and his whole group have been treated as if they had no existence. Their acting-area has been totally 'differentiated' in the players' technique from the acting-area at the lower end of the hall. But in what follows – without the opening of any curtain and without any entrance being required – his presence is suddenly confirmed, and the differentiation of the two acting-areas has tacitly ceased.

This action is so simple – indeed it might be called a 'non-action' – that scholars have tended to overlook it. But simple as it is, it is an absolutely vital piece of theatre technique without which this most simple scene would not have been possible. And it is, for all its simplicity, capable of leading to an increased employment so wide as ultimately to reach the situation which drew out Sir Philip Sidney's scorn, when he wrote his famous passage in *An Apologie for Poetrie* about the readiness of audiences to accept a stage 'Where you shall have "Asia" of the one side, And "Affrick" of the other. And so many other under kingdoms that the Player, where he commeth in, must ever begin with telling where he is; or els, the tale will not be conceived'. Medwall had not reached those lengths; but there is to be continually more advanced employment of the convention as we proceed. Even in the present passage there is a second use of it which is still more instructive and which will receive attention in its place.

Now putting this aside, I turn to the second important matter, to see what takes place after World has broken his long silence and come into the action, leaning forward to speak to Man and those who are standing by his side. I would recall that Nature has left; her chair is empty in the distance, and the others have made their passage down the hall, with Sensuality lagging behind, and are standing respectfully in World's presence, having announced their business.

World is most smoothly courteous to them; he murmurs –

> Syrs ye be welcome / to vs hartely
> your messagye ys / to vs ryght acceptable
> Be ye assured / there ys nothyng erthly
> to vs so ioyfull / ne yet so delectable
> As to be acquaynted / wyth parsons honorable
> Namely souch / as ye seme to be [. . .]

B.ii.*rev.*

> Mankynde syr / hartely welcom ye be
> ye are the parsone / wythout faynyng
> that I haue euermore / desyred to se
> Come let me kys you. [. . .]

And then there is that full-stop. It is a very rare punctuation mark in this script, and bears an extraordinary dramatic significance. World has broken off in mid-speech. What he sees as Man steps forward gives him deep concern; he resumes –

> [. . .] O bendycyte
> ye be all naked / [. . .]

(He is horrified lest Man should catch cold!)

> [. . .] alas man why thus
> I make you sure / yt ys ryght perylous

This deliberately calculated pause, and what is to follow it, serves once again to show what a striking significance was attached in Interludes to the expression of ideas through costume. This extended far beyond the fashions and styles worn by the actors, and included the changing of costume to express changes of status and changes of heart. Several writers have remarked on this (among them T. W. Craik, with two chapters on the subject in *The Tudor Interlude*), particularly pointing to the use by Interluders of costume to express character and to symbolize qualities. Undoubtedly this is of great importance; but there is yet another side. The employment of costume for the purposes they mention might be called a *dramatic* usage (in the literary sense of the word), in that it can assist in expounding and clarifying a plot. But costume may have a purely *theatrical* usage; it can assist the performance itself and embellish the action of the players – it can support that action, broadening it or pointing it, it can assist the player as it whirls round him, or as it hangs still. And in this aspect costume was for the early Interlude its only decorative element. The background of the hall may have offered a glimmering surround, and the panelling of the screens a quiet foil to the actions, but it was the costume itself that brought out the movement and lent the colour to a scene, and underlined the gestures of the actors. The care and expense lavished at this time over the costumes at court entertainments, together with the whole organization of the wardrobe of the Revels, prove how highly dresses were regarded. And the eagerness with which Interluders would gain possession by fair means or foul of used court costumes shows how they themselves valued the significance that clothes could add to a performance.

But it was not only in the costume worn by a character that the theatrical significance lay; it was also in the act of putting on a costume during a passage in the show – it was in the action of *robing* in itself.

A particular theatrical condition comes up for consideration here. It is in practice extremely difficult to put on a complicated garment quickly during the action of a scene; so much may go wrong, and there is a very real risk of dropping the atmosphere in the enforced pauses that cannot be wholly avoided even by the most adroit player. Fear of the pauses tends to make the player hurried, and to hurry on a voluminous garment before an audience is to invite trouble.

It therefore follows that any technique of play-presentation which customarily makes use of assuming or changing costume during the action is almost certain to resort to a deliberate featuring of this business, that is to say of doing it ceremonially and with all the necessary care – in a word, slowly.

This particular use and treatment of the ceremony of robing is one of the most memorable conventions of the Japanese *Noh* stage. Not one garment is assumed there without the most restrained timing, and without deliberate care given to the precision of every fold; if required, an assistant is brought on to ensure near-perfection. The play is held up until the requirements are satisfied, and the result of this frank capitalizing of the difficulty of robing on the stage is that it becomes no longer an embarrassment but one of the very attractions of a performance.

When World, now, sees Man naked, the purpose of the garments that were brought in at the beginning of the play is immediately clear. But how might the Interluders handle a situation which, as I have been at length to show, presents such problems? At first there is some bye-play; Man is a little resentful of World's implication. He says stiffly –

> I thanke you / but I nede none other vesture [. . .]
> Gyltles of syn / and as a mayden pure
> I were on me / the garment of innocencye

And at once, of course, this is the cue for the careful 'nurse' at Man's side, whose name is Innocency, to improve the occasion. She speaks up with –

> ye [*yes*] hardely were [*wear*] that garment contynually
> It shall thy body / suffysantly sauegard
> From stormy weder [. . .]

A clearly Spartan philosophy! World at least would seem to think so for one can almost see him turning to look at her under his eyebrows as he slides out the reproof –

> Be pece / fayre woman ye ar not very wyse
> Care ye not / yf thys body take cold [?]
> ye must consyder / thys ys not paradyse [. . .]

He next goes on to make a very shrewd comment upon conventionalism. He observes that

> Whose so lyueth here / [. . .]
> [. . .] must nedys / do as the worlde doth [. . .]
> Aud folow the gyse that now a day goth [. . .]

And who doth the contrary / I wyll be playne
He ys abyect / and dyspysed vtterly
and standeth euer baneshed / from all good company

He embroiders the moral and tells Man that once a body is committed to live on this earth –

B.iii.   [. . .] he must hym selfe apply
          To worldly thyngs / and be of suche condycyon
          As all men be / [. . .]

He speaks with as much authority as ever Reason could do, and gives Man no opening for further objection, but straightway initiates the robing ceremony –

          Take thys garment / man do as I you byd

The turn aside towards Worldy Affeccyon must now follow, and the gown must be lifted off his arm and held out to Man.

          Be not ashamed / hardely to do yt on

(World watches as the arms are put into the sleeves, and he can 'hold the stage' by his close attention until the moment comes for –)

          So lo / [. . .]

(he looks, then turns to Worldly Affeccyon;)

          now thys gurdell / [. . .]

(and pauses as the girdle is unfolded and held out)

                    haue gurd yt in the myd

(If I am accused here of being too imaginative in my effects I would point out that there is not another line in this whole play that has *two* successive pause-strokes in, as this particular line has. And that I think justifies my reading; but more of these strokes later. Then –)

          And thys for your hed / [. . .]

(again the stroke, and the likelihood of World's turn to point to the cap)

               go set yt vppon

(and he would seem to lean back with a smile, and his head on one side –)

          By the charge of me / you be a goodly on
          As euer I saw / syth yt I was borne
          Worth a thowsand / that ye were beforne.

And here there is no doubt that he pauses, for we have unmistakably one of the rare full-stops in the script. He is evidently very well pleased with what he sees for he suddenly waxes jovial, and begins a new paragraph in his lines:

> Gyue me your hand / be not in fere
> Syt down / as ye ar borne to occupye thys place [. . .]

It is not clear where Man sits – whether on a footstool placed at World's feet, or whether World rises to take his hand and now motions him into his own chair. At any rate he feoffs Man with all the world. Man is deeply impressed and grateful, and professes his good motives in this life. Reason is listening and takes the opportunity to express the hope that he never does anything other than what he now promises. Innocence cannot resist the moment to press the point home, despite the fact that World is still looking down his nose at her, and she urges that Man must abstain not only from the 'dede / but also from theassent' since 'ye may not be cleped innocent . . . yf onys ye assent/to foly in your mynde'. But World cannot let this pass unchallenged; he tells her –

B.iii.*rev.* Thys ys an harde word / syster that ye haue spoken . . .
> But thynk ye goddys / commaundement broken
> For a lyght tryfull [. . .] [?]
> Alas haue ye suche a spyced conscyence [. . .] [!]
> Leue yt woman leue yt. For yt ys nought . . .

And with that he turns to Man. This again is a definite, specified movement, for the direction is in the margin: 'loqui – ad ho.' – He speaks to Man.

The pace of the action now slows down for a longish conversation in which World gives Man some advice on settling-in to his new country with its new manners, and recommends that his first action should be to get rid of his rather dubious followers and take counsel instead 'Of well enured men / such as haue growne In worldly experyence'. Innocence is thus dismissed and 'goeth out'. No direction is given for Reason, but it would appear that at some point he too leaves. World recommends that his own retainer, Worldly Affeccyon, become Man's servant, and that Sensuality be retained. He then asks if he can do anything more before he goes. Man says no, and World presumably then exits, though there is no direction for him to do so. Worldly Affeccyon leaves next, and thus Man and Sensuality stand discussing what has just passed and the spectacle dies down to just these two talking by World's vacated chair.

They discuss very briefly. Sensuality has only four lines, and then the great moment of the early section of the play, from the theatrical point of view, takes place; but the opportunity offers here for a note or two on what has already happened.

The sex of Innocence seems to be a matter of uncertainty. On the one hand World distinctly addressed this figure as female when he said 'Be pece / fayre woman'; on the other hand when, later, World recommends Innocence's dismissal he uses the words –

C.i.   [. . .] I wyll aduyse you
        to put thys man / from your company
        I tell you / euery man wyll despyse you
        As long as ye / be ruled by innocency

Again, after Innocence's departure, Sensuality says –

        Let hym go to the deuyll of hell
        He ys but a boy [. . .]

There would clearly seem to be an inconsistence in the script here, or perhaps an overt recognition that the 'maiden' was in fact played by a boy.

But it is clear that the printed text does in fact contain errors. On folio c.i. *rev.* it seems certain that some of the speech-ascriptions are wrong or out of place; for among other things World seems to speak after he has apparently gone out, but the speech so ascribed to him is without any doubt only suitable to Man's lips. Moreover, World is given two consecutive speeches in direct succession, without any reason for such an abnormality. This is a textual matter and scarcely concerns presentation, but I suggest that World's second speech on this page really belongs to Man; that his third and fourth speeches belong to Worldly Affeccyon; and that World's exit is to be understood after Man's first speech on that page, at the line 'And send you well to spede'.

A curious trick of the printer concerning speech ascriptions may be remarked here. It is the occasional, but not consistent, placing of the name of the character speaking *not* opposite the first line of his speech, but opposite the last line of the preceding speaker's speech. At first this may bring a little confusion, though in practice one is helped because the printer usually precedes the opening line of a speech with a paragraph sign.

Another textual matter that I ought perhaps to touch in more detail than I have done so far is the mid-line stroke. This may not be entirely a matter of theatrical presentation and thus is perhaps out of my province; there is however this to be said. I have made the suggestion that this mid-line stroke is the sign for a pause. There is no doubt, I think, that in many lines this is true. But the pause demanded by the meaning is of varying length in various lines, and in some lines there seems to be no need for a pause at all. The stroke, then, might be held to be primarily a feature of versification, marking the caesura of each line, and thus a matter for the writer or reader but not for the actor.

On the other hand however, this is certainly not always true since, as we have seen, a line may on occasion have *two* strokes in it; these are clearly not versification marks and equally clearly, they are there as pause marks. Again, some lines have no stroke at all, though this is rare in the earlier part of the play (but very much more common in the later part, as will be seen). Any line which has no stroke does seem, as one considers it in spoken delivery, to be a line that would be spoken quickly, or at least with no suggestion of a pause in it.

A passage illustrative of the above impressions comes on folio c.i. *rev.*, during a business talk between World and Man:

> Syr at few wordys / I you exhorte
> Syth that ye be come to your own
> Cast your selfe to bere suche a porte
> That as ye be / ye may be knowen
> Eke yt ys necessary / for that behoue
> that there be made / some maner of puruyaunce
> Whereby / ye may bere out your countenaunce
> Wyll yt lyke you therfore / that I suruey
> And se thextent / of all your land [. . . *etc. etc.*]

But a far more significant indication that the strokes may relate to the actor's presentation is that generally speaking they occur only in the grave speeches; their absence is remarkable in the speeches of the caricatured, or comic, characters, and of course these speeches are likely to have been delivered at the quicker speed of colloquial speech, while the graver parts would use a more deliberate, or at least impressive and dignified, pace.

The system of mid-line strokes does, then, offer some indication of variation in the rhythm of the play as the audience would hear it spoken in the hall.

To resume once more. The sensational step in the presentation is now introduced as follows: Sensuality is agreeing to assist Man in the arrangement of his new household and in the recruitment of proper companions for him. He says—

C.ii.   [. . .] I shall take the enterpryse
    Of all suche maters / and loke where I fynde
    any man of pleasure / on hym set your mynde [. . .]

and then he immediately catches himself up and interrupts what he was saying with –

    Lo wyll ye se lo / here cometh one

(the repeated 'lo' is particularly effective in calling attention; and he adds, rather mysteriously –)

    Euen the last man / that was in my thought

At which, Man looks in the direction indicated and then asks,

    What ys he.

– Sensuality finishes the broken line with –

    ye shall se anon

– and begins to describe the individual that he sees, the text now running as follows –

    a well drawen man ys he / and a well taught
    That wyll not gyue hys hed for nought
    And therto goodly / as ye shall se in a day
    As well apparelyd / at eche poynt of hys aray
PRY. CO. Who dwelleth here / wyll no man speke [. . .]

– and a long speech follows. But before looking at it, what is implied in the above?

To recapitulate the steps covered in the above lines: Sensuality begins by saying he will help Man, and among other things will try to find him a 'man of pleasure' to be his companion. At the moment of speaking his eye is caught by a movement in the crowd at the lower end of the hall near the screens, and he looks and sees a new figure thrusting his way through. This figure he recognizes with some surprise as the last person he expected to see. He calls Man's

72

attention to him and Man turns to look but does not recognize him, and asks who he is. Sensuality tells him to wait a moment and see. He then goes on to describe the figure as a well set-up man, well educated, one that 'will not give his head for nought', as fine a fellow as one could wish, and all dressed up to suit.

Now, for the long space of 105 lines there is no more speech or action whatever from Man or Sensuality. The whole play moves over to the newcomer. He dominates the scene with a lone soliloquy, and from the words of this soliloquy it is quite clear that he speaks almost the whole of it without showing any recognition whatever of the presence of the other two characters who have watched his entrance with such interest from the upper end of the hall.

Here then is another example of the temporary 'differentiation' of the general acting-area into two separate and isolated areas. But the isolation in this case is not complete as it was at the opening of the play, for in the present situation the two players in the first area are able to continue to see and watch what is happening in the second area, while the player in that second area plays his whole scene quite independently of them. Thus it is in effect a one-way isolation. It continues until the moment arrives when it is necessary for the new character to meet the others; and then, almost with the effect of an invisible curtain being lifted, the two areas are merged into one again.

Provided such a convention can be convincingly handled and made clear to the audience, it is obviously of considerable value to a playwright presenting a developing complex situation on the floor of an ordinary room.

It is perhaps useful to add at this point that we are able, on the evidence of material that comes later, to form a picture of this new figure in very great detail. He offers a vivid contrast in appearance to the characters so far seen in the action. These latter have all been dressed in relatively sombre, long robes, with their hats possibly squarish in effect, low-crowned and with rolled brims. The newcomer is in tights, to use a modern word, that is to say he wears *hose*, and hose of contrasting colours, striped and flashing beneath a very short-skirted doublet, with a brief cloak swinging from his shoulders, and with exaggeratedly full sleeves. He has long, golden, silken hair, with possibly a fore-and-aft pointed hat and a sweeping feather in it. His general colour is a staring scarlet. Behind him we have to picture a small boy struggling along under the weight of two great, heavy double-handed swords.

73

But even more important than this, is one particular line near the beginning of his speech which comes in the following context. The character himself has been cryptically described in the margin, by the words 'pry. co.' which I interpret as *Pryde cometh in*. He jostles the unsuspecting watchers in the screens entrance, pushing through them and striding in to the acting-area as if it contained no one in the world but himself. As he comes forward, what he says is:

> Who dwelleth here / wyll no man speke
> Is there no fole nor hody peke
> Now by the bell yt were almys to breke
> Some of these knaues brows
> A gentylman comys in at the dorys
> That all hys dayes hath worn gylt sperys
> And none of thys knaues nor cutted horys
> Byddys hym welcom to house.
> Wote ye not how great a lord I am [. . .]

It is worth breaking in for a moment here. These lines are important in two respects; first, they show that there is a complete change in the timing of the action, because in them, and in the long speech that follows, there are only four mid-line strokes. It is therefore all spoken pretty rapidly after the first exclamation, 'who dwelleth here', and the arrogant look round in the startled silence which pretty certainly followed. Another pause for effect comes after 'welcom to house' where Pride shows his contempt for the company, and where we have a clear full-stop.

The second point is of greater significance. One line in this speech seems to me to offer a key to the main problem of this opening part of the investigation, and its importance is, I believe, fully confirmed by later evidence. It is, 'A gentylman comys in at the dorys'. The discovery of the use in the plural of this word 'dorys' – or doors – adds final confirmation to something which is really inescapable; that the entrance used by players as they came into a Great Hall was the entrance in the screens. The word is in the plural precisely because there was a *pair* of such doors in any normal lay-out of screens. And there was no comparable pair of doors anywhere else in the hall.

In case a question should occur here, it is relevant to point out that the word 'Door' is defined in the *O.E.D.* in two main ways; as a movable barrier on hinges to close a passage into a room – but also as having the meaning in Middle English of the opening or passage into a room, that is, a doorway. The example quoted of this use is

Shakespeare's 'They . . . met the iealous knaue their Master in the doore' (*Merry Wives*, III.v.103). And so the phrase, 'comes in at the doors' is fully applicable to the openings in the screens whether they were clear open doorways, as they were in the early period, or whether they were closable by hinged leaves, as they did become but only after the period of this study.

A further small point about the duality of these doors comes later in the play; it occurs when, after a talk with Bodily Lust, Gluttony hurries Man off to a tavern, leaving Bodily Lust behind alone. Now to him there suddenly enters Wrath with the demand –

G.ii.*rev.*   Wherebe these knaues that make thys aray

– and Bodily Lust replies to him –

Mary they be gon that other way [. . .]

What can be meant by *that other way*? It cannot, I think, be avoided that if a character on entering is told that another character has gone out by another way then there must be two doorways available. There were two such doorways in the normal screens.

This reference of Pryde's to coming in at the 'doors' (in the plural) is not the only one of its kind. In Skelton's *Magnyfycence*, about 1516, one character calls to another 'Hens thou haynyarde, out of the doors fast' (see later p. 195).

Pryde's long speech, as he stands at the far end of the hall just in front of the screens, and speaks down the length of it taking in everyone present, is an interesting one and deserves the quotation of a few extracts. It affords a very vivid picture of the presentation of an Interlude. Following on his first outburst of indignation at his reception, he enlarges on his nobility. But then, by a natural transition, he turns from his splendid ancestry to his splendid clothes, and now his tone changes to one of satisfaction:

C.ii.   How say ye syrst [? *syrs*] by myne aray
             Doth yt please you ye or nay [. . .]

– and he goes on to describe in detail his 'staryng colour of scarlet red', his long hair hanging down below his ears and shining 'as bryght as any pyrled gold', his doublet and short gown with wide sleeves, his dagger, and his two swords which –

C.ii.*rev.*   To bere theym my selfe yt were a payne
             They ar so heuy that I am fayne
             to puruey suche a lad [. . .]

and thus we find that we must add to the picture he is creating for
us, the figure of his small boy struggling under a brace of 'two hand'
swords, and he bestows several scurrilous witticisms on the child.
Then he goes on 'to do that I com fore', namely to seek 'some
newelte'; in particular he has heard of a stranger lately come to this
'contray' who is disposed to be a householder, and into whose
affairs he now proposes to 'threst in one hand'. He says he has
recently met with Sensuality and feels, after discussion with him,
that 'The mater ys cok sure'. Then at length he suddenly stops; he
has at last seen the others. To his lad he says

C.iii.   Ey good lord what man ys that [?]
                   Fathers soule thys ys some great wat

The precocious youngster replies –

                   Thys ys he that ye seeke

– much to his doting father's delight, who beams and invites the
audience to

                   Se thys brat
                   Thys boy ys passyng taunte
                   Com behynd and folow me
                   Set out the better leg I warne the

And so action is introduced again, and the two begin to stride up
the hall to accost the others. The boy starts off –

                   yes in the best wyse trust ye me

– and adds in French

                   ale seygniour ale vouse auant

and Pryde says as he comes up,

                   Salut to you syr.

Man replies –

                           & to you also
                   Whens are ye [?]

But Pryde is circumspect and does not give anything away yet. He
contents himself with –

                   I shall tell you or I go
                   But fyrst wold I speke a worde & no mo
                   wyth thys saruant of yours

Sensuality of course feigns surprise, and queries –

C.iii.*rev.*   Wyth me syr. Wolde ye speke wyth me

– and we may be certain that Pryde tries to draw him aside and keep this matter private, as he puts a question just to make sure there is no mistake:

ye for god are ye not Sensualyte [?]

Sensuality can't deny it –

yes surely.

Pryde (with meaning),

ye such a gentylman ye seme to be

Sensuality bows in non-committal politeness

your pore saruaunt at all howris

and the plot thickens. That I have not been drawing unjustifiably on imagination in the above, there now comes proof in a delightful acting-direction and a remarkable piece of speaking to follow it:

Then Pryde speketh to Sensua. / in / hys
ere that all may here.
Syr I vnderstand that this gentylman is borne to great
fortunes and intendeth to inhabyt herein the contrary.
And I am a gentylman y^t alway hath be brought vp wyth
great estatys and affeed wyth them and yf I myght be
in lyke fauour wyth this gentylman I wold be glad
therof / & do you a pleasure.

And we realize that to convey this notable communication into his ear (so that, however, all may hear) Pryde has adopted direct prose – possibly he might claim the first prose speech in English secular comedy. His last line, after the significant pause at the stroke, is a triumph of insinuation. There is now a sharp exchange of dialogue from one to the other; Sensuality begins:

Where ys your dwellynge [?]
PRYDE   I dwell her by
SENSUA What ys your name [?]
PRYDE   Pryde
SENSUA Pryde?
PRYDE   ye sykerly
But I am cleped worshyp comenly
In placys where I dwell.

SENSUA Worshyp [*!*] now in fayth ye saw [*? say*] trew
        ye be radix viciorum. Rote of all vertew
PRYDE ye ye man ye wolde say so yf ye me knew
SENSUA Turd I know you well
        Syr ye are welcom as I may say [. . .]

– and with that aside-line and the following cover-line we must for space' sake, if for no other, leave these two most plausible rogues with, I think, little doubt of the effect they could bring to the scene if they had skill enough to take advantage of it.

The scene as I envisage it at this point is of Man a little out of the picture, standing inconspicuously somewhere near the High Table end of the acting-area, with Pryde and Sensuality talking intimately together having pointedly drawn a certain distance away from him, thus standing possibly somewhere between the high table and the mid point of the hall. The two plotters come to the end of their consultation, with Pryde anxious to prevent the scheme looking too obviously premeditated:

C.iiii.   But syr abyde here on[*e*] thyng
                I wyll not be knowen that yt ys my sekyng

– and Sensuality agreeing, in a speech beginning with three lines whose particular printing-arrangement is worth noting:

SENSUA No more wold I for. xl. shelyng
        Let me alone hardely
SENSUA Syr yf yt please you here ys come a straunger
        That neuer was aquaynted wyth you ere
        Somwhat shamefast and halfe in fere [. . .] (*etc.*)

We have thus found another example of two consecutive speeches from one character. But here it would seem that this variation from the normal is correctly printed, and was arranged in this way for a purpose. The purpose is obvious; it is to indicate that Sensuality breaks off his *tête-à-tête* with Pryde, leaves him, walks to where Man is standing, and opens a fresh conversation with Man. After a few lines in recommendation of Pryde, he ends by asking Man –

        Wyll yt please you that I hym call
C.iiii.*rev.*   To speke wyth you. MAN. byd hym com. SEN. I shall
        Syr wyll ye come nere.
SENSUA Syr byd hym welcome for the maner sake [. . .]

78

Again consecutive speeches. Thus, what happens is that Sensuality first asks Man's permission to summon Pryde; then Man replies by bidding him send Pryde to him. This Sensuality agrees to do, and he turns away, walks to Pryde and invites him to approach; then he turns back again to Man and asks Man to make Pryde courteously welcome. During this brief return of Sensuality to Man, Pryde perhaps gathers himself together for his momentous interview and, it may be, gives his small boy a sign to clear out of the place and leave him unencumbered. For we must remember that the boy has walked across the hall with Pryde, but has had no speech or acting-direction allotted to him since his meeting with Man; but he does not enter into the action of the play again and, at some point round about this present situation, he presumably trots down the hall under the burden of the two great swords (offering much amusement to the audience) and, having thus made his little contribution to the entertainment of the show, goes off through the crowd at the screens and so, amid smiles and hand-pats, away.

Such points as this of the exit of the small boy are relatively unimportant to playwrights (even to this day). What is important to them is the idea behind the introduction of such a figure, the occasion of his entrance, and the success of the brief moment of amusing relief he can bring. Then he is, quite understandably, forgotten. It is the business of the performers themselves how and when to get rid of him. Questions of this sort are always cropping up in rehearsals, as players – having to face a situation in real fact, not its conception in running imagination – see that a character or a property having served its purpose is now in the way, and that arrangements must therefore be made for conveniently getting rid of him or it. These are the kind of details that, however important theatrically, may never get recorded in a dramatic script.

Sensuality ends his speech to Man by confirming Pryde's suitability and by saying that no man knoweth the world better than he. Thereupon Man speaks out towards the approaching Pryde and says,

> Syr ye be welcom to thys place

Pryde, with affected graceful courtesy and apology, says,

> I thanke you syr / but I do you trespace
> to come thus homly.

– and Sensuality finishes his broken line with a tart comment that

79

must have been spoken aside: and then lifts his voice in his next
line to second his master's welcome –

> ye a parlous case
> God wote ye are welcom heder [. . .]
> Go nere to hym and talk your fyll
> I leue you togeder
>
> He goeth forth

The mechanics are quite clear here, and the suspense and interest
of the intrigue are very well preserved by the writing. Sensuality
shows the audience his private opinion of Pryde, covers it by his
apparent welcome to him, underlines the summons to him to come
near and then, once Man and Pryde are together, he retires from
their encounter, walks down the hall, and goes out. Man now
draws his breath and asks,

> Now syr what haue ye to say to me

There follows next a relatively long scene where Pryde worms
his way into Man's confidence; and he does it with striking effi-
ciency, both up and down, including arguments against the sway
of Reason couched in terms of subtle psychology. He ends with
disparaging the clothes Man is wearing and says he is behind the
fashion. This goes on until, at length, Sensuality comes striding
down the hall again, this time with Worldly Affeccyon by his side.
Sensuality detaches Man from the conversation, in which Pryde is
gradually making him feel a weak fool, and proposes that Man
should come with him – leaving Pryde and Worldly Affeccyon to
handle 'all thys gere' on their own and to 'deuyse . . . a new fassyon'
in clothes for Man – while he himself takes Man off to 'some
tauern'. Man assents and excuses himself to the others with,

> D.ii.   [. . .] I pray you syrs do your dylygence
> For thys aray and spare none expence
> and for a whyle I wyll go hens
> And come agayne shortly
>
> Here Man and Sensualyte go out.

One may picture them walking down the hall side by side, parting
the crowd at the screens and disappearing into the entry.

Pryde now fills in for a space. He outlines at some length the
detail of the new dress he will devise, and Worldly Affeccyon
laughs aloud at the prospect; but he adds a doubt whether reason

80

may not interfere. Pryde replies that he need not be afraid, but to make doubly sure he will bring Man –

D.ii.*rev.*   [. . .] shortly in acquayntaunce
             Wyth all the company of myne affyaunce [. . .]

(that is, the other Six Vices,)

             Than shall ye se hym vtterly dospyce [*despise*]
             Reasons counsell [. . .]

and immediately on this, Sensuality returns from the tavern having clearly overheard the last words, and says,

                 Nay nay syrs care ye nothynge
                 That mater ys sped well and fyne
PRYDE   Is yt so. SENSUA. ye by heuen kyng.
                 Euen as we sat togeder at the wyne
W.AFF.   Thou shalt haue goddys blessyng and myne
                 but ys yt true [?]
SENSUA ye syr by thys day
                 Our mayster and Reason haue made a great fray
PRYDE   How so [?]

– and to this pertinent question, whose answer all the audience must be agog to hear in detail, Sensuality gives a long and vivid description of how two bright girls, Kate and Margery, descended upon them as they sat drinking, how Man mysteriously began to change colour and then rose from the board to go lie down on a bed –

D.iii.   and prayd me for the maners sake
             That margery myght com hold hys hede [. . .]
             And so she hath hym vndertake
             To make hym hole / in an houre or twayne
             whan soeuer he hath any suche soden payn
             What yt meaneth I wote neuer [. . .]

The insinuation, the brightness and liveliness of this reported scene are equal to those of any 'messenger's speech'. Especially interesting is the introduction it effects for us to a very simple example of the convenient condensation of time. The whole dialogue since Man's exit with Sensuality has taken only 53 lines (including the ingeniously inserted diversion on the matter of Man's new dress) but it has sufficed for an epoch-making passage of events in Man's expanding life. But more is to come. Pryde does not see how all this is to the point – where does the quarrel with Reason come in? Sensuality explains:

> Mary Reason [. . .]
> Cam euen to vs as we sat so drynkyng
> And gaue our mayster an hete [? *hit*] worth an hangyng
> Bycause that margery sat on hys kne [. . .]

– surely an extremely ill-judged action in the circumstances from such a person as Reason of all people! As might be expected he immediately precipitated a tavern brawl, swords were drawn, and Reason had his head broken – this despite, or perhaps because of, Sensuality's running in to part them and deliberately confusing the combatants.

Worldly Affeccyon listens with amazement and amusement –

D.iii.*rev.*   But can our master play the man now [?]

– and Sensuality avers that he most certainly can, and warns them –

> Medyll ye no more wyth margery
> For by cokkys precyouse body
> If our mayster may yt espy [. . .]
> That ye vse her company
> I tell you he wyll be angry
> He ys so full of ielosy
> As euer I knew man [. . .]
> He ys now as famylyer
> Wyth bodely lust as euer ye were
> ye and therto as great a swerer [. . .]
> Knew I neuer of hys age
> A man of better corage
> To do all maner of outrage
> After our desyres

– and he goes on to describe how Man has also called Pryde's kinsmen into his favour, namely

D.iiii.   Enuy wreth glotony and couetyse
          Slouth and lechery become to hys seruyce

All this has apparently happened, or been communicated to Sensuality, between his exit with Man to the tavern and his return to relate these events. We recognize his story as the old, old one of all the Morality plots, but it is told with a gusto and a colour now that certainly give a new life to it.

After an additional description of the familiar trick of changing the names of all the vices to their opposites so that Man should not recognize them, Pryde decides all is well and turns to leave the others and go out to see to the bespeaking of Man's new garments.

The First Part of the Interlude is now approaching its conclusion; and the playwright has soon to round it off neatly. He makes Pryde finish by saying (of Man),

D.iiii.*rev.*   And yf he come hyder whyle I am hens
                   I pray the [*thee*] excuse myne absens

This leaves two to dispose of; and one of them, Sensuality, is quick to take a cue, turning to Worldly Affeccyon with –

                 ye and myne also

Pryde checks his going and asks

                 Why [,] wylt thou go wyth me [?]

– and Sensuality neatly answers,

                 Wyll I q*uod'*a ye parde
                 It ys accordyng for Sensualyte
                 Wyth Pryde for to go

No exit-direction follows, but clearly Worldly Affeccyon is now left alone. He speaks twenty lines of satisfaction in the situation, with some thoughts on how to confirm it, and then he concludes that it is high time that he also went off to find out how his master is getting on, and –

                 He goeth out and Reason cometh in.

(Whether or not Reason has a bandage round his head after the tavern brawl we are not told, but with players so conscious of the significance of costume, it would not be unlikely.) Reason, of course, bewails the whole situation, reminding us

E.i.   [. . .] at the begynnyng
                 that Nature comytted me to hys seruyce

– thus callyng to our attention that so much has happened since those quiet minutes at the beginning of the play when Nature left the scene, and Man and his friends went up the hall to the World – and so much of the vivid and unexpected has intervened – that we had almost forgotten them. Reason now plans to win Man back but as he speaks Man, almost unexpectedly, pushes through the by-standers, half-turning to demand of them –

E.i.*rev.*   I say syrs where ys wurshyp can ye tell [?]
                   In thys place I left hym last

('Worship', we should remember, was the alias assumed by Pryde.)

Now there is a brief 'coda' interpolated before the imminent conclusion. We watch to see how it is handled.

The answer to Man's question does not of course come from the bystanders, nor does it come from Reason who is in the Place though presumably standing somewhat distant from the screens, but from Worldly Affeccyon – rather unexpectedly, because some short time back he was quite clearly directed to go out. Presumably, therefore, he now calls through the screens-crowd, perhaps from the entrance opposite to the one Man has just entered by, and says that Pryde (*i.e.* Worship) is busy ordering the new garments which he described before he went, and if they turn out as well as he suggested then Man will cut a fine figure.

But Man is now suddenly struck with a gnawing doubt –

               ye but what wyll Reason say
               Whan he seeth me in that aray

Worldly Affeccyon quickly retorts,

               Reason. Mary let hym go play
               To the deuyll of hell [. . .]

– which implies that he does not see Reason waiting a short distance away. But Man feels he can't really do a thing like that, and speaks his doubts. Worldly Affeccyon replies with less skilful flattery than Pryde would have done, so that Man stiffens and rejects both him and Sensuality into the bargain; Worldly Affeccyon presumably goes, and Man turns to seek Shamefastness, who then makes a personal appearance saying that if Man wishes to have his acquaintance he is ready to wait on him. Man replies,

E.ii.   [. . .] and glad am I now of your comyng
               Prayng you wyth hart entere
               whan I haue nede thus to com nere

and Shamefastness agrees to stand ready to answer such a call when it comes and then 'He goeth out'. So he entered the hall only for a brief moment and, it seems, principally to indicate to the audience that more of the story might be ready for them on another occasion.

Now at last Reason, who has stood on the fringe of the Place observing all this, comes forward and begins the final dialogue with Man. Man asks,

> Hard [*heard*] ye all thys mater [. . .] [?]

Reason replies,

> yes that I dyd in very ded

– so that he witnessed the above scene between Man and the other two yet none of the three was conscious of his presence. Man is now profoundly contrite and asserts with the very best intentions –

E.ii.*rev.*
> But now haue I refused vtterly
> All suche maner of cumpany
> and thys haue I done veryly
> Of myne own mocyon

Reason replies to the effect that –

> yf ye be contryte as ye pretend
> God ys mercyable yf ye lust to craue [. . .]

Man repeats how sorry he is. Reason says they will never part again. And then –

> And for thys seson
> Here we make an end
> Lest we shuld offend
> Thys audyence / as god defend
> It were not tobe don
> ye shall vnderstand neuerthelesse
> That there ys myche more of thys processe
> wherein we shall do our besynes
> and our true endeuure
> To shew yt vnto you after our guyse
> whan my lord shall so deuyse
> It shalbe at hys pleasure

> > Thus endeth the
> > fyrst parte

It is interesting to enquire why these early Interludes should be written in two so distinct parts. Was it because on all occasions when a play was given at a gentleman's house, it was convenient to have one part played on one occasion and the other at another – either later the same day, or after a day or two's interval? If this were, for some reason, always the custom (and I cannot clearly see why it should have been), why was it that Medwall took the trouble to add what I have called a 'coda' to a situation that was already far better, as an interesting break-off point, without it? To leave Man in full career in his misdeeds without any near prospect of his reform would seem a better temptation to induce people to hear a second instalment, and would make the audience look forward in anticipation to learn what form the inevitable retribution would take. But Medwall deliberately rounded off his section with Man's (temporary) repentance – even dragging in, a little unconvincingly, this fresh figure to motivate it – that of Shamefastness. Thus he gives rather a sense of termination to his play than an expectation of more to come; and he has to put the promise of a resumption into the mouth of one of the characters in the form of a direct announcement to the audience.

But it is to be observed that Medwall's construction is such – whether he intended this or not – that the play could be given as written and described above (that is in two parts with an interval between), but *also* so that it could be cut in half and one part only given, if a shorter one-session show was preferred. In that case the little 'coda' which he adds to the First Part would be justified as a rounding-off of the preceding matter, in such a way as to present the improving moral, even if the audience were never to have any chance to witness any further instalment.

How far early Interlude-writers were required to offer to their players such an option for either short or double-length presentations we do not at present know. But it is certain in this resepct that when John Rastell (who was the printer of *Nature*) later wrote his own Interlude, entitled *The Four Elements*, he offered a specific scheme of cutting, whereby the performance, which he reckoned at one-and-a-half hours complete, could be reduced to three-quarters of an hour on occasion (see below p. 205). But he also added that 'if ye list, ye may bring in a disguising' – so that there seems to be some sort of Procrustean condition laid upon playwrights about this particular period.

The Second Part of *Nature* is not so much a new movement in the story as the old movement played again with variations. The essence of the action is the preparation for a battle between Reason and the forces that Man has gathered round him in his new estate, namely the Seven Vices. The ultimate battle does not take place before us but is handled with a bright twist of wit, and quite unexpectedly. But first there are some diversions.

Reason opens with a long speech to Man likening the life of mortal creatures to the siege of a castle, and ends –

E.iii.*rev.*	ye remember as I suppose well I now
	How yt ys not fully .iii. dayes past
	Syth ye me promysed [. . .]
	[. . .] to be obedyent

(Note the reference apparently to the length of the interval.) Man agrees. Then Reason 'goeth out & Sensua. cometh in.' Sensuality with double cunning professes to offer sympathy to Man on a great misfortune and ends by bursting into tears ('Then he wepyth'). He explains it is because since Man has listened to Reason again, all his old acquaintance are so sorrowful without him – especially Margery who –

E.iiii.	[. . .] hath entred into a relygyouse place
	At the grene frerys hereby [. . .]

Man is overcome with remorse; he tenderly murmurs 'Alak good lytell wenche . . .', and asks if she is as closely held there as other nuns be. He listens innocently as Sensuality discloses that the place in question is a brothel. Man feels he would very much like to go and see her but is put off by the entrance of Bodily Lust and Worldly Affeccyon. Bodily tells him of a new place of pleasure –

F.i.		[. . .] the smorterst place
		that euer ye saw wyth eyes
MAN	What thyng ys yt yong or old [?]
BODYLY	What euer yt be yt ys able to be sold

– and he goes off to try to make arrangements for Man's visit there. Now follows a nice detail of cynical but human character-study. Worldly Affeccyon slyly observes to Man that –

F.i.*rev.*		Now wyll margery make great mone
		bycause ye com not. MAN. ye[a] let her alone
		I am not her bond man parde
		She hath dysappoynted me or now
W. AFF.	Yet [. . .]
		Send her word [. . .] yf ye do not so
		She wyll so morn [. . .]
MAN	[. . .] Thys answere wyll I deffar and spare
		tyll I be certayn
		what answere bodyly lust shall bryng
		Of thys other praty new thyng [. . .]

87

Seeing his distraction, Worldly Affeccyon swiftly takes the opportunity to try to pick up another man's leavings, and has the effrontery to enquire –

> Wyll yt please you that I go to mergery
> in your stede

At that Man has enough virility to be startled into indignant jealousy –

> [. . .] that shall thou not do

– at that moment Bodily returns from his errand. He has to admit it was a fruitless one because,

F.ii.   I could not speke wyth her [. . .]
                   [. . .] they be a slepe euerychone [. . .]
MAN.   How knowest thou wether they be a slepe or no
BODYLY Mary she her selfe told me so
                   whan I rapped at the dore
MAN.   It semeth she was not a slepe than
BODYLY No she was a bed wyth a strange man

This puts a new complexion on things and Man swings round with –

F.ii.*rev.*   Lo worldly affeccyon now mayst thou se
             Thy counsell was nought that thou gauest me [. . .]
             therfore now let vs go
             And resorte agayn to our old hostes [. . .]
                             Then they thre go out & Pryde
                             cometh in.

Pryde addresses the audience with –

> Syrs remember ye that thys other day
> Man promysed me euen in thys stede
> that I shuld wyth hym dwell [. . .]

Thus he again suggests that the First Part was performed some days earlier. He goes on to say that he has heard a report that Man has gone back to Reason again, and so he decides to put Sensuality on to him once more. Upon which Sensuality must enter because Pryde asks him where Man is, and Sensuality replies –

F.iii.   He ys besy harke in your ere
                 wyth lytell margery ye wote where [. . .]

Sensuality goes out and, in a short time, Sloth has come in and is speaking with Pryde. They exchange some joking comments on the change in name that each of the Vices has engineered. And then comes a remarkable passage in this typical technique of involving the audience. Sloth asks if Pryde knows where Man is. Pryde does know, but what he in fact does is to turn to the spectators with the words –

F.iiii.   Now must I to the stewes as fast as I may
                 to fech thys gentylman [. . .]

– then he pauses and looks round the spectators with a twinkle –

                 [. . .] but syrs I say
          Can any man here tell me the way
          for I cam neuer there

Then comes the resounding piece of cheek; since, obviously, there can be no reply from the spectators, Pryde singles one poor unfortunate out and tackles him directly, with obvious effect –

          ye know the way parde of old

There may have been a laugh and a crimson disclaimer from the man fixed on, but Pryde goes on without any mercy –

          I pray the tell me whyche way shall I hold

– and then, making capital of the poor fellow's discomfiture, he turns aside and exclaims in pretended disgust –

          wyll ye se thys horson cocold
          I trow he can not here [*hear*]
          Now yt were almes to clap the on the crown

and whether or no he advances upon the bystander with upraised hand we cannot tell for fortunately at that very moment there comes the direction, 'Then cometh in man and worldly aff.' Man quickly sizes up the situation, and from his lines has obviously heard some of the dialogue, for he calls –

          Why [,] be there any cocoldys in town [?]

Pryde replies, with the first two lines possibly spoken aside, as follows:

          ye I durst hold theron my gown
          that there be a score [–]
          but for god I cry you mercy

> For by my fayth I wyst you not so ny
> Had I wyst yt I ensure you faythfully
> that word I wold haue forbore

– and so the bright jollying goes on. At length Man and Pryde decide to go off and inspect the making of the new clothes, and another piece of remarkable effrontery follows. Before leaving they say to Worldly Affeccyon 'abyde thou here'. He is thus left alone. He replies –

G.i.   Mary I shall wyth all myne hart
       thys good fyre and I wyll not depart

(Obviously he refers to the real fire burning in the hall fireplace, whether that fireplace is, as in an old hall, in the centre of the floor or whether it is, according to the newer fashion, one built under a chimney in the side wall of the hall. He continues –)

> For very cold myne handys do smart
> It maketh me wo bygon

(Now comes the piece of effrontery; he snaps at a bystander –)

> Get me a stole [*stool*] here may ye not se
> Or ellys a chayr wyll yt not be
> thou pyld knaue I speke to the [*!*]
> How long shall I stande [*?*]

Again, very fortunately there is an interruption; Glotony has come in and seen the situation, and he calls out contemptuously –

       Let hym stand wyth a foule euyll
       [. . . . .] deuyll [*part line missing*]
G.i.*rev.*   wyll ye se lo / euery dreuyll
       Now adayes I warand
       Must commaund as he were a kyng
       Let hym stande on hys fete wyth bredyng

But there is no hard feeling, and they exchange compliments and pick up the dialogue. The next gag comes shortly after; Glotony is speaking to Bodily Lust, who comes in after Worldly Affeccyon departs to seek his breakfast; Glotony is discussing food and ends his speech with –

G.ii.   For hote drynkys and delycate refeccyon
       Causeth flesshely insurreccyon
       ye know yt as well as I

– but the voice that answers is not Bodily Lust's; it is the unexpected voice of Man, who has obviously entered and overheard.
The two turn to him and pause in transfixed silence! Now the
amusing gag begins; Glotony turns covertly to Bodily and asks in a
changed tone –

> What gentylman ys thys can ye tell [?]
> BODYLY Wotyst thou neuer [?]
> GLOTO. No by the bell
> I saw hym neuer byfore
> BODYLY Is yt our mayster
> GLOTO. Nay by the rood
> It ys not he [,] woldyst thou make me wood

What has happened is clearly that Man has returned, no doubt
feeling a very fine fellow in his new clothes, and out to impress the
others. But they in their turn are out to make other game of him;
their reception is not only unbelieving but *mournful*! 'Why' (asks
Man) 'Bycause I haue chaunged myne aray'? They reply 'Nay' and
give a different and quite unexpected reason – namely because he
looks so thin and ill! His sojourn with Reason has not suited him!
They compassionately decide to take him in hand and get him to an
inn again. He goes with Glotony, telling Bodily to wait behind for
the coming of the rest of his company.

This really amounts in fact to a mustering of Man's troops, and
such warlike preparation is not at all to Bodily's taste – he soliloquizes –

G.ii.*rev.*

> I had leuer kepe as many flese
> Or wyld hares in an opyn lese
> as vndertake that

– whereupon he is interrupted by Wrath, breaking in all warlike and
crying –

> Wherebe these knaues that make thys aray
> BODYLY Mary they be gon that other way

– and then he implies that he did not at first recognize Wrath because he was 'thus defensybly arayd'.

Bodily Lust's last line is not entirely clear. I have already quoted
it as evidence for the double screens-entrance. As I see it, Wrath in
his war-gear comes in by a door. But it is implicit that he has met no
one on his way. He then calls for certain people, namely the 'knaves

that make this array'. The word *array* can mean (according to the
O.E.D.) an arrangement in line or ranks, especially martial order;
therefore I suppose he is asking for the persons who are preparing
for the battle – that is to say, for Man and his party. But since Man
has just gone out, and since Wrath manifestly did not meet him as
he came in, then the argument is for two doors; and thus for the
hall screens once more.

Wrath would now appear to storm off in search of them, leaving
Envy behind to speak with Bodily Lust. Envy has not been mentioned before, and Bodily who is very disinclined for battle annoys
him by proclaiming –

G.iii.   I wyll not com where strokys be [. . .]

and then he attempts to scuttle away. Now again there follows a
curious involvement of the audience; Envy cries out in rage to the
bystanders at the door –

G.iii.*rev.*   Hold hym in syrs I you requyre

– but (of course) in vain –

                         alas wold ye not at my desyre
                         Do so myche for me [. . .] [?]

There follows some bye-play in which Man returns and too clearly
sees that most of his company are going to desert him. There are
some entrances and exits, and then Man goes off with Glotony and
Wrath leaving Envy to continue his grumbling; then –

H.i.   Goddys body here cometh Pryde
                        as crank as a pecok [!]

– and Envy tells Pryde that Man has taken Pryde's office away
whereat Pryde, who has spent much on horses and gear, runs off to
hide.

Then Sensuality makes an appearance again and hears from Envy
a speech about the conflict. This speech gives a strange impression
that the battle (which Pryde has so conveniently missed) has taken
place – or even that it is still taking place at that very moment. And
one is led to be sharply interested in the issue; will Man be betrayed
by his forces? The tumultuous comings and goings create an atmosphere of impending climax. And thus what follows comes as a
complete surprise; Envy is saying –

		But now in ernest Sensualyte
H.ii.		tell me whan thys fray shalbe
		I pray ye hartely SENSUA. What agaynst Rea[*son*]
H.ii.*rev.*	ENUY.	ye the same
	SENSUA	Tushe they be agreed in payn of shame
		and good cumpany they kepe
	ENUY	Agreed q*uod*'a / in the mare name
		Mary syr that were a game
		to make some of vs wepe [*!*]
	SENSUA	Wepe or laugh man so yt ys
		and who trow ye ys the causer of thys
	ENUY.	Who [*?*]
	SENSUA	Age the deuyll hym quell
	ENUY.	Why ys age now com in place
	SENSUA	Ye . . . and what trow ye more
		thys age hath done
	ENUY.	What [*?*]
	SENSUA	By my fayth he hath brought in Reason [*!*]
		In suche wyse that at no season
		Nothyng can be wrought
		But Reason must be called therto [. . .]

This is really the end of the dramatic part of the Interlude. The two leave to try to find their fellows, and then a far graver atmosphere descends as Man enters and meekly humbles himself before Reason. After this, each of the Virtues comes in and addresses Man improvingly. He finally desires to be led out to speak with Repentance. Reason resumes and fills in till Man returns; he concludes –

I.iiii.		O here cometh / he that I loke for
		Syr haue ye done as I wylled you to do
	MAN.	ye that haue I don [. . .]
	REA.	[. . .]
		and greter reward / thou shalt therfore wyn
		Than he that neuer in hys lyfe dyd syn [. . .]
		Then they syng some goodly ballet.

The names of the players.

Nature.	Wreth.	Lyberalyte.
Man.	Enuy.	Chastyte.
Reson.	Slouth.	Good occupacyo*n*.
Sensualyte.	Glotony.	Shamefastnes.
Innocencye.	Humylyte.	Mundus.
Worldly affeccyo*n*.	Charyte.	Pacyence.
Bodyly lust.	Abstynence.	Pryde.

I have tried to make clear various details that I think played a part in a presentation of *Nature*; before I leave the play I would like to refer to an occasion when it was possible to put the parts together to make something nearer the living effect. In 1969 the Central Office of Information arranged a British Week in Tokyo. Part of this consisted of a Shakespeare Exhibition in the Keio Department Store. As a prelude to this I made four exhibits to suggest the sources of the Shakespearean stage.

Each of these exhibits consisted firstly of an actual, untouched photograph of some contemporary setting blown up to five feet by four feet. This blow-up was next faced with a series of three transparent sheets with four-inch intervals between them. On these sheets, various figures were sketched to animate the scene and show a play in action. The first of these exhibits showed an episode at the beginning of *Nature*, and it is reproduced in Pl. 2. The moment is when Sensuality exclaims at Nature – 'What . . . haue I none intresse aswell as reason / or innocency . . . thus am I set a syde . . .'

The setting chosen for the photographic background here was the end of the Great Hall at Haddon Hall, Derbyshire, showing the screens which date from about 1475. In order to give as nearly as possible a three-dimensional impression of the depth of the hall, and thus of the acting, the farthest sheet contains only the distant figures near the screens – that is to say the groups of standing spectators and the figure of Nature in her seat. Next, on the centre sheet are figures about the centre of the hall, showing Man with his nurse, Innocence, by his side and Reason behind her; on a slightly larger scale (as being farther up the hall) is the protesting Sensuality; to the far left and right are glimpses of diners seated at the side tables. On the nearest sheet are seen the figures at the upper end of the hall; chief of these is World looking down on the scene from his chair, and Worldly Affeccyon standing behind him bearing the garments with which to clothe Man in his arms. As well as these, there are shown (somewhat conventionally) indications of some of the principal diners who would be seated at the High Table on the dais.

The whole thus makes an attempt to people an actual place with impressions, or 'ghosts', of the figures who might have been present at the performance, and to dispose them in regard to the spatial features of that place as the evidence of the Interlude suggests.

The remaining three exhibits in this series will be described in later parts of this book.

5 *Fulgens and Lucrece*

The other play of Medwall's is in a lighter vein. The sole surviving copy is now in the Henry E. Huntingdon Library and its title-page reads:

> Here is conteyned a godely interlude of Fulgens Cenatoure of Rome. Lucres his doughter. Gayus flaminius. & Publi*us* Corneli*us*. of the disputacyon of noblenes. & is deuyded in two p*a*rtyes / to be played at ii. tymes. Co*m*pyled by mayster Henry medwall. late chapelayne to ye ryght reuerent fader in god Johan Morton cardynall & Archebysshop of Cau*n*terbury.

On the title-page of *Nature* Medwall had been described as 'chapleyn' to Cardinal Morton, in *Fulgens* it may be noticed he is 'late chapelayne'. The play is clearly specified as being in two parts, and the phrase 'to be played at ii. tymes' suggests an interval between the parts longer than the ten or fifteen minutes usual today; on this see above pp. 85–7

Below the title there is printed a woodcut of two figures; some consideration needs to be given to this (see Fig. 4). The picture has been assessed in two very different ways. It has been welcomed as a unique item of evidence showing two precise pieces of theatrical costume for two specific characters in fifteenth-century drama; and it has been totally discredited as a mere item picked at random from a stock of printer's decorations all designed quite independently of any text. This was a general custom; to give some examples – the blocks used by Wynkyn de Worde, the printer of *Hyckescorner* (c. 1513), show two pages of figures (see Figs. 6 and 7). None of those on the first page has anything to do with the play, but the central figure in the top row on the second page shows an old man wearing a long gown and a cap; above him is a scroll in which is printed the name 'Pyte'; this is one of the characters in *Hyckescorner*.

Yet this same block was also used by the printer of the 'Lambeth Palace' fragment of *The Interlude of Youth* (c. 1528), as can be seen in Fig. 9, for the righthand figure of the trio at the opening of the script, but this time with the name-scroll left blank.

Again, the block of the left-hand figure of this 'Lambeth Palace' trio was used once more by the printer William Middleton as the left-hand one of the three figures in his edition of *The Foure PP*, see Fig. 13. Again the scroll is above the head, but again it is empty.

Further, the block of the right-hand figure in *The Foure PP* was used again as the right-hand figure of the William Copland edition of *The Interlude of Youth* (c. 1560), see Fig. 11. Once more the scroll above is blank.

Again, there is among the blocks in *Hykescorner* a figure labelled 'Perseue.' (Fig. 7, lower right), but though Perseverance is certainly one of the characters in the play, he is specifically described there as wearing the dress of a priest or doctor, while the block shows a figure in knightly armour with a helmet, sword and halberd. Thus there is little doubt that the blocks of figures used generally to decorate the printed editions of Interludes were arbitrarily chosen.

All the same, returning now to the particular block in *Fulgens*, a third assessment can be made of the picture. Even if it has no direct connexion with what the actors looked like, it must have a certain indirect connexion that is too important to be discounted because, however this woodcut originated, it must represent a

FIG. 4. The woodcut from the title-page of Medwall's *Fulgens and Lucres*
(published sometime before 1520)

96

couple in normal period dress more or less contemporary with the date of the printing of the book.

But beyond this there is a still more important point; the printer of this book was John Rastell. This is important because in the first place Rastell (c. 1475–1536) was himself a man of presumably some culture, since he married Sir Thomas More's sister, Elizabeth, and Sir Thomas More was pretty closely associated with the ways of players since in his young days he would 'sodenly sometymes stepp in among the players, and never studyinge for the matter, make a parte of his owne there presently amonge them' (see Roper's *More*); moreover More had been a page in the court of Cardinal Morton as Medwall had. But in the second place and more importantly still, Rastell himself was very closely associated with the theatre; besides being the author of at least one good Interlude, *The Four Elements* (and some say of *Calisto and Melibea* also), he devised ornamental roofs at the Field of the Cloth of Gold (1520), erected a pageant by Paul's Gate in 1522 with a dome and a cloud with an angel in it, and designed another pageant at Greenwich in 1527 with an astronomical subject, called *The Father of Heaven*; and he seems to have had a stage built in his own garden (on this see below in Section 12). But possibly most remarkable of all in this connexion is that he with his wife and a taylor actually made costumes for players, and ran a sort of hiring agency for such things. (Also, though it is not relevant to the above, Rastell's daughter, Joan, in her turn married an Interlude-writer and player, John Heywood himself.)

It seems then that Rastell's knowledge of theatrical matters was both a wide and an intelligent one. With this in mind, picture him in his printing establishment choosing, or being responsible for the choice of, a suitable block to decorate *Fulgens* – a play by the man who had been chaplain at that same court where his own brother-in-law had been page. Rastell would scarcely have chosen or sanctioned a block that was conspicuously unsuitable to the play – he would, for example, be very unlikely to have passed it if he knew that the performers in *Fulgens* had worn classical Roman costume. However, I grant that this reasoning alone might be insufficient to justify spending further thought on the matter; but there is yet another consideration.

A contemporary document such as this cannot avoid conveying a certain amount of significant information to a serious student. To take a modern analogy; suppose the book of some play of the year 1900 were found by a historian three centuries hence, with nothing

97

in the way of illustrations but a random advertisement at the end showing a picture of a contemporary lady in her corsets. It might be quite conclusively proved by scholars that that advertisement had nothing directly to do with the characters in the play. But it would still remain a fact that any designer basing on that advertisement and capable of reading its information could produce a costume-design for a presentation of that play which would not be entirely lacking in historical correctness. In one essential it would be more accurate than many period costume-designs are – that is, it would be correct in silhouette line.

In the same way, though the two figures on the title-page of *Fulgens* may not have been drawn with any intention of representing persons in the play, there is no doubt that the designer who based two dresses for a revival of *Fulgens* upon them would not be committing a solecism.

The only risk would be if Rastell had, because the play dealt with the past, deliberately chosen a picture of two people in a style many years earlier than the date of the play. But this is not so; a simple period-costume assessment of the fashions shown sets the year about 1495 or 1500.

Thus, I believe the lady's costume can be accepted as something that Lucrece might have worn. The man's costume is less likely to suit the dignified Fulgens, but it would be very fitting for one of the suitors, with its gay feathers.

Accepting the above, in what surround should the figures be imagined? The old Hall at Lambeth Palace is no longer as it was in Cardinal Morton's time, but the figures may be visualized against the nearly contemporary screens of Haddon Hall as for the performance of *Nature*. Concerning the particular screens here, it is likely that they had originally been more in the form shown in Fig. 3, that is in three distinctly separate sections possibly connected at the top simply by a cross-beam spanning the hall. The gallery in the present hall at Haddon is supposed to be a little later than the screens themselves. The point is worth noting as a possible influence on the development of Interlude presentation; in the earlier period screens were generally without galleries, but sometime in the late fifteenth century the entry passage behind began to be roofed over and the top adapted as a gallery, and as a consequence the contemporary Interluders might have to work in surroundings that varied from hall to hall. In some they would find no gallery, in others they might be tempted to modify their show and make use of this new upper feature. But it would clearly be, in the event, a matter for choice. So, with such a background picture in mind I turn to the text of the play.

Ostensibly its main subject is the great debate which the title-page well names 'the disputacyon of noblenes' – or, whether true nobleness lies in high birth or in humble virtue. In fact, however, the actual disputation is limited to some 400 lines in the second part of the play; nearly all the remainder is a gay romp around the events that led up to that disputation.

I have used the facsimile edition of the unique Quarto published in the Henry E. Huntington Facsimile Reprints, No. 1, with introduction by Seymour de Ricci (New York, 1920).

The opening of the play is as carefully studied for effect as that of *Nature*, though the effect is by entirely opposite means. The picture of the bustling banquet hall with its audience is the same, but there is no quiet placing of a pair of seats followed by a long prologue including the silent World. Instead it opens with an entrance as forceful as Pryde's was; straight away a fellow bursts through the throng at the screens jostling the bystanders and striding out on the hall floor, and he shouts 'Ah! For God's will . . . .!' – an ejaculation deliberately calculated to make everyone break off gossiping and stare at him. Then he asks in feigned surprise 'What mean you sirs to stand so still?'

It is interesting that no name is given to this character. He is neither an impersonation of some quality nor does he stand for anyone in the story. He is a perfectly ordinary anonymous man, ordinarily dressed. He is indicated by the letter 'A', and his fellow who enters later is indicated similarly by the letter 'B'. The text of the opening lines is –

Intrat A dicens.

> A For goddis will
> what meane ye syrs to stond so still

What response this might evoke from the bystanders, stimulated and amused by its effrontery and already flushed by their banquet, one cannot be certain. But the frequency of such kinds of address in Interludes suggests that the performers were quite prepared to stand up to whatever backchat they evoked. The actor here might have called out the first of these two lines from the passage behind the screens, then pushed through the crowd round the door during the second line, and, disengaging himself from them, walked out, into the body of the hall for his following lines:

> Haue not ye etyn & your full
> And payd no thinge therfore

After pausing to let that sink in, he changes from attack to a sort of grim encouragement –

> I wys syrs thus dare I say
> He that shall for the shott pay
> Vouch saueth. that ye largely assay
> Suche mete as he hath in store

– a gesture to the High Table as he indicates who in fact is 'paying the shot'. (The special full-stop after the word 'Vouch saueth' is pretty certainly an actor's note to leave a fractional pause there, so as to give him an effect to play with in the rest of the line.) He now goes on:

> I trow your disshes be not bare
> Nor yet ye do the wyne spare
> Therefore be mery as ye fare
> ye ar welcom eche oon
> Unto this house with oute faynynge
> But I meruayle moche of one thinge.

Again a suggestive full-stop in mid-sentence. A pause here would certainly stimulate attention as he glanced round the faces before he went on. (The allusion to 'this house' and to the 'welcom' are closely parallel with Mankind's allusion and welcome to Mercy in our first play, and would suggest, I believe, a similar setting and atmosphere.) He then proceeds to say why he marvels, namely:

> That after this mery drynkynge
> And good recreacyon
> There is no wordes amonge this presse
> Non sunt loquel[a]e ne*que* sermones
> But as it were men in sadnes
> Here ye stonde musynge
> where aboute I can not tell
> Or some els praty damesell
> For to daunce and sprynge

The editors, Boas and Reed, remind us that the Latin quotation is from *Psalms* xix – 'The heavens declare the glory of God; and the firmament sheweth his handywork. Day unto day uttereth speech, and night unto night sheweth knowledge. *There is no speech nor language*, their voice is not heard.' So the quotation would be a calculated piece of licence for a Cardinal's hall, amounting near to blasphemy.

The frequent references to spectators who are standing may have a particular significance. Clearly most of the spectators in the body of the hall and at the High Table would be sitting since as yet their 'disshes be not bare', but for a special banquet such as we shall find this is, many more people would have to be accommodated, and would have to eat when and where they could. These, as I have said, might stand congregated round the screens entrances. The player has already alluded to them as he came in through the screen doors. But now he would appear to have strolled right round the hall, broadcasting his comments indifferently in a sort of circular tour (such as we find characters making on a larger scale in *The Castle of Perseverance* played in a Round), and at this point he will have neared the screens and the standing crowd again. He ends with four particular lines that are not only a build-up for the next step in the action, but afford the justification for what I have just pictured. He says – facing the standing and 'musynge' people whom he has accused of looking for a dancing girl, and snapping out suddenly at one of them:

> Tell me what calt is it not so
> I am sure here shalbe some what a do
> And I wis I will know it or I go
> Withoute I be dryuyn hens

Clearly these lines might indicate he is on the point of going out again. They might evoke a ripple of general amusement as well as an embarrassed grin from the man so discourteously addressed as 'What d'you call it'. But how does it continue? The man naturally cannot answer. But another actor can, and he is directed to enter at this precise point. He is the man called 'B', and he it is who will take it upon himself to answer A's question.

Such a confrontation is certainly more effective if the two actors are relatively close to one another, than if one of them had been at the top of the hall while the other had just entered down at the screens. This new actor is very specially dressed, as we shall see. The text continues –

Intrat B.

[B.]   Nay nay hardely man I vndertake
           No man wyll suche mastryes make
           And it were but for the maner sake

> Thou maist tary by licence [. . .]
> Among other men and see the pley
> I warand no man wyll say the nay.

So A is not after all going out. I take it that the second and third lines in this speech mean something like: No one will go so far as to drive you away, if only because it would not be good manners. But the especial interest of this speech as I see it is in the engineering of the last two lines.

It may be difficult at first to credit the players of this early period with that agility of mind, quickness of pick-up and ear for contrived effect that a modern music-hall artiste has; this is partly because so many authorities have implicitly belittled the Interluders' abilities by referring to their theatre as crude, vulgar and primitive. But I see no justification whatever not to suppose that here these two would not make the most of this opportunity; and so, when B rounds off his answer with, in effect – 'No one is going to throw you out' – he is offering an admirable cue for A to reply swaggeringly 'You needn't tell me. I'd like to see them try!' ('I thinke it well euyn as ye say That no man wyll me greue') – and then suddenly catch his breath. Through his swagger there has sprung to his mind what B really meant in his last-but-one line; and he concludes with a sort of double-take –

> But [. . .] I pray you tell me that agayn
> Shall here be a play. [?]

– and B's reply could not be crisper or in a neater syncopation of response; he simply says, 'ye for certeyn.' And the full-stop is in the original text.

Now the whole atmosphere is free to change; an idea has been planted in A's head to the effect that it would greatly amuse him to get a chance to see this play. Another significant full-stop comes after his next line as he resumes –

> By my trouth therof I am glad and fayn.
> And [= *if*] ye will me beleue
> Of all the worlde I loue suche sport
> It dothe me so myche plesure and comfort
> And that causith me euer to resort
> wher suche thing is to do

This is a particularly interesting speech. It is incontrovertible evidence that the present play, *Fulgens*, could not have been by any means a unique example of 'suche thing', for A loved such sports and 'euer' reported to watch them. It is indeed sad to think that there are so few other plays to survive. A offers us a witness to the one-time frequency of such shows and, at the same time, an advertisement for playgoing thrown in gratuitously; and his point will be repeated later.

The next two lines bring a further delight; speaking perhaps in a silkier tone now as one who feels considerably impressed, A asks –

> I trowe your owyn selfe be oon
> Of them that shall play

– but this is sharply disclaimed by B with, 'Nay I am none.' Then after pulling himself up in resentment, as the check of the full-stop here suggests, he goes on –

> I trowe thou spekyst in derision
> To lyke me ther to.

Now A hastens to apologize, and the reason he gives for his mistake adds a gay piece of colour to the picture –

> A. Nay I mok not ye well
> For I thought verely by your apparell
> That ye had bene a player
> B. Nay neuer a dell.
> A. Than I cry you mercy.
> I was to blame / lo therfor I say
> Ther is somyche nyce aray
> Amonges these galandis now aday
> That a man shall not lightly
> Know a player from a nother man
> But now to the purpose wher I began
> I see well here shalbe a play than.

I think one thing is certain; whether the playwright was a shrewd craftsman or just wrote by chance – whether the actors really made as much of the lines as I have suggested or whether they reeled off their speeches dully and let them all fall flat – there is still material here for the most sparkling and sophisticated nonsense. It would surely have been a little odd for it not to have been relished! But to continue; B replies –

> ye that ther shall doutles
> And I trow ye shall like it well

A. It semeth than that ye can tell
 Sumwhat of the mater
B. Ye I am of counsell
 One tolde me all the processe

What could be more engaging than meeting someone who really
had inside information from behind the scenes! A's and B's heads
must now come close together:

A. And I pray you what shall it be:

Again the full-stop. B draws his breath to impart, and this scene of
bye-play now draws to its conclusion:

B. By my fayth as it was tolde me
 More than ones or twyse
 As fare as I can bere it awaye
 All the substaunce of theyr play
 Shall procede this wyse.
  when thempire of rome was in such floure
 That all the worlde was subgett to the same
 Than was there an nobill senatour
 And as I remember fulgens was his name
 whiche had a doughter [. . . *etc. etc.*]

From this point onwards, a new test is laid upon the players; the
test of switching from sharp dialogue into a very long solo speech
without allowing the atmosphere to drop or the audience's attention to wander. B now gives his summary of the play in no less than
eight 7-line stanzas – 56 lines of solid speech. One is reminded of
the story put about by Payne Collier that 'The fyndyng of Troth' by
'Mayster Midwell' was so long 'yt was not lykyd . . . the Kyng departyd befor the end to hys chambre.' There are certainly passages
in *Fulgens* where a modern actor would be happier to make some
cuts.

These 56 lines do nothing to advance the action. They merely
describe the situation as it will be at the opening of the play. Their
whole gist is contained in one of the stanzas which says, concerning
Lucrece's two suitors, that public opinion –

Hade both these men in lyke fauour & reuerence
Supposing they had bene of lyke condycion
yet this seyd woman of inestimable prudence
Sawe that there was some maner of difference
For the whiche her answere she differred & spared
Tyll both theyre condycions were openly declared

Not only is the situation at the opening of the play described in this long speech, but even the final decision that Lucrece is to make between her two suitors is anticipated so that in fact nothing of the plot is left to be unfolded. It is clear that Medwall had no particular interest in that aspect of a dramatist's technique which involves keeping an audience in suspense until an eventual *dénouement*. His dependence was purely on the interest to be evoked by the chain of incidents on the way to a conclusion that was pre-decided. And these incidents are almost all limited to surprises in the behaviour of A and B towards the actors, as the story is presented. The first of these surprises is that A thoroughly disagrees with the conclusion of the plot as B explains it – namely, that Lucrece chooses the poor but virtuous suitor –

> By my fayth but yf it be euyn as ye say
> I wyll aduyse them to change that co*n*clusion
> What [*!*] wyll they afferme that a chorles son
> Sholde be more noble than a gentilman born [. . .]

– but eventually he washes his hands of the matter and consoles himself with the thought that –

> . . . there can no man blame vs two
> For why in this matter we haue nought to do

With this B agrees and then, incidentally, makes reference to an individual who is apparently a Master of Ceremonies on this occasion:

> we no god wott no thing at all
> Saue that we come to see this play
> As farre as we may by the leue of the marshall

There was then some measure of control of entry by an official on these private occasions. B continues by saying that he has

> [. . .] sene by fore this day
> Of suche maner thingis in many a gode place

– thus giving the impression of being quite a seasoned playgoer, and confirming thereby that though *Fulgens* may nowadays be considered to be the earliest surviving secular comedy in English, yet in its own time there were and had been many more of its kind. A and B nod their heads over this, and then come to the conclusion that the audience will not have any reason to be offended whichever way the verdict goes at the disputation because –

> [. . .] why shulde they care
> I trow here is no man of the kyn or sede
> Of either partie / for why they were bore
> In the cytie of Rome as I sayd before
> Therefor leue all this doutfull question [. . .]

– and the argument is thus peacefully reconciled.

Immediately after this there is a break in atmosphere and the formal anticipation of an entrance to come; B exclaims –

> Pees no moo wordes for now they come
> The plears bene euyn here at hand.

– A replies, and the two go on talking for another twelve lines before the direction comes in the text – 'Intrat Fulgens'. This delaying of an entrance, or to put it more accurately this calling attention to an entrance several lines before the character has come in, is a striking characteristic of Interlude technique, and it continues right into the full Elizabethan drama. Without the knowledge of the conditions imposed by the screens it might seem meaningless; but having realized these, it is very easy to appreciate the sudden sensation and turning of heads and backing out of the way on the part of the crowd by the doors that must inevitably have heralded the coming of a new character into the hall. It would be almost impossible for the actors on the floor not to react to this sensation and to the hold-up. All entrances would be at least slightly delayed, and so it would be impossible in these conditions for any player to make a sudden dramatic appearance with perfect timing because, unless the screens entrances had been clear, no player could tell to a second how long it would take to come through. It would be equally difficult to make an 'unexpected' entrance. In consequence of all this it would be inevitable that the players should try to get the effect from an entrance by some other means than its timing; one such means is used here – the anticipated, or heralded-and-delayed entrance. In much the same category is the 'Yonder-he-cometh' entrance which marks Elizabethan technique, and which developed from this, as will be shown in later plays. The lines here which fill in before the actual entrance are not uninteresting; A looks towards the screens and says

> So thei be so selp [? *help*] me god & halydome
> I pray you tell me where I shall stand.
> B. Mary stand euyn here by me I warand
> Geue rome there syrs for god a vowe
> Thei wold cum in if thei myght for you.

A.   ye but I pray the what calt tell me this
     who is he that now comyth yn.
B.   Mary it is fulgence the senatour.
A.   ye is: what the father of the forseide virgyn.
B.   ye forseth he shall this matere begyn.
A.   And wher is feyr doughter lucrece.
B.   She cometh Anon I say hold thy pece.

Intrat fulgens dicens. [. . .]

Note that this is a change from *Nature*; there there were no entrance directions in the whole play; here already three entrances have been clearly directed.

What happens now to A and B, who have no exit directions, appears from the sequel to be that they gather on the side to 'watch' the play, and either join the group at the screens or sit together on the edge of one of the tables. They are now out of the action for 160 lines.

During this period there takes place an entirely different section of the play, and one conceived in the convention of rhetoric. With this convention I think we today might feel less at home than with the previous colloquial dialogue of the comedians A and B. We are much less used to rhetoric in acting than the audiences of the late fifteenth century were or, indeed, than audiences continued to be until into the Georgian period. There may be here the beginnings of the technique that was to lead to Heroic Drama, for heroic drama could not have come into existence without the rhetorical delivery. However these thoughts might turn out, one thing is clear; Fulgens could not have held the audience's attention if he delivered the particular speeches here given to him in terms of current prose; they must have been 'lifted' in some way. The remarkable thing from a modern actor's point of view about his opening speech is its length. I have pointed out how the player, B, was tested with an unbroken speech of 56 lines describing the plot of the play to come; his task was relatively light compared with that of Fulgens. Fulgens has to come in and, starting cold, address to the spectators an opening speech of no less than thirteen consecutive 7-line stanzas, a total of 91 lines in which he adds practically nothing of interest to what we have heard already.

Some idea of Fulgens' task as he takes the floor alone with spectators surrounding him on four sides can be suggested by the following fragments, reducing the 91 lines to 16. He opens with a pious prayer:

107

Euerlastyng ioy with honoure and praise.
Be vn to our most drad lord & sauyour
whiche doth. vs help & [. . .]
[. . .] of his grace is euer indifferent
All be yt he diuersely commytteth his talent.
To some he lendith the sprete of prophecy. [. . .]
To some litterature and speculatyf science [. . .]
when I consider and call to my remembraunce
The prosperous lyfe that I haue all wey [. . .]
       [. . .] well may I [. . .] pay
Grete prayse and thankes to the hye kynge [. . .]
Than haue I a wyfe of gode condicyon [. . .]
[. . .] I haue a doughter in whom I delight [. . .]
She is so discrete and sad in all demeanyng [. . .]
And also she is now of gode & ripe age
To be amannes fere [*mate*] by wey of mariage [. . .]

– and then at length the essential last three lines –

It was the chief cause of my hider cummyng
To haue a communication in this same matere
with on[e] Cornelius cam there non suche here [?]

Since Fulgens is alone, this direct question must be addressed to
the spectators: Has Cornelius been here? It is the cue for the next
step in the action of the play, the entry of Cornelius, the rich and
idle suitor, with an apology –

                    Intrat publius Cornelius dicens
yes now am I come here at the last
I haue taried long I cry you mercy.

They politely hedge round the main subject of marriage for a
while but Cornelius reaches it at length, only to hear Fulgens declare that he cannot fully answer for his daughter –

For me semyth it were ryght expedient
That we know therein her mynde before
Or euer we shold commune therof any more [. . .]

– a kindly recommendation which Cornelius accepts a little grudgingly. He urges Fulgens to put in a good word for him with
Lucrece. Fulgens agrees to essay 'her mynde therin', and presumably goes out. Cornelius is left apparently feeling a little inadequate
for the situation, but through this inadequacy he paves the way
for the resumption of the action, for he says to himself –

> Now a wise felow that had sumwhat a brayne
> And of suche thingis had experience
> Such one wolde I with me retayne
> to gyue me counseile and assistence [. . .]

and thereupon he makes that special and personal appeal to the spectators which I have already noted as being essential to my reconstruction – he asks the audience in general

> So many gode felowes as byn in this hall
> And is ther non syrs among you all
> That wyll enterprise this gere

(but obviously there follows only silence, because he concludes:)

> Some of you can do it if ye lust
> But if ye wyl not than I must
> Go seche a man ellis where
>
> Et exeat.

A and B would seem to have let this opportunity pass unseized; for Cornelius has turned and walked out of the hall on his quest for a helper without their attracting his notice. But immediately he has gone B springs into action, to be quickly restrained by A –

> B. Now haue I spied a mete office for me
> For I wyl be of counsell and I may
> with yonder man
>
> A. Pece let be
> Be god thou wyll distroy all the play

B retorts, with some reason, that 'the play began neuer till now' and reaffirms his intention. A enquires in some distress

> A. And what shall I do in the meane while
> B. Mary thou shalt com in anone
> with a nother pageant
> A. who I
> B. ye be saynt Johan
> A. what I neuer vside suche thing before

We are here introduced to an unusual application of this curious English word, 'pageant', it is used as equivalent to 'episode'.

The *O.E.D.* is reticent about the derivation of the word, remarking that its ultimate origin is obscure. Among the earlier readings, however, is the Anglo-Latin form, *pagina*. The word 'page' (in the sense of one side of a leaf in a book) is also from the

Latin *pagina*; and among the definitions of 'page' is 'An episode, such as would fill a page in a written history.' It is most likely then that Medwall is using this word 'pageant' correctly, in this early sense, so that B would be saying to A, 'You shall come in soon in another episode.' In the sequel B goes on to tell A to 'abide here still' while he himself goes off to make his bargain with Cornelius, first adding:

> B. when thou seest me com in ageyn
> Stond euyn still and kepe thy contenaunce
> For when Gayus flamyneus comyth in
> Than must thou thy pageaunt begyn

Shortly after, B has the direction, 'Exeat', and A is left to soliloquize for 16 lines, after which 'Intrat fulgeus lucres & ancilla & dicat.' – so the great moment to which A had looked forward has now arrived and there come from the screens, the 'feyre doughter' Lucrece and her father and her maid, called here Ancilla, but otherwise Joan.

The action now turns to a dialogue between Fulgens and Lucrece in which Lucrece refuses (but not altogether disingenuously) to make any decision about the suitors that shall not be in reference to her father's advice, and he equally waits upon her choice. After their talk, he has the direction, 'Et exeat.' Lucrece bids him farewell and there follows an unusually explicit direction for her to turn over in her mind how she will deal with this matter: 'Et facta aliqua pausation*e* dicat lucres.' After making some pause, then, Lucrece begins to speak her thoughts to her maid, but is suddenly cut off in mid-sentence by the maid saying:

> AN. Peace lady ye must forbere
> Se ye not who cometh here
> LU. who is it wot ye ere [*ever*]
> AN. It is gayus flamyneus parde [. . .]

Again, therefore, capital is made of a delayed entrance. The newcomer is the less rich but more worthy of the two suitors (and Lucrece's favourite). The maid has time to catch sight of him and to announce his name while the crowd round the entrance is still hiding him from Lucrece, who is thus supposed not to recognize him, whereas of course she knows him very well. Then, in the moments still intervening before Gaius's complete entrance, Lucrece has time to exclaim – 'Ey gode lorde how wyste he For to fynde me here'! (Intrat gayus flam.) He comes with a compliment on his lips beginning 'yes gode lady where so euer ye go . . .' thus implying that he has heard her last words. There follows typical cross-talk in which Lucrece at length, after refusing to say anything definite about her choice, states that she will refer the matter again to her father and yet – rather delightfully – she reveals her mind for a moment with a nice remark –

> For if he like you aswell as I
> your mynde in this behalf shalbe sone easid [. . .]

Gaius is satisfied. Lucrece goes out with her maid, leaving him alone. And A's 'pageant' is now ready to begin as this direction indicates – And let Lucrece go out; then let A, accosting Gaius Flaminius, say to him thus –

> Et exeat Lucres. deinde A. acced*ens*
> ad Gayum fla. & dicat ei sic.
>
> Syr ye seme a man of grete honoure
> And that moueth me to be so bolde [. . .] [*etc.*]

The word *accedens* is interesting; it is an unusually precise word suggesting that, after Lucrece and her maid have gone out through the screens, A comes into the action not by a formal entrance (since he has gone out) but by slipping forward from that part of the crowd with which he had merged earlier, and going up to Gaius and accosting him – possibly walking across some considerable space of the floor before he does so.

Once in conversation, he frames a warning about the risks of trusting to 'feyre wordes' and insinuates himself into Gaius's service as a go-between in a speech which clearly shows he has overheard Gaius's talk with Lucrece. Moreover, he shows that B is not far distant, for he calls to him to witness his good character –

> I haue no more acqueyntaunce with in this hall [. . .]
> Syr wyll not ye for my trouth wndertake

– to which B immediately agrees, thus proving that he was present in the crowd all the time. Gaius accepts A on this testimonial and puts him directly to work by entrusting him with a message for Lucrece; then, 'Et exeat gayus flam.' The two now congratulate each other on having both entered into service. B tells A how comfortable his new position is and gives some interesting details of the sumptuousness of Cornelius' wardrobe. Their gossip is brought to a halt with their realization that they both ought to be going about their respective masters' businesses.

We have now reached the 837th line of the 1432 lines which go to the First Part of the play; just over the half-way point. From now to the end of the Part there is no action whatever concerning the plot except a brief proposal for a meeting between Lucrece and Gaius at the end; all the action is restricted to the comedy of A and B and their relations with Joan, Lucrece's maid. Included among all the rest is a comic duel between them for her favours, taking the form of some sort of grotesque cock-fight in which their arms are bound, and staves put 'thorow here' – but without any further explanatory detail.

In this long passage of comic business there are a number of details relevant to the presentation technique. For instance, near the beginning, at l. 833, A leaves B alone, but we do not find the usual Latin direction 'exeat'; instead we have a quite unusual direction, and in English – 'Avoyde the place A.' This is followed some twenty lines later by another English direction, again in unusual form – 'Come in the maydyn' – referring to the entrance of Joan. It seems particularly interesting to find here a phrase that is quite out of the ordinary in this play and yet one which is so like the typical entrance-invitation in a Mummer's Play, such as for instance, 'Come in Saint George'.

During the scene when Joan and B are together, there is another example of direct audience-address. A is making urgent advances to the maid who is however parrying them with success; she says, 'ye do but mocke To speke to me of ony wedlocke And I so yonge a mayde'. He picks on the word and demands insinuatingly 'Why[!] are ye a mayde[?] She returns with, 'ye[a] ellis I were to blame'. Then he asks –

> where by wote ye [*i.e. How do you know!*]
> [*She*] Mary for I ame
> [*He*] A[*h!*] that is a thinge
> Here ye not syrs what she sayth
> So resonable a cause there to she layth
> [*She*] A straw for your mockynge [. . .]

They are alone together at this point, so his appeal – Do you hear sirs, what she says! – must have been meant for the audience's delectation. One notes that in all the references to the spectators so far in this play, they are addressed as 'sirs'; the conclusion might be that no women were present. But as will be seen later it would be a wrong conclusion.

According to our standards the Interluders were unusually conscious of the audience; or, perhaps the comic players took unusual advantage of their presence. Today in a love scene on the stage, it is tacitly accepted as an essential that the players pretend they are alone with no spectators looking on. But in *Fulgens,* when A returns and finds that the maid has been left alone with B for a significant time, he expresses a fear that B may have made undue progress with her from his point of view! he says—

> A.   Haue ye two be to geder so longe [. . .]
> Mary then all is wrong
> I fere me [. . .]
> B.   Nay nay here be to many wytnes
> For to make ony syche besynes
> As thou wenest hardely

So the situation is nicely turned, and the close circle of spectators round the floor brought intimately into the show once more.

After the cock-fight alluded to above, where the two rivals' arms were tied up, Joan goes out leaving them in the lurch and still helpless, having duly slapped each of them first. Then Gaius comes in, and after some bye-play releases them. He asks A if he has delivered the message he was given to take to Lucrece; and concludes with the question – 'Spakyst thou with her'? A in replying apparently draws him aside out of earshot of B, before saying –

> ye syr dowtles
> And this is her intent
> Sche commaundyth hyr to you [*etc*].

– and he goes on to say that Lucrece will arrange a special meeting 'this nyght . . . Or to morow' at which Gaius will be told what choice she has made. The reason for supposing that A leads Gaius aside to tell him of this arrangement involves a rather complicated editorial maze. It lies in the following facts. There is no exit-direction marked for B at this point (though Boas and Reed invent one which will be discussed below), and yet B does not speak again for 34 lines, and at the end of these lines there is – somewhat surprisingly – the following direction from the second part of which it is clear that he *enters*. The direction reads –

> Et exeat gaius & A.   Intrat B.

– that is to say, 'Let Gaius and A go out. B comes in.' There is already a difficulty here in the first part, for 'exeat' is a singular verb and yet seems to be used to apply to two people. Such renderings are however found in Interludes, and may be no more out of order than it is for us today to say 'They both exit'. The main point is that B is clearly directed to enter although he has not had any previous direction to go out.

It is to be supposed, I think, that B must have politely withdrawn or been left aside at the moment when Gaius and A moved away for their private conversation. But after their exit he must come into the action again. This would imply a brief example of 'differentiation'.

The next curiosity is that after this exit of Gaius with A, and after the direction to B to enter, B speaks ten lines and is immediately replied to by A *who has just gone out.*

This might seem at first to be a misprint. But there is an explanation; namely that Gaius and A in fact go out as directed, that B's short speech of ten lines is a soliloquy, and that A after seing Gaius as far as the door and into the entry, returns undirected, and comes back again into the action in time to reply to B's speech.

What makes it almost certain that A did go out with Gaius for a brief space is that during the ensuing conversation between B and A, A expresses a fear that his master will give him a beating 'Because I haue ben so long a way Oute of his presence'; but B replies that he has information that there will be no beating, at which A asks naturally enough, how he knows, and is given the reason as follows –

> A. Nay. nay.
> I haue harde so muche syth I went hens
> That he had lityll mynd to thyn offens
> B. I pray you tell me why
> A. For as I brought my mayster on hys way
> I harde one of lucres men say
> That thy mayster hathe ben
> All this houre at her place [. . .]

– so A directly states that he 'went hens', that his purpose was to bring his master 'on hys way', and that in doing so he picked up a piece of information from one of Lucrece's men that Cornelius had been busily engaged at her house and would not have noticed A's absence. The suggestion clearly is that he picked up this piece of information just outside in the entry from a man he met as he was seeing Gaius on his way. This may involve a little 'condensation of time' – gaining such specific information in a space of ten lines of soliloquy – but it is a much less extreme use of the convention than can be found in later Interludes, for example in *Pacient Grissill*.

To turn back now and take up the Boas and Reed treatment of this passage; in their edition of *Fulgens* the curious direction is shortened and made to read '*Et exeat* gaius. *Intrat* B.', thus leaving out the reference to A altogether. But this would appear to deprive A of his chance to go out and get his information from Lucrece's man – and this he states he did do. Earlier in this sequence, Boas and Reed had (as was noted above) inserted an invented direction, '[*Exeat* B]' at their line 1286 – that is to say at the point when A first drew Gaius aside to impart his message. The editors rightly enclose this direction in square brackets to show that it is not in the original. Their justification for this interpolated direction is given in a footnote which reads as follows (the letter 'Q' in the footnote is a reference to the original Quarto edition of the play);

> S.D. *Exeat* B] *as the dialogue between* Gaius *and* A *from ll. 1287–1324 has to do with* A's *errand to* Lucres *and as after l. 1324 Q has* Et exeat gaius & A. Intrat B, B *evidently goes out after l. 1286.*

Thus, in order that A may give his message privately to Gaius, their reading is that B leaves to the extent of making a full exit, not just a drawing to one side. Now A and Gaius have their conversation and the point arrives at which the direction comes for Gaius and A to go out. This direction they change to apply only to Gaius; and here they insert another footnote;

> S.D. *Et exeat* gaius] *Et exeat* gaius & A Q. *But* B *evidently addresses* A *in l. 1325.*

– so justifying their cutting the reference to A's exit on the grounds that ten lines later he has to be speaking to B.

I would suppose, on the basis of the analysis I have given, that all this is unnecessary and that the whole passage could be performed as I have indicated without any alteration of the original Quarto text.

To go on now to the speeches and the information they contain. There are two examples of the Interluders' acceptance of the presence of the audience and of their making a feature of that presence instead of trying to pretend it away.

The first is at l. 1313. Gaius has asked A what persons will be present at the disputation, when Lucrece shall make her choice between the suitors; A answers that firstly Fulgens will be there –

> And publius cornelius hym selfe also
> with dyuerse other many moo
> Besyde this honorable audyence [. . .]

– the honourable audience, then, will be held to be as much present on that occasion as the actors, and they are to form a body of witnesses to Lucrece's decision.

The second example comes shortly afterwards, almost as if confirming the first. At l. 1329, when B in his soliloquy is remarking ruefully on the drubbing he got from Joan, he adds that –

> . . . the strokys be not so sore
> But the shame greuyth me more
> Sith that it was done
> Be fore so many as here be present [. . .]

A final point of interest in the First Part is a reference to the time of day of the performance. A says that Lucrece, in fixing the meeting at which she will give her decision –

> . . . hathe appoynted hym to be here
> Sone in the euynyng a boute Suppere
> An than he shall haue a fynall answere [. . .]

Concerning this occasion, A tells B –

> I wold not for a swan
> That thou sholdest be hens at that season
> For thou shalt here a reyal disputacyon
> Bi twext them or they haue do

(and then comes the interesting afterthought –)

> An other thing must be considred with all
> These folke that sitt here in the halle [. . .]
> Thay haue not fully dyned
> For and this play where ones ouere past
> Some of them wolde falle to fedyng as fast
> As thay had bene almost pyned
> But no forse hardely and they do [.]
> Ussher gete them goode wyne therto

> Fyll them of the best
> Let it be do or ye wyll be shent
> For it is the wyll and co*m*maundement
> Of the master of the fest
> Bnd [*And*] therfore we shall the matter for bere
> And make apoynt euyn here
> Lest we excede a mesure
> And we shall do oure labour & trewe entent
> For to play the remenant
> At my lordis pleasure
> > Finis prime partis

The concluding lines are noticeably like those which ended the First Part of *Nature*.

Part One of *Fulgens* is here shown to be written for performance during an interval between courses in a midday meal or dinner. Part Two is to follow 'in the euynyng a boute Suppere', and with it the occasion which Lucrece had appointed for the ceremony of selection of suitors or, as Medwall calls it, the 'disputacyon of noblenes'.

Part Two contains 921 lines, a little over half the length of Part One. This might seem to imply that one could interrupt a midday dinner at much greater length than one could an evening supper. But there is a qualification to be made; it is that Part Two includes a separate entertainment of indefinite length in the form of some kind of dance.

The structure of this Part is relatively simple; there is an introductory scene for the two comedians (ll. 1–130), a long gag about a bungled message involving Cornelius, B and Lucrece (ll. 131–355), the disputation of nobleness itself (ll. 356–807), and a conclusion (ll. 808–921).

In the opening, A rushes in in great haste 'For fere that I sholde come to late' and repeats the general argument of the play, going on then to justify the mixture of comedy with plot as follows:

> This was the substance of the play
> This [? *that*] was shewed here to day
> All be it that there was
> Dyuers toyes mengled yn the same
> To styre folke to myrthe and game
> And to do them solace
> The whiche tryfyllis be imp*er*tinent
> To the matter principall

> But neuer the lesse they be expedient
> For to satisfye and content
> Many a man with all
> For some there be that lokis & gapys
> Only for suche tryfles and Japys
> And some there be a monge
> That forceth lytyll of suche madnes
> But delytyth them in matter of sadnes
> Be it neuer so longe

How serious the last remark is we cannot be sure, but if it is meant seriously it would show that some spectators actually delighted in long, grave speeches.

As this introduction goes on, A implies that his relation to the other actors has changed. In Part One he took pains to pretend that he had no connexion with them, but in this Part he speaks quite directly 'Of me and my company' (almost as if he were their leader or, perhaps, their vice) and of their aim to 'content The leste that stondyth here'. Then he realizes that in his enthusiasm he has lost the thread of what he began to say:

> By godis mercy where am I now
> It were almys to wrynge me by the eare
> By cause I make suche degression
> From the matter that I began
> whan I entred the halle

Then (after this reference once more to the Hall) he goes on to remind the audience that they are to see Lucrece and her two lovers come in –

> To dyffyne thys question
> whether of them ys the more noble man [. . .]

Now he begins to berate the absent players for being late and works the old gag of pretending the show is being held up; ending –

> Let me se what is now a cloke
> A[*h!*] there com*m*yth one I here hym knoke

– from which we learn that a newcomer to a hall might have to knock before being admitted, and this would seem at first to conflict with our earlier picture of entering freely through the screens, hampered only by spectators. But I believe that what is intended

118

here is a suggestion that this visitor is in fact coming in from out-doors, and is knocking not for entrance from the screens-passage to the hall, but at the outer door for entrance from the open air to the screens-passage. For such knocking to be heard in a hall through the noise of supper it might well be that,

> He knokythe as he were wood

Then A adds to the audience –

> One of you go loke who it is

Boas and Reed, in a note on this line, say 'here again the audience is brought into the action, as one of its members opens the door to a player'. In my opinion such an idea is directly contradicted in the next speech, which is from B (who is the newcomer who has just knocked); he comes in and exclaims crossly to A –

> Nay nay all the meyny of them I wis
> Can not so moche gode
> A man may rappe tyll his naylis ake
> Or ony of them wyll the labour take
> To gyue hym an answere

This would surely seem to mean that no one among the audience did take the 'labour' to answer the door; the whole thing is merely a gag. Moreover, I think that from a player's point of view it might be detrimental to their show to allow the audience to be 'brought into the action' in any physical degree; the audience could be referred to, questioned, abused, ordered about and so on to al-most any extent, but only if the greatest care were taken to see that they did not in fact reply or respond with anything more than laughter or perhaps back-chat; and even the latter would be osten-sibly ignored by the player unless he saw he could safely make good use of it. To allow an audience any chance to take over the action and have an influence on it would be risky in any theatre (unless as a deliberate effect). To create the illusion that such a thing was just on the point of happening might be amusing, but there the actors would normally draw the line.

A reproves B tartly with –

> A. I haue grete maruell on the
> That euer thou wylt take vpon the
> To chyde ony man here [. . .]

119

The cross-talk rises to a quarrel –

> B.   Kockis body syr [. . .]
> I am com hedyr att this season
> Only at thy byddynge
> And now thou makyst to me a quarell

But they are as quickly reconciled. And they turn to discuss the arrangements for the forthcoming disputation; which reminds B that his master, Cornelius –

> [. . .] hath deuysyde
> Certayne straungers fresshly disgisyd [. . .]
> For to be here this nyght also

– and immediately A jumps to the point about these 'strangers' –

> A then I se well we shall haue A mum*m*ynge

B confirms this, and then

> Mary here he co*m*myth I haue hym aspyde
> No more wordis stonde thou a syde
> For it is he playne

With this now familiar convention of the heralded entrance (no knocking here, we notice), Cornelius comes in and begins to open the general action of the plot. In his dialogue with B he gives him a verbal message to take to Lucrece. Then he leaves and Lucrece enters; B gives her the message in a bungled and ingeniously bawdy form, and is properly rebuked by her. At length he goes out covered with shame. Now A in turn comes to Lucrece with a message from the other suitor, Gaius, which he too bungles almost as extravagantly but making use, this time, of an amusing direct appeal to the audience; he says to Lucrece on behalf of Gaius –

> And here he sendyth you a letter
> Godis mercy I had it ryght now
> Syrs is there none there a mong you
> That toke vp suche a wrytyng [?]
> I pray you syrs let me haue it agayne

– which brings, of course, the comment from Lucrece,

> ye ar a gode messanger for certeyne [. . .]

A leaves, and Cornelius next enters with his servant, B, and is told by Lucrece that he must play fair in the coming disputation. Now,

to fill in the time before the disputation begins, Cornelius proposes
to present his 'device', and asks her accordingly –

> whyle that these folke dothe tary this wyse
> wyll ye see a bace daunce after the gyse
> Of spayne. whyle ye haueno thynge to do

She agrees, and he says to B –

> Go sone and bidde them come thens a none
> And cause the mynystrells to come in beffore

To this B has a curious reply –

> Mary. as for. one of them his lippe is sore
> I trow he may not pype he is so syke
> Spele vp tamboryne ik bide owe frelike
> > Et deinde corisabunt.

We have, then, the accompanists for a Spanish base-dance summoned in the Flemish language. Boas and Reed attribute both
novelties to visits being made at the time by the Ambassadors of
Spain and of Flanders. The Latin direction signifies 'And then they
shall dance'.

When the dancers have finished their dance, Lucrece is prompted
to enquire about their nationality –

> were they of Englonde or of wales

but gets the reply from B that –

> Nay they be wylde Irissh portyngales . . .

Then B is sent off to look after the dancers' refreshment (rather like
Polonius). Now an unusual direction follows, and then a speech
showing that a certain action has taken place for which we have had
no direction:

> Dicat lucres.
> Lo here thys man ys come now
> Now may ye in your matter procede
> ye remember both what I sayde to you [. . .]

The word 'both' clearly implies that the man who 'ys come now'
is Gaius. The two suitors are thus now present before her, and all
is ready for the disputation to begin.

(A curiosity to be noted here is that there is no sign now, or at
any point in Part Two, of Fulgens himself; unless of course

he is in attendance on Lucrece, but undirected, and silent through-out.)

Lucrece outlines some preliminaries; among them (rather oddly) that she wishes that when her decision is made it shall not be told to any other persons than the two suitors. They agree. Then Cornelius says,

> Than wyll I begynne

and Gaius,

> I holde me well content

Cornelius now speaks without a break from l. 441 to l. 535, cataloguing the nobility of his ancestors and turning aside to cast aspersions on Gaius' family. Lucrece quickly checks him for thus infringing the rules of the disputation; there is a sharp ruffling of feathers and then Cornelius resumes from l. 543 to l. 584. This makes, in all, a 135-line speech during which no action is taken and nothing new introduced (with the exception of the above interruption) to vary the subject. No doubt an audience used to and interested in the art of rhetoric could take all this; but there is little to it beyond rhetoric. Cornelius at last ends,

> Now say what / ye wyll syr for I haue all doo

and Gaius takes up,

> with ryght gode will I shall go to
> So that ye will here me with as grete pacience
> As I haue harde you / [. . .]
> And what so euer I shall speke in this audience
> Eyther of myn owne merits or of hys insolence
> yet fyrst vnto you all syrs I make this request
> That it wolde lyke you to construe it to the best

– thus he is to direct his speech (as Cornelius did not appear to do) partly to the audience. He goes on from l. 585 to l. 705, that is for 120 uninterrupted lines. He attacks Cornelius unreservedly (and unchecked by Lucrece), accusing him of all bestial and voluptuous living, 'of theftis and murdres euery day', of sloth and 'cowardy and other excesse' (all this without Lucrece uttering a word of restraint!). Having torn the man's reputation to threads, he concludes –

> Now lucres [. . .] considre [. . .]
> whiche of vs twayne ye will rather alow
> More worthy for nobles to marry with you

She is about to reply when Cornelius, rather understandably, claims the right to answer the above charges; but his claim is arbitrarily disallowed.

Then Lucrece springs the one surprise of the evening. So far things had been going just as forecast; every character has done just what he or she proposed to do, and the end would appear to be a foregone conclusion. But, instead of announcing her promised decision between the two men, Lucrece introduces what seems to be a subterfuge to put them off again. She says she wants time to collect witnesses to the truth of what each has said. Thereupon the evil (and hard-done-by) Cornelius complains –

> Let me not now depart in vayne
> Not knowyng theffect of my desyre

– but Lucrece decrees,

> Syr all though it be to you a payne
> yet must ye do so euyn both twayne
> Eche of you depart hens to hys owne place [. . .]
>   [. . .] my sentence
> I shall go write it [. . .]
> And than to eyther of you both shalbe sent
> A copy of the same [. . .]

Rather lamely, they agree; and Gaius asks,

> well lucres will ye co*m*maunde me ony seruyce

She replies –

> No seruyce at all syr why say ye so
> Our lorde spede you both where so euer ye goo
>   Et exeant pub. cornelus et
>   gaius flam.

(Note that in this instance the verb is in the plural.) And so we reach the end of the action part of the plot. There is now an oddly-engineered conclusion. On being left alone after her rather off-hand dismissal of the men, Lucrece turns to the audience and proceeds to offer a justification for what she has done, beginning –

> Now som mayde happely. & she were in my case
> wolde not take that way that I do intend
> For I am fully determyned with godis grace
> So that to gaius I wyll condyscend

But at the same time she (being a good Conservative) adds she will still respect Cornelius' blood, though his 'condicyons be synfull and abiect'. Then suddenly, perhaps a little awed by her temerity, she makes the appeal to the spectators –

> I pray you all syrs as meny. as be. here
> Take not my wordis by a sinistre way

– and immediately upon her request comes an interruption which completely disregards her words; for B, whom we have forgotten through all this, cries from the fringe of the spectators,

> yes [. . .] I shall witnes bere
> where so euer I be [. . .]
> How suche a gentylwoman did opynly say
> That by a chorles son she wolde set more
> Than she wolde do by a gentylman bore [*born*]

but Lucrece protests she did *not* say that –

> For god syr the substaunce of my wordis was this

– and she repeats that she would choose virtue rather than blood *if* blood were not accompanied with 'gentil condicyons'. B immediately takes her up and puts case that a born gentleman might also –

> Haue godely maners to his birth accordyng

– and poor Lucrece is rather forced into a corner and has to admit that

> Suche one is worthy more lawde and praysyng
> Than many of them that hath their begynnyng
> Of low kynred ellis god forbede
> I wyll not afferme the contrary for my hede
> For in that case ther may be no comparyson
> But neuer the lesse I said [. . .]
> That gaius flaminius shall haue his intent
> To hym onely I shall myself apply
> To vse me in wedloke [. . .]
> So that to cornelyus I wyll neuer assent [. . .]

and so she announces to B, rather imperiously –

> ye be hys seruaunt syr go your way
> And report to your mayster euyn as I say

But B, careful for his skin, very prudently replies

> [. . .] do it your selfe for me
> I promyse you faythfully
> I wolde my mayster had be in scotland [. . .] (etc.)

– by the time he has reached the end of his protesting, however, Lucrece has gone. She does not speak again.

Instead, A insinuates himself once more, a little breathlessly, into the action, and asks,

> what now syrs how goth the game

– this presumably to the audience in general, since he uses 'syrs' in the plural; but then he speaks directly to B –

> what is this woman go [*gone*]
> B.   ye ye man.
> A.   And what way hathe she takyn

(so he has not been present during Lucrece's last conversation with B, and does not know the result of the disputation. B replies –)

> That she wolde nedis haue hym for his vertue [. . .]
> A.   Vertue what the deuyll is that

– but B admits that he cannot tell what virtue is any more than A can; all he can do is to insist, waving to the audience-witnesses –

> But this she said here opynly
> All these folke can tell

Whereupon A somewhat unexpectedly turns round and asks – and there is no indication whether he speaks rhetorically or whether he actually addresses some watching lady spectators who have slipped into the men's assembly –

> How say ye gode woman [? *women*] is it your gyse
> To chose all your husbondis that wyse

B tries to moralize on what the audience's views may be, and begins to issue a sour warning to the married men, when A cuts him suddenly short with –

> Tusshe here is no man that settyth a blank
> By thy consell [. . .]
> Speke therof no more [   ]
> But what shall we twayne do now
> B.   Mary we may goo hens whan we lyst [. . .]
> A.   why than is the play all do [*done*]
> B.   ye by my feyth and we were ons go
>   It were do streght wey

But A is still not happy; he would wish that this matter should have another conclusion. B retorts,

> ye thou art a maister mery man
> Thou shall be wyse I wot nere whan

He says that the question of nobleness is now fully defined by a woman's mind – what more could one have? And he draws towards the conclusion with –

> [. . .] And though the matter that we haue playde
> Be not percase so wele conueyde [. . .]
> yet the auctour therof desyrith
> That for this season
> At the lest ye will take it in pacience
> And yf therbe ony offence . . .
> It is onely far lacke of co*n*nynge
> And not he / but his wit ru*n*nynge
> Is there of to blame
> And glade wolde he be / and ryght fayne
> That some man of stabyll brayne
> wolde take on hym the labour and payne
> This mater to a mende
> And so he wyllyd me for to say [.]
> And that done [,] of all this play
> Shortely here we make and end

I would remind readers that I have been concerned above only with the evidence that this script offers to help in visualizing the character and technique of an early Interlude performance, and of the 'toyes mengled yn the same To styre folke to myrthe . . .' I do not want to seem to suggest that there is not in the text a very great deal that would stand much more study than I have given, particularly matters of a literary character, and such as refer to the thought of the times. But all this I leave to the specialists in order to keep myself to the one subject of presentation which has been studied much less frequently.

6 *The World and the Child*

Before returning to *Mankind* there is one other early play which offers in a small degree some relevant considerations. It is the anonymous *Interlude of the Worlde and the Chylde*. Craik dates it about 1508;

it is thus placed just over a decade later than the presumed date of *Fulgens*. But two things about the play make it seem very much more primitive than the lively work of Thomas Medwall. The first is its ancient alliterative verse; the second is a matter which will have to have some consideration in detail; it is a reference to 'seats' again, but in an old form of the word reminiscent of the references to seats in *The Castle of Perseverance* back in c. 1425.

For example, in *The Castle* (l. 836) there is Covetyse's invitation to Mankind to

> sit up ryth here in this se

and in *The World and the Child* there is this announcement from Mundus in the opening speech (l. 22)

> Lo here I sette semely in se

– and it is remarkably similar again to World's line in *The Castle* (l. 458)

> Now I sytte in my semly sale

I have given my reasons in *The Medieval Theatre in the Round* for believing that the 'se' referred to in *The Castle* was a *seat* or throne placed on a high scaffold with possibly a drawable curtain in front. There might be five or more such scaffolds situated at intervals round the perimeter of the open Place, each dedicated to the use of one particular character in the play. A technical Latin term for such a scaffold as a whole was *sedes*, a seat.

The enquiry that one is naturally prompted to make by these notable similarities of wording is, do they imply a similarity in presentation? If so, then we might have to accept that an early Interlude could on occasion be performed in a Round, or at least in a round formation. This in turn might suggest that there was some development by which the circle of scaffolds characteristic of the medieval performances in Rounds was adapted in Tudor times to indoor usage by setting a corresponding circle of seats, or chairs, on the floor of a hall.

With a hope of discovering whether this, or any prt of it, is true I turn to the text of the play.

It is available in facsimile in the *Tudor Facsimile Texts*, No. 135 (reproduced in 1909 from a 1522 edition in Trinity college Dublin). The printer was Wynkyn de Worde. The title-page reads:

Here begynneth a propre newe Interlude of the worlde and the chylde / other wyse called [Mundus & Infans] & it sheweth
of the estate of Chyldehode and Manhode.
Mundus.

The pair of square brackets is in the original. Below this is printed
a woodcut of a king sitting under a canopy, crowned, in robes, and
with a mitre and orb, see Fig. 5.

of the estate of Chyldehode and Manhode.
Mundus.

FIG. 5. From the title-page of *The Worlde and the chylde* (published 1522)

The action of the play can be divided into five episodes of varying lengths. Each consists of one dialogue. The five dialogues are
between Man on the one hand (under various names according to
the stage of his life) and on the other hand one of four other characters, Mundus, Conscyence, Foley and Perseueraunce – Conscyence
appearing in two of the dialogues, the second and the fourth:

128

Episode 1,	Mundus and Man	288 lines
Episode 2,	Conscyence and Man	242 lines
Episode 3,	Folye and Man	188 lines
Episode 4,	Conscyence and Man	32 lines
Episode 5,	Perseueraunce and Man	235 lines
	Total	985 lines

As will be noticed Episode 4 is much shorter than the others, and it is somewhat in the nature of a *reprise*.

No entrance or exit directions of any sort appear in the script.

No indications occur in the lines which give any guide at all to the occasion or place or character of the performance, saving the reference already mentioned to seats, and certain statements in the dialogue that a number of changes of costume are effected.

Episode 1 – Mundus and Man

The play begins directly with Mundus speaking:

fol.A.i.*rev.* Syrs seace of your sawes what so befall [. . .]
For I am ruler of realmes [. . .]
My selfe semely in sale I sende with you to be
For I am the worlde [. . .]
The floure of vertu foloweth me
Lo here I sette semely in se
I commaunde you all obedyent be
And with fre wyll ye folowe me

INFANS
Cryst our kynge graunte you clerly to know [. . .] etc.

Infans, the Child, continues his speech addressing the audience, not Mundus; but I must pause here for a moment to look at the situation with the 'seat' problem in mind.

There is no sign that Mundus makes any ceremonial entrance or walks from any screens to take his place before he speaks; yet by his l. 22 he makes that remark which I have noted and which seems quite impossible unless he were in fact at that point definitely installed in a chair. It is clear that his line means in effect 'Look here at me sitting finely in my seat', and such a line can scarcely make sense if he is not sitting finely in a seat. The abruptness of his statement might almost suggest a curtain was drawn and he was discovered. But we have not so far had the slightest grounds for supposing any such thing could take place in an Interlude in a hall.

129

Admittedly such a curtain could be used in *The Castle of Perseverance*, for the technique of that play was suited to the uncurtaining of scaffolds to discover characters seated aloft. The essential question at this moment is, How far does this help us to decide the present problem? Could chairs, in any postulated circle in a hall, be somehow provided with curtains for discoveries (as, for instance, the throne depicted on the title-page of this play might have been)?

Apart from obvious practical difficulties of masking, one is very hesitant to believe such a thing. What reason is there to justify this hesitation?

Possibly one reason for the hesitation lies in the very opening line, with its clear demand of the audience to stop chattering. This suggests an entrance rather than a discovery. It would in practice be disastrous to deliver such a line if, upon a curtain opening to discover Mundus, the audience immediately dropped into interested silence! I feel that the line is not theatrically suggestive of a discovery!

There seems then, so far, no positive evidence for picturing the opening of this Interlude, save that Mundus must have made some sort of entrance into the hall, that a seat must have been placed ready for him, possibly near the lower end; and that he might walk round the hall to deliver the first part of his speech, in which he describes himself, to various sections of the audience in turn. Then, during the latter part, he might have reached his chair and have sat, as he announces, in preparation for receiving the next character to come.

The next character is named 'Infans' in the script, but he is not addressed by this name in any line in the play. He is given a special name by Mundus, but this is only the first of several renamings he is to suffer during the action.

'Infans' begins by addressing not the seated Mundus but the audience in the place. He makes a somewhat bitter beginning:

> [. . .] Now semely syrs beholde on me
> How mankynde doth begynne
> I am a chylde as you may se
> Goten in game and in grete synne [. . .]

– and he goes on to picture the pain and peril of birth. From the point of view of presentation there is here one positive hint – namely, that he is in some way dressed as a child, for he uses the expression 'as you may se'. Two possibilities are open; either he was a grown-up actor in some way visibly presented as a child, or he was an actual child from the players' company – one recalls the definition of an Interluders' troupe as 'four men and a boy'. But there is a qualification to be made about each of the alternatives suggested.

First, it was probably more difficult in those days to represent that a man was a child merely by his dress, for the simple reason that a child's dress then was in all main features merely a smaller version of a grown-up's dress – there was no characteristic that one might 'see' to convey at once that the wearer was a child. So for the moment one rejects the idea of a grown-up actor pointing to his costume as he spoke this line.

Taking the alternative that the part was played by a real child, the problem is that in successive episodes this child is seen to grow to boyhood, manhood and old age. Also this part is the longest and most important in the play. Could it then have been given to a child? Perhaps, if the child could at some suitable point hand over his part to a more adult player. Is there any indication of a point in the script where he could go out for such a purpose?

Later in his opening speech, Infans again refers to his appearance; he is talking of how he had to leave his mother and –

A.ii.   Now in to the worlde she hathe me sent
                Poore and naked as ye may se
                I am not worthely wrapped nor went [. . .]
                But powerly prycked in pouerte
                Now in to the worlde wyll I wende
                Some comforte of hym for to craue
                All hayle comely crowned kynge
                God that all made you se and saue

MUNDUS
Welcome fayre chylde what is thy name

'Infans' says that his mother used to call him 'Dalyaunce'. Mundus is amused, but asks –

But my fayre chylde what woldest thou haue

INFANS
Syr of some comforte I you craue
Mete and clothe my lyfe to saue [. . .]

131

MUNDUS

A.ii.*rev.*   [. . .] These garmentes gaye I gyue to the
And also I gyue to the a name
And clepe the wanton in euery game
Tyll .xiiij. yere be come and gone
And than come agayne to me

WANTON

Gramercy worlde for myne araye
For now I purpose me to playe

MUNDUS

Fare well fayre chylde and haue good daye
All rychelesnesse is kynde for the

– and then from l. 77 to l. 123 little Wanton is apparently left on his own, and he plays his boyhood through.

There seems to be no doubt that in the above, three actions must have taken place; the coming of the child to the World, the dressing of the Child, and the parting of the Child from the World. There is no indication of where Mundus gets the clothes from. How far then are we justified, on the example of *Nature*, in supposing they were brought in at the opening of the play by Mundus himself or by an assistant? It is possible, but this is not by any means the only ceremonial change of clothing in the play, and one asks where at this moment are all the other garments which will be used in the sequel?

Another point concerns the parting of the Child from the World. If these farewells are meant seriously, then Mundus's line is emphatic enough to suggest the idea that he himself makes an exit here. Or he may remain sitting, and merely wave his hand to little Wanton as the child turns away and begins to play. This would involve the 'invisible dropped curtain' effect, differentiating the acting-area into two unrelated places.

Wanton's short playing-scene of some 45 lines is of considerable interest. It appears to be the accompaniment to a mime. He says –

I can many a quaynte game
Lo my toppe I dryue in same
Se it torneth rounde [. . .] (*etc. etc.*)

These particular words can scarcely have been spoken without either a mime of top-spinning or actual business with a real top. There is another consideration; this passage might be very effective indeed if played, apparently artlessly, by a bright child-player, but it could never have had the same appeal if the lines and business had been entrusted to the voice and actions of a full-grown man. If this is a sound argument, then it is essential to look for some point later when the real child can exit and be replaced by a grown man.

The speech goes on to list many other pastimes of the child, not excluding a few fairly brutal ones; and then it draws to a particular conclusion. Wanton, speaking directly to the audience, ends with –

A.iii.   But syrs whan I was seuen yere of age
               I was sent to the worlde to take wage
               And this seuen yere I haue ben his page
               And kept his commaundement
               Now I wyll wende to the worlde ye worthy emperou[r]
               Hayle lorde of grete honour
               This .vij. yere I haue serued you in hall & in boure
               With all my trewe entent

                     MUNDUS
               Now welcome wanton my derlynge dere [. . .]

This speech is a notable example of the Interlude's condensation of time; years pass before our eyes. But there are other details. One is forced to see Wanton breaking off his games and straightening himself and turning to address the audience directly. In his statement that he was seven years old when he was sent to the World, he gives the age of the child who entered in the opening scene. Mundus's line, 'tyll .xiiij. yere be come and gone' is now seen to mean 'till you are fourteen years old'.

The action now develops; at fourteen years the child is to become a youth. Mundus continues his speech with –

               [. . .] A newe name I shall gyue the here
               Loue lust lykynge in fere [. . .]

('in fere' would mean 'in truth' or 'in very fact'). The youth, now named 'Lust & Lykynge', suggests that this change in character is again accompanied by a change in costume for he says he is –

A.iii.*rev.*   . . . proudely apperelde in garmentes gaye
               My lokes ben full louely to a ladyes eye
               And in loue longynge my harte is sore sette [. . .]

But there seems to be no opportunity whatever up to this point at which the child could have gone out and been replaced by an older actor. However, it is still quite possible that, with a little licence, a boy of, say, ten or eleven could impersonate a child of seven and also a youth of fourteen; and presumably there is less call upon miming in the youth episode than in the child episode.

Later in this same speech Lust-&-Lykynge suffers another development; he now says,

> But syrs now I am .xix. wynterolde [. . .]
> Now I wyll go to the worlde
> A heygher scyence to assaye [. . .]

– and a few lines later –

> All hayle mayster full of myght
> I haue you serued bothe day and nyght
> Now I comen as I you behyght
> One and twenty wynter is comen and gone

– so the condensation of time continues; and the problem of the child actor adequately representing the age he is pretending grows more acute. There is still no chance for an exit to allow substitution. Mundus next has a 28-line speech beginning,

> Now welcome loue lust and lykynge
> For thou hast ben obedyent to my byddynge [. . .]
> A.iiii. And myghtly I make the a man
> Manhode myghty shall be thy name

and he goes on to enumerate seven kings who serve him – the familiar Seven Vices – and recommends Manhode to worship them. Manhode promises; and Mundus goes on once more to a robing ceremony:

> A.iiii.*rev.* Now manhode I wyll araye the newe
> In robes ryall ryght of good hewe [. . .]
> And here I dubbe the a knyght [. . .]

The ceremonial might be rich here. Manhode thanks him. Mundus pronounces a farewell again. And now – at last – comes a speech that gives Manhode a chance to go out. He says,

> Now I am dubbed a knyght hende
> Wonder wyde shall waxe my fame
> To seke aduentures now wyll I wende
> To please the worlde in gle and game

Clearly the above would allow of very colourful presentation; there is both costume and ceremonial. Having now reached this climax in the development of the action I believe, for the reasons given, that the boy who has played Infans under the guises of Dalyaunce, Wanton, Lust-and-Lykynge and at length reached Manhode, and who has thus represented a passage of fourteen years, from the ages of seven to twenty-one, with four changes of costume, goes out. If so, this must all have been a pretty splendid opportunity for a boy-player to have been offered.

Granted that the reconstruction is correct thus far, then it explains the next passage, which otherwise is a puzzle. Mundus speaks for 21 lines, addressing the audience but saying nothing significant that he has not said before. It is no more than a typical vaunt from a character announcing himself on his first entrance. Mundus simply describes himself. He begins,

> Lo syrs I am a prynce peryllous yprobyde
> I preuyd full peryllous and pethely I pyght [. . .]

It looks very like a fill-up, and it is to be presumed that that is just what it is, giving opportunity for a change of atmosphere to prelude the re-entrance of Manhode in a new phase. It ends –

> [. . .] I haue ladyes bryghtest in bourys
> Now wyll I fare on these flourys
> Lordynges haue good daye

With this speech his contribution to the play is done, for he is no more heard of. Presumably he rises at last from his seat, makes his way to the door and goes out.

The next speech is from Manhode. It opens exactly as if he made an entrance (thus confirming our reconstruction) with a typical address to the audience:

> Peas now peas ye felowes all aboute
> Peas now and herken to my sawes
> For I am lorde bothe stalworthy and stowte [. . .]

Remark the new note of mature arrogance. It would appear, thus, that during Mundus's previous and final speech, the boy who had gone out drops his part – and perhaps his 'robes ryall ryght of good hewe' – and hands over to an older player who then takes on the rest of the play at grown-up level.

This soliloquy, or address to the audience, continues for 50 lines.

During the vaunting, Manhode makes one reference to his dress which may or may not suggest that instead of assuming the boy's costume he has put on a new one; he says,

> I am ryall arayde to reuen vnder the ryse
> I am proudely aparelde in purpure and byse
> As golde I glyster in gere [. . .]

Thus we must picture him gleaming in purple and (apparently) bice green, or blue-green. And then he comes to his conclusion with a significant passage in curiously concise versification:

> Where is now so worthy a wyght
> A wyght
> ye as a wyght wytty
> Here in this sete sytte I
> For no loues lette I
> Here for to sytte

Thus we suppose him stepping up to the seat vacated by Mundus and confirming his new greatness by actually taking Mundus's place there. What is to happen next?

Episode 2 – Conscyence and Man

The next development is a speech by a new character named Conscyence. He is unlikely to have been present during all the preceding action, and we therefore imagine him making an entrance. He begins with the usual address to the audience –

> Cryst as he is crowned kynge
> Saue all this comely company [. . .] (*etc.*)
> For conscyence clere it is my name [. . .]

After 29 lines Manhode suddenly interrupts him and demands –

> Say how felowe who gaue the leue this way to go
> [. . .] Say thou harlot whyder in hast

> CONSCYENCE
> What let me go syr I knowe you nought

A rather nice reversal of the common convention! From this it would appear that Conscyence was on his way out again and was passing Manhode's chair, when suddenly he was hailed and stopped by Manhode, whom he had ostensibly not seen till now. They argue. Conscyence remarks,

[. . .] No [;] conscyence clere ye knowe ryght nought
And this longeth to a knyght

MANHODE
Conscyence what the deuyll man is he [?]

CONSCYENCE
Syr a techer of the spyrytualete

MANHODE
Spyrytualyte what the deuyll may that be [?]

CONSCYENCE
Syr all that be leders in to lyght [. . .]

– and so forth. In spite of all Manhode's attempts now to drive him away, Conscyence stays, and gradually weakens Manhode's belief in all his seven servant Vices one by one. In desperation Manhode cries,

B.ii.   Fye on the[e] false flaterynge frere

and thus indicates that Conscyence is clad in some sort of religious gown or friar's habit. The last Vice to be considered is 'Couetous' and, somewhat to Manhode's surprise, Conscyence swings round to praise that figure –

For couetous I clepe a kynge
Syr couetous in good doynge
Is good in all wyse
But syr knyght wyll ye do after me
And couetous your kynge shall be

This is a sufficiently crafty surprise to seize the attention of Manhode and at the same time cause all the audience to prick up their ears for what is coming. But in the sequel Conscyence explains that he means 'Covet good deeds!' Manhode bewails,

B.ii.*rev.*   What conscyence sholde I leue all game and gle [?]

and Conscyence moderately replies,

B.iii   Nay manhode so mote I thye
              All myrthe in measure is good for the [. . .]

and so forth. But –

B.iii.*rev.*   Syr in euery tyme beware of folye [. . .]
              Now fare well manhode I must wende

Thus we are prepared for the exit of Conscyence, leaving Manhode still presumably sitting and definitely inclining now to virtue. He soliloquizes for 31 lines, until the next interruption comes.

Episode 3 – Folye and Man

Now a fresh figure comes in – a fresh one and a vulgar one. He cries,

B.iiii.   What hey / how care awaye
                 My name is folye I am [? *am I*] not gaye
                 Is here ony man that wyll saye naye
                 That renneth in this route [. . .]

– what he is driving at is (perhaps deliberately) not immediately made clear; but he suddenly notices Manhode sitting there –

                 A syr god gyue you good eue

(Notice 'good eue', implying the performance is at night – though Mundus had said 'good daye' as he went.) Manhode is, however, scandalized by his manners and rebukes him –

                 Stonde vtter felowe where doest ye thy curtesy preue

                              FOLYE
                 What [!] I do but clawe myne ars syr be your leue

                              MANHODE
B.iiii.*rev.* What stonde out thou fayned shrewe

                              FOLYE
                 By by [? *my*] faythe syr there the cocke crewe [. . .]

After this sufficiently scurrilous introduction, he is asked by Manhode whether he can practise any handicraft. He replies,

                 Ye syr I can bynde a syue and tynke a pan
                 And therto a coryous bukler player I am
                 Aryse felowe wyll thou assaye [?]

thus, at one and the same time, he shows us that Manhode is still seated, and challenges him to a sword-and-buckler fight. This is at first refused. But he taunts Manhode till the latter in desperation leaps up crying,

C.i.   Defende the folye yft you maye
                 For in feythe I purpose to wete what thou art
                 How sayste thou now folye hast thou not a touche [!]

– so they have drawn and engaged, and Manhode has claimed a
touch with his sword. But Folye turns and appeals to the crowd of
spectators to disallow the point –

> No ywys but a lytell on my pouche
> On all this meyne I wyll me wouche
> That stondeth here aboute

After this the two make up. Folye reports how he lives in England,
and in London, and moreover was born in Holborn –

> And with the courtyers I am betaught
> To westmynster I vsed to wende

> MANHODE
> Herke felow why doost thou to westmynster drawe [*?*]

> FOLYE
C.i.*rev.*   For I am a seruaunt of the lawe [. . .]

– and he tells Manhode of his adventures, with several satirical
overtones. But Manhode finds out that his name, beside being Folye
is also sometimes Shame. At this he is put on his guard again, and he
repulses him; but Folye won't go away. At length Folye makes a
curious proposal which appears to imply that he will slough off the
shameful side of his nature and wrap it up and throw it away. His
words are,

C.ii.*rev.*   Syr here in this cloute I knyt shame
         And clype me but propre folye [. . .]

At any rate the stratagem, whatever it is, works; Manhode is satisfied and proposes a drink on the bargain. Folye has an aside to the
audience telling them exactly how he will treat Manhode once he
has him thoroughly drunk. Manhode, however, is still apprehen-
sive of being found out by Conscyence, but he puts the thought
aside and agrees to go to Eastcheap to the Pope's Head to take
wine. Before going he decides, for prudence' sake, to assume a
different name. Folye of course has now a discarded name to spare
which he kindly lends to the unthinking Manhode – the name of
'Shame'. They are in a hurry to set off. Manhode urges Folye to go
first and show him the way. Folye urges Manhode not to linger
behind and concludes with an exit couplet almost worthy of the
great Elizabethans –

C.iii.*rev.*   Folye before and shame behynde
                Lo syrs thus fareth the worlde alwaye

and then he must go out. But Manhode is left to speak another 13
lines and – rather effectively – in a changed rhythm of verse; as an
example –

>   Now I wyll folowe folye / for folye is my man
>   Ye folye is my felowe and hath gyuen me a name [. . .]

C.iiii. & now haue good daye syrs to london to seke folye wyll I fare

and he runs to the door – but only to be suddenly called back by a
newcomer, probably coming from the opposite door (see below).

Episode 4 – Conscyence and Man (resumed)
    The newcomer is, of course, Conscyence, and he demands –

>   Saye manhode frende whyder wyll ye go

They argue. Manhode breaks away and runs after Folye. Conscyence
left alone turns to the audience with –

>   Lo syrs a grete ensample you may se
>   The freylnes of mankynde [. . .]
>   That manhode is forthe with folye wende

He adds that there is nothing for it but that he should go to seek
out Perseueraunce, a new character, to help, and he concludes,

C.iiii.*rev.*   Fare well lordynges and haue good daye
                 To seke perseueraunce wyll I wende

– and thus he must clearly go out.

Episode 5 – Perseueraunce and Man
    The next passage is a speech from Perseueraunce himself. This
speech follows immediately upon Conscyence's exit, without any
break at all in the script. It begins with the usual formal greeting by
a newcomer to the audience –

>   Now cryst our comely creature [*creator*] clerer tha*n* crystal clene
>   That craftly made euery creature by good recreacyon
>   Saue all this company that is gathered here by dene [. . .]

I pause to remark that it is fairly clear that the entering Perseueraunce could not, as he came in, have met with the departing Conscyence. If the two had met, obviously Conscyence, who was de-

parting expressly to look for Perseueraunce, must have hailed him and explained what he wanted to see him about. But Conscyence has gone out for good, and he takes no further part in the play. Even if we are to suppose a moment or two to elapse in blank silence after Conscyence's exit, with the Place left empty (not, by the way, a good piece of technique theatrically), it might still seem unconvincing to have Perseueraunce enter at the same door, affecting not to have noticed him outside – particularly as he was the very man Conscyence was looking for. This one small fact is, I think, the only contribution offered in the lines of the play to our query about where it might have been presented; for the action suggested above would be consistent with presentation in a hall with its screens and their two entrances – thus allowing one character to go out as another came in by the other door, and preserving the appearance that one could not have met the other.

However this may be, the action continues with Perseueraunce announcing his name and saying he has come to try to help to free mankind from their vices, and –

> Therfore in this presens to cryst I praye
> Or that I hens wende awaye
> Some good worde that I may saye
> To borowe mannes soul from blame

The inference to be taken from these lines is that he is to pause in this place for a short while to see if he can help. He would appear to be a deliberate character in his speech, for he has one line with two pause-strokes in it; he prays –

> This company / counsell / comforte and glad
> And saue all this symylytude that semely here syttes

Then we may suppose he quietly draws aside to the fringe of the action to await events.

Now the last new figure enters. Whether it is in fact a new actor, or whether Manhode has had time, during the 46 lines of Conscyence's and Perseueraunce's last speeches, to change his dress and assume a grey beard and wig and appear once again, we do not know. But, however it was, the next speech is given as follows:

> AGE
>
> Alas / alas / that me is wo
> My lyfe my lykynge I haue forlorne [. . .]

141

– and he tells his story. A few lines later, the words –

> Than conscyence clere comely and kynde
> Mekely he met me in sete there I sate

clearly refer to Conscyence's re-entrance at the beginning of Episode 2, and fully confirm that at that point Manhode was sitting.

Age goes on to tell of his unfortunate experiences in London, ending up in Newgate Prison. Now he has a cough, he staggers, he groans, he doesn't care what happens to him.

Perseueraunce now steps forward from the crowd and greets him, listens to his tale of trouble and then gives him a new name – this time, Repentaunce. He comforts him with reminders of others who had failed but are now saints 'in heuen clere'. There follows a little sermon on the Five Wits and the Twelve Articles of Faith. Age (alias Repentaunce) gratefully thanks him, turns and calls the audience to 'take all ensample' by him. And finally Perseueraunce adds,

> And therfore withoute ony dystaunce
> I take my leue of kynge and knyght
> And I praye to Jhesu whiche as made vs all
> Couer you with his mantell perpetuall
> > Amen

In resumption; I think on the whole that the puzzling problem about sitting on seats which I raised at first is not to be interpreted as meaning that *The World and the Child* was presented as *The Castle of Perseverance* was. But on the other hand I do think there is a reason for seeing a meaning behind the similarity in phrasing; I would suppose it to imply that certain early Interludes were very definitely framed on the kind of presentation-technique that had gone before in the Middle Ages, and that *The World and the Child* is an instance of the retention of the old terms but of the employment of them now for a new set of circumstances namely, presentation indoors. And from this, one would deduce that the shape Medwall gave to *Nature*, in his use there of chairs, is a perfectly traditional shape, showing a growth from the medieval technique of outdoor Moralities to the Tudor technique of indoor Interludes. As a further example of such a development, I would recall the use of the medieval term 'Place' in these early Interludes.

7 *Return to 'Mankind'*

Now that it has been possible to establish in the last three chapters some picture of what the presentation of an Interlude must have been like at the end of the fifteenth century, I can return to *Mankind*, some thirty-odd years before, to see if any of its problems seem nearer solution.

In the first place it seems reasonable to say that in action, in idiom, and in general construction the two Medwall Interludes are close to the style of *Mankind* – close enough to permit the idea to be put another way; namely, that *Mankind* would seem more suitably classed as an early Interlude than as a late Morality of for instance the type of *The Castle of Perseverance*. We know that *The Castle* belonged to a tradition of outdoor presentation; *Nature* and *Fulgens*, as I have shown, belong as certainly to a tradition of indoor presentation. (*The World and the Child* may offer an example of the merging of the first tradition into the second.)

With this in mind, any hints in *Mankind* that might point to indoor presentation acquire much more authority. My opinion, therefore, about the presentation of *Mankind* is that, rather than being an inn-yard play, it is in every way consistent with the presentation method of *Nature*, *Fulgens*, and probably with that of *The World and the Child*. This would imply that it was performed in a hall before screens.

If this is so then there can now be little doubt that the places of entrance for the players, which seemed at first so puzzling, were in fact the doorways in the screens. This is supported by Nought's reference to leaving by a door.

Following this up, the situation in which Newgyse, Nought and Nowadays deliver their three eight-line gibes (beginning at l. 238, see p. 27 above) without entering, can be perfectly well explained by supposing them calling out these lines in mocking tones from the concealment of the entry passage and hidden behind the groups of spectators standing round the two entrances to that passage in the screens. And so the mystery of where the voices came from, which Mankind seemed to express, arose from the fact that those voices would sound almost as if they came out of the audience – or at least the fiction that they did so could be sustained by the players. This would again be consistent with the suggestion of 'barracking' that these particular three speeches have.

The audience at the screens end of the hall would consist of the 'humbler' elements of the audience; it would thus be not unlike the 'gods' of a modern theatre. Thus again there is justification for the barracking to seem consistent, coming from the screens.

To expand this. As we saw, Adams decided that the clowns spoke 'from behind', but did not specify from behind *what*. He merely inserted his own direction, 'speaking from behind'. With his suggestion we can now agree if we may read it as 'from behind the audience' – or, to speak more accurately, from behind that part of the audience that was standing at the lower end of the hall crowding round the screens entrances.

It might be that the three scurrilous figures kept pretty nearly invisible during the whole episode, by standing in the entry behind the screens. There they would be safely protected from the action in the Hall Place – and helped in this by the press of bystanders at the two doorways – yet at the same time they themselves would be in complete touch with that action, and able to interpolate ribald comments on it as from the audience's standpoint, with exciting and infectious freedom. On cue, each one severally might thrust forward, elbowing those bystanders, deliver his interruption, and slip back out of sight behind the amused spectators, without the actors in the Place seeming to have the faintest idea where the words came from.

On a raised platform-stage, such as a booth stage, this action would be impossible, and any substitute effect could not be as entertaining; but the one arrangement where the effect might have its full value theatrically is the arrangement I have proposed at the hall screens.

I would suggest that such lines as that from Nowadays when the knaves come in for their song – 'Make rom, s*ers*,' (l. 324) – is pretty nearly final proof of the idea.

With regard to the second point mentioned on p. 26 – the theory offered there of differentiation of acting-areas – I have little hesitation, after considering the action of *Nature* and *Fulgens* in detail, in claiming that this theory is confirmed as one of the fundamental elements in the technique of Interlude presentation.

Finally, the fact that there are no entrance-directions can now be reconsidered. One might perhaps have been inclined at first to explain their absence simply by supposing that the writer of the play was too early in history to have an interest in such things, and that the script is too primitive for such niceties. But that would be to disregard the fact that there are (though not consistently) directions for exits. Therefore such matters were at that date certainly recognized.

One reason why entrance-directions are lacking though exit-directions are present may be that in a hall there could never be any question about the place where entrances would have to be made – it was inevitable since there was only one place possible, the screens – and that this being so the character's name at the head of a speech was all that was needed to indicate that he was 'on'. This would be quite understandable if the players were accustomed to congregate up to the moment of their entrance in the Entry where the doorways would be immediately available, and where incidentally they might not necessarily even be hidden from the audience; the screens and their doorways with the entry behind would perfectly serve this custom.

The presence of exit-directions, on the other hand, would be explained by the fact that a quite different condition applied to exits since, once in the acting-area or the middle of the hall floor, a player would be some way removed from any entrance door, and could not simply merge into it as he could emerge out of it, or as he could merge into the encircling crowd, but instead would have to make a direct action so as to go across the floor until he reached it. You would *see* an actor begin to exit; but you would not normally see him begin to enter (unless he made a special point of drawing your attention) until he was already well through the crowd of bystanders.

Contemporary Court Staging 1511 onwards

On scenic 'Houses' ∽ Court Pageant Technique

8 *On scenic 'Houses'*

Any consideration of the methods of presenting plays in the pre-Shakespearean period must include some reference to the methods of presenting court-shows in that period; the reason is that methods used at court might have influenced the method used by Interlude players in their ordinary performances in private houses or public halls. If such influence can be proved at all, it is certainly of importance to find out how great it was.

A considerable amount of information on court shows begins to be available from the year 1511 onwards, and so it fits here in our chronological scheme.

There is however a preliminary warning. The typical court shows, at least into the period of Henry VIII, were not Interludes nor indeed anything that could be called dramatic plays at all; they were chiefly masques or 'disguisings', which specialized in spectacle and not in dramatic plot. The distinction is as great as that between sumptuous cabaret and regular repertory theatre today. They may therefore have been set quite differently.

It seems to me that the understanding of the technicalities of play presentation before Shakespeare has sometimes been confused by failing to keep a proper distinction here, and by taking for granted that the quite elaborate and expensive preparations made for typical court shows would inevitably be those adopted for travelling plays. I stress *typical* court show with the masques in mind, but admittedly, during Henry VIII's reign, and more so in Elizabeth I's, plays as well as masques were given at court. My point is that the immense amount of setting information that has come down to us from the early Revels Accounts of the court is primarily concerned with masques. When in the later part of the period the information begins to include references to plays as well, it is almost certainly to a specialized form of play-presentation only, which was devised for command performances under the instruction of the Master of the Revels. But this specialized form may obviously not have the slightest reference to the way in which the same plays were presented on normal occasions outside the court. Above all, caution is needed over the question of the use of *houses* in the setting of Interludes. This is where a particular confusion comes in, and it seems very necessary to break off here to see, if possible, how it arose and what is its extent.

These 'houses' later came to be widely-used items of setting in court shows. Their nature is still a matter for much controversy; they seem to have been scenic buildings of very widely varying natures set up on the masquing-hall floor. But whatever they were, they do not seem to be mentioned in accounts before about 1570, that is to say, not until the last few years of the period under discussion in this book. They *may* of course have been in use earlier but any guess at their employment before the 1570s should be tested with care, and any suggestion that 'houses' were used in play presentation outside court occasions will need particular examination.

The confusion I mentioned concerns the question of the use of 'houses' as backgrounds in the setting of Interludes. Craik puts the difficulty in a nutshell when he comments on certain remarks by Chambers with the words, 'As for the use of a background of "houses" I think that there was less of it than Chambers is prepared to assume, . . .' (*The Tudor Interlude*, p. 11).

Thus the question, now, of *what* Chambers was prepared to assume needs to be examined again in detail to see if by any chance the confusion could stem from him. Before turning to Chambers there are some other remarks by Craik in which he ventures to express similar reservations.

On his p. 10 he refers to certain variations in types of setting and adds, 'most of them are discussed by Chambers whose evidence I wish to weigh afresh in some instances'.

Again, in a long footnote to his p. 13 he says,

Chambers (*The Elizabethan Stage*, III, 24 5) has suggested that 'houses' are required for *Jacob and Esau, The Marriage of Wit and Wisdom, Misogonus, The Conflict of Conscience, Three Ladies of London*, and also (III, 28) for *Tom Tyler* and (III, 38) *Patient Grissell*. In some of these plays I believe that no 'houses' are required; in others, fewer than Chambers postulates.

– and he goes on to detail his own views about the staging requirements. I think it is important to note that these particular plays are all later by some half-century than anything I have discussed so far.

After these comments it seems necessary to make a careful review of all Chambers really says on this matter.

As a preliminary, I venture to say that it often seems to me that the almost unbelievable quantity of material in the four volumes of *The Elizabethan Stage* frequently obscures – and even contradicts – the occasional direct statements that Chambers makes about the methods of presentation which are indicated in that material. For instance, it may very well be that the mass of information in the section of Volume III entitled, rather confusingly, 'Staging at Court' obscures the fact that on p. 23 Chambers says clearly, 'My inference is that the setting of the interludes was nothing but the hall in which the performances were given.' That is a clear general statement to be kept well in mind.

Now, to see what he says in detail about the setting of Interludes: he begins by classifying briefly some forty-five (III, 22), and he says (and I now take upon myself the risk of misrepresenting him by a necessary summarizing; also I venture to mark with an asterisk certain significant points) –

> Subject, then, to the exceptions, the interludes . . . call for no changes of locality . . . The action proceeds continuously in a locality, which . . . is referred to, . . . as 'the place' * . . . [III, 23] In exterior plays some kind of a house may be suggested in close proximity to the 'place'. . . .

Now the general impression which Chambers might seem, at first reading, to give in this passage is that he imagines that *some kind of a house* was actually represented in close proximity to the 'place'. But upon further reading this apparently turns out to be a misleading impression; for two lines later he continues –

> There is no obvious necessity why these houses should have been represented by anything but a door . . . My inference is that the setting of the interludes was nothing but the hall in which performances were given, . . . And I think that, apart from interludes woven into the pageantry of Henry VIII's disguising chambers, the hall contemplated was at first just the ordinary everyday hall, after dinner or supper, with the sovereigns or lords still on the dais, the tables and benches below pushed aside, and a free space left for the performers on the floor, with the screen and its convenient doors as a background . . . The actors . . .

would have had to rub shoulders all the time with the inferior members of their audience. And so they did.

With all of this there seems – after the conclusions reached so far in this present book – no reason whatever not to be in full agreement. But then on p. 24 a new paragraph begins and here, as I think, the misleading impression already noted might seem to be confirmed – particularly for any reader who has not kept in mind the very just opinion on Interlude-presentation expressed immediately above. The new paragraph reads (again in summary) –

> I come now to nine interludes which, for various reasons, demand special remark. In *Jacob and Esau* (>1558) there is coming and going between the place and the tent of Isaac . . . the tent of Jacob, and probably also the tent of Esau. In *Wit and Wisdom* (>1579) action takes place at the entrances of the house of Wantonness, of the den of Irksomeness, of a prison, and of Mother Bee's house, . . . In *Misogonus* (c. 1560–77), the place of which is before the house of Philogonus, there is one scene in Melissa's 'bowre' (ii. 4, 12), which must somehow have been represented. In *Thersites* (1537), . . . Mulciber, . . . 'must have a shop made in the place', . . . Similarly, the Mater . . . 'goeth in the place which is prepared for her', . . . These four examples only differ from the normal interlude type by * some multiplication of the houses suggested in the background, and probably by some closer approximation than a mere door to the visual realization of these.

The last three lines might certainly be read as negativing, or modifying, the previous statement that the 'houses' would not have been represented 'by anything but a door'. Such a reading would seem to be further confirmed in what follows (from p. 25):

> . . . Four other examples do entail some change of locality. Much stress must not be laid on . . . *The Conflict of Conscience* (>1581) and . . . *Three Ladies of London* . . . But in *The Disobedient Child* (c. 1560) some episodes are before the house of the father, and others before that of the son in another locality forty miles away. In *Mary Magdelene* (<1566), again, . . . two localities were indicated on opposite sides of the hall or stage, . . . You may call this 'multiple staging', if you will.

The two phrases, 'on opposite sides of the . . . *stage*' and 'multiple *staging*' are hard to reconcile with his remark on p. 24 that 'Of a raised stage the only indication is in *All for Money*, a late example . . .'. To continue; there is a reference to *Godly Queen Hester* as 'in most respects quite a normal interlude' but no suggestion that any house is required there. But later, on his p. 27, Chambers picks up the story of houses again;

> I come now to the group of four mid-century farces, . . . so far as scenic setting is concerned, they do not diverge markedly from the interlude type. Nor is this surprising, since Renaissance comedy, like the classical comedy upon which it is based, was essentially an affair of continuous action, in * an open place, before a background of houses. *Gammer Gurton's Needle* requires two houses, . . . *Jack Juggler* one, . . . *Ralph Roister Doister* one, . . . *Tom Tyler*, . . . has a slightly more complicated staging. . . . there is at one point a transition from exterior to interior action. . . .

There follows next a curious sort of disclaimer which seems at first to weaken all the theory apparently put forward earlier; Chambers now says that not one of the plays he has so far considered can be held with certainty to have been presented at court! Does he imply that if they were not presented at court then any question of their employment of 'houses' would not arise? –

> I am of course aware that the forty-four interludes and the four farces hitherto dealt with cannot be regarded as forming a homogeneous body of Court drama. Not one of them, in fact, can be absolutely proved to have been given at Court. Several of them bear signs of having been given elsewhere, . . . Others lie under suspicion of having been written primarily for the printing-press, . . . and it is obvious that in such circumstances a writer might very likely limit himself to demands upon stage-management far short of what the Court would be prepared to meet.

It seems to me obvious that there certainly is grounds for misunderstanding here. Chambers states clearly that he sees no obvious necessity for any house to 'have been represented by anything but a door' and goes on to picture the hall 'with the screen and its convenient doors as a background' for the performers; yet he states equally clearly that several Interludes differ from the normal type by 'some multiplication of the houses suggested in the background' and even by some closer approximation than a mere door to 'the visual realization of these'! And, even more strikingly – '. . . Renaissance comedy . . . was essentially an affair of continuous action, in an open place, before a background of houses.' But perhaps it is that the difficulty arises from the turn of speech he uses, in 'houses *suggested* in the background'. For *suggested* can mean either represented actually by some suggestive scenic device such as a piece of scenery;

or, not represented at all but 'merely *suggested* as a background' by certain speeches in the dialogue of the play. And there is no positive indication which Chambers meant.

An added difficulty is that 'howses', as I have indicated, is a quite definitely employed, technical term to designate certain pieces of scenic building specified in the Accounts of the Revels Office of Queen Elizabeth I, but only, so far as I know, after about 1570. I have in mind the sort of item quoted under 1571 as being among 'The Contentes of this Booke', viz. 'the apparelling, disgyzyngge, ffurnishing, ffitting, Garnishing & orderly setting foorthe of men, woomen, & Children; in sundry Tragedies, Playes, Maskes, and sports with their apte howses of paynted Canvas * & proprties incident . . .' Some very brief account of such 'howses' has been given in my *The Seven Ages of the Theatre*, p. 145, and in *Changeable Scenery*, pp. 26, 29.

Whether Chambers had in mind anything so elaborate as this kind of 'howses of paynted Canvas' when he talked of the 'houses suggested in the background' of certain Interludes is not certain; but the conclusion is that several later writers have taken it that he had. And eventually disagreement has followed. It seems that the best line to take in the circumstances is to review some court-show methods and note carefully how much there is in these, as well as in the Interludes to be considered in the latter part of this book, to indicate *positively* that 'howses' were used; and to refrain from supposing their use unless such positive evidence is found.

I end this summary of what Chambers was 'prepared to assume' by returning to that remark of Craik's which opened the puzzle, quoting it now in full with its significant final lines which offer a helpful lead-on to the next party of my study. He says –

> As for the use of a background of 'houses' I think that there was less of it than Chambers is prepared to assume, and that it is confined mainly to Elizabethan court interludes of a professedly spectacular nature.

There are two other preliminary matters which have an important bearing on the relationship between the theatre of the court and the theatre of the commoners. The first concerns the effect made on the popular theatre by the performance at court of plays by companies of boy players. H. N. Hillebrand discusses this effect at considerable length in an essay called 'The Child Actors' (University of Illinois, *Studies in Language and Literature*, XI, Feb. 1926). The essay concerns the importance of the work of the boys from the choir schools and of those of their masters who wrote plays for them, specifically in the period between 1515 and 1580.

These boys' companies and their plays came into existence to give entertainments at court. The aim of Hillebrand's essay is, in the author's own words, to put forward 'a stimulating and in many ways a surprising discovery' which is, that these sixty-five years of the English theatre in fact 'belong' to the children (p. 283), and that so far as concerns the drama of that time 'the children . . . led it' (p. 264).

I am not concerned here to question the extent to which this is true but to put forward one point; that, even if these children led the drama, it may not necessarily follow – as Hillebrand rather implies – that the methods they used for setting their plays similarly 'led' the common Interluders, when they in their turn presented shows in private halls throughout the country.

There is no doubt that some of the plays shortly to be considered were written primarily for boys' companies to perform. There is also no doubt that, as Hillebrand shows, a play presented by a boys' company at court might be associated with certain pretty elaborate resources of setting. But what has to be decided, after a consideration of some of the court methods is, What facilities had the common players of the early sixteenth century for carrying items of that sort of setting over the country with them?

The second preliminary matter I want to introduce is certain striking evidence that court procedure can exert a limitation on common players that may prompt them to hostility against court ways, even though it might have to be a concealed hostility. This evidence is supplied by that experienced man of the theatre, Colley Cibber. Fortunately there is something ageless about the experiences of a common player before the public, and though Cibber was born nearly seventy years after Elizabeth I died, his experiences of playing at court must have been close enough to those of James Burbage. In Chap. XVI of *An Apology for His Life* (Everyman edition, p. 280) Cibber contrasts a court show with a public show. He announces –

A play presented at court, or acted on a publick stage, seems to their different auditors, a different entertainment. Now hear my reason for it.

I pause to note that he considered this to be so significant a matter that he put a full stop here, as drawing his breath before proceeding to his point. Cibber always wrote in long paragraphs, and sometimes the many just elements of reasoning within his sentences are so run together that one may easily tend to overlook their separate value, so I will take the liberty to break into a new paragraph at each of his full stops. He goes on –

> In the common theatre, the guests are at home, where the politer forms of good breeding are not so nicely regarded; every one there falls to, and likes or finds fault, according to his natural taste or appetite.
>
> At court, where the prince gives the treat, and honours the table with his own presence, the audience is under the restraint of a circle where laughter, or applause, rais'd higher than a whisper, would be star'd at.
>
> At a publick play they are both let loose, even till the actor is, sometimes, pleas'd with his not being able to be heard, for the clamour of them.
>
> But this coldness or decency of attention, at court, I observ'd, had but a melancholy effect upon the impatient vanity of some of our actors, who seem'd inconsolable, when their flashy endeavours to please had pass'd unheeded; their not considering where they were, quite disconcerted them; nor could they recover their spirits, till from the lowest rank of the audience, some gaping John, or Joan, in the fullness of their hearts, roar'd out their approbation;
>
> And indeed, such a natural instance of honest simplicity, a prince himself, whose indulgence knows where to make allowances, might reasonably smile at, and perhaps not think it the worst part of his entertainment.

It is of the essence of the theatre that this uncurbed reaction – even if it is from 'some gaping John or Joan' and provided it is from 'the fullness of their hearts' – can in fact *recover a player's spirits*. As Cibber continues; the presence of this reaction can make it more easy for even His Majesty to smile, and enjoy the show the better, while this experience of the reaction of the spectators around him will contribute not 'the worst part of his entertainment'. Cibber embroiders this –

> . . . it must be own'd, that an audience may be as well too much reserv'd, as too profuse of their applause; for tho' it is possible a Betterton would not have been discourag'd . . . those of less judgement may sink into a flatness, in their performance, for want of that applause, which from the generality of judges, they might, perhaps, have some pretence to; and the auditor, when not seeming to feel what ought to affect him, may rob himself of something more that he might have had, by giving the actor his due, who measures out his power to please, according to the value he sets upon his hearer's taste or capacity.

These are impressive words from a man experienced in practice. It is worth remembering in passing that Betterton himself was not too distantly linked with the Interluders who are the subject of this book, since he had learnt his actor's job under Davenant, who was a contemporary of the two younger Burbages, whose father was that very member of Lord Leicester's Men who in 1576 built the Theatre. Cibber goes on with a reference to the feelings of his own company on their appearance at court, which begins;

> But, however, as we were not, here, itinerant adventurers, and had properly, but one royal auditor to please; . . . the rest of our ambition had little to look after; . . .

Notice the wording – 'as we' (the players) 'were not, here' (that is, at court), 'itinerant adventurers' . . . But the Interluders *were* itinerant adventurers, and when they were not at court my belief is that court methods were not the methods they would use with another public than 'one royal auditor to please' – or to foot their bill. And there we must leave Cibber in mid-paragraph.

9 *Court Pageant Technique*

To emphasize the different atmosphere between house and court (if indeed it needs further emphasis), I may take a passage from Harleian MS 69, quoted by Hillebrand, concerning the court entertainment at the marriage of the ill-fated young Prince Arthur to Katherine of Aragon as early as 1501. The passage is particularly worth including here since it indicates that at court the guests might banquet together first and then remove from the banquet hall into another chamber for the entertainment – whereby, of course, any arrangement of elaborate preliminaries for a show would be facilitated; the preparations for such an entertainment might include elaborate furnishings and decorations quite separate from the setting for the performance itself. But the show proper would begin 'when that his Grace was come and his welbeloved company of Nobles' had entered with him. Here, straight away, is a major difference from the occasions I have reconstructed so far, in which the common players entered a private hall where supper had just been, or was still being, taken. At the marriage of Prince Arthur to Katherine there were several pageants; concerning the last –

Against that his grace had supped the goodly hall was addressed and goodly beseene and a Royall Cupborde sett thervppon in a baye windowe of ix. or x. stages and haunces of height, furnished and fulfilled with rich and goodly plate of gould and of silver and guilt and in the upper part of the hall a Cloth of gould carpet*tes* and Cushions for the King*es* noble M*ai*es*tie* whither when that his Grace was come and his welbeloved company of Nobles [? *there*] entred in a pleasant disguising conveyed and shewed by a glorious towne or tabernacle made like a goodly Chapell fenestred full of light*es* and brightnes [;] within this Pageant or tabernacle was another standing Cupboard of rich and Costly plate to a great substance and quantitye this throne and pageant was of two stories in whose longer [? *lower*] were viij. goodly disguised Lordes Knight*es* and men of honor and in the upper story and particion viij. other fresh ladyes most strangely disguised and after the most pleasurefull manner, thus when this goodly work was approached vnto the Kinge presence and sight [–] drawen and conveyed vppon wheeles by iij. woddose ij. before and one behind and on either side of the said [? *pageant*] homely mermaides one of them a man mermaide the other a woman the man in harnesse from the wast vpward*es* and in every of the said mermaides a Childe of the Chapell singing right sweetly and with quaint hermony [–] descend[*ed*] these viij. pleasent gallante men of honor and before their coming forth they cast out many quicke conyes [*rabbits*] the which ran about the hall and made very great disport*es*. after they daunced many divers goodly daunces and forthwith came downe the viij disguised Ladyes and in their apearance the[*y*] let flye many white doues and byrdes that flewe about the hall and great laughter and disport they made. These Lordes and Laydyes coupled together and daunced a long season many Courtly roundes and pleasant daunces. After that the Earle of Spaine and a Ladye of the same Countrey daunced two base daunces and went vp againe. . . .

All this is clearly so far from the atmosphere implied in the Interludes I have examined up till now as to belong to a different world. And yet that different world *was* one into which 'itinerant adventurers' might, by command, penetrate. Adult Interluders did on occasion perform at court; indeed Henry VIII retained more than one such company of his own. Such players would undoubtedly see men like William Cornish, Master of the Chapel Children, freely ordering in 1516, fifteen yards of stuff for a gowne and a bonnet for himself, and two yards for a doublet for one of his child players, and another twelve yards for a mantle and bishop's surcoat and a bonnet and girdle for himself, and seven ells spent by his 'avyes' for short sleeves 'wyd hangyng out at ye hand and other plac*es*' for other of the boys

– all for a performance of Cornish's own play *Troilus and Pandar* (now lost). And they would possibly know that on that particular occasion there was a castle of timber fix(ed) and fast in the King's hall, which was designed as a setting for a masquing entertainment quite different from Cornish's play, but before which he and his boys apparently gave their show, since their play preceded the masquing and the castle was 'fix and fast'.

Such things the itinerant adventurers might certainly know about. But it would seem to me that the playing-tradition they generally pursued, and upon which some of the younger of them were eventually to build their own playhouse, was not – and was *deliberately* not – in essence concerned with settings of that court kind; even if for no better reason than that such settings, in their fix-and-fast-ness would take away all their mobility as itinerants. But since such court methods must have been known to some at least of them, a short time must be spent on some of the astonishing details of those methods.

The staging of shows at court is a wide subject and one that certainly calls for separate and detailed study of the very considerable amount of evidence about it which survives in rolls of accounts and such things. I shall content myself here with certain references to later summaries of the evidence rather than attempt a study of the original evidence itself. I turn to the domestic state papers collected by J. S. Brewer under the title of *Letters and Papers of the Reign of Henry VIII*. There, in Vol. II between pp. 1490 and 1517, we find a section of 'Accounts of Revels etc. drawn up by Richard Gibson at the King's order', dating from 28 February 1510 onwards. I do not intend to suggest that Brewer's presentation of the material is at all an ideal one; he resorts too often to summarizing passages in his own words. But what he has done is very convenient for my present purpose, and I use him while freely acknowledging the truth of Hillebrand's remark that 'Extracts from the *Revels Books*, somewhat impaired by inaccuracies, have been printed in . . . Brewer and Gairdner's *Letters and Papers of Henry VIII*.'

Though there is a bewildering uncertainty about how scenic properties in general were used in early plays, and even about how much they were used at all, yet there is on the other hand, odd though it may seem, a great deal of detail about how such scenic properties were made. It would obviously be out of place to speak of the crafts of *scenery* or *scenepainting* in sixteenth-century England because no one painted scenes. But already by that period the skill, of an astonishing number of specialists were devoted to the making, and consequently to the painting, of those many things that can be classed under the heading of theatrical properties. Almost anything that the wit of man could devise might be specifically designed – that is, have a particular method of construction thought out especially for it which was suitable for building it in a royal hall, or for bringing it into a hall, on wheels or by bearers, and for its use by performers in a show.

Design was entrusted to men specially appointed to the work and, once designed, the properties were constructed by a wide variety of skilled craftsmen. Seamstresses were available for sewing, papier-mâché workers for all sorts of details, plasterers, metal-workers, gilders, carpenters, carriers, wire-drawers, embroiderers (to say nothing of furriers, glovers, etc.) and, of course, painters.

Our insight into the details of their techniques comes from lists of purchases. For instance, there were bought for shows at court in the year 1511 and shortly after, among many thousands of other items, the following – extracted almost at random:

Earthen vessels,

Hogs' bristles for painters,

'Pink' for tempering the colours. This would be one of those strange uses of the word *pink* such as survive today in the name 'Dutch pink' which is a yellow; the reference in *The Oxford English Dictionary* (whose date of '1634' we can now put back at least to 1511) gives: 'A yellowish or greenish-yellow pigment or "lake" obtained by the combination of a vegetable colouring matter with some white base, . . . also *pink-yellow* = yellow lake. *Brown p., French p., Dutch, English; Italian p.*' It is useful not so much as a pigment in itself but for tinting, or modifying, other stronger pigments.

Vinegar,

Candles for night work,

Charcoal for heating the colours. These would be size colours, that is to say *distemper*; and the painters made their own size, for we find '2 bushels of leather shreds sodden for size'.

A beechen log for a pouncing block; that is a surface for preparing a pattern for transferring by piercing its outlines with a series of pin-holes, so that powder might be dusted through them, leaving the outline on the material to be painted.

Canvas, for many purposes (including aprons for painters),

Many varieties of paper; coloured, grey, silver, shiny; for many purposes including cutting up for leaves of trees, and moulding for masks:

Horn glue,
Gum arabic,
'Orsade' or arsidew, or gold foil, and scissors for cutting it,
'29,000 spangles',
Crossbow thread,
Red and white lead,
White varnish,
Many varieties of raw pigment such as Spanish brown, orpiment,
vermillion, saffron, verdigris;
Shears,
Flour for paste,
Oil,
Tallow,
Iron wire,
Soap, for greasing pageant wheels,
Pack needles,
Wax for setting the leaves in trees,
Rushes,
Ostrich feathers,
Nails and tacks in great number and variety,
Coals for heating the workshops,
'Forlokks' and bolts of iron for setting pieces of timber together.

From all this one can set up in one's mind an entertaining enough picture of what was involved in the preparation of a show at court, but what one cannot do is decide just how much of this expensive activity was available to a strolling Interluder. Presumably anything of it *could* be taken advantage of provided he so desired, but in practice one is inclined to suppose that very little of it would be really indispensable. If so, then we must, when we think of the presentation of an early Interlude, be reluctant to see in it any wide use of 'mounts' and 'houses'. The Interluders had most probably to get along in general without such things.

To return to consideration of the elaboration of court shows; a 'joust of honour' was held at Westminster by the King on 12 February 1511, for which there was constructed within the house of Blackfriars a forest. We are not given in the sequel all the details to satisfy our curiosity about this forest, but there are sufficient facts to fill in the corners of a pretty elaborate picture. To being; it was drawn by two animals, a lion and an antelope; the forest must therefore have been on wheels. The beasts were 'conducted with men in wodwoos' apparel', that is 'woodwoses' or wild men of the woods, and later a measurement is given for this forest of '26 ft.

long, 16ft. broad, and 9ft. high'. It must therefore (if I am forming a correct picture of it) have required much more power to draw it along than could be provided by two artificial animals. So other men were possibly concealed beneath it. (How it got through doors is another matter.) Brewer's description now goes on as follows:

> The forest had artificial 'hawthorns, oaks, maples, hazels, birches, fern, broom and furze, with beasts and birds embossed of sundry fashion, with foresters sitting and going on the top of the same' [*The phrase 'going on top of' the forest seems strange at first; presumably the implication is of a high platform as a basis for the trees, 'on the top of' which platform there were foresters both sitting and walking about.*] 'and a castle on' [*presumably 'in' and reaching above the trees,*] 'the said forest, with a maiden sitting thereby with a garland,' [*Now the description turns to the animals drawing it,*] 'and a lion of great stature and bigness, with an antelope of like proportion after his kind drawing the said pageant or forest, conducted with men in wodoos' apparel, and two maidens sitting on the two said beasts; in the which forest were four men of arms, riding, that issued out at time appointed; and on every of the 4 quarters of the forest were the arms of the four knights challengers. . .'

About the construction of this forest there are given the following facts, though the interpretation of them is our hazard.

There were bought '78 alder poles for the body of the forest and great beasts . . .' The leaves of the boughs were apparently made from part of a great quantity of 'green sarcenet' totalling '542 yards', from which a couple of other separate items were also taken. Sarsenet is 'a very fine and soft silk material now used chiefly for linings' (*O.E.D.*). The details are:

> 'Green sarcenet, for the "boos" (? boughs) of the forest, 26 ft. long, 16 ft. broad, and 9 ft. high, 153 yds.; lining a pavilion for the King, 42 yds.; for 12 hawthorns, 44 yds.; 12 oaks, 44 yds.; 10 maples, 36 yds.; hazels, 32 yds.; 10 birches, 32 yds.; 16 doz. fern roots and branches, 64 yds.; 50 broom stalks, 58 yds.; 16 furze bushes, 33 yds.; lining the maiden's sleeves, $2\frac{3}{4}$ yds.; total, 542 yds.'

It is not uninteresting to note that this may be a pretty exact description, because the order of the trees and plants here is precisely the same as the order in the preliminary description quoted at the beginning.

It would seem that this soft silk, or sarsenet, when used for the leaves, was stiffened with paper pasted behind, for there were bought '7 reams of white Geen paper, for lining the sarcenet, that the leaves were made of, and for covering the rocks.'

Much paste must have been needed for such a purpose and for papier-mâché work, and we note an item of '5 bushels of wheat flour for paste'.

There were also 22 yds. of yellow sarsenet 'for broom and furze flowers'.

Beside all this, real foliage was used, for example '6 fir trees' and 'Holly boughs, fennel stalks, broom stalks, &c. planted with sarcenet flowers and leaves'.

An astonishing further item is '2,400 turned acorns and hazelnuts'.

The costumes of the woodwoses or wild men are particularly interesting. They appear to have required 48 yds. of 'Russet sarcenet for the 4 woodwos' garments, shred like locks of hair or wool'. And to this is to be added '9 ells' of 'Canvas of Normandy' 'for lining the 4 woodsys apparel'. For the concealment of their faces there were '4 vizors for the woodwos who conducted the forest'. There was provided also 'Ivy for the woodwos' heads, belts and staves', and in addition a more puzzling '2 doz. green "schyng" payer for mixing with the ivy on the woodwos' heads and staves' [? green shining paper]. And finally the name of the man who made 'the apparel for . . . the woodwos' is given – it was (not inappropriately) Edmond Skill.

(The shredded sarsenet over lining, for their coats, reminds one distantly of the shredded 'papers' of the traditional Mummers.)

Another item for which it is informative to collect the details is the pair of beasts which drew the pageant. I have already noticed that some of the '78 alder poles' were earmarked for their construction. In addition 16½ ells of canvas of Normandy were used 'for the lion and olyvant'. (It must be that the scrivener was confused here, and wrote 'olyvant' for 'antelope', as he does at another point in these accounts, but in the latter instance he has made a written correction to 'antelope'.) Their faces were papier-mâché masks, for there were obtained '10 bundles of crown paper for moulding beasts; the faces of the lion and entelope &c.' The lion was particularly splendid in gold, with '5 doz. of gold paper for the castle and the body and legs of the lions [*sic*]'; and both animals were brightly and correctly 'langued' with '1 lb. vermilion for the mouths of the lion and antelope'. The main bulk of their colouring may have come from '1 lb. of Spanish brown for colouring the beasts'. But the antelope was not entirely without his glory also, and he had his share of 'Gold for gilding the antelope's horns, crowns, etc.'

A special touch must have been provided by '4 lbs. of iron wire . . . for the lion's and olyvaunt's tails' – again the elephant is mentioned but in all other instances but one it is an antelope. The means by which the animals drew, or were feigned to draw, the pageant is also revealed in the item of '6 backs of tanned leather . . . for the chains that the lion and the antelope drew the forest with'. And lastly there is the very remarkable item of '118 lbs. orsade for flossing and casing the lion, &c.' costing the considerable sum of £5.18s. Arsedine is one of the most ancient and most widely used elements of theatrical effects and also one of the most variably spelt; it turns up as orsedyne, orsedew, arsdew, arsidew, and as here orsade. It is an alloy of copper and zinc which gives a glittering imitation gold. But to find one hundred and eighteen pounds of it required for a lion, even with etceteras, is hard to believe. Something may depend of course on what 'flossing' and 'casing' are. 'Flossing' would appear to be 'to make shining' in some way, and 'casing' perhaps 'to cover', but the amount and weight still seem excessive.

It is perhaps not surprising that information is lacking from such lists as these; on the other hand it is equally remarkable to see occasionally what curiously intimate pieces of surprise information can and do creep through that one would never expect. The ultimate fate of this forest pageant is described; after use it was either carted to, or left in, Westminster Great Hall and there, for some reason not stated but presumably because they were attracted by it, a crowd of looters went for it. Among them were certain persons who, one would have hoped, might have been under closer discipline, namely members of the King's Guard itself. They were admittedly not alone in this for with them were what the account notes bitterly as 'other gentyllmen'. It is surprising to see how such persons given an opportunity are quite unprincipled, like those who reach into an unprotected model at an exhibition and wrench, break off and carry away by force the costume figures that have been laboriously incorporated in it. All this happened to the pageant in Westminster Great Hall and it happened, apparently, despite the fact that men had been set to keep it when it was there. The King's Guards and the gentlemen nevertheless broke some of these poor men's heads and threw the rest of them out of the building; and the result was that when the authorities came for it, there was nothing left of the pageant to use again or put in store for the King, but the bare timbers . . . The wording of the passage as given by Brewer is:

Thys forrest or pagent after the ewsans had into Westmester Gret Hall, and by the King's gard and other gentyllmen rent, brokyn, and by fors karryed away, and the poor men that wer set to kep, theyr heds brokyn two of them, and the remnant put ther from with foors, so that noon ther of byt the baar tymbyr cum near to the King's ews nor stoor.

The entertainments on this occasion were fairly elaborate. The jousts (for the first day of which the above forest pageant was made) went on for two days, 12 and 13 February, 'And for the second day were provided and made 4 rich pavilions, one crowned, the other three with balls of bornd gold.' Some details of these pavilions can be gleaned from the ensuing accounts, but there is little more practical information. (They were however better guarded, for after the above account of the looting of the forest; – 'The second day the 4 pavelyons wer savyd to the Kyngs ews [*use*], and profyd [*profit*] with meche payn.') But after the jousts of the 12 and 13 February the King ordered a revel to be held at night in the White Hall, Westminster, and a pageant was prepared called 'The Golden Arber in the Arche yerd of Plesyer'; of this there are some striking details. The arbour itself was –

set with wrethyd pilers of shynyng porpyll, kevyrd with a type in bowd gold, with fyen golld, raylyd with kostly karousing and ther over a vyen of syllver beryng graps of goold; the benchys of thys erber seat and wrowght with kyndly flowers, as rosys, lyllyes, mary gollds, gelofers, prymroses, kowslyps and seche other; and the orche yerde set with horenge trees, ponygarnet trees, happyll tres, per trees, olyvf trees, the porter [? *portal*] of thys orchyerd in bowght and gylld; and with in thys arber wer syttyng xii. lords and ladyes, and without un the syds were viii mynstrells with strange instruments, and befoor un the steps stood dyvers persoons dysgysyd, as Master Sub Deen, Master Kornyche, Master Kaan and other, and un the top wer the chylldyrn of the chappell syngyng, so that oon thys pagent was xxx. persons, weche was marvelus wyghty to remevf and karry, as yt dyd bothe up and down the hall and turnyd round.

Items in the relevant list of expenses are given as:
'2 Beer car wheels and one upright wheel for carriage of the pageant . . .
'16 moulds for pears, apples and oranges and 1 lb. cotton . . .
'4 lbs. black soap for anointing the pageant wheels and joints . . .

'Rushes to strew the house . . .

'Mending the floor broken by weight of the pageant . . .'

Clearly such a scale of spectacle could not be even contemplated by Interluders on tour.

On 9 March 1511, there was at Greenwich a pageant called *The Dangerous Fortress*, 'built like a castle with towers and bulwarks, and fortified with ordnance . . . "and un the dongone of the sayd plaas, 2 kressets brynning with lyght . . . and un the wall or for part of the sayd dongon a rossyer reed and wyght [*a rose tree of red and white roses*] of sassenet, well and kunnyngley cut and wrought, kround with a kroun of golld . . ."' etc. etc.

The relevant expense list shows that 'polen wax' was used at the foot of the 'rosier' or rose tree, and for setting the leaves on it. Also that the guns and 'hagbochys' of the castle were of turned wood.

An especially interesting item here, though an obscure one, is quoted by Brewer as 'A rope used for the "travas" in the hall at Greenwich, and stolen during the disguising' (as indeed so much else was). But it is the significance of the word 'travas' that is tantalizingly obscure. I shall have something to say of this on a later occasion; here I merely note the reference to such a thing as early as 1511, and take it to be some sort of curtain.

A similarly elaborate pageant seems to have been arranged for 1 June 1512, embodying a fountain, but the accounts are mutilated.

The notes for the pageant of 6 January 1513, conclude with a valuable indication of the amount of time and work involved in building and painting for one show. It was entitled *The Ryche Mount*; the scenic item was a 'rock or mountain of gold and precious stones with flowers and a burning beacon on the top, drawn by two "myghty woordwossys or wyld men" '. This mount was made to open. There were bought 28 lbs. of verdigris for colouring it. There was iron work and timber work in it; and 18 carpenters worked for '22 days and divers nights', and no less than 28 painters 'for 23 days and divers nights', upon it. It would seem very certain that no ordinary company of Interluders could have afforded to pay for such a considerable item of labour.

On 6 January 1515, there would appear to have been a difference of some significance; the device was entitled *The Pavyllyon un the Plas Parlos*, and this pavilion is not stated to have been drawn in but was 'on a "pas" or stage, of crimson and blue damask'. What is to be understood by the word 'pas'? (For a suggestion, see below, p. 433). The description continues:

With a gold crown and a bush of roses on the top, and hung with blue tartron. At the 4 corners, 4 brickwork towers, a lord in each . . . On the pageant, 6 minstrels . . . At the foot, 2 armed knights . . . Also gentlemen of the chapel, viz., Mr. Kornyshe, Mr. Krane, Mr. Harry of the Chapel, with the children. These gentlemen first declared the intent of the pageant by process of speech, then entered 3 armed knights . . . 'with noise of drombyllslads, in fierce manner, making a goodly tourney; then 6 wodwos entered suddenly and parted the tourney; after which departure the 3 knights un rescuing the four knights and their ladies [*sic*],' . . . 'They descended and danced before the presence of the King's grace and the Queen's grace, and after returned unto the said pageant, the which with press was spoiled.'

The accompanying notes include '8 lb. verdigris, and 1 pottle pink, for coloring the paper for the woodwos coats', and '6 quarter staves', and 'Ivy and holly for the woodwos apparel'. Also, '51 yards red and blue tartron, used on the pageant, "which tartron in the press of people was cut away, rent and torn by strangers and others, as well the King's servants as not, and letted not for the King's presence."' There were employed '8 carpenters, 4 days and 2 nights, at 8d. a day or night.' Mr. Cornish and many others 'kept' the garments they were provided with.

The pageant for 9 May 1515 was apparently not completed, for 'the King's purpose changed', but it would have been remarkable even in this series. It was 'to have been called "the Palys Marchallyn," in length 36 ft., in breadth 28 ft., in height 10 ft. The house in 4 separate parts, joined in one, and every piece of timber set together with "forlokks" and bolts of iron. On the house 10 towers "embattled, kestyd, inbowyd, dormanddyd and other works by joiners, carpenters and carvers wrought and made." The house framed passant to be borne by men.'

At Christmas 1516, came the particular occasion to which some reference has already been made when Cornish and his boys performed *Troilus and Pandar* with a castle fixed in the hall. Brewer affords an example here of what may be lost by summarizing the words of an original; he speaks of a 'castle of timber in the King's hall' whereas the original reads

a castel of tymbyr fyx and fast in ye Kyngs hall,

which contains valuable extra information; it shows that the castle was not wheeled in but was built, and fixed solidly beforehand, for the spectators to come in and see as they sat down. Thus it is a dis-

tinctly premeditated setting, and therefore different from the effect
of impromptu deliberately exploited by such Interlude-writers as
Medwall.

For Epiphany, 8 H.VIII (Brewer is not clear as to the year, but
1516 or 1517), there is a little information about a slightly different
kind of pageant; namely, a railed garden. The show was called
'"the Gardyn de Desperans"' and:

> It consisted of a garden railed with banks of artificial flowers, as mari-
> golds, rose-campions, daffodils, 'flosmownds', columbines, 'byttayne'
> flowers, roses, eglantines, holly oak and other plants. 'In the midst of
> the said pageant a pillar of sinaper and rowyllyd with gold; and on the
> top of the said pillar, six parted anticks embowed; and in the said antyks
> so dormand and embowed, set with stones and pearls, a roseyar of red
> roses and pomegranates richly inorned and korwnyd with gold of
> great bigness; also all the rails of the said garden were covered with
> gold. Of which garden Master Cornish showed by speech the effect
> and intent, inparelled like a stranger in a gown of red sarcenet, and a
> coat of arms on him, his horse trappered with blue sarcenet, and so
> declaring his purpose. Also 2 children of his inparell, in purple satin of
> Breges for his purposes, and after himself inparelled as well in black
> sarcenet as green sarcenet, for the accomplishment of the intent of the
> revels.' In the garden were 6 knights and ladies walking, the former in
> purple bonnets and garments, the latter 'in purple and cut works on
> white sarcenet and green, embroidered with yellow satin,' and with
> damask gold head attire. The pageant was brought towards the hall
> with noise of minstrels; which ended, it retreated, and the personages
> descended and danced before the King, the Queen and the Court . . .
> The broken frame of the pageant remains in the Prince's Wardrobe.'

Summarizing, there were

> for 1511, a Forest
> 1511, an Arbour
> 1512, a Fortress, also a 'travas'
> ? 1512, a Fountain
> 1513, a Mount
> 1515, a Pavilion, also a 'pas'
> 1515, a Palace (proposed)
> 1516, a Castle
> 1516 or '17, a Railed Garden.

Looking at this summary one asks, in view of the question earlier:
Which, if any, of these could be called a 'house'? The name given
here to a construction carried in or brought in on wheels seems to

have been 'pageant'. It is perhaps possible that the Castle of 1516, which was 'fixed and fast' and not wheeled in, might be termed a 'house'. But it is particularly to be stressed that up to this time the word 'house' itself has not been specifically used in the records. It is true that there will be much use of it in the Revels of Queen Elizabeth I, but so far it is not apparently in technical use at court for a scenic background.

I do not want to go into the question here of what the term 'house' precisely means, but simply to notice that there is so far no apparent justification for using it. For the Interludes next to be discussed it will be necessary to watch in order to find if and when the need for such a term begins to arise.

Apart from the problem of 'houses', one thing, however, can be established from these notes on court shows; namely, that Interluders might well be keenly on the lookout (just as Master Cornish obviously was in regard to his 'children' and 'gentlemen') to exploit court methods when the chance was offered to them, or actually to get possession of such items of costumes and so forth as they could possibly lay their hands on, whether legitimately or illegitimately.

Further, it would not be incorrect, I think, to deduce from the above that by the early sixteenth century, though a few of the Interluders may have been rough enough fellows with little idea of the finer points of theatre, yet others were as shrewd, far-seeing and ambitious for their work – in a word, as sophisticated – as any man at all experienced in court procedure might be expected to be. But it must have been equally true that the source of riches of the common Interluders would lie not in a fat exchequer to lavish on trimmings, but in a store of comment on life and people, together with a very close experience of how to use words and actions so as to put over these comments to a watching audience in the form of public entertainment; that is to say, how to create dramatic actions – entrances, confrontations, suspense, audience-address, exits – that would effectively embody the situations of the characters they created.

If this be a correct opinion, then the essential point is not whether common Interluders did or did not know of court methods. In all likelihood they did, and were not particularly inclined or qualified to use such methods – because they had already created a technique of expressing a dramatic situation through acting and not through elaborate setting; and second because, since touring conditions would make elaborate setting difficult anyhow, they preferred to exploit and develop their acting technique rather than weaken it by relying on assistance from such things as scenic houses.

It is from such a deliberate taking-advantage of their situation that Interluders (as I see it) produced the particular conventional technique of presentation that they did when at length they opened their own (and Shakespeare's) playhouse, to which they apparently did *not* take the technique of court setting, however available it was to them. Or to be accurate, I should perhaps say: they only took single elements of that technique when they decided it would be effective to their dramatic presentation to do so.

10 *Hyckescorner*

In resuming the main story there is a need now to remember that some of the surviving printed Interludes may have been originally written for boy actors, with court resources in mind, and that they may therefore carry signs of presentation methods which belonged only to the court. But on the other hand the possibility equally exists that the playwright of a court Interlude may have carefully revised his text before printing, to remove any court-setting problems so as to make his book more widely saleable to travelling players.

A reader is rarely informed whether or not a given printed Interlude was first written for court performance, but there may be some evidence in the text to help. For example, a large cast with little doubling suggests a boys' play at court in its assumption of a larger pool of players available; on the other hand a play with a small cast – or with a large cast, but arranged to allow of much doubling, and perhaps prefaced with the announcement that four (or so) may play it – is likely to be written (or adapted) for a professional company.

There are some strong suggestions that certain Interludes written for court were afterwards printed for general performance outside. For example, the Interlude of *Damon and Pithias* (c. 1565) has the announcement in the printed edition of 1571 that the text is as it was when played before the Queen by the Children of the Chapel – 'except the Prologue, that is somewhat altered for the proper vse of them that hereafter shall haue occasion to plaie it, either in Private, or open Audience'. Again, in *The Conflict of Conscience* (c. 1572) there is a note in the printed edition of how the doubling of the parts may be arranged 'for such as be disposed either to shew this comedie in priuate houses or otherwise'.

The next two Interludes in provisional order of date are *Hyckes-corner* and *Magnyfycence*. Both are curiously irregular about exit- and entrance-directions; some are in Latin, some are in English; sometimes they are inserted, sometimes not marked at all. They seem to be treated as of less importance than they would be in a modern play script. On the other hand, though they are not always marked as such, there is a very strong tendency to indicate them by the lines of the speeches. That is to say, an entrance is commonly anticipated some lines in advance by a character already in the action; and an exit is often preceded by a farewell speech or a statement of intention to leave.

Hyckescorner is particularly notable in this respect for it contains no directions of either sort from beginning to end; and so, the entrance-heralding lines and the walk-off lines are especially significant. I have used the text of c. 1512, reproduced in Tudor Facsimile Texts in 1908.

This edition opens with two pages of woodcuts (see Figs. 6 and 7). As I have already indicated at the beginning of Section 5 on *Fulgens*, the cuts on the first page (Fig. 6) have no apparent connexion with the play at all, and are purely printer's decorations. The figures on the second page (Fig. 7) do at first sight seem to be more promising since each bears a name in the scroll above, and each name is that of one of the characters in the play. But there is no real connexion beyond the names for, as I have said, Perseueraunce is shown in armour whereas the play distinctly states that he is dressed as a priest, a doctor, or a friar; while the figure labelled 'Pyte' is used again, without the name, in the Lambeth Palace fragment of the Interlude of *Youth* (Fig. 9). The central figure in the lower row, bearing the name of 'Hyckscorner' himself, is almost the same as the central figure in the William Copland edition of *Youth* (Fig. 11), where it is clearly labelled 'Youth'. But it is curious to note that though in every detail of pose and dress these two figures are almost identical, yet the line-work in which they are rendered is quite different; they must come from two different blocks cut by possibly different blockmakers but copied from the same original drawing.

For the purpose of review it is convenient to divide the script into three actions or episodes.

In Episode 1, three grave characters named Pity, Contemplation and Perseverance meet and discuss the evils of the times (5 pages);

FIG. 6. The first illustrated page at the opening of *Hyckescorner* (no date)

FIG. 7. The second illustrated page at the opening of *Hyckescorner*

In Episode 2, three ribald knaves, Freewill, Imagination and Hickscorner, meet, gossip and quarrel. To them comes one of the grave characters, Pity, who is mocked and left fettered (12½ pages);

In Episode 3, Pity is released by his two companions, and two of the knaves are converted; of the third knave we hear no more (15½ pages). The mechanics of the action are as follows:

Episode 1 – Introduction and Meeting
First Pity (Pyte) speaks and must, therefore, enter. He addresses himself to the audience and says,

> Now Jhesu ye gentyll yt bought Adam fro hell
> Saue you all soueraynes & solas you sende
> And of this mater that I begynne to tell
> I praye you of audyence tyll I haue made an ende
> For I saye to you my name is pyte [. . .]

– and he goes on to describe how he once stood with the Virgin Mary at the crucifixion. He ends,

> And now here wyll I rest me a lytell space
> Tyll hyt please Jhesu of his grace
> Some vertuous felyshyp for to sende

Here is clearly a possible reference to an impending entrance. Pity now presumably retires a little but does not go out. Immediately there follows an entrance speech from Contemplation. He does not at first notice Pity but begins with an address to the audience; he describes briefly Christ's suffering, and gives his name –

A.ii.*rev.*   [. . .] I am perfyte contemplacyon [. . .]

Then Pity accosts him, and thus presumably emerges from his retirement, saying –

> God spede good broder fro whens came you now

This is simply a normal speech by a stranger in a new country speaking to a resident. But the resident has apparently come that way with a specific purpose, for he answers –

> Syr I came frome perseueraunce to seke you
> PYTE.   Why syr knowe you me
> CONTEM. Ye syr and haue done longe your name is pyte [. . .]

Later, after some exchanges, Pity courteously remarks –

> I thanke god that we be mette togyder
> CONTEM. Syr I trust yt perseuerunce shortly wyll come hyder

PYTE.　　Than I thynke to here some good tydynge
CONTEM.　I warant you brother that he is comynge

And so, after this particularly good example of the anticipated entrance, it is, surely enough, Perseverance who has the next line. It begins a twenty-line speech addressed once more to the audience, during the whole of which Perseverance does not apparently yet notice the presence of the other two characters, for he ends:

A.iii.*rev.*　　Now to this place hyder come I am
　　　　　　　To seke contemplacyon my knynnesman [*sic*]

At this, Contemplacyon presumably comes forward for he says,

　　　　　　what brother perseueraunce ye be welcome
PERSEUE.　And so be you also contemplacyon

The three now acknowledge each the presence of the others. Contemplatyon introduces his new-found friend, the traveller Pity, to Perseverance with

　　　　　　Loo here is our mayster pyte
PERSEUE.　Now truly ye be welcome in to this countre
PYTE.　　　I thanke you hertely syr perseueraunce [. . .]

and Perseverance goes on to ask him what news there is abroad. Thus, all is smoothly, neatly and courteously engineered in the manner of a normal chance meeting in a street or in a private house – where of course there would be no 'entrances' or 'exits'. The three continue in polite conversation, bewailing the evil of the times, until Contemplacyon pulls up with a sigh, saying:

A.iiii.　　　　Now god that euer hath ben mannes frende
　　　　　　　Some better tydynges soone vs sende
　　　　　　　For now I must be gone
　　　　　　　Fare well good bretherne here
　　　　　　　A grete erande I haue elles where [. . .]
　　　　　　　Theder wyll I hye me shortely
　　　　　　　And come agayne whan I haue done

He does not state what this great errand is, and one supposes it merely exists as a reason to get him out of the action. There appears to be some slight confusion in the lines now. The three are preparing to depart to clear the place for the next episode. It is to be supposed that Contemplacyon's line 'Fare well good bretherne here' is not addressed to his two companions (for one of them is to go out with him) but to the audience in general. Following the last line of his speech is a remark from Perseverance –

> Hyder agayne I trust you wyll come
> Therfore god be with you

It is not quite clear to whom this second line is addressed, but presumably it is not (like the first) addressed to Contemplacyon, for Perseverance and Contemplacyon are on the point of going out together; therefore it must be either to Pity, or again to the audience. Contemplacyon now speaks once more –

> Syr nedes I must departe now
> Jhesu me spede this daye

– addressed it seems to the remaining character, Pity, the visitor from abroad. Next, Perseverance has one line, and with it concludes the scene; he says,

> Now brother contemplacyon let vs go our waye

– and so it seems obvious that he and Contemplacyon now leave together, parting from the visitor, Pity, and go out by one of the doors into the entry. Pity himself is not accounted for, but since it would appear that he does not go with the others we may suppose him leaving by the second door as they go out by the first. Without two doors and the arrangement suggested, this end to the scene would apparently be unworkable. At all events what follows is a totally new episode.

Episode 2 – Quarrel and the Fettering of Pity
A completely fresh character now calls through the bystanders to the audience in general –

A.iiii.*rev.*   Aware felowes and stande a roume
How saye you am not I a goodly personue [*sic*]
I trowe you knowe not suche ageste [. . .]

– and he gives his name as Frewyll and goes on for thirty-six lines, including a gag about money he has lost in a brothel. He finally shouts for his 'felowe' Imagynacyon:

How Imagynacyon come hyder . . .
IMAGY.   What how how who called after me
FREWYLL.   Come nere [. . .]
Where haue ye be so longe

Thus there is again a sort of 'hidden' entrance; that is to say, a second new character has now apparently made his way in as Frewyll did, but has remained concealed among the bystanders so that Frewyll could not see him in the shadows from the torches, and has to call out for him and summon him to 'come nere'. This newcomer, whose name is Imagynacyon, now joins Frewyll and tells at some length of his own adventures with a tavern wench, and finally asks –

> But frewyll my dere broder
> Sawe you not of Hyckscorner
> He promysed me to come hyder

– but there is no news of this Hyckscorner, and the same technique is employed again of an apparently 'hidden' entrance but, this time, one with a difference in that the implied entrance does not in fact, for the moment, take place; the audience is led to expect it, and then deliberately put off by its non-occurrence. The two in the place resume their conversation and discuss the state of affairs current in Newgate Prison. Imagynacyon says he is so accomplished in the thief's craft that

> Yf my handes were smyten of I can stele wt my tethe

– and so forth. At length they again look round for Hyckscorner, and Imagynacyon chaffs the bystanders with –

> Some of these yonge men hathe hydde hym in
> theyr bosomes I warraunt you

– a line which does not scan with the rest, and in view of the small letter 't' at the beginning of 'theyr', one wonders if the line is really a line of prose thrown in among the rest for a gag. This idea has some confirmation in that the speech immediately following is not a reply from Frewyll but is a resumption of the same speech by Imaginacyon, though with a fresh ascription to head it:

> IMAGYN. Let vs make a crye that he maye vs here

The frequent repetition of the idea that a figure is lost or hidden, or cannot be seen for the time being, would accord very well with the picture I have tried to present of the crowded dimness of a torch lit hall in a country house. In some places it might have been as difficult to see one's neighbour as in a modern darkened cinema.

Then Frewyll responds to Imagynacyon's proposal with the call –

> How how hyckscorner appere

Now at last the deferred entrance is made, and there comes a speech from Hyckscorner himself. He presumably pushes through the crowd, and his speech is a curious one –

Ale the helme ale vere shot of vere sayle vera

Frewyll helps us a little to understand it by his next line which is,

Cockes body herke he is in a shyppe on the see

– and Hyckscorner replies –

God spede god spede who called after me

Thus it is clear that Hyckscorner is a seaman, or at least is from a boat; and his 'ale' is presumably to be read 'a-lee'. The whole line is an echo of a sailor's orders.

Hyckscorner describes with some scurrilous detail a satirical voyage, and eventually proposes that the three of them should go stealing and whoring. But Frewyll soon slanders Imagynacyon, and these two quarrel. Hyckscorner intervenes but is threatened also. Imagynacyon turns on him and it would appear the two become locked in a bout of rolling fisticuffs. During this Frewyll apparently stands discreetly back to observe them, and laughingly addresses the audience with the colourful speech:

B.i.   Lo syrres here is afayre company god vs saue
For yf ony of vs thre be mayre of london
I wys y wys I wyll ryde to rome on my thom

And then, concerning the combat –

Alas a se is not this a grete feres
I wolde they were in a myll pole [*? pool*] aboue the eres
And than I durst warraunt they wold departe anone

('departe' equals 'become separated'). From presumably the bottom of the scuffle Hyckscorner's voice is now heard calling,

Helpe helpe for the passyon of my soule
He hath made a grete hole in my poule

He (or Frewyll; the text is not clear here) then appears to break away and run for refuge into the crowd at the doors, for Imagynacyon shouts –

Ware make rome he shall haue a strype I trowe

– and at that point the struggling, jostling group by the doors is broken in upon by an unexpected figure. It is Pity returning, and he calls –

Peas peas syrres I commaunde you

At this sudden intervention of the voice of authority the three leave their quarrel to unite against Pity. They slander him while Frewyll slips out to find a pair of gyves to fetter him. The abuse continues, the gyves are brought in, Pity is fettered by the legs, and a 'halter' is found to bind his hands as well. Pity continues to preach bravely the while; he begs them to remember God and their own imminent deaths. But Frewyll pertly and blasphemously retorts –

B.ii.*rev.*   What dethe and he were here he sholde syt by ye
                 Trowest thou that he be able to stryue wt vs thre
                 Nay nay nay

– and they all three depart to go to Shooters Hill to rob travellers, Frewyll exclaiming –

Byshrewe hym for me yt is last out of this place

We picture a scampered exit and collisions with the crowd; and then Pity is left alone.

Episode 3 – Pity released; Two Knaves converted

Pity, sitting in his gyves with arms bound, delivers a long speech to the audience. At the end of it there is no anticipation of the entrance of the next characters – they come in unheralded, and speak at once in dismay –

B.iii.*rev.*   CONTEM. what mayster pyte how is hyt with you
              PERSEUE. Syr we be sory to se you in this case now

Pity explains his plight, and the others loose him both 'the fete and the handes'. Contemplacyon advises Pity to go after Frewyll and Imagynacyon, arrest them and imprison them (Hyckscorner is not mentioned). Pity agrees and goes, with –

B.iiii.   Now fare wele bretherne and praye for me
                 For I must go hens in dede

Perseverance bids him good bye with

Now god be your good spende [*? speede*]

– and Contemplacyon similarly –

And euer you defende whan you haue nede

And then it is – rather surprisingly – Frewyll who speaks next. This would seem another very good reason for the existence of two doors, for Pity has just departed, specifically to look for Frewyll, and if Frewyll came in immediately by the same door that Pity left by, it would appear ridiculous that Pity had not seen him.

I therefore believe that when Pity went out on his errand he left by door A, while his two friends conveniently merged themselves in the crowd for the moment, leaving the floor clear; and that thereupon Frewyll's voice was heard through the crowd round door B (and through the sudden chattering, perhaps, of that crowd concerning the scene they had just witnessed), as he breaks into the action once more with the lines –

> Make you rome for a gentylman syrs and pease
> Duegarde seygnours tout le preasse
> And of your Jangelynge yf ye wyll sease
> I wyll tell you where I haue bene
> Syrres I was at the tauerne and dronke wyne [. . .]

. . . and he tells how he was caught stealing but was rescued through a cheat arranged by Imagynacyon. He is dancing and delighting in his freedom when, suddenly, he must see the other two, for he stops with –

> What whome haue we here
> A preest a douctoure or elles a frere

– and so Perseverance (who speaks next) must now step out from the shadows into the action again with Contemplacyon. The above lines by the way give a very good idea of what he looks like and how he is dressed – like a priest, doctor or friar (notice that this is in contradiction of the title cuts which show 'Perseue' as a knight in armour). He gravely exclaims,

> [. . .] of thy lyuynge I reed amende the

– and Frewyll (rather interestingly) retorts with an indirect reference to the French familiarity of speech called *tutoyer*. He says:

> Auaunt catyfe doost thou thou me [. . .]

– and the two fall to lively argument. Frewyll defies both him and Pity, but Perseverance replies –

C.i.*rev.*   Naye naye thy grete wordes maye not helpe the
         Fro vs thou shalte not escape

– and Frewyll, presumably in a tight corner both physically and metaphorically, cries about him –

> Make rome syrres that I maye breke his pate
> I wyll not be taken for them bothe

And Contemplacyon now speaks; whom we have pictured coming out from among the bystanders close behind Perseverance. These two indulge in a ding-dong dressing-down of Frewyll – amounting to a verbal brain-washing. Two-against-one prevails in the end, despite Frewyll's wriggling and false reasoning. Battered down by their picture of his death and damnation soon to come, he cries –

C.iii.*rev.* Now of all my synnes I axe god mercy
Here I forsake synne and trust to amende

And – as is typical of the Interludes – Contemplacyon thereupon gives him a change of clothing. Where he gets it from is not explained; presumably he walks out to fetch it from the entry –

C.iiii. Holde here a newe garment [. . .]

– and they press their lessons home, concluding –

> But loke that thou be stedfaste
> And let thy mynde with good wyll laste
> IMAGY. Huffe huffe huffe who sent after me [. . .]

And thus we are switched, with no warning at all, into a new atmosphere created by the sudden return of Frewyll's old companion-in-evil – Imagynacyon. He apparently does not see the others; he is in high feather and asks the audience –

C.iiii.*rev.* But syrres wote ye why I am come hyder [. . .]
Saue ye not of my felawe frewyll [. . .]

– and then he peers about him in amazement!

> What felawe is this that in this cote is fyled
> Kockes deth whome haue we here
> what Frewyll myn owne fere
> Arte thou out of thy mynde . . .

– and he proclaims his astonishment at the sight of the reformed and reclothed Frewyll. The other two grave figures, who seem to have momentarily escaped his notice in the shadows, now turn their awful persuasion upon him too; and at length under the added pleas of Imaginacyon he gives in also. And he makes the same request –

179

> I wyll do syr euen as you wyll
> But I praye you let me haue a newe cote [. . .]
> No thynge drede I so sore as deth [. . .]

Perseverance complies:

> Holde here is a better clothynge for the

– and he arranges for the future reformed lives of the two, and their bliss-to-be in heaven. He reaches his conclusion with –

> Unto the whiche blysse I beseche god almyghty
> To brynge there your soules that here be present
> And vnto vertuous lyuynge that ye maye applye
> Truly for to kepe his commaundemente
> Of all our myrthes here we make an ende
> Unto the blysse of heuen Jhesu your soules brynge
> AMEN

But of the eponymous hero (?), Hyckscorner, we hear, strangely enough, not another single word.

11 *Magnyfycence*

With *Magnyfycence* (c. 1516) we come into a somewhat different atmosphere. *Mankind*, *The World and the Child*, and *Hyckescorner* are all anonymous, and though the title-pages of *Nature* and *Fulgens* give the name of Thomas Medwall as author we have little more information about him. But the author of *Magnyfycence* is well-known and distinguished as a poet, a man who was a university laureate and who has now a recognized place in English literature: John Skelton (c. 1440–1529). Besides being the writer of some of the wittiest, most human, and most technically original sixteenth-century poems, he was a rector and a reformer attacking the morals of his fellow-churchmen, and particularly the magnificence of Wolsey. But especially to the present subject, he appears to have written more than one play though only this one is known to have survived.

One of the lost plays is recorded by Thomas Warton, the author of *The History of English Poetry*, 1774, who says he saw a copy printed by Wynkyn de Worde in 1504. According to him it was entitled *The Nigramansir*, 'a morall Enterlude and a pithie and plaid before the King and other Estatys at Woodstoke on Palm Sunday' (see Henry Morley, *English Writers*, vii, p. 180; but see also the scepticism of R. L. Ramsay on this, in his E.E.T.S. edition (extra series No. 98, 1906) of *Magnyfycence*, footnote on p. xix). Two other of his plays would seem to have been his 'sovereign *Interlude of Virtue*', and his 'comedy Achademiss called by name' quoted by him in his poem, *The Garland of Laurel*. Of the two latter we have no evidence of performance, but of *The Nigramansir* Warton says it was played at court; and the conclusion would be that Skelton had at least some experience of a play in presentation as well as of a poem in writing.

The title-page of *Magnyfycence*, in the facsimile edition of The Tudor Text Society (Old English Drama, No. 71), reads

> Magnyfycence,
> A goodly interlude and a me-
> ry deuysed and made by
> mayster Skelton / poet
> laureate late de-
> ceasyd ∴

No attempt will be made here to discuss the plot of this fairly elaborate play in detail. Briefly it concerns eighteen characters (but could be played, according to the preface in R. L. Ramsay's edition, by a company of five actors); these characters are listed on the final page as –

Felycyte.	Clokyd colusyon.	Good hope.
Lyberte.	Courtly abusyon.	Redresse.
Measure.	Foly.	Cyrcumspeccyon
	Aduersyte.	Perseueraunce.
Magnyfycence.	Pouerte.	
	Dyspare.	
Fansy.	Myschefe.	
Counterfet counte.		
Crafty conueyaunce.		

(The last-but-one name in the first column is, in full, Counterfeit Countenance.)

The plot shows how the three first-listed characters combine to try to ensure proper balance in Magnyfycence's court life, and how he himself is confused and betrayed by those below in the first column together with all those in the second column; and finally how he is saved by those in the third.

There is a certain difficulty for a reader of *Magnyfycence* that would not exist for a spectator at an actual performance. This matter is not uninstructive, for it lights up one of the great advantages of theatre in action as against a script studied at a desk. The difficulty is the similarity of four of the characters' names, leading to an impression of confusion; they are, in modern spelling, Counterfeit Countenance, Crafty Conveyance, Cloaked Colusion and Courtly Abusion. In the speech ascriptions these are abbreviated to –

> Coūterfet coū.
> Crafty conuey.
> Cloked colusyō
> Courtly abusyō

It clearly would require a more than usually attentive reader to attach the proper character to each of these four, and to keep those characters unerringly distinct throughout his whole reading. Particularly does it make difficult the clear picturing of such brief extracts of dialogue as I must be reduced to here, in a short review of the practicalities of the play. The sense of confusion that the reader (as against a spectator) must experience may tend to make him judge the play as obscure and ill-written. This would be a very unfortunate judgement.

However, what is so very significant about all this is that in a living performance the spectator would not be contemplating a group of abstract epithets, but a quartet of very lively and very distinct human beings – he would not say 'Now, who is speaking? Ah, Courtly Abusion! Now which of them is Courtly Abusion?...'. He would in fact *see* that the speaker was that particular one of the four characters that had a certain gorgeous manner, with a 'bush' of hair, a rippling robe, a flowing sleeve, and who glittered all in gold. There would be no mistaking him. To every spectator that man would be *that man* – with a character entirely his own, whether they forgot his name or remembered it.

Cloaked Colusion would be, again, quite distinctly recognizable because of his appearance; as well as having a convenient nickname, Sir John Double-Cloak, he would be memorable because he 'weareth a cope' or 'cap[e]' to wrap him from the world; and he carries his nose in the air 'hawking for a butterfly'.

Crafty Conveyance is a doubtful piece of official work, probably well acquainted with conveyancing. His alias is 'Sure Surveyance' and he is Master Surveyor at Magnyfycence's court.

Finally, False Face (or Counterfeit Countenance), a forger, is the first of the four to appear and he carries a forged letter.

The acting-directions in *Magnyfycence* are unusually detailed.

There are many points about them that make them worth considering on their own, and to read them through in order gives a not inadequate introduction to the whole action of the play. It will therefore be useful to extract them and consider them now. There is however one qualification; some of them are in English and some in Latin. It is not easy to decide the reason for this mixture, but what is worth noting is that Skelton was a pretty accomplished Latinist and anything he had to say by means of a relatively unusual Latin phrase is possibly of significance and worth translating. But translation is not easy; if Skelton was a good Latinist then we must blame the printer for certain misprints that make the meaning sometimes very hard indeed to interpret.

I propose to list these acting-directions in order, in two columns, putting the Latin ones in the left-hand column, and the English in the right. Against each Latin direction I put, in italics in the right-hand column, an approximate English equivalent. (My own Latin is very far from adequate for this specialized task, and I must record here how very deeply indebted I am to Mr. R. E. Latham, editor of the *Medieval Latin Dictionary*, for his full discussions with me about the problems involved.)

The directions are as follows, numbered in order of their appearance in the text, and each bearing a Roman numeral after it to indicate the folio on which it occurs in the printed edition.

1. Hic intrat Measure. (fol. ii) — [*Here Measure enters.*]
2. Hic intrat magnyfycence. (iii) — [*Here Magnyfycence enters.*]
3. Ita*que* measure exeat locu*m* cum lybertate et maneat magnyfycence cu*m* felicitate. (iiii) — [*Then let Measure go out from the place with Lyberty and let Magnyfycence remain with Felicity.*]
4. Hic intrat Fansy. (iiii) — [*Here Fansy enters.*]
5. Hic faciat tanqu*am* legeret litteras tacite: Interim superueniat cantando counterfetcountenaunce suspenso gradu q*ui* [?] viso magnyfycence sensū [? *sensim*] retrocedat ad te*m*pus post pusillu*m* rursum accedat coun terfetcountenaunce prospectando & vocitando a longe et fansy animat [? *annuat*] silentium cum manu. (v) — [*Here let him (Magnyfycence) act as if he were reading the letter to himself: In the meantime let Counterfet Countenaunce run in trolling and tripping [;] when he sees Magnyfycence let him stealthily draw back for a moment [then] after a brief space let Counterfet Countenaunce again approach, looking on them and speaking from a distance, and let Fansy motion silence with his hand.*]

6. Hic discedat magnificens cum fansy et intrat cou*n*terfet countenaunce. (vi)

[*Here let Magnyfycence depart with Fansy and Counterfet Countenaunce enters.*]

7. Hic ingrediatur fansy properantur [? *properanter*] cu*m* crafty conueyau*n*ce cum famina multa [? *famine multo*] adiniucem [? *adinvicem*] garrulantes tandem viso cou*n*terfet countenau*n*ce dicat crafty co*n*ueyau*n*ce. (vii)

[*Here let Fansy walk in quickly with Crafty Conveyaunce chatting together with much talk, at length on seeing Counterfet Countenaunce let Crafty Conveyaunce say;*]

8. Hic ingrediatur cloked colusyon cum elato aspectu deorsum et sursum ambulando. (viii)

[*Here let Cloked Colusyon walk in with a lordly expression and stride up and down.*]

9. Hic deambulat. (ix)

[*Here he promenades.*]

10. Hic ingrediatur courtly abusyon cantando. (ix*r*)

[*Here let Courtly Abusyon come in singing.*]

11. Et faciat tanqu*am* exiat [? *exuat*] beretrum [? *berettum*] cronice [? *ironice*]. (ix*r*)

[*And let him make as if he doffs his cap mockingly.*]

12. Here cometh in Crafty conueyaunce poyntyng with his fynger and sayth. Hem colusyon. (x)

13. And so they go out of the place. (x*r*)

14. Courtly abusyon alone in the place. (x*r*)

15. Here cometh in fansy craynge stow stow. (xi)

16. Hic ingrediatur Foly quesiendo [? *quatiendo*] crema et faciendo multum feriendo tabulas [? *taburas*] et similia. (xii*r*)

[*Here let Foly walk in shaking a bauble and making much ado of beating drums, and so on.*]

17. Here cometh in crafty conueyaunce. (xiiii)

18. Here foly maketh semblaunt to take a lowse from crafty conueyaunce showlder. (xiiii*r*)

19. Here crafty conuaunce putteth of his gowne. (xiiii*r*)

20. Here foly maketh semblaunt to take money of crafty conueyaunce saynge to hym. (xiiii*r*)

21. Crafty conueyaunce alone in the place. (xvi)

22. Here cometh in Magnyfycence with Lyberte and Felycyte. (xvi*r*)

23. Here goth out Crafty conuayaunce. (xvi*r*)

24. Here cometh in Fansy. (xvi*r*)

25. Here goeth out felycyte / lyberte / and fansy. (xvii)

26. Magnyfycence alone in the place. (xvii*r*)

27. Here cometh in courtly abusyon doynge reuerence and courtesy. (xviii)

28. Here cometh in cloked colusyon with mesure. (xix)

29. Hic introducat colusion mesure magnyfycence aspectant[?*e*] vultu elatissimo. (xx)

[*Here let Colusyon bring Mesure forward, Magnyfycence staring with a very lordly look.*]

30. Here mesure goth out of the place. (xx*r*)

31. Here goth cloked colusyon awaye and leueth Magnyfycence alone in the place. (xxi)

32. Here cometh in Foly. (xxi)

33. Here Fansy cometh in. (xxi*r*)

34. Here goth foly away. (xxii)

35. Here cometh in aduersyte. (xxii)

36. Here magnyfycence is beten downe and spoylyd from all his goodys and rayment. (xxii)

37. Here cometh in pouerte. (xxiii)

38. Hic accedat ad leuandum magnyfycence et locabit eum super locum stratum. (xxiii)

[*Here let him approach to lift up Magnyfycence and he shall lay him on a 'spread place'.*]

39. Difidendo [? *diffindendo*] dicat ista verba. (xxiv)

[*Hopelessly* [or ? breaking off] *let him say these words;*]

40. Here magnyfycence dolorously maketh his mone. (xxiv)

41. Hic aliquis buccat in cornu a retro post populu*m*. (xxv)

[*Here someone blows a horn at the back behind the people.*]

42. Here cometh in Crafty con-ueyaunce Cloked colusyo*n* with a lusty laughter. (xxv*r*)

43. Et cum festinacione discedant a loco. (xxvi*r*)

[*And let them hastily depart from the place.*]

44. Hic intrat dyspare. (xxvi*r*)

[*Here cometh in Dyspare.*]

45. Hic intrat myschefe. (xxvii)

[*Here cometh in Myschefe.*]

46. Here magnyfycence wolde slee hymselfe with a knyfe. (xxvii)

47. Hic intrat Goodhope fugienti-b*us* dyspayre & myschefe repente good hope surripiat illi gladio [? *gladium*] & dicat. (xxvii*r*)

[*Here Goodhope enters while Dys-pare and Myschefe take to their heels* [;] *let Goodhope suddenly snatch the sword from him and say;*]

48. Hic intrat Redresse. (xxviii)

[*Here cometh in Redress.*]

49. Magnyfycence accipiat indu-mentum. (xxviii)

[*Let Magnyfycence receive the gar-ment.*]

50. Here cometh in sad cyrcum-speccyon sayenge. (xxviii*r*)

51. Hic intrat perseueraunce. (xxix)

[*Here cometh in Perseverance*]

Before coming to particular problems there are three general comments to make on this list.

Firstly there are the several uses of the word 'Place' (these occur of course only in the English directions). There are six of them, see nos. 13, 14, 21, 26, 30, 31. The common use of this word as a par-ticular technical expression in medieval theatre I have already dis-cussed at length in *The Medieval Theatre in the Round*. There, on p. 235, I suggested a definition of 'Place' (or *platea*, or *placea*, or 'plain') in the following terms; 'the area on which the audience stood [or sat] before a raised stage or stages'. And I added that 'the actors might descend to it as part of their technique whenever necessary, and use it on occasion for considerable passages of action'.

It is clear now upon reading the Tudor Interludes that the term suffered some development in the late fifteenth and the sixteenth centuries; not only a 'considerable passage' of the action but the whole of it now evolves in the Place, and now (so far as we have reached at present) no raised stages are required. I have put forward my reasons for supposing that with indoor Interludes the word was retained and used in much the same sense as formerly but now particularly applied to the floor of a Great Hall as a whole; that is to say, for defining (as before) an area where both audience and players were. Perhaps there is now to be felt a slight modification in that the tendency seems to be to contract it to mean that part of the floor which could be claimed as the acting-area, but of course there was no demarcation of any such area. Thus, the earlier definition might be brought up to date by rewording it as 'The area where the actors played and where also the audience sat or stood to watch, i.e. the hall floor.' With all this Skelton's use of the word 'place' is entirely consistent.

But it is of some interest to see that Skelton, the Latinist, did not use the Latin word for Place which was usual in medieval times – that is, *platea* or *placea*. He may perhaps have considered such a usage to be dog-Latin. Instead, when he has occasion to refer to the thing in Latin he uses the word *locus* (e.g. Nos. 3 and 43). This is surprising since in medieval usage the word *locus* seems rather to have applied to a *sedes* or scaffold on the perimeter of the Place proper.

The second general comment is that Skelton is unusually careful about the Latin words he uses for what we might call entering and exiting. Besides the normal *intrat* (used eight times) and *exeat* (used only once), he has *superueniat* ('let him come up to'), *retrocedat* (retire), *accedat* ('draw near' – used twice), *discedat* ('depart' – used twice), *ingrediatur* ('walk in' – used four times), *introducat* ('bring in'). In addition are the words *maneat* ('let him remain') and *deambulat* ('he walks about').

The third general comment is that Skelton, the Latinist, uses nearly all the above verbs in the subjunctive mood ('let him' so-and-so) with the two exceptions of the term *intrat*, which is curiously always in the indicative ('he enters'), and the one occasion of *deambulat* ('he promenades').

Certain particular notes are due on individual directions:

In No. 5, two words seem corrupt and have been amended to *sensim* and *annuat* respectively as indicated. *Cantando . . . suspenso gradu* is perhaps too freely translated by 'trolling and tripping' but the meaning is otherwise not exactly clear. A very puzzling question rises over the phrase that reads in the original *q̄ viso magnyfycence*. To expand the contraction to *quo viso* would seem unlikely, for this would imply that it was Magnyfycence himself who saw Counterfet Countenaunce and then drew stealthily back, not the other way round – and the sense of the scene is quite against this since the dialogue shows that Magnyfycence has no idea who has just entered at that point. Ramsay, in his edition of *Magnyfycence*, expands as *qui viso* which is no doubt right. The phrase 'after a brief space' (*post pusillum*) has in the Latin that extra touch of the idea of diffidence which would suggest that Counterfet Countenaunce was meant to look, to check, to half-turn, then turn back and look again – in other words it is equivalent to saying in modern theatre slang, 'after a brief double-take' – which is a piece of business that can always be relied upon for a small laugh. The whole of this direction is of the greatest interest as being one of the fullest and most minute acting-directions in all early drama. The situation when it occurs will be described below.

In No. 7 three emendations to words, as shown, seem necessary to correct what must be misprints.

In No. 11 the meaning is very obscure, and the emendations and translation are given tentatively.

In No. 16 both *crema* and *tabulas* are very difficult to translate. There is little, if any, evidence for the former word meaning 'bauble', and the rendering is a suggestion. Also *tabulas* (meaning 'boards') is a puzzle. It could mean 'castanets' or something similar; the alternative *taburas* is again a mere suggestion.

In No. 38, *super locum stratum* is one of the biggest puzzles of all. Some editors give 'upon a bed'. This I discuss separately.

In No. 39, *diffindendo* is a hazardous suggestion. It makes sense. But *difidendo* as printed could mean 'defiantly' in a medieval context, yet this seems not to fit the situation in the play. At best one can do no more than claim that *diffindendo* is just conceivable. Ramsay here takes the step of emending to *discedendo*, 'as he departs'.

Turning now to the action. No acting-direction is given at the opening; the play begins simply with a speech from Felycyte, who stresses the comforting support given in a changeable world by the possession of wealth, and he identifies himself therewith under the name of 'welthfull Felicite'. To him there comes a second character saying,

> Mary welthe and I was apoynted to mete
> And eyther I am dysseyued or ye be the same

– to which Felycyte replies,

> Syr as ye say [;] I haue harde of your fame
> your name is lyberte as I vnderstande

Thus the exposition of the situation is much like that in *Hyckescorner*
so far. The two figures greet each other. In their conversation
Felycyte argues that liberty must be subject to measure, 'For lyberte
at large is lothe to be stoppyd'.

To them, a third character comes; this time there is an acting-
direction and, like all the acting-directions in the first nine folios
of the play, it is in Latin (after fol. ix., some directions are in Latin
and some in English). The direction is simply –

> Hic intrat Measure.

Measure joins the discussion and the three at length reach the conclusion that –

> There is no prynce but he hath nede of vs thre
> welthe with measure and plesaunt lyberte

– and immediately Measure says,

> Nowe pleasyth you a lytell whyle to stande
> Me semeth magnyfycence is comynge here at hande
> Hic intrat magnyfycence.

Again I notice the 'heralded' or anticipated entrance which, as
was remarked concerning *Hyckescorner*, is particularly suggestive of
performance in a hall with screens; it would be far less suitable on
any form of stage that resembled ours of today, because of course a
player on our stage can *not* see another player when he is 'coming
here at hand' – but only when in fact he *has* come fully in.

This technique of heralded, or anticipated, or deferred entrance –
or entrance deferred for notice to be called to it by actors already
present – can have very different variations in detail. Several are to
be found in this play and it may be helpful to collect a few.

Thus, at the bottom of fol. vii.*rev.*, Counterfet Countenaunce
suddenly interrupts himself in mid-dialogue with –

> Cockes woundes se syrs se se

– and the reason for his crying 'See! See!' is that just then a completely new character has come in at the end of the hall and is
walking to and fro with his nose loftily in the air ('Hic ingrediatur
cloked colusyon cum elato aspectu deorsum et sursum ambulando').
He is, as the lines later show, wearing a heavy 'cope' or cape, symbolic of his name. Here is the perfect opportunity for a laugh for
any comedian; and to improve the situation the newcomer is clearly

not meant to notice the others farther down the hall in the flickering torchlight, so they can make the most of him. Fansy murmurs in amazement,

> Cockes armes what is he [!]

and Crafty Conveyance bursts out with a giggle –

> By cockes harte he loketh hye
> He hawketh me thynke for a butterflye

The third one among the watchers acts a little more politically; he approaches the haughty figure directly, exclaiming –

> Nowe by cockes harte well abyden
> For had you not come I had ryden

And only then does Cloked Coluyson lower his gaze, notice them and begin to speak.

Thus we have a new character entering and not, for some time, taking notice of characters already present. Such an entrance might fairly be classed with the convention I have noticed earlier and called 'differentiation of acting-area'.

A reversed form of the technique described is when a character in action refuses to notice a character entering. For example, on fol. x., there is a scene in which Cloked Colusyon is being importuned on a certain matter and has agreed to undertake to 'do somwhat' about it, when suddenly there comes the direction (and, for the first time, in English) –

> Here cometh in Crafty conueyaunce poyntyng
> with his fynger and sayth. Hem colusyon

At this, the character who is importuning Cloked Colusyon immediately exclaims,

> Cockys harte who is yonde that for the dothe call

Now, unfortunately, there rises a textual problem; the next speech, which is only a single line, is obscure. Let me for the moment ignore it. The line which follows after it is quite clear; it is a continuation of the above speech and reads

> Cockys armys he hath callyd for the twyce

– and there seems no doubt that Crafty Conveyance must have 'hemmed' again. In reply, Cloked Colusyon says firmly,

By cockys harte and call shall agayne
To come to me I trowe he shalbe fayne

Thereupon, Courtly Abusyon (who is the character that has been importuning Cloked Colusyon, but whose name I have concealed up till now in an attempt to keep confusion from becoming worse confounded) remarks that Cloked Colusyon seems to be acting very high-handedly; his line is,

what is thy harte pryckyd with such a prowde pynne

– and eventually Cloked Colusyon deigns to notice Crafty Conveyance's presence and to give him some sort of attention.

What is to the point at present is that we see how a character can effectively ignore the entrance of another character if it suits him to do so, even if the character entering has made deliberate signs to try to attract his attention, and what is more, that such a piece of business can be put over to the audience as being convincing. This sort of technique may, of course, be met with on a modern stage, but there it is conspicuously something that falls short of conviction, however much one suspends disbelief in it. Nevertheless, in a presentation taking place on the floor of a crowded hall, under flickering torchlight, and with the two doors of the screens encumbered with bystanders, the technique is not only acceptable, but is indeed a case of exploitation of the medium.

For the reader's information, the line withheld above as a textual problem is –

Nay come at ones for the armys of the dyce

The problem is, who speaks it? In the original the speech is ascribed to Cloked Colusyon; it does not seem immediately to fit him, and in the edition of *The Complete Poems of John Skelton*, by Philip Henderson (reprinted 1966), the editor has ascribed the line to Crafty Conveyaunce, though without remarking the fact nor offering his reason. He may well be right, but our concern must be with the technique, and the textual problem here does not affect it.

To resume; something of the same sort of technique is to be found on fol. xi., where Fansy comes in during a long soliloquy by Courtly Abusyon; but Abusyon carefully finishes his speech before heeding the interrupter and even then fails to recognize him immediately. The lines read as follows (Abusyon speaking):

> [. . .] wherfore I preue / a tyborne checke
> Shall breke his necke
> > Here cometh in fansy craynge stow stow.
> All is our of harre / and out of trace
> Ay warre and warre / in euery place
> But what the deuyll art thou / that cryest stow stow

– whereupon Fansy (conceivably threading his way through the by-standers) mockingly rejoins:

> what whom haue we here Jenkyn Joly
> Nowe welcom by the god holy

– and only then does Abusyon profess to recognize him with –

> what fansy my frende howe doste thou fare

Another example is on fol. xxi.*rev*. By this particular part of the plot, the character Fansy has for strategic reasons assumed the alias of 'Largesse'. The situation shows Magnyfycence listening to a tall story from Foly, when Foly suddenly breaks off what he is saying with –

> Se syr I beseche you largesse my brother
> > Here Fansy cometh in

Fansy's entrance is thus anticipated both by Foly's remark and by his sudden change of subject.

A difference occurs again on fol. xxii. Here Magnyfycence has been finally betrayed by all his old servants, and Fansy is mocking him, saying –

> [. . .] it was I all this whyle
> That you trustyd and fansy is my name
> And foly my broder that made you moche game
> > Here cometh in aduersyte

This direction marks the entrance of a new and baleful figure; in this instance there is no doubt that Magnyfycence sees him immediately for he exclaims –

> Alas why [? *who*] is yonder / that grymly lokys

– but Adversity himself does not yet speak, and still takes time to come up to the others, so giving Fansy a chance to exclaim in reply –

> A dewe for I wyll not come in his clokys

– and then presumably he slips aside, leaving Magnyfycence alone to murmur –

> Lorde so my flesshe trymblyth nowe for drede

as the baleful figure comes down on him. Then, at length –

> Here magnyfycence is beten downe and
> spoylyd from all his goodys and rayment:

And only after this does the grim new character begin to speak:

> I am aduersyte that for the mysdede
> From god am sent [. . .]

In fol. xxviii., is another example of the simple, heralded entrance. Here Goodhope is comforting Magnyfycence, and is saying–

> Then shall you be sone delyuered from dystresse
> For nowe I se comynge to youwarde redresse
> > Hic intrat Redresse

– and Redresse then greets them.

On fol. xxviii.*rev.* there is the same sort of heralded entrance once again; Redresse has proved powerless to correct mankind on his own account and so he welcomes the entry of a fresh character to help and reinforce him –

> But redresse is redlesse and may do no correccyon
> Nowe welcome forsoth sad cyrcumspeccyon
> > Here cometh in sad cyrcumspeccyon sayenge [. . .]

Finally on fol. xxix., Magnyfycence's new friends are advising him on the better conduct of his affairs, and one of them, Redresse, remarks –

> Vse not then your countenaunce for to counterfet
> And from crafters and hafters I you forfende
> > Hic intrat perseueraunce

– but before taking any notice of the newly-entered Perseverance, Magnyfycence first takes time to reply to the above speech saying patiently

> Well syr after your counsell my mynde I wyll set

– and it is not he but Redresse, who then greets the new character who has just entered, with –

> What brother perceueraunce surely well met . . .

In the brief interval, Perseveraunce has presumably been walking from the entry through the door into the hall and down the floor to the other characters.

In my opinion all these particular passages are indications of a form of actor's entrance different from the form of entrance we think of today as associated with the stage; they all have the common quality of *delay* in some form or other. Today, on the other hand, an actor's entrance is almost inevitably in the nature of a sudden, an instantaneous, or momentary thing; he opens a door in the side wall of the scene immediately verging on the acting-area and at once comes in. Or he appears even more suddenly coming on between two wings. It is not irrelevant to notice that we have never quite got used to the suddenness of actors' entrances between wings – we are still, like Charles Dickens, left 'in an unpleasant state of uncertainty as to whether they were supposed to walk straight through the wall of a . . . room . . . or whether the . . . room had been left . . . with no walls at all at the side'. (See article in *All the Year Round* for 31 Oct. 1864.) This 'unpleasant state of uncertainty' would not have obtained in the Interludes.

Again, I may go much further back in our history than Dickens, and picture the primitive booth stage of the fairground or of the Flemish *Kermis*, with its curtain to back it. The entrances were made, in general, round or through that curtain. Entrances of this kind are also sudden, and cannot very convincingly be anticipated. Therefore a stage of that kind would not, I suggest, lend itself readily to the technique of entrance implied in the Interludes under consideration at present.

But (and again in my suggestion) a situation that would exactly suit such a technique is that of the hall screens with their doors into the entry. Moreover, there is one line in this play which I believe offeres a confirmation of this point of view.

On fol. xx. *rev.* a group of characters, intent on betraying Magnyfycence, have discredited his good friend, Measure, and are on the point of getting him dismissed from Magnyfycence's court. Measure defends himself in a final brief speech of some dignity, and then there comes the direction – 'Here mesure goth out of the place'. This is perfectly clear and the significance of the word 'place' in this context has been referred to above; what happens next however is that the triumphant Courtly Abusyon hurls a last contemptuous line after the departing Measure; and that line is:

Hens thou haynyarde out of the dores fast

'Haynyarde' is a useful term of abuse, presumably derived from the French *hainer*, to hate; but the main interest of the line is its use of the phrase 'out of the dores', and in particular of the word 'dores' in the plural. It offers a suggestive reminder of the line which we noticed in *Nature:* 'a gentylman comes in at the dorys'. It seems very unlikely that in both these examples the word 'door' would be used in the plural unless justification existed in some contemporary custom. Since the screens in a Great Hall of that date normally afforded two such openings for what Margaret Wood refers to as the 'two-way service' of meals, I am inclined to believe that this explains the use by Interlude-writers of the word 'doors' in the plural, and confirms again that these writers envisioned the screens as the backing for the action in early Interludes.

Another passage of *Magnyfycence* contains a different matter and needs considering in some detail. It is on fol. v., and this is what leads up to it: There are three characters in the action at the moment; Magnyfycence is in conversation with Fansy, while Felycyte looks on. Fansy is objecting to Magnyfycence's decision to allow himself to be ruled by Measure, and to make his point Fansy has changed his name to 'Largesse' and under this alias is tempting Magnyfycence to open his purse *without* measure. He is observing, somewhat tactlessly, that Magnyfycence is too careful, and his argument runs –

> what auayleth lordshyp yourselfe for to kyll
> with care and with thought howe Jacke shall haue gyl
> [. . .] couetyse hath blowen you so full of wynde
> That colyca passyo hath gropyd you by the guttys

Magnyfycence is, understandably, annoyed and gives him short shrift –

> [. . .] you are nothynge mete with vs for to dwell.
> That with your lorde and mayster so pertly can prate.
> Gete you hens I say by my counsell
> I wyll not vse you to play with me checkemate

This sharp rebuke brings Fansy to a more respectful tone, and he turns to another matter –

> Syr yf I haue offended your noble estate
> I trow I haue brought you suche wrytynge of recorde

> That I shall haue you agayne my good lorde
> To you recommendeth sad cyrcumspeccyon
> And sendeth you this wrytynge closed vnder sele

This timely production of a mysterious letter, of course, intrigues Magnyfycence, but at the same time it annoys him because the letter had not been produced sooner. He remarks,

> This wrytynge is welcome with harty affeccyon
> why kepte you it thus longe:

Magnyfycence now wants to see what is in the letter, but he wants to read it in peace, and so what he does is first to send Felycyte off home, saying to him as he goes –

> I shall come to you myselfe I trowe this after none

– and he turns to Fansy (alias Largesse) with the remark –

> I pray you larges here to remayne
> whylest I knowe what this letter dothe contayne

There must follow now a fairly elaborate piece of business. Felycyte having been sent out, Fansy presumably draws obediently aside to allow Magnyfycence an opportunity of perusing the letter to himself. This is the situation when suddenly there appears a noisy intruder among the people by the door; it is Counterfet Countenaunce singing as he comes. But at the sight of the other two he stops dead and checks his impulse to advance and greet Magnyfycence, because he can see that it is not a propitious moment. He draws back to allow him a little time to finish reading his letter. Perhaps he turns to go. And then after a sort of double-take he checks, turns back, examines the situation again, and from a certain distance presumably gives a loud 'ahem!'. This immediately prompts Fansy to turn to him surreptitiously and motion him to silence; he probably puts a finger to his lips but says no word. Then he turns his back on him again. This reduces the importunate Counterfet Countenaunce to hissing in a stage whisper – 'what fansy fansy'! But this sound does catch Magnyfycence's ear and he looks up from his reading and asks –

> who is that that thus dyd cry
> Me thought he called fansy

Fansy replies with the equivalent of, Oh, it's nothing – just a Dutchman! –

> It was a flemynge hyght hansy

But Magnyfycence is not convinced and now perhaps looks round, only to find the place to all appearances empty, because Counterfet Countenaunce has dodged back among the crowd, and he insists –

> Me thought he called fansy me behynde

– and Fansy tells him –

> Nay syr it was nothynge but your mynde
> Bur nowe syr as touchynge this letter [. . .]

– and the scene now proceeds steadily for some 65 lines while Fansy describes the risks he took and the expense he went to to bring the letter – angling for a tip. At length Magnyfycence says,

> Let vs departe from hens home to my place [. . .]
>> Hic discedat magnificens cum fansy et
>> intrat counterfet countenaunce.

As they go, then, we find the still-lurking Counterfet Countenaunce popping his head in again, presumably from the opposite door, and hissing after Fansy as he is departing–

> what I say herke a worde
> FANSY. Do away I say the deuylles torde
> C.COU. ye but how longe shall I here awayte
> FANSY. By goddys body I come streyte
> I hate this blunderyng that thou doste make

There is clearly little love lost between these two at that moment! After Fansy has followed Magnyfycence out, Counterfet Countenaunce has the place to himself and takes the opportunity to come fully in and deliver a two-page soliloquy.

The particular point, now, about the whole above passage is that its details are not in any way an elaborate fiction by the present writer; they are all exactly prescribed in a long Latin acting-direction inserted after Magnyfycence's line 'whylest I knowe what this letter doth contayn'. I have already quoted the direction as No. 5 in the list above, and an English equivalent is there given beside it. It offers a minute catalogue of the actions upon which I have built all the details of the scene in my description. There could scarcely be found a clearer demonstration of the fact that it was possible for Interluders to undertake the most precise and extensive passages of business in their presentation technique; and moreover for playwrights to know this and to write directions for such business as they worked out the drafting of their scripts.

Finally I want to return to consider more fully the curious Latin direction (no. 38 on the list) instructing Poverty to approach and lift up Magnyfycence and lay him *super locum stratum* – upon a 'spread place'.

At first it occurs to one to wonder whether this action of laying a character on a 'place' which is 'spread' with something could have any ultimate source in that ancient practice (which for instance the Mummers employed) of spreading a cloth or groundsheet over the place where a figure was about to fall. The assumption would then be that the players had some proper regard for the preservation of the costumes they wore. But here Magnyfycence had fallen before Poverty came to him, so the sheet or whatever it was may have here another purpose than that of keeping his clothes clean.

The passage comes towards the end of the play (on fol. xxiii. out of the total of thirty), where Magnyfycence has been degraded and is suffering the sharpest retribution for his extravagancies, and it contains in my view some of Skelton's bitterest and finest poetry. It begins with Fansy abandoning Magnyfycence in utter contempt, and being replaced by the grim figure of Adversity by whom Magnyfycence is beaten down and spoiled from all his goods and raiment. Adversity then has a long speech of some 80 lines of scathing condemnation ending with a warning to the audience to 'Take hede of this caytyfe that lyeth here on grounde', and with the summons called over his shoulder –

> Howe / where art thou come hether pouerte
> Take this caytyfe to thy lore [*i.e. instruction*]

(So Magnyfycence is already stretched out on the floor at this point.) Now Adversity gives place to Poverty, who enters with full character-acting and possibly, as I shall show later, dragging something with him. He soliloquizes –

> A my bonys ake my lymmys be sore
> Alasse I haue the cyatyca full euyll in my hyppe [. . .]

– and so forth, ending,

> Nowe must I this carcasse lyft vp
> He dynyd with delyte with pouerte he must sup
> Ryse vp syr and welcom vnto me
>> Hic accedat ad leuandum magnyfycence et
>> locabit eum super locum stratum.

Here the significance, at least, of this 'spread place' becomes a little clearer, even if its physical nature so far does not; this 'place' signifies the domain of poverty whereto Magnyfycence is now 'welcomed' and at which he must henceforward 'sup'. Can any other detail about it be found?

In the passage which immediately follows, Poverty describes at some length the circumstances of the life that Magnyfycence now will have to follow. He does so in terms that suggest he may well be illustrating in actions, as far as possible, the conditions he is describing. For instance Magnyfycence is prompted to say, among much else –

> Alasse that euer I was so harde happed
> In mysery and wretchydnesse thus to be lapped [. . .]

– which may or may not suggest that Poverty is drawing a cover about him where he lies. Poverty adds,

> ye syr nowe must ye lerne to lye harde. [. . .]
> Nowe lap you in a couerlet full fayne that you may. [. . .]
> Nowe must ye lerne to lye on the strawe [. . .]
> ye syr yesterday wyll not be called agayne
> But . . . nowe go I wyll begge for you some mete [. . .]
> I wyll walke nowe with my beggers baggys
> And happe you the whyles with these homly raggys

It seems unavoidable that what Poverty must do at this point is gather his begging-bag to go search for food, taking care before he goes to bend down over Magnyfycence and tuck the 'rags' he is lying on more closely round him. Something amounting almost to a proof of the above suggestion comes later on fol. xxiv. *rev.* where, after Lyberty has entered without seeing Magnyfycence lying there, and has soliloquized satirically, he is interrupted by an exclamation from the shadows, at which he cries –

> what a very vengeaunce I say / who is that
> what brothell I say is yonder bounde in a mat

The last four words seem to offer final evidence about the so-called 'spread place'; it is somewhere where old rags and probably straw in some form have been laid down. Thus it appears that *super locum stratum* might signify a little area, a *locus*, or strewn place – even perhaps a pallet in the sense of a poor or mean straw bed.

If this is so the significance of the 'spread place' is to act as a symbol of poverty by a sort of metonymia, putting the pallet for the hovel, and in this sense it would be very comparable to the allusive skeleton properties used on the Japanese Noh stage (see for example Fig. 17).

The last point is relevant in that it may contain the hint for solving the final problem about the 'spread place' – namely, how it got there. It would surely have been inconsistent to have a mean pallet or its equivalent lying on the Hall floor throughout the play – and inconsistent (at any rate to the more logical and less imaginative western mind) to have it brought in at need by a 'stage assistant'. But it would be perfectly in order for Poverty to drag something of this sort in with him as he entered speaking his first doleful soliloquy, and for him to drop it a few lines before he spoke to Magnyfycence, so that later he could lift him and lead him back to lie on it.

Before leaving *Magnyfycence* it is worth noting how much our knowledge of Interlude presentation or – to use a modern term – of Interlude 'staging' has broadened since the discovery of *Fulgens* at a sale in 1919. Ramsay's preface to the E.E.T.S. edition of *Magnyfycence* offers a good example of the old views; on p. xliv of that preface, which was issued as far back as 1908, he includes a brief section headed *Stage and Costumes*. He says there that the script is (and I put certain words in italics for comment later), 'strikingly poor in its indication of scene and *staging*'. He states that 'a great many of the most necessary directions have been omitted', and those that remain are 'explicit . . . as to gestures', but 'contain almost no allusion to the *stage-setting*'.

This general dearth of references to 'staging' or 'stage-setting' would nowadays be taken as probably having a significance, and as meaning that there might have been *no* stage, nor stage-setting. But faced by the dearth, Ramsay goes on to form the conclusion that 'what we can learn about its mounting is principally by indirect reference'. He then makes a series of just and useful deductions on this basis; namely, that 'the play was evidently intended for a closed and comparatively small room, and apparently at night', and that 'there would seem to have been two exits (called "dores")'. But then, beside these conclusions that are all verifiable from the text, he also speaks of the use of the 'usual term "place" or "locus" applied *to the stage*' in the directions. In fact there is no evidence that either term, 'place' or 'locus', ought to be understood as having anything to do with any *stage*. But he finally confirms this picture with the observation that – 'Since there are never but four actors present together *on the stage*, a small *platform* would have sufficed.'

The change that the publication of the text of *Fulgens* has made is simply a matter of narrowing down. Already by 1908 Ramsay had seen the implication in the use of the word 'dores' in *Magnyfycence*, namely, that the performance was intended for a room. *Fulgens* added the information that the room most suitable was the Hall.

Yet there stuck fast a legacy from the Victorian investigators – the unavoidable idea that a play must be presented *on a stage*. This idea of a raised platform for the actors is not, as I have tried to show, even indirectly referred to in *Magnyfycence* at all; nor is there, in any play script until the 1550s, any use of the word 'stage'. There is on the other hand every reason to believe, from the many references to entering through the spectators, that a stage was either not in use or, if it were, that it was something of a character or shape such that the actors still had to make their entrances through the group of spectators who stood by the screens. What that character or shape might be (or whether it even existed), it seems pointless to guess until one finds some clear reference to it in a script. It seems safest to restrict any picture to the evidence available; and that means that the actors should be pictured as performing on the hall floor until positive evidence comes up that they performed on some other surface – or even that they might perform a *part* of the show on some other surface.

To make myself quite clear, what I intend is not any definite statement that raised stages were never used until the 1550s. Indeed there are a few scattered suggestions of their use a decade earlier, as I shall go on to show, but not in connexion with Interludes played in private halls (see Section 27). What I do intend is that an open mind should be kept about the presentation of Interludes *in private halls* until clear evidence comes to hand. But equally an open mind must be kept about the fact that the surviving evidence is not complete, and that there yet may be found proof of the use of stages earlier.

The main point is not to assume them; but to follow the development of the presentation of Interludes in private halls as closely as the available facts in the scripts allow. And there are still some score of plays to be looked at before 1550.

12 *Rastell's 'Stage'*

The Four Elements is a play by John Rastell, provisionally dated about 1517. It is convenient here, before considering it for evidence about presentation or 'staging', to take up the rather curious matter hinted at near the opening of Section 5 on *Fulgens*, namely, the stage that Rastell is reported to have had built in his garden. His house was at Old Street in Finsbury Fields, and his lease of that house began in 1524, while he died probably in 1536, so the matter of the stage in the garden would belong to somewhere early in the second quarter of the sixteenth century, not many years after the presumed date of writing of *The Four Elements*. I therefore take the opportunity of fitting it in here.

This matter of the stage might be of quite considerable importance. More than once in this book I have noted occasions when authorities have spoken of 'stages' in connexion with Interludes (for example, pp. 22, 47 and 200), and I have queried their use of the word since I believe that, on the evidence offered so far by the plays themselves, there has been no reason to justify the introduction of such an item into the technicalities of early sixteenth-century presentation. But if in fact this stage of Rastell's in his garden can be confirmed, it would seem to be historically of prime significance in any study of the 'staging' of plays; indeed in his *Early Tudor Drama* A. W. Reed makes a particular point of this; he refers to it as 'the earliest stage known to the historians of the Tudor drama' – surely a matter of the first importance! What now is the evidence available about this stage?

It appears to be confined in a certain group of legal papers containing the Pleadings in a case in the Records of the Court of Requests, described as 'John Rastell *v.* Henry Walton' (the lawsuit is published in H. R. Plomer's transcript in *The Transactions of the Bibliographical Society*, vol. iv, and reprinted in *An English Garner of fifteenth-century prose and verse*, edited by E. Arber in 1903, vol. 5, p. 307, where it is introduced by A. W. Pollard).

Despite the subtitle of *The Garner*, the lawsuit is of the sixteenth century. Pollard comments in his introduction that the

> particular details about Rastell's stage in his garden, the classes from which actors were drawn, the value of the dresses they wore, the practice of hiring the dresses out, and the rather puzzling distinction made between stage-plays and interludes[1], are all of considerable interest

Concerning the matter of Interludes he has the following very attractive suggestion in a footnote:

> ... Stage-plays were acted in the summer, interludes in the winter, the cost of hiring dresses being apparently from three to five times as great

for a stage-play as for an interlude. My own interpretation is that the distinction has nothing to do with the plays acted, but solely to the place of performance, interludes being acted indoors and stage-plays in the open air, where the dresses were exposed to greater damage.

The case itself consists chiefly of a dispute about payment for the hire of theatrical costumes and curtains made and let out by Rastell, and in fact the references to the stage are only incidental and very slight. The first, indeed, is entirely inconclusive; it comes in the Deposition of William Knight who appears to have supported a sort of counter-claim by Walton for expenses due to Walton himself from Rastell. Knight was 'of London, latten founder, of the age of 56 years' and we are told that he

> saith that Walton did make of new for stages and stage players as much as by estimation, esteemed by this deponent and William Sayer at 50s. in board, timber, lath, nail, sprig and daubing, which the said Rastell should have paid to the said Walton . . .

This is unfortunately very inadequate as information. Indeed but for the second reference, which is only slightly more communicative, it would convey practically nothing. The second reference is in a Deposition by Nicholas (not William) Sayer 'of London, skinner, of the age of 49 years or thereabouts' who

> saith that he and William Knight were desired by the said Rastell and Walton, being at the Mitre in Cheap, to view such costs as the said Walton had done in making of stage for player [*sic*] in Rastell's ground beside Finsbury, in timber, board, nail, lath, sprig, and other things. Which they esteemed and judged at 50s. that Rastell should pay to the said Walton to render such garments as he had in his keeping to the said Rastell.

The result of the suit is apparently not preserved and, so far as I have been able to find, that is all we have on which to shape a picture of the stage in Rastell's garden; and it seems to come very near to being of no practical value at all. At most we may say that between 1524 and 1536 there is mention of a 'stage for player in Rastell's ground beside Finsbury' and that it, whatever it was, was built of timber, lath and (the only contribution from the first Deposition) 'daubing' – which latter term, if it means mortar or clay used as roughcast, suggests a solider erection than one would have supposed. But that is the extent of our information about this 'earliest stage known to the historians of the Tudor Drama'.

13 *The Four Elements*

Magnyfycence was an instance of the taking-up of the developing Interlude form by an outstanding and original poet. The next play in the provisional date-list, Rastell's *The Four Elements*, is an instance of the taking-up of the Interlude form by an omnivorous student of the new sciences. It might even be called a popular lecture with trimmings.

Some introduction to John Rastell has already been offered in the preliminary notes to *Fulgens*, of which Rastell was the printer (see p. 97). Since Rastell was a printer he must have had opportunities to see several manuscripts setting out the discoveries of the new scientists, and these would be chiefly written in Latin. The new sciences obviously intrigued him, but so also did the new idea of propagating them in English instead of Latin, and thus in a form which might have a popular appeal. He expresses himself strongly about knowledge being of little value if it is pursued only for money and without regard for the common good. For, as he writes –

A.iii.*rev.*   [. . .] all clerks afferme that that man presysely
whiche studyeth for his owne welth pryncypally
Of god shall deserue but lytyll rewarde
Except he the com*m*yn welth somwhat regarde

– and –

[. . .] for a com*m*yn welth occupyed is he
That bryngyth them to knowlege yt yngnora*n*t be.

The title-page of his Interlude clearly shows how deeply the possibilities of the new sciences impressed him; and since he had that particular close acquaintance with plays and players that I have noticed above, it is not surprising that he chose drama as the popular form to embody them. It would not be inapt to see him as an ancestor of writers of Science Fiction.

This is his title-page: (Quotations are from *The Nature of the Four Elements*, Tudor Facsimile Texts, 1908, edited by John S. Farmer. The original, the only known copy, is in the British Museum '643b. 45, *impf*'; the preliminary page or pages are missing, also eight leaves in the middle, and the conclusion.)

A new iuterlude and a mery of the nature of the .iiij. elements declarynge many proper poynts of phylosophy naturall / and of dyuers straunge landys / and of dyuers straunge effer[?*c*]ts & causis / whiche interlude yf ye hole matter be playd(e) wyl conteyne the space of an hour and a halfe / but yf ye lyst ye may leue out muche of the sad mater as the messengers p*a*rte / and some of naturys parte and some of experyens p*a*rte & yet the matter wyl depend conuenyently / and than it wyll not be paste thre quarters of an hour of length.

Here folow the namys of the pleyers.

The messengere / Nature naturate / Humanyte Studyous desire / Sensuall appetyte / The tauerner / Eyperyence / yngnoraunce / Also yf ye lyst ye may brynge in a dysgysynge.

Here folow dyuers matters whiche be in
this interlude conteynyd.

Of the sytuacyon of the .iiij. elements that is to sey the yerth the water the ayre and fyre / & of theyr qualytese and propertese / and of the generacyon & corrupcy*on* of thyngs made of ye co*m*myxion of them

Of certeyn *con*clusions pr*u*ynge yt the yerth must neds be rou*n*de & yt [*that*] it hengyth in ye mydds of the fyrmame*nt* / & yt it is in cir-cu*m*fere*n*ce a boue .xxj.M. myle

Of certeyn *con*clusions pr*u*ynge that the see lyeth round vppon the yerth.

Of certeyne poynts of cosmography / as how & where ye see [*sea*] coueryth ye yerth / & of dyuers strau*n*ge regyons & landys and whiche wey they lye / and of the new founde landys and ye maner of ye people.

Of the generacyon and cause of stone & metall and of plantis and herbys.

Of the generacyon and cause of well spryngs & ryuers / and of the cause of hote fumys that come out of the of ye [*sic*] yerth / and of ye cause of the bathys of water in the yerth whiche be p*er*petually hote.

Of the cause of the ebbe and flode of the see
Of the cause of rayne snowe and hayle
Of the cause of the wyndys and thonder
Of the cause of the lyghtnynge of blasyng sterrys and flamys fleynge in the ayre

There is much that could be discussed in this title-page – indeed, almost every Interlude affords material for a full study on its own – but as far as concerns the particular subject of presentation, the reference to length of performance-time and to the option of cutting the script deserves notice.

This play, we learn, may be presented to last either for an hour and a half, or for forty-five minutes. In other words one may cut it to half if one desires. To do this it is suggested one would leave out much of the 'sad matere'. Examples of what is to be considered as sad matter are: the Messenger's part, some of Nature's part, and some of Experience's part. How much, is left apparently to the players' discretion. But once the cuts are made it is claimed that the remaining matter will still 'depend conveniently', or hang together consistently – as far, apparently, as entertainment is concerned.

Following upon this the prospective presenter is informed, just after the names of the players, that if he list he may bring in a disguising. This may be a reference to the inclusion of a noble masque should the play find its way to performance at court, or it may be simply an indication like that in *Fulgens* that a troupe of professional dancers could be introduced if opportunity offered. At any rate the main point is that the show could be lengthened or curtailed to suit almost any occasion. This certainly seems to suggest that the performance of at any rate some Interludes might vary considerably from one occasion to another.

It is also worth noting that some evidence is given as to the rate of speaking that might be used in an Interlude. The number of lines in *The Four Elements* was originally probably a little under 2,000 (deducting some three or four pages which contain music only, and allowing the addition of some 16 pages for the section now missing). Speaking at some 30 seconds per 10 lines we arrive at 6,000 seconds, or 100 minutes, for the whole, which gives just over an hour and a half.

The rate of 10 lines in 30 seconds is a steady, not particularly hurried rate; it is an acceptable average speed and would allow for a little quickening in some passages and, in others, for pauses to permit of moments of business. The speed of speaking in Rastell's Interlude would therefore seem to be normal according to modern custom.

The Messenger's speech (where the first cuts can come) is the opening speech; and admittedly it is a very long one, though with much of potential interest to a thoughtful and attentive audience. It ranges over nearly 150 lines. If this were spoken with significant pauses and at a moderate speed it might occupy something approaching eight minutes.

Besides its introduction to certain items of natural science which are to be enlarged upon in the play itself, the speech contains an interesting plea for the sciences to be expounded in the English language. The Messenger remarks that the author

A.ii.   [. . .] hath oft tymes ponderyd
          what nombre of boks in our tonge maternall
          Of toyes and tryfellys be made [. . .]
          And few of them of matter substancyall.

But he believes, significantly,

A.ii.*rev.*   [. . .] that our tonge is now suffycyent
          To expoun any hard sentence [. . .]

– and that the 'clerks in this realme',

          [. . .] myght yf they wolde in our englyshe tonge
          wryte workys of grauyte somtyme [. . .]
          For dyuers prengnaunt wytts be in this lande
          As well of noble men as of meane estate
          whiche nothynge but englyshe can vnderstande

As it is, he claims, the English writers simply limit their efforts to writing books –

          Some of loue or other matter not worth a myte
          Some to opteyn fauour wyll flatter and glose
          Some wryte curyous terms nothyng to [*the*] purpose

– but he takes this as justification to exclaim –

          why shold not than the auctour of this interlude
          Utter his owne fantesy and conseyte also
          As well as dyuers other now a dayes do

Perhaps the chief matter in this opening speech that touches our subject is Rastell's implied opinion towards the end on how an Interlude should be written. After describing the many items of natural philosophy to be touched on, the Messenger concludes –

A.iiii.   whiche matter before your presence shortly
              In this interlude here shall be declaryd
              without great eloquence *in* ryme rudely
              Because the compyler is but small lernyd
A.iiii.*rev.*   This worke with rethoryk is not adournyd
              For perhappis in this matter muche eloquence
              Sholde make it tedyous or hurt the sentence [.]
                But because some folke be lytyll disposyd
              To sadnes / but more to myrth and sport
              This phylosophycall work is myxyd
              with mery conseytis to gyue men co*m*fort

And occasyon to cause them to resort
To here this matter / wherto yf they take hede
Some lernynge to them therof may procede
    But they that shall nowe this matter declare
Openly here vnto this audyence
Beholde I prey you see where they are
The pleyers begyn to appere in presence
I se well it is tyme for me to go hens
And so I wyll do / therefore now shortly
To god I commyt all this hole company

– which in itself is yet another good example of what I have called a 'heralded entrance', since it clearly suggests that the players are beginning to come in sight even before the Messenger has finished his prologue.

What the players do as, and immediately after, they begin to appear is fortunately told to us in a definite and unequivocal acting direction, though in Latin. There are three characters; they – or two of them – are bringing in a particular property. The first character is the curiously named Natura Naturata (spelt Nature Naturate on the title-page), the other two are called Humanity and Studious Desire respectively and they are carrying *figuram*. The Latin reads: 'Hic intrat natura naturata Humanyte & Studyous desire portans figuram'. This *figura*, as the text later suggests, would appear to be a diagram illustrating the surface of the earth – a map or globe. It is presumably carried in by the two last players and set down just inside the entrance so that all the assembly may see it. I venture to suggest that, if the previous conclusions are correct, one would be justified in visualizing this property as now standing somewhere just in front of the centre portion of the screens between the two doors. This, of course, presupposes that the performance was planned to take place in a hall. Is there any evidence for this?

There would appear to be categorical evidence at four separate points in the play. All come near the end. First (on folio E.iii.) Sensuall Appetyte says,

> [. . .] I shall bryng hydyr [. . .]
> [. . .] lusty bludds to make dysport [. . .]
> That all the hall shall ryng

Second (on folio E.iii.*rev.*), the same character says again,

> I shall brynge them in to this hall

Third (on folio E.iiii.) Yngnoraunce says of the audience,

> For all they that be nowe in this hall
> They be the most *parte* my seruaunts all

Finally (on folio E.iiii.*rev.*), there is the acting direction, 'Then the daunsers with out the hall syng this wyse'.

Returning now to the action of the play. With the map of the world set up, Nature lectures Humanyte on the conservation of matter and the construction of the universe (incidentally not at all inconsistently with modern ideas!). Humanyte responds. Possibly Nature demonstrates on the map or diagram of the world, as the lines suggest:

> Marke well now how I haue the[*e*] shewyd & tolde
> Of euery element the very sytuacyon
> And qualyte, wherfore this fygure beholde
> For a more manyfest demonstracyon

Nature next introduces the third character, Studyous Desire, to be Humanyte's guide, and announces, 'well than for a season I wyll departe[. . .]' stressing that the 'fygure' shall remain to be referred to. No exit direction is given but the following dialogue is confined to Humanyte and Studyous Desire, and it is to be supposed that Nature goes out.

Now Studyous Desire takes the floor and is about to embark on a discussion of the plant world when Humanyte brings variety into the discourse by checking him, and saying that before he goes on he himself wants to be better assured about certain statements of Nature's which he cannot believe – as for example that the earth, with its seas upon it, is round. They argue. At length, after successfully proving some things, Studyous Desire finds the pressure too great and announces that he is about to go off and fetch a fresh character, by name Experyens, who, among other things,

B.i.*rev.*   [. . .] by his scye*n*s
　　　　Can tell how many myle the erthe is a bowte [. . .]
B.ii.　　yf ye wyll I shall for hym enquere
　　　　And brynge hym heder yf I can hym fynde

Humanyte replies dutifully and eagerly,

> Then myght I say ye were to me ryght kynde

And Studyous Desire, no doubt gathering his robe round him with some dignity and smoothing one or two ruffled feathers that Humanyte has upset with too much questioning, prepares to sweep out, saying,

> I shall assay by god that me dere bought
> For cunnyng is the thynge yt wolde be sought

– and walks straight into a newcomer!

This collision is in the middle of the seventeenth page of the script; some twenty minutes have passed, or getting on for a quarter of the play. It is not surprising that Rastell feels it time to shake something out of his sleeve. The next lines of the dialogue are sharp and immediate enough to justify modernized spelling; the newcomer cries –

> Well hit! quoth Hickman, when he smote
> His wife on the buttocks with a beer pot [. . .]

– so there clearly is a collision at the door! The newcomer continues –

> Aha now god euyn fole god euyn
> It is euen the[e,] knaue that I mene

(so Studyous Desire, understandably, is dumbfounded. Note the slight suggestion that this would be an evening performance. In the hesitation, the fresh character – who cannot surely be Experyens! – asks)

> Hast thou done thy babelyng

Studyous Desire finds his tongue to gasp –

> Ye[a,] peraduenture what than [?]

– and the newcomer with placid insolence –

> Than hold downe they hede lyke a prety man & take my blyssyng [. . .]

– and he launches into a speech of folly, finally quarrelling with Studyous Desire and advising Humanyte to beware of him. He announces that his name is Sensuall Appetyte, and puts up a skilful parody of the earlier speeches, proving himself equally useful to man. Studyous Desire retires (no exit-direction). Humanyte agrees that he does in fact feel ready for some distraction and refreshment; so Sensuall Appetyte suggests a tavern and makes a nice Freudian slip of the tongue –

> And yf that I euer forsake you
> I pray god the deuyl take you

– at which Humanyte sharply exclaims,

> Mary I thanke you for that othe [*!*]

– and Sensuall Appetyte recovers himself with –

> A myschyfe on it my tonge loo
> wyll tryp somtyme what so euer I do
> But ye wot what I mene well

Humanyte says, Let it pass, and asks if the other knows where there is a good tavern. To this Sensuall Appetyte is immediately able to reply (with some truth if he is near the screens passage with the buttery beyond) –

> Mary at the dore euyn here by

– and he calls for a Taverner, who replies first from outside and then, on advancing, demands leave of the bystanders in the usual way to come in through them –

> Beware syrs [,] how [*!*] let me haue rome
> Lo here I am what seyst thou [*?*]

After several very light-hearted exchanges, a meal with some gay company is bespoke, and the Taverner goes ahead to get it ready while the others follow. We then have the direction, printed as follows –

> Exeat Sen. & Hu.   Intrat Exper*iens*. & Stu.

It is pretty clear that Humanyte and Sensuall Appetyte must not walk straight off into the very arms of Studyous Desire and the fresh character Experiens, whom Desire has been so long a time finding, for they would then be immediately stopped. But of course the two entrances in the screens would come into perfect use here, allowing a simultaneous entrance and exit but with no meeting.

Rastell is now presented with the task of picking up the serious purpose of his play once more, after mixing in his merry conceit to give the audience comfort. He does so by springing a question right away; it comes from Studyous Desire and amounts to: How many miles to Jerusalem? Experience, a great traveller, takes the floor (as it were with a glint in his eye upon seeing the *figura* or map in the background). He replies: and the dialogue is so to the point here in showing Rastell making use of the map to help the exposition that it is worth quoting at length:

> From hens theder to goo
> Syr [,] as for all suche questyons
> Of townes to know the sytuacyon
> How ferre they be a sunder
> And other poyntes of cosmogryfy [,]
> ye shall neuer lerne then [*them*] more surely
> Then by that fugure yonder
> For who that fygure dyd fyrst deuyse
> It semeth well he was wyse
> And perfyte in this scyens
> For bothe the se and lande also
> Lye trew and iust as they sholde do
> I know by experyens
> STU. who thynke you brought here this fygure
> EX. I wot not
> STU. Certes lorde nature
> Hym selfe not longe a gone
> Whiche was here personally
> Declarynge hye phylosophy
> And lafte this fygure purposely
> For humanytes instruccyon
> EX. Dowtles ryght nobly done
> STU. Syr this realme ye knou is callid englande
> Somtyme brettayne I vnterstonde
> Therfore I prey you poi[n]t with your hande
> In what place it shulde lye
> EX. Syr this ys ynglande lyenge here
> And this is skotlande yt Joyneth hym nere [. . .]

And in this way he goes on, crossing the Channel, touching France, Spain, Italy . . . Iceland . . . the great 'Occyan', so great –

> C.i.   [. . .] that neuer man
> Coude tell it sith the worlde began
> Tyll nowe within this .xx. yere [. . .]

– Westward beyond; to a country so large of room, much longer than all Christendom, to which not long ago some men of this country went but had cause to curse their mariners, . . . else Englishmen might have been the first that there should have taken possession, . . . with a description of the primitive inhabitants, their mineral, their timber, their fisheries, their dress.

Then he picks up again, turning to the East; to the Mediterranean and the Turks; to Africa, to India, to 'Catowe' and – still pointing on the map – 'Towardes the newe landis agayne'. Then to the

Southern Hemisphere 'whiche we knowe nothynge at all'. Then suddenly Studyous Desire interrupts him:

C.iiii.   *Et subito studyouse desire dicat.*
          Pese syr no more of this matter
          Beholde where humanyte co*m*meth here

At this point, Humanyte and Sensuall Appetyte re-enter with the Taverner, discussing what supper shall be ordered to follow the dinner they have just eaten. After some three pages of gags not without a spice of indelicacy, the Taverner leaves. Now Humanyte suddenly notices Studyous Desire; and Sensuall Appetyte notices (and immediately dislikes) Experiens. These last two cross swords verbally and Sensuall Appetyte leaves. The three others heave a sigh of relief, and immediately Studyous Desire takes up once more the problem of the earth being round. Humanyte says that he can understand how the earth is round from east to west, but not how it can be round from north to south. This Experiens of course demonstrates, at some length and to Humanyte's partial satisfaction. They are just on the point of going into another proof by means of some occular demonstration, when the script breaks at folio C.viii. *rev.*

The next part of the script is on folio E.i. When the dialogue resumes, a new character is speaking, by name Ignorance, spelt without the adenoidal 'n' which marks his name in the list of players. He would seem to be something like a Vice in the show; he proclaims,

          I loue not this horeson losophers [. . .]

He is speaking with Sensuall Appetyte, who is claiming to have slain certain Englishmen that are servants of Ignorance. Comic business is made of this, and then Sensuall Appetyte asks him if he knows where Humanyte may be. Ignorance answers,

E.i.*rev.*   I wot neuer except he be
          Hyd here in some corner

– at which Sensuall Appetyte looks round, presumably among the audience by the doors, and exclaims,

          Goggys body and trew ye sey
          For yonder lo beholde ye may
          Se where the mad fole doth ly

213

Humanyte is with some difficulty got to his feet and explains he is hiding for fear, but is told it is really because he has been driven mad by 'this folyshe losophy'. They ask him if he was merrier in the tavern than with the philosophers, and Humanyte ruefully admits he was.

We cannot tell what has happened in the missing pages, but Humanyte is now in pretty poor shape, and is not interested even in going to the tavern again. So Sensuall Appetyte hits on the bright idea of bringing entertainment to him – 'lusty bludds' to dance – and, after he is recovered, getting him to the tavern and a wench once more. Humanyte blearily agrees. Sensuall Appetyte promises to go at once and bring 'them in to this hall', and be himself their 'chefe marshall'. Then he presumably goes out to fetch the dancers.

Ignorance approves the suggestion and says 'all these folke' in the audience have been made weary by Experiens's arguing, adding that 'they that be nowe in this hall / they be the most *p*arte my ser-uaunts all / and loue pryncypally disportis' . . . And then the promised entertainers are heard outside –

E.iiii.*rev.* Then the daunsers with out the hall syng this wyse and they with in answer or ellys they may say it for nede.

Now follow three pages of musical staves with the notes and words of the song and some indication that care has been taken to fit the whole ingeniously with the action. The dance follows, led by Sensuall Appetyte with the direction –

Than he syngyth this song & daunyth with all And euermore maketh countenaunce accordyng To the mater & all ye other annswer lyke wyse.

The carefully organized fun rages fast and furious, but there is some disappointment expressed at the lack of a minstrel. The ac-commodating Sensuall Appetyte hurries off to the tavern again to try to find one. Then Ignorance sings a nonsense song based on a Robin Hood ballad. At the height of it Nature appears and begins to rebuke Humanyte in reasonable terms, chiefly warning him that if he will learn no science he will not advance but be like Ig-norance . . . And the script breaks off, unfinished.

A comment in looking back on *The Nature of the Four Elements*; the First Part may be said to be in what closely resembles modern 'lecture technique', not only because of the subject-matter, but also from the visual point of view. There is the principal demonstrator,

Nature, and there are two assistants, Humanyte and Studyous Desire; in addition there is the equivalent of the blackboard or projection-screen for illustrations, the *figura*. The resemblance is close enough for one to use the term 'demonstration technique' rather than lecture technique – keeping in mind that one meaning of *demonstrare* is 'to point out', as with the finger, and another is 'to represent'. I would add that even the costumes would not greatly differentiate this Interlude from a modern formal lecture, for what could be a more fitting dress for Studyous Desire than a university gown – and for Nature than a Master of Philosophy's robe! The essential point is that the play is consistent with 'demonstration technique'.

Having established this, I want to notice – without at present going deeper than merely noticing – that the particular set-up designed for lectures in demonstration technique which can be seen today in a typical university hall is comparable in general principle with the kind of set-up I have so far visualized for Interludes (see Fig. 8). It differs in certain details of course, but we are dealing only with early Interludes just now. One difference is that in *The Four Elements* there is no allusion to a rostrum for the 'demonstrator'. But it is precisely that very useful auxilliary that the evidence will show was later introduced as a presentation-aid into such Interludes as *Pacient Grissill* and many which followed. This I hope to prove in Part Three of the present book.

FIG. 8. A comparison between the conjectured setting of Rastell's *The Four Elements* and a modern lecture hall

All I suggest at this moment is that the set-up suitable to early Interludes appears not unlike the set-up found suitable for a lecture hall in a university today; and I think the similarity has a logical explanation in that the form of 'demonstration technique' characterizes, in some measure, both the modern lecture and some early

Tudor Interludes – both are concerned to point out or to represent certain ideas or opinions not, like the modern stage, to show 'scenes' or to reproduce portrayals of plots from fiction. It seems to me to be true that not until the introduction of scenery into the theatre did this 'demonstration technique' of the Interludes give way to the visual representation of stories in 'stage-settings'.

The next two sections cover the decade 1520 to 1529. To this period the chronological list ascribes ten plays:

> *Youth* c. 1520
> *Witty and Witless* c. 1521
> *Love* c. 1525
> *Calisto and Melebea* c. 1527
> *Of Gentylnes and Nobylyte* c. 1527
> *Weather* c. 1527
> *Godly Queen Hester* c. 1527
> *Johan Johan* c. 1529
> *The Pardoner and the Friar* c. 1529
> *The Foure PP* c. 1529

I propose to take these ten plays slightly out of chronological order for two reasons. The first is that one of the plays, *Godly Queen Hester*, introduces a certain feature that seems to me to open a new era in Interlude presentation, and I shall reserve it for separate study in Section 23; the second is that of the remaining nine plays no less than six are by – or are attributed to – the same man, John Heywood. This is unparalleled in the present history and so it seemed worth taking these six out of the chronological sequence and dealing with them in Sections 17 to 22, so that all Heywood's work could be grouped together.

This leaves three plays for consideration at present – *Youth*, *Calisto* and *Gentylnes*. I would however point out to the reader what appears to be a rather interesting fact which the ordering might otherwise conceal – namely that the second of these, *Calisto*, is considered to be contemporary with the *Godly Queen Hester* of Section 23, and that both are contemporary with the middle period of Heywood's plays, *Weather*, in Section 19, all being dated about 1527.

To begin now with *Youth*.

Thenterlude of youth,

FIG. 9. *The Interlude of Youth*; woodcut from the title-page of the so-called 'Lambeth Palace' fragment (c. 1528)

14 Youth

The anonymous *The Enterlude of Youth*, dated by Craik c. 1520 (reproduced in 1909 in Tudor Facsimile Texts from the edition printed by William Copland about 1560), is from the presentation point of view a very simple play. It amounts to little more than an exchange of argument between Riot and Pride on the one hand, and Humility and Charity on the other, as to which pair can persuade Youth to follow them. A very brief entry is made by Pride's sister, Lechery. There are one or two direct addresses to the audience – 'A backe felowes and giue me roume Or I shall make you to auoyde sone' (A.i.*rev.*), and 'Abacke galautes and loke vnto me' (C.i.*rev.*) and a rather humble farewell to the spectators at the end: 'We thanke all this presente Of their meeke audience'.

The only suggestion of any particular action is that when the argument is at its height, Youth seems to be freely moving about the

Thē̄terlude of youth.

FIG. 10. *The Interlude of Youth*; woodcut from John Waley's edition of c. 1557

hall while Riot and Pride try to out-talk Charity and Humility, and occasionally one or the other walks over to Youth to make a point; for example, 'I will vnto him gone And se what he wyll saye' (C.ii.*rev.*). As in *Hyckescorner*, one of the characters (Charity) is fettered and so would have to be provided with a seat.

There are some examples of what I have called 'heralded' entrances (which I have suggested are proofs of acting before screens), but this convention has already been exemplified in much greater variety in *Magnyfycence*. In passing, it is perhaps worth recalling that *Youth* is the Interlude which especially illustrates the freedom with which printers' decorative figures were used, as mentioned at the beginning of Section 5. There have survived three separate examples of *Youth* by different printers and all have different figures at

FIG. 11. *The Interlude of Youth*; woodcut from John Copland's edition of
c. 1562

the opening. The first is the so-called Lambeth Palace fragment, dated about 1528, which shows three figures – two men and a woman (Fig. 9). Each has a name-scroll above but all three scrolls are empty. Of the two men one is used again in *The Foure PP* (Fig. 13) and the other in *Hyckescorner* (Fig. 7). The second example is John Waley's edition (c. 1557) which has one single block showing two figures labelled respectively 'Charitie' and 'Youth' (Fig. 10); neither seems to fit the script – particularly Charitie who is depicted as carrying a long bow and an arrow, while Youth has a halberd. And the third example is the William Copland edition (c. 1562, see Fig. 11) which has three separate figures, all male, of which the first has a scroll with the name 'Charite' (?) in it and shows a bearded old man in cap and full gown; the second is a young man labelled 'Youth', but with the scroll cut away from round the name,

219

and it shows a figure that seems to be reproduced from the same original drawing as that for *Hyckescorner* (cf. Fig. 7); and the third shows a middle-aged man with a scroll above but no name in it at all. He is the same as is printed also in *The Foure PP* (see Fig. 13).

15 *Calisto and Melebea*

The comedy generally called *Calisto and Melebea* (though the name is not on the title-page) presents several uncertainties. It is, at present, supposed to date from about 1527. It is anonymous, but reckoned by some (for example A. W. Reed in *Early Tudor Drama*) to be by John Rastell. It is not called an Interlude on the title-page but 'A new commodye . . . in maner of an enterlude', though the significance of this particular form of description is not made clear (on this matter see later, Section 25). It has a small cast of six characters, and was thus probably for professional players. It is partly a translation of the famous Spanish story of Celestina but with an altered, moral ending.

In the opening part, the technique of presentation seems to be very close to what we have seen before; exits and entrances are not consistently marked, but when they are not, the lines of the dialogue nearly always supply, by themselves, a full explanation of the action. But quite soon in the play there is a situation which is handled in a new way, suggesting a step forward in technique.

The title reads,

> A new commodye in englysh in maner
> Of an enterlude ryght elygant & full of craft
> of rethoryk / wherein is shewd & dyscrybyd as
> well the bewte & good propertes of women /
> as theyr vycys & euyll condicions / with a morall
> conclusion & exhortacyon to vertew

At the end of the play we read,

> Johēs rastell me imprimi fecit
> Cum priuilegio regali

In what follows, the edition used is that in the Malone Society Reprints, taken from the unique copy in the Bodleian Library, assigned to about 1525 or 1527. It is checked with the Tudor Facsimile Text reproduced in 1909.

The play opens with the young lady, Melebea, bewailing to herself the importunity of young men; and in particular how she herself is, as she puts it, cumbered by the dotage of Calisto. She avows –

A.i.*rev.*   [. . .] he shall neuer that day see
            Hys voluptuous appetyte co*n*sentyd by me

A paragraph-sign here marks a break in her soliloquy, and she next begins to make some preparation for 'heralding' an entrance. She says –

            wyst he now that I were present here
            I assure you shortely he wold seke me
            And without dout he doth now inquere
            wether I am gone or where I shuld be
            Se / is he not now come I report me
            Alas of thys man I can nener [*never*] be ryd
            wold to cryst I wyst where I myght be hyd

– and the next line is spoken immediately by Calisto. There is no entrance direction but after such an unmistakable indication in the preceding lines, and since he now speaks himself, it is obvious that he makes an entrance and no direction is needed. As in earlier examples, there are at least three lines (those at the end of Melebea's speech) during which the new character has time to clear the entry and walk some distance down the hall.

He accosts Melebea at once and praises her fulsomely, but she has little use for him and says so in no uncertain terms, ending –

A.ii.   And I promyse the where thou art present
            whyle I lyff by my wyll I wyll be absent

                                        Et exeat

And so the direction for her to exit is quite clearly stated, and in this situation is obviously needed, for Calisto next speaks five lines of abject grief which might otherwise have been equally addressed to her face as to her departing back. The direction is clearly inserted to put us out of doubt.

The next development in the situation is indicated by a greeting speech from a new character; his line is –

            Dew gard my lordes and god be in this place

At which Calisto exclaims 'Sempronio!' and the new character answers at once 'ye syr'. Here again there is no entrance direction, but the action is equally clear.

There might be, perhaps, a momentary feeling of puzzlement at Sempronio's words 'my lordes' in the plural, since there is only one other actor present when he comes in, but of course his greeting is addressed not to his master Calisto (whom he possibly does not immediately see), but to the assembled spectators through and among whom he now comes. Calisto's exclamation of his name brings the two men together and at the same time helps to inform us who the newcomer is. Calisto pours out his woes unreservedly to his man, and then says –

> I pray the sempronio goo fet[ch] me my lute
> And bryng some chayre or stole with the[e] [. . .]
> Hy the sempronio hy the I pray the

Sempronio's action now is entirely indicated by the lines of the dialogue and no direction is needed; he says –

> Syr shortly I assure you it shalbe done

and Calisto dismisses him with –

> Then farewell cryst send the agayn sone

– and goes on to speak four lines of mournful soliloquy, after which Sempronio has the lines –

> Tush syr be mery [. . .]
> How sey you haue I not hyed me lyghtly
> A.ii.*rev.*   Here is your chayre and lute [. . .]

– and so the action is completely clear; he must go to the entry, pick up a chair and lute and return. Neither exit nor re-entrance direction is needed.

Calisto sits, but finds the lute out of tune and goes on to repeat his woes to Sempronio. At long length Sempronio proposes to enlist the help of 'a neyghbour a moder of bawdry That can prouoke the hard rokkys to lechery' (A.iiii.), in an attempt to overcome Melebea's defence. The bawd is the famous Celestina.

It is at this point that the new step in technique begins to be taken. The situation as I have visualized it at this moment is that master and man are somewhere in the hall, possibly near the centre, and (unless some development has taken place of which there is no indication) Calisto is still sitting, with his lute on his knees or beside him. Sempronio is standing and has just told his master of the bawd. Next, Calisto eagerly asks,

A.iiii.*rev.*   How myght I speke wyth her sempronio

Sempronio's reply is clearly a preparation for exit; he says,

> I shall bryng her hydyr vnto this place [. . .]

and thus he makes perfectly clear that he is about to go and look for her. After a few lines Calisto hurries him with –

> But alas sempronio thou taryest to long

Sempronio then says 'Syr god be with you', and Calisto 'Cryst make the strong', and the next line is spoken by Calisto to himself; so clearly Sempronio has already gone. Calisto continues his soliloquy for seven lines; and then he makes an unexpected change of subject. He presumably rises from his chair, and he says the following:

> To pas the tyme now wyll I walk
> Up and down within myne orchard
> And to my self go comyn [*commune*] and talke
> And pray that fortune to me be not hard
> Longyng to here whether made or mar[*re*]d
> My message shall return by my seruannt sempronio
> Thus farewell my lordys for a whyle I wyll go

(Now immediately a new character, called 'C', speaks –)

> C. Now the blessyng that our lady gaue her sone
> That same blessyng I gyue now to you all
> That I com thus homely I pray you of pardon
> I am sought and sendfore as a woman vniuersall
> Celestina of trewth my name is to call
> Sempronio for me about doth inquere
> And it was told me I shuld haue found hym here
>   I am sure he wyll com hyther anone
> But the whylyst I shall tell you a prety game [. . .]

No exit or entrance or any other direction whatever marks this passage.

There seems to be only one way to understand it. Calisto is not needed any more for the present; in fact he is in the way. The next concern of the plot is to reveal what success Sempronio is to have with Celestina the bawd. But the obstacle in the way of our finding this out directly is that Sempronio has already left us and gone out to look for her.

What is needed is, either for us to follow Sempronio and see him deliver his message to her; or for us to be transported to where Celestina is so as to witness Sempronio's approach and hear what he says and how she replies. Obviously neither of these things can happen, for they would involve moving the audience and transporting it from one place to another. An alternative might be considered; namely to move the action or to *change the scene* of the action. This, to the best of my present knowledge, is the first time such a situation has been faced in the present study of the development of pre-Shakespearean presentation-technique.

It is not easy to see how the author of the play might have visualized this passage when he wrote it. It might be he saw it as an innovation. It might equally be that a number of previous Interludes, now lost to us, had already introduced similar situations and handled them in the same way. Be that as it may; what does seem inescapable is that in the present play, the speech of Calisto's quoted above is a deliberate move to make him go out of the hall or the Place, but go in such a way that he can be thought of as only temporarily retired from the action, not as having concluded some action. The lines 'To pas the tyme now wyll I walk Up and down within myne orchard' are a piece of engineering that has nothing to do with the plot itself but only with the mechanics of presenting the plot. The 'orchard' has no place as such in the story but – since one of the doors to the outer air at either end of the entry did, in actual fact, often lead to a courtyard or orchard or vegetable garden – it might have a very positive place in the real practicalities of the action. Were this the only passage of the sort in Interlude-writing it might be dismissed without more comment, but an almost exactly similar line is to be found, in the contemporary play *Godly Queen Hester* (see Section 23) and it is used there for precisely the same purpose, to effect the temporary retirement rather than the complete exit of a character.

Calisto here, then, rises, bids farewell to the audience and concludes pointedly *'for a whyle* I wyll go'. He must presumably take his lute and chair with him.

Then the next action is the entrance, straight away and pretty certainly from the other door, of the new character Celestina; and she greets the audience in the usual way of a player coming into a crowded hall and says, among other things, that she has heard Sempronio is enquiring for her. (Why did she not wait at home for him!) Then she goes on to say she had expected to 'haue found hym here'. And finally she settles herself comfortably with the reflection 'I am sure he wyll come hyther anone', and goes into a long descriptive story about her profession, extending over some 60 lines. At the end of it she says,

[. . .] no mo word*es* of this
For this tyme to long we spend here amys
                                        Intrat sempronio
S. O moder Celestyne I pray god prosper the
C. My son sempronio I am glad of our metyng
    And as I here say ye go aboute to seke me [. . .]

There is no heralded entrance here; Semprono's coming interrupts
the soliloquy and therefore needs an entrance-direction. It is the
first entrance-direction in the play.

They begin to talk, and Celestina quickly jumps to what is wanted
of her; and then Sempronio suddenly silences her with –

Peas for me thynkyth Calisto is nye
                                        Intrat Calisto et parmeno

It seems clear that, however much novelty there might be in
what I have ventured to relate in some sense to a 'scene-change',
there is still no intention in the playwright's mind of indulging in
any fictitious conception of representing a 'place-where'; it would
be impossible to say *where* Celestina is supposed to meet Sempronio
– for example, in a street, or at her house – and consequently it is
not at all out of place for Calisto to come, with his other servant
Parmeno, straightway upon them immediately he returns from his
'orchard'. The main thought in the playwright's mind is still that
these are players in a hall giving an entertainment; they are not
imagined as pretending to be in some fictitious place any more than
Medwall supposed his two characters, A and B, in *Fulgens* to be
attending Lucrece's court in a fictitious Rome. I would suggest that
this frankness and freedom about the 'scene' of action was one of the
factors that were to make the technique of Shakespeare's playhouse
what it became.

Immediately upon the entrance of Calisto with his new companion, Calisto informs us of the companion's name by exclaiming
'Parmeno'! – and Parmeno asks 'what sey you'? Calisto replies
delightedly –

                                        wottyst who is here [?]
        Sempronio [!] that reuyuyth my chere

But Parmeno is very down-to-earth, and has no illusions about
Sempronio's companion; he answers –

It is sempronio with that old berdyd hore [. . .]

– and Calisto immediately reproves him with a significant line,

> Peas I sey parmeno or go out of the dore

– a line which could scarcely have any meaning (since, as we have seen, no sense of 'place-where' is involved) unless it were a direct reference to a door in the screens.

After this, the dialogue seems to become somewhat confused. Calisto obviously resents Parmeno's suspicions of old Celestina. But Parmeno's contempt for her only grows; he abuses her to his master in her presence and she appears to invite him sarcastically to go on. Sempronio reproves him for his frankness. Trouble seems to be brewing. Then Calisto turns to smooth Celestina and praise her. Her reply is to say, not to him but to Sempronio, that kind words mean little; she prefers deeds – or money. Sempronio apparently conveys this message to his master, who then says –

> [CA.] Then come on sempronio I pray the wyth me
> And tary here moder a whyle I pray the [. . .]
> S.   Go ye before & I shall wayt you vppon
> Farewell mother we wyll come agayn anon

This seems to be a clear enough exit speech; and apparently Calisto then goes out followed by Sempronio to fetch money, leaving Parmeno with Celestina. But no direction is given through all this.

Parmeno turns now to the audience and invites them to observe how Calisto is about to be fleeced; but Celestina blandly requests him to sing with her, to a tune of her own choosing (!). A marginal direction follows – '& cantant'. Afterwards Parmeno, in spite of the revulsion he feels for her, appears inclined to take her advice to encourage his master.

Next, there is an entrance. There is nothing in the dialogue to herald it; it is a sudden entrance, and hence it requires a direction –

B.i.*rev.*   Hic iterum intrat calisto

– 'Here Calisto comes in again', and he comes in quickly because he is bringing the money to give Celestina –

> Moder as I promysed [. . .]
> Here I gyfe the an .C. pesis of gold

She takes the hundred pieces of gold, speaks four lines and is off! Calisto sends Sempronio after her 'To remember & hast[e] her in euery thyng'. (Thus, Sempronio must have come in again when

226

his master brought the money.) And Calisto also asks him to send Parmeno to him as he goes, with the rather puzzling line –

B.ii.   Then go & byd parmeno come I pray the

– puzzling because Parmeno is, so far as the indications go, still present. The supposition would seem to be that Parmeno drew aside (possibly in disapproval) at Calisto's entrance with the gold, and is now invited into the action.

During the whole of the above there is still no fresh entrance or exit direction.

Parmeno now offends Calisto once again, who then goes out: 'Et exeat calisto' – and, strangely enough in this strange passage of the play, that is the last we see of Calisto! Parmeno has a short soliloquy, deciding finally that he had perhaps better appear to humour his master; and then –

B.ii.*rev.*   Hic exeat parmeno et intret melebea

This, then, is another simultaneous exit-entrance direction like that in *The Four Elements* (see p. 211) and, similarly, would be far less effective if only one door were available. But if, as Parmeno goes his way through one door in the screens, so Melebea enters, a little nervously, through the other, then the play is sustained without any sense of collision.

And Melebea does in fact enter nervously. Her first line is to the bystanders –

I pray you came this woman here neuer syn [?]

– and the bystanders must have been as puzzled, as we; so Melebea continues as she slowly comes forward –

> In fayth to entre here I am half adrad
> And yet why so / I may boldly com in
> I am sure from you all I shall not be had
> But iesus iesus be these men so mad
> On women as they sey / how shuld it be
> It is but fables and lyes ye may trust me

– and immediately following on this attempt to reassure herself comes this second entrance-direction

Intret Celestina

C. God be here in

M. who is ther

C. wyl ye bye any thred [?]

– and the classic scene of Celestina tempting Melebea in the guise of a hawker now follows. It lasts for over 260 lines and ends with Melebea expressing willingness to go some way to ease Calisto's ache . . . 'Et exeat melebea.' Celestina gloats for 14 lines and hurries off to give the glad news to Calisto.

Now a further surprise follows; we have this direction (or speech ascription, centralized) –

Danio pater melebee

– and speaking in soliloquy Danio, Melebea's father, tells of an ugly dream he has had, and the rest of the original story is abandoned to give the play a new moral ending, where Danio talks to his daughter about her narrow escape. . . . Technically, however, there is nothing further of interest – except perhaps the rather unusually long Latin direction to Melebea as she listens –

Hic melebea certo tempore non loquit sed uultu lamentabli respicit

16 *Of Gentylnes and Nobylyte*

Two or three times in the review of *Calisto and Melebea* the suggestion has offered itself that that play seemed to be breaking new technical ground. It is to be repeated that it avoids taking directly the name of 'Interlude', and that instead it calls itself a 'new comedy in English'. It seems that the intended implication is that it is a play owing something to foreign sources – such as the Latin or the Spanish – and is for that reason called a 'comedy', but that it is recast into the English language and, in the recasting, is set down according to a certain traditional English style or manner – namely, the *manner* of an Interlude.

But why did the writer employ this phrase? What could be the significant difference between (*a*) an Interlude, and (*b*) a comedy written after the manner of an Interlude?

It may or may not be by chance, but the only other script among the Interludes which bears in its title a similar qualification is ascribed to the same year as *Calisto* – about 1527. It is called *Of Gentylnes and Nobylyte*. It is generally regarded as anonymous, though sometimes attributed to John Rastell. And it describes itself as 'A dyaloge . . . compilid in maner of an enterlude'.

These two odd descriptions which are so like each other and so

unlike anything else in the whole run of Interludes, come together
in the same year. It would seem on the face of it to be pure chance.
And yet one cannot help remarking that that year comes just at the
point in history where the general term 'Interlude' begins to be replaced, or supplemented, on title-pages by new terms such as
firstly, 'play' and then, later, 'comedy' and, later still, 'tragedy'. The
possible significance of this calling of Interludes by other names
will be considered again in Section 25.

Of Gentylnes and Nobylyte is in all other respects as far removed
from *Calisto* as any play could be; it has no dramatic plot at all and
in fact the best description of it is that given on its own title-page
(see Malone Society Reprints, 1949) where it is simply –

> A dyaloge betwen the marchau*n*t the knyght & the plowman dys-
> putyng who is a verey gentylman & who is a noble man and how men
> shuld come to auctoryte / compilid in maner of an enterlude with diuers
> toys and gestis addyd therto to make mery pastyme and disport

By 'diuers toys' is probably meant the two pitched quarrels
which arise between the disputants, one in the first part and one in
the second part of the 'dyaloge'. There are no acting-directions
with the exception of the following – 'Here the plouman co*m*mith
in with a short whyp in hys hand & spekyth as folowith', and later
the Latin 'Et verberat eos' and another similar direction to 'beat
them'. Beside the whip, nothing seems required for a performance –
except the hall itself as it has been visualized up till now.

Six Plays Attributed to John Heywood
1521–1529

Witty and Witless ∽ *Love* ∽ *Weather* ∽ *Johan Johan* ∽ *The Pardoner and the Friar* ∽ *The Foure PP*

Of the six plays sometimes attributed to John Heywood, three are at present attributed confidently; namely, *A play of loue* (c. 1525), *The play of the wether* (c. 1527), and an untitled dialogue known under the name of *Witty and Witless* (perhaps as early as 1521). The three other plays occasionally attributed to Heywood but on less certain ground are, *Johan Johan, Tyb his Wife, and Sir Johan*, and *The Pardoner and the Friar*, and *The Foure PP*, all datable c. 1529.

Most of these plays are simpler in dramatic construction than those I have described. None of them has a great deal of plot, and some are mere dialogues though their wit, verbal ingenuity and suitability as scripts for entertainment are often of the first quality. In the matter of technical presentation they only occasionally offer material for detailed discussion.

17 *Witty and Witless*

Of the dialogue known under the title of *Witty and Witless* there exists a manuscript copy in the British Museum (Harl. 367). The handwriting is not at all easy to decipher. There is a complete Facsimile in Tudor Facsimile Texts, folio series, published in 1909.

So far as I am able to judge there is no acting-direction of any sort included. The text is simply an argument or disputation between John and James, and later Jerome, on the nature of common sense or ability in wit.

18 A Play of Loue

A playe of loue, reputedly the next earliest in date (c. 1525) is
described on the title-page as (see Tudor Facsimile Text, 1909) –

A newe and a
mery enterlude concernyng pleasure and payne in loue,
made by Jhoñ
Heywood.

The players
names.

A man a louer not beloued.
A woman beloued not louyng.
A man a louer and beloued.
The vyse nother louer nor beloued.

There is practically no passage in the text which throws any light
at all on the presentation, and there are no acting-directions whatever beside a few relating to exits and entrances – save one. That
one, however, happens to be almost the oftenest-quoted direction
in all Interludes, and certainly it is among the most surprising.
A brief account of the action is useful to lead up to this direction.

The action opens with no direction but with a speech from 'The
louer not beloued'. It amounts to some 63 lines and chiefly describes
his unrequited love for a lady; but the opening stanza gives the
player a very good opportunity to make an unusual entrance. He
says,

A.ii.   Lo syr [*sirs*], who so that loketh here for curtesy
And seth me seme as one pretendyng none
But as vnthought vppon thus sodenly
Approcheth the myddys amonge you euerychone
And of you all seyth nought to any one.
May thynke me rewde perceyuyng of what sorte
ye seme to be, and of what stately porte.

So he must have entered the Hall silently and slowly, making the
most of the chance of a long pause to draw attention to himself as a
curiosity. He goes on to apologize for his vacant manner:

[. . .] some tyme my selfe may cary me
My selfe knowyth not where, [. . .]

He bewails the pain he feels from his unrequited love. And then, to him 'The woman belouyd not louyng entreth' (A.ii.*rev.*).

They debate whose discomfort is the greater. Their exchange is witty but lengthy, and might well give great amusement to an audience accustomed to rhetoric, and appreciative of fine-pointed argument. At length the two agree to go and look for an arbiter to judge their debate. They have taken up some 245 lines to this point; then, 'Here they go both out and the louer belouyd entreth with a songe'.

He expatiates on his happy lot. Then to him, 'Nother louer nor loued entreth' (B.i.*rev.*) – he is a whole-hearted man free from both the joys and the pains of love. He is also the member of the cast who, on the title-page, is alluded to as the 'Vyse' of the company. He jeers at the Lover-loved, and claims that he himself is far happier. They dispute, and Lover-loved goes, as the others did, to find an arbiter for this second debate. Next, Neither-lover-nor-loved has one of the longest soliloquies in our whole study, running to nearly 300 lines, and telling the audience the story of how he outwitted a maid who then outwitted him, so that both stayed heart-whole; and he very glad of it. Then, once more, 'The louer loued entreth' (C.ii.), and says he has found two arbiters, not one, and introduces the precise couple that opened the play.

Now these four indulge in bewildering word-play discussing how to judge which of one couple has the more pain, and which of the other couple has the more joy. How long the audience could have kept up attention is not certain. But at length Neither-lover-nor-loved (the Vice) asks Lover-loved if he never feels any pain, either small or much, through love. The answer is 'No'. At this Neither-lover-nor-loved breaks the atmosphere of the play with an unexpected action; he suddenly says he has forgotten a book! And that he must go out and fetch it. Thereupon Lover-loved exclaims: 'He is gone' – and turns, proposing to give judgement between the two sad ones, and quite confident that his own case is now proved because of his opponent's retreat, and that he himself is thus shown to be the happier of the two glad ones; he asks that the others should confirm his victory so that he may go to his lady and rejoice with her.

It is just at this moment that the famous acting-direction occurs:

D.iiii.*rev.*   Here the vyse cometh in ron*n*yng sodenly aboute
the place among the audyens with a hye co-
pyn tank on his hed full of squybs fyred
cryeng water . water / fyre fyre / fyre / wa
ter / water / fyre / tyll the fyre in the
squybs be spent.

There are several points worth notice in this unique direction. First, one is perhaps a little surprised to see that it is an entrance-direction specifically for the *Vice*, and that it directs *him* to come in when only a few lines before, in the preceding exit-direction, it was Neither-lover-nor-loved (not called the Vice) who was directed to go out. But the lines undoubtedly prove that now the same character is back again, though only here in the whole script is he called the Vice. Except for the note in the list of characters on the title-page, there is nothing elsewhere in the text to suggest that the character named 'Neither-lover-nor-loved' is to be necessarily identified with a Vice. One may suppose perhaps that, of the four (or so) men making up a typical early band of Interluders, the particular one whose job it was to take the Vice-parts was the one to whom this character, with his trick-clowning entrance, would be allotted.

Next, the emphasis on the entrance being a 'ron*n*ying' one is particularly sensational in days when artificial light was by means of naked flames. The horror of clothes catching fire must have been ever present – as it was for instance, so fatally, on the occasion when four woodwoses had their costumes caught accidentally by a by-stander's torch before Richard II in 1393, and were burnt to death.

Further, the putting together of the two phrases 'aboute the place' and 'among the audyens', in such a way as to imply that the one could include the other, is a warning to those who suppose that the word 'place' referred only to the acting-area and did not also include a considerable audience-area. This firework figure was clearly intended to jostle the onlookers – if, indeed, they had not already fallen back in dismay!

Again, the reiteration in disjointed words of calls for help is admirably calculated to produce the highest effect possible out of this piece of theatrical sensationalism.

Finally, the reference to the squibs being fired in a 'hye copyn tank' on the Vice's head is not a primitive fire-precaution by which the risk from the sparks might be confined in a *copper tank*, as is implied by F. S. Boas in Chap. 5 of *The Cambridge History of English Literature*. Consultation of the *Shorter O.E.D.* will put this right at once; there we see *copintank* (1508) to be a sugar-loaf hat. Planché, in his *Cyclopaedia of Costume*, takes us a little further. Under 'copotain' we are referred to 'Hat', and there we read that

> A hat called a copotain, capatain, and coptankt hat was worn in the reign of Elizabeth and her successor. Gascoigne, in 'Herbes' (p. 154) has
>
>> 'A copthank hat made on a Flemish block;'

and also in his Epilogue, p. 216.

> 'With high copt hats and feathers flaunts a flaunt.'

Whatever tediousness the audience may have felt over some of the earlier speeches, it seems pretty likely that they would now be well stirred up with this last sudden and unexpected piece of business.

The process of the play is now quickly taken up again. Lover-loved calls out in surprise 'water *and* fire?', and the Vice explains,

> Nay water for fire I meane

and Lover-loved replies, presumably laughing,

> well thanked be god it is out nowe cleane
> Howe cam it there

In the Vice's reply we learn the meaning of this strange episode – and also of his former apparent uneasiness about his lost book. He says that while he had gone to fetch the book he chanced on a house which was on fire and 'burned pyteously'. But the people were all concerned for a 'goodly' lady who lived in that house. Whereupon he ran –

> thyther to haue done some good
> And at a wyndowe therof as I stood
> I thrust in my hed and euyn at a flush
> Fyre flasht in my face and so toke my bush

– at this, Lover-loved is assailed by a horrid thought and interrupts with a demand in sudden trepidation – 'What house?' The Vice replies, very specifically, 'A house paynted with red okre [. . .]' – and of course the fat is in the fire indeed, for poor Lover-loved realizes it is his own lady's house; and he is immediately in an agony of apprehension. He apparently dashes towards the door, for the Vice, bubbling with laughter, says he 'is gone clere', and continues in a triumph of mockery, calling after him that

E.i.   My lady your leman one vntertakes
             To be safe from fyre by slyppyng through a iakes

– and then, so that he may make sure for himself, 'The louer loued goeth out'.

The Vice's mocking continues as he explains it is all a put-up job to prove how much more pain Lover-loved can be afflicted with than he who neither loves nor is loved. The Lover-loved apparently now returns (though with no direction) and the argument is taken up afresh, and hairs are split at full length, till after it all judgement is finally made (one) that Lover-not-loved and the lady, Loved-not-loving, both suffer equal pain; and (two) that Lover-loved and Neither-lover-nor-loved both experience equal happiness.

Prynted by W. Rastell
M.ccccc.xxxiiii.
Cum priuilegio Regali.

19 The Play of the Wether

The title-page of the Tudor Facsimile Text of 1908 reads –

The play of the wether
A new and a very
mery enterlude of
all maner we-
thers made
by John Heywood,

The players names.
Iupiter a god.
Mery reporte the vyce.
The gentylman.
The marchaunt.
The ranger.
The water myller.
The wynde myller.
The gentylwoman.
The launder.
A boy the lest that can play.

There is one particularly interesting problem of presentation in *The play of the Wether*, and that is – What is implied, in the dialogue, about the nature of the seat occupied by Jupiter during the action? This particular seat is directly referred to as a throne, but it seems to be a throne of such a kind that some characters in the play can see Jupiter on it, and talk to him directly, while others can be denied access to him, are unable to see him, and must say what they have to say not to Jupiter but to his servant. The problem is: How could Jupiter in this throne be accessible at some times in the play and inaccessible at others?

What happens in the play is as follows. Jupiter in a superbly jovial opening speech explains how four of the gods – those of frost, sun, rain, and wind – have each complained that the others are interfering with their weather, and so they have appealed to Jupiter to make some orderly judgement among them: 'wherefore', says Jupiter,

A.iii.   [. . .] we hyther are dyscendyd
      [. . .] to satysfye [. . .]
      All maner people whyche haue ben offendyd
      By any wether [. . .]

– and Jupiter decides to issue a proclamation that he will set up a court personally to listen to any complaints or claims about weather.

He then appeals to the audience for a volunteer to make public his proclamation –

      wherfore eche man auaunce and we shall se
      whyche of you is moste mete to be our cryer

Of course, no one in the audience moves, but instead there enters an actor to take the part of the volunteer.

So far, there is no indication at all of how Jupiter comes in in the first place, or whether he stands or sits for this fairly long preamble of nearly a hundred lines.

The character now entering is called Mery Reporte, and his entrance-direction and opening lines are –

                              Here entreth Mery reporte.
      MERY REPORTE
A.iii.   Brother holde vp your torche a lytell hyer
      Now I beseche you my lorde loke on me furste [*etc*].

Here, then, is the line that I discussed above on p. 54 in the introduction to Medwall's *Nature*, with its implications regarding the

236

lighting of the hall, and the use made of the lighting by a player on such an occasion.

Mery Reporte, after introducing himself to Jupiter, now undertakes the job of being his cryer. What is next to follow is that eight characters are to come in, one by one, to plead for the kind of weather that best suits their needs to the exclusion of all other sorts of weather. But Jupiter gives his new servant some special instructions about how the suitors are to be treated, for they are not all to be received in the same way' –

A.iiii.   [. . .] suche as to the may seme moste metely
we wyll thow brynge them before our maieste
And for the reste that be not so worthy
Make thou reporte to vs effectually [. . .]

Neither the precise reason for this distinction, nor the way it is to be worked, are so far made apparent. Mery Reporte however agrees and then turns to go out, making as he does so a particularly striking address to the members of the audience standing at the doors:

Frendes a fellyshyppe let me go by ye
Thynke ye I may stand thrustyng amonge you there [/]
Nay by god I muste thrust about other gere
                        Mery report goth out

There now follows the most curious passage in the play. Jupiter has seven lines of soliloquy and then Mery Reporte is to come in again. During these seven lines Jupiter announces,

Now syrs we haue thus farre set forth our purpose
A whyle we woll wythdraw our godly presens
To enbold all such more playnely to dysclose
As here wyll attende in our foresayde pretens

The meaning here is not entirely clear at first; I take it to be something like: 'We will withdraw for a while so as to encourage all such as are going to attend here for the enquiry we have proclaimed, to put forward their views the more clearly (or frankly).' He then adds the final three lines which are even more obscure:

A.iiii.*ꝛeu.*   And now accordynge to your obedyens
Reioyce ye in vs wyth ioy most ioyfully
And we our selfe shall ioy in our owne glory

To add to this obscurity there is a marginal direction printed alongside the opening four lines –

*At thende of this
staf the god hath a
song played in his
trone or Mery re
port come in.*

For the moment I will leave this puzzle to look at what happens in the sequel. Upon Mery Reporte's re-entry he has another striking speech to the spectators, playing up his new dignity for all he is worth –

> Now syrs take hede for here cometh goddes seruau*n*t
> Auaunte cartely keytyfs auaunt
> why ye dronken horesons wyll yt not be
> By your fayth haue ye nother cap nor kne
> Not one of you that wyll make curtsy
> To me that am squyre for goddes precyous body
> Regarde ye nothynge myne authoryte
> No welcome home [*!*] nor ['] where haue ye be[*en?*'] [. . .]

– and he goes on into a comic satirical list of the places he has been to. All this amounts to a fill-up of some thirty lines to serve as a diversion and a preparation for the entries of the first suitors. These are to be as follows:

The Gentylman, who seeks calm, dry, clear weather for hunting;

The Merchant, who wants strong, favourable winds for his ships, veering so as to speed them best;

The Ranger, or forest keeper, who also wants strong winds, but for the reason that they bring him windfalls which are his perquisites;

The Miller, who wants no wind, but only rain to swell the rivers and drive his mill;

The Wind Miller, who wants no rain, but brisk winds to turn his mill sails;

The Gentlewoman, who wants neither sun to tan her skin, nor frost, nor winds to wreck her beauty, but close, temperate weather;

The Launder (actually a Laundress), who wants sunshine to dry her washing;

And finally a little Boy (the smallest that can play the part), who wants frost for his bird snares and snow for snowballs.

The first comer, the Gentylman, makes a sensational entrance. Immediately on the last line of Mery Reporte's speech comes the direction, 'Here the gentylman before he cometh in bloweth his horne'. There is, then, a trumpet call from the entry passage (just as there will be at the opening of *Jacob and Esau*). Mery Reporte cries, 'Now by my trouth this was a goodly hearyng' and proceeds to some considerable bawdry about horns. The Gentylman announces that he comes 'to sew [*sue*] to the great god Iupyter'. Mery Reporte replies 'Mary[!] and I am he that this must spede'; and they exchange banter. Then Mery Reporte says (and these four lines come entirely unbroken, and without any direction, in the script):

B.i.
> But stande ye styll and take a lyttell payne
> I wyll come to you by and by agayne
> Now gracyous god yf your wyll so be
> I pray ye let me speke a worde wyth ye

> IUPYTER.
> My sonne say on let vs here thy mynde

The curiosity of the passage now becomes evident; Jupiter has gone out (or 'withdrawn'), but he has left word with Mery Reporte that the more seemly suitors are to be brought before him, and the rest 'reported' to him. Mery Reporte has now checked the first suitor and said, in effect, 'Wait till I come back' – and has *immediately* spoken directly to (the absent?) Jupiter and been replied to by him.

How was this presence-absence, visibility-nonvisibility of Jupiter worked? Mery Reporte continues to Jupiter –

> My lord there standeth a sewter euen here beynde
> A Gentylman in yonder corner [*etc.*]

Eventually Jupiter replies, 'let hym appere', thereupon Mery Reporte summons the Gentylman: 'I pray you come nere', and then – and then only – can the Gentylman see and speak to Jupiter. He presents his suit and later apparently goes, but without any exit-direction.

The next suitor is the Merchant (with an entrance-direction). His treatment is much the same, as the lines explain –

Entreth the marchaunt.

MARCHAUNTE.
> [. . .] brynge me yf ye can before Iupiter [. . .]

> [MERY REPORTE.]
> yes mary can I and wyll do yt in dede
> Tary and I shall make wey for your spede
> In fayth good lord yf it please your gracyous godshyp

B.ii.*rev.*
> I muste haue a worde or twayne wyth your lordshyp
> Syr yonder is a nother man in place [*etc.*]

239

So again, the Merchant cannot see Jupiter nor apparently can Jupiter see him. But Mery Reporte (and, it seems, the audience) can see both. Jupiter agrees to receive the Merchant, and Mery Reporte turns to look for him – only to find he has disappeared! (Or mingled perhaps with the audience.) And he exclaims, 'why where be you shall I not fynde ye'? But the Merchant is immediately discovered and presented to Jupiter. After which Mery Reporte shows him out, chatting to him, and there is the direction '*Exeat marchaunt*'.

But the third suitor, the Ranger, is treated very differently. He also cannot see Jupiter; now, however, Mery Reporte refuses to allow him an audience – or even to take a message to Jupiter. So the Ranger goes out again, and the Water Miller next comes in (both the exit and the entrance have specific directions).

This fourth suitor, the Water Miller, boldly threatens to go through to the God, but Mery Reporte checks him and reproaches him for his manners. Argument rises. But still the Water Miller cannot see Jupiter, nor does Mery Reporte make any appeal to Jupiter on his behalf.

Intervening in their argument comes the fifth suitor, the Wind Miller, with the direction – 'Entreth the wynd myller' – and in his opening conversation with Mery Reporte there is a line that seems to offer a slight hint about the mystery of the throne; the situation is that immediately on his entrance the Wind Miller, a very outspoken and downright character, plunges into his complaint –

B.iiii.*rev.*   How is all the wether gone or I come
              For the passyon of gode helpe me to some

– he is getting nothing but useless rain and no wind, his trade is ruined! He exclaims at the end,

              And now at thys tyme they sayd in the crye
              The god is come downe to shape remedye.

It is upon this that Mery Reporte makes answer with the following remarkable line –

C.i.   No doute he is here euen in yonder trone

and this is immediately followed by –

              But in your mater he trusteth me alone

– in other words, Jupiter is present right enough, and present in a throne which is itself perfectly visible and can be pointed to – 'euen in *yonder* trone' – and yet he cannot be seen in that throne, and he is not available for any direct address from the Wind Miller who can reach him only by passing a message through Mery Reporte. It is almost certain therefore that here Jupiter is reckoned as invisible, and this would mean – either that the Wind Miller *makes pretence* that he cannot see him though Mery Reporte and the audience can; or that the throne, or rather its occupant, can be temporarily concealed in some way, as for instance by a curtain.

I am inclined to favour the latter idea on the grounds that such a curtainable *sedes* had been a regular feature of the preceding Moralities (to this I will return in a moment).

As the action proceeds Mery Reporte, instead of applying at once to Jupiter, introduces the two Millers to each other, and sets them to dispute their claims between themselves. A long debate ensues; so long in fact that Mery Reporte 'goth out' and leaves them arguing. They continue to do so with many interesting technicalities about their crafts for some 150 lines, but neither of them sees Jupiter. At length Mery Reporte returns and sidetracks the argument with a little bawdry, but ends with the promise (and promise only) that he will speak for them both to Jupiter. With that, 'Both myllers goth forth' (C.iii.*rev.*).

The sixth suitor is the Gentlewoman; she obviously takes Mery Reporte's fancy and he decides to treat her more intimately. But she is only interested in speaking to Jupiter, and so Mery Reporte goes back to his earlier tactics, telling her to wait while he himself goes to Jupiter –

C.iiii. Stande ye styll a whyle and I wyll go proue
whether that the god wyll be brought in loue
My lorde how now loke vppe lustely
Here is a derlynge come by saynt Antony [*etc.*]

But Jupiter preserves his dignity, saying reprovingly –

Sonne that is not the thynge at this tyme ment
If her sewt concerne no cause of our hyther resorte
Sende her out of place / but yf she be bent
To that purpose / heare her and make vs reporte.

Thus Jupiter has not heard her previous speech, and she for her part has had no inkling that Jupiter was there on the spot. Mery Reporte now turns back to her with –

Maystres ye can not speke wyth the god

GENTYLWOMAN

No why?

MERY REPORT

By my fayth for his lordshyp is ryght besy [. . .]

– and he goes on with a piece of foolery. But she gets no sight of Jupiter; instead the Laundress comes in to interrupt them.

She is the seventh suitor. She gives Mery Reporte as good as she gets, and sets the Gentlewoman by the ears. But both leave at length without seeing Jupiter.

The last suitor is the small Boy. Mery Reporte hears his suit but does not take him to Jupiter, and the Boy goes out again. One small point is offered during the Boy's speech; he says that he and his comrades had heard –

D.iii.   That my godfather god almyghty
             was come from heuen by his owne accorde
             This nyght to suppe here wyth my lorde [. . .]

Here is not only a clear implication of an evening performance, but also, apparently, a nice little pseudo-innocent gesture of compliment to the Master of the House in the picture of God coming down 'to suppe . . . wyth my lord'.

After the Boy has made his plea for frost and snow, and left the place, Mery Reporte soliloquizes briefly, and then decides –

[. . .] I wyll shew the god all thys procys
And be delyuered of my symple offys
Now lorde accordynge to your commaundement
Attendynge sewters I haue ben dylygent [. . .]

– and thus he is immediately in Jupiter's presence again, and detailing at length the various claims that have been detailed earlier to him. Still the question remains: How does Jupiter become visible to him in a way that is consistent with his having been invisible to the last six suitors? The use of a curtain would seem almost certain.

The action is now nearly at an end. Jupiter hears from Mery Reporte about all their cases, congratulates him on his diligence, and bids him fetch in all the suitors together, to hear the verdict. 'Mery report goth out'. Jupiter chats to the audience for seven lines, and 'Mery reporte and all the sewters entreth'. Jupiter's verdict is that each shall have the weather he wishes – for *some of the time*! They are all delighted with such wisdom, and Mery Reporte ends with –

God thanke your lordship lo how this is brought to pas
Syrs now shall ye haue the wether euen as yt was

Jupiter concludes –

[. . .] and in meane tyme we shall
Ascende into our trone celestyall.
Finis.

No exit-direction is given. The only hint in the whole play as to
how this business of the equally accessible and inaccessible Jupiter
was worked is of the slightest; when, near the beginning of the
play, Mery Reporte went out to make proclamation of Jupiter's
court, there were two consecutive directions as I have said, first –
'Mery report goeth out', then – '*At thende of this staf the god hath a
song played in his trone or Mery report come in.*' Jupiter then spoke the
next lines which were

Now syns we haue thus farre set forth our purpose
A whyle we woll wythdraw our godly presens [. . .]

He speaks another five lines and then – What does he do? Immediately he has finished Mery Reporte comes in again and begins to
chaff the audience, clearly *by himself.* But of Jupiter we hear no
more till Mery Reporte asks leave to introduce the Gentylman to
him, which is some 56 lines ahead.

The second part of the two directions is very strange. To begin,
the word 'staf' is a puzzle; it might perhaps have originally been
'state' – and in any case it may be a misprint – but neither 'staf' in the
sense of 'stave of a song', nor 'state' in the sense of 'chair of state'
is entirely satisfactory. But apart from all this there is the remarkable statement that Jupiter should have 'a song played *in* his
trone'. 'Trone' must mean 'throne'; but the mystery is how could a
song be played *in* his throne? The suggestion presents itself that the
throne, or the surround to the throne, might have been a relatively
large construction – the picture which comes to mind is of a seat
up a couple of steps with a canopy above, and perhaps curtains
hanging from it at the sides which could be closed or opened (a
perfect example of such a surround is to be seen in Fig. 40). Then
the musician could perform on the lower step within the embrace
of the curtains. And if the curtains were drawable they might be
used to conceal or reveal Jupiter on cue and so provide a solution
to the main puzzle. (One remembers the King's line in *The Pride of
Life*, a Morality of about 1400 – 'Draw the cord sire streynth, rest

243

I wol now take. *et tunc clauso tentorio* . . .' etc.) But there is unfortunately no certain confirmation of such a thing here. As far as direct
evidence goes, all we can fairly do is call attention to this further
example of the existence of a convention in Interludes whereby a
figure is enabled to become withdrawn or hidden. The most useful
thing that can be said is that we have had a warning in this play that
a *withdrawing space* (and hence, by reversal, a *discovery space*) might be
implied in certain Interludes.

The fact that all the cast appear together at the end of the play
shows that there was no doubling of parts, and therefore indicates a
larger company than the four or so players that seem to have made
up a group of professional Interluders at this particular period; it
is thus possible that *Wether* was written for performance by boy
players at court, and therefore might have called upon special resources of setting.

20 *Johan Johan, Tyb, and Sir Johan*

Of the three other plays attributed to John Heywood, but about
the authorship of which there has been some controversy, the one
chiefly calling for notice here is –

A mery play
betwene Johan Johan the
husbande / Tyb his
wyfe / & syr Jhān
the preest.

It was 'Impryntyd by Wyllyam Rastell / the. xii. day of February
the yere of our lord. M. ccccc. and. xxxiii.' The edition I have used
is the Tudor Facsimile Text, No. 114 (1909), reproduced from the
earliest known edition in the Pepys Collection, Magdalene College,
Cambridge. The play is reckoned to have been written about 1529.

From the point of view of presentation, this play is noteworthy
in coming nearer to creating an atmosphere of real place for its
setting than any play so far. But the place whose atmosphere is
created is simply an ordinary dwelling-room with a hearth, where a
meal is prepared, a guest invited, and the meal eaten; in other words,
though the setting is so clearly defined, it is in fact the same setting
as the setting of the actual performance (provided this took place

in a domestic hall). So, again we find that the 'scene' of the play is – the place of the performance; no fiction is involved. The only difference, if it can be called a difference, is that the scene of the play here could be a relatively humble room not a great hall, though it is completely possible that the situation portrayed might happen in any stage of society.

The action in itself is so simple as to be not so much a play as a mere music-hall sketch – to use a modern comparison. It concerns a jealous husband with a wife who frequents the company of a priest whose reputation the husband suspects. She cajoles the husband into inviting the priest to a meal; but she then tricks her husband into being distracted by other business, so that in the end he has no part in the meal, while she and the priest enjoy themselves to the full without him.

To effect the presentation of this action, the playwright uses what appear to be three different, or 'differentiated', acting-areas; first, the part of the living-room where the table is laid; second (in a sort of interlude), the door to the priest's house; third, the fireplace of the same living-room which is of such a character that a person involved in business at it is prevented from taking part in the meal at the table – though at the same time he can, in the intervals of his business, see what is happening at the table; while those at the table can address remarks to him and yet also proceed privately with their own business. The convention is clearly designed to make the most of the situation in a way best suited to divert an audience.

Johan, the husband, opens with a long soliloquy bloodthirstily proclaiming how he would beat his 'gaddynge' wife, 'were she come home Unto this my house' (A.i.). In this phrase he clearly indicates the notion that the place where he is speaking is his house, and thus he sets 'the scene', as I have suggested above.

Eventually his wife overhears him and begins to speak; she must therefore now enter, though there is no direction for her. Johan immediately loses his aggressive bombast, and fawns asking if it were not –

A.ii.*rev.*   [. . .] well gest of me
          That thou woldest be come home in safete
          Assone as I had kendled a fyre
          Come warme the swete tyb I the requyre

This business of referring to the presence of a glowing fire is essential to the action as will be seen later; what is involved is making

245

dramatic capital out of an object that is actually available at hand in reality, namely the fire on the hall hearth. Where this hearth would be might vary; in old halls such as that at Penshurst the hearth was, and still is, in the centre of the hall floor; in later halls, as building skill developed, chimneys could be contrived in the walls, and the fireplace was then in the centre of one of the two side walls.

If this performance took place in the winter season, as so many indoor entertainments did, then the fire would be alight; and Johan might actually be making it up at his wife's entrance. There follows now much bye-play, with asides from both of them to the audience; finally Tyb says she has been helping to make a pie, for the ingredients of which the Priest has paid. This pie she now produces. Johan eagerly proposes to set it on the hearth to warm up. Tyb then boldly suggests that the Priest ought to be invited to come in and share the pie with them. Johan strenuously objects to the idea of a sharer but is pressed into reluctant agreement, though he abuses the Priest under his breath the while, whereupon Tyb demands (A.iii.*rev.*), 'What is that that thou hast sayde' – and Johan, to cover up, tells the following lie which is to lead to a significant development:

> Mary I wolde haue the table set and layde
> In this place or that I care not whether

and she immediately takes him up on that remark with – 'Than go to [,] brynge the trestels hyther'. This Johan is now committed to do, and he begins by putting off his gown so as to work more freely. He brings in some comedy here by not being able to decide whether the gown would be safer in one place, or clearer of the dog's fouling in another – whether it might get scorched if he left it near the hearth, or whether it might not be wisest to entrust it to a spectator; but he decides that the particular spectator is 'so nere the dore he myght ron away'. It is scarcely necessary here to point out that such a line could only have meaning if some of the spectators were actually situated by the doors of the hall, and thus were for all practical purposes within the action itself. Johan eventually chooses one of the more reliable-looking of the audience – and bids him scrape the dirt off the gown while he is looking after it!

He is on the point of going when Tyb calls him back to 'Set vp the table' (A.iiii.). This he must presumably now do in actuality while she talks, for she concludes her speech with 'Nowe go thy ways'. Then he starts off but immediately returns in order to bid her

246

see that her 'candelstyk*kes* be not out of the way' – we thus have to
picture the scene by candle-light. He turns away but she calls him
back once more, this time to 'lay the table'. He does this quickly
and turns away again; she once more calls him back to 'brynge
hether yender stole [*stool*]'. When all seems ready he claims that the
pie by the fire is burning; then she sends him to wash two cups
(note, only two, not three; she seems already to be scheming). Once
again he starts off, but again is called back, this time to look and see
if 'there be any ale in the pot'. He goes once more but is once more
checked in order that he may 'brynge hyther that breade' (A.iiii.*rev.*).

It would seem certain that all this comic business must have been
actually performed, and all the properties mentioned must have
been actually produced and set in place according to the lines; but
they are all of such a nature as to be found readily in any kitchen.

When this business is finished, the moment comes when the
change in the 'scene of action' takes place. The lines now run as
follows (Johan is concluding a speech with a proverb) –

> He must nedes go that the dyuell dryueth
> How mayster curate may I come in
> At your chamber dore without ony syn

> SYR JOHAN THE PREEST
> Who is there nowe that wolde haue me
> What Johan Johan / what newes with the[*e*]

So Johan the husband must have left the area where the table had
been set, and gone muttering to another part of the hall and
knocked, or feigned to knock, at a door.

At this point one must try to plot the positions in the hall (see
fig. 12). The fireplace will be either central (A) or in the middle of a
side wall (B). In some other part of the hall – or at least in a position
slightly removed from the fire, as we shall see later – the trestles,
board and stools, etc. must have been set; the alternatives are somewhere between the hearth and the high table (C), or between the
hearth and the screens (D). Johan must now go away from these
two areas and approach the screens, pass through the spectators
there, and knock, perhaps on the post flanking one of the screens
entrances (E). The 'scene' has (if we care to think that way) been
changed. Tyb will remain quiet, now 'differentiated' at the table
(C); Johan is entering into a dialogue with the Priest.

There is a longish exchange at the Priest's door before the Priest allows himself to be persuaded out. At length he consents. Johan apparently hurries back now to the table leaving the Priest to follow more slowly. As soon as Johan is within range of the table acting-area (C), Tyb is on to him to go and fetch water. He goes, possibly to door (H), and so it is that when the leisurely Priest comes at length to the table he finds Tyb alone. She greets him with –

B.ii.
    Welcome myn owne swete harte
    We shall make some chere or we departe

Wherever Johan now is as he fetches water (perhaps from the actual kitchen), he can see this meeting between the two, but apparently he cannot hear the words, for he slips in the lines –

    Cokkes soule / loke howe he approcheth nere
    Unto my wyfe [. . .]

Then, after a short speech of satisfaction, the Priest breaks off to warn Tyb –

    But peas no more / yonder cometh thy good man

Tyb immediately demands the water from Johan. But Johan lets it be seen that (as an acting-direction indicates) 'he bryngeth the payle empty'. There is a hole in it!

Now Tyb and the Priest make capital of this and offer him wax with which to stop the hole; but Johan replies that the wax (which comes from two candles the Priest happens to have with him) is too hard to work. At this, the climax to the action comes: the two send Johan to warm the wax at the fire – that is, into an area where his relation with the other two must be interrupted, and where some independence can be understood between what happens in the one area and what happens in the other. The subsequent business is simply that, delayed and distracted by this errand, Johan does not get one chance to have bite or sup at the table while the others enjoy themselves to their hearts' content. He frequently tries to break in, but as often is sent back to his job. He can, all the time, turn and see what is happening at the table for he exclaims to himself –

B.ii.*rev.*
    And is not this a very purgatory
    To se folkes ete / and may not ete a byt

– and yet the couple at the table can use the convention to take their own pleasure in the intervals when he is bent over the fire and the smoke, for Tyb mocks at him to the Priest with –

> Loke how the kokold chafyth the wax that is hard
> And for his lyfe / daryth not loke hether ward

And Johan, solus, bewails –

B.iii.

> I burne my face / and ray my clothys also
> And yet I dare nat say one word
> And they syt laughyng / yender at the bord

Much is made of this tart comedy, where the situation of course asks to be played up to the full. The Priest enlarges on his opportunity and tells Tyb three distinctly dubious stories while they eat. These Johan hears and he comments bitterly upon them, but can do no more about it.

At length Tyb and the Priest get up from the table with –

B.iiii.

> [. . .] then ryse we out of this place

– and the Priest adds –

> And kys me than in the stede of grace
> And fare well leman and my loue so dere

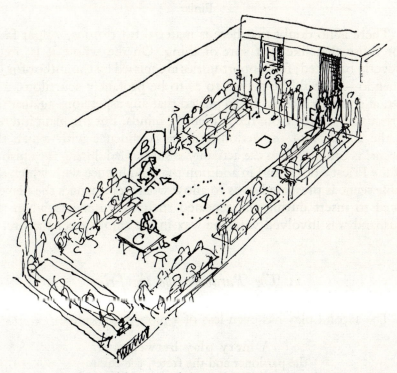

FIG. 12. Conjectural lay-out of the action in Heywood's *Johan Johan*

249

They now come to the fire to put a final mock upon Johan. But Johan has reached his limit and he ups with his pail and smashes it on the floor. Tyb upbraids him; Johan cries to her in rage –

B.iiii.*rev.*   [. . .] come no nere
                  For by kokk*es* blood / yf thou come here
                  Or yf thou onys styr / toward this place
                  I shall throw this shouyll full of colys in thy face

– so he is near the fireplace right enough! Then he turns on Sir Johan, and comes to blows with him –

> Here they fyght by the erys a whyle & than
> the preest and the wyfe go out of the place.

Johan is left alone. What is he to do? How is he to be given an exit? He suddenly asks himself what the two may have gone away to do together! and cries –

> [. . .] I wyll hye me thyder
> To se yf they do me any vylany
> And thus fare well this noble company.
>   Finis.

There is no doubt that here is material for riotous, vulgar farce for those that like that sort of thing. On the whole it is pretty cleverly balanced; few opportunities are missed by the author for in-nuendo – it could be played so as to be profanely scurrilous, and yet, at a pinch, it could be so played that any aspersions against the Priest rose simply from the audience's minds. But the main interest is the actuality of the action and the confidence with which the 'scene' is broken when the actuality is suspended during the episode at the Priest's door, and in addition the bold licence with which the table scene is presented so as to allow whatever nuances the players liked to insert during the repeated snatched moments when the husband was involved with the wax in the smoke over the fire.

21 *The Pardoner and the Friar*

The second play has even less of a plot; it is headed:

> A mery play betwene
> the pardoner and the frere / the curate
> and neybour Pratte.

I quote from the Tudor Facsimile, No. 125, made in 1909 from a copy, printed by William Rastell and dated 5 April 1533, in the Pepys Collection, Magdalene College, Cambridge.

There are three features that are interesting theatrically. First, a visiting Friar enters to preach a sermon, but is interrupted by an itinerant Pardoner equally out to display and describe his relics and to collect any fees he can. The technically rather difficult gag is introduced of making the two speak fairly long speeches but with their individual lines alternating between the two of them, so creating an atmosphere of ludicrous confusion.

Secondly, concerning the Pardoner's relics; these are pretty certainly actually brought in in a bag and produced as they are described, for the Pardoner refers to –

> [. . .] these holy relyques / whiche or I go hens
> I shall here shewe / in open audyence

They consist of a sufficiently satirical collection, comprising
  – a bone 'of a holy Jewes shepe' to cure animals' diseases;
  – a 'mytten' for a sower to wear;
  – the 'blessed arme [?] of swete saynt sondaye';
  – the 'great too [*toe*] of the holy trynyte', a cure against toothache;
  – Our Lady's 'bongrace / which she ware with her french hode';
  – 'Of all helowes / the blessyd Jaw bone';
  – 'of saynt Myghell / eke the brayn pan' as a cure for headaches.

He specifically denies the contemplation of these relics to any women 'that hathe done syn', so presumably he expects there to be some women in the audience.

Eventually the two quarrel, and the Pardoner turns to the spectators to borrow a sword, with –

> I say some good body / lende me his hengar
> Than the fyght

Thirdly, in the heat of the fight a curate suddenly enters with the rather surprising revelation that they either are, or are pretending to be, in a church; for he reproaches them with –

> That euer ye came hyther / [. . .]
> To polute my chyrche

I am not certain whether a parson would in those days lend his church to a performance of this particularly satirical sort nor, even if he did, whether he would assent to being caricatured by a player at the climax of the performance. At all events, the actor playing the Parson pretends to summon help from the audience with the line –

Neybour prat / com hether I you pray

– and so the fourth player is called in for his small part, and the two try to eject the disturbers.

ℭ The playe called the foure PP.

ℭ A newe and a very mery enterlude of
.A palmer.
A pardoner.
A potycary.
A pedler.

Made by John Heewood

FIG. 13. Title-page of Heywood's *The Foure PP*, published c. 1545

The final twist is that the Pardoner and the Friar prove too good for the Parson and Prat, and give them a thorough drubbing before they depart on their ways – leaving the curate and his neighbour to join in hurling maledictions after them.

22 *The Foure PP*

The last play has some similarities with the one just discussed. Its title-page reads–

The playe called the
foure PP.
A newe and a very mery enterlude of
A palmer.
A pardoner.
A potycary.
A pedler.
—Made by John Heewood—

It was 'Imprynted at London in Fletestrete at the sygne of the George by Wyllyam Myddylton.' It is undated (c. 1545); it may be read in Tudor Facsimile, No. 32, made in 1908 from the British Museum press-mark C.34, e.43.

The Palmer and the Pardoner enter and argue which is the easier way to salvation – through pilgrimage or by buying 'pardons'. They are so busy talking that they scarcely notice the Apothecary, who comes to prove them both false – or at least ineffectual – since he and his drugs are most effective at freeing souls from bodies, and until that happens neither salvation nor damnation can operate. The Pedlar overhears and joins in.

The remainder is but argument and dialogue – some of it still shrewd and fresh – but no development or event occurs to help us to further our knowledge of presentation. All the same we may be grateful to encounter, in the Pardoner's tale of his visit to hell, a gay piece of invention sometimes extracted and offered as an example of 'the short story' in early English literature.

Part Two 1527–1553
The Travers

Godly Queen Hester ∽ *Thersytes* ∽ *The Problem of Defining an Interlude* ∽ *Wit and Science*

23 *Godly Queen Hester*

The last six Heywood-attributed plays made scarcely any demands at all in the matter of technical presentation, but each of the three plays that now follow presents some new element or problem in setting. All three probably belong to the second quarter of the sixteenth century.

It is possible, I think, to see some development in technique taking place, and certainly to see that the method of simple Interlude-presentation in a private hall, which I have described up to now, has to be supplemented in certain ways.

The three plays are the anonymous *Godly Queen Hester* (c. 1527), the anonymous *Thersytes* (c. 1537) and John Redford's *Wit and Science* (c. 1539); the last not to be confused with either the anonymous *The Marriage of Wit and Science* (c. 1567) or the anonymous *The Marriage of Wit and Wisdom* (c. 1579).

Godly Queen Hester introduces an entirely new element in setting; *Thersytes* introduces a new placing of an element of setting; and *Wit and Science* raises two curious problems – first, that of an apparent third entrance, and second, that of a 'mount'.

The plot of *Godly Queen Hester* is a simple one. I have used the edition by W. W. Greg of the 1561 quarto, published as vol. 5 of W. Bang's *Materialen zur Kunde des älteren Englischen Dramas*, Louvain, 1904. The title-page reads

A newe enterlude
drawen oute of the holy scripture
of godly queene Hester, verye necessary
newly made and imprinted, this pre
sent yere. M.D.LXI.

Com nere vertuous matrons & women kind
Here may ye learne of Hesters duty,
In all comlines of vertue you shal finde
How to behaue your selues in humilitie.

The names of the players.

The prologue	Pryde
King Assuerus.	Adulation.
iii. gentlemen	Ambition.
Aman.	Hardy dardy
Mardocheus	A Jewe.
Hester.	Arbona.
Pursueuant.	Scriba.

The virtuous address immediately below the date is either ill-chosen or grimly humorous; for Queen Hester's behaviour to her oppressor is the reverse of humble since she plans and accomplishes his destruction. It is also the first direct implication that I have found that a deliberate address might be made to a female audience, or to the women of the audience primarily – unless the passage is a mere attempt at advertisement.

The play has some 1180 lines. The first 337 lines show King Assuerus (that is, King Ahasuerus or Artaxerxes) electing one of his subjects, Aman by name, to be his chancellor; and later taking to wife the Jewess, Hester (that is, Esther of the Bible). Lines 338 to 580 consist of a long discussion in which Pryde, Adulation and Ambytion show how corrupt Aman's chancellorship becomes and how the Jews are oppressed by him. Lines 581 to the end show Aman's attempt to refute his accusers, with his desperate move to discredit the Queen, her triumph over him, her saving of the Jews, and his final execution.

A curious intrusion into the latter half of the play is made by the very unbiblical character of Hardydardy who offers a vice-like low-comedy commentary, much as A and B did in *Fulgens*.

The plot, as I have said, is simple but the acting-directions are of an interest so great that I believe they can be taken to show a complete step forward in the presentation-technique of Interludes; because of this the development of the story needs to be studied in detail.

The script opens with a title: 'The enterlude of the vertuous and godly Queene Hester' and then follows directly a speech-ascription, centred in mid-page:

THE PROLOGUE

His opening speech is brief, containing only 14 lines, and in them he says that divers philosophers have disputed wherein the greatest honour lies, whether in riches, in noble blood, in wisdom, in power. . ., and concludes with the following two lines, after which there comes immediately the first of the very curious directions –

13.   Ouer this some said, that vertuous demenoure
             To bee excellent, and of moste honour.
                  The kyng sitting in a chaire speaketh to his counsell.

– and the King's speech begins straightway:

          Of these my lordes we woulde be glad to here,
          Which is most worthy honoure to attayne [. . .]

In general, the purpose in this opening is quite clear and workmanlike; the subject is raised – What makes the most honourable statesman? And the King enquires of his lords which one of them they think fittest to be promoted to such a position of honour.

The directness of this opening and its coming so sharply to the point within twenty lines seem to suggest a playwright who had a pretty clear idea of what he was doing, and was out to do it with no fumbling. And yet the direction, 'The kyng sitting in his chaire speaketh to his counsell', seems at first sight just the opposite; it seems unexpected, cryptic and incompetent. How did the King get to his chair? How did his lords-in-council get to him? There is no answer, so far, to these questions, and any attempt to explain them must be left until later in the play.

To continue: after the King has spoken for 7 lines he is answered by one of his lords. This lord's speech is headed with a speechascription centred in the middle of the page as is usual for speechascriptions in this particular play. It reads –

PRIMUS GENEROSUS.

– and then comes the speech itself consisting of 14 lines in which this particular lord argues that it is the quality of *virtue* that is most deserving of honour; and the discussion will be taken up in a moment by 'Secundus Generosus' and 'Tertius Generosus'. But at this particular point opposite the first line of Primus Generosus's speech there occurs, squeezed up in the right-hand margin, clear of the main text, the three words –

                                      The first
                                      gentleman

All the speech-ascriptions that follow – for Primus Generosus, Secundus Generosus and Tertius Generosus – are centred in the usual way, and no English reference to any second gentleman or third gentleman occurs after this in the margin. The above-quoted marginal note seems then to have no purpose.

The script continues with the three noblemen gravely quoting the classics in support of their views about honour and the necessity for virtue. To virtue they add justice, for where justice 'fayleth in the prince . . . The common weale decayeth . . .' The King thanks them for their counsel, and ends by particularly observing that a prince must see that his 'lieutenaunt' also should be just –

98.   That no ambicion nor couetise [. . .]
            Doe erect his corage, for to play checkmate
            For though it be as well as it may neede,
            It shall be thought nay, I assure you in dede
            Sir what is your name and progeny?

This last line appears to be nothing whatever but a complete *non sequitur*. Putting aside the question whether some other lines are missing, let me try to reconstruct the situation. The King apparently switches suddenly from theory to action and seizes unexpectedly on one of his courtiers, almost in mid-sentence, demanding his name and family. Clearly 'progeny' is meant to be 'ancestry' (perhaps formed from 'progenitor'). This courtier turns out to be (though there is no previous indication of this) called Aman, for the lines continue –

AMAN.
I am Aman sonne of Amadathy,
Of the stocke of Agag borne lyniallye,

ASSUERUS.
your learnyng and reason pleaseth vs well [. . .]
So that [. . .]
we make you our chaunceloure [. . .]
Seε ye doe iustice and trueth euer approue
Or to your destruction, we shall you soone remoue

But opposite the first line of Aman's speech there is in the margin another of the explanatory notes, and it is certainly unexpected as well as explanatory. It reads –

One of
y gētyll
mē must

answere
whyche
you will

The narrowness of the margin obviously sets a quite embarrassing restriction upon the clear setting out of notes of this sort, and one can easily realize they must be as succinct and abbreviated as possible. At first, therefore, one sees no reason for the printer's involving himself in this troublesome restriction for the sake of a note that seems to have no more importance than this one.

Then upon consideration one might be inclined to see a company of players perhaps saying at the opening of Aman's speech, 'Yes, but who is Aman and where does he come from?' And being answered, 'He is one of the courtiers already present.' 'Oh; then which one?' 'It doesn't matter which one; any of them would do.' 'I see; then we'ld better make a note of that in the margin.' And the marginal note got printed.

The question why was Aman not directed to 'enter' with the counsellors in the first place when the King 'entered' could perhaps be answered if the number of counsellors was not fixed to begin – that is, if it was left undecided in order that different companies of players could introduce different numbers of actors as the King's counsellors according to the resources of man-power they had available. Especially might this be applicable if the company or companies for which the play was written belonged to large groups such as a school or chapel choir. Later directions seem to support this idea, as will be seen.

As it is, it appears that Aman was in fact one of the 'generosi' who entered, in a way still unspecified, with the King. This would mean that the court consisted of two 'gentlemen' unnamed and a third called Aman. But under the names of the players on the title-page we read distinctly that there were 'iii. gentlemen' and also, separately, Aman, thus making four courtiers. On the other hand the whole picture may have been different, for a little later there is a marginal note reading 'Here entrith Aman with many men awaiting on hym'. What is meant by *many men* cannot be guessed, but it would seem to suggest, 'an indefinite number of actors according to what you have available'. There is nothing to forbid our supposing that Assuerus's courtiers may have been similarly indefinite in number at the opening of the play. After all it is a very typical problem in preparing a new play for presentation, to decide how many supers you can manage.

With all this, it is still remarkable to see from the note now under discussion that it did not seem to matter which of the 'gentlemen' was to answer with Aman's lines, but that it could be 'whyche you will'. It is, I think, clear that it may pay to examine these marginal notes with particular care.

To resume: the next three lines in the script are from Aman. He says,

113.   My duty is more nowe then euer it was,
         Truly to serue youre moste noble grace,
         Both nyghte & day, here and in euery place.

                                                    (et exeat)

And thus, with an abruptness which again seems unexpected, he goes out.

One thing can be said for this technique; however puzzling it may appear at first sight, a remarkable amount of business has been got through in one hundred and fourteen lines of dialogue; and in action there is no reason at all to suppose any of it would not be perfectly clear to a spectator watching. But how it is all likely to have been managed we still have to seek.

The action is now free of the somewhat troublesome Aman for the present. The King is still presumably 'sitting in a chaire', and now about to address his indefinite number of counsellors once more. He is as cursory about his business as before; he says,

     My lordes [. . .]
     we are comfortles, for lacke of a Queene [. . .]
     therfore youre counsells firste had, to marry we do intend

Primus Generosus answers this with a proposal to 'peruse this realme' and gather a great number of fair maidens –

                         [. . .] that we may make reporte
            Vnto your grace, then may ye be sure
            To chose the beste, [. . .]

Assuerus responds to this with an immediate recall of his new chancellor –

                         ASSEWERUS
            Call to vs Aman our trusty chaunceler.

                         AMAN.
            If it please your grace I am here,

262

– from which it is obvious that Aman must now reappear (and thus the purpose of his earlier exit is made still more uncertain). However, any doubt about his action now is removed by the marginal note which I have already quoted, and which gives us a fragment more information:

> Here en
> trith A-
> mā with
> māy mē
> awaitīg
> on hym.

The extra information is of course this puzzling statement that he has *many men* with him. Perhaps his purpose in going out was to gather them. The vagueness of the specification clearly – and possibly intentionally – leaves it open whether to suppose two or twenty men. Again, the number is probably meant to be dependent upon the man-power available. And once more the suggestion of such a pool of personnel as might be found in a school comes to mind.

It is worth observing that the margin-width is such as to limit the lines of these side-notes to eight or so letters only, so we cannot expect to avoid abbreviations and unusual breaks in words.

The next matter is important enough to be set out in full. After Aman's response to the King's summons, Assuerus says to him,

132.   Aman this is the councel of my lordes all,
That our officers in hast we shoulde sende
To pervse this region vdiuersall
From the begynnynge vnto the ende
To seke faire maidens, where so thei may be kende
And of most goodly personages that maye be sene
To the intent among them we may chose a quene
This is our minde, more to speake it shal not nede,
In all that ye may, see it bee done in dede.

– directly upon this there comes an acting-direction in English but not printed in the margin. Instead it occupies the right-hand part of a normal line, just as did the opening direction about 'the Kyng sitting in a chaire . . . ' This new direction is again in the nature of a surprise for which we have had no preparation; it reads –

> Here entreth Mardocheus and a maiden with him.

This new character goes on to announce his name and what he is, and to introduce the maiden, who is his brother's daughter, Hester. He then tells Hester of the King's decree and offers her some advice on how to behave if she should be the one chosen to be queen. This obviously means that neither the King nor any of his court can still be present; the conversation is clearly a private one and, as it were, taking place in a spot quite different from the King's court. In other words there is what would be called today a 'change of scene'. But it would be to beg the question if this term were applied too freely to what now happens in the action; because we do know quite definitely what did happen, and it is *not* a 'change' of 'scene'. This information is contained in another of the marginal notes, and its contents offer the most striking news concerning presentation in this whole play. The note reads –

Here the
kynge en
tryth the
trauers &
aman go
eth out.

That, then, is what occurred before Mardocheus entered with Hester and talked with her; and that is the means by which these two were given an empty Place to talk in. But the main surprise in this direction is of course the new item in setting which is referred to. It is necessary to see now with what certainty it can be defined, and how far it helps to explain the above puzzling passages. This item is a 'trauers', by which is to be understood a 'traverse'. What is a traverse? To begin let me dispose of a possible confusion. The word traverse might be thought to be another name for that item which has already become so important in the setting of Interludes namely, the screens across the hall, through the intervals between which I have argued the actors go out and come in. But this last direction specifies two distinctly differentiated actions. Aman *goeth out* (presumably through the screens); but the King is *not* said to go out – he is said to *enter the traverse*.

I have shown that space is at a premium in these marginal notes because of the limited width of the margin, and therefore it is to be supposed that if the printer could have adequately served the purpose of the direction by printing 'Here the King and Aman go out' he would have done so. But he did not. Despite the cramped space, he took the pains to make it clear that Aman went out but that the

1. An impression of the dimness of a torchlit hall (by Richard Southern and Iris Brooke)

2. *Sensuality:* 'Thus am I set a syde . . .' (*Nature*, Haddon Hall)

3. 'Here the kynge entreth the trauerse'
(*Godly Queen Hester*, Penshurst Place)

4. A public outdoor performance in an inn-yard
(The New Inn, Gloucester)

5. The opening procession 'passing by' the stage
(*The Coblers Prophesie*, Trinity College, Cambridge)

6. A traverse in the Chinese Classical theatre (*ta-chang tzu*)

King did something different – that he, by implication, *did not go out*. If he did not go out, then the traverse could not be the screens, for to go through the screens would have been to go out – just as surely as Aman went out. What then did the King do and why? He 'entered a traverse' instead.

The 'why' of this move may be easier to explain at first than the 'how'. In several passages in the ensuing play a character coming into the action from some business at a distance, has to appeal to the King. Conversely, at other passages characters have to speak when the King is not present (this situation is not unlike that with Jupiter in Heywood's *Weather*). It would distinctly assist the action if the King could be spoken to sometimes, but could also be conveniently hidden away at other times, yet without his having to make numerous exits and entrances. This is the kind of situation that has come up often in Interludes; namely, the need for a means of *temporary withdrawal* that should be different from the regular and more final means of exit offered by the screens-openings themselves.

At this point it is worth recalling what I have said already about the scene of action in Interludes; any serious study of them suggests that if one allows oneself to think of this scene of action as one thinks of the 'scene of action' of a modern play – that is to say as the place where the plot is *supposed* to take place instead of where the actual performance *is* taking place – then the whole nature of the presentation of an Interlude will be missed.

The action of an Interlude was emphatically not conceived as an imitation or re-presentation of some outside event supposed to be happening, or to have once happened, elsewhere, but as the entry into one's room of a group of players who came in and presented a story or a diverting argument *in one's own room*. It was indeed, from the presentation point of view, something more like having a home charade than going out to a theatre performance. The technicalities of setting were provided, or accepted, with the purpose of helping the players in presenting such a performance, not so as to turn part of one's room into the semblance of some other place. So long as the galvanizing and vivid custom of direct audience-address persisted, no other conception of the scene of action of a play could of course ever be entertained, for direct address to spectators *must* belie any fiction that the action is taking place somewhere where there are no spectators!

This realistic attitude about a theatrical presentation – that it is a theatrical presentation and does not pretend to give an illusion of a real-life event – remains of course up to the highest period of Elizabethan drama. There is no stage-direction in *Hamlet* reading 'the scene; a graveyard', instead we read, as we would in an Interlude, simply 'enter two clowns' and nothing more.

The upshot of this is that whatever a traverse might be in *Godly Queen Hester*, it would not *represent* a King's Palace, and would not have to be made to look like a palace in any way. It would *be* a traverse, functional not representational. What is required for the King is simply a place of concealment – in the modern sense of the word, a screen. Stated in these terms one can perhaps see why, although the actual Tudor screens typical of a Great Hall might be present, there might yet also be needed a subsidiary screen that could be used in a different sense – not as a means of exit (which would be too final), but as a means of temporary concealment or retirement from the action, and otherwise not very different from the screens themselves – even, in practice, a sort of small duplication of them. What might such a thing be like?

Before attempting an answer, a reference to *The Oxford English Dictionary* offers some help. A 'Traverse' is defined as *something that crosses*, with a derivation from *trans*, 'across' and *vertere*, 'to turn'. Of the many variant meanings given there, two seem to me to be particularly useful. First, under meaning 13: 'A curtain or screen placed crosswise, or drawn across a room, hall, or theatre.'

I hesitate a little over the *Dictionary*'s use of the word 'theatre' here. There is given an example of this use dated 1589 (see below). By this date there had admittedly been three theatres built in London – the Theatre, and the Curtain in Shoreditch, and the Rose on Bankside – but none of these so far as is known was capable of having a curtain 'drawn across' the *theatre* proper. If we are meant to understand 'stage' for 'theatre', the picture might seem a little more acceptable but then, of course, there would rise the objection that the Elizabethan stage (again, as far as is known) emphatically did not have any curtain *drawn across it as a whole*. And any smaller curtain across only a part of the stage, e.g. in the sense of drawing across to close an 'inner stage', is still a matter of very heated controversy, which I would prefer to look at in another place. Suffice it for the moment to settle that the idea of a 'traverse' as something that might be 'drawn across', in a theatre or on a stage, is certainly what the *Dictionary* accepts. It may be, of course, that the *Dictionary* uses the word 'theatre' here in the sense of any place where a performance is given; in that case a traverse might be a curtain drawn across on the floor of a Great Hall, or across part of the floor of a Great Hall (and independently of any stage), when an entertainment was given. The example of this usage in 1589 which the *Dictionary* quotes is from Puttenham's *English Poesie*, l. xvii (Arb.) 51, and reads in full, 'The floore . . . had in it sundrie little diuisions by curteins as trauerses to serue for seueral roomes where they might repaire vnto and change their garments and come in againe, as their speaches and parts were to be renewed.'

There is also a meaning given under sense 14, which is useful: 'A small compartment shut off or enclosed by a curtain or screen in a church, house, etc.; a closet.' There are two examples of this, the first; – '1526. *St. Papers Hen. VIII.* l. 172. Aftyr his first Masse was done, I wente unto hym, withyn his travesse'; the second: – '1536. Wriothesley *Chron.* (Camden) l. 46. The King . . . then went into the traves that was made for him at the alters end.' All three examples have clearly the sense of a private temporary retiring place.

Next I turn to the relevant footnote to l. 140 inserted by Greg in his edition of *Godly Queen Hester*; it reads.

> 140 side note. *trauers*. Grosart erroneously describes this as 'a closet behind a screen'. The 'traverse' was a curtain, opening in the middle, which hung across the stage. To enter it was to go off the stage through it. Skelton in his *Bowge of Courte*, l. 58 (Dyce l. 32) uses the form 'traues' in the sense of 'curtain' independently of its technical stage use.

Skelton's lines, as given in Philip Henderson's edition of 1964, are, in full,

> [. . .] Then should ye see there pressing in apace
> Of one and other that would this lady see;
> Which sat behind a traves of silke fine
> Of gold of tissue the finest that might be,
> In a throne which far clearer did shine
> Than Phoebus in his sphere celestine.

Greg's footnote is perhaps a little final in its tone. Grosart's 'error' (Dr. A. B. Grosart was editor of an 1873 reprint) might not be an error, if by his words, 'a closet behind a screen', he meant 'a covered space behind a curtain' – which it is not impossible he did mean. On the other hand, Greg's own definition as 'a curtain . . . which hung across *the stage*' (my italics) suffers very seriously in one respect, because I have not up to this point found the slightest indication of anything being used in Interludes which was called a stage.

And therefore to speak of a 'technical *stage* use' of the word *traverse*, before the word *stage* itself was used as a technical term, may be objected to as misleading.

It seems certain that Greg's note means that he considered this traverse as being upon a stage; for a little later he has a further interesting footnote relative to the marginal direction coming at l. 203 in the script. This direction reads 'Here Aman metythe the*m* in ye place'. Greg's note about the term 'place' is:

> 203 side note. *place*. According to Collier 'the open space where the performers stood'. The term 'traverse' l. 140 implies that the play was intended for representation on a stage of some sort, so 'place' would apparently mean merely 'stage'. Whether it had any more technical meaning, I do not know. *cf. Thersytes*, l. 21. s.d. . . . and Skelton, *Magnificence*, l. 241, s.d.: 'Itaque *Measure* exeat locum' etc.

(I discuss the references to Place in *Magnyfycence* and *Thersytes* in Sections 11 and 24 respectively.)

There is an almost palpable sense of indecision in Greg's note. I think it is there because the facts themselves are not decisive. The quotation from Collier seems to be given grudgingly (and I think justifiably so, for in my view the 'place' was not restricted to the open space where the performers stood). But the statement that 'The term "traverse" implies that the play was intended for representation on a stage . . .' is what gives one especially to hesitate.

I feel very reluctant to believe that the term 'traverse' does so necessarily imply a stage; why should it? It is almost certain that the two *Dictionary* references to Henry VIII's traverses carried no implication of any stage. Nor did Skelton's reference in *The Bowge of Courte*; and to claim that Skelton uses the word 'independently of its technical stage use' is sheer begging the question unless a 'stage use' can be established as early as this. There seems to be nothing in either the *Dictionary* definition of a traverse or the use of the word in general to suggest that a traverse could not be set up on the floor as naturally as it could upon a 'stage'.

To argue that a traverse could only be set up on a stage, or that it implied the use of a stage, may obviously lead to the still less defensible belief, suggested by Greg, that '"place" would apparently mean merely "stage"'. It is quite clear from the direction in *A play of loue* that a player could run about the place *among the audience* (see p. 233). 'Place' could not here mean 'stage'.

The final impression of indecision is, very fairly, given in Greg's concluding statement – 'Whether it ["place"] had any more technical meaning I do not know.' I have tried, above and in *The Medieval Theatre in the Round*, to define that more technical meaning, and it seems to me that the facts do not at any point whatever support the idea that a 'stage' need necessarily be involved at all when a traverse is mentioned, or when the Place is mentioned; and I think a whole confusion has come about through what I have, justly or unjustly, called the Victorian opinion that any theatrical performance at any period must inevitably have taken place on a stage.

I make this point at length because it seems to me that it should be almost axiomatic that any play in which the actors call for 'room', or free passage, before entering cannot have been performed upon a stage. The only way that the two incompatibles, 'stage' and appeals for 'room', could be reconciled would be if spectators were themselves on the stage. And of such a custom there is no evidence until the Elizabethan public playhouses, with their particular stages, were built.

Now after this preliminary, it seems necessary to sum up and to see how the above-discussed view that the traverse was something associated necessarily with a stage may have arisen.

Firstly it does seem correct to say that there exists an acceptance of the word 'traverse', on occasion, as a theatre term and one that means a 'curtain drawn across' in some way. It could perhaps be said to be something hung up for a theatrical occasion to go behind, or as a means to afford cover for something or someone. Given the existence of an independent meaning of the word as a curtain forming a screen, what was it like when used theatrically? And, incidentally, how did it come to have this close association with a *stage* that has so obsessed the Victorian commentators and their successors?

A visual example of such a thing used as background to a performance could be taken from almost any representation of a booth stage at a Flemish *kermis*, though admittedly most such pictures date from a slightly later period than *Queen Hester*, and of course they are not English in origin. The earliest of these is probably a water-colour in the library at Cambrai, and dates from about 1542 – say some twenty years after *Hester*. Especially when such booth stages show signs of belonging to one of the Rederijker societies is their evidence interesting in the present connexion, because the development of the Rederijker stages during the later part of the sixteenth century was not unlike the development from Interlude technique to Elizabethan playhouse technique that I am examining in this book. Indeed, as Renaissance fashions in decoration crept in, the booth traverse developed into something remarkably like the later hall screen and subsequently the Elizabethan tyring house façade. The Cambrai water-colour would appear to show a Rederijker performance because of the presence, over the centre of the traverse, of a device closely resembling the badge of a Rederijker society.

Fig. 14 is an attempt to generalize the characterstics of a booth stage. It is made to combine the features of the Cambrai water-colour with those of an exceptionally clear picture of a *kermis* stage in a painting by Pieter Balten now in the Rijksmuseum in Amsterdam. (For a reproduction of the Balten stage see my *The Seven Ages of the Theatre*, plate 4.)

At all events, just such a curtain as is shown in this figure, in two parts hung by hooks from a rod and capable of being entered through the join in the middle, is what we should call a *traverse* in the modern theatre today, though ours usually slides on a 'railway' not a rod, and can be opened by working-lines.

I would be prepared to say, on the evidence available at present, that the 'trauers' mentioned in the marginal note in *Hester* is likely on three grounds – on the grounds of technical suitability to the requirements of the script, on the grounds of contemporary meanings of the word, and on the grounds of near-contemporary paintings – to have been a fairly small two-part curtain, perhaps some eight feet high and some six to ten feet wide in all, hung on a rod supported on two uprights, and set up on the floor about a couple of feet in front of the centre element of the screens, so as to leave the two regular screen-entrances free for the servants and the general spectators and also for the more final comings and goings of the actors on occasions when they were supposed to leave the Place entirely. The traverse would thus supply a sort of temporary refuge when an actor was not concerned in the immediate action but had to be ready to be drawn back into that action later. A further point; as I have shown, such a traverse curtain was a simple thing and quite innocent of any pretence at illusion. It is not to be thought of as *representing*, say, a castle – or even a room in a castle. It was a simple traverse.

But how did the player get into it in the first place? And how did he get out of it if the play ended while he was still concealed behind it? The answers would be very simple; he merely walked, quite frankly, from or to it by means of the screen doors, with no thought

FIG. 14. An assembly of the main features of a booth stage (from Pieter Balten, c. 1550, and the Cambrai Library water-colour c. 1542)

whatever that it was necessary to conceal his action. He could move as simply and as frankly as the elaborate figure of a Kathakali actor walks into position behind his *therissila* or 'traverse' curtain, and leaves it afterwards.

In the Kathakali theatre of South India, two simply-clad assistants bring on a length of brightly-coloured silk, some 12 ft. long and 8 ft. wide, that is to serve as this *therissila* curtain. It is innocent of any fixing. The assistants merely hold it up by its top corners above their heads and let it hang between them. Then, from whatever place he happens to be, the actor to be discovered unhurriedly walks across without any concealment, passes behind the curtain and stands at the back of it. There may then follow some elaborate preliminary business of shaking the curtain (the *tiranoku*, or 'curtain-look'), but at cue all that happens is that the assistants simply drop the curtain to the ground, so discovering the actor, and then gather it up to one side and walk away with it. The whole episode is entirely successful dramatically, and the visible getting-into-place of the actor creates no distraction at all. For further information see G. A. C. Pandeya, *The Art of Kathakali*, 2nd edn., Allahabad, 1961.

Of much the same nature dramatically is the *ta-chang tzu* curtain used on the Chinese classical stage on certain special occasions, see Pl. 6. This is slightly more developed in that it has its own upright supports and cross-piece, but it is openly carried on by stage hands in the same way, and may be quite simply supported by bracing the uprights with a couple of ordinary chairs.

It is not out of place to point out here that the normal background to the Classical Chinese stage on which this traverse curtain is set is, in practical essentials, remarkably like a hall screens, even to possessing two specific and traditional doors for entrance and exit.

Such an actors' traverse-curtain has in fact been introduced into theatres all over the world. It is not far from the truth to say that it is the first item of scenic equipment they invented – apart, of course, from their costumes. But what I am now concerned with is to establish in as much detail as possible what a traverse may have been in Tudor England. There is one further piece of evidence, I believe, concerning its size.

Suitably enough we owe this evidence ultimately to John Rastell. It is to be found in the Pleadings of the law case referred to on p. 202 in which Rastell attempted to get satisfaction from Henry Walton in respect of the hire-price for a number of theatrical costumes, etc., which Rastell had had made. In the opening Pleading, after an itemization of the garments themselves ending with, 'two caps of yellow and red sarcenet', we read:

> and two curtains of green and yellow sarcenet.

Later, there follows among the papers a more detailed inventory. In it, concerning the above we read:

> 'Item   Two caps, of yellow and
>   red sarcenet . . . .   3s. 4d.
>   Item Two curtains, of green
>   and yellow sarcenet . . 20yds. 1s.

Thus we learn the length of material estimated in the two curtains. This was apparently considered a not unimportant matter in establishing the justice of the amount claimed, since the question was asked of three separate witnesses (but without result); for later in the papers, in the Deposition of one, George Mayler, he said 'that he knew the said garments . . . for he hath occupied and played in them . . . And he saith that he hath seen the curtains of sarcenet, but how many ells they contained he knoweth not, but it was worth 40d. every ell.'

Similarly, in the Deposition of a certain George Birch who, with 'his company', played in the garments, we read that 'He saw the curtains of sarcenet but how many ells they were he knoweth not, but every ell was worth 3s.'

In the Deposition of John Redman who also had played in the garments, we find that 'the curtains of silk were fresh and new'.

There is then clear indication that this pair of curtains was familiar to the players who hired the costumes, though they were unwilling to commit themselves about the size. Thus we return to the item in the inventory which lists them as containing 20 yds. In what width of material might these 20 yds. come?

Looms were relatively limited in size in the sixteenth century, and we may take as a likely figure the width of 23 ins. Very roughly this would give us an area of 60 sq. ft. for each curtain and, for the pair, we might not be far out in visualizing them as making a whole some 12 ft. long by 10 ft. high, divided in the middle.

This is very much what a study of the representations of traverses in the Flemish *kermis* pictures would lead one to expect.

At this point it seems helpful to introduce the second in the series of four exhibits from the Tokyo Shakespeare Exhibition. This is not because I believe my solution is final and to be set down for the record, but that I feel it incumbent upon me to explain as fully as possible what I think a traverse was and looked like, even if only so that others may more easily correct the picture where it is wrong.

For this scene I took as background a photograph of a more elaborate screen in a larger hall, that at Penshurst Place in Kent, see Plate 3. On the farthest perspex sheet, against the photograph, are painted the distant spectators standing before the screens and in the entrances, with a few of the seated spectators at the table along the far side of the Hall; but particularly on this sheet was painted the traverse curtain itself in front of the centre screen, with the figure of the King about to go through the curtain into concealment behind it. On the centre sheet is painted a suggested figure of Aman bowing as the King leaves; shortly afterwards to straighten up and himself move to his exit and go out through the crowd at one of the screens doors. On the nearest sheet are painted some of the high table spectators and one of the audience at the end of the near side table. The purpose of this reconstruction is particularly to illustrate the difference between going out by entering a traverse, and going out by exiting at a screens-door, and to establish as nearly as possible

273

what the appearance of a traverse in an Interlude in a Great Hall may have been.

To return to *Hester*. Much about the presentation now becomes clearer. The King's entrance 'sitting in a chaire' at the beginning of the action can be simple. The player of the King walks behind the traverse and seats himself until its curtains are drawn open at the moment when the group of counsellors comes in from the doors in the screens. The scene now runs smoothly until the exit of Aman to organize the search for the maidens. Naturally he 'goeth out' of the hall to perform this duty. The King does not; he has to await the return of his embassage. Thus he 'entryth the trauers', returning to his chair, and if the curtains had been open they might now be closed again upon him. The remaining courtiers, whatever their number, and the 'many men' waiting on Aman, must leave by one of the screen doors, and then the Place is, for the moment, empty. Next, from the other door come the two new figures, Mardocheus and Hester; and the action can now continue with the dialogue between them. It is of course dramatically important that these two characters are not, as yet, in the King's presence, for to them there still has to come the King's messenger to tell them of the King's search for a bride.

Mardocheus is describing himself and his ancestry and introducing his niece to the audience. His lines make it quite clear that he knows about Assuerus's quest and, moreover, that he is aware that Hester has been 'appoynted for one' among the other maidens; with this in mind he begins to advise her on the fitting behaviour for a king's wife. Hester is most dutiful in her agreement with what he says:

186. It is my whole mynde and hartye desyre
      That same to fulfyll, as reason shall requyre.

PURSEUAUNT.
I haue here of maydens a fayre companye [. . .]

– and so, though there is no direction about his entrance, the Purseuaunt must now walk into the hall and intercept their conversation bringing behind him a train consisting (theoretically) of all the attractive girls in the country save one – Hester. There is no doubt about the intention here, since beside his own statement we have another of the marginal notes to emphasize the point. It reads –

Here en-
trith pur
siuante
with ma
nye may
dens

What we must imagine by this 'many maydens' is as uncertain as in the note on Aman's 'many men'. But it is clear that something other than the limited resources of a travelling company of four men and a boy would be needed here. And since the crowd is now of maidens and, by definition, attractive ones, it seems highly likely that a school of young boys was taken as being at hand. (They can be made up very nicely as 'maidens'.)

The Purseuaunt, surrounded as he is by the crowd, does not at once see Mardocheus and Hester. His lines are to the audience

> I haue here of maydens a fayre companye [. . .]
> which to the king I thynke [. . .]
> For to present, [. . .]
> Saue before wyth Mardocheus the Iew,
> I muste speake for Hester, that is so fayre of hew.

Then it is that Marocheus steps forward and says over the maidens' heads 'She is here redy . . .'. Purseuaunt answers,

> Then shall I brynge her the kynge vntyll.
> Come on lady Hester, and followe me
> To the kynge shall ye goe with youre [? *our*] cumpany.

Now follows immediately another piece of interesting dramatic condensation; the next speech is from Aman and he says to the Purseuaunt, 'haue ye these maydens broughte For the kynge . . .'. Surely this can only suggest that the Purseuaunt with his train is now understood to have come to the King, and therefore that he must have left Mardocheus? There is no indication what happens to Mardocheus, but we must believe he goes out by one of the doors, while Hester joins the train. But there is on the other hand a clear statement about Aman's action, a side note reads

Here A-
man me-
tythe the*m*
in ye place

– He therefore must have entered by the other door as Mardocheus left by the first, and walked thence to the (presumably stationary) group who are supposed to be on their way to the King; and thus he meets them there in the middle of the floor. They exchange official greetings and Aman concludes with the order –

> Se that ye follow vs wyth youre hole cumpany.

PURSYUAUNT.
210.   As ye haue sayed so shall it be.

Next, the unexpected (if I may still call it such, for the technique is now becoming familiar) happens again; Aman simply goes on speaking without any apparent break but now addressing the King. He says,

211.   Pleasyth it youre grace, [. . .]
we haue made serche [. . .]
For goodly maydeus [. . .]
And of them haue founde in myne opynyon
A number ryght fayre [. . .]

But there is no direction for the King to enter!

What we *are* given, to show us a way out of the difficulty, is another of the valuable side notes, reading –

Then thei
go to the
kynge.

Where is the King? Earlier he entered into – and must therefore be still within – the traverse. I suppose either that its curtains are now opened to discover him (whether worked by assistants or by his own hand), or that on Aman's words the King simply lifted the curtain aside and stepped out, leaving it to fall back again.

Being a person very much to the point, he asks briefly,

218.   Are they also of suche competent age
Of suche demeanour and grauitie,
That they be fytte for oure mariage

Aman says yes. The King walks among them, savouring. And then he says to one of them, obviously Hester –

> But ye fayre damsell of the highest stature, [. . .]
> Of all this companye of most fynest nature.
> Tell vs your linage, . . .

Hester, being an orphan, does the best she can and concludes with a prayer that her foster-father may be befriended by the King. Thereupon – and very interestingly – we have –

ASSEWERUS
251.   Call in Mardocheus, that we may see his face.

MARDOCHEUS.
I am here to attende vpon youre grace.

I think there is no question here of Mardocheus's having remained in the action after Hester had left him, in order to be ready to come now to the King, or that he held himself at the King's elbow for this summons; I believe instead that he did leave the action fully, and that the King's order to 'Call in . . . ' was in fact an order, and resulted in one of his court (or, if they were straitened for number, Aman himself) going down the Hall and out, to find Mardocheus and bring him in. At all events, Mardocheus now picks up the dialogue with the King and praises Hester. The King questions her to find out her ability, and she shrewdly observes that a Queen should counsel her King and be capable of taking his place at home in time of war, and that she should therefore be as able and as well instructed as he. She discourses on good government. At length the King sends her to his 'waredrobe' to be attired – 'her selfe as for her ladyes all'. And he ends with two lines that have by now quite a familiar ring to them:

336.   And we for a season thys busynesse wyll cease,
                 And oure selfe repose for our pleasure and ease

                                                    Here de-
                                                    partith yᵉ
                                                    queene &
                                                    Aman &
                                                    all ye mai
                                                    dens.

– and the Place is once more empty. But we should notice that there is no specific indication of the King's departing, nor of where he goes.

There now follows what is in a way another surprise; it is a sort of *entr'acte* to use a modern term. Some way has to be found by the playwright to get on to the climax of the story and yet to justify that climax. What he has to show is how bad Aman's chancellorship did in fact become.

The line he takes is to bring in three completely new characters to explain events; they are different even to the extent of being abstract personifications, much in the same way as the characters of the early Moralities. Their names are Pryde, Adulation and Ambition. They occupy 243 lines of dialogue, just about 100 lines less than have been used already to open the play. Their whole function is to show that all pride, adulation and ambition have been annexed, as it were, to Aman's usage so that they themselves are left relatively beggared. In fact this reduction of their status is dramatically stressed in the acting-direction which opens this section of the play; it is not a marginal note but a direction within the lines of the text and it reads,

> Here entreth Pride syngynge
> poorely arayed.

I do not think 'poorely arayed' is the name of the song that Pride is singing. I think he enters poorly dressed and humming a mournful tune. He has a purpose in this; namely to draw attention to his sad state. This is shown in his opening lines –

338.   To men that be heuy [. . .]
                        [. . .] with their mouth thei sing,
            Though thei wepe in their hart.

Later he explains to the spectators –

368.   Syrs my name is pryde, but I haue layde asyde,
            All my goodlye araye:
            ye wynne [*ween*] I lye, there is a cause why,
            That I goe not gaye.
            I tell you at a worde, Aman that newe lorde,
            Hathe bought vp all goood clothe,
            And hath as many gownes, as wonld serue ten townes . . .

And similarly with the other two, who come in to complain with him. Only the latter of these, Ambition, has a direction to enter: 'Here entryth Ambytion' (l. 449). But they make together a very good job of discrediting Aman; and finally they bitterly make their wills, leaving everything they stand for to the man who has already got it nearly all. In disgust they conclude –

ADULATION.
577.   Let vs beginne with singynge, and conclude with drinkynge,
            It is the newe gyse:

AMBITION.
Then let vs beginne a songe, that wyl last euen as long
As hence to the tauerne dore.

(Et exeunt.)

On the whole, it is a very colourful piece of detraction. The margin
now confirms that –

Thei de-
part sing
yng, aud
Aman en
treth.

Note very carefully that there is no direction whatever for the
King to enter here; and yet as the three go out by one door to
their tavern, and as Aman enters immediately afterwards by the
other door, Aman's very first lines are –

AMAN.
581.   Moste noble prynce, and of highest wysedome [. . .]
[. . .] great malice I do sustayne, [. . .]
[. . .] I can not longe endure.
The sclaunderous reportes (etc. etc.)

– and he ends 30 lines of resentful complaint with, 'Let me be re-
moued another to haue my place', before the King replies tactfully
to him.

I do not think there could be a better proof that the traverse
was in fact the thing which I have described. Pride and his two
friends had the Place to themselves as they made their moan, and
the King was *not* present and *did not* hear them. They go out; and
immediately Aman comes in (with a clear entrance-direction) and
makes his moan also, and the King now (without any entrance-
direction) *is* present and listens to Aman's whole speech and at
length answers him. And the King all this while has neither gone
out nor come in! He is regally the chief figure, yet not a single direction concerning him has been given since l. 337, when he said he
would repose himself for his pleasure and ease.

I suggest that there is no doubt whatever that he is provided with
some sort of place of retirement which saves him from any exits or
entrances, which takes him out of the action when he is not needed,
and which allows him to be immediately present the moment he is
appealed to. This place of retirement was the traverse.

Now to continue with the action of the play, to see whether confirmation of this can be found.

The King answers Aman's complaint with sympathy – 'we know ryght well the wordes enuious to be . . .' – and finally makes a decree which gives Aman still greater power over the Jews –

625.   [. . .] for youre comforte [. . .]
            we make you lieutenaunte to rewle Israell,
            Take heare these robes see ye do them weare,
            Eke this golden wande in youre hande to beare, . . .

– so, in the Interlude tradition, he invests Aman in both senses of the word, presumably bringing the new garments from behind the traverse. And Aman accepts.

Thus, for the moment all is well. What follows now is of considerable interest. The King expresses his satisfaction at the termination of the interview, with two lines that are so familiar and at the same time so unexpected, that one's mind immediately goes back to the earlier examples which they resemble. What he says (l. 634) is –

            For a season we wyll to our solace
            Into our orcharde or some other place,

Firstly, the lines remind us of his earlier speech at l. 336 –

            And we for a season thys busynesse wyll cease,
            And oure selfe repose for our pleasure and ease.

And secondly, they remind us even more forcibly of a speech in another play altogether which at the time particularly caught our attention (above, p. 223); this was in *Calisto and Melebea* when, in a closely parallel situation, Calisto said –

            To pas the tyme now wyll I walk
            Up and down within myne orchard [. . .]
            Thus farewell my lordys for a whyle I wyll go

In *Calisto* there was unfortunately no clear indication of what Calisto then did. All that could be safely said was that he must have made some sort of a withdrawal since the lines immediately following introduce a new and separate passage of the play. The mention of the 'orchard' seemed curiously specific as if it had some sort of deliberate reference to the real topography of a Tudor Hall – either for the purpose of suggesting the actual place to which Calisto went, or to give verisimilitude to an otherwise rather contrived exit. Here in *Hester*, it is to the orchard again that the King proposes to go on the occasion of another equally contrived exit.

The question immediately rises here, as it did in *Calisto*: is there any indication of what in fact, not in theory, the player now does? And there is.

The moment is one where the action of the play is suddenly to be given a diversity by the author's bringing on a completely new character with as little relation to the real plot as A and B had in Medwall's *Fulgens*. This character is given a name to go by, rather than the mere capital letters that designated Medwall's couple, but it is as little in tune with the Bible names as their's were in tune with Roman names; it is 'Hardydardy'.

To recapitulate briefly the possible movement of the figures at this point; the King has heard Aman's complaint, both have been standing, let us say, about the middle of the Hall. The King then retires a little to the screen-end to fetch, or to order, the robes for Aman. He remains near the screens as he watches Aman, standing about the centre, assume the robes. The King then announces the intention of going to his orchard, and Aman is momentarily left alone – but only momentarily, for Hardydardy comes in and begins to walk down the Hall muttering a string of wryly comic proverbs to himself. There is now to follow a scene in which Hardydardy insinuates himself into Aman's confidence as a prospective servant. The question at issue in the above was: what are we to visualize the King doing after his orchard speech?

As I said, we have not far to seek, for the question is precisely answered by a marginal note in the script. It reads –

Here the
kynge en
treth the
trauerse
& Hardy
dardy en
treth the
place.

It is now possible to fill in the blank in my picture of the movement of the figures. As Aman finishes robing, standing about centre, the King, nearer the screens-end, turns, states his intention of going to the orchard or (with a curiously unregal vagueness) to 'some other place' and simply puts aside the traverse curtain and goes behind it (alternatively, it may be opened for his passage by a servant and closed again when he is inside).

This done, Hardydardy's voice is immediately heard, and he enters, threads through the crowd at the door and begins his garrulous passage down the Hall to the newly-resplendent Aman.

It is worth noting that the word 'entreth' in this marginal note is employed twice but means two completely opposite things – to *go out* (or 'enter' the traverse) and to *come in* (or 'enter' the Place).

What follows now is that Hardydardy and Aman converse for some 50 lines, by which time Hardydardy has succeeded in convincing Aman of his ability to speak 'merrily' enough to justify Aman's taking him into his service. Aman tells him so, and then goes on with a particularly significant speech:

> AMAN.
> well ye can speake merely wherwith I am contente
> Sirs [*Sir*] tarrie you a seasone se that farre ye not walke,
> I will to the kinge secretly to talke.
>> Moste victorius prince & of higheste honour
>> Primate of the worlde and president chefe, (etc. etc.)

– and Aman goes on for some 60 lines with a speech of courtly adulation, blending skilfully into a proposal to exterminate the Jews and to have a royal edict sent out to that effect.

It is quite clear here that Aman must leave Hardydardy in the Place, for he goes to talk *secretly*, and since he goes to talk secretly with the King, he must go to the traverse and open it – or call to the King with his line, 'Moste victorius prince . . .', and have the King step through the traverse to listen to him.

The next development is that the King quickly agrees to Aman's proposal (and incidentally again uses the Interlude's symbolic gesture-language by giving Aman for token a ring and seal), and then Aman turns away and raises his voice in the summons –

774.   The Pursiuauntes call to vs shortely.

> PURSYUAUNTES.
> If it lyke you we are here

Here the King leaves the situation to be dealt with by Aman, and either goes out, or retires again behind the traverse – in view of his next action later, his retirement is the more likely – and there come into the Hall 'Pursyuauntes' in some number undecided – presumably anything from one upwards according to resources. Aman gives them letters (apparently already written) and sends them (or him) off to deliver the letters to the rulers of the local towns and cities. Aman, left behind, speculates grimly on the approaching end of Mardocheus, and then Hardydardy emerges from the fringe with some shrewd and mocking comments, adding that it has already got about that Ambition, Adulation and Pryde have bequeathed all their qualities upon Aman. Aman shrugs this off and dismisses Hardydardy with a now-familiar excuse –

809.   well ye are verely, disposed merely,
                      Now for to talke.
                      And I am suerly minded secretely,
                      For my solace to walke.   Et exeat.

– a speech and punctuation difficult to interpret at first, but the final direction is perfectly clear. It is not a marginal note but within the lines and, as would be expected, it does not make any reference to any traverse but is a clear statement that Aman goes out in the normal way by the exit in the screens, and so, for the time, he leaves the action.

There immediately follows now a second direction within the lines –

                                      Here entreth a Iew and speaketh.

Now another movement of the plot, equivalent to a 'change of scene' takes place. We have to forget the proximity of the King and are transported for the moment to the Jewish quarter. Already the Jews there have heard the edict to exterminate them; and 'Another Iewe', and then 'An other Iew', both come to add their dismay to the first. To them again, we suddenly find Mardocheus speaking; and then, even more surprisingly, Hester. Presumably she enters now in royal robes and from one of the screen doors like her countrymen, but no direction occurs at all at this point. She says she has heard their lament and has decided to petition first God and then the King, 'A meane to fynde, for to sauegarde ye all', and then the remarkable next line –

860.   Call in the chapell to the intent they maye
                   Syng some holy himpne to spede vs this day

– and a marginal note confirms this–

than the
chappell
do singe.

283

Greg has a footnote that does not quite clearly let us see what is in his mind; he says,

860. *chapell* = choir, chorus. Collier has the astonishing note: 'This stage-direction shows, in all probability, that the performance was by the Chapel Royal, or at least that they assisted, and sang here out of sight.'

After the hymn there is no direction about what happens, but presumably the Jews go out when the singing stops, and leave Hester. She offers a brief prayer for success in her attempt to obtain the King's mercy. Perhaps she kneels there alone.

The next development, again quite unheralded, is a speech from King Assuerus. It has some interesting details. He begins by addressing Hester directly, but presumably he does not enter and certainly he does not go to her. I think therefore that he speaks from the traverse, which is thus either drawn aside to discover him, or through which he steps. He asks Hester her purpose, praises her, and bids her '[. . .] approch nere to this place, [. . .]' (he cannot therefore have moved towards her. But the purpose of his summons is interesting also in view of a theory that any form of physical embrace was absent from Interludes, for he goes on, '. . . That we may kisse you, and in our armes embrace', and that this is no mere figure of speech this marginal note exists to show –

here thei
kysse.

Then he again asks her her wishes.

Now follows what seems to me the most difficult passage of all in this play to interpret. Hester's reply ends –

880.   [. . .] I besech your grace, with heart most entier
              That it may please you this day to dine with me
              Eke my lord Aman I woulde be glad to see
              At the same banket for to take repaste

                        ASSUERUS.
              Call vs in Aman that we may go in haste,

                        AMAN.
              I am here ready to atende vpon your grace.

At this point a marginal note tells us that –

Here
must bee
prepared
a banket
in ye place

– the lines proceed straight away –

ASSUERUS.

Then let vs go while we haue tyme and space.
Lady Hester our moste beloued Quene,
So pewer and so exauisite is thys repaste,
Both of wine and meate that no better may beene,
youre mirth eke and manners so pleasaunte to attaste,
That for to departe we make no maner haste, [. . .]

What I believe must happen here is this: the embrace must take place near the traverse, for the King summons Hester to him. She proposes the banquet. Then the King calls either to one of his courtiers, if any are present, to fetch Aman; or if the players are too few to allow any courtiers, no harm is done, for there is almost certain to be a real page or two among the bystanders at the screens and the order can be perfectly delivered as to him; of course he would not be rehearsed to respond, but that again would not matter since, immediately the order was given, the actor Aman, waiting in the entry, would hear it and take his cue to come in. This we suppose he now does, and stands waiting on the King's other hand.

There must now be, if we are to follow the marginal direction, some moments of bustle; through the screens a couple of servants (either from the actors or from the household) must bring in a table and three seats. The most likely setting of the table would appear to be up-and-down the Hall so that the King can sit at its screens-end, facing up the Hall to the High Table. Hester can sit on his right and Aman (possibly a few inches farther away than Hester) on his left. The table set and the servants cleared, the King gives his invitation, 'while we haue tyme and space' after the bustle, to sit. They sit (see Fig. 15). They pretend to fall to. Next the King addresses a compliment to Hester, condensing time, to suggest the banquet is over but showing they are not yet to rise from it . . . Now the lines proceed, perhaps – if the players know their business well – in an atmosphere of growing tension. The King goes on, 'wherfore as we sayde we wolde ye shoulde demande' whatever she will. Hester then rises and makes a careful speech, working up to the climax –

285

910.   This I do aske [. . .]
       That throw all your reame both east and west
       As manye as bee of the Iewyshe nation,
       your grace wil them pardon at my supplication
       Assurynge you I am of that nacion, [. . .]

– the situation is clearly becoming a very uncomfortable one for Aman. The King furiously asks who is responsible for the outrage against his Queen and the Jews. And then Hester denounces Aman to his face in no uncertain terms, taking nearly 20 lines over it. Here is a chance for Aman to act if he wants to. He has no single word to say through all this. The King exclaims how convincing Aman had seemed, but Hester takes to pieces Aman's arguments against the Jews one by one. Still Aman does not speak. Finally (l. 971) the King turns on him – 'O kaytiffe moste crafty o false dissembler [. . .]' (etc.).

Then at length Aman responds. His action is puzzling. He addresses himself (with some wisdom) to Hester, not the King. He begs mercy. He puts the argument that the greater his offence the more credit she will gain by forgiving him. But she is not to be

FIG. 15. Conjectural arrangement of the action in *Godly Queen Hester* at the line – 'So ex*q*uisite is thys repaste'

cajoled. And then he must make some positive action, for the King exclaims that Aman

998.   [. . .] the quene wylt oppresse, we beinge presente
         what nede we call for euidence moore

– and the impression given is that Aman approaches the Queen physically and maybe lays violent and imploring hands on her. The King goes on without more ado –

> Make him sure and fast and therto bind him sore
> we will that oure counsell shortlye deuice,
> How we shalbe bestow him accordynge to iustice

Then into the ruins of the feast, with possibly a seat overturned, there comes a completely new figure, the Jew Arbona (or Harbonah). He seems to burst in from the crowd and he calls out –

> There is in the house of thys traitour Aman
> A paire of galowes of fiftie cubites hie
> Vpon them he had thought either now or than
> To haue caused Mardocheus to die.

FIG. 16. Conjectural arrangement of the action in *Godly Queen Hester* at the line – 'Leade him hence'

And Assuerus orders (see Fig. 16) –

> Leade him hence, and vpon them by and by
> See that ye hange him, and so stoppe his breathe
> without fauoure see he snffer deathe.

They presumably drag him out. In the confusion now, the irrepressible Hardydardy speaks to the King –

1010.   Other folkes be tardye, as wel as hardy dardy
        By this reckeninge
        A syr besyde belles, bacon and somewhat els,
        Must nedes haue hanginge.

(Greg puts in a helpful footnote here, ending ' . . . I therefore take "A syr" as the subject, meaning "a lord".') The atmosphere is now relieved while the King and Hardydardy bandy bawdry.

During the interchange, Hardydardy gives us another example of the usage of the word 'pageant' that we noticed on p. 109. He says, since Aman has gone to be hanged on the gallows he had meant for Mardocheus, that (l. 1051) 'now he is faine him selfe for certaine, To play the fyrste pagente' upon them.

Arbona now speaks again,

> If it please your grace this traitoure Aman,
> we haue put to deathe as was youre cummaundyment.

– so he has been out with Aman, hanged him, and returned again.

Assuerus gives all Aman's goods to Hester. She asks with filial thoughtfulness that Mardocheus, her uncle and foster-father, be remembered. And Assuerus promises that –

1075.   we wyll him aduaunce accordynge hys parage,
        Holde Mardocheus here is our rynge and seale, [. . .]

– so that Mardocheus must have now come in once more. And once again the bestowal of a new dignity is symbolized by the bestowal of symbolic objects.

Hester, now, with a clear business head for protocol, turns to another thought –

> I beseche youre grace at my suppl ycation,
> The precepte [. . .]
> Againste me and all the Iewishe nation,
> May be reuoked [. . .]

– and continues at some length. Curiously, she would appear to be

sitting during this (possibly still at the banquet table ?) for Assuerus
answers her –

1103.   Stande ye vp Lady, and approche ye neare
      your petition we graunte it gladlye,

(The 'approche ye' suggests that he had probably withdrawn to
stand before his traverse to dominate Aman's removal.)

 Hester is as quick apparently, as Aman was, at having documents
ready to hand, for she replies at once –

     Than if it please your graee to heare,
     This epistle is made to the sealyng readye.

Then, since the document was a historically important one, we
are allowed to hear its contents by a means explained in a marginal
note –

            Here the
            Scrybe
            doeth re-
            de ye King-
            es letter.

It is a dignified document of over 40 lines. The King seals and dis-
patches copies of it to every city. Her purpose achieved Hester now
considerately asks, 'May it now please you your selfe to repose', but
the King first has something to say. He addresses the audience and
points a moral –

1162.   My Lordes by this fygure ye may well se,
      The multitude hurte by the heades necligence,

Hester caps the moral; and Assuerus draws to a conclusion with –

1176.   Let vs then cesse thys conuocatione,
      And this tyme dyssolue this congregation.

       HESTER
    That lyke as here they haue lyued deuoutly,
    So god graunt them in heauen to lyue eternally,

       ASSEWERUS.
   To the which we committe all this company,

       FINIS
  Imprynted at London by Wyllyam Pickerynge
   and Thomas Hacket, and are to be solde at
       theyre shoppes.

Concerning my review of *Godly Queen Hester* I venture to make the following claims:

1. That the play could not be performed as it stands without the use of the traverse.

2. That with the use of a traverse such as I have described, the presentation of the play is possible in every detail, given the acceptance of normal Interlude conventions.

3. That the form I have described for the traverse is (a) consistent with such usages of the word as it is understood to have, and (b) consistent with the curtain used contemporaneously by actors in other circumstances; for example, on booth stages.

4. That the main item about my traverse which is lacking in proof, is the matter of its position before the centre screen. I can support this only on the grounds of there being nowhere else satisfactory to put it, and that it serves its purpose best there. It could not, I think, be placed asymmetrically to one side of the Hall because it would interfere with the tables. It could not be placed near the High Table end because it would mask the action, and would not of course conceal from the High Table any actor meant to be concealed by it. Furthermore it would be more difficult for an actor to reach. These grounds seem sound enough.

5. That we know from this play that a traverse had by c. 1525 been introduced into the presentation technique of at least some Interludes.

24 *Thersytes*

Thersytes does bring up an entirely fresh subject for consideration, but it is one about which it is very difficult to come to a positive conclusion; all the same it is of such obvious importance that every effort should be made to picture it correctly. This fresh subject is an item of setting specially placed *in the acting-area* for the performance.

The anonymous *Thersytes* (c. 1537) may be a university play (see for example, Craik, p. 13), but one passage in the script offers some surprise, for in it an address is made quite unquestionably to one of the audience as a woman, and apparently to another as a 'lyttle pums', once 'a mayd' (see below, p. 301); and one may be surprised to find women and girls in a sixteenth-century university audience, but of the actual circumstances of such a performance there is admittedly little information. Was this play written for students to act? If so, it is presumably a coincidence that the cast is exactly designed for four men and a boy – one of the men taking the part of a woman; in other words, that it follows a typical professional pattern.

The title reads –

A new Enterlude called
Thersytes
Thys Enterlude Folowynge
Dothe Declare howe that the
greatest boesters are not
the greatest
doers.

The names of the players
Thersites   A boster.
Mulciber   A smyth.
Mater   A mother.
Miles   A knyght.
Telemachus   A childe.

Tudor Facsimile Text, No. 106, printed 1912, reproduces a unique copy in the Devonshire Collection from about 1550.

Whether the play was performed at a university or not, the lines show that the entrance of the players was the same as the entrance of players in any ordinary early Interlude; that is, they come in upon the normal floor, pushing through the audience. Thus, a straightforward hall-setting before screens is implied.

The play opens with a direction reading, 'Thersites commeth in fyrste hauinge a clubbe vppon his necke'. He boasts, and commands the spectators to step aside: 'abacke, geue me roume, in my way do ye not stand'. He explains he has lost all his harness, or armour, and must get more, and therefore he is looking for a blacksmith to make some for him, and he ends, 'But nowe to the shop of Mulciber, to go I wyll not faile'.

There next follows the novelty which demands an extension to the kind of picture I have built up so far. On the old basis one might have supposed that Thersytes, having come in normally through one of the screens entrances, would now simply turn and approach the other door in the screens to get to Mulciber's 'shop' or smithy. But intead there follows, immediately on his line, a direction of an unusual kind. It reads –

> Mulciber must haue a shop made in the place and
> Thersites co*m*methe before it sayinge a loude
> Mulciber, [. . .]
> Come foorth [. . .]

This is all there is upon which to try to base a picture of this novelty – the direction that 'Mulciber must *haue a shop made in the place*'.

So far as I am aware, no indication exists in any previous Interlude of the need for any scenic item in the Place, which phrase apparently means 'out on the floor of the hall'. So far, the information provided in earlier plays has pointed only to chairs or stools being set in the Place; but now it is indisputably stated that a 'shop' must be 'made in the place'.

The word 'made' may here mean one of two things; either that the shop had been built, or made, in the Place before the guests assembled and was there for them to see and to speculate upon until the play began; or else that assistants came into the hall when the guests were already present, and put up or *made* the shop in the Place with the spectators looking on. There is nothing to indicate which is meant. But this does give me occasion to point out that (as will be seen later in, for example, *Susanna*) the latter interpretation is by no means outside the bounds of possibility. And such a procedure need be no more against the conventions of theatrical art here than it is in the technique of the nearly contemporary Japanese Noh plays.

Before going on, it may be useful to recall that in the conventions of the Noh drama – which are in many ways not unlike Interlude conventions – it is customary, when a 'scenic object' such as a cottage or a temple or some similar property is needed, for the assistants to bring on to the stage quite openly a light wooden framework (classed under the generic heading of *tsukuri-mono*, lit. 'made thing', or 'construction') suitable to the object and to place it in position for the action (see Fig. 17A, B and C). If this object were intended to have something or someone concealed in it – for example, a demon or a swordsmith – the framework would have been covered with a cloth which could be removed at need (17C). An actor can walk in, concealed in the curtained framework, as the assistants carry it on.

I do not wish to suggest that I suppose there was any direct interchange of technical ideas between medieval Japan and England; I simply note that another contemporary theatrical civilization came upon precisely the same need for a temporary construction as is

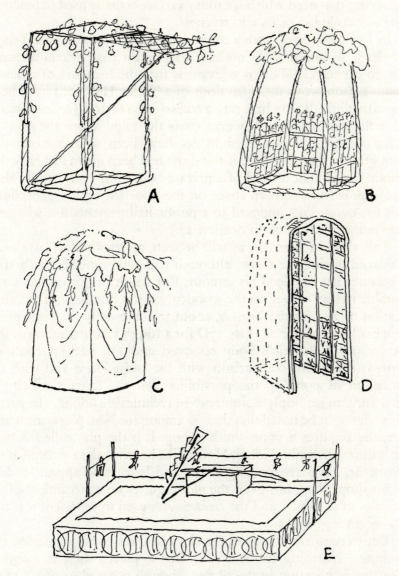

FIG. 17. Four Japanese *tsukuri-mono* (built things), or *saka motsu* (fictions) and one English 'built thing'. A. a wicker gate in *Hajitomi*; D, a hut in *Iori*; C. a mound in *Sumidagawa*; D. a bower in *The Spanish Tragedy*; E. a swordsmith's shop in *Kokaji*

apparently present here in *Thersytes*, and has produced a way of satisfying that need which we today can see actually used in practice, and so can judge of its effectiveness.

In Japan of course such a construction is set up on a raised stage whereas, so far, there is nothing to suggest that Interludes were played on stages. What is relevant is that the bringing of a blacksmith's shop on to the open floor of a Tudor Hall need have been no more difficult than bringing a *tsukuri-mono* on to a Japanese stage. (A reflexion that does however cross the mind about the shop in this connexion is that it might not have been so easy to have it brought out into the Place if the show had been given in a crowded public Guild Hall instead of a private house, for there would then not appear to have been space on the floor for such a procedure; but the conditions imposed in a public-hall presentation will need separate consideration in Section 27.)

This shop in *Thersytes*, as will be seen, appears not to have been removed during the show, although it is quite finished with after Thersytes has obtained his armour. But was it in this respect comparable to the 'bower' in the woodcut on the title-page of the 1633 edition of *The Spanish Tragedy*, about which exactly the same problem has been raised? See Fig. 17D for a rough reconstruction of this bower (with Horatio's body removed and the back portion restored) drawn for comparison with the *tsukuri-mono* and with the intention of pointing the possibility that the close similarity in structure might imply a similarity in technical handling. (In parenthesis it might be noted that there is among the Noh plays one which actually requires a swordsmith's shop. It is the play called *Kokaji*. In it the swordsmith Kokaji Munechika has to make a sword for the Emperor. He prays for help to the god Inari, who appears to him in his shop. Here, however, the plot requires no concealment of the interior of the shop, and the *tsukuri-mono* used to represent it is that shown in Fig. 17E.)

But to return to *Thersytes*; the shop here raises other puzzles. For instance, returning to the words 'in the place', there is a sort of positive implication in the phrase, though not a clear one. On reflexion it seems that it cannot be taken as meaning simply anywhere in the Place for, if I have visualized the set-up correctly, it will be obvious that the available space on the hall floor would be limited to certain positions because of the presence on that floor also of the audience. It would be unlikely to have been set right down at the lower end of the hall because of the crowd of standing spectators there by the doors, through which the entering actors had always to pass. The other three sides of the hall were also occupied, this time by the guests sitting at the tables. Mulciber's shop must, then, have been in the Place to the extent of standing well in it and away from any wall since all four walls were crowded. Fig. 18 shows what I have in mind. In these circumstances the shop must have been a free-standing building, either near where the diagrammatic shape, A, is in the figure, or in some other position in the open part of the floor.

But it is possible to go a little further. There is one other consideration in the matter of the position of the shop. If Thersytes speaks his 21-line entrance-vaunt somewhere at the far end of the hall near the screens, and concludes with, 'But nowe to the shop of Mulciber, to go I will not faile', and if in addition there later follows a direction saying, with regard to the shop, that Thersytes 'commethe before it', then there is a strong implication that he begins

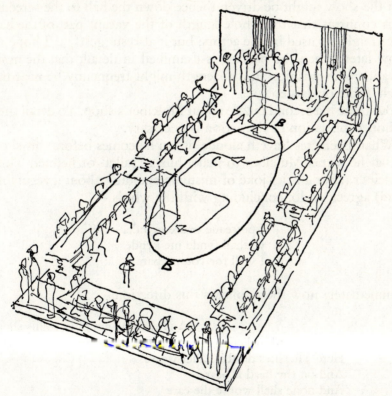

FIG. 18. Study of the probable main actions in *Thersytes*, with the position of the blacksmith's shop

some little way away from it, makes his proposal to go to it, and then takes the necessary action – that is walks across such distance as there is before he 'commethe before it'.

In terms of modern orthodox theatre, one might think of such an action as being inevitably *across* a stage, that is from side to side (see the arrows at A). But there is no reason why the Interluders should have had this frontal view of the 'stage picture'; I have given fairly strong evidence that they did not regard their Hall-Place in the same directional way; instead they took possession of the whole central floor strip from end to end. Thus a possible alternative position for the shop is at or about the point C in Fig. 18; and such a position is more likely than one about the point A in the figure.

In Section 27 I shall give some further evidence about the end of the hall players might prefer in given circumstances; one item from Palsgrave's *Acolastus* will show that a play might be performed in part before the dais at the upper end, where the High Table was, and that the show might be driven thence down the hall to the screens. This confirms that the whole length of the vacant part of the hall floor might be used by the actors; but it also suggests, as I hope to show later, when the passage is examined in detail, that the most advantageous position in that length might frequently be near the High-Table or dais end.

But there is a second puzzle about Mulciber's shop. To detail this, a short explanation of the action is necessary.

What Thersytes 'sayeth aloude' when he comes before this shop is that he wants Mulciber to make him a 'sallet' or helmet. This, Mulciber (after a brief joke of misunderstanding about a vegetable salad) agrees to do, concluding with the words –

> I perceaue youre mynde.
> ye shall fynde me kynde
> I wyll for you prepare

– immediately now there follows this direction –

> And then he goeth in to his shop,
> and maketh a sallet for hym [;] at the laste he sayth.
> Here Thersites do this sallet weare
> And on thy head it beare
> And none shall worke the care
> Then Mulciber goeth into his shop,
> vntyll he is called agayne.

What has been involved so far is that Thersytes walked to Mulciber's smithy and called him; Mulciber came out and greeted him; Thersytes gave his order for a helmet; Mulciber retired into his smithy, made the helmet and then came out with it, gave it to Thersytes with a recommendation, and finally retired into his smithy once more.

Thersytes is now left alone in the Place, where there is only one thing to be seen beside himself, and that is the shop into which Mulciber has just disappeared. About the nature of this shop and its appearance and how far it conceals or reveals Mulciber at this point, we now need to learn as much as possible. Thersytes left alone begins to speak. He pronounces a boasting soliloquy about his own valour now that he is equipped with his new helmet. Then, after some 18 lines he is struck by a sudden fresh thought, and calls –

> But Mulciber, yet I haue not with the do
> My heade is armed, my necke I woulde haue to
> And also my shoulders with some good habergyn . . .

(A 'habergeon' is defined in the *O.E.D.* as 'A sleeveless coat or jacket of mail or scale armour, originally smaller . . . than a Hauberk, but sometimes apparently the same as that.' And under 'hauberk' we read 'A piece of defensive armour, originally for neck and shoulders; but early developed into a long military tunic, usually of ring or chain mail'.)

And so Thersytes may perhaps walk a little away from the shop – probably back down the hall a few steps – while he speaks, but then he must break off at this new thought and turn on his heel to go back and summon Mulciber again.

The lines continue immediately with Mulciber's reply; but this reply does not now involve any comic misunderstanding as the first one did, nor is Mulciber given any direction now to go into his shop to make this habergeon, and 'at the laste' bring it out completed. He simply says straight away without any direction, or apparently any business –

> Bokell on this habergyn [*etc.*]
>> Then he goeth in to his shoppe againe

– so he must come out at once with the required habergeon and thereupon return. Thersytes now vaunts once more, this time for 48 lines. Then he suddenly bethinks himself again –

> But Mulciber, yet I must the desyre
> To make me briggen yrons for myne armes

297

– and he goes on to say in another 18 lines how he will then be equipped to climb even to heaven. ('Briggen irons' is not given in *O.E.D.*, but a 'brigandine' is 'body armour composed of iron rings or plates, sewed upon, and covered with, canvas, linen, or leather . . .' The word is cognate with 'brigand'.) Mulciber immediately replies to this –

> Haue here Thersites briggen yrons bright . . . etc.

He must therefore come out again. He makes a short speech and then bids Thersytes farewell. But after thanking him elaborately, Thersytes has yet another thought –

> but yet Mulciber one thinge I aske more
> Haste thou euer a sworde now in store? [. . .]

Mulciber replies (and thus he had probably retired and now appeared yet again) –

> Truely I haue [. . .]
> [. . .] here it is, gyrde it to thy syde
> Now fare thou well, Jupiter be thy guyde

Thersytes shakes hands, and –

> Mulciber goeth in to hys shoppe againe,
> and Thersites saith foorth

– and he now picks up his vaunts again. But of Mulciber we hear no more in the whole play.

There can be no question from the above but that the shop is a fairly considerable item in the setting of the early part of the play. To recapitulate the action-directions in this particular episode; the first came after the joke about the 'salad', and there are two informative phrases in it. It says of Mulciber that 'he *goeth in* to his shop'; then, after making the sallet for Thersites, '*at the laste* he sayth'. Thus he is directed to go *into* the shop to make the sallet – he does not make it outside, and therefore he must make it in some degree of concealment. Then after he has made the sallet, there come the words '*at the last* . . .' before he begins to speak again. These particular words would imply that some more-or-less considerable space of time has to be left for Mulciber to seem to make the sallet. Was he visible or invisible for that time?

It might seem to us today a good opportunity for this 'stage-wait' to be filled with some mimed smithing-business at a forge and anvil. But the bringing of so many practicable, or pseudo-practicable, properties into the Place as well as the shop itself, seems to offer both practical and artistic problems. The need could be completely met if the inside of the shop were in fact not visible, and if Mulciber disappeared through the flap of a sort of small tent or draped framework. The wait during the manufacture of the helmet could then be amusingly enough filled up by sounds and by Thersytes' reactions to these. But, however such details might have been suggested, one thing seems fairly clear: that Mulciber *disappeared* into the shop, and thus that it was of a nature to conceal him.

The next direction, after he has given Thersytes the sallet, is that Mulciber should go into his shop *until he is called again*. This strengthens the idea of concealment. When he *is* called again, it is to produce the habergeon. The habergeon apparently comes out of stock, for he is given little time in which to pretend to make it – only 3 lines from Thersytes. After giving it to Thersytes – and obviously having to appear again to do so – the next direction for him is 'Then he goeth in to his shoppe againe.'

Now follows Thersytes' long soliloquy, and during it he calls Mulciber by name once more. On both this occasion and the last there is a comma after the name 'Mulciber' in his speech. Such punctuation is typically rare in the script and would appear to have particular significance as indicating a pause. But Mulciber this time does not make an appearance at once; Thersytes asks for the 'briggen yrons', presumably calling through the wall of the shop, and Mulciber's response follows as much as 19 lines later, when he (appears and) brings the 'briggen yrons' and describes their quality to Thersytes for 20 lines.

In this speech he incidentally gives us a perhaps unexpected detail about Thersytes' appearance; he remarks –

> Would not thy blacke and rustye grym berde
> Nowe thou art so armed, make anye man aferde

Thersytes, then, is wearing a ferocious false beard.

There comes now no direction to Mulciber for the next and last item, the sword which Thersytes asks for. But the lines are unmistakable without any direction, for Mulciber says –

> Truely I haue suche a one in my shoppe
> that wil pare yron as it were a rope
> haue, here it is, [. . .]

– he must, then, break off, step into his concealment for a moment,

299

and then come out again with the sword to give to Thersytes. They shake hands and 'Mulciber goeth in to hys shoppe againe' – and that is the last we hear of him.

What happens to him thereafter? Whether he sits there concealed until the end of the play or whether, as a Japanese Noh player might, he quietly walks out at a propitious moment, and makes his way down the hall to an exit, there is no indication. But one thing does seem certain; that the 'shop' formed some sort of concealment, and that the interior was thus not visible.

To summarize the very sparse information to be derived about this shop in the Place:

(1) It was *in* the Place; it was not on a stage, and it was free-standing on the floor, and not against a wall.

(2) It could be entered, and its occupant could be concealed in it.

(3) Apart from point (2) above, there seems no indication of what the shop looked like; it might have tended to one or the other of two widely opposite extremes – it might have been a mere curtained booth, or it might have been a full, four-sided, framed canvas erection with a door, painted to represent a house in a style conceivably like the houses shown in the side extensions of some of the Strasbourg *Terence* illustrations of 1496. We have not the slightest evidence to accept either alternative.

(4) However much we do *not* know, we do know one thing; that from about the year 1537 onwards, a 'shop' could be 'made in the place' for a play performance.

(5) Small and indecisive as all this information is, there arises one other – possibly even more hazardous – thought; is this shop the first example to come up in this study of a 'house' or 'mansion'? So far as I am aware, the first clear reference to scenic 'houses' comes about 1571 in the Revels Accounts for Queen Elizabeth's court. I have already referred to Craik's comments on Chambers' views about houses being used as the 'background' for Interludes (see above, p. 147). There I noted that the Interludes mentioned as requiring houses all date *after* 1550. Is this shop in *Thersytes* an early 'house'? – Or were the later, court 'houses' developments from some previous curtained framework or scaffold of which this shop is a rare, precocious example?

(6) One last consideration. Is any understanding of the problem of placing such a property in the acting-area likely to be helped by the well-known print of Baltazar de Beauioyeulx's *Balet comique de la Royne* (1581)? At least, this shows, in a later and highly sophisticated

300

form, a layout of the Place where a scenic grove or bower stands in much the same sort of position as was conjectured above for Mulciber's shop.

For the rest of the play: What Thersytes says after Mulciber has retired finally into his shop is interesting. It is a bold joke with the audience; at first, normally enough, with the men present, but then, taking somewhat more licence, with the women. The gist is as follows (Thersytes speaking):

> Nowe I go hence, [. . .]
> I wyll seeke aduentures, [. . .]
> If there be any present here thys nyghte

(Note the allusion to the time of day)

> that wyll take vpon them with me to fighte
> Let them come quickly, [. . .]
> how say you good godfather, [. . .]
> Dare ye aduenture wyth me [. . .]

– and the old man who is picked on, having presumably laughingly refused, Thersytes continues –

> Go coward go hide the [. . .]
> What a sorte of dasterdes haue we here [. . .]

– then, turning to a woman –

> What saie you hart of gold [. . .]?
> Will you fighte with me? [. . .]
> Fye blusshe not woman, I wyll do you no harme
> Excepte I had you soner to kepe my backe warme

Then I presume he turns to another and younger woman –

> Alas lyttle pums why are ye so sore afrayd?
> I praye you shew how longe it is? sence ye were a mayd
> Tell me in myne eare,

There is obviously a pretence at a whispered colloquy here; then to all the audience –

> – syrs, she hathe me tolde,
> That gone was her mydenhead, at thrustene [*thirteen*] yeare olde [*etc.*]

Finally –

> Well, let all go, whyε? wyll none come in
> With me to fyghte [. . .]
>
>   The mater commeth in.

301

There is no indication that this entrance of the Mother is of any unusual kind, and one takes it for granted that she enters normally by the screen doors; but her exit, as we see in a moment, is directed in a very unusual phrase. In the meantime she tries to prevent Thersytes setting off to battle; she says –

> Here is none I trowe
> that profereth you a blowe
> Man woman nor chylde [. . .]

– and at length the moment for her protesting exit arrives, and –

> Then the mother goeth in the place
> which is prepareth [*sic*] for her.

This certainly is a cryptic direction. There is apparently no information at all to help us to understand what is intended by this going 'in the place which is prepareth for her'. 'Prepareth' is an odd misprint for 'prepared' (if indeed it be such), for a misprint usually consists of replacing a correct letter by an incorrect one, but to replace a 'correct' letter by two other letters is odd. Again, 'goeth in' where one would expect 'goeth into' is strange. But however it is, the words do seem to indicate that the Mother disappears for a time, or at least withdraws from the action. And the subsequent script bears this out.

Having used the word 'withdraw', and in view of what now happens, I am reminded of the 'trauers' of *Godly Queen Hester*. There was a withdrawing-place put up (or 'prepared') for an exactly similar sort of action – a temporary, but not final, retirement. It is then conceivable that this direction means, 'goes in[to] a traverse which has been put up for the purpose'. Otherwise, why does the direction not say simply 'She goeth out', just as her entrance-direction said simply that she 'cometh in'? Presumably because she is not intended to go out any more than King Ahasuerus went out in the *Queen Hester* direction; Aman went out but the King went into the place prepared for him. And he went in there instead of going out, for exactly the same reason as the Mother in *Thersytes* – because in a short time there would be a need to be present in the action again.

After six more lines of boasting from Thersytes there comes another direction, equally unusual but fortunately not equally cryptic – 'Here a snaile muste appere vnto him, and hee muste loke fearefully vppon the snaile'. This snail must have been an amusing and also ingenious property. It was presumably moved by the small boy of the company crawling underneath; but it was elaborate enough to have working, retractable 'horns' for later Thersytes is directed to '[. . .] fighte then with his sworde against the snayle, and the snayle draweth her hornes in'.

The fourth adult character, a soldier, enters during this passage – 'here Miles cometh in' – and watches the fight contemptuously. On the approach of the snail, Thersytes calls for his servants to bring shield and spear, but no one appears despite his repeated cries.

After being threatened with the sword the snail apparently withdraws, though there is no direction.

There is plenty of room for such clowning in the 'ring' of space between B and B in Fig. 18; and clowning is a fair name for all this business. It is in fact much the sort of thing that one might see performed by clowns in the ring of any circus nowadays. Indeed what takes place in Interludes is often closer to the atmosphere of the circus and the technique of circus performances than it is to any dramatic conventions that we are used to in a modern theatre; and therefore it is not surprising that the physical surroundings as visualized here resemble the circus ring more than the stage.

Now the Soldier advances –

> And he begynth to fight with him, but Thersites must ren awaye, and hyde hym behynde hys mothers backe sayinge.
>
> O mother mother I praye the me hyde
> Throwe some thinge ouer me and couer me euery syde

It is for this reason, then, that the Mother did not go out. Thersytes appears to have run some considerable distance to escape the Soldier, for the Soldier loses sight of him and calls –

> Come foorth if thou dare, and in this place appere . . .

so he does not realize that Thersytes is hiding behind the Mother, and at length he asks her –

> Thou olde trotte, seyst thou any man come thys waye

– and she says No. The Soldier goes out; and the Mother says –

> Come foorth my sonne [   ]
>
> Then he loketh aboute if he be gone or not, at the last he sayth [. . .]

– there follow boasting challenges behind the Soldier's back. Next, 'Then cometh in Telemachus bringinge a letter from his father

Ulisses'. Here, then, is the boy of the company again but now in a new character. The letter is a request from Ulysses that Thersytes will persuade his Mother to charm Telemachus clear of the worms. This, after some protesting, she is made to do. Then, after much bye-play, Telemachus goes, and we have the direction – 'The mother goeth out' and this time her direction is quite unequivocal; it is a simple exit. Now Thersytes is left to revile her behind her back for the audience's amusement. The Soldier next returns unexpectedly and takes him up on his words, until –

> [. . .] then he muste stryke at hym, and Thersytes muste runne awaye and leaue his clubbe & sworde behynde.

The Soldier closes the play alone, with a pious address to the audience.

About this point in the chronological sequence a brief note is due concerning the works of John Bale, since they fall chiefly between c. 1532 and 1538. But his plays have already received much study chiefly because of their particular literary, religious and historical significance (for example in W. T. Davies, the Oxford Bibliographical Society's *Proceedings*, V (1940) as regards his life etc., and in J. S. Farmer, *Dramatic Writings* (1907), for the plays). I shall take advantage of this existing work to conserve my space for other Interludes that have received less attention.

25 *The Problem of Defining an Interlude*

Two special problems in *Wit and Science* are (1) *three* ways of access and (2) a *mount*.

But before looking in detail at the problems it will be useful to consider whether it is right to take this play as being directly in the line of tradition of the typical Interludes such as it has been studied in the earlier part of this book. The question involved is one which has for some time been lurking in the background and which now seems particularly to be forced to attention. It arises here because the first pages of the only manuscript of *Wit and Science* (the play was never put into print) are missing and there is therefore no means of knowing whether it might have been called an Interlude on its opening page or not. On the final page there is written simply, 'Thus endyth the play . . .'

Something of what may be involved here has already been hinted at in the discussion of *Calisto* in Section 15. The matter must now be examined in more detail; what leads up to it is as follows (It might be helpful to turn to the list of Contents at the beginning of this book during what follows, for that list has been specially prepared to show the descriptions that were originally given to the plays.):

So far there have been some eighteen plays discussed in this book. Of these the first one has no classification, or none that has come down to us (*Mankind*). The next seven, however, are definitely described as Interludes either on the title-page or at the end (*Nature, Fulgens, World and Child, Hyckescorner, Magnyfycence, The Four Elements* and *Youth*). So far, then, no question about the type of the plays seems to arise.

But the next play, *Calisto,* had a different sort of wording in its sub-title; it was called 'A new commodye in englysh in maner Of an enterlude'. Was there a difference between an Interlude and a Comedy *in the manner of* an Interlude?

The next title on the list is the disputation entitled *Of Gentylnes and Nobylyte.* This is described with the same unusual qualification as was *Calisto*; it is 'A dyaloge . . . compiled in maner of an enterlude . . .'. Is there any distinction implied between a plain dialogue and a dialogue compiled in the manner of an Interlude? Presumably the latter might be a dialogue written specifically to be acted as a play, or to be read with the action of a play in mind. But then why was this particular dialogue said to be compiled in the manner of an Interlude and not simply in the manner of a play?

Of the six 'Heywood' plays three revert to the simple description of Interlude. These are *Love, Weather* and *The foure PP.* The exact wording relating to the last of these is 'The playe called the foure PP. A newe and a very mery enterlude . . .' which at least offers us one morsel of confirmation in that it makes it clear that, whatever an Interlude was in detail, it was something that contemporary opinion could also accept as being a 'play'. For the remaining three of the Heywood group the description 'Interlude' is not used; *Witty and Witless* is not titled; the other two are simply described as merry plays – 'A mery play betwene the pardoner and the frere . . .' and 'A mery play betweene Johan . . .[*etc.*]'. But there is no indication whether the omission of the classification 'Interlude' is significant or not.

The next two plays present no problem for they are again clearly classified as Interludes (*Hester* and *Thersytes*).

Thus, to summarize so far; out of these eighteen plays, two are uncertain, twelve are clearly called *Interludes*, two are called comedy (or dialogue) *in manner of an Interlude*, and two are simply called *plays*. To bring the list up to date, the play next to be considered, *Wit and Science*, though its opening, together with any description that might have been there, is lost, yet has in the colophon at the end the words 'Thus endyth the play of wyt & science'. For what this is worth, then, the evidence points to its being regarded as a play and not as an Interlude. What bearing might this have?

Perhaps a few words of anticipation should be allowed before I go on. Of the later plays the following will all be found to be described as Interludes:

The Four Cardynal Vertues c. 1541, *Impacyent Poverty* c. 1547, *Nice Wanton* c. 1550, *Lusty Juventus* c. 1550, *Respublica* 1553, *Jack Juggler* c. 1553, *Wealth and Health*, c. 1554, *Disobedient Child* c. 1560, ?*Enough is as Good as a Feast* c. 1564, *The Trial of Treasure* c. 1565, *King Daryus* c. 1565, *Mary Magdalene* c. 1566, *Horestes* 1567, *The Marriage of Wit and Science* 1567, *Like will to Like* c. 1568, *New Custom* c. 1570.

It is clear from this list that the classification of 'Interlude' continues to be used for several decades. On the other hand there are some curiosities in this period; for instance John Bale (who was admittedly a law unto himself) calls *God's Promises* (1538) 'A Tragedy or Interlude . . .'. The anonymous *Jacob and Esau* c. 1550 is a 'Comedie or Enterlude'. *Ralph Royster Doyster* c. 1553 is interesting in that the Prologue refers to it as 'Our Comedie or Enterlude which we intende to play' and five lines later as 'this our Enterlude'. *Gammer Gurton's Needle* c. 1553 is a 'merie Comedie'. *Pacyent Grissill* c. 1559 is a 'Commodye'. *Apius and Virginia* c. 1560 is a 'Tragicall Comedie'. *Tom Tyler* c. 1560 is an 'old Play'. *All for Money* c. 1560 is 'a moral and pitieful Comedie' but is also referred to in the lines as 'a pleasant Tragedy'. *Gorboduc* 1561 is reckoned a tragedy. *The Pedlers Prophecie* c. 1561 is undescribed. *The Longer thou livest* c. 1564 is a 'Pythie commedie'. *Damon and Pythias* c. 1565 'a Tragicall Commedie'. *Supposes* 1566 'a Comedie'. *Gismond of Salern* c. 1566 is pretty certainly a tragedy. *Liberality and Prodigality* c. 1567 is a 'comedie'. *Cambises* c. 1569 a 'lamentable Tragedy'. *Susanna* c. 1569 is a 'Commody'. *Misogonus* c. 1570 probably a comedy. *The Conflict of Conscience* c. 1572 a 'commedie'. *Tyde taryeth no Man* c. 1576 is a 'merry commody'. *Common Conditions* c. 1576 is a 'pleasant Comedye'. *The Three Ladies of London* 1581 is a 'comoedy', and *The Three Lords and*

Three Ladies of London c. 1589 is called rather unexpectedly 'A Morall'.

And so, looking at all this, there would seem to be four main possibilities of classification: (1) an Interlude; (2) a play *in manner of* an Interlude; (3) a play *or* Interlude; and (4) something not called an Interlude at all but a Comedy, or Tragedy (or both).

In an attempt to read some logical reason into this, it will be noticed that in the earlier part of the period the term 'Interlude' was a general and probably the only term. About 1657 comes something – a comedy or a dialogue – which is said to be *in the manner of* an Interlude. And about the same time we first find the word 'Play' being used alone. There seems to be suggested a gradual but progressive blurring of the distinct meaning of the word 'Interlude'. Then by 1550 or so comes the first play which is specifically noted as a 'Comedie *or* Enterlude', an apparent alternative – as if by then any difference was in effect beginning to be forgotten.

If by chance the above distinctions can be proved significant, would it be reasonable to ask: What was the original difference between an Interlude and a Comedy, such that there could be on the one hand a sort of comedy which was shaped like an Interlude (e.g. *Calisto*), and on the other hand a sort of comedy which was presumably *not* shaped like an Interlude (e.g. *Gammer Gurton*)? And was there in between these a third sort of comedy which could be classed by *either* name, Comedy *or* Interlude (e.g. *Jacob and Esau*)?

To attempt to answer this frankly fantastic question is of course to face the problem that has baffled all historians – What was an Interlude? And I do not think a positive answer is yet possible. But the following reflexions based on the study made so far in this book may not be irrelevant. To begin, it seems clear that 'Interlude' is an older usage than 'Comedy' or 'Tragedy'. Next, if we allow that the early examples reviewed above were all performed in halls at some sort of feast or meal, then it would seem that the definition of an Interlude as a show given at an interval in, or as the accompaniment to, a feast is likely to be a proper one.

I think that here it is worth pointing to the inconclusiveness of the *Oxford English Dictionary* definition of 'Interlude' which shows the uncertainty that surrounds the word's meaning. The definition reads,

A dramatic or mimic representation, usually of a light or humorous character, such as was commonly introduced between the acts of the long mystery-plays or moralities, or exhibited as part of an elaborate entertainment; hence (in ordinary 17–18th c. use) a stage-play, esp. of a popular nature, a comedy, a farce. Now (after Collier; see quot. 1831) applied as a specific name to the earliest form of the modern drama, as represented by the plays of J. Heywood.

Concerning 'stage-plays'; there seemed in the sixteenth century to be a tendency (for example, in the Pleadings in the Rastell *v.* Walton case) to distinguish between the Interlude and the stage play, as was pointed out at the beginning of Section 12. If this were true then, according to the *Dictionary*, the distinction had disappeared 'in ordinary 17–18th c. use'.

The most confusing part of the definition is, however, the earlier part describing the Interlude as 'A dramatic . . . representation . . . such as was commonly introduced between the acts of the long mystery-plays or moralities'. This seems to me confusing because in the whole of my study of early British theatre I have never found so far as I can remember any evidence to suggest, even vaguely, that between the 'acts' (whatever that can mean) of the Mystery-plays, any kind of 'dramatic representation' was – or could be – 'commonly introduced'. It cannot be meant to imply, for example, that between the separate plays of the York Mystery Cycle (of which there were some forty-eight), there was presented anything even remotely resembling *Fulgens and Lucrece* – which is unescapably described as an Interlude. Or that *Mankind* (if we allow it to be an Interlude) might be presented in the middle of *The Castle of Perseverance*. If so, how could the Interlude references to feasts indoors be reconciled with the obviously outdoor performances of the Mystery plays or Moralities?

The only possible occasion I can think of which could be in any way fitted into the *O.E.D.* definition is in *Ane Satyre of the Threi Estaitis*. There, half-way through the 1552 version of this Scottish Morality, the main actors of the play vacate their seats and give place to the comic *interlude* of the Carle, who climbs up the ladder to the king's scaffold to sit in his chair (l. 1941), and then has the ladder cast away so that he has eventually to leap off the scaffold (l. 1953). But this interlude is an integral part of Lyndsay's script, *not* a separate dramatic representation 'commonly introduced'.

The quotation from J. P. Collier referred to at the end of the definition is from his *History of English dramatic poetry*, II.384, and reads, 'John Heywood's dramatic productions . . . are neither

Miracle-plays nor Moral-plays, but what may be properly and strictly called interludes'. But it brings little enlightenment.

To return now to the idea of an interlude in feasting such as is clearly intended in the early plays *Nature* and *Fulgens*: in this connexion it is to be remembered that *Nature* and *Fulgens* must not be thought of as the earliest Interludes ever to be presented – they happen to be the first two, after *Mankind*, to survive, but it was clearly stated by B in *Fulgens* that the kind of show which was then about to be presented to the audience was by no means anything of a novelty for, as he said, he himself had 'sene byfore this day Of suche maner thingis in many a gode place'.

Accepting the feast idea – or, to put it a little more exactly, the idea of some special occasion when the person who could afford it might choose to celebrate a birth or an anniversary before invited guests (in modern terms, to throw a good party) at which eating and drinking were properly supplemented with entertainment – it seems not unreasonable to see an Interlude as being originally an entertainment for acting that was designed in a particular way; namely, so as to be capable of presentation in the centre of a hall-place, between the side tables, with the players' entrances and exits all contrived through the screens-doors and through the crowd clustering about them. I might go further and say that these conditions would lie inevitably upon the writer of an Interlude; they would be incumbent upon him; if he did not observe them his play could not be acted as an Interlude in a hall. Again, from the point of view of setting (or of 'staging' to use a later word in deference to the term used in the title of this book) the writer would have to conceive his show so that it could be presented without any scenic demand that might interfere in any way with the arrangement or conduct of the feast in the hall, whether by causing physical obstacles to the service of the food, or by disturbing the atmosphere of a domestic party through the introduction of any object that might distract attention during the initial part of the meal, or anticipate the surprise of the show before it began. A play written for such conditions would have to be a specialized composition.

If this be acceptable, then the term 'comedy in manner of an Interlude' might now be understood as applying to a particular form of play in an up-to-date (i.e. probably classical or Renaissance) style, but shaped broadly on the accepted Interlude lines so as to be consistent with hall performance.

Following this idea, the still later term 'comedy *or* Interlude' might then mean simply that the play was of the 'new' style but bore an alternative traditional title because Interlude at feasts were still in fashion, but were tending to give way to novelties.

And 'comedy' or 'tragedy' used alone would imply the success of the 'new' style, with the implication that any one-time distinction was becoming ignored or forgotten, or because there was an attempt to break away from the tradition.

But still, official documents with their ancient word-usages might find it politic to allude comprehensively to 'Comedies, Tragedies and Interludes'.

All this is vague enough and one would not expect it to apply strictly. But one thing does seem clear; that 'Interlude' as a term had once a distinct meaning and one that stuck in people's minds, but it was a meaning which, about the time of the spread of Renaissance fashions to England, gradually lost its distinctness and, under the influx of the new comedies and tragedies (though these owed much to it technically at the outset) became first a synonym for them, and then a mere survival retained out of a sort of affection for what had once been.

Despite this progress, however, I am inclined to think that the line of development to the Elizabethan playhouse and its techniques was, fundamentally, the line that began with the professional players in house-halls.

It is worth noting that some confirmation of this general idea is offered in F. S. Boas's conclusion, expressed in *University Drama of the Tudor Age* (1914, p. 11), concerning the Latin terms used to describe plays at various periods in university records. He says that

> the verbal distinctions [between plays] in the Magdalen accounts are very suggestive. In 1486, 1487, and 1495 'ludus' (or 'lusores') is used; in 1502, 1512, and 1531 'interludia' is substituted; in 1532 'ludus' reappears in 'ludus baccalaureorum'; in 1535, 1539, 1540, 1541, and 1544 'comedia' and 'tragedia' take the place of the earlier terms. Without unduly pressing the phraseology, it is a fair inference that we see reflected in it the broad lines of transition from the morality to the interlude and thence to the comedy and tragedy of classical origin or inspiration.

Something further that follows from all the above is that if the attendance at a banquet was large and formal, as it might be at the royal court, and if because of this it became the custom to remove from the banqueting hall to another room to witness a performance, then the scenic restrictions that had governed ordinary Interludes would no longer apply, and thus that even an Interlude by orthodox professional players, if presented at court, might be equipped with certain special scenic devices for that particular occasion – that is, devices totally different from anything used in the normal presentation of that Interlude by those same professional players in their travelling round less exalted hall banquets.

The upshot of this is that one solution to the three-ways problem in the play *Wit and Science* might be that the script was conceived in a more independent style – not strictly on the lines of an Interlude – and that it was intended for presentation in a place other than a domestic hall – for example a special chamber at court. In that case it might well have been provided with scenic devices of a kind not yet discussed, but which would in fact allow of a group of characters entering at one opening and still having two other openings available to choose between when making their exit.

It might be tempting to say without more ado that the very existence of this problem is sufficient proof that *Wit and Science* was not presented before a two-door screen; and that the mention, later on, of a 'mount' clinches the matter and finally argues the presence of scenery. This would be to fall in with the idea of 'houses' being used as the background for Interludes, to which I have made some reference in my review of *Thersytes*, and in Section 8.

But as I have suggested, I feel that the fact that so many Interludes – even those which we can presume were originally written for court use – were printed for normal purchase is some argument against this. I realize that we are poorly informed about what sort of persons they were who bought printed plays, or manuscript copies of plays. Many may have bought them for ordinary reading in a study, and I confess there is little direct evidence that plays were bought by travelling companies for their own acting use. The nearest I have found are such remarks as in *The Four Elements* concerning the possibility of any presumed performers cutting the play to suit their occasion (see above p. 250), and in the later *Damon and Pythias* (c. 1565) concerning 'them that hereafter shall have occasion to plaie it, either in Private, or open Audience' (see above p. 168). Again we have (see p. 533) the kind of thing implied behind the statement in the still later *Conflict of Conscience* (c. 1572) that its eighteen roles could be performed by no more than six players – or 'deuided into six partes most conuenient for such as be disposed either to shew this Comedie in priuate houses or otherwise'. The possibility suggested in these quotations that plays could be adapted for presentation in various situations seems to be justified, and I think enough can be presumed to make it interesting to ask if an apparently difficult situation in a printed play could in fact have been adequately presented in the Interlude technique as I have so far outlined it. This is particularly important if I am to show that the elaborate presentation-technique of the full Elizabethan playhouse could have sprung from the methods of the professional Inter-luders using domestic hall screens; for the scope of the situations presented in full Elizabethan drama is of course immense.

And this brings me to the thought that any suggestion about *three ways of entrance* might prove to have some bearing on the con-troversy over the 'third' or 'middle' door on the Shakespearean stage. This 'third door' conception is clearly such a highly provoca-tive subject for argument today, in regard to any reconstruction of the tiring-house façade of the Elizabethan public playhouse, that any situation in an early Interlude which might seem to foreshadow it demands particularly fine dissecting.

So, before dismissing the problem of the three ways it is only fair to ask, since we are still at an early point in presentation-develop-ment, whether any handling of this puzzling situation might be possible if by any chance the play came to be presented in a hall with screens, in the manner of a traditional Interlude. The following attempt is made to answer this question.

The mechanics of the situation at the moment of the problem can be very simply outlined as follows: a group of three characters taking part in a certain quest enter the acting-area, thus inevitably using, and so putting behind them and out of availability, one way of access. They pause for a moment uncertain how to proceed on their quest. One of them then asks, 'Now syrs cu*m* on whyche is the way now / Thys way or that way / . . .'. What two ways can the actor now point to as 'thys' and 'that', seeing that the way they have just come in by is ruled out because they could not advance on their quest by going out the way they came in! This is the general prob-lem; I now turn to the play to see how the problem comes about.

26 *Wit and Science*

John Redford's *Wit and Science* exists in a 'seriously defective' manuscript copy (British Museum Additional MS. 15233) which

was discussed and printed in modern type in the Malone Society
Reprints in 1951, edited by Arthur Brown. There are twenty characters, of which twelve are central to the plot and eight are more or
less incidental. Of the twelve main characters the relatively high
number of four are specifically female and one other is a child.
All this suggests a choir-school boys' play. The characters may be
described as follows:

> Reson, the father of the maiden, Science,
> Instruccion, his servant,
> Experyence, his wife,
> Science, his daughter,
> Honest Recreacion, a female friend.

Opposite these are:

> Wyt, a young man betrothed to Science,
> Confydence, a messenger of Wyt's,
> Studye, Wyt's servant
> Dylygence, Wyt's servant.

On the 'dark' side of the plot are:

> Tedyousnes, a demon,
> Idelnes, a woman,
> Ingnorance, a child.

And there enter incidentally as a pair of singing choruses, of
unspecified sex:

Cumfort	Fame
Quycknes	Favor
Strenght	Ryches
	Woorshyp

– and the isolated figure of

> Shame (non-speaking).

At the opening (that is, after the missing early pages), Reson, the
father of the maiden, Science, is speaking. He is giving a mirror to
his servant, Instruccion, to deliver to young Wyt who is in love
with Science. Other characters appear to be present at the moment,
but we do not know who because of the missing pages. The
earliest direction reads:

l.10   / heere all go out save
                                            resone

Presuming a production before screens in a hall, we will suppose
them going out by door A. Reson, left alone, now soliloquizes
telling the audience why he has approved of Wyt's being affianced

to his daughter. He ends by saying that he is proposing to go and ask Honest Recreacion ('an honest woman' who 'dwelleth here besyde') to help to console and preserve Wyt. If she dwells 'here besyde', she cannot be far away; and when he goes to her, Reson presumably simply leaves by door B. There is no exit-direction, but after his speech there follows directly a marginal note informing that –

confydence
cu*m*th in wt
a pycture
of wyt

Confydence is one of Wyt's servants. He comes presumably by the first door, that is door A, carrying this portrait which is a love token from Wyt to Science, and which he is about to deliver to her. He opens by asking the audience the time of day:

43.   / ah syr what tyme of day yst who can tell
               the day ys not far past I wot well [. . .]

– so he feels justified in taking a moment's rest, and improves upon the occasion by looking at the portrait and describing it. He thinks it will win the lady's heart and prepares to go on his way to her and further the suit.

It is worth bringing up this curious repetition (which is found in several other plays) of the trick of addressing the audience in the singular as 'Sir', instead of in the plural as 'Sirs'. Editors have frequently amended the scripts to turn such singular uses of 'Sir' into 'Sirs', alleging a printer's error. But it is not impossible that the scripts are correct, and that on these particular occasions the player did not broadly issue a sweeping appeal to the spectators as a whole, but resorted to that particular element of 'cheek' or intimacy, which seems characteristic of Interluders in those days, and deliberately singled out *one* individual member of the spectators only, and got a laugh by addressing him directly and in particular, dropping his voice seductively as he did so. A good deal of effect could come from such a piece of general licence.

At all events, Confidence here concludes –

               [. . .] ye shall see now who lyst to marke yt
               how neatly & feately / I shall warke yt

– then he must go out (though there is no direction) and presumably, since he is going to seek Science, he would go through door B recently used by her father, Reason. The Place is now empty.

Next begins the difficult passage about the three ways. A marginal direction introduces it –

Wyt cu*m*th
in / wtout Instruc
cion / wyth study &c

This seems a muddle to begin with, but it becomes clear; it simply means that Wyt comes in specifically *without* Instruccion (for Instruccion has to follow up later) but *with* Studye, and also with Studye's fellow-servant who is the '&c' and whose name is in fact Dylygence. They will all presumably use door A since Confydence has just gone out by door B. Opposite this direction comes Wyt's first line, as quoted above –

65.   Now syrs cu*m* on whyche is the way now [. . .]

(the group here probably pauses uncertain, near the door and looking round about (see Fig. 19). Wyt continues with his question –)

             . . . thys way or that way / [. . .]

The three ways are thus specifically implied – the way they have come in, and the two other ways between which they have to choose. If an elaborate setting at court were what was in question, then almost any solution to the problem might be possible and we could get little further towards any definite sort of picture; but if we take the alternative of a normal screens setting with a small central traverse, then we can begin to make up such a picture by asking where Wyt would be standing and how he might gesture as he spoke.

He will be standing a little inside door A facing up the length of the hall, with his two servants immediately behind him, both of them looking curiously and a little apprehensively past him at the prospect. The traverse, which I have presupposed, will be immediately on Wyt's left hand.

Having pictured the situation, it is clear that the alternative ways could now be clearly and distinctly pointed to by Wyt; one is straight in front of them up the length of the hall, the other is across the front of the traverse and out through door B. Fig. 19 suggests Wyt's gestures as he speaks, motioning with his right hand up the hall, and indicating the alternative with his left hand across the traverse. The fact that no actual practicable exit could be reached by proceeding up the hall towards the High Table is of no logical

Fɪɢ. 19. 'Whyche is the way now: thys way or that way . . .'? Redford's
Wit and Science

significance at all; the sense of a choice of ways at a cross-roads is all
that is important to express, and this can be done simply by taking
advantage of the liberty offered by a non-specific setting where,
since no 'ways' are represented, a gesture can call one or two – or
more – into existence. In short, with Interlude technique there is no
need to portray the ways. Can this theory now be at all confirmed?
This is what follows:

Wyt stops a moment as indicated by the stroke in the text, then
continues his speech looking back over his right shoulder at the first
of his servants as he asks –

[. . .] / studye how say you

– but Studye is in a dilemma; the question is too much for him, he
does not answer and feigns to consider. So Wyt next turns his head
the other way and says over his left shoulder to his other servant –

speake dylygence whyle he hath bethowghte hym

Dylygence is thus forced to make the answer; he says, pointing
across the hall to the left of Wyt (that is past the traverse and to the
opposite door) –

/ that way belyke [. . .]

(and then justifies himself with what would be an obvious truth)

> [. . .] most vsage hath wrowht hym

for, of course, since players had so often before come in at one screens-door and crossed to leave by the other, that would clearly be the way that most usage had earmarked.

Wyt and Dylygence may perhaps now take a step in the indicated direction. But Studye is immediately uneasy and holds them back:

> / ye hold your pease best we here now stay
> for instruccion [. . .]

(this character, Instruccion, is the one whom Reson had dispatched to follow Wyt and deliver to him the safeguarding mirror. Studye finishes his line –)

> [. . .] I lyke not that waye

But Wyt exclaims impatiently, possibly with a contemptuous 'Huh!':

> / Instruccion / [. . .]

– and adds, to show how little he thinks of Studye's advice –

> [. . .] / studye / I weene we have lost hym

At this point there is a disturbance at the door behind, and the 'lost' figure whom they are discussing immediately enters to take up the tale –

Instruccion
cu*m*th in

– and take up the tale he certainly does! He roundly berates Wyt for running 'thus styll owt of syghte' and orders –

77. cu*m* back a gayne wyt for I must choose ye
 as esyer way then thys or ells loose ye

Note the clear command to come *back*! Wyt, however, is not so easily brooked; he is not going to go back on his steps. He gestures forward past the traverse again, and demands –

> / what ayleth thys way / parell here is none

But Instruccion holds him back and explains that in fact peril *does* lie that way in the form of Wyt's greatest enemy – the monster called Tedyousnes. On hearing this, however, Wyt is delighted;

317

nothing more is needed to confirm him in that path, for he longs to win his spurs by defeating precisely that particular enemy for his lady Science's sake. Instruccion redoubles his arguments against such temerity; he says that Wyt is not well enough equipped yet for such an encounter –

106.   [. . .] pas not thys way I tell you trew
     WYT   / whych way than
  INSTRUCCION / A playner way I told ye
                  out of danger from youre foe [. . .]

(that is, 'I told you before of a safer way round'). He will then probably point back the way all four had come, as if to tell them to pick up a totally different road. But Wyt is adamant, and Dylygence offers to lend him a weapon to help him. Instruccion now turns and appeals to the reluctant Studye. And Studye replies –

126.   my hed akth sore I wold wee returnd

Wyt snaps –

          thy hed ake now I wold it were burnd
          cum on walkyng may hap to ese the

– and he urges his two servants on towards the far door B. When they are halfway towards it Instruccion calls after them in despair –

          & wyll ye be gone then / wythout mee

Wyt is laconic –

          / ye by my fayth except ye hy ye after [. . .]
                  exceat wyt study & dylygenc

– thus they would cross in front of the traverse and go out at door B; and Instruccion murmurs after them –

          / well go your way [. . .]

and, as I believe, he turns to go back again by the other door and report the position to Reson; and so the Place is empty.

In this manner, it seems, the whole passage could be entirely and convincingly presented without resort to any form of imported scenic elements whatever.

All the above fits so easily into the kind of picture I have proposed that I feel there is some chance of the picture being not incorrect; but it is possible that the sequel will offer further confirmation of what I have suggested; and in any case the development is interesting in itself.

I have pictured an empty Place after the exits of Wyt, Dylygence and Studye by door B, and the retirement a moment later of Instruccion through door A. There remains nothing to see then but the silent traverse curtain. Next follows this direction –

tedyousnes
cum*th* in wt a
vyser over hys
hed /

His lines are particularly significant. He asks:

146.   [. . .] what kaytyves be those /
                            that [.. .]
                                [. . .] thus dysese me /
                            out of my nest /

He has even seen who the caitiffs were, for he goes on:

                    that wyt / [. . .]
                    yt is he playne
                    that thus bold / doth make hym
                    wythowt my lycence /
                    to stalke by my doore /
                    to that drab syence /
                    to wed that whore /

Three things seem clear from this: (1) that Tedyousnes has over-heard the entire passage, or at least has heard their voices as they talked, and was disturbed (or 'dis-eased') by them; (2) that he was in his 'nest' when he overheard them; and (3) that the characters who spoke had, without his leave, *stalked by his door*, or passed across in front of his nest. It may be chance, but there is no doubt that an arrangement that would fit perfectly with all these three points and strengthen the preceding scene would be if Tedyousnes's nest were behind the traverse, whence he 'came in' by poking his vizarded head through the curtains.

There is certainly no proof in the text that this is the answer; but what I am rather seeking to show is that, whether or not the scene had been elaborately set for an original presentation at court, the script as written could have been played in Interlude technique by strolling players, if the need arose – and without altering a single line or modifying a single direction. What I am concerned to establish is not how a given script must have been presented in detail on the occasion of its first performance, whether at court or not, but

319

how far it was possible for ordinary, common, travelling, professional Interluders to use the screens technique to present such scenes effectively without resorting to impractical additional properties or 'houses', and without mutilations of the text.

We have next a delightful piece of horrific nonsense much in the strain of Tityvillus's exhibition in *Mankind*. Tedyousnes breaks off and sets to work to entertain the audience by getting himself in good fettle for beating the despised Wyt into the dust. To begin he exclaims –

170.
> I am not halfe lustye /
> thes iontes / thes lynkes /
> be ruffe / & halfe rustye /
> I must go shake them /
> supple to make them /

– and he clearly cavorts extensively in what appears to be a panoply of devil's accoutrements, wings, horns, tail, mask, etc. – so extensively in fact that he imperils the bystanders near the traverse, and he warns them –

> stand back ye wrechys / [. . .]
> make roome I say /
> rownd evry way /
> thys way / that way
> what care I what way /
> before me / behynd me /
> rownd abowt wynd me
> now I begyn
> to swete in my skin
> now am I nemble
> to make them tremble
> pash hed / pash brayne [. . .]

– and he war-dances through an imagined encounter with his disturbers –

> where art thow wyt
> thow art but deade
> of goth thy hed
> a the fyrst blo
> ho ho ho ho

Then, quite suddenly, he presumably puts his finger to his lip, stops dead, listens, then sinks to the floor in an amorphous heap of 'invisibility', for just at that moment we have the interrupting marginal direction –

wyt spekyth
at the doore

What Wyt speaks is simply a call to Studye. I picture him standing still outside, not yet advanced into the acting-area but checking in the entry, and thus speaking 'at the door' to his servant. Studye replies. Wyt asks him crisply how his headache is and learns that it continues. He then turns to Dylygence and asks him if he is ready to fight. Dylygence assents. Studye protests. Wyt tells both he needs only their moral support, at which they say they are ready; and Wyt concludes –

218.   / I axe no more studye cu*m* then goe

– which I take to mean 'come then, let us go on into the hall'; and they then enter bravely.

At this precise moment the audience is offered a deliciously horrible thrill by a movement from the sunken figure on the floor, and a direction reads –

Tedyiousnes
rysyth vp   / why art thow cu*m*

They fight and –

here wyt fallyth
downe & dyeth

The others flee, and Tedyousnes soliloquizes in triumph before stalking off victor, with the significant words spoken over Wyt's body –

236.   [. . .] now ly styll kaytyv / & take thy rest
            / whyle I take myne / in myne owne nest

exceat tedy

If in fact his 'nest' was as I have suggested within the traverse, then he has simply to step in and conceal himself behind the curtain.

Wyt is revived by Honest Recreacion and three friends of hers, and several entertaining passages of the plot now follow, including a comic school-scene with a dunce, that is almost reminiscent of Will Hay's music-hall act. With most of this we need have no concern – any problems are simply normal problems of conventional presentation. But there is in it one acting-direction that introduces a new phrasing and does seem very puzzling indeed. The situation is as follows:

Shortly after Wyt is revived, he is left alone in the Place with the lady, Honest Recreacion, and he is suddenly affected by her charms and makes a decided pass at her; she prudently reminds him of his commitment to Science and (perhaps less prudently) puts him off by suggesting they should dance together. But she observes, quite symbolically, that if he should do so he must first doff his long-skirted coat which he had donned to go and see Science –

312.　　　　　　　　　[. . .] ye must excyle
　　　　　　　　　　　this garment cumbryng

Wyt agrees, saying –

　　　　　　　　　　/ In deede as ye say
　　　　　　　　　　this cumbrus aray
　　　　　　　　　　woold make wyt slumbryng

Honest Recreacion is in two minds about the rightness of this action for she observes –

　　　　　　　　　　/ yt is gay geere
　　　　　　　　　　of science cleere
　　　　　　　　　　yt seemth her aray

But Wyt is cavalier; he tosses it aside, with –

　　　　　　　　　　/ whose ever it were
　　　　　　　　　　yt lythe now there

– and Honest Recreacion, perhaps in spite of herself, can do no other than give the order –

　　　　　　　　　　/ go to my men play
　　　　　　　　　　here they dawnce / & in the mene
　　　　　　　　　　whyle / Idellnes cumth in / & sytth downe
　　　　　　　　　　& when the galyard is doone / wyt sayth
　　　　　　　　　　as folowyth / & so falyth downe in
　　　　　　　　　　　　　　Idellnes lap

– and he refuses to get up! Whereat there is a slanging match between the two women, Idelnes and Honest Recreacion, until eventually the latter takes herself off in disgust –

424.　　　　　　　　　[. . .] syns wyt lyethe as wone
　　　　　　that neyther heerth nor seeth I am gone /　　　　　　exceat

The position now is clear: Idelnes had come in at the screens, had sat down near the doors, and Wyt is now lying luxuriously in her lap, where he in fact sinks into an exhausted slumber. Idelnes croons –

434.   [. . .] well whyle he sleepth in Idelnes lappe
                idelnes marke on hym shall I clappe [. . .]

– and she blacks his face. Then she thinks further of 'an other toye', and whistles for her 'boye' called Ingnorance. He comes. There follow some 150 lines of schoolroom farce while she pretends to teach him to spell; but ultimately she makes Ingnorance, the fool, with his 'cote, hoode eares' and 'kokscome', change clothes with Wyt. After the change the boy runs out in delight and Idelnes frisks her heels and leaves the poor, unconscious hero lying alone in the Place near the screens, 'cuniurd from wyt vnto a starke foole'.

Confidence next comes in seeking Wyt, but cannot see him and leaves disconsolately. (We realize that the exhausted Wyt must be practically invisible at the end of the torchlit hall.) Later the lady Science and Experience her mother enter and discuss Wyt's defection. They too do not see the sleeping figure. They perhaps stroll up the hall past him as they talk, and Experience warns Science to give Wyt up and seek a lover elsewhere, concluding –

720.   & make ye warrantyse another way

There now follows the unusual acting-direction. It reads –

wyt cum̃th be
fore

– and he immediately says (showing that he has overheard them) –

        / But your warrantyse warrant[?s] no trothe
        fayre ladye I praye you be not wrothe [. . .]

The essential question is, What do the words 'Wyt cometh before' mean?

In this context it is perhaps not too difficult to offer some provisional answer; but the answer depends on the picture which I have made of the placing of the three figures being a correct one – and I have no proof that it is. But if it were true, then 'Wyt cometh before' would mean that Wyt rose from where he was lying, in the background near the screens, walked up the hall to where the two women were talking facing up towards the dais, overtook them, made a turn and, coming between them and the High Table, faced them with his back to the dais, and began to speak from in front of them. I can see no other interpretation of the action of Wyt's 'coming before' than that he came before – or in front of – the women, speaking from the viewpoint of the master of the house at the High Table – or of a sovereign upon the state if it were a court performance.

I have had a particular purpose in trying to clarify this odd phrase 'cometh before' because there is a similar usage in a later Interlude which is even more puzzling, and if the present episode can be found to throw light on the later one, the time spent on it will be worth while.

I now go on to the moment when the rehabilitated Wyt sets out on his second attempt to pass Tedyousnes's domain. The problem there raised comes from the reference to a 'mount'. This reference is held by some writers to imply a built piece of scenery in the style of the revels at court.

The situation develops as follows, opening with this acting-direction –

Instruccion cumth
in wyth / wyt / study /
& dylygence

Instruccion says to Wyt –

953.   Lo syr now ye be entryd agayne
    toward that passage where dooth remayne
    tedyousnes your mortall enmy

– and asks him if he is ready to try his hand again or would prefer to walk 'alytell abowte'. Wyt is eager to try his new sword. Then Instruccion makes the announcement that contains the problem; he says –

964. / then foorth there / & turne on your ryght hand
    vp that mownt before ye shall see stand [. . .]

In my view it will be seen on studying these lines that instead of affording evidence that any mount is visible, their implication is rather the reverse – that the mount *cannot* be seen from where the characters are; Instruccion tells Wyt that he must *go forth* to see it, and moreover go forth *there* (as if by that far door). On top of this, only when he is 'forth', or outside, is Wyt to turn to his right and look; the implication is that he should look along the entry-passage behind the screens towards a fictional mount. Finally, Wyt is told

that he *shall* see the mount stand before him, but only *after* he has
taken those movements – not that he *could* see it from where he then
was. And therefore, though a mount is most certainly specifically
mentioned, there is not only no suggestion that it is visible, but
there would in fact have to be some alteration in the lines if it were.
That an actual property mountain might or might not be justified
in some elaborate court performance is outside the present consideration.

Instruccion's speech now continues with some special advice to
Wyt, but advice that is unfortunately cryptic for us, and may refer
back to some passage of the play now missing. What he says is –

> but heere ye / yf your enmye chance to ryse
> folowe my cowncell in anye wyse
> let studye & dyligence flee ther towche
> the stroke of tediousnes & then cowche
> them selves as I told ye / ye wot how /

This is not clear. But Wyt apparently does 'wot how' for his reply is –

> / ye syr for that how marke the proofe now

– which unfortunately helps us only a little further – but it at least
has a pretty strong flavour of being an exit line, and I believe that
Wyt is in effect saying, 'Yes I remember what you told me about
them, and now we will go out and prove it'. And they go. But what
Instruccion had told Wyt about Studye and Dylygence 'couching'
themselves is not, so far as I can see, to be discovered; possibly they
are to perform some sort of decoy action in the fight. Whatever is
meant by Wyt's reply, Instruccion accepts it.

Then as Wyt and his two men leave, Instruccion immediately
goes on to say –

972.   / to marke it in deede / heere wyll I abyde
> to see what chance of them wyll betyde

(This would seem to clinch the matter of their exit. But he now
gives us a glimpse of enlightenment about the reason for mention-
ing a mountain; his speech continues –)

> for heere cumth the pyth lo of this jornaye
> That mowntayne before which they must assaye
> in [? *is*] cald in laten mons pernassus
> which mowntayne as old auctors dyscus
> who attaynth ones / to sleepe on that mownt
> ladye science / his owne he may cownt [. . .]

– so the mount is Parnassus and has a symbolic justification. The whole of the above speech is in the tone of an explanatory soliloquy to the audience to fill in while Wyt and his two servants have gone out. The speech continues with –

> but or he cum there / ye shall see fowght
> a fyght wt no les polycye wrowght
> then strenghth / I trow If that may be praysed

His last remark seems to be the beginning of a fresh thought – indicated by the capital letter for 'If' – which is then broken off by an interruption. The statement that 'ye' shall see the fight fought would seem addressed not to Wyt but to the audience. Then we should have to read the verb 'see' as a piece of poetic licence, for what follows seems to be a fight taking place entirely out of sight. The lines continue with a good reason for an interruption; it is a great shout from Tedyousnes, out of sight –

983. TEDIOUSNES / oh / ho / ho
INSTRUCCION / hark
TEDIOUSNES / out ye kaytyvss
INSTRUCION / the feend is raysyd
TEDIOUSNES / out ye vilaynes / be ye cum agayne
              have at ye wretches
WYT   fle syrs ye twayne
TEDIOUSNES   thei fle not far hens
DYLIGENS / turne agayne studye
STUDYE / now dylygence
INSTRUCCION / well sayde holde fast now
STUDYE / he fleeth
DYLIGENCE / then folowe
INSTRUCCION   wyth his owne weapon now wurke him sorow
              wyt lyth at reseyte
TEDIOUSNES / oh / ho / ho
   dyeth
INSTRUCION   hark he dyeth
              where strength lackth policye ssupplieth
              / heere wyt cumth in & bryngth in the hed vpon
              his swoorde & sayth as folowyth

– and mutual congratulations ensue. An added complication now comes, in what follows, for to them there now enters Confidence ('confidens / cumth runing in'). He announces that Science approves the victory, and Wyt – quite understandably – wonders how she comes to know anything about it; and Confydence explains –

1012. / vpon yonder mowntayne on hye
     she saw ye strike that hed from the bodye [. . .]

Now, this is ambiguous; it could mean that Science was standing upon a (different) mountain and looked from it at the combat (so involving us in further scenery – real or imagined). |Or, it could simply mean that Science saw Wyt fight *upon* the mountain, that is upon Parnassus, whither we know he went, in which case no actual mount need be concerned at all.

The suggestion is sometimes made here that the elevated place from which Science was said to have watched the fight could have been represented by a normal feature of the (later) screens; namely, the minstrels' gallery above. No doubt this may be so, but it is not essential. There is nothing in the lines that makes it necessary for Science actually to be seen watching from a mountain.

Some business is now made with the typical robing of Wyt in a new 'gowne of knoledge'. Then he gives Confydence the severed head which he has just won and bids him go and present it to Science upon which Confydence presumably goes out, but in four lines he 'cumth runnyng in' again with the announcement that –

1030. / my ladye at hand heere dooth abyde ye
     byd her wellcum / what do ye hide ye

– and there follows the detailed direction:

here wyt / Instruccion / studye / & digigence syng wellcum my nowne ['*Welcome, mine own*'—*the name of their song*] / & syence / experience / reson / & confidence cum in at / As ['*As*' *is the opening word of the second stanza of the song whose words are given in a supplement to the play*] & answer evre second verse & when the song is doone / reson sendyth instruccion / studye & dyligence / confidens out / & then standyng in the myddell of the place / wyt sayth as folowyth

– and he welcomes Science. It is interesting to see that the playwright takes care that Wyt should be situated at the most advantageous spot in the hall for his climax – that is to say at 'the myddell of the place'.

There is some brief moral exchange about treating his bride well, and at length Reson sums up with a pious wish for joy for the King and Queen, and –

1125.   Heere cumth in fowre wyth violes & syng
          remembreance / & at the last quere all make
          cursye & so goe forth syngyng
          Thus endyth the play of wyt & science
          made by master Ihon redford /

The purpose of this longish analysis is to do little more than offer the opinion that as technique develops the Interlude and the play become less distinct; that Interludes by distinguished professional companies might receive summonses to command performances at court; and that successful court plays originally written for large casts of boy players from the chapels, and for more elaborate scenic resources too costly and cumbersome to be travelled, might soon come to be adapted by skilful professional Interluders, and taken into their repertory for simplified presentation in halls with screens.

If this were the case, then any shrewd playwright having his play printed would be deliberately non-committal about technical scenic details, knowing that those who bought his play would have to make their own arrangements according to circumstances.

Presentation in Civic Halls etc. 1538 onwards

27 *The Evidence of Civic Accounts*

In the year 1538 comes the first, chronologically, of a series of fragments of evidence about a different side of the staging of plays before Shakespeare. It is convenient to take these fragments together though the later ones reach well towards the end of the century. They concern performances in places other than the Great Halls of Tudor houses or the court. They are drawn from various municipal records of towns to which travelling companies came not to perform in private, but before the general public in some civic building such as a Guildhall, and they give us a little information about the preparations made in the hall on such occasions for these Common Players.

The term 'common player' is particularly important to the subject of this book. I remember that when Sir Bernard Miles held one of his public meetings in the early days of the Mermaid theatre in Lower Thames Street in the City of London (where formerly no, or few, theatres were allowed), he read out the relevant document of entitlement from the Council of the City. In it an old wording was preserved; and we heard that the permission for the theatre was given to one 'Bernard Miles, a common player . . .'. This brought a ripple of amusement from the modern audience, but the phrase is valuable. It means of course a player to the commonality, the general public, and as such becomes in the event a term really for pride.

This book is specifically concerned with the presentation-technique of common players, or players to the general public, as against that of the nobles at court who played for their own entertainment, or that of the choir children who played at court for the nobles' entertainment. To some extent my study of the players' work up to now has been under a limitation, because it has dealt only with private, as against truly public, performances, that is to say, with performances in private houses, where the entertainment

329

would inevitably have been given under some degree of protection, or at least in an atmosphere slightly biased out of respect for the host. What I want now to try to find out – though the material is lamentably scanty – is what sort of conditions obtained when the common players were exposed to the common people and had to give their performance free of all protection, depending entirely on their own success or failure with a paying audience. This is another way of asking: What were the conditions when real professionalism in the theatre began? In my opinion this, and not any circumstance of court procedure, would ultimately stand at the root of the development that was to lead to Shakespeare.

It must be made clear straight away that the companies of common players would have to face quite different playing conditions and make quite different preparations from what were involved when an Interlude was given at a festal celebration in a private house.

It is not impossible that the sudden spurt of Interlude writing at the end of the fifteenth century came about because of the popular custom of celebrating a family occasion with a private play. The custom would encourage Interluders because private shows would afford them a more favourable atmosphere for refinements in technique than the rough-and-tumble of one-night stands before random audiences of the general public. Compare, for instance, the difference between the general picture conjured up by *Mankind* and that of Medwall's plays. On a private occasion the patron would be inclined to take the side of the players, and would obviously encourage them to provide the best entertainment for his guests, and so enhance his own prestige – especially if these guests were sophisticated men. In a private house, therefore, some sort of recognized discipline would exist in the audience which, provided the players justified themselves at all, would make their show easier if only out of good manners to the host. It would indeed be – as Medwall suggested in *Fulgens* – a captious sort of guest who booed a performance that he had not only paid nothing for but had been well feasted to watch. Thus shows in private houses might to some certain extent have had an encouraging and refining influence on Interlude writing.

But shows before the general public would rather tend to harden and sharpen the technique, if they did not indeed merely coarsen it. For a performance before the common public would be a more hazardous experience; the local authorities themselves, unlike the host in a private house, might be very reluctant at having to allow the 'licentious players' there at all. They would be far less inclined to exert a protecting influence. The general public would be always capable of taking undue advantage of the licence of the occasion and (not having the religious atmosphere of a Mystery play to restrain them) might express their reaction by wrecking the appointments of the hall. If they did not like a play they would certainly not simply contain themselves and walk out, as the King might.

There may therefore have been a period when the custom of giving plays at private feasts encouraged writers to refinements that public shows alone would not have encouraged; and the combination of the two styles in judicious proportions could set them well on the way to the standard of technical craftsmanship that was achieved by the time Shakespeare came.

To define now the physical differences between the conditions at a private performance and those at a public show. Before everything else, the surround of dining-tables would not be there, and so the whole business of accommodating the audience would have to be settled quite differently. This is particularly important since if the audience-accommodation were different, then the acting-area might have to be completely different to fit in with it. It is true that a typical Civic Hall or Guildhall might or might not include tables in its normal furniture, but such things would obviously have to be cleared out of the way before any public play performance, since they might be pretty roughly treated if they were left. Again, a Town Hall would not be equipped like a domestic Hall for serving meals regularly day after day; anything of that sort would be limited to an occasional banquet given by a Guild or some such. And so the Kitchens, and consequently the Entry and the Screens, would not necessarily have the same importance. The dais across the upper end of the Hall might perhaps be fairly common, but about this dais at the upper end I shall have something to say later.

Supposing now a company of players arranging with the civic authorities to play in such a hall, as the records show they frequently did, how would they present their play?

They would have no open floor down the middle of the hall such as I have visualized for private performances because, in the absence of dining-tables, the spectators would no longer be confined mostly to the sides and ends as they were in a house; they could crowd anywhere over the floor in a hall that had been emptied to receive them. What steps are the players to take to make this cleared and unspecialized Place more possible for them to play in and for the spectators to watch in?

So far as their playing was concerned, they might consider using the dais as an acting-area. But there is a qualification; a normal hall dais is not in itself so suitable for a performance before a crowded public audience as it might seem. Though we find little evidence about whether such an audience generally sat or stood – or, if both in what proportions – yet if it – or any considerable part of it – stood, then a typical hall dais would be too low to be of much use to the players. They would need a platform somewhere round five feet high to gain any real visual advantage from it before a standing audience; and a dais was usually only twelve or eighteen inches – in this resembling a 'pas' or 'footpace', that is a surface elevated one pace, or step, up. Any experience of playing in halls today shows that a platform lower than about three feet is of little use to actors even with a seated audience – unless the auditorium or hall floor is raked, which of course it could not normally be in any civic hall planned for general use. I will bring in a separate piece of evidence below (see p. 341) which I think confirms my opinion that players would only rarely use the dais.

Speaking broadly, there would be little then as there is little now in a Town Hall to be really helpful to a show, once the authorities had cleared it of anything that the players or a demonstrative crowd might damage – nothing except the protection of the shell itself against the elements. Otherwise we must begin by reckoning it a dark and empty interior.

In what follows I shall take a number of items which offer help in answering these problems from the lists of extracts from civic accounts assembled by J. Tucker Murray in his *English Dramatic Companies*, 1558–1642 (1910), but first I begin with a somewhat different and rather unexpected item.

In a topographical book by Chas. John Palmer, published in 1872 and entitled *The Perlustration of Great Yarmouth, etc.*, is a quotation from a lease dated 1538 (vol. 1, p. 351); it concerns a 'house and game place', and enjoins that the lessee must, in regard to theatre players –

> permit & suffer all such players & their audience to have the pleasure & use of said house & game place, at all such times as any interluds or plays should be ministered or played at any time; without any profit thereof to him or his assigns to be taken.

This document is dated 1538, that is to say one year after *Thersytes* and one year before *Wit and Science*. In addition, then, to the Guild and other Halls which might be occasionally taken for play performances there was, by 1538 at least, one house specifically used for the 'pleasure' of Interludes and plays available to both players and audiences 'at all such times as . . . interluds . . . should be . . . played'. Not only did such a house apparently exist at Yarmouth, but its use might be had without 'any profit' being 'taken'. This would seem an early example of civic subsidy of the theatre; but, alas, it helps us little in the problem of how such a place might be arranged inside.

I turn now to Tucker Murray's extracts beginning at his p. 361 with some from the Chamberlain's Accounts at Norwich.

In 1541–2 we find this for 'wytson weke' –

Itm payd for sedge to strow the Halle ther when the prynces players playd an enterlude ther, ii^d [;] dryncke for the players – ii^d [;] to ii laborers that fetchyd barrells and tymber and made a scaffold then— ii^d . . . . vi^d

This seems to me an item which can justly be said to mark an epoch in the present study. It says that on occasion the hall was definitely strewn with rushes for a performance; 'sedge' is applicable to any rush-like or flag-like plants. It says that it was a company called the Prince's Players that performed and that they performed something called an 'enterlude' there, but there is no suggestion that the performance was given during a feast – though we learn incidentally that the players were provided with drinks by the Town.

But the final detail is the one that is of sufficient interest to start a new chapter in a history of presentation – it says that two labourers were hired to fetch barrels and timber and with them to make a scaffold on that occasion. (It may be noticed that each of these three details, sedge, drinks, and scaffolding, is valued at the same amount.) What now is to be deduced from the words 'barrels and timber for a scaffold'?

A potential trap here is that there seems little to indicate whether this 'scaffold' was built to accommodate the audience or the actors, whether to be a grandstand or a stage. It seems necessary to turn aside for a moment to make some definitions.

The root derivation of the word 'scaffold' is obscure; it appears to be related to the modern French *échafaud*, and possibly to the

Roman *excatafalcum* and our own 'catafalque', which latter word is, however, of unknown origin.

Reference to the *O.E.D.* gives us first a number of variant spellings: scaffot, skefold, shapfold, skafell -oll, etc. There follow eight senses for the word, of which two are relevant to theatrical usage, the fourth and the fifth.

sense 4 reads:

> *specifically*: A platform or stage on which theatrical performance or exhibition takes place; *especially*, in early use, a temporary stage on which a mystery play was performed. *Obsolete* except *in historical use*.

Two examples of usage in this sense are – (from about 1386) Chaucer's *Miller's Tale*, l. 198. 'Somtyme . . . He pleyeth Herodes on a scaffold hye.' And (from 1565, not far from the time we are now considering) Cooper's *Thesaurus*, under the word 'scena', 'Orestes oftentymes represented on scaffoldes in playes.' This then clearly enough establishes the usage of 'scaffold' to mean an actor's stage.

But sense 5 reads:

> A raised platform or stand for holding the spectators of a tournament, theatrical performance, etc. Also, a gallery in a theatre or church. *Obsolete*.

One example given is from Bellenden's *Livy* (1533): 'Thai war constrenit to mak public setis and scaffaldis in commoun placis quhare playis war devisit.' And this equally clearly establishes a usage of the word signifying a place for spectators from which they can view a stage.

(A brief digression offers itself here; the additional note in the second definition is perhaps a little surprising. It does not appear relevant to the present subject of performances in Town Halls, but it may be useful to remember it and I repeat it – 'Also, a gallery in a theatre . . .'. Some help about this particular usage may be found, rather unexpectedly, under the much more unusual word 'scaffolder' in the *O.E.D.* This is defined as 'An occupant of the gallery at a theatre. *Obsolete*.' – and the example quoted from Bishop Hall's *Satires* refers to an actor who can ravish 'the gazing Scaffolders'. The quotation is dated 1597. But I feel inclined to take this definition a little cautiously; I do not think it must be understood as a proof that a theatrical scaffold could normally be a theatre *gallery*. It would more commonly be a 'stand' built up on the floor of a Place, perhaps not unlike church pews or a jury-box in a magistrate's court.)

To resume; the *Dictionary*'s contribution to our problem is simply that the term 'scaffold' may imply equally a 'stand' to accommodate spectators or a platform for actors to play on. Have we any choice in the above reference?

There are two considerations which suggest that the latter meaning may perhaps be the one intended in the Norwich item. First, the word is found in a later account (see below p. 339) distinctly qualified as 'a skaffold for players to playe on'; thus there is no doubt that it meant a stage on that occasion. Second is the fact that the scaffold we are now considering is stated to be made of timber and *barrels*; this almost certainly implies some structure with the barrels used underneath as supports. There are several reasons why the players might choose barrels for use as supports: because they were firmly built; because they were convenient to borrow from a local inn; because they could be adapted as supports without much carpentry; and because they could be returned afterwards relatively undamaged. But there is also another reason: that they are in uniform sizes and would therefore be useful as supports for a flat, or level, structure such as a floor. Thus a stage, rather than an audience stand, is suggested since a stand for spectators would be more likely to be stepped and not level.

It might, however, be objected that barrels could be used in the construction of a stepped audience stand, provided rows of different sizes of barrel were used; but this suggestion, beside seeming a little over-ingenious, is unlikely since a stepped audience stand made on the support of rows of barrels of different sizes would not be secure unless the timbers of the planking were nailed firmly to the barrels. Since the barrels must have been only borrowed, and would therefore have to be returned undamaged – and particularly, *unpierced* – any idea of using them as supports for audience accommodation seems put out of court. And so, after consideration, I am inclined to understand by 'scaffold' in the present item, a raised playing-stage made out of planks laid on barrels.

If this is so, then the raised stage in this reference is the first one to be definitely hinted at in the present study; or to be more exact, the first to be definitely hinted at in a contemporary reference as against the unconfirmed, and unconfirmable, hints sometimes found in editors' remarks.

Let me now go back to the arrangement of the public hall generally; clearly the kind of arrangement that I have built up for shows at meals in private houses would not do. But all that is available in this first item from which to build any alternative picture is the dark, empty rectangle of the building, into which timber and barrels have been brought to make a scaffold – but whereabouts, or of what shape or size, is not yet clear.

The next reference comes in the same *Accounts* from Norwich, and the following year (1542–3). Now the company is the Earl of Arundel's Men, the season is Michaelmas, the show is again referred to as an Interlude, and the hall where it was played is now clearly specified as the Assembly Chamber of the Guildhall:

> Itm pd to the Erle of Arnedells players who playd on myhelmes day in the begynnyng of this accompt an enterlude in the sembly chamdyr of ye guldhall vi^s viii^d

A curious touch of actuality is added concerning this occasion which brings a note of colour to the picture of a possibly little-used building in the autumn season before the days of central heating. On this occasion a separate item was paid for perfume for the chamber, which savoured 'sore' ('sore' may mean 'sourly', or 'strongly'). This may have been partly because it had been shut up and not ventilated, but we also have a specific reason added; the strong smell was of burnt soot from the adjacent prison chimney ('. . . the stronge savor ther by reason of a chymney in the *prison* whereoff the Swote was brent').

The item continues with a payment to a labourer who swept the chamber and who also made a scaffold – this time not upon barrels, but upon the forms there (' . . . a labourer yt swept ye chambyr and made a skafold vpon the fourmes there'). This presents a further problem; a scaffold upon forms would presumably be lower than a scaffold upon barrels, but its use and position are still unclarified; it might have been the basis for a 'box' for special spectators, or it might have been a stage made high enough by being built on the dais – but more of this possibility later.

An item from the following year (1543–4), at Norwich again, tells us that six labourers 'caryed xii long popill planks from the comon . . . to the como*n* Halle to make a skaffold for an Interlude to be played ther . . .'. Notice that the phrasing here tends more to imply that the scaffold was for the Interluders than for the audience and is thus a stage not a stand. The company was 'My lord of Sussex men'. By 'popill' is meant, I think, 'poplar', since poplar is naturally a timber obtainable in long lengths and is especially suitable for planks. It is particularly interesting to notice that we are here taken a very small step nearer to estimating the size of this scaffold. We have no indication of the width of the planks, but in those days they could be relatively wide; twelve inches is a legitimate average guess. In that case, since there were twelve planks, one or other dimension of the scaffold (width or depth) is likely to have been round about twelve feet, supposing the planks to have been layed side by side.

The next item of information comes from Canterbury. Again it concerns the year 1542–3. It uses now quite clearly, and for the first time in this present study, the actual word *stage* and not scaffold, and it suggests that, on some occasions at any rate, such a stage was not necessarily made up from borrowed materials because in this instance, once it was finished with, the materials were sold – 'Receyved of Master Batheise for the hole stage of the play to hym sold xlˢ.'

At this point I have to turn aside again for a definition. I spent some consideration on the word 'scaffold'; it is only fair, upon meeting this, the earliest use of the word 'stage' to come in the present study, that it should be treated in the same way.

In some respects the present book is a history of the introduction of the raised stage into theatrical presentation. I pointed out at the beginning (intending something more than a paradox) that an incidental event in the development of the staging of plays before Shakespeare was the introduction of the stage. Certainly some pains should be taken here to find out what a stage, in common acceptance, is.

The *O.E.D.* reveals a considerable range of meaning under the general head of something to stand on. The first division, in the sense of storey or level, has five sub-variants. The next two meaning-divisions do not directly concern us (one is a step in the ladder of virtue!). The fourth division has the sense of 'A raised floor, platform, scaffold', and the first of eight sub-variants here is interesting enough to note: 'A floor raised above the level of the ground for the exhibition of something to be viewed by spectators. Now *rare* or *obsolete*. Cf. 5a.' This leads to the fifth meaning-division where '5a' reads –

> The platform in a theatre upon which spectacles, plays, etc. are exhibited, esp. a raised platform with its scenery and other apparatus upon which a theatrical performance takes place.

Two of several examples of usage at the end of the article are particularly relevant here; the first from R. Robynson's edition of More's *Utopia* is dated 1551 – 'Whyles a commodye of Plautus is playinge, . . . yf yowe shoulde sodenlye come vpon the stage in a philosophers apparrell.' And the second from Puttenham's *English Poesie* is dated 1589 – 'When Tragidies came vp they deuised to present them upon scaffoldes or stages of timber.' The word is an adaptation from the French *étage*, and ultimately comes from the Latin *stare*, to stand.

There is confirmation here that stage and scaffold are, in some contexts, synonymous. But the main point is that a stage is essentially a raised thing; it must be different from the floor or the ground level. Hence the word should never be confused (as some authors do) with the word Place.

In 1546–7 the Norwich accounts record another small but valuable point about the 'skaffold', this time concerning its position; it was 'at the ende of the halle'. Tucker inserts the word '[far]' before 'ende', in square brackets but does not say whether the word is in brackets because it is obscurely written in the original, or whether it is in brackets because to speak of *the end* of a hall was to imply the 'lower' portion or part farthest from the High Table. But, as a later extract will show (see p. 341), the far end of the hall is in fact the more likely end. I will return to this later.

The particular reference here continues with an item to diverse men who 'removyd the tabyles trustylls & fforymes & set them agayne when all thyngs was done'. So we are once more reminded that care was taken to clear the hall of any valuable things before a show, and that consequently these had all to be replaced afterwards.

From Norwich again, in 1548–9, there is a brief entry that may or may not be significant – namely, 'to a carpente yt made certen skaffolds'. If these were for a play-performance it would appear that, since they are in the plural, the reference must be either to two or more separate audience-stands, or to a stage and one or more audience-stands. A further detail is offered in the fact that 'the reward was payd by master mayer' – presumably to the players – and immediately after there is the item: 'but payd to ii men yt kept the dores iiiid'. Thus we learn that door-keepers were employed.

The next item is from the Bailiff's Accounts at Shrewsbury in 1556 when the bailiffs were required 'to set forward' [which may simply mean 'to put in hand' generally, or it may have a more specific intention in the sense of 'to arrange for the *setting* of', thus anticipating such a usage as the 'orderly setting foorthe' of court entertainments that we find in the Revels Accounts in 1571] 'the stage play this next Whitsontide for the worship of the town, and not to disburse above £5 about the furniture of the play'. Some specific care must therefore have been taken over the arrangements for such shows, though a clear limit is here set to the expense. It is further worth noting that the presence at the show of 'the worship of the town' pretty certainly implies that something beyond mere standing-room would need to be provided, for some at least of the audience would expect to sit in comfort.

Next, in the Chamberlain's Accounts of Gloucester from the years between September 1559 and 1568, there are several items, one of which has already been referred to as unmistakably proving that the scaffold mentioned was a stage and not a spectator's stand. The first item (1559–60) is for 'money payed for an hundred of borde-nayles to make a scaffolde in the bothall for the Quenes Majesties players', and also paid 'to John Battye, carpinter and his fellowe for the makinge of the said scaffolde'. Thus we have the name of an early stage-carpenter and mention of his mate. From the year 1561–1562 the same source gives us the first indication about lighting such shows; it records a payment to a Mr. Ingram for 'a pounde of candelles at the same playe' – and shortly after this a payment for a 'bankett made to the seid players and for makynge of a scaffold in the Bot hall'. Similarly in 1562–3 is an item for 'the makynge of the skaffold at the Bot hall & for nayles there'. In 1564–5 money was paid 'for tacking of the same Scaffold away agayne'. The final item from this group is the particularly informative one; it contains the confirmatory evidence for the scaffold being a stage, and a further very small piece of information about the construction of such a scaffold. The first reads, 'paid to Battie for C and iii quarters of elme bourdes for a skaffold for players to playe one'. The second, 'Alsoe paid to hime for a piece of tymber to sett under the bourdes'. Some slight advance towards understanding how the stage scaffold was constructed is offered here in the specification of *boards* for the players to play on, and then, as a separate item, *timber* to set under the boards. One visualizes the barrels first as a general support, then *timbers* in the form of battens or joists laid across the barrels, and then a flooring of *boards* laid over these again to provide the playing surface – the boards being almost certainly nailed to the timbers with the 'board nails'. Obviously the boards could not be nailed directly to the borrowed barrels without risk of damaging them. If there were no nailing at all they would be insecure. But to batten them out by nailing them to cross-timbers beneath would provide a firm surface for the barrels to support.

339

How significant this suggested distinction between 'boards' and 'timbers' may be is not greatly cleared up by the next item which is from Maidstone in 1568; it refers to a payment for 'layeing the tymb^r off ye stage together'. Whether this is to be understood as being confined to the battens under the stage floor, or as applying to the whole structure is unclear.

Going on now to 1564-5, there is an item from the Norwich accounts for 'Torches to show light in the Chappell when they played'. The provision of torches is itself a confirmation of the need for light that has already been mentioned. But in addition, it is just such a reference as this to a chapel, which makes one the more inclined to consider the curate's line in *The Pardoner and the Friar*, about 'polute my chyrche', as being possibly factual, for in the Norwich reference it is specifically '*in* the Chappell' that the players played.

The next two items come from the Chamberlain's Accounts at Nottingham for 1571-2. The first again concerns the borrowing of material; it records a hire charge for the boards for a stage or scaffold – 'to William Marshall for bordes that was borowed for to make a scaffold to the Halle when the Quen's Maiestyes players dyd play'; and the second is interesting in referring not to a performance in a public Town Hall but to one in what is once more, presumably, a private house – 'to Maister Harpham for ale when the Quen's plears dyd play at his howse'. The sum appears to be sixteen shillings, which is exactly 48 times as much as the amount of the hire-cost of the scaffold boards in the preceding item, which was 4d.

Another contribution towards the question of the size of a scaffold may be contained in an item from St. Ives in 1573 which reads, 'receivyd of Wm. Trinw^{th.} for sixe score and thre foote of elme bordes in ye playing place'. If these boards were a foot wide, then 123 (6 × 20 + 3) feet of them would furnish a stage some 12 ft. by 10 ft. in size. But we are not told, unfortunately, any more than that the boards were 'in the playing place'. They could conceivably have been used for other purposes than making the stage floor. Especially is the matter in doubt here because the sum mentioned is 6d., and in the following item the sum of 1s. 6d. is mentioned as 'recieyed of harrie bayne for bordes'. If these were also from the playing place, it might mean either that the stage was considerably larger, or simply that other timber than that for a stage was involved – for example, the timber used in audience-stands.

At Bristol in 1573-4, the Treasurer's Accounts mention a payment to 'My Lord of Leycesters players at thend of their play in the Yeld hall at the comedm^t of Mr Mayer & the Aldermen' – and the sum is Twenty Shillings. But in the next item, exactly the same sum is paid 'for taking down the table in the Mayors house and putting it up agayne after the said players were goune'. It seems strange that it should have cost as much to remove and replace a table as to pay for a performance by Lord Leicester's Men (of which company James Burbage himself became a member somewhere about the year 1574).

The consequences were, however, worse in 1577–8 with the same company, because after the payment made to them 'at the end of their play in the Yeld Hall before Mr Mayor and the Aldermen and for lynks to giue light in the euenyng & the play was called Myngs', there was an additional item involved 'for men, one party 3 days one 2 days, for mending the bord in the Yeld hall and the doers [*doors*] there, after my L of Leycesters players who had leave to play there'. Thus any pains taken to guard the hall furniture were probably fully justified.

Another hint of a different place for performance comes in 1589–1590 from Gloucester, where the Queen's players are recorded as playing 'in the colledge churche yarde', so an open-air performance must have been involved.

To go well beyond the period with which I am concerned now, there is an item from Worcester which fits particularly well with the above. It relates to between 1600 and 1622, and is from the Audit and Chamber Order Books, as follows –

> Item – yt is ordered that noe playes bee had or made in the upper end of the Town-hall of this city, nor council chamber used by any players whatsoever, and that noe playes be had or made in yeald by night time, and yf anie players be admytted to play in the yealdhall, to be admytted to play in the lower end onlie, upon paine of 40s to be p^d by Mr Mayor to the use of the citie if any shal be admitted or suffered to the contrary.

I want at this point to turn aside to consider a separate piece of evidence at which I have already hinted and which is relative first to the dais and second to the end of the hall which was customarily used for performances.

It seemed particularly important to reserve this piece of evidence for special consideration because it has appeared to be capable of interpretation in two diametrically opposite and contradictory ways. The passage is one from the opening of Palsgrave's translation of the Latin play by Fullonius entitled *Acolastus*. This translation dates from 1540. It can be studied in the Early English Text Society's edition of 1937 (No. 202, old style), pp. 17–18.

Craik quotes the passage in reference to a particular remark he makes in *The Tudor Interlude* on his p. 10. The remark itself is a very just one – 'There is little evidence that raised platforms were set up in halls for interludes before the second half of the sixteenth century.' Craik adds, however, a note at this point and the note reads as some qualification of the above remark; it says that –

From John Palsgrave's denial [note, *denial*], in the prologue to *Acolastus* (1540), 'that we wold for our new inuentions dryue the comedies of Plautus and Terence frome the hyghe deasse, downe behynde the skryne', it appears that a staged dais might occasionally be used, unless the image is wholly figurative (the original Latin has merely '*velut simul de ponte deiectis*'). Chambers notes that the staged dais was a rarity: E.S., III, 23, I, 228–9.

I think this needs some further consideration. I understand Craik to say that Palsgrave's reference to a 'hyghe deasse' (or high dais) suggests that a *raised stage* might occasionally have been used before 1540. There is possibly a slight qualification due concerning my interpretation, on the grounds that a 'staged dais' is not a very clear term, but since the note concerns a mention of 'raised platforms' in the text, I suppose this is in fact what he means. If the above is correct then Craik takes Palsgrave's 'hyghe deasse' to mean a raised stage.

But a quite different interpretation is possible. In the first place I think there is an intrinsic objection in the general situation itself, which rules out any possibility that a raised stage is implied in any play we have studied so far, for I take it as axiomatic that a script wherein the actors are given speeches appealing for room and for space to come in, *cannot* have been written for a raised stage, since such speeches either imply entrance through the audience or they mean nothing at all.

Only one qualification can possibly be raised against this; it could conceivably be imagined that a *small* raised stage might be built between the screen doors, which the players could only reach by entering through the doors in the usual way, passing through the surrounding bystanders, and then stepping up on to it.

This particular arrangement is not in itself an impossible one (far from it, as we shall see later); but it is an arrangement that does not accord easily with Palsgrave's image of driving a play from a *high dais* down behind the screen.

What in fact Palsgrave is writing at this point is an explanatory construing of three lines from Fullonius. He writes to explain the Latin meaning to students. Fullonius's three lines are –

> . . . *probatis fabulis*
> *Plauti, atq: item Terentij, velut simul*
> *De ponte deiectis.*

Palsgrave now glosses this as follows, and I insert the Latin words into his construing –

> [*probatis fabulis*] The approved fables i [*.e.*] comedies [*Plauti, atq: item Terentij*] of Plautus and also of Terence [*velut simul*] beinge as it were at ones or togyther [*De ponte deiectis*] throwen downe from the brydge

– and now he goes on to explain the meaning of this passage in his own words –

> as who saith, that we wold for our new inuentions dryue the comedies of Plautus and Terence frome the hyghe deasse, downe behynde the skryne, or cast them out at the cartes ars (as thinges which now wax unprofytable, by reson of theyr great ancientie) or dyscharge them from bearyng any maner offyce any longer,

– and now he concludes by explaining the words 'throwen downe from the brydge' through a reference to a Latin adage which he prints in the margin opposite this passage – '*Adagium. Sexagenarios de ponte deiicere*' – as follows:

> for this adage toke his begynning for bicause that the youth of the Romayns vsed to cast old men down from the brydge, whan they wold haue theym lese theyr voyces.

It seems to me that the words in the above – 'dryue the comedies of Plautus and Terence from the hyghe deasse, downe behynde the skryne' – evoke, and are intended to evoke, a different picture, and that instead of referring to any kind of raised stage whatever, the words mean in fact, 'To drive the comedies of Plautus and Terence down from *the upper end of the hall* (where such comedies could be performed in the most advantageous position, just before the High Table), and thus *away from the dais* (on which the high table stood), down the hall's length to the opposite or lower end where the screens were, and finally out through the doors there and so *behind* the screens into the entry itself and thus out of sight.'

And so I take it that the kind of performance that Palsgrave must obviously have seen before 1540, and which he had in his mind when he conceived this image to explain the meaning of the words *De ponte deiectis*, 'Thrown down from the bridge', was not a kind of performance upon some high stage from which the players could be *cast down*, but was a kind of performance where the players found their best playing-place to be just before the dais at the upper end of the hall. And indeed I have already supposed they must have done so from my study of *Mankind* where there is the direct approach to 'the good man of this house', and of *Nature* where Man travelled from Nature up the hall to World at the 'high' end.

My opinion is that Interluders knew as well as did the players of *The Castle of Perseverance* that some positions in their total acting-area were more favourable than others. And that, just as the players of *The Castle* recorded that 'ye myddys of ye place' must not be occupied by spectators because it 'shal be ye best [position] of all' for playing in, so the Interluders knew that the best position of all – at any rate for intimate playing to affect the master of the house in a Tudor Hall – was directly in front of the dais at the 'high' end or upper end, and that any withdrawal in the direction of the lower end, where the screens were, was in the nature of a retreat and eventually a mingling with the crowd, and an exit.

But at a performance before the general public in a Civic Hall the dais at the upper end would not be occupied by any goodman at his High Table. All the same an appropriation by the players of this end would still be frowned upon for reasons I have given. Thus the players at a public performance might 'be admytted to play in the lower end onlie, upon paine of' a fine.

At this lower end, then, I conclude their stage-scaffold was in general erected.

One footnote ought to be added to this section; in the various Civic Accounts there is to be found clear evidence that the public paid to see these performances, or at least that they were asked to contribute to a 'gathering'. For example, the account for 1546–7 at Norwich begins

> Imprimis gaf in reward to the qwenys players who playd an Interlude at the comon Halle on the tewysday in the vi[th] weke after myhelmas whose matter was the m[r]ket of myscheffe – x[s] . . .

(Thus we have an interesting record of the name of the Interlude played, though no script of a play of this name has been found. But the main point is here in what follows:)

... of the whyche was gatherd amonge the pepyll ther – vi^s iiii^d and so was payd by the accomptant iii^s viii^d

thus we apparently have an example of the Chamberlain's office undertaking to cover a deficit in the receipts at the door.

The sums gathered naturally varied considerably. For example, the Parish Record Book of St. Ives for 1573 lists the receipts for six days of playing, and they vary between 12/- and £4.10.11 –

1st day of the play received					xii^s	
2nd „ „ „ „				„	i li xii^s ii^d	
3rd „ „ „ „				„	iiii li x^s xi^d	
4th „ „ „ „				„	i li xix^s vi^d	
5th „ „ „ „				„	iii li ii^s	
6th „ „ „ „				„	iii li i^d	

What Civic Accounts unfortunately tell us very little about is how public performances were arranged when they took place in the open air. It is certain that there were such presentations because of records of shows in crofts, or in 'pightells', or in 'folds'; all of which refer to outdoor enclosures. It is also certain that at least as early as about 1540 there did exist in neighbouring countries a particular form of stage for the presentation of open-air plays at markets and fairs. This is the form of stage which I have referred to as a 'booth stage'; and there are detailed pictures of it from the Low Countries. The problem is to find any clear evidence that this form of stage was used in England about the same period. It would perhaps seem inevitable that there must have been a stage-form of this sort used here, but as far as I have been able to find out, the nearest that can be got to anything positive, so far as Interludes are concerned, is confined to supposing that the booth stage possessed features that would serve, if required, the same purposes as the hall-screens did in indoor presentation. This can be to some extent claimed as feasible; but that is about as far as any enquiry seems able go at present.

But now, ignoring this unfortunate hiatus in knowledge, I have, before I close this chapter, to consider the matter of illustration. And it seems most convenient, in default of any record of an indoor public performance of this date, to introduce the third of my four exhibits from the Shakespeare Exhibition in Tokyo, which shows a public outdoor performance in an inn-yard (Pl. 4).

The photograph used as the basic setting was one showing the

New Inn at Gloucester, taken before its recent modernizations. In this particular yard there are reputed to have been performances by sixteenth-century travelling players.

The first overlay-sheet near the photograph was painted with the spectators in the rooms overlooking the yard and with those standing near the far wall; on the middle sheet was painted the stage and booth with the actors and the standing audience in the centre of the yard; the nearest sheet showed the backs or profiles of persons supposed to be sitting in a room on the near side of the yard and looking out over the action.

Beside the disposition of the spectators, two other items have to be conjectured: the position of the stage, and the character of the stage.

The position of the stage has been chosen at the middle of one of the 'sides' of the yard leaving the 'ends' free for access; in the end farthest from the spectator is seen the carriage-way from the street by which vehicles arrived at the inn-yard. Though some specialists have suggested that the stage would be set up at that end instead of along one of the sides (cf. W. J. Lawrence, with Walter Godfrey, in *Pre-Restoration Stage Studies*), I have ventured to put my stage as shown. The argument for the alternative of a stage at the end seems to be based on the opinion that the carriage-way opening might have been employed by the players as a sort of off-stage area from which to make their entrances. But it seems to me that this idea is rather based on the supposition, formerly widely held, that a largish recess at the back, called the 'inner stage', was a regular feature of the Elizabethan public playhouse, and that this must therefore have had some similar predecessor when plays were performed in inn-yards. The carriage-way would be an obvious candidate for such a predecessor. But I am more inclined to the recent views (as stated, for example, by Dr. Richard Hosley in 'The Discovery-space in Shakespeare's Globe', *Shakespeare Survey*, vol. 12) that the so-called 'inner stage' and its effects could have been realized in practice by means other than a recess in the tiring-house wall, and that they are more likely to have had their ancestry in the booth with its traverse in front, such as is seen in the many Dutch fairground pictures. If I am right in this, then I think the carriage-way to the inn-yard would have been left free for spectators' access; and the stage would therefore be set up at the side of the yard and not at the end.

I have already hinted at my source for the character of this stage – namely the fairground stages of the Dutch pictures – but two particular features of it seem important to notice here; first, its height, and then the curtains at the back.

The height of an open-air stage is dependent on the fact of a standing audience, moreover a standing audience that may crowd fairly close about the performance. In such circumstances the actors could not be properly seen unless they were raised. And they must be raised higher for a standing audience than for a sitting audience, especially for a sitting audience whose nearest members sat at some clear remove from the stage. And so I have made the platform in this reconstruction some 5 ft. high.

The traverse curtain fronting the booth at the back of the stage is there to conceal the off-stage space – whether that off-stage space were used as a dressing-room or property-room, or merely as a place to come in from. Since it is a curtain in two halves joining in the centre, entrances can be made, (1) round either end, in which case they correspond to the two screen-door entrances in a hall; or (2) through the join at the centre, in which case they correspond to entrances through the 'travers' in a hall – indeed, if my theory is correct, they would be in fact the same thing because an entrance through the centre of a traverse is the same whether the traverse is indoors or out.

And so, not only is every major feature of a Hall-and-screens presentation provided but – working, in the reverse direction – the traverse arrangement as I have shown it could be easily set up in any empty hall which had no screens, so providing it temporarily, with the features of a fully-equipped Hall with screens.

There remain two additional points. First, 'upper scenes' could be played from a ladder against the back of the traverse bar. Second, – and it seems best to put this in the form of a question – Could the players in any way use this arrangement to present episode such as Man's passage along the hall-floor from Nature's chair at one end to World's chair at the other? Or – more particularly – could they handle the curious situations that I still have to describe in *Pacient Grissill, Apius and Virginia, Horestes* and *Susanna*, where characters seem to appear *beside* the stage, and to act upon ground level while another action goes on simultaneously but independently on the stage itself? Or again, to put the matter at its extreme and revert to techniques long past instead of anticipating techniques to come; could players on the sort of stage that I have shown present, say, in 1550, an action such as that of Herod in the Coventry Cycle when he raged on the pageant *and* in the street also (see below p. 442)?

In fact the answer to these questions is quite positive. They could do any of these things on this stage. In the first place they could set a flight of steps against the stage-front and descend by this into the yard when they required. But in the second place they could do more; they could retire into the booth, leave it by a concealed opening in the curtain at the back, and climb unseen through an adjacent window into the inn itself; walk round by corridors inside to a convenient door, enter with as much ceremony as they wished into the yard, cross the yard with full effect through the spectators, and either mount the stage as a personage 'from a distance', or go out of the yard by an opposite door without mounting the stage at all – having presented to the audience a processional interlude in the action.

Developments to Mid-16th Century
1541–1553

The Four Cardynal Vertues ∽ *Impacyent Poverty* ∽ *Nice Wanton*
∽ *Lusty Juventus* ∽ *Jacob and Esau* ∽ *Respublica* ∽ The
'Yonder he cometh' Convention

Sections 23 to 27 have brought some complications into the
picture of the development of Interludes; not only have private
Interlude performances in domestic halls begun to show innova-
tions in technique, but the evidence of the Civic Accounts has proved
that raised stages could be used in presentations in public halls, and
this may have had some reflexion on the methods of ordinary
domestic Interludes after about 1550.

The present sections, 28 to 34, cover two reigns. In 1547 Henry
VIII died and was succeeded by (1) the young Edward IV who
reigned for six years, and then was followed in 1553 by (2) Mary who
died in 1558. The first four Interludes assigned provisionally to this
period are *The Four Cardynal Vertues* (c. 1541), *Impacyent Poverty*
(c. 1547), *Nice Wanton* (c. 1550) and *Lusty Juventus* (c. 1550). These
four may be treated fairly briefly; they show few signs of any
notable development in method, and seem rather to belong to a
relatively early phase of the form.

28 The Four Cardynal Vertues

Of *The enterlude of the .iiii. cardynal vertues* we possess only the last
four leaves, which were discovered in the binding of an old book
in 1950 and were described by Frederick S. Boas in *Theatre Notebook*,
vol. 5, no. 1 (Oct.–Dec. 1950).

The pages contain confirmation of two points of Interlude technique; the symbolic investment with new garments of a character

349

who changes heart (Justice says to Fortytude, 'as our brother be thou shall In token wherof take this crowne ryall With this robe and garment gay . . .'); and secondly, a reference to the place of performance (Fortytude towards the end of the play recapitulates his actions in the earlier part saying, '. . . and ye have in mynde Of my fyrste commynge into this hall For then aduersytye men dyd me call . . .').

But at the very end of the play is something arousing particular attention. The colophon is –

Thus endeth the enterlude of the .iiii.
cardynal vertues, & ye vyces contrarye to them.
Imprynted at London in Fletestrete
at the sygne of ye George by wyl
lyam Myddylton

and there then follows a woodblock. The block (see Fig. 20) shows a scene where a fool in an ass-eared hood is haranguing two men in a town square, or a wide perspective street of houses. It might seem that here is the information so desperately needed – namely, a pictorial record of the appearance of a Tudor Interlude in actual performance. Unfortunately experience with earlier blocks in printed plays leads one to feel no surprise at reading, in Boas's article quoted above, that the block 'is identical with that in section 34 of Wynkyn de Worde's 1517 English edition of Brant's *The shyppe of fooles.*' The reason for its presence here is simply that 'Myddylton may have chosen this particular woodcut from the great variety in *The shyppe of fooles* to illustrate an interlude directed mainly . . . against . . . worldly power and possessions.' There seems no justification for supposing the block shows the action of any Interlude; and I think there is still less justification for reproducing it as is done in Phyllis Hartnoll's *A Concise History of the Theatre* over the caption 'A scene from the *Interlude of the Four Cardinal Virtues*', and adding a comment in the adjoining text that 'Heywood's Interludes, and those of Rastell and Redford, . . . were probably given in a setting of houses on each side of a street which owed something to Renaissance Italy.'

I will leave further consideration of this idea of a street of Renaissance houses as the setting of early plays till the note on *Gammer Gurton's Needle* in Section 35

FIG. 20. The woodcut on the final page of *The Four Cardynal Vertues*

29 *Impacyent Poverty*

The title-page of the second play in this group reads –

A Newe In
terlude of Impacyente pouerte
newlye Imprynted
M. C. LX.
Foure men may well and ease
lye playe thys Interlude.

Peace and Coll hassarde and Con
scyence, for one man.
Haboundaunce and mysrule for
another man.
Impaciente pouerte, Prospery-
te, and pouerte, for one man
Enuye and the sommer for another man.
T.R.

The colophon reads –

Imprinted at London, in Paules
Churche yearde at the Sygne of
the Swane by John Kynge.

351

I have used the edition in Tudor Facsimile Texts, No. 47, reproduced from the sole copy in the British Museum (C34, i, 26).

The following points are worth extracting from the text, mostly as confirmation of matters already discussed in greater detail above.

Near the beginning of the play is a clear reference to the performance taking place in a hall; the character called Peace concludes a scene with the main character called Impacient Pouerty and, as they leave, Haboundaunce makes an entrance, as usual addressing the audience. Peace ends his speech:

> Then let vs departe for a season
> yf ye nede I wyll be your protection   Exiunt ambo
> HABOUN. Ioye and solace be in this hall
> Is there no man here, that knoweth me at al [. . .]
> Haboundaunce is my name [. . .]

Another good example of audience address comes on folio C.ii, where Impacient Pouertie, now transformed in his circumstances and dress, and renamed Prosperitie, enters while Envye is speaking. Envye greets him by his old name, then apologizes:

> I crye you mercye I was to blame
> To call you by your olde name
> yet all these people thynke ye are the same [. . .]

– which is a pleasant way of ensuring that the audience are not misled by the new costume. And there are other examples of this direct audience-address. At the end of their dialogue Prosperitie leaves with the old excuse –

C.ii. *rev.*   A lyttle season I wyll from you goo
                         To solace me wyth some recreacyon

Envye sneers at him behind his back, and then a marginal direction gives a hint of yet another usage made of the screens to achieve an effective entrance – this time for a new character named Mysrule. Envye's lines at this point are:

> [. . .] To brynge hym to mysrule I holde it beste
> For he can soone brynge it to passe
> Now what rutterkyn haue we here   Here mysrule
> I wolde he were oure subchauntere   syngeth wtout
> Bycause he can so well synge   comminge in.

and then Mysrule enters and begins to speak. So what happens is that he begins to sing 'off', he is heard and commented upon, and only after that does he enter through the screens into the action. Envye and Mysrule now plan together how to seduce the rehabilitated Prosperitie – but suddenly they notice Prosperitie himself returning, and Envye whispers sharply –

> Peace whyst I se hym come
> PROSPE. God saue al thys honourable companye [. . .]

– so Prosperitie gives the typical entrance-salutation though he went out only a page and a half ago!

In the next turn of the action the opening character, Peace, re-enters to try to save Prosperitie, but Envye and Mysrule together set on him with a particular effect suggested in the direction –

> (And here they face Peace out of the place)

– this presumably means that they grimace fearsomely at him and force him backwards; after he goes, Envye scoffs –

> Howe saye ye, was not thys a good face
> To dryue a knaue out of the place
> MYSRULE [. . .] Thou loked as thou hadde bene madde

The Place is again referred to later in the play when a character called Coll Hassarde has won all Prosperitie's goods from him at game-play, and has promised to share the winnings with Mysrule, but then quarrels and refuses. So Mysrule, with Envye trying to check him, attacks Coll Hassarde and –

> Here they fyght and runne all out of the place
> And then entreth prosperite poorely and sayeth

– but after his brief 7-line soliloquy, Mysrule returning from the chase, cries,

> I am so angry I wote not what to do
> That yonder knaue scaped from me so

Poor Prosperitie is later reduced to Povertie again, and resumes his old name. He is abandoned by his recent companions and is then apprehended by the Somner who takes him out for chastisement. And then

> Here entreth ye somner agayne, & pouerte
> foloweth him with a candell in his
> ha*n*d deoyng penau*n*ce aboute the place.
> And them fayth [*then sayth*] the somuer.

353

> Rowme syrs auoydaunce
> That thys man maye do hys pennaunce
> POUER.   Now haue I my penaunce done
> SOMNER. Nay thou shalt aboute ones agayne

Here, then, is a quite clear demonstration of an Interluder using the whole of the available hall-space for his action, and even spreading wide enough to justify another character's appealing to the audience to give him wider space still as he circles for the first time and afterwards is made to circle 'ones agayne'.

Peace next comes in to help; he reclothes Povertie who then assumes the name Prosperytie once again. Peace turns to the audience with –

> Soueraynes here may ye se proued before you al
> Of thys wanton worlde the great fragilyte [. . .]

– and Prosperytie adds,

> Withe the supportacyon of thys noble audyence
> we haue here shewed thys symple enterlude

and the conclusion follows, with a prayer for the Queen.

In recapitulation; the phrase 'about the place' is, I believe, a fair justification of the definition of 'Place' as I outlined it above on p. 187, and it is additionally useful in suggesting how a character in an Interlude might take possession of a whole floor space and perambulate round it in a piece of business – in this instance particularly effectively since he is carrying a candle through the dimness of the hall.

30 *Nice Wanton*

Nice Wanton (c. 1550) is probably for children to perform at court. It exposes the evils of playing truant from school, includes a fairly technical dice game, has a trial scene with a judge sitting to take the verdict of a jury, and references to going out by separate ways; but all could be handled smoothly in the normal Interlude technique.

I use the Tudor Facsimile Text edition (No. 82) copied in 1908 from a text of 1565 in the British Museum (BM C.34, *i.* 24). The title-page with its moral verses is as follows:

'Nice Wanton'

A pretie Enterlude
called Nice Wanton
Wherin ye may see,
Three braunches of an il tree:
The mother and her Children three,
Two naught and one godly.

Early sharp that wilbe thorne,
Soon il that wil be naught:
To be naught better vnborne,
Better vnfed then naughtily taught.

Et magnum magnos, pueros puerilia decus.
Players.
The messenger

Barnabas.	Iniquitie, bayly arrant.
Ismael.	Xantippe.
Dalila.	Worldly sham [*shame*]
Eulalia.	Daniel the Judge.

Imprinted at Lon
don at the long Shop adioyning vnto Saint
Mildreds Church in the Pultrie, by
John Allde.

There is a typical heralded entrance early in the play, which also gives some slight suggestion of the opening atmosphere; the two 'naughty' children, Ismael and Dalila, have displayed their vices and have quarrelled with their 'godly' brother, and so a neighbour called Eulalia determines to inform against them to their over-fond mother, Xantippe. She is speaking alone in the place and ends (fol. A.iii) –

I will go shew their Parents neighbourly:

– then she stops and adds,

Neuer in better time their mother is heerby.
God saue you gossip / I am very fayne,
That you chaunce now to come this way:

– thus heralding the entrance of Xantippe.

Later, there occurs one of the most remarkable instances in all Interludes of time-condensation (fol. B.i.*rev.*); the villain of the piece, Iniquitie, leads the young girl astray, but they eventually quarrel over the share-out of gaming winnings and Dalila says to him,

355

> Yea by the masse they shall box you for this geer:
> A knaue I found thee, & a knaue I leue thee heer.

and she flounces off in disgust. There then follow no more than 7 lines of soliloquy from Iniquitie while she is gone, ending with a conventional farewell to the audience:

> I wil tary no longer heer,
> Farwel, God be with ye.

at which he too goes out, leaving the Place empty. But next follows straightway the entrance of an oddly pathetic little figure, as indicated in this remarkable marginal direction (which is partly cropped in the original but is to this effect) –

Da | lila
co | mth in
ra | gged,
he | r face
hi | d bea-
rin | g on
a s | tick.

– she immediately says,

> Alas wretched wretch that I am, [. . .]
> My sinewes are shrunk, my flesh eaten wt pocks, [. . .]

– thus she has run through a whole youth-time of sin in seven lines.

Her godly brother, Barnabas, is the only one who will take pity on her and he promises (fol. B.iii) –

> I wil clothe and feed you as I am able.
> Come sister go with me you haue need of releef.
>
> > They goe out.

Immediately upon their exit there comes in a new character, with Iniquitie beside him, now acting the part of his officer or bailiff –

> Daniel ye
> Iudge &
> Iniqui.
> ye Bayly
> errand
> come in
> the Iudge
> sitteth.

Daniel, the judge, must therefore have had a chair set for him. He says (and it is interesting to notice his reference to 'the Kings maiestie' when the final lines of the play offer compliment instead to 'the Queenes royall maiestie' alone, suggesting that the play itself is of an earlier date with a revised ending composed for Queen Mary) –

> As a iudge of the countrie heer am I come,
> Sent by the kings maiestie iustice to doo: [. . .]
> I tary for the verdit of the quest ere I go.
> Go bayly, knowe whether they be agreed or no /

Iniquitie answers 'I go my Lord . . .', but what he in fact does instead is try to bribe the judge in an aside, as the marginal direction shows ('He telleth him in his eare yt all may hear'), to exercise a favourable judgement on Ismael, the 'wicked' brother –

> [. . .] I beseech your Lordship be good to him: [. . .]
> if your Lordship would be so good to me:
> As for my sake to set him free.
> I could haue twenty pound in a purse:
> Yea and your Lordship a right fair horse,
> Wel woorth ten pound.

DANIEL. Get thee away thou helhound. [. . .]

And later Iniquitie is seized, protesting, and put alongside Ismael: 'They take him in a halter & he fighteth'. He has eleven lines of struggling vituperation, then the judge cries –

B.iiii. Away with them bothe lead them away: [. . .]   they lead
> If no body heer haue ought to say: them out.
> I must go hence some other way.

– and 'He goeth out'. The words 'some other way' seem to suggest very strongly that the Judge leaves by the other door in the screens, not the one the prisoners left by.

The conclusion of the play is crisp and bitter and contains one vivid line about the eventual fate of Ismael; a fresh character is brought in to sum up the situation, under the name of 'Worldly Shame', and he says to the audience, reviling Xantippe –

B.iiii.*rev.* Now sir[s], Dalila her daughter is dead of ye pocks;
> and her sonne hangd in chaines & waueth his locks.

A little later Xantippe herself walks in to this sad scene and Shame heaps reproach upon her for not controlling her children –

C.i. The cause of their death is euen very you

357

There now follows a particularly interesting direction which be-side stating the action which the player must take, actually quotes the word-cue on which that action must come, namely, 'The cause of their death . . .' –

> At the cause of their death she would swoun.

– then Shame exclaims in contempt 'Wilt thou swoun? . . .' and leaves her.

She recovers and echoes his grim lines about the fate of her two children –

> My fair daughter Dalila is dead of the pocks,
> My deer sonne Ismael hanged vp in chaines:
> Alas the winde waueth his yelow locks, [. . .]

She is so distracted that 'Shee would stick her self with a knife', but 'Barna*bas* co*m*meth in' and reproves her and checks her hand. He points his mother to better ways and sends her out to 'comfort my father', adding –

C.i.*rev.* I haue a little to say I wil come by and by.
Right ientle audience by this enterlude ye may se,
how dangerous it is for the frailtie of youth . . .

– and so on and so forth. Eulalia makes a brief entrance to support his homily, and then Xantippe returns to add a last word, then 'Heer kneel down.' and they pray for the Queen, and then sing.

31 *Lusty Juventus*

The Interlude called *Lusty Juventus* (c. 1550) is by R. Weuer or Weaver; I have used Tudor Facsimile Text No. 70. The title-page reads

> An Enterlude called
> lusty Iuuentus,
> Lyuely discribing the frailtye of youth:
> of nature, prone to vice: by grace
> and good counsayll, trayne-
> able to vertue
> : :
> The names of the players.
> Messenger.
> Lusty Iuuentus.

> Good Counsell.
> Knowledge.
> Sathan the deuill.
> Hypocrisy
> Felowship.
> Abhominable lyuing.
> Gods mercifull promises.
> Foure may play it easely, taking such partes
> as they thinke best: so that any one take
> of those partes that be not in
> place at once

The note at the end of the list of players is interesting.

Lusty Juventus offers a typical example of heralded entrance near the opening; a character called Good Counsell is talking to the central figure Lusty Juventus, or Youth. He concludes his speech as follows, while a marginal direction informs us that at the moment Knowledge is entering –

A.iiii. Beholde youth now, of whom reioyce we may,
　　　For I see knowledge of God, and verity stand here behind,
　　　He is come now to satisfy your mynde,
　　　In those thynges which you will desyre,
　　　Therfore together let vs approch him nere,

– thus the first two, Youth and Good Counsell, are some way up the hall when they see Knowledge, and they turn and go down to greet him. In his reply Knowledge says ' . . . Now good christian audience, I will expres my name . . .'

Later, an even more distinct example is provided. During a dialogue between a somewhat comic Devil (who provides the only light relief in this sombre play) and his son Hipocrisy, in which the downfall of Youth is plotted, the lusty young man himself appears in the entry, and Hipocrisy breaks off and then puts a bold face on the situation and goes to accost him with false heartiness:

　　　　　　　　　　　　　　　　　　　　　Youth entreth.

C.ii.*rev.*　HIPOCRISY. What Maister Youth,
　　　　　　　Well I met by my trouth,
　　　　　　　And whether away?
　　　　　　　You are the last man
　　　　　　　Whych I called on,
　　　　　　　I sweare by thys day.
　　　　　　　Me thought by your face,

> Ere ye came in place
> It should be you:
> Therefore I dyd byde
> For your comming, this is true.

The plot is that Youth should be subjected to the seductive charms of a young lady rather ponderously named Abhominable Living. Youth is eager to meet her, and abandons a 'preaching' meeting in favour of an introduction to her through the intermediary of Felowship. Abhominable Living is a servant in a house where her free hours are only 'betwene eyght and nine, / And then her maister & misters wil be at the preaching'. Felowship and Youth approach 'her house' and pause. Felowship explains that –

D.iii.   She wyll come her selfe anone
             For I told her before where we would stand,
             And then she sayd she would becke vs with her hande
IUUENTUS. Nowe by the masse I perceiue that she is a gallaund
             What wyll she take paynes to come for vs hether?
HIPOCRY. Yea I waraunt you, thefore you must be familier wt her
             When she commeth in place, [*etc.*]

Now the young lady utters a sudden whispered speech. Where she speaks from is not indicated; it might be the other screens-door, it might even be the gallery above:

> Hem, come away quicklye,
> The backe dore is opened I dare not tarry,
> Come felowship come on a waye.

Youth falls for all this, and as a consequence receives a long dia-tribe from Good Counsell, which is typical of its kind but which contains one line worth noting:

E.iii.   [. . .] The tyme were to long now to recite
        What whordome, vncleanes, and filthy abomination
        Is dispersed [*?*] with youth [. . .]
        To aduance your flesh, you cut and iag your clothes, . . .

The interest lies in the fact that jagging was not used as a form of decoration after about 1475; it would thus seem to have been a curious accusation to make in the mid-sixteenth century, and it suggests that the play is at least an adaptation of an older one, if it is not in fact itself ascribable to an earlier date than 1550.

Hazlitt in his edition of Dodsley has a crisp description of this particular Interlude; he calls it 'didactic to a fault' – and that is not far wrong.

32 Jacob and Esau

The previous four Interludes were relatively simple in matters of technical presentation and therefore were treated briefly. The one now to be considered, *Jacob and Esau*, c. 1550, has certain problems which demand that it should be taken in more detail.

I have used the reprint in the Malone Society Reprints edited in 1956 by John Crow. The editor makes some points in his Foreword that have a bearing on the presentation; the first of these is particularly interesting because it notes the division of the play into acts and scenes (*Jacob and Esau* is one of the earliest examples of an Interlude so divided), and points out that 'The construction and the division into acts and scenes suggests the author's acquaintance with the humanistic religious drama of the sixteenth century'. If this is so, then it is also possible that he would know of the theories of the time about the classic stage with its entrances; the one on the actor's right for characters coming from the near neighbourhood, and that on the left for characters coming from a distance. This could have a bearing on a query raised in the following study of the play.

Six copies of the 1568 edition are known. The title-page reads:

A newe mery and wittie
Comedie or Enterlude, newely
imprinted, treating vpon the Historie of
Iacob and Esau, taken out of the .xxvij.
Chap. of the first booke of Moses
entituled Genesis
The partes and names of the Players
who are to be consydered to be Hebrews
and so should be apparailed with attire.

1 The Prologe, a Poete.	7 Hanan, a neighbour to Isaac also.
2 Isaac, an olde man, father to Jacob & Esau.	8 Ragau, seruaunt vnto Esau.
3 Rebecca an olde woman, wife to Isaac.	9 Mido, a little Boy, leading Isaac.
4 Esau, a yong man and a hunter.	10 Deborra, the nurse of Isaacs Tente.
5 Jacob, a yong man of godly conuersation.	11 Abra, a little wench, seruant to Rebecca
6 Zethar a neighbour.	

Imprinted at London by Henrie
Bynneman, dvvelling in Knightrider streate,
at the signe of the Mermayde
Anno Domini. 1568.

This is the first of the nine Interludes that Chambers grouped together for special remark, as I have indicated in the review of his opinions at the beginning of Section 8 (see especially p. 149 above). His reference in full is as follows (*Elizabethan Stage*, III, 24–5):

> I come now to nine interludes which, for various reasons, demand special remark. In *Jacob and Esau* (>1558) there is coming and going between the place and the tent of Isaac, before which stands a bench, the tent of Jacob, and probably also the tent of Esau.

A little later he goes on to say that this is one of the plays that –

> differ from the normal interlude type by some multiplication of the houses suggested in the background, and probably by some closer approximation than a mere door to the visual realization of these. There is no change of locality, and only an adumbration of interior action within the houses.

I have already pointed out the possible sources of confusion that seem to lie here. Craik remarks on this passage that 'Chambers states that three tents – of Jacob, Esau, and Isaac – are wanted' (and it cannot be denied that Chambers does seem to do this). Craik himself now adds his own view – 'The play could in fact be staged without scenery, but I think a "house" representing "the tent", with Isaac's bench standing before it, is desirable' (see his Note 24 to p. 13 of *The Tudor Interlude*). All this seems to me a good example of the difficulties that lie in the way of any attempt to reconstruct the presentation methods of the Interlude when considered from the point of view of a normal, semi-professional troupe of common players. There are admittedly difficulties in reconstructing a presentation by common players of *Jacob and Esau*, but I propose to put both the views aside for the moment and go through the play examining these difficulties afresh in the light of the knowledge of Interlude-presentation gained so far in this study.

The play was very probably intended for performance by children. It is a fascinating play, with some of the subtlest character drawing to be found so far in the Interludes, and one speech of outraged fury from Esau that is colourful enough for the great Elizabethans themselves. But my special concern in the present study must be confined to the problem posed by the many references to *tents*.

Naturally, such a word (recalling the *tenti*, or *pulpita*, or 'scaffolds' of the Mysteries) turns the minds of some writers to the possibility that these tents might be representational built 'houses' on the lines either of medieval scaffolds or of the later scenic 'mounts' and 'houses' of the Elizabethan Revels Accounts. This is clearly an important matter to settle in any study of the development of play presentation before Shakespeare.

But before taking up in detail the references to tents, I would like to see how far an explanation may be offered of that remarkable observation on the title-page, immediately following the words, 'The partes and names of the Players'. In effect the observation is that since the characters in the play are Hebrews they are to be treated as Hebrews even to the extent that – and this is the remarkable conclusion – they should be 'apparailed with attire'.

I think there can be little doubt about the intention of the phrase, though it reads strangely; it simply means 'dressed in costume' – that is, not in ordinary dress but in the *costume* (or customary clothes) of the Hebrews.

It is true, of course, that any ordinary dress is in fact *costume* if it consists of clothes customary to whomsoever is wearing it. But we have come to use the word as meaning not ordinary dress but special dress. In this connexion the observation on the title-page is particularly interesting because it belies the school of thought which holds that all early plays were performed in ordinary, contemporary clothes and that no early players had any sense of special costume. I have already tried to show that Interluders could have a very particular sense of the significance of costume; but this reference gives a clear and additional proof that the actors of the mid-sixteenth century were not only not content to let their Bible characters go in any clothes that might be seen in their own streets, but that they sought to dress Hebrews *as* Hebrews – or at least to *apparel* them, in the sense of equipping them in a suitable way (probably the word is from the Latin *adpariculare*, to make equal or fit), and further to apparel them with *attire* (which seems to be a word of unknown origin).

There is one other thing about the opening of *Jacob and Esau*, before I go on to take up the considerable problem of the tents. It concerns an indisputable piece of evidence about the place of performance being a Hall, and about the effect that could be made by an actor entering the Hall through the screens. The opening of the play – after some 20 lines from the Poet as prologue – is marked with a direction in the margin reading:

> Ragau entreth with his horn at his back,
> and his huntyng staffe in hys hande, and
> leadeth .iij. greyhounds or one as may be gotten.

This would be effective enough, and the suitability of such an entrance in such surroundings is obvious; but the full effect possible in the circumstances is caught in another direction some 50 lines later, reading:

> Here Esau appereth in sight, and bloweth
> his Horne, ere he enter.

The words 'appereth in sight . . . *ere he enter*' are immediately significant. Nowhere else could a player appear in sight *before he entered* save in an arrangement such as that provided by the screens with their doorways into the entry-passage beyond. Not only did Esau come into sight along this passage, but he paused there a moment 'ere he entered' and, framed in the door, unslung his horn and blew a blast upon it that was (as the text later shows) enough to wake the neighbours – to say nothing of rousing up the excitement of the guests in the torchlit hall and putting them all agog for the show. It would be as arresting an opening to a play as the piece of impudence at the beginning of *Fulgens*.

Having mentioned this acting-direction, I turn to the references to tents. The best way of reviewing these is to list them in order and to take each in turn.

(1) The first reference is a very simple one; in the list of characters on the title-page Deborra is described as 'the nurse of Isaacs Tente'. This has a certain implication – namely, that the word *tent* is used here to apply to a family dwelling, so that 'Isaacs Tente' signifies something housing not only Isaac and Rebecca, but also their nurse, and probably their servants Mido and Abra, and possibly one at least of their sons, Jacob. (To Esau's dwelling I shall have to give some special consideration in a later reference.)

(2) The next reference is at l. 58 where Ragau, the hard-worked servant of Esau the hunter, complains that '. . . we disease [*disturb*] our tent and neighbours all With rising ouer early eche day . . .'. But this clearly need not be a reference to any specific visible scenic tent; the line is simply referring to 'our household and the neighbours'.

The question rises, did Ragau mean by '*our* tent' a tent which belonged only to Esau and his family; or did he mean a larger, general tent that housed all of them – not only Esau, but Isaac and all his family as well – includnig incidentally Jacob? This is a crucial question, but it is difficult to answer. It will be necessary to see if any hints can be gathered in the rest of the play.

(3) At l. 101 Esau remarks disparagingly of his brother Jacob that, he 'must keepe home I trow, vnder mothers wing, To be from the Tentes he loueth not of all thing.' Here 'Tentes' must refer to the village or encampment in general and not to any specific property tents that might be represented in the action. There is also another suggestion behind the lines here; that Jacob, since he must be 'vnder mothers wing' all the time, may in fact still live in Isaac's family tent. Of Isaac's tent I shall have more to say later.

(4) The next reference is at l. 119 when Ragau, echoing his master's disparagement of Jacob, says, 'Jacob shall keepe the Tentes tenne yeare for Ragau' – in other words, he's a stay-at-home and may remain so for all Ragau cares. But again no hint of a practicable tent.

(5) Next, at l. 132, a neighbour called Hanan complains of the noise Esau makes with his hunting horn so early in the morning that 'no neighbour shall in his Tent take any rest'. Again this is a reference free from any implication of a scenic 'house'.

(6) At l. 158 Hanan is contrasting the characters of the two brothers to his friend Zethar and says of Jacob that he is God-fearing and 'keepeth here in the Tentes lyke a quiete man' instead of being wild like Esau. Again an innocent and general reference.

(7) Next, at l. 259 is a reference that demands a little more study. Jacob at this point is being persuaded by his mother Rebecca to take part in the famous deception that will bring him his elder brother's birthright; at the end of the conversation he leaves her with the words, 'I will againe to the Tent. Well you bee. *Exeat Iacob.*' This seems more explicit; the tent is mentioned and the announcement of going 'to' it is immediately followed by an exit-direction. This suggests that something representing the tent must be there, into which Jacob walks. It might be a scenic property, or simply a screens door. Also, the words, 'I will *againe* to the Tent' rather imply that on his entrance earlier in the scene Jacob had come out from that same 'tent'. When one refers back in the text to check this, it is to find that Jacob's entrance is preceded by Rebecca's line, 'Come forth sonne Jacob, why tarriest thou behinde?' – to which Jacob, stepping forward, then replied, 'Forsoth mother, I thought ye had sayd al your minde.' And she – 'Nay, come I haue yet a worde or two

more to say. . . .' etc. This goes to confirm the suggestion above that there is something standing for a tent in which a character can wait 'behind' while another character enters.

(8) The next reference offers confirmation that Jacob lives with his mother and father in their 'tent', for Rebecca says of him that he – in contrast to Esau – 'liueth here quietly at home in the Tent', l. 364. This seems a specific reference.

(9) The next reference is particularly important. It is contained not in a speech but in a marginal direction. Opposite l. 621 we read:

> Esau entring
> into Iacobs tent
> shaketh Ra-
> gau off.

The situation at this point is that a hungry Esau has prevailed upon Jacob to agree to give him a meal. The equally famished Ragau follows the two brothers to the tent entrance (whatever it may be), hoping for some part in the meal, but Esau 'entring into Iacobs tent' to eat, pushes Ragau away. This particular phrase, 'into Iacobs tent', has perhaps led some investigators to believe that Jacob must have had a separate, practicable tent for them both to go into; but we have already seen that it is pretty certain that Jacob in fact lives with his family in Isaac's tent, and thus that the action described in the direction would take place at the entrance to Isaac's 'tent'. This tent has still to be defined, but for the moment I merely note that what is apparently a clear reference to a specific tent for Jacob is not necessarily so at all.

(10) The next reference has a curious puzzle in it. It comes at l. 673, where Isaac's small guide-boy, Mido, tells Ragau afterwards how the meal in the tent went off, and he says that Ragau could have had no chance of a share in it because Esau 'praide Jacob ere he did begin, To shutte the tent fast that no mo gestes come in.' One can perhaps use the phrase *to shut* a tent, in the sense of closing the tent-flap and tying it, but the words seem more suggestive of a door; and so a theory might perhaps offer itself once more that the 'tents' were represented by the screens-doors.

(11) The next reference is again a very important one. After the meal and after having sold his birthright, Esau comes out again and orders the hungry, waiting Ragau to accompany him on a walk. Ragau refuses. Then Esau changes the command to: 'Then go see all be well in my parte of the tent.' *In my part of* the tent might imply

that Esau (as well as Jacob) lives in Isaac's tent or in part of that tent; and thus that, after having eaten with Jacob in Jacob's part of the tent, he then came out and sent his servant to see that all was well in his own part of the tent.

(12) Next, at l. 971, the old, blind Isaac has had a talk with his son Esau and has asked him to find some venison for a meal; Esau agrees to go out to hunt for some, and the old man concludes, 'Then helpe lead me home, in my tente that I were set. And then go when thou wilt.' This again points to a specific, visible place for Isaac's tent and home.

(13) The next reference comes from the little serving-maid Abra, at l. 1083. Here she replies to an enquiry from her Mistress Rebecca as to whether she has washed her dishes properly – 'There is not one foule peece in all our tent I wene.' The phrase *our* tent confirms that Rebecca and Abra live in the same tent, which is of course also Isaac's.

(14) Next, at l. 1094, Rebecca reinforces Abra's statement about cleanliness with, 'let no foule corner be about all the tent' – again, obviously Isaac's tent.

(15) At l. 1113 Abra continues and proudly proclaims that, in view of the forthcoming feast of venison with which Esau is to supply his father – 'I will not I trow be found such a sluttishe beast, That there shall any filthe about our tent be kepte', but that she will sweep it 'both within and without'. Once again a reference to 'our' tent and surely to a specific one. An accompanying direction in the margin here says, 'Then let her sweepe with a brome . . .' and she sings a song as she sweeps.

(16) Not only Abra but, as we saw, Deborra also belongs to this 'tent', and at l. 1163 Deborra the nurse says, after some words about the little girl, 'But it is time that I into the tent be gone. . . .'

(17) Later, when the trouble really begins to brew, Jacob and Mido enter from the fields with a young goat with which to supplant Esau's venison; and Jacob sees his mother waiting eagerly for them. As he approaches he exclaims, 'But loe I see my mother stande before the tent' (l. 1196). Again a specific reference to a specific tent, and again that of Isaac.

(18) At l. 1253, after Mido has gone in to wait on Isaac, Jacob – who is left outside – says to himself, 'I were best also to get me into the tent.' Again the same 'tent'.

(19) Then, rather significantly, the next reference is from an angry, fuming Esau who realizes at length what he has been tricked

out of, and cries (l. 1547), 'But as for these misers within my fathers tent, . . . I shal coyle them till they stinke for pain'.

(20) And finally, at l. 1697, Isaac, the old man, weary at all the politic forbearance which the situation has demanded of him, says, 'Now will I departe hence into the tent againe.'

These are all the references. They are twenty in number, and in all of them there is no mention of any tent that demands portrayal as a specific, visible object – except one; and that is the 'tent' of Isaac. Of the twenty references, five are merely general (nos. 2 to 6 inclusive), one is, for the moment, puzzling (no. 11); all the other fourteen settle down into references to one 'tent' – Isaac's.

What else now does the text offer about this dwelling of Isaac's that has not already been brought out in the list of references given above?

Something may be learned from the actions of the characters using this tent. Strictly speaking I think this object, whatever it is, should not be confidently called a tent at this point; all that can be said of it is that it is something standing for Isaac's tent. Therefore I shall use the word in quotation marks for the present, signifying 'that which is called Isaac's tent'. There is however no reference anywhere else in the text of the play (save one alone) to anyone else's tent, therefore it may simply be called 'the tent'. (The unique other reference is in the acting-direction no. 9 about Esau entering 'Iacobs tent', which however I have argued is the same tent as Isaac's.)

Not unnaturally the chief information about the method of using Isaac's 'tent' comes in Isaac's own lines. And the first such reference is a somewhat puzzling one; at l. 271 the blind Isaac says to his small guide-boy, 'Leade me forth of doores'. This direct allusion to doors in the plural exactly suggests the use of the screens entrances upon which I have laid so much emphasis in earlier chapters, and might thus be held to confirm the hint mentioned in reference no. 10. But I think there can be no doubt that here the phrase occurs quite simply, and means no more than 'lead me out-of-doors, into the open air'. It is admittedly a stretch to speak in these terms of leaving a tent, but the expression is so idiomatic as to be acceptable as natural in the context.

This context runs in full as follows: At the opening of I.iv. we have the first speech from Isaac in the play. The previous scene has ended by Jacob bidding farewell to his mother, Rebecca, and leaving her in the Place. His last words to her were those quoted in reference no. 7, 'I will againe to the Tent. Well you bee *Exeat Iacob*.' The new scene now opens with Isaac speaking:

269. ISAAC. Where art thou my boy Mido, when I doe thee lacke?
     MIDO. Who calleth Mido? here good maister Isaac.
     ISAAC. Come leade me forth of doores a little I thee pray.
     MIDO. Lay your hande on my shoulder, and come on this way.

It may be important to notice that these lines (whether the speakers are at the moment visible or concealed) occur almost immediately after Jacob's apparent exit into the same 'tent', and that the speakers soon come out into the open from that very 'tent'. Thus it might be that we shall find there are more entrances than one to this 'tent', in view of the unfortunate collisions that would otherwise occur at such moments of nearly simultaneous going in and coming out.

This may be the moment to remember the puzzle in reference no. 11, when Esau speaks of *my* part of the tent, because that puzzle could now be explained by supposing Esau had his own entrance to the family tent, as Jacob his brother seems also to have had. This would mean that we have to retain for checking the idea that Isaac's 'tent' had three possible entrances.

To resume; now Rebecca alone in the Place speaks four lines to herself, praying for Jacob's success. After this Mido, without seeing her, next continues,

> Syr, whyther would ye goe, now that abroade ye be?
> ISAAC. To myfe [*my wife*] Rebecca.
> MIDO. Yonder I doe hir see.

– so that now they are 'abroade', or clear of the 'tent', and Rebecca in the Place is now visible to Mido. She, however, does not see them and continues her prayer for two more lines. After this, Mido says to Isaac,

> Yonder she is speaking, what euer she doth say:
> By holdyng vp hir handes, it seemeth she doth pray.
> ISAAC. Where be ye wife Rebecca? where be ye woman?
> REBECC Who is that calleth? Isaac my good man?
> ISAAC.A. [*sic*] Where be ye wyfe Rebecca, lette me vnderstande?
> [The 'A' has obviously dropped from 'Rebecca' in the line above.]
> MIDO. She commeth to you apace.
> REBECCA. Here my lorde, at hande.

And Isaac now discusses his blindness with her. I have quoted at some length here because the successive speeches build up into some sort of picture; the first four lines of the scene, from l. 269 on, might perhaps be spoken in the concealment of the 'tent'. There is such a change of atmosphere on Mido's question, 'whyther would ye goe, *now* that abroade ye be?' that it would seem that some particular piece of business had been effected during the four lines of Rebecca's prayer, such as the negotiating of the 'tent' opening by Mido, with blind Isaac's hand on his shoulder, before they came out together into the open Place. Once out, they do not at first see Rebecca – true to Interlude tradition – while she in turn does not see them, in spite of their conspicuous entrance, until even later.

The scene now is a longish one, and at the end of it Isaac concludes the discussion with his wife with the words –

439.   Well, nowe go we hence, little Mido where art thou?

and after a short comedy scene from Mido, Isaac repeats,

    Well, come on, let vs goe.

– and Mido asks –

    And who shall leade you? I?

– and Rebecca says –

    No, it is my office as long as I am by. [. . .]

– and, though there is no direction for them, they must then leave the Place for the end of the first act, and so presumably return into the tent.

Much the same sort of business is repeated at the opening of III.i.; here it is Esau who comes into the empty Place saying it is a long time since he saw his father, but he immediately interrupts himself with – 'But he commeth forth, . . .' and Isaac's voice takes up –

    On leade me forth Mido, to the benche on this hand, [. . .]

Mido replies,

    Here syr this same way, and ye be at the benche now,
    Where ye may sit doune [. . .]

– and then Isaac asks after Esau. Mido offers to go and look for him and so, clearly, Esau is not visible to him yet. Then Esau speaks; Isaac recognizes his voice, Esau confirms, and then Mido has the rather curious lines –

    Here he is come now inuisible by my soule:
    For I saw him not till he spake harde at my poule,

('harde at my poule' would imply 'just behind my head'). Isaac orders him –

    Now go thou in Mido, let vs twoo here alone.

At the end of their discussion Isaac says to Esau,

971.   Then helpe lead me home, in my tente that I were set.
           And then go when thou wilt.

Another interesting sequence concerning Isaac's 'tent' comes in IV.iii. and iv. Rebecca has 'come to see if Iacob be gone a fielde yet,' and, finding he has, decides to check with Abra the maid that all things be in readiness for his return with the food for Isaac. She calls, 'Abra, where be ye Abra?' Abra answers, 'Here within maistresse.'

At this point I might pause to remark on this curious theatrical usage of the word 'within'. (Linked with the same usage are such phrases as 'to go in' and 'to go out' and 'to come out' or 'come forth'.) We have had some introduction to this matter in a general way in *Hester* where the King *entereth* the traverse at the same time as Aman *goeth out* – both terms indicating, in effect, an exit. The action of leaving the scene may be expressed in opposite ways: 'to go in' in the sense of going in to the screens or to a booth or tiring-house at the back of the acting-area, or 'to go out' in the sense of the classic word 'exit'. Similarly, an action or speech occurring 'off' may either be termed 'within', or – equally commonly – 'without'. But by Abra's 'within' there is no doubt, I think, that she means 'within the tent'; had she spoken from the entry outside the screens, she would have said, 'Here without', on the analogy of Aman's going *out*. As it is her 'within' is more reminiscent of the King's entering, or going *within*, his traverse.

Rebecca's response to Abra is 'Come forth', and after a short delay the maid comes out, possibly with a broom, and says she has been washing up the 'vessells' and now there is 'not one foule peece in all our tent'. Rebecca tells her to 'make a great fyre' and other preparations; Abra turns, but Rebecca cries, 'Nay, soft, whither away? I haue not yet all done.' and orders spices and herbs to be fetched, adding 'let no foule corner be about all the tent' (l. 1094). Abra promises and asks, 'Is there any thing else but that I may go now?' Rebecca says, 'Nought' and six lines later, 'Now will I go in to see . . . mine olde husband,' so she must enter the 'tent'. Abra, left outside, snatches the broom and gives the lines quoted above at reference no. 14:

> I will not I trow be found such a sluttishe beast,
> That there shall any filthe about our tent be kepte,
> But that both within and without it shall bee swepte.

371

Then follows a song and the marginal direction 'Then let her sweepe with a brome, and while she doth it, sing this song, and when she hath song, let her say thus'. Her words are –

Now haue I done, [. . .]
Now but for fetting mine herbes I might go play.

– and she calls Nurse Deborra, who answers, 'What is the matter? who calleth me . . .?' Thus Deborra must come out of the tent; and then Abra hands the broom to her and adds that she herself 'must to the gardine . . . to fet hearbes . . .' and she runs out, presumably (since she is going away from the tent to some nearby garden) by one of the screens-doors. Deborra, left behind, reminisces for a moment and then says 'it is time that I into the tent be gone.' So she too goes, but now into the 'tent'.

The next scene, IV.v., is Abra's alone; she returns and has 16 lines beginning 'haue not I dispatched me quickely?', and later adding 'But to tary here thus long, I am muche to blame', and then she clearly goes into the tent with her herbs. Immediately she does this, Rebecca enters to open IV.vi. with the line, 'I come to see if Iacob do not returne yet,' – and there is again a suggestion that she might have to come from the 'tent' by another entrance if she is to avoid collision with the energetic little Abra. There is scarcely more than the slightest flavour of such a thought on this particular occasion, but the idea does definitely grow that this 'tent' might need to have two or more entrances.

Jacob now enters and it is at this point that he sees his mother standing before the tent. He must have come in by a screens-door, since he comes from 'abroad', having captured a kid in the fields.

The situation at the end of IV.viii. is particularly impressive. Rebecca has dressed Jacob's arms in the hairy, skin 'gloves' to deceive his blind father into thinking he is the hirsute Esau, and she tells him 'the meate by this time is ready . . . Take thy time, and assaile thy father when thou wilt.' Jacob, covered with shame at the trick, says 'Goe before, & I folow: but my chekes will blushe red, To be sene among our folke thus apparailed.' Then they must both go into the 'tent'. But *immediately* upon this follows IV.ix., which begins with Isaac summoning Mido as usual to conduct him out 'to sitte abrode, and take th' open aire', and Mido answers, 'That shalbe well done, the weather is very faire.' It is thus almost impossible to imagine that this quiet movement of Isaac and Mido *out* of the 'tent' could have immediately followed the entries of Rebecca and of the disguised and blushing Jacob *into* the tent, *by the same entrance*! This is finally clinched when, only four lines later, Jacob comes out of the 'tent' again saying 'Where is my most dere father?' – and then answers himself with – 'as I would haue it, Taking the open ayre, here I see him sitte.' The case for more than one entrance to this 'tent' seems indisputable. Later in the scene, Jacob leads Isaac back in to the fateful meal.

Again in the next scene, IV.x., Rebecca enters and describes how the meal is going on within the tent. She gives a brief 6-line interim report to the audience and then says, 'But I will in to harken how the thing doth frame.' The line is explicit; she is about to re-enter Isaac's tent – but immediately Mido runs out, warningly, crying 'Come in dame Rebecca' – and Abra unexpectedly adds 'My maister Isaac is comming foorth streight way.' On which, Rebecca concludes, 'He shall not finde me here in no wise if I may.' And immediately Isaac and Jacob come out to the bench to begin the next scene. Rebecca could not in these circumstances have gone in by the same entrance as her husband and son were coming out by!

It will, I think, not require any more evidence to confirm (1) that Isaac's tent is represented in some practical way; (2) that no other tent need be represented; (3) that whatever object stands for Isaac's tent must be big enough to conceal some five or six people at a time; and (4) that it must have at least two – and preferably three – entrances.

It will also be obvious to a reader who has followed this whole study so far, that an object already exists in the tradition of Interlude presentation (as I have constructed that tradition) which entirely fulfils all these requirements – and that is the traverse.

Turning to Fig. 21, the central opening could be used for all entrances of Isaac, either by his parting the curtains slightly and stepping through or if need be by drawing them wider apart and so effecting a 'discovery'. Equally, the spaces either side the pair of curtains as a whole, could be used as side entrances in a sense that would allow independent entry into the main 'tent' – or, as Esau put it in reference no. 11, into 'My parte of the tent'.

Further, this traverse as shown in the figure is of a size adequate to conceal, or to be understood as concealing, the requisite number of actors. If, however, a different system were used, and separate free-standing tents were built in the nature of 'scenic houses', then

373

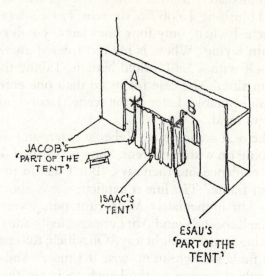

JACOB'S
'PART OF THE
TENT'

ISAAC'S
'TENT'

ESAU'S
'PART OF THE
TENT'

FIG. 21. A suggestion for a simple hall setting of *Jacob and Esau*

it seems to me quite obvious that the amount of space that they would take up in any normal domestic Tudor Hall, where a banquet was being served with the play as an Interlude, would be quite insupportably objectionable.

Thus, in conclusion, I find reason to agree with Craik (in the footnote to his p. 13) that this play 'could in fact be staged without scenery, but I think a "house" representing "the tent", with Isaac's bench standing before it is desirable' (but with the proviso that for 'house' we may read 'traverse') – rather than take Chambers' view that three tents – those of Jacob, of Esau and of Isaac – are wanted.

After *Jacob and Esau*, the next play listed by Craik is Sir David Lyndsay's *Ane Satyre of the Thrie Estaitis* in 1552, originally performed in a shorter version in 1540. This shorter version is now lost. From the point of view of the present study this is especially to be regretted because the earlier performance was probably an indoor one, and may have been closer to the tradition I have been discussing; whereas the later version falls outside it as being certainly an outdoor performance and probably more in the presentation tradition of *The Castle of Perseverance* than that of the Interludes.

33 *Respublica*

Respublica as the title-page says was performed in 1553 before the newly enthroned Queen Mary; it was thus – at any rate at its first presentation – not a common Interlude but a play designed for court performance and by boys.

In respect of this staging of plays at court there is a preliminary point that seems of special importance. Magnus in his Introduction to the Early English Text Society's edition of the play (Extra Series XCIV, 'from Mr. Gurney's unique Macro MS. 115', published 1905) quotes a number of documents from 1553, the year of the production, containing various warrants from Queen Mary for material to be delivered to performers by the Master of the Royal Wardrobe or by the Master of the Revels. A typical opening to these documents runs somewhat as follows:

> We woll and commaund you vppon the syght hereof furthwith to provide and deliuer vnto the berer hereof, for . . . a play to be playde before vs . . . suche necessary stuffs . . . as hereafter folowith . . . etc., etc.

That is a typical opening; now to the material specified in the body of the warrant to be delivered to the players; in one warrant the material is specified as –

> . . . suche shewtes of Apparrell in as ample and large maner as other owre musitions heretofore have byn accostomed to haue at the lyke Feastes . . .

– in another, as –

> . . . theis *p*arcills of Sylke Followinge . . .

– in another –

> . . . all suche nessessary stuff and other thing*es* as
> hereafter folowith . . .

and then follows a list of garments and items of dress. Then again –

> , . . all suche necessarie garments and other things . . .
> as shal be thought mete and convenyent . . .

– and once more (this time relating to Nicholas Udall) –

> . . . such apparell . . . as he shal thinke necessarie and requisite for the furnisshinge and condigne setting forthe of his devises before vs . . .

The significant point, as it seems to me, which is suggested in these quotations is the stress laid upon costumes, as against any scenery, in the preparation of these earlier court entertainments. In the later Records of the Revels Office under Elizabeth I there is on the other hand much mention of, for example, 'howses', mounts, and mechanical devices such as pulleys and clouds; but in these earlier warrants from Queen Mary's time, the subjects covered are almost wholly confined to clothes. So far then the indication is that the dressing of the court plays at this date was more important than what we should today call their 'setting'; and even in the last warrant quoted, where the 'condigne setting forthe' of devices is mentioned, the specific item necessary for that setting forth is 'apparell'.

A further preliminary point about this boys' presentation of *Respublica* comes in the contrast of two different writers' viewpoints. On the one hand it is interesting to see that Schell and Shuchter, the editors of the edition of the play printed in *English Morality Plays and Moral Interludes*, say (p. 235):

> It is probably misleading to think of *Respublica* as having contributed to the development inr damatic form, for it was played, as far as we know, only at Court and only in the special occasion mentioned in the Prologue, and it was never printed . . . [it was] meant for performance by children.

And at the other hand we have to put Hillebrand's enthusiastic insistence (referred to above on p. 152) that the plays of the child actors at court were the most formative influence on the drama of the period 1515 to 1590. Thus can different conclusions be drawn from the same evidence.

The opening page of the manuscript reads:

> A merye enterlude entitled Respublica, made in the
> yeare of oure Lorde 1553, and the first yeare
> of the moost prosperous Reigne of *our* moste
> gracious Soverainge, Quene Marye the first: /

> The partes and names of the plaiers.

The Prologue.	a Poete	
Avarice.	all*ias* policie,	The vice of the plaie.
Insolence.	„ *Authoritie,*	The chief galaunt.
Oppression.	„ *Reformation,*	an other gallaunt.
Adulation	„ *Honestie,*	The third gallaunt.

People.   representing the poore Commontie.
Respublica.   a wydowe.
Misericordia. ⎫
Veritas.   ⎪
Iusticia.   ⎬ fowre Ladies.
pax.   ⎭
Nemesis.   the goddess of redresse *and* correction. A
                    goddesse.

The especial feature I now want to examine in the present context of technical presentation is the method used in this play for handling the entrances and exits of the players so as to link the scenes together. This feature is common in Interludes but it is particularly well-suited for study in *Respublica*, since the author has consistently used what was then a relatively new convention, based on the study of the classic drama, of dividing his script into acts and scenes. Generally he takes the entry of a character as the occasion of the beginning of a fresh scene, so that a 'scene' is, in copybook fashion, the subdivision of an act, marked by the entrance or departure of one or more actors.

In this particular interpretation of the word 'scene', the writer does not make each of the scenes in an act a separate self-contained unit, with a deliberately constructed beginning and end; instead, he rather links the scenes together arranging a deliberate and special 'transition' between them, so that the characters at the end of one scene notice, or in some other way herald, the coming of the character or characters who are to take part in the next scene. These 'transitions' are something like a bridge passage in music, arranged to effect a modulation from one key to another. But the main thing about them is that they are clearly a contrived effect with a purpose; the purpose being to accord with, and accommodate, that particular form of entrance where players come into a hall from the screens-entry through the bystanders, and so are forced to make not an instantaneous entrance but one deliberately phased over some number of seconds of time – occasionally a considerable number. In brief, it is a convention designed to suit performers using screens-doors. This 'transition effect' is employed only between scene and scene; between act and act there is a complete break with no transition.

What I propose, therefore, to do now with *Respublica* is to review it noting each of these scene transitions in turn, and afterwards to add a comment on the convention and its relation to the later Elizabethan playhouse technique.

The play opens with a soliloquy in the form of a Prologue by the Poet; we learn that the season is Christmas and that the players are 'boyes' performing to an adult audience – 'We children, to youe olde folke . . .'

The transition between the Prologue and the first scene is quite a simple one but, all the same, obviously designed; the Poet says in conclusion,

57.   Nowe, yf yowe so please, I wyll goe & hither send, /
         That shall make youe laughe well, yf ye abide thend. /
                          Finis /

There is no exit-direction but since the Poet uses the words 'I wyll goe . . .' of himself, and 'yf ye abide . . .' to the spectators, there is almost certainly an exit; thus leaving the audience to await what follows.

59–122.   *Actus primi, scena prima.*

And what in fact follows is that the character who is distinguished in the list of players as 'The vice of the plaie' now greets the audience. He is called Avaryce (and during the play he will assume the alias of 'Policie'). He comes in crying, 'Goddygod' to everyone, 'Goddiggod to yowe all', and proceeds with a soliloquy outlining the gist of the plot to come. He makes pointed reference to his need to fill certain 'purses *that* hang att my bakke', and goes on to mention a 'store' that he has got tucked away accumulating at home. This store brings him to the device employed as the transition to the next scene; it is his falling into sudden panic lest he has left his 'Cofer Open' so that the hoard may be rifled. And he runs off to find out; he has a clear direction '*Exeat*'.

We are thus left ready for the next scene. This particular transition was, thus, abrupt and unusual; the Place is left empty for a moment. Then we presumably hear certain voices 'off' singing rowdily; there was nothing in Avaryce's last words to prepare us for this, and – perhaps for that reason – we find the new scene open with one of the relatively rare entrance-directions in the play; as follows –

123–154.   *Actus primi, scena secunda.*
              ADULACION, INSOLENCE, OPPRESSYON. / *Intrant Canta*[n]*tes.*

No words are given for their song and it is perhaps delivered outside in the hall entry, and continues only so long as it takes the three

characters to come through into the Place. At all events, the first line
of the scene is part of a speech from Adulacion, who exclaims,

> Oh noble Insolence, if I coulde singe as well,
> I wolde looke in heaven emonge Angells to dwell.

– and some badinage follows. The three rogues now explain that
their intention is to take advantage of Respublica and swindle her
out of all she and her realm possess. They speak of the absent
Avaryce as the fittest to counsel and lead them in this scheme, and
in so doing they set on foot what is one of the most elaborate
and artfully engineered transition-effects in the whole play. It
begins in this way: Oppressyon is speaking and says of Avaryce:

> he knoweth where & howe that Money is to be hadde,
> And yond*er* he cometh, me thinketh, more then half madde.
> [*Intrat* Aver. /

155–342.   *Actus primi, scena tertia.*

This is as clear an instance as could be wished of a 'heralded'
entrance. But it is perhaps worth pausing a moment before going
on to what follows, in order to try to see the operative sentence
with a fresh eye. It is the sentence which I have used as the title of
my next section – 'Yonder he cometh'. It has become so hackneyed
a line that we are inclined to overlook the particular implication
behind it. What, as I see it, is implied when one bears in mind the
evidence presented so far in this study is that the entrance in question is one which though it is made quite openly is, in some respect
or another, an entrance remote from the acting-area where the other
characters have been speaking – remote either by reason of being
simply some little distance away from them, or by reason of being
partly obscured – so that the character entering cannot be fully
seen at first but only glimpsed.

In this particular instance there is also another quite different
purpose; namely the indication, before he fully appears, of the
newcomer's mood – he is 'more then half madde'. But the essential
words for our present purpose are 'yonder he cometh'.

I am well aware that the objection might be raised that I am
reading more into a simple statement than it contains. But such an
objection, I feel, would be based on an idea that the line is no more
than a typical actor's line carelessly thrown in but signifying
nothing. Has it not indeed become almost a joke of Shakespearean
ham – 'Yonder he comes!' instead of 'Here he is!'

But if the Interluder really meant 'Here he is!' why did he say 'Yonder he comes'? I think the answer is an obvious one; the Interluder did not say, Here he is! because 'he' was *not* 'here' at that particular moment; 'he' was in the process of getting there; he was still 'coming', though coming quite obviously, and he would be there as soon as he had threaded his way through the crowd and reached the spot where the other actors were. This is an inevitability because of the conditions of performance in Interludes presented in a hall; and since those conditions existed, they were accepted and exploited. The continuity of the action was maintained by such acceptance, and the situation was turned into a means of quickening the dramatic interest.

Whatever may be the truth of the above, there is no doubt that what follows now is one of the best examples in all Interludes of the effect of 'differentiation of acting-area', or of one character proceeding with his own scene quite oblivious of the remarks of the other characters to whom he had just entered – even, as in this case, while they make repeated and unsuccessful attempts to address him. The situation here goes on for 30 lines, as follows:

Avaryce, as soon as he is fairly entered, begins a 12-line speech of extravagant relief at having been in time to prevent his store being rifled. Then Insolence says to his two companions –

> Let vs speake to hym and breake his chafing talke.

– but it is to no purpose, for Avaryce rattles on. Next, Oppressyon tries to catch his eye –

> Lett vs call to hym *that* he maye this waye Looke.

Note that the suggestion in 'call to hym', and 'this waye Looke' (with a capital L), is that Avaryce is still some little distance from them and completely oblivious of them. And he continues to talk to himself. Then Adulacion takes his turn to try to reach him with a fine greeting –

> All Haille our Fownder & chief, Mr. Avaryce.

Still not a wink of notice from Avaryce, who goes on talking to himself. So Adulacion tries yet again –

> when ye see yo*ur* tyme, looke this waie yo*ur* frend*es* vppon.

– but again Avaryce continues to himself. In fact, Adulacion has to make two more separate attempts of the same sort before at last Avaryce is prompted to demand irritably (l. 180) –

Whoo buzzeth in myne eare so? [. . .]
what clawest thowe myne elbowe, pratlinge merchaunte? . . .

– so they are now in touching distance. Some sort of contact having now been made, the beginning of a conversation is attempted, but it is still some lines yet before any real exchange is possible. At length the four knaves plot together to get service under Respublica, and eventually to ruin her.

This is a long scene, but there is one more scene to follow before the end of the first act. The transition between these two scenes is an odd conceit. The present scene ends with Avaryce telling the other three to be all in readiness for a call from him to come and join Respublica's household; Oppressyon and Insolence specifically indicate that they will come to him at the very first summons he may make. Then follows an unusual direction: '*they go foorthwarde, one after other*'. The general intention here seems clear enough; namely, that 'they' (that is, as the text shows, Insolence and Oppressyon, with Adulacion hanging a little behind) begin to go out one by one, but the adverb 'foorthwarde' is puzzling. It is unlikely to mean 'go forward' since as we have seen the Interluders did not act in any particular directional sort of way; the likelier meaning is 'go forth', but modified to imply 'forth toward' the exit door, as if about to leave, but not quite out. The lines confirm this, for Adulacion, bringing up the rear of the file, says to Avaryce as he passes him –

Doe but whistle for me, and I comme foorth with all.

And Avaryce acknowledges this with –

That is well spoken. I love suche a towarde twygg.

It is then that the odd transition begins to take place; the three rogues are traipsing off in single file to the doors at the far end of the hall, and Avaryce (having been told to whistle for them when he wants them) watches them go. The picture could be quite a mildly amusing one for the audience to look at, and to be made to suppose by it that the situation was now over. But next comes the surprise; there is a simple direction for Avaryce, following his last line as he watches them go; it is '*he whistleth*'. Immediately now Adulacion responds with – 'I comme, fownder.' – and Avaryce calls –

And co*mm*e on, backe againe, all three, come backe agayne.
INSOL. Owre founde*r* calleth vs backe.
OPPR.   retourne then amaigne.

It is pretty clear that each departing figure stops in his tracks,
turns on his heel, and all simultaneously begin to walk back again –
which, well timed, could easily turn the mild amusement into a
laugh.

The implied exit, then, was a pretence, and the careful effect of
winding up a scene was a planned deception. And so the transition
to the next scene (which is not really a new scene at all, but a continuation of the last) becomes a joke, for no sooner are the players
walking out than they are walking in again.

It is not uninteresting to notice that in Magnus's 'Analysis of the
Action' of this play, he says of the above episode, 'The scene closes
in a pantomime picture, in which the Vices (who faithful to medieval precedent are mainly clowns) drill round and round the stage
in comic discipline.' This is on the whole very fair; but the Vice is
generally a single figure (as the list under 'the Names of the Plaiers'
shows him to be here), and in character he is very much more than a
mere clown; but chiefly, I believe the whole situation just described
can almost be said to owe its very existence to the fact that it was *not*
conceived for a raised stage. It would be far more effective when
presented on a hall floor and exploiting the screens entrances and
the surrounding spectators.

Now at length we come to what is treated as the last scene of the
first act; immediately after Avaryce's summons to the other 'gallants' to come back again, we have the heading –

343–438.   *Actus primi, scena quarta.*

Now Avaryce launches into a new piece of comic business with
the words 'Com*m*e on, syrs, all three'; this consists simply of the old
Interlude gag of providing each character with a new name to hide
his true self. The scene runs for just under 100 lines and concludes,
significantly enough, with no transition, so preparing the way by
a complete break in the action for a fresh act. Avaryce finishes his
lines by saying he is about to go out and find Respublica and, when
he has found her, he will, at 'a tyme convenient', 'saie and dooe that
maie bee expedient'. The finality of this sort of scene-ending is of a
quite different nature from any previous one and distinctly marks
the end of an act. The directions show that the three lesser gallants

go off first ('*exeant*'), and that the Vice follows them after his final line ('*exeat* Avar.')

461–460.   *Actus secundi, scena prima.*

The new act opens normally, as an independent unit, with the first appearance of Respublica herself; there is no transition or anticipation of her entrance. The first scene is very short and consists simply of her 20-line soliloquy on the troubles of state that beset her. At the end of it, however, there is a transition, but one with a new touch. It consists of an acting-direction reading as follows:

> *Intrat* Avar. *cogitabund*us *et ludibund*us.

– which is to say, in effect (if I might venture such a translation), 'Enter Avaryce, musing and acting a gag'.

461–533.   *Actus secundi, scena Secunda.*

What Avaryce is musing and gagging about is the clutch of empty purses under his cloak – 'Alas, my swete bag*es*, howe lanke and emptye ye bee . . .', and so forth. This is all spoken in one part of the Place while Respublica, quite oblivious of his entry and his speech, goes on with her soliloquy in another, their speeches alternating; until Avaryce suddenly observes her and pulls up short – immediately on his guard lest he expose his motives . . .

> Hahe! who is that same *that* speaketh yond*er* in sight?

(notice how 'yonder in sight' suggests that she is now visible to him but still some little way apart from him)

> Who ist? Respublica? yea, by the Marye Masse. [. . .]
> Hide vp these pipes. Nowe, I praie god she bee blynde:
> I am haulf afraide leste she have an yei behynde.
> we must nowe chaun*n*ge *our* Coppie: oh, lorde, whowe I fraie
> lest she sawe my toyes & harde whatt I dyd saie.

– and he cloaks up. But she goes on, still oblivious of him, till he makes a spoken reference to his alias of 'Policie'; this word she catches, and it makes her turn to see who and where he is. Only after that does she add (a little pathetically) –

> I praie youe: come to me if youe be Policie.

Then at length he comes closer to her, and normal dialogue begins. The whole transition between II.i. and II.ii., has taken 20 lines.

Towards the end of II.ii., Avaryce tells her that he will go and

fetch his three confederates so as to introduce them to her, and he has
an exit-direction. Respublica speaks a few lines while he is away,
and then the transition to the next scene begins. This time it is quite
a simple one, and it is explained by the direction '*Intrat* Avaricia
adducens Insol. Oppr. *et* adulac.' (enter Avaryce bringing in Insolence,
Oppression and Adulacion), and while they are all approaching
Respublica across the floor she has time to murmur –

> And behold where he is returned againe seens:
> he Shewith himselfe a man of diligence.

Then the new scene begins.

534–597.   *Actus secundi, scena tertia |*

The transition continues; as the four advance they discuss Respublica among themselves, but without her hearing them although
she has already seen them! It is interesting to notice, also, that the
three knaves whom Avaryce is now bringing in do not apparently
see Respublica at first, for after a crack from Adulacion about her,
Avaryce hisses a quick rebuke at him –

> Ye quadrible knave, wi' ye ner vse modestie?
> Thowe dronken whoresone – doest thowe not see nor *perceive*
> where Respublica stand*es* readie vs to receyve?

But she clearly does not catch the drift of their words, for she
murmurs to herself –

> what talke have the*ye* yond*er* emong them selves togither?

(What a relish these small choirboys could have had in all this
intrigue!) Adulacion now presumably peers through the shadows,
and sees her, for he whispers eagerly –

> I have spied hir nowe. Shall I first to hir thither?

– but Avaryce snatches his arm and checks him –

> Softe; lett me *present* yowe.

All this time Respublica is wondering at them in her corner and now
she says to herself that she will have to encourage them to approach–

> I weene thei be in feare:
> Polycye, approche & bring my goode frend*es* nere.

– and after a line or two they at last advance and Avaryce says to her,

> Madame, I have brought you*e* these men for whom I went.

384

– and the scene now gets under way smoothly and clearly with nice engineering and considerable effect, having made capital out of the lapse of time dependent on any full entrance of a group of characters into the hall.

And now, towards the end of this scene, Respublica goes out leaving them to consult among themselves how to improve (as she hopes) her affairs. Behind her back they make their decision, which is to sing a song, the name of which is given in the direction, and go their ways – '*Cantent. "Bring ye to me & I to ye," etc., et sic exeant.*' This leaves the Place empty, and there is no transition now to the next scene – which is clear indication of the end of another act.

598–610.   *Actus tercia, scena prima.*

The third act opens like the one before it with a short scene in which Respublica appears alone; she delivers a soliloquy of 12 lines ending –

> Loe where Cometh Honestie: he wyll the truthe tell.

– again a heralded entrance for Adulacyon (alias Honestie) to come in and open III, ii.

611–636.   *Actus tercij, scena secunda.*

Adulacyon begins with a couple of lines to himself gloating on the first perquisites he has managed to rake in from Respublica's estate, and then he suddenly comes to his senses and sees that he is in her presence –

> Bones, heare is Respublica, what vse I suche ta[l]ke?

– and he changes face and goes to meet her.

After a couple of dozen lines a transition is again arranged with the heralding of the entrance of a new character. This is a rough, shrewd, goodhearted peasant called People, representing the populace over which Respublica rules. Adulacyon is properly suspicious of his shrewdness, and is annoyed at him for interrupting his schemes:

> RESPUB.   [. . .] but loe, yond*er* cometh People.
> ADUL.   I had thought as soone to have mette here Paules
>   steeple.

637–751.   *Actus tercij, scena tertia.*

People is very direct. He sees Adulacyon at once but does *not* apparently see Respublica. He speaks in broad stage dialect:

> Whares Rice-puddingcake? [. . .]

Adulacion immediately tries to pull his leg; he protests he does not know the name. People is not to be put off, for he knows that 'this waie she came'. Respublica draws herself up in her shadows and orders with rather faded dignity, 'lett my people come to mee', and only then is People able to come and lay his troubles before her.

Towards the end of this scene, Respublica and People have the direction 'exeant', and the transition to III.iv. falls to Adulacion with the following lines –

> But nowe I wolde Avarice [. . .]
> [. . .] were heare [. . .]
> And Loe where Avarice comth, a woulff in the tale!
> (as the *proverbe* saithe) what dothe he after hym hale?

– and so the action is now off again, to a new phase.

752–775.   *Actus tercij, scena quarta.*

What Avaryce is in fact 'haleing', or hauling, is his clutch of now-filled money bags. As usual the first lines are a monologue to himself, or rather to the 'swete bags' – and he does not see Adulacion for 7 lines as he is dragging them in along the floor. Then suddenly he is aware of him and immediately on his guard:

> what nowe, brother Honestie? what prye ye this waie? [. . .]
> looke of from my baggs [. . .]
> ye can see no grene cheese / but yo*ur* teethe wyll watier /

But his fear is lulled, and the two begin to descant on the ill-gotten gains, when Adulacion says –

> But looke, who cometh yond*er* puffing and tuffing?

(again 'cometh *yonder*', not 'cometh *here*'). And with this very simple and direct transition we come to –

776–827.   *Actus tertij, scena quinta.*

The new, bustling figure is Oppressyon; he comes in and straightway reports his own gains to the other two. After some 50 lines Adulacion thinks he hears Insolence clearing his throat outside:

But softe, peace! me thinketh, I here hym hem and hake:
If we mete here all fowre, we shall some ordre take.

Thus there is again a smooth, simple transition of the usual kind –

828–969.   *Actus tercij, scena sexta.*

Insolence now appears and greets his three cronies directly,
without any hesitation or intervening soliloquy. Avaryce is again
afraid his friends will dip into his money bags, and insists on their
standing 'a goode waie hence', while he tells them how he filled the
bags. After various digressions Oppressyon, Insolence and Adulacyon run out (*'exeant currentes'*), leaving Avaryce who addresses himself to his money bags once more, and finally drags them out (*'exeat'*).
The scene and act are now over, and there is no transition.

970–985.   *Actus quarti, scena prima.*

The fourth act opens, like the others, with the appearance of Respublica in a short soliloquy; she wonders how People is faring and
would talk with him; then, sure enough –

And loe, as I would wishe, he approcheth hether.
                                              Intrat people.

986–1001.   *Actus quarti, scena secunda.*

They meet at once and fall into dialogue straight away, for
People's condition is urgent and grave. They mention the need to
discuss the situation with 'Policie', *i.e.* Avaryce. Immediately then
the convenient formula of transition is repeated yet again by
Respublica saying, 'I see hym yond*er* appere: . . .'.

1002–1050.   *Actus quarti, scena tertia.*

Avaryce (or Policie) appears in a conciliatory mood, but People
blames him roundly for bringing the state near to ruin. Avaryce asks
their permission to go and fetch his fellows to help in their general
defence. The transition now has an interesting variant; Avaryce
would seem to go out though there is no direction, then –

1051–1168.   *Actus quarti, scena quarta.*

Avaryce, Insolence and Oppressyon appear and begin (a little
surprisingly, since he is there present) with an outspoken plot to
get rid of People; they are of course taking advantage of the convention that any opening lines need not be heard by those characters
already in the Place. Insolence's question as they are coming in is:

Couldest thowe by no meanes make the peasaunte afearde?
AVAR. No, but anon I trowe we shall his Masship trym;
Conveighe hir awaie / & than all wee three chide hym, [. . .]

but Respublica does not hear their actual words, and only declares, 'I here Policies voyce'. At last, however, they all meet, and there follows a longish scene of strenuous argument between the five characters, at the end of which Respublica is persuaded to tell People 'to hope a while longer' for any improvements in his living-conditions; and then she departs (*'exeat* Resp.') leaving the four to continue the argument among themselves. People is roundly attacked by the rogues and then sent out (*'exeat'*). Insolence follows to go home (*'exeat'*). Oppressyon in his turn, to 'go abrode' (*'exeat'*). And finally Avaryce goes to see who has been hanging about his door (*'exeat'*). This brings the end of the scene and the end of the act, and therefore there is no transition.

1169–1208.   *Actus quinti, / scena prima.*

The last act has ten scenes. There is a straight opening like those of the previous acts, but the soliloquy is this time from a new figure, not Respublica, but Misericordia or Mercy, who tells of God's mercy and how she has been sent to comfort Respublica and to help redress her affairs. Then the transition to V.ii. is brought about by her saying of Respublica,

> & Loe, me thinketh, I see hir appere in place,
> of frendshipp devoyde / & of succoure destitute.
> I will heare hir and than geve wordes of solace.

(Note how the old phrase 'in [the] place' persists; and also how she clearly proposes to listen unseen at first.)

1209–1338.   *Actus quinti, scena secunda.*

Respublica now appears, but does not see Mercy, and speaks 12 lines of lamentation upon which Mercy intervenes with 'Now I will speake to hir'. They discuss Respublica's situation and Respublica then turns to herald an entrance by saying,

> but yond cometh one of them, *that* doe me governe.

Avaryce now appears, oblivious of them and cursing certain citizens who are trying to reduce his profits. Mercy asks, 'what talketh he?' (so she can see him but not hear what he says), and Avaryce checks at her voice and stealthily asks, 'who speaketh yond, Respublica?' (so he can hear her though not recognize her voice). Eventually he is introduced to Mercy, and then changes his tone to fawning. Mercy now leaves ('*exeat* Mia.'). Avaryce, alias Policie, bids her a polite farewell –

> Good Misericordia now / and Ladie mooste deare, –

– and then explodes in rage behind her back and turns on his heel:

> Christe blister on yo*ur* harte; what Make your heare? –
> RESPUB. Come backe, Policie.
> AVAR.   I come.
> RESP.   whither woulde ye nowe?

– and an uncomfortable passage follows, broken by the entrance of Adulacyon who wants a word in private with Avaryce. The rogues are in great concern; they exchange whispered confidences together and Adulacyon leaves ('*exeat* Adul.'). Respublica is suspicious and asks what they were talking about (so she has not heard what they said). Avaryce hurriedly leaves ('*exeat*'), and '*Intrant Mis*ericordia *et* veritas.' Respublica has prayed for this interruption, and remarks,

> behoulde een with the worde speaking, where thei bothe bee.

This line ends the scene and forms the quick transition to –

1339–1394.   *Actus quinti, scena tertia.*

Mercy and Truth exchange a few words as they come in about Respublica's position, before they see her, and then Mercy greets her with, 'How nowe, Respublica? have I not been Long hens?', and the three ladies get down to a detailed examination of the troubles of the times. Truth reveals the tricks of the four swindlers. Mercy announces that two new characters, Justice and Peace, are on their way with help, and then Mercy makes the transition to V.iv. with,

> I will leave youe here with my syster Veritee.
> And learne of their coming wyth all celerytee.

– but Truth interposes –

> ye nede not; For I knowe thei bee nowe veraly here,
> And beholde they begynne alreadie to appeare.

Thus we have an indication that a supernatural figure could even *sense* an impending entrance! and beyond that we have the extremely interesting and significant implication in the phrase 'begynne alreadie to appeare', that entrances of this kind might indeed be events extending over several moments of time.

1395–1430.   *Actus quinti, scena quarta.*

Now Justice and Peace, the two who have just come in, greet each other – '... leat vs twoo systers kisse / In token of oure ioyn-ynge ...' – which is pretty certainly indication that they have entered simultaneously but by opposite doors (to use an Elizabethan phrasing), and that they now meet in the Place. After the greeting Truth says, 'Leat vs meete theym, Sister Misericordia/' and these two now advance and Respublica is presented to Justice and Peace. At the end of a short scene Mercy proposes to celebrate this 'blys-full renovacion' with an old and well-known Interlude device:

> Nowe, Sisters, goe wee and Respublica with vs
> to be Newe appareled otherwyse then thus.

– and so they go out, singing as they go ('*Cantent*, The mercye of God, *et exeant etc.*').

There now follows a complete break as if we were to enter a new act. One supposes the author might have been daunted by the number of scenes still to come, and so proposed a sixth act but re-frained from calling it such because of classic tradition. So there is no transition, and we have –

1431–1484.   *Actus quinti, scena quinta.*

This is opened by Avaryce, alias Policie, coming in and bitterly reviling the beggars in the streets who cry to him, 'geve, geve, geve, geve'. And then he checks with –

> But who cometh yond? Honestee? he cometh in haste?

Adulacyon, alias Honestie, appears and as usual does not at first see Avaryce, for he cries,

I seke Policie.
AVAR.   here, boye.

– and then the two exchange their bad news in great perturba-tion; Adulacyon is sent off with a message to the other two swind-lers ('*exeat*') and Avaryce suddenly pulls himself up with the shocked realization –

> And loe, where Respublica appereth in sight.

Intrat Resp.

– again a phrase suggesting a gradual, or partly obscured entrance; he does not say 'comes' but 'appereth in sight'. Then:

> She is nowe att [? *hand*] hyr Nymphes bearing vpp hir traine;
> I will stande a syde, & Lysten a worde or twaine.

So there is little doubt what he himself does, though the first of the lines is not entirely clear, and in this way the transition is engineered to V.vi.

1485–1576. *Actus quinti, scena sexta.*

Respublica, probably in some regal state now with attendants (Nymphes), appears and begins to fuss over the exposed villainy of her councillors. In this she is overheard by the listening Avaryce who, after a few lines, insinuates himself into her discourse (incidentally congratulating her on the appearance of her new dress!). But Respublica is now no longer to be hoodwinked, and at length she dismisses him ignominiously (*'exeat'*). She then announces that she is on the point of going to join the four Ladies – when the transition to V.vii. is effected by means of the direction, *'Intrat* People', and she just has time to say while he makes his way towards her –

> But loe, heare cometh people; I will nowe tourne againe
> And firste knowe of his goode state by a woorde or twaine.

1577–1614. *Actus quinti, scena septima.*

Any dialogue between them is, however, still deferred for a few lines. People is hesitant and looks round without at first seeing her; the scene thus opens with Respublica's puzzled enquiry –

> what standith he prying? dareth he not entre?
> PEOPLE. Shoulde vaine zee my ladie: but I sdare not venter.
> RESPUB. Shrinke not backe from me, but drawe to me, my deare frend.
> PEOPLE Chill virst knowe an ye bee alone, zo God me mende.
> RESPUB. Come, here bee non but thie frends, me beleve.
> PEOPLE. well than, chil bee zoo bolde to peake in by yo*ur* leve.

All of which offers an excellent example of the capital deliberately made by Interlude-writers of the situation which gave rise to the 'remote' or 'obscured' entrances, and which is the subject of this present section.

People describes his recent poor condition and his present improvement since the Four Ladies took over. Respublica persuades him to stay behind here on his own and face his old oppressors, while she goes out (*'exeat'*); upon which, the transition to V.viii. is effected by People's saying nervously –

> [. . .] & azee, praie, if zome of om comnot yond*e*r;
> choulde my ladie had byd ner zo lytle longer. /

1615–1662.   *Actus quinti, scena Octava.*

If Respublica took her train of 'nymphes' (whatever the word indicates) with her as she went, it might have made some sort of a processional exit. But this processional exit would have lost part of its effect if on leaving she had run into the three rogues, who now enter to open V.viii.; and thus it would seem, I believe, most likely that she and her train departed by one door while the rogues came in, looking about them, at the other. They are looking for their leader, because Insolence begins with –

> where is Avarice, howe? he doeth not nowe appeare.

Oppressyon checks him with –

> But see where People staundeth. /

– and Insolence, a couple of lines later, adds –

> Let vs speake vnto hym. People, wherefore and why,
> like a loytring losell standeste thowe heare idelye?

Then they set about abusing People until Adulacyon breaks off with –

> but see where Avarice cometh rennyng veraie faste.
>   *Intrat.* Avar.

As he runs in he exclaims to the audience in general that he cannot find his mates (so he does not at first see them). But they call his attention to themselves, and then he upbraids them and washes his hands of them; they are at loss to know what to do. In quick lines they blame People, then Avaryce cries, 'thei come. we are caught', and the transition follows with a gay piece of licence by Avaryce deciding in desperation to try to turn the situation into a song and dance, so that –

1663–1814.   *Actus quinti, scena Nona.*

– as the Four Ladies come in with Respublica, and as Truth exclaims,

> Heare theye bee all fower. This is an happie chaunce. /

– so Avaryce comes out with –

> Take eche Manne a ladie, sirs / & leate vs goo daunce.

He wriggles in every way possible, but Justice is bent on arresting them all. An elaborate and witty scene of accusation and defence follows but Avaryce is unfrocked, and so his swollen purses are revealed; the others also have to doff their 'vtmost robes eche one', and so expose their true selves. Truth rules that Nemesis must be brought in.

The transition now to the final scene is probably as follows, though in the excitement of the climax the script lacks any acting-directions; Justice says to People,

> Than, people, while we ladie Nemesis doo fett,
> all these offend*ours* in thie custodie we sett,
> theim to apprehende & kepe tyll wee come againe.

It is almost certain, then, from these lines that the Ladies go out. If so, then we have the lively picture of a nimble and gloating People, like an eager sheepdog, striving to keep four desperate knaves, all near their wits' end, from breaking away and escaping. There are only five lines of exclamation here, but possibly a great deal of scurried checking and dodging, before People effects the transition with the lines –

> stande styll, skitbraind theaff, or thy bonds shall be coilled.
> yond bee thei comyng Nowe, che warte, that will tame ye.
> A zee, art thowe gon too? com*me* backe & evill a thee.

– and just as they are getting out of hand the last great entrance is made with –

1815–1939.   *Actus quinta, scena de[cima]*.

– and the forbidding figure of Nemesis appears, blocking all escape. There are now eleven figures in the action, offering a pretty effective climax in a full hall under the torches. Nemesis summons Respublica, 'Come foorth, Respublica . . .', and Respublica comes out from behind the others and identifies the malefactors. People has shrunk back before all these magnificent characters for Nemesis asks him,

> People, whie aret thow bashefull & standest so farre?

– and a comic moment is given to exploiting his fear of presumption at joining such august company. The rogues are indicated (with gloating comments from People), and judgement (tempered with mercy) is given. Nemesis leaves on other business, People apparently takes out Avaryce, Insolence and Oppressyon, though no specific direction is given, and Respublica thanks God while Peace, Truth and Justice salute Queen Mary, and then –

Cantent | ex exceant |

Finis |

34 *The 'Yonder he cometh' Convention*

This convention of what I have called the 'heralded entrance' had the very considerable effect on Elizabethan dramatic technique that I have hinted at more than once in the earlier part of this book. An almost indefinite number of examples could be quoted. To choose two –

In *Othello*, III. iii, Iago and Aemilia are speaking –

IAGO.   [. . .] Go, leaue me.   *Exit Aemil.*
    I will in *Cassio's* Lodging loose this Napkin,
    And let him finde it. Trifles light as ayre,
    Are to the iealious, confirmations strong,
    As proofes of holy Writ. This may do something.
    The Moore already changes with my poyson:
    Dangerous conceites, are in their Natures poysons,
    Which at the first are scarce found to distaste:
    But with a little acte vpon the blood,
                        Enter Othello.
    Burne like the Mines of Sulphure. I did say so.
    Looke where he comes: Not Poppy, nor Mandragora,
    Nor all the drowsie Syrrups of the world
    Shall euer medicine thee to that sweete sleepe
    Which thou owd'st yesterday.
OTH.   Ha, ha, false to mee?
IAGO. Why how now Generall? No more of that. [. . .]

The four lines beginning 'Looke where he comes:' are notoriously difficult to make convincing on a modern picture-frame stage. What can Othello do all this time? Why does he not exclaim at once? But in an Interlude presented in a Tudor Hall they would not only have occupied the time and action that a player would need for striding in from the entry, through the door and the crowd of bystanders, out to the floor and on to the open centre, but they would also have made of that short interval a vivid dramatic effect, and so allowed an intensification of the mood of the entering character by the comment possible to the character already in the action.

It is particularly interesting in this instance to compare the folio and the quarto readings; I have quoted above the words of the folio, but I have placed the entrance-direction for Othello at the line where it comes in the quartos – which is a line earlier than in the folio. Thus, in the quarto readings, the silent interval after Othello's entrance is in fact five, not four, lines long and fits as I have shown above.

Second, to take an instance of an entirely different sort; when in *As you Like it*, II.vii, the Duke Senior at table in the forest wishes to have proof that the mournful Jaques has grown musical, he says naturally enough,

> Go seeke him, tell him I would speake with him.

But on that line of naturalism there follows a line from the First Lord, to whom the order had been given, that seems unnatural, awkward and even discourteous on a conventional modern stage, namely –

> *Enter Iaques.*
> 1. LORD. He saues my labor by his owne approach.

Again, this line would fit with some small dramatic effect into Tudor-Hall conditions; and again, it must appear that its presence in a public-theatre play indicates a similarity of conditions between playhouse performance and Interlude performance.

In short; this convention of the Interluders sprang from the two-door entrance system of the screens. That it persisted on the Elizabethan public stage is, I think, a very strong argument for believing that the two-door entrance system of the Elizabethan public playhouse, as illustrated in De Witt's drawing, developed from the two-door entrance system of the Interluders in Tudor Halls.

It is of course to be expected that this convention will become modified as time goes on – like any living technique – and there comes a point when under the conditions of the public playhouse stage only a trace of it remains. An indication of how the length of entrance-heralding speeches gradually decreased in Elizabethan times is given in *A New Companion to Shakespeare Studies* (1971) in the essay on 'The Actors and Staging' by Daniel Seltzer, pp. 46–7.

He describes there the convention by which an actor 'sees the entrance of another and comments on it, covering . . . the new actor's approach to the acting-area', and adds the following observations on the chronological development of this convention:

> In the earlier period – up to, say, 1580 – this form of delivery covered . . . on an average, six lines. Usually these lines involved some descriptive comment on the approaching . . . character, delivered either to another person already on the stage or, in many cases, to the audience. The average number of lines used in such 'anticipatory' or 'covering' address in the period up to 1605–6 is closer to three lines . . . and . . . the average seems to drop off still more in plays written between 1606 and the closing of the theatres. The use of the convention itself seems to decrease; in Shakespeare's *Pericles, Cymbeline, The Winter's Tale, The Tempest,* and *Henry VIII,* and in Shakespeare's and Fletcher's *The Two Noble Kinsmen,* the average number of lines used in this category of address is only two – and such address occurs infrequently.

Part Three 1553–1576

The Rise of the Stage

Diversions from Interlude Tradition
1553–1560

Ralph Royster Doyster and *Gammer Gurton's Needle* ∽ The
Problem of the University Stage ∽ *Jack Juggler* ∽ *Wealth and
Health* ∽ Four Special Directions ∽ *Pacient Grissill* ∽ *Apius
and Virginia*

---

35 'Ralph Royster Doyster' and 'Gammer Gurton's Needle'

The first and simpler part of this review is over. From now on there
begin to come developments of several kinds. The need will be
to ravel out one clear thread and follow it through the maze of new
departures during the next twenty-five years up to the fixed event
of the first Theatre.

The novelties are all signs of a remarkable expansion in the form
of plays – new outlooks; experiments by new groups of people in
new contemporary forms expressive of themselves; importations
of new fashions of thought from abroad recast in terms of British
manners; wider explorations into character study; perfectings of
the language form into an immensely flexible medium.

I have already noted above that in the development of English
plays of Interlude form through the second quarter of the sixteenth
century a certain group had branched away and adopted methods
of presentation that were different from those of the earlier travelling Interluders; those plays were the Choir Boys' plays written
for performance at court.

Now in the third quarter of the century a different group once
more is to be found rising to importance which also employs new
methods – adult plays this time, and produced by the gentlemen of
the Inns and the Universities.

Much play-presentation had, of course, already taken place before at the two Universities (see Boas, *The University Drama of the
Middle Ages*), but this had been usually in Latin and not, so far as
one can see, based on any native tradition.

399

The plays I now have in mind are *Gammer Gurton's Needle*, and a little later, *Gorboduc, Supposes* and *Gismond of Salern*. With these can be associated *Ralph Royster Doyster*, and it will be convenient to include also under this heading *Misogonus* while we are dealing with developments. All these plays are characterized by using a method of presentation that, in one respect or another, apparently differs from the Hall and Screens method of the Interluders. To begin, not one of these plays is called an Interlude (except only *Ralph Royster Doyster*); *Gammer Gurton* is a 'Pithy, Pleasaunt and merie Comedie', *Gorboduc* (otherwise called *Ferrex and Porrex*) is a 'Tragidie', *Supposes* 'a Comedie', *Gismond of Salern* a tragedy; for *Misogonus* we have no contemporary description since there remains only a mutilated manuscript but it is certainly something quite different from an Interlude, both in its greater length and in its dramatic detail. Further, all these plays (save perhaps *Ralph Royster Doyster* and *Misogonus* – and about these we are not sure) were definitely performed upon stages. *Gammer Gurton* (and conceivably *Misogonus*) were performed at Universities; and *Gorboduc, Supposes* and *Gismond* at Inns of Court.

The difficulty with all these is that each seems likely to have been presented in a style of its own, and not owing much to any immediate precedent. Each was probably 'experimental theatre'. Consequently, since we lack parallel examples from which to draw details to fill in gaps and afford comparisons, any conception of the presentation has to be made up from material in each play considered by itself; and there is a strange amount of uncertainty and contradiction here.

Ralph Royster Doyster (c. 1553) seems perhaps the least revolutionary of this group so far as presentation style goes, however much it may have of innovation in dramatic style. It still bears the old description of 'Enterlude' quite uncompromisingly, and its action is such that it could be played either on a booth stage or in front of hall-screens with equal facility; but there is nothing in the script to confirm that a stage was in fact used.

Gammer Gurton, Gorboduc, Supposes and *Gismond*, however, were all performed on stages, but about the nature of these stages, and particularly how the action was set upon the stage as regards background, they are all in one respect or another provocatively indefinite. It seems best therefore not to deal with each in detail but to take the most provocative and set out the general problems, which in principle are equally relevant to the others.

Gammer Gurton is by far the most puzzling play of the group and it is worth studying separately and in some detail. It will serve to introduce us to the problems of the others; but it will unfortunately offer, like them, little enough to help solve those problems.

Summing up what we know about *Gammer Gurton's Needle* it is the first English play which states definitely of itself that it was played at a university. (We may ascribe earlier plays to universities but only on uncertain grounds.) In the same way – and this is more important to our present study – it is the first play that states that it was played 'on Stage'. Finally, it does not call itself an Interlude but a Comedie. The great question here is, was this 'comedie' something of a new kind? If it were, was it presented in a new kind of way – that is, somehow differently from an Interlude before hall-screens? Let me repeat that I do not think enough direct evidence can be found to decide the point and I must warn the reader that I shall not be able to offer a solution here. But a proper course seems to be to consider what possibilities there might be.

The question arises partly because the play has an academic quality and shows a certain recognition of classic Latin precedent – for example it is, like *Respublica*, divided into five acts with their scenes. Yet nothing could be less academic and more English than the action and the dialogue nor, I think it can be said, more in the manner of an Interlude. I take it that the dialogue and action of this play are so well known that there is no need here to describe the plot in full detail. The title-page reads in Tudor Facsimile Text, No. 34:

A Ryght
Pithy, Pleasaunt anp me
rie Comedie: In-
tytuled *Gammer gur-*
tons Nedle: Played on
Stage, not longe
ago in Chri-
stes
Colledge in Cambridge
Made by Mr. S. Mr. of Art
Imprented at London in
Fleetstreat beneth the Conduit at the signe of S. John
Euangelist by Tho-
mas Colwell

(1575 on colophon)

The names of the Speakers
in this Comedie.
Diccon the Bedlem.
Hodge Gammer Gurtons seruante.
Tyb Gammer Gurton's mayde.
Gammer Gurton.
Docke [*sic*] Gammer Gurtons boye.
Dame Chatte,
Doctor Rat the Curate.
Mayster Baylye,
Doll Dame Chattes mayde.
Scapethryft mayst Beylies seruante.

Mutes

God Saue the Queene.

The two outstanding pieces of information are in the statements 'Played on Stage', and played 'in Christes Colledge in Cambridge', but what we are not informed is: where in Christ's College. It would seem tempting to take for granted that the performance must have been in the Great Hall of the College, and so base a reconstruction of the setting on the screens of that particular Hall. But, first, the place is not certain and, second, if it were certain, the Great Hall at Christ's College has been completely reconstructed in modern times. So we are forced to compromise; and all that can be offered about the possibility of the lost Hall's being the place is the unsatisfactory knowledge that in 1636 – that is three quarters of a century later – when Charles I and his Court were entertained at Christ Church (in Oxford, not Cambridge) with Strode's *Passions Calmed*, the performance was in 'the Common Hall', as Anthony à Wood tells us and 'It was acted on a goodly stage, reaching from the upper end of the Hall almost to the hearth place, . . .' That is to say (and this is disturbing to any earnest reconstruction) that the stage for *Passions Calmed* appears to have been at the opposite end of the hall to what we have supposed the Interluders were most used to. But this is, of course, in the days when scenery was first being used.

There is one very tenuous note in *Gammer Gurton* about the place, and it would seem to confirm the Great Hall; in II.i when, after Diccon's announcing to the credulous Hodge that he is about to conjure up the actual presence of the Devil to find where the Gammer's needle was lost, Hodge is rendered so nervous that he has to cry in despair –

> By the masse cham able no longer to holde it,
> To bad iche must beraye the hall.

– and out he has to run. Notice that he does not fear to 'beraye' (or let us say, splash) the stage or any 'scenery'; it is the Hall. And so there seems no doubt that the performance was in a hall, and one where the actors were close enough to the actual walls; and yet a question rises to mind – how could he have berayed the hall if he were standing on a stage? Could he have left the stage to go out by a door?

The script has a quite remarkable number of references to doors. But it is very difficult to decide whether these relate to the traditional screens-doors, or to practical canvas doors in constructed scenic houses. There is nothing to indicate positively whether the play was presented as a late Tudor Interlude or as an early revival of the type of a Roman Comedy. The references to doors in the lines can be listed as follows:

In I.i, Diccon's opening speech begins with a reference to Gammer Gurton's house and contains these words,

> Many a myle have I walked, [. . .]
> Yet came my foote neuer, within those doore cheekes, [. . .]
> That ever I saw a sorte, in such a plyght
> As here within this house appereth to my syght [. . .]

– and he describes the tumult he has just seen inside, where the inmates are hunting for the lost needle. The reference is indeterminate; practically nothing about the nature of the door is given. At most, one might suppose from the words 'within this house' that the actor gestured towards a visible building. The unusual word *cheekes* catches attention in passing; there are similar references later to door *posts*.

Later in the same scene Diccon describes leaving the house with the words, 'out at doores I hyed mee'.

Towards the end of I.iv, Gammer Gurton answers a question about where she has been with two interesting lines:

> Within the house, and at the dore, sitting by this same post
> Wher I was loking a long howre, before these folke came here,

The insistence on the door post is surely evidence that some visible door was there to point to; but whether an ordinary screens opening or something else is still not to be decided. In the second line there is a curious reference, apparently to the audience; and the picture is conveyed that the old woman had been searching the ground a full hour before the audience had taken their places. (Whether we dare infer from this that the audience had dined elsewhere and only came 'here' into the hall just before the show began, I hesitate to say.)

Near the beginning of I.v, Cocke, the house boy, remarks on the sight of Hodge inside the house trying to light a candle-end at the fire, and exclaims to Gammer, 'if ye will laugh, looke in but at the doore', and follows with a descriptive speech implying that the interior of the house (whether real or imagined) is something that the audience cannot see.

There is a variant wording in II.iv where Diccon tells Gammer that he saw Dame Chat, the opposite neighbour, stoop and pick up something 'euen at this gate'. Is this gate something different from a door? In her reply Gammer avers it must have been her needle since she had been sitting 'euen by this poste'.

In III.i Hodge, in a soliloquy, decides he will 'not now go to the doore againe with it (*? the needle*) to meete;' but that if he had light enough he would mend his breeches himself with an awl and thong straight away.

At any rate, Gammer enters (III.ii) and he tells her to go and demand her needle of Dame Chat, adding (perhaps a little surprisingly) 'Go to her gammer, see ye not where she stands in her doores'. The plural form may hint at one of the screens-doors, or it may be simply idiomatic. But it confirms that the door of the other house, that of Gammer's opposite neighbour Dame Chat, is also visible and that at that moment she herself is standing at it.

After the Gammer has crossed to speak to her, Dame Chat demands, 'Why art thou crept fro*m* home hether, to mine own doores to chide me'; Gammer retorts that Dame Chat had herself stolen across previously and stolen the needle 'euen from my doore,' . . .

During the fight which takes place between the two women there is a curious piece of bye-play from Hodge which requires a moment's study. I lead up to this curiosity with the following: at l. 21 in this scene, Dame Chat interrupted her vituperations against the Gammer with an unexpected exclamation, 'Come out Hogge' – unexpected because Hodge was already present. So she could not mean to summon him out of the house; and the line may mean 'Come out of the way (and let me get at her)', which seems confirmed when Gammer echoes with, 'Come out hogge, and let haue

404

me right' – perhaps meaning 'Let me have right of way'. Then the conflict continues. After several exchanges Dame Chat cries –

> I trow drab I shall dresse thee.
> Tary ye knaue I hold the a grote, I shall make these hands blesse thee
> Take ye this old hore for a mends, [. . .]

– and so forth. Now, the middle line here, being addressed to 'thou knave', must be addressed to Hodge since 'knave' is a male epithet (being derived from German *Knabe*, a boy). So presumably she turns on him for a moment; and equally presumably he runs away, so prompting her to call 'tary'. But two lines later he is shouting 'Where is the strong stued hore . . .?' And thus he must have dodged out of the way and then returned. It is now that the curiosity mentioned above comes, in the remainder of his speech; he continues,

> [. . .] chil geare [*I will give her*] a hores marke,
> Stand out ones way, that ich kyll none in the darke:

To whom is this last line addressed? There are present only Hodge and the two women – and the audience. If then the warning line is addressed, as seems unavoidable, to the audience then it follows that some spectators are in very close proximity to the action – close enough to seem to risk being struck. But how could that be if the players were on a stage? We seem offered a very strong suggestion that this episode is taking place on the floor at the screens-door close to the bystanders, in the typical Interlude way. But much is obscure here. How far away had Hodge run? What had he come back with? Note the striking phrase 'in the darke', conjuring up a picture of confused excitement in the torchlit hall.

Dame Chat, however, sees him clearly enough, and confirms with her next line that he has just been away, for she exclaims: 'Art here agayne thou hoddy peke', and goes for him with a spit.

Now the reference to the door comes.

Hodge cries to the house-boy of Gammer's house: 'Let dore stand Cock, . . .' – that would seem to mean, 'leave the door open so that I have a way of retreat'. Then to (presumably) Dame Chat: 'Why coms [*comest thou?*] in deede?' – and again to Cocke – 'Kepe dore ye horson boy'. Dame Chat still comes on. Hodge still retreats; and then prepares to rush home. He presumably runs into his house for he now calls, 'take heede Cocke, pull in the latche'.

Dame Chat helps us to reconstruct this action by her next line: 'I faith sir loose breche had ye taried, ye shold haue found your

match' – so obviously he did not tarry. But he goes on shouting
encouragement to Gammer Gurton, apparently from the protection of the house. Perhaps he speaks over the top of a half-door.
But the Gammer is beaten down to the ground and left, and she
cries sadly, 'A hodg, hodg, where was thy help, when fixen had me
downe'.

Later in the play, when Dame Chat is relating this episode to
Diccon, she helps us a little further over the details. She says of
Hodge –

> And thadst seene him Diccon, it wold haue made ye beshite the
> For laughter. The horsen dolt at last caught vp a club,
> As though he would haue slaine the master deuil Belsabub,
> But I set him soone inwarde.

So we learn that Hodge had in fact gone out, and gone to fetch a
club, but to little purpose for she soon 'set him inwarde' again.

All this seems to indicate a fairly substantial business with the
doors, and either to contradict that they were only screens-openings,
or to prove that screens-doorways could at that date be furnished
with closable door-leaves that had latches to them!

To take up the door references once more. At the opening of
III.iv Gyb the cat is said to be 'gasping behind the doore' – this
would suggest just *outside* the door if it is a screens-door, or just
inside the door if it is a scenic door into a 'house'.

A little later in the same scene Doctor Rat is reported as having
found Hob Filcher's 'naule' (or awl) 'hard beside the doore poste'.

In IV.ii Hodge, retailing the course of events, says that Gammer
Gurton had 'sat her downe at this doore' when the needle was lost,
and that Dame Chat had picked it up 'euen here at this gate'. (Could
it be that a front garden before the house is indicated?)

Finally, when in V.ii the Bayley is examining into the case, he
sums up: 'This is the case, you lost your nedle about the dores'.

The evidence of the doors, then, seems indecisive; they may have
been practicable doors built in two separate scenic house-fronts, or
they may have been the screens-doors.

But, leaving the doors aside, there is one practical element in
the setting that it does not at first seem possible could have been
managed with normal screens, and that is the hole in Dame Chat's
house-wall that Dr. Rat got caught in. The evidence offered in the
lines about this hole is as follows.

First: in IV.ii, Diccon asks Dame Chat a question in order to find out if there is any place about her house where a thief could slip in –

> Have you not about your house, behind your furnace or leade:
> A hole where a crafty knaue, may crepe in for neade?

– and she replies –

> Yes by the masse, a hole broke down, euen wi*th*in these ii. dayes.

The riddle is: what is a 'furnace or leade'? And why should Diccon think it likely that there might be a hole behind at that point? Some commentators insert a note here to the effect that a 'leade' is a pot or cauldron. There seem two objections to this; first, that the word 'leade' is made to rhyme with 'neade' (that is, not with 'Ned'), and second, that a hole 'behind your furnace or *cauldron*' does not seem to make any particular sense at all. But if we follow the rhyme and pronounce the word 'leed', not 'led', then we find that the dictionary, instead of directing us to any sort of metal utensil, will offer for consideration the term 'mill-lead' in the sense of 'something that leads' – for instance, 'an artificial watercourse' or a channel, or even a path; indeed the word 'duct' might best suit. And so we might be prompted to enquire whether there was, anywhere about a Tudor cottage, a 'lead' or duct in this sense connected with the fireplace. And in fact there may be such a thing.

Some Tudor houses still have inside the fireplace a rectangular opening, cut clear through the back wall into the open air some two or three feet above the hearth level. It is roughly about 18 in. long by 12 or 13 in. high, and is closed by an iron door hinged in the thickness of the wall and secured by a bolt on the inside. Its purpose is apparently to act as a smoke-lead if the chimney is not drawing well. It may be that this is what Diccon alludes to as a hole, or lead, 'behind your furnace'.

Dame Chat replies that there is such a hole, and then remarks further that this hole had recently had some of the stones or bricks round it broken away – thus, presumably, making the iron door fit less well and the hole, therefore, more suitable to climb through.

The second piece of evidence in the lines about this hole comes just as Diccon leads the unfortunate Dr. Rat to the particular spot later in the same scene and says to him –

> Follow me but a litle, and marke what I will say,
> Lay downe your gown beside you, go to, come on your way:
> Se ye not what is here? a hole wherin ye may creepe
> Into the house, and sodenly vnwares among them leape, [. . .]

This all seems to fit in with the above suggestion. But a few lines later Diccon adds –

> Go softly, make no noyse, give me your foote sir John, [. . .]

This, now, seems to create a difficulty; the request 'give me your foote' is so reminiscent of holding a person's foot to give him a 'leg up' over a high wall that it seems inevitably to suggest that the hole must be well up in the air – certainly higher than a smoke-lead. But I think that the intention of the words is not to give Dr. Rat a lift to something he could not reach by himself, but to hold his foot firm so as to give him something to push against horizontally as he worms his way into a lowish opening that (even with a brick or two 'broke down') would not be a great deal bigger than his body was thick.

The third piece of evidence is valuable as confirming the above suggestion. It comes in V.ii, when Dr Rat is recapitulating his experience before the Mayster Baylye. He tells Dame Chat how Diccon –

> [. . .] said ful certain, if I wold folow his read
> Into your house a priuy way, he wold me guide and leade, [. . .]
> And set me in the backe hole, [. . .]
> And whiles I sought a quietnes, creping vpon my knees,
> I found . . . etc., etc.

– and he goes on to describe how he was beaten about the head from inside the house. But the point is that he has said he crept in *upon his knees*, as he might well do through a smoke-lead but not through a hole high in a wall.

And now, reviewing all this very circumstantial and specific evidence, how could this essential piece of comic business have been presented as far as concerns the hole that was the occasion for it? How was the hole provided? In what way did the students or staff of Christ's College arrange to have this hole contrived for the actors? The answer to these questions would obviously have a great influence on any conception one might make of the details of the staging. But before the problem can even begin to be considered as a whole the great problem of the nature of the two houses must be looked at.

With regard to Gammer Gurton's house there is no particular reason in the script why any of it should have been actually represented, except the door and the doorposts. The interior is certainly presented to us, but only by report. We know it is supposed to have two storeys because Hodge is said to go upstairs, but we do not see him. Again, the house is understood to be thatched, since there is a fear lest Hodge's candle should set light to the straw. But in all this there is no positive need for anything beyond a door to be really presented. The deduction might tend to be, then, that for this house a screens-opening would adequately serve all needs.

With regard to Dame Chat's house, the door is equally important for we see her standing just outside it; but of presumably even greater importance dramatically is the hole in its wall, which we have just discussed; thus the argument seems to run: Gammer Gurton's house could be entirely adequately represented by a screens-door. But Dame Chat's house must, it seems, be represented by something more if the hole is to be practicable. But if Dame Chat's house is represented in any detail it would seem highly likely that Gammer Gurton's house must be equally representational to match. And so we should be committed to two houses.

Accepting this for the moment; how might the siting of these two practical houses have been arranged on a stage?

But first – even nearer to the essential problem – where would the stage be sited?

The problem about the placing of the stage can be simplified to a plain alternative; was it before the screens or not before the screens? If it were not before the screens then it could have been almost anywhere – at the other end of the hall or not in a main hall at all – and arranged in almost any manner. This would take it out of the range of study here, since we would lack any sort of comparison or tradition with which to think about it.

If on the other hand it were before screens, then at least we can take a typical contemporary set of screens as a basis, and contemplate what possibilities of arranging a stage in front of them seem to arise.

There is a point to be made in passing here. It is obvious that a stage-before-screens would be closer to the tradition of the Interluders as I have outlined it in this book – that is to say it would be so if we suppose that the main tradition which the Interluders followed was of performances in Tudor Halls. But if on the other hand the tradition they mainly followed was of less formal performances in the occasional Public Halls where scaffold-stages had to be put up without any reference to a screens background, then their main tradition would be of a stage independent of screens. I do not however think it was, for this reason: a stage independent of screens

409

can have no background except the chance wall it is built against, or a traverse curtain. Yet De Witt's drawing of an Elizabethan public playhouse shows a specific wall behind the stage, with doors in the position of screens-doors. Moreover, the tradition of Elizabethan public-playhouse playwrights was to handle the entrances of characters in the same way as they had been handled by Interlude playwrights writing for entrances through screens. Thus, though the stage-without-screens was equally familiar to travelling Interluders, it does not seem to have been the tradition they favoured when the public playhouses came to be built.

(This is always supposing (a) that all playhouses were planned by the successors of the Interluders, and (b) that the earliest playhouses were built to the same pattern as the one De Witt drew.)

The tradition seems therefore to run most directly through the stage-before-screens channel. If so then the unrelated stage is the break-away form. And thus, if *Gammer Gurton's Needle* were played on a stage with no screens, its style would be outside the main tradition of the Interludes; whereas my interest here is to trace the tradition from Tudor-Hall presentation to public-playhouse presentation. Therefore I shall consider the presentation of *Gammer Gurton* and the other stage plays on the basis of a stage built before screens, because I want to see what difficulties would then arise when we tried to put the traditional form of Interlude against a background, or setting, of houses on such a stage.

Before beginning this I must try to collect any other pieces of evidence that may remain in the script relevant to the matter of its presentation.

First, it is clear that however important the entrance of players from those two houses may be, there must still be one or more other entrances which are quite independent of the houses. This means that we are facing a new style in which two doors are not enough; there must be at least a third entrance. The instances of this need are as follows –

1. Hodge's exit in fear, at the end of II.i, before the conjuring up of the Devil; since he says he might beraye the hall it seems likely that he runs out of the hall altogether, not into either of the houses. Thus he must use a third door.

2. When in II.iii Hodge returns again, he must come back by the way he ran out, this means he could not enter from a house.

3. At the end of this scene he leaves again, and now in order to go to Sym Glover's shop; so he cannot go into his own house.

4. At the end of Act II, Diccon says he is leaving to visit friends in the town, and so his exit cannot be into one of the two houses.

5. Hodge opens Act III by coming in from Sym Glover's shop, so he cannot enter from a house.

6. Near the end of III.iii, the Gammer sends Cocke to fetch Dr. Rat 'at his chamber, or els at mother Bees' – so Cocke must leave by an exit other than the two houses.

7. Near the beginning of III.iv, Cocke returns from his errand and so must come in by the entrance he left by in III.iii.

8. Dr. Rat, on entering in the beginning of IV.i, comes from the village to the houses, so cannot enter from either house.

9. At the end of IV.ii, Dr. Rat goes out back to the village to fetch the Bayley, that is to say he cannot go into either house.

10. At the opening of V.i, Dr. Rat and the Bayley enter; this must again be from a door other than one of the house doors.

It is proved, then, that at least one entrance besides the doors into the two houses must be available. What follows from this is that, if the play were presented before the screens, then the houses could scarcely have been placed so as to obscure the screens-doors.

Leaving now the matter of the extra entrance or entrances, there is a very curious passage at the beginning of II.iv which seems to add to the puzzles. The situation is that Diccon opens the scene alone on the stage, having seen Hodge go out to Sym Glover's shop at the close of the previous scene. Diccon begins with a couple of lines that seem a direct address to the audience, but they conclude with the last thing we should expect; here is the sequence –

DICCON. Now this gere must forward goe, for here my gammer
        commeth,
        Be still a while and say nothing, make here a litle romth.
GAMMER. Good lord, shall neuer be my lucke my neele agayne to
        spye:
        Alas the whyle tys past my helpe, where tis still it must lye.
DICCON. Now Jesus gammer gurton, what driueth you to this
        sadnes:
        I feare me by my conscience, you will sure fall to madnes.
GAMMER. Who is that, what Diccon, cham lost man: fye fye.
DICCON. Mary fy on them yt be worthy, but what shuld be your
        troble . . .

The surprising point is of course that Diccon should apparently call for the audience to make a little 'room' for the entrance of the Gammer if she is (as the script proves) supposed to be entering from her house, which must surely be on the stage! It is to be admitted that the meaning of the whole sentence is wide open to doubt; 'make here a little romth' may mean 'make her a little room' to come in, or 'make a little room here (for her)' – or 'romth' may mean something other than 'room', though what I cannot tell. The note which Creeth gives here in his edition in *Tudor Plays* is: 'This kind of injunction to the audience to make room for players to enter was frequently necessary in plays performed in halls and innyards; it is interesting that it should be written into the text.' And he quotes instances of the use of the expression from *Mankind, Fulgens, Cambises*, and even by Falstaff in *1 Henry IV*. But however 'interesting' the writing in of the injunction may be, the puzzle of why it was written in – whether for a purpose or for a purposeless reminiscence – remains unsolved. Or rather, the only solution would be if the play were in fact acted traditionally with entrances through the screens – and this seems already ruled out by the presence of the stage and the houses. Or could there be an arrangement that would reconcile all these?

An additional curiosity in the above is that, after her entrance, the Gammer's first words are in a mumble to herself and only as Diccon speaks again does she notice him and ask 'Who is that'?

This is not the only puzzling passage related to one of Gammer Gurton's entrances. At the end of I.iii, Hodge is invoking vengeance on Gammer's household, when the old woman appears, and he exclaims,

> Se where she com̄meth crawling. come on in twenty deuils way.
> Ye haue made a fayre daies worke, haue you not?

The word 'crawling' applied to her coming is suggestive of someone on a height looking down at another below. But of course it is equally applicable to someone entering slowly.

One matter concerning the presentation on which we are not left in doubt is the matter of the dim lighting of the hall. In I.v Hodge asks for a candle to be set before he can seek and grope for the needle. At the end of the same scene, Gammer says,

> Our candle is at an ende let us all in quight
> And come another tyme, when we haue more lyght.

In III.iii, during the fight Hodge calls (as has been noticed), 'stand out ones way, that ich kyll none in the darke'. And in V.i, the Bayley reminds Dr. Rat that you cannot tell an honest man 'when he meets you in the darke' as Dr. Rat was met. Later in V.ii Dr. Rat confirms this by saying that Dame Chat could not distinguish him because she had no light. Finally at the end of V.ii, when Hodge discovers the needle in his own breeches, he cries 'Go neare the light Gammer' to find it.

But now, how much farther may one go in presuming the character of the two houses?

36 *The Problem of the University Stage*

One view may be considered at this point; the view that the houses may have been Serlian in appearance, that is to say designed on the lines of the scenic houses which Sebastian Serlio had described and illustrated in the theatrical section of his book *Architettura* of 1545. The argument behind this view would be that *Gammer Gurton's Needle* must have been written by a classic scholar, or at least one versed in the new Renaissance learning, and hence he might well have known Serlio's work. This view requires examination for a moment.

It is to be admitted that the influence upon certain English playwrights in the sixteenth century of the classic drama of Terence and Plautus is a real one; it is clear, for instance from such lines as the Prologue's in *Ralph Royster Doyster* –

> The wyse Poets long time heretofore
> Under merrie Comedies secretes did declare [. . .]
> Suche to write neither *Plautus* nor *Terence* dyd spare
> Whiche among the learned at this day beares the bell.

– to say nothing of the insistence upon this point by all the scholarly commentators. But I do not see evidence that those early Tudor playwrights who were familiar with Terentian or Plautan plays were necessarily able to form any clearer picture of how they were originally staged than we are today.

It seems to me doubtful that a learned Tudor schoolmaster would be as familiar with the practical work of the recent Italian architect, Serlio, as he would with the literary work of the ancient and revered Latin dramatists. Even if he were, what reason would he have to associate the Serlian court settings with the plays of classic Rome? It seems to me, indeed, that the contrary is more likely to be true; if he read his Terence in the Lyons edition of 1493 he would almost certainly visualize the plays as being performed most suitably against a traverse curtain, or an arcade with curtains in each opening like those shown in the illustrations to that edition. And the same is true if he read the Venice editions of 1497, 1518, 1524 or 1545. While if he read him in the Strassbourg edition of 1496 he would probably have been as puzzled about what the settings were intended to be as we are to this day. In any case, what reason would he have to set aside all these illustrations from the classic authors themselves, in favour of a new scheme of scenery devised for expensive entertainments at ducal courts?

It was Inigo Jones, half a century later, who went to Italy to find and import the Italianate ideas of setting; but it is noticeable that Inigo Jones himself began his work on the setting of the earlier court masques (c. 1600) not directly with classical precedent but with essays in the style of the medieval 'house', brought up to date in nothing save its decorative treatment (see for example his House of Fame in Ben Jonson's *Masque of Queenes*). Despite the availability to him of Serlio in the original of 1545, or in the English translation of 1611, he did not produce full settings on a truly Italianate plan till after his visit to Italy in 1613.

The students and staff at Christ's College, Cambridge, may well have been – or had among them a few individuals who were – up-to-date students of the new Renaissance humanism in drama, and the presentation of dramatic spectacle. But would they have drawn on this knowledge to set a play like *Gammer Gurton*? They may have done so, but if they did they must have produced from among themselves a really historical innovator because no one in the history of Britain had, so far as we know, done such a thing before.

But it is clearly impossible to decide such a matter by argument. I would prefer to take a different line with the thoughts that arise here; that of making a sort of pictorial test of all the various possibilities that it seems might have been used when presenting a play upon a stage in a university hall and – at any rate so far as *Gammer Gurton* is concerned – presenting it with something, however tentative, in the nature of 'scenic houses'. This will not attempt to offer a solution to the *Gammer Gurton* problem but simply to provide a set of considerations by which to judge what might be involved in this and the other related plays. And, following on the line of study I have begun in the previous pages, I shall suppose the

FIG. 22. The dimensions and proportions of a university hall screen contemporary with *Gammer Gurton's Needle*, based on St. John's College, Cambridge

stage being put up at the screens-end of the hall, to test the problems that arise.

For this purpose I take as a physical basis (since Christ's College Hall is no longer in its original form) a nearly contemporary college hall, that of St. John's College, Cambridge, dating from about 1511–16. We know that plays were presented in this hall, and at least one of them upon a stage, for *The Pilgrimage to Parnassus* was done there in 1599, and *The Return from Parnassus, Part One,* in 1600, with *Part Two* in 1602. In the last play there is a direction referring to *the corners of the stage.* The general features of the screens-end, with dimensions, are shown in Fig. 22

To begin, I set up for the sake of argument a smallish scaffold-stage with two houses of a Serlian character upon it, see Fig. 23. The stage is 3 ft. high and 16 ft. 8 in. wide, leaving 6 ft. 6 in. either side to the walls of the hall. The houses would have to be no more than 5 ft. wide each, to leave an acting-space between them of 6 ft. 8 in. All this is pretty cramped. Moreover the screens-doors are

FIG. 23. The St. John's College screens with a stage and Serlian 'houses' before the doors

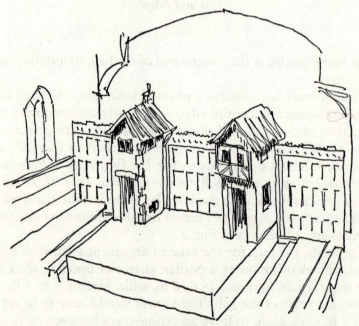

FIG. 24. The same screens with 'satyric' or rustic houses

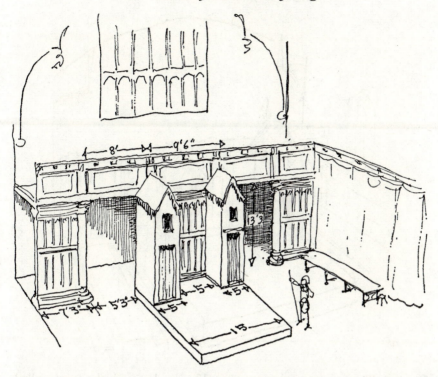

FIG. 25. The problem of stage and houses considered in a large hall based on Hampton Court hall dimensions

completely blocked, which means two things; that no service of any meal could be undertaken (though the meal could perhaps have been served in another hall on that occasion), and also, which is more important, no exits can be made by actors save through the houses, and as I have shown, other exits are in fact called for in the script of *Gammer Gurton's Needle*. But a major objection so far as this play is concerned is that the style of the houses on the Serlian pattern is quite unsuitable to the humble style of the cottages in the play.

I turn next to Fig. 24, keeping all the general details of Fig. 23 but changing the style of the houses to the 'rustic' cottages shown in Serlio's Satyric Scene or in Inigo Jones' *Florimene* setting. Here at least some sort of representation of Dr. Rat's hole could be made without too much inconsistence. But the majority of the objections still stand.

FIG. 26. The same arrangement as in Fig. 24, but with the stage pulled
forward clear of the screens

In Fig. 25 I turn for a moment from a medium-sized college
hall to the Great Hall at Hampton Court to see how it might be
possible in such more spacious surroundings to place a small lower
stage, or footpace, so as to accommodate two narrow houses, and
yet not obstruct the screens-doors. It will be clear that since the
centre screen is only 9 ft. 6 in. wide, the arrangement would be practically impossible unless the stage and the houses encroached on
each 8 ft. opening to the extent of some 3 ft. This would just allow
two 5 ft. houses with a space of 5 ft. clear between them. For other
notes on 'footpace' cf. Sections 9 and 39.

In Fig. 26 one solution is offered for freeing the screens-doors;
namely, by pulling the stage forward from the screens so as to stand
clear leaving a small passage, some 4 ft. wide, between its back and
the screens behind it.

In Fig. 27 a new arrangement is suggested with a low stage (now
only a footpace) but one reaching entirely across the hall, and bear-

FIG. 27. A low wide stage, with the houses against the side walls

ing the two houses at either extreme end of it so clearing the screens-doors, and at the same time offering not too great a step for the pages and waiters to negotiate if and when they had to serve a meal. Here a short length of table-space at the sides has had to be sacrificed. This might seem possibly the most workable suggestion so far if we are to accept the idea of practical houses on a stage.

There is just one possible qualification to the last figure. In Fig. 28 I show what is in most respects the same arrangement, but with the difference that the houses stand now on the hall floor, and the stage – still a low footpace – occupies only the space in front of the centre screen. So far as all practical actions go this is the arrangement that most nearly accommodates all the data in the text of the play.

Now to go farther afield, leaving the conception of practical built houses; what other conceivable arrangements could be put forward for the presentation of a play of this sort in the hall? One possibility is the 'normal' Interlude arrangement posited in the

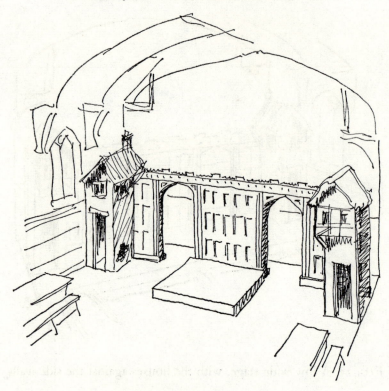

FIG. 28. The stage reduced to fit the centre screen, with the houses now
on the floor

earlier part of this book; this is shown in Fig. 29. Now we would
have to resort to the compromise that Dr. Rat's hole in *Gammer
Gurton* was represented (much less effectively) by lifting one of the
bottom corners of the traverse curtain. The entrances from the two
houses would have to be made round the ends of the traverse.

For good measure let me add two other conceptions. In Fig. 30
is a scaffold stage on barrels, such as might have been erected in a
public Guildhall; and in Fig. 31 is a replica of an indoor stage such
as that which Adriaen van de Venne showed in his print in the
Tafereel van de belacchende werelt of 1635. This is admittedly much
later in date but it has the slight advantage of showing at last a kind
of stage for which we have positive pictorial evidence. Here two
rows of audience might sit on the stage-right, with an orchestra on
the stage-left. (Cf. Fig. 40.)

FIG. 29. The effect of setting with only a low small stage and a traverse

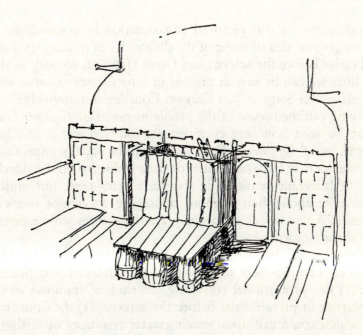

FIG. 30. The stage made of boards and barrels, with a curtained booth

FIG. 31. The kind of stage pictured in Van de Venne's print (compare
with Fig. 40)

Two results of this pictorial consideration of possibilities are,
first, to give an idea of some of the difficulties of putting up a stage
and houses before the screens in a Great Hall and, second, to show
how little we can be sure at present of how *Gammer Gurton* was in
fact 'played on Stage . . . in Christes Colledge in Cambridge'.

Having outlined some of the problems raised by *Gammer Gurton*
it may be seen how any consideration of *Gorboduc* at the Inner
Temple, or of *Supposes* at Gray's Inn, will be equally unprofitable.
Such shows may have had much or little influence on the development of Interlude tradition in the years 1560–1576, but until we
know more about their methods of staging we cannot assess that
influence. A few words about the plays themselves will be given in
their chronological order.

Summing up: the most that can be said generally is that in the
period about 1560 there seem to be three classes of play presentation: (1) the professional travelling Interluders' tradition devised
for playing in private halls before the screens; (2) the Court tradition which could call upon much greater resources of setting for
its own masque entertainments, and almost certainly imposed

something of that more elaborate tradition upon Interluders when they brought their plays to court – but imposed it to an extent that at present is not definable; (3) the probably quite novel methods of the Inns of Court and the Universities where innovation, as against tradition, in setting seems likely to have been the rule, and with which kind of theatre the Interluders probably had little to do.

Of these three classes the first, since it was the tradition of professional players, is the one that is likely to have had most influence on the eventual form of the professional playhouse.

What I want to do therefore in the rest of this book is to follow the professional Interluders' tradition as closely as possible, particularly in respect of any new technical developments that come into that tradition before the building of The Theatre in 1576, but at the same time keep some track of university and court developments particularly where those show any sort of innovation that might conceivably influence the Interluders.

37 Jack Juggler

The next play in the provisional chronological list, *Jack Juggler* (c. 1553), is probably not a professional play, for it is clearly described on the title-page as 'A new Enterlued for chyldren to playe'. It appears to be written – or at least printed – so as to be consistent either with presentation in a hall, or with something a little more elaborate if the 'chyldren' happened to be members of a school, or with considerably more elaboration if they were members of one of the royal choirs and summoned to perform at court.

No 'scene' is indicated but there are references to a gate, and suggestions of a house exterior. There is nothing in the action that could not be adapted to presentation with the screens, one door serving for entrances from the house and the other for entrances from the street. On the other hand a form of simple 'house' could well have been set up in three dimensions for a court presentation.

But what is difficult in picturing such a court production as I have just suggested is not how entrances from the house were worked – which would be obviously through the house door – but how, since these could be effected so realistically, the other entrances from the neighbouring streets could have been managed in such a way as to escape an impression of inconsistence. The later Revels Accounts (after 1571) frequently specify houses for plays, and even 'houses' sufficient to stand for towns, yet there is nothing to show that such houses were more than single constructions standing somewhere on the floor. No hint exists of any painted representational background for them; nor is there any suggestion of a grouping of houses so as to form a street (such as Serlio describes), or of any way of representing some place different from the house from which a player might enter, when he was supposed to approach the house as from a street. The presumption seems to be that he simply came into the hall by a normal door and walked across the floor to the house, without any effect of illusion.

However the above may be, it is clear in *Jack Juggler* that the spectators were as real a part of the show as in earlier Interludes for they are frequently addressed directly; they are personally given 'good evening' to; and when Master Bongrace and Jenkin Careaway are enquiring where Jack Juggler has got to, Jenkin hazards, 'He is here among this company for forty pence'. This does seem to imply that he could get easily among the audience from the acting-area, and insofar, it tends against the idea of an illusionistic stage.

38 *Wealth and Health*

Coming next in the provisional chronology after *Jack Juggler* is *An enterlude of Welth, and Helth, very mery and full of Pastyme, newly att his tyme Imprinted* (composed about 1554); it is anonymous. The subject is a typical plotting and quarrelling of knaves to gain service with people of influence, wealth and health, much on the lines of other Interludes. The cast is advertised as being so distributed that 'Foure may easely play this Playe' so it might well be for a company of professionals. There are seven roles. There is a clear suggestion of hall performance in the exit line of a character called Lyberty: 'Farewell I wyll get me out of the doore . . .'. There are the usual instances of characters coming in and speaking for several lines before noticing the presence of characters already in the place. One such example is where Remedy and Helth are alone, discussing the ill-treatment they have had from Wit and Wyll, and Remedy suddenly cries that he hears them coming. They then presumably stand aside, for as Wyll comes in he says, 'Cum in wit for here is no body. We may be bolde and talke largely' – and they go on talking oblivious of the two watchers till they have accused themselves inextricably.

The opening of the play consists of a curious trick almost exactly like that to be found later at the opening of *King Daryus*; in it Welth and Helth enter singing and afterwards Welth says, of the audience –

> Why is there no curtesy, now I am come
> I trowe that all the people be dume
> Or els so god helpe me and halydum
> They were almost a sleepe.
> No wordes I harde, nor yet no talking [. . .]
> What ayles you all thus to syt dreaming
> Of whom take ye care? [. . .]

Compare the opening speech of *Daryus* on p. 482 below. Again in *Damon and Pythias*, there is indication at the opening of a silent watching audience, see below, p. 484. It occurs to one to wonder whether, since the spontaneous effect of an Interlude is now becoming, as I suggest (see p. 465), a thing of the past, the audiences, humbly bowing to the dignity of the Prologue, tended to sit hushed and all ready for the play to begin, instead of being interrupted by him in mid-gossip as they had been in earlier times.

39 *Four Special Directions from 'Grissill', 'Apius', 'Horestes' and 'Susanna'*

After the *Welth and Helth* of c. 1554 there comes a gap of five years in the chronological list before the next play, *Pacient Grissill*. The last years of Queen Mary's reign may of course have seen some new plays but no record of them remains; and *Grissill*, ascribed to c. 1559, becomes the first play in our list to belong to the reign of Queen Elizabeth I. It opens a new phase both in technical presentation and in output.

From *Grissill* in c. 1559 up to the building of The Theatre at Shoreditch in 1576, there come some twenty-five new plays. Some of these are, naturally enough, much on the old pattern which I have described in the earlier part of this book, and they bring little in the way of staging that is new. Some are strikingly different, and I want to concentrate on these in what follows, though each of the others will have some mention in its place.

The striking difference is the clear use in acting-directions of the word *stage*. I have of course given some evidence for the employment of stages before this date, but the particular point is that now the word begins to be used specifically in scripts, with directions regarding the way the stage was to be used.

It will help if I take four directions of this particular kind, as samples, and consider these to begin with.

The first is the direction, 'Go once or twise about the Staige, . . .' from *Pacient Grissill* (c. 1559).

The second is, 'Here let Virginius go about the scaffold' from *Apius and Virginia* (c. 1560).

The third is a direction to a general and his band of soldiers to 'marche a bout the stage' from *Horestes* (c. 1567).

The last relates to the two notorious Elders who spied upon Susanna, 'Here they go afore into the Orchard, and Susanna and her two maydes come vpon the stage' from *Susanna* (c. 1569).

These quotations have one thing in common – all refer to the new element, the stage. It is the main purpose of this present section to extract what evidence there is concerning the nature of this stage.

The first matter that might help to explain the nature of this stage is a certain curious flavour in the verbal expression 'to go about' as used in the first two references. It might be thought that 'to go about the stage' simply means that the actor should take a turn, to and fro, upon it. But there is an inescapable feeling that if this is all the expression means then these two first directions are so pointless as to be unnecessary. In other words, in the particular circumstances where each occurs in the script there seems nothing particular gained by directing the actor not to stand still, but to walk about on the stage instead. So, in my view a different meaning for the phrase will have to be found which has some theatrical significance. This may influence the conception we make of the nature of the stage, when we come to it.

It is necessary to describe the acting-situations where these directions occur in some detail.

I take first the reference in *Pacient Grissill*: 'go once or twise about the Staige'. The situation where it occurs is as follows: Grissell has been stripped and turned out by her husband and sent back 'naked' to her father's humble home. There she meets him and two abstract characters called Patience and Constancy. These two promise to dwell with her and her father, Janickel, and all prepare to go off into her home. This passage now follows, reproduced at length from the text. (I have quoted it first without comment, as it stands, although it will not explain itself; but it is useful to show how obscure an Interlude text may be to a reader not previously prepared with some conception of the presentation methods. The vital line is marked with an asterisk, and notes on the other details will follow immediately after the extract. There are some inverted letters in the original and these I have preserved.)

1817   GRISSELL.   So, now if you please let vs depart.
        IANICKELL.   I graunt to go hence with all my hart.
        PACIENCE.   And I Pacience, on you will attend.
        CONSTANCI.   In stormes tribulous coustancye shall you defend.

                                                  Exiunt

        DILIGENCE.   From my Lord *Marquis*, euen now I am sent,[1]
                Who euen now is iornied to Bullin Lagras,
                To featch whom [*home*] his new spouse a Lady
                    excelent, [. . .]
                But at this season accordinge to my Lords com-
                    maundiment,
                Which with humillitie I will bringe to perfecsion,
                As it becometh euery seruant to be dilligent,
                So as I am charged, I will giue Grissill here of intel-
                    lecsion
                Harke, me thinkes I here hyr voice delectable,[2]
                Suerly to vertue, this Lady was tractable,
                How God be here, who resteth in this place.[3]
        GRISSELL.   My poore Father and I this is a plaine case.
                *Go once or twise about the Staige,[4] let Grissill
                  Singe some songe, and sit Spinninge.[5]
                    A songe for Grissill, when the
                    Messinger commeth to hir.
        GRISSELL.   How greatly am I bounde to prayse
                My God that syts in Throne,
                Which hath asswaidged by prouidence,
                My anguishe and my mone. [*etc. for two stanzas.*]

Notes

1. Since Grissell and the other three characters have just been directed to exit, it is to be understood that the Place is left empty for a moment, and then from another door there enters the messenger called Dilligence, sent by the Marquis. At first he soliloquizes.

2. At this point towards the end of his speech he must hear the voice of Grissell singing or speaking. She herself is now presumably

preparing to enter from the door where she and the three others recently exited.

3. At the end of his speech he apparently offers her a salutation and asks (though the line is not entirely clear) who is dwelling in that place, and to this she replies.

4. Next follows the particularly notable direction, 'Go once or twise about the Staige'. It is not perhaps absolutely certain whether this direction is intended for Grissell or for the Messenger, but the very strong presumption is that it is for the Messenger, and I shall take it in this sense in what follows.

5. Now, or about now, Grissell has clearly returned, probably singing and carrying a distaff ready to spin. She has either carried in a stool as well or she finds one provided on the stage, for she is definitely instructed to sit. If she is not already singing she now begins to sing.

The uncertainty about the exact timing of these actions, expressed by the alternatives above, arises because it would seem most effective if this double direction, which is here condensed in one place, were really split up so as to apply its two parts to separate lines. Thus (taking one possibility) the first direction to go about the stage may apply to the Messenger as he says 'Hark, me thinkes I here hyr voice', so that in effect he would withdraw from the door he is approaching because he hears her speaking within. In this case what would follow is that he makes the comment on Grissell's tractability to himself, and then calls out his greeting aloud and is answered by her from within. Only then would she appear, come on to the stage, and sing.

But there is an alternative; Grissell may enter after the Messenger's line 'I will giue Grissill here of intellecsion', and seat herself and begin singing and spinning straight away as if unconscious of his approach. He would now possibly stroll 'about' the stage listening; and then his later line beginning 'suerly to vertue . . .' would fit in between the two verses of the song as a comment aside, while his greeting and question would follow separately as the song ends. Grissell's reply would now naturally follow. This admittedly means altering the position of the verses of the song in the text so that the first stanza came as Dilligence said 'I here hyr voice . . .', and the second one after his 'suerly to vertue, this Lady was tractable' – the rest of the dialogue continuing unbroken. But some justification for this may lie in the otherwise rather curious two lines about the song which are printed separately from the direction proper; they say 'A songe for Grissill, *when* the Messinger commeth to her' as if the song, though printed later all in one place, was intended to be rendered as the Messenger begins to come to her.

The next line in the script after this is from the Messenger –

1863 God save the Grissill, and sheild the from care,
My Lord Marquis, doth him to the commend, [. . .] etc. etc.

– and he gives her his bitter news, for which see the review of the whole play later.

My second reading of the passage would make for a better theatrical effect at a peak moment of the play. But if in fact it is the true reading, it may help to show the reason for this unusual direction; it may be deliberately inserted to indicate to the Messenger that he is not to interrupt Grissell during the singing of her pious song – which is almost an act of devotion – but that he must, while she sings, keep away from her and walk instead a few times *about the stage*.

It is now that the problem of what is meant by the two words 'about' and 'stage' becomes crucial.

I want to make some attempt to list the possibilities. This will mean considering the various shapes that a stage might take in the present context, and then seeing how the phrase 'to go about' that stage might vary in respect of the various shapes.

I have already introduced some of the possible variants in stage-shape during my discussion of *Gammer Gurton*, but I was chiefly concerned there with asking in what ways stages could be combined with scenic houses. Now I can get rid of the complication of the houses, and consider the uncumbered stage in relation to the movement of players. I shall be using again some of the stages proposed in the *Gammer Gurton* enquiry, but to begin I want to examine the possibilities of a stage shape that is somewhat different from anything described in that set of sketches.

It is a shape, however, that will probably be more familiar to a modern; it is a waist-high platform right across the hall. Except that I do not propose anything quite as deep, it is just the sort of stage that one might meet today in any ordinary general-purpose drill hall or recreation centre. It is shown in Fig. 32.

Before considering this arrangement with reference to the direction in *Grissill* I want to pause to look at two other significant matters.

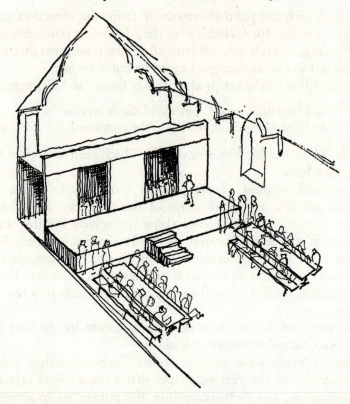

FIG. 32. 'Going about the stage', (I) the effect of a 'modern' platform set
up across a Tudor hall

First, how practical is this particular shape of stage, and how
likely is it to be suitable to a troupe of Interluders performing in
the hall of an ordinary Tudor house?

On considering carefully, several objections to it will become
obvious.

In the first place a stage of this shape, though at first sight seeming perhaps perfectly suitable to performances such as we are inclined to visualize today, does in fact form a serious obstruction in
the path of Tudor players. It would entail two flights of steps up
from the entry passage, one at each door, before any actor could
get on to the stage area. In the smaller type of hall, the doorways
themselves might not be sufficiently high to allow a clear entrance.
In any case an entrance up steps is never considered a good entrance
for effect by an actor. The inconvenience of these steps up would be

430

as great, or even greater, for the servants carrying in dishes for the meal in the hall; for those servants it is obvious that, having ascended the stage, they would need to carry the dishes down again by other steps in front before they could reach the hall floor.

What is perhaps not so immediately obvious is that the latter point could be equally objectionable to the players if – as we believe from the earlier part of this study – they were in the habit of performing part of their actions in the middle, or even at the upper end, of the hall floor.

But there is another essential point where this arrangement runs counter to the traditions we have found to be characteristic of Interludes; that is that spectator-clusters at, and particularly just in front of, the entrance doors are almost ruled out. They could only form if the spectators were allowed to climb the steps from the entry, and themselves stand on the stage – an uncomfortable isolation for any but exhibitionists.

This form of stage, in effect, would tend to limit the general action of a play to the lower end of a hall; but I have established that Interluders were used to taking in the whole available floor area up to the High-Table dais.

Next, I want to come to another sort of consideration altogether concerning a stage of this shape in a Tudor Hall.

Any reader who refers to an article entitled 'The Origins of the Shakespearian Playhouse' by Richard Hosley, in *Shakespeare Quarterly*, XV, no. 2, p. 29 (1964), will notice a particularly striking fact; the arrangement shown above in Fig. 32 is in essence identical with Figs. 1 and 2 in that article. Dr Hosley's two figures show diagrammatically a 4 ft.-high stage erected in front of the 40 ft.-wide screens of, firstly, Hampton Court Great Hall and, secondly, of the hall of the Middle Temple. The two diagrams are then compared with a third, drawn to the same scale, which shows an estimated lay-out of the tiring-house façade of the Swan Playhouse based on a careful assessment of the dimensions suggested in De Witt's drawing.

A result of comparing the three diagrams (as is done in detail in the article – to which the reader is recommended) is to find so striking a parallel in essential features and dimensions as to support very strongly a theory that the tiring-house façade of the Elizabethan playhouse may have been derived from the Tudor screens.

Now, I have taken some space to show that the arrangement in my Fig. 32 is unsuitable for an Interlude performance in a hall; it might therefore be supposed that this unsuitability invalidates Hosley's theory of the origins of the tiring-house façade.

In fact this is not so. I believe on the other hand that it is the very accumulation of disadvantages in the arrangement shown in Fig. 32 that would have led Burbage to design a public playhouse stage which, while retaining all the familiar and useful features of the hall-screens, would at the same time overcome the disadvantages. And the one outstanding feature of the Elizabethan playhouse for which we find no precedent at all in Interlude procedure is the great wide and high platform projecting out into the middle of the yard.

The disadvantages illustrated in Fig. 32 may have engendered the pressures which forced the Elizabethan stage to rise out of the Interlude hall.

Turning now back to my original purpose with Fig. 32; what action would players be involved in on such a stage by a direction to 'go about' it?

The answer seems very simple. It would be the action shown by the arrows in Fig. 33 – or some minor variation of it. That is to say, Grissell would enter at, say, door A, take – or go to – her stool probably about left-centre, and sit. The Messenger would then enter at door B, come forward, turn to his right or left, walk as far to one side as the stage allowed, turn, and walk back again. And what good would that do?

Whether he walked in front of her, or behind her, or up and down beside her, or all round her, he would in my opinion do no more than create a distraction. Certainly, I cannot possibly see any dramatic or theatrical purpose behind the action sufficient to justify the special insertion into the script at this point of the present direction to the Messenger.

I would be prepared slightly to modify the objections to this stage if we allow some period to be reached where performances grow more elaborate – as for instance in the seventeenth century, at court and with scenery – and where the banquet was enjoyed beforehand and in a separate hall, with the audience repairing after it to a special entertainment-chamber for the show. In those circumstances the stage could be even higher and deeper than this one. But for an Interluders' presentation in a domestic hall at the period under consideration now, this stage seems pointless and over-elaborate, and any direction to 'go once or twise about' it to have no significance at all.

But the details of the Elizabethan stage façade are outside my

FIG. 33. 'Going about the stage', (II) the movements of Grissell and the Messenger as conditioned by the stage in Fig. 32

present province, and I leave them to Hosley's study, having merely called attention here to the similarity with his expressed views. And so, with the Playhouse still more than a decade away I return to consideration of the problems that are rising to confront Interluders now that they have incorporated stages into some of their presentations.

For this I want next, as with the *Gammer Gurton* sketches, to put forward some alternative shapes and ask what improvements or otherwise they offer. I begin with Fig. 34. Here there is only one difference from Fig. 32: the stage is lower. But the practicalities are immediately improved. I show in the figure something amounting once more to a footpace, but stretching now across the full width of the hall. What I intend by the term 'footpace' (a similar term 'pas' has already been mentioned on p. 163 above) is indicated in the *O.E.D.* where for meaning 2b we read – 'a raised portion of a floor: e.g. the step on which an altar stands, 1580'. Again, under 'pace' (whose derivation is from the past participle of *pandere*, to stretch) at meaning IV (special senses) we read – '1. A step of a

stair or the like; a stage, a platform. See also Footpace, Halfpace.'
Among the meanings for Halfpace is – 'A step, raised floor, or
platform on which a throne, a dais, etc. is to be placed or erected.'
This use of a 'footpace' removes several of the objections noted in
Fig. 33, by reason of the stage now being lower. The spectators
can perhaps be felt to cluster slightly more acceptably at the doors
now. They might even conceivably mount the stage to watch – but
they would then break the cohesion of the natural spectator-crowd
as a whole, for all could make one unit at floor level if the stage were
not there. However, the banquet-service would be facilitated, and
the making of entrances by the actors would be simplified because
of their having to ascend only one step. Nevertheless, in spite of all
this the problem of 'going once or twise about the Staige' is not
brought any nearer improvement; there is little possibility of any
significant change in the actions suggested in the last figure (compare the arrows in Figs. 33 and 34).

Fig. 35 attempts another solution. It returns to the higher stage
but reduces width, so that normal access through the doors is now
possible though partly restricted; the waiters could serve the meal,
but the actors would still need to have steps to reach the stage
from the entrance level of the hall floor. Steps placed at the side of
the stage (see the steps drawn in thin lines in the figure) are still
objectionable as creating obstructions once again. Steps at the front
require a fairly circuitous path to get from the entry door round and
up the platform. The go-once-or-twice-about problem is not eased
by the movements suggested by the arrows.

The general character of the stage in Fig. 35 is similar to that
shown in Figs. 23 and 24 save that it is considerably narrower and,
of course, lacks the scenic houses. It could, on the other hand, quite
suitably take a traverse curtain across the back, of the sort shown
in Fig. 29, or even a complete, shallow booth like the one in Fig. 30.
And, just as in Fig. 26 the stage was pulled forward to clear the
screens, so could the stage in Fig. 35 be pulled forward, and it would
thus tend to make access slightly easier to the hall. But if it were so
pulled forward, it is very clear indeed that any traverse or booth
erected at the back of it would entirely obstruct all sight of the action
for any spectators at the lower end of the hall, and this would
put it out of court for all presentations in the Interlude tradition.

The final and chief point against Fig. 35 is that the idea of going
about the stage, in the sense of walking to and fro upon it, is reduces
to even more manifest pointlessness and distraction. This, it seemd

FIG. 34. 'Going about the stage', (III) the movements as conditioned by
a low footpace instead of a high stage

FIG. 35. 'Going about the stage', (IV) the effect on movement of a small
high stage

to me, is obvious enough in the figure as it stands, but when one realizes that in the third direction in my list – that from *Horestes* – Horestes *and his band of soldiers also* are directed to 'marche a bout the stage' it surely begins to verge on the ludicrous! But the *Horestes* problem has still to be considered.

At present I want to make a further and final suggestion; just as the high stage of Fig. 33 became more suitable to both Interluders' requirements and servants' comfort when its height was reduced, so in Fig. 36 I show the effect of reducing the height of the stage of Fig. 35 to an ordinary footpace. Now all the traditional Interlude demands can be met, and there is something more; the going-about-the-stage problem takes on a new meaning and for the first time ceases to imply a distraction, but instead makes dramatic sense.

FIG. 36. 'Going about the stage', (V) the effect on movement of a small central footpace; the Messenger now walks on the hall floor

436

In all the figures before this, the word 'about' was understood in an adverbial sense as qualifying the action of 'going' on the stage; and the actor was thus pictured as being upon the stage, and going about, or walking to and fro, *on* it. But 'about' might be used prepositionally to imply a different relation between the going and the stage; it would then mean that the stage was 'gone about', or encompassed, at floor level.

Of course, such a meaning would not be possible with the orthodox stage familiar to us today. But if instead we see the sort of stage in the figure – one placed well clear of the hall walls at the sides, and narrow enough to free the screens-doors at the back – then the whole thing becomes not only possible but effective. With the sort of arrangement I show in Fig. 36, action can be presented *either* on the floor as in the old tradition, *or* on the stage, or *on both*, according to what makes the most significant picture.

The justification for alternative meanings is quite clearly to be found in the *O.E.D.*; there under 'Go' (sense VII, 69), we find the first alternative, the compound 'go about' used adverbially. But the full grammatical expression would more correctly be 'to go about *upon* the stage'. That wording would be unequivocal and had it been used in the direction it would certainly have ruled out any possibility that the Messenger could be imagined anywhere else but on the stage.

But in the *O.E.D.* there is also (under sense VI, 49) a purely prepositional use of 'go about', with the quite distinct meaning of 'encompass'. Two early examples of the usage are given; one from the Gloucester Rolls of 1297 – 'The see geth (*goeth*) him al aboute, he stond as in an yle'; and one from Palladio on Husbandry in 1420 – 'Another with a diche aboute ygoon is'.

I am very well aware of the logistical problem here. All I am able to prove is that 'going about' might have two meanings. I have not yet proved beyond doubt which was intended in the *Grissill* direction. I am prepared to find that the same phrase means one thing in one play, and the other in another. But even in this, some readers may feel I go too far, and that the sense of encompassing the stage at floor level cannot be accepted at all. I ask their careful attention to the further references in the remainder of this book.

While I am on this subject of the usage of the word 'about' in the sixteenth century, there is another example that is worth mention. In his statement of the dimensions of the Old Banqueting Hall at Whitehall, Holinshed (*Chronicles*, 1587) speaks of the building being 'a long square, three hundred thirtie and two foot in measure about'. We know that each of the three successive halls on this site was approximately the same size – that is roughly 120 ft. by 53 ft. At first then Holinshed's figure seems completely in error, for one is inclined to read his meaning as '*approximately* 332 ft. [long]'. But of course that is not his meaning; he is saying that the hall is 332 ft. *in perimeter* – or measured all round about. Which is close enough to $120+53+120+53 = 346$ ft. to satisfy any enquirer. The point is that Holinshed's use of 'about' signified a peripheral measurement not an approximate measurement. And so, I believe, the Interluders' use of 'about' could signify a movement round the stage's periphery and not a movement upon its surface.

To return to Fig. 36; it shows a small squarish stage, only one step high, set before the centre screen and leaving the screen-doors practically clear. It allows, in all respects, the gathering and disposition of spectators as in earlier Interlude presentation. The meal service is unrestricted. The actors can enter the hall floor in their customary fashion, and use the extent of it generally. When action on the stage is required they have simply to step up one step.

Particularly can this arrangement be interesting and effective in the *Grissill* scene. The Messenger now enters alone at door B just after Grissell's exit with her father at door A. He enters in the traditional and customary way, through the spectator-cluster by the door, and on to the hall floor (but does *not* mount the stage). He walks forward, and as he walks he speaks a soliloquy informing the audience of his erand to Grissell. His is clearly a 'Messenger's speech' bringing news from a distance to the audience, and he rightly walks among them, on their own floor, to deliver it, speaking to everyone around. He thereby creates, or reaffirms, his acting-area as *the place of someone arriving from a distance*.

As he strolls and talks, he suddenly hears Grissell's voice from door A (which she has entered as her home), and he pauses in his walk and comments.

This is the cue for her to enter with her distaff and stool. She simply and quietly mounts the stage (as the arrow shows) and sits. She has now produced a 'differentiation of acting-area', because she does not see the Messenger; he is not in her world, while she is still 'at home', and she begins to spin there and sing.

Naturally, this could create a very effective picture. Still more naturally, the Messenger would not interrupt it nor step up into her acting-area; he remains 'outside'. Thus it is, I think, that he is told to 'go once or twise about the Staige' – but now as is shown by the arrows in the figure. Similarly, Grissell is told to 'sit Spinninge'.

After the song, he dissolves the separation of the acting-areas; he steps up into her world, she raises her head and sees him; he greets her and asks who lives there . . . And so the show goes on in the way I shall describe later.

It seems to me after consideration, and taking into account all that has already been learnt about Interludes, that this is the only acceptable solution to the problem of going once or twice *about* the stage. And it is perhaps interesting to remark the similarity in principle between this Fig. 36 and the earlier Fig. 28, which itself seemed to offer the best solution to the *Gammer Gurton* problem.

So far then as concerns the problem in the stage-direction in *Grissill*, the arrangement shown in Fig. 36 seems the most satisfactory. Later, when I have looked at the other three references, I will come back to the plays themselves and go through their whole action in detail for situations which seem to confirm or reject the kind of stage I have proposed. At present I would remark that this is the first instance of what are to make up a whole series of indications, becoming more and more insistent as they accumulate, that *when the Interluders used a stage they used it in a way that was in some respect different from what we imagine today.*

I go on to consider next the similar puzzle that occurs in *Apius and Virginia*, in the passage quoted second in the list above. I take the form of stage I have suggested for *Grissill* in Fig. 36 as the basis for reconstruction to see if it will seem adequate for the situation in this new play. I may say that the standard of the verse in this play perhaps condemns the writer as a poet, but it is of course no proof that he was also a bad or ignorant stage manager.

The situation in the action when the reference occurs is as follows; a plot has been laid by the lustful ruler Apius and his courtier Claudius to get the young lady Virginia from her father Virginius by trickery, in order to seduce her. The details having been agreed, the plotters leave the Place and her father comes in alone: 'Enter Virginius' He tells the audience that he suspects evil because of certain omens he has seen, and concludes by heralding an entrance with these words,

D.i.*rev.*   I enter will Judge Apius gate, reiecting care and mone:
          But stay Virginius, loe, thy Prince doth enter into place,

Oh sufferant Lord, and rightfull Judge, the Gods do saue
thy grace,

Here entreth Judge Apius and Claudius.

They enter from the 'gate' (or door) 'into place', so it would seem
that they must come in on the floor level, and then they would
presumably mount the stage to Virginius. Apius there delivers six
lines of polite welcome to Virginius, but also informs him that he
must meet an accusation. Virginius has six lines of response (including the remarkable couplet, 'If ought I haue offended you,
your Courte, or eke your Crowne, / From lofty top of Turret hie,
persupetat me downe:') and Apius thereupon calls on Claudius to
speak out. So Claudius says (I give the passage in full without in-
terruptions, as with *Grissill*, reserving comment for the end, and
marking the essential line with an asterisk):

CLAUDIUS.

Thou sufferant Lord, and rightfull Judge, this standeth now ye case,
In tender youth not long agone, nere sixtene yeares of space,
Virginius a thrall of mine, a childe and infant yonge,
From me did take by subtell meane, and keepes by arme full strong
And here before your grace I craue, that Justice be exstended,
That I may haue my thrall agayne, and faultes may be amended

VIRGINIUS.

Ah Gods that guide the globe aboue what forged tales I here,
Oh Judge Apius, bend your eares, while this my crime I cleare:
She is my child, and of my wife her tender corpes did springe,
Let all the countrey where I dwell, beare witnesse of the thing.

Apius and Claudius go forth, but Apius speaketh this.[1]

Nay by the Gods not so my friend, I do not so decree,
I charge thee here in paine of death, thou bring the maide to mee:
In chamber close, in prison sound, the secret shall abide,
And no kinde of wight shall talke to her, vntill the truth be tride:
This doo I charge, this I commaund, in paine of death let see,
Without any let, that she be brought, as prisoner vnto me: Exit.
*   Here let Virginius go about the scaffold[2]
Ah fickle faule, vnahppy dome, oh most vncertaine rate,
That euer chaunce so churlishly, that neuer staide in state:
What Judge is this: what cruell wretch? what faith doth Claudius
finde?
The Gods do recompence with shame, his false and faithles minde:
Well home I must,[3] no remedy, where shall my soking teares,
Augment my woes, decrease my ioyes, while death do rid my feares

Here entreth Rumour.[4]

440

Come Ventus come, blow forth thy blast,
　　Prince Eol listen well,
The filthiest fackte that euer was,
　　I Rumor now shall tell: . . .

[Rumour speaks on for twenty-four more lines, explaining Apius's intention to deflower Virginia under pretence of questioning her privately; then Virginius, apparently hearing this,[5] has the following speech:]

VIRGINIUS.

O man, O mould, oh mucke, O clay, O Hell, O hellish hounde,
A faulse Judge Apius wrablinge wretch, is this thy treason found:
Woe worth the man that gaue the seede, wherby ye first didst spring
Woe worth the wombe yt bare the babe, to meane this bluddy thing:
Woe worth the paps that gaue ye sucke, woe worth the Fosters eke
Woe worth all such as euer did, thy health or liking seeke:
Oh that the graued yeares of mine, were couered in the clay

　　　　　　　　　　　　　　　　　　Here entreth Virginia.

Notes

1. The action involved here would seem to be as follows: after the accusation is made by Claudius, Claudius and Apius are directed to 'go forth'. This is a little surprising because, immediately afterwards, Apius has a further speech to Virginius. The suggestion is that they make *as if* to go out (possibly stepping off the stage to go to the door, cf. Fig. 36), but then Apius checks, turns back where he stands, and addresses a further six ominous lines to Virginius before turning again to leave. After that he has a separate, and this time unmistakable direction to exit.

2. Now comes the direction to Virginius to 'go about the scaffold'. (I take it that 'scaffold' means 'stage'.) It is easy to understand that Virginius is disturbed by this open threat to his daughter's honour, but this alone seems an insufficient reason to direct him specifically to pace to and fro. He might rage, admittedly, but to order him to stride about as he rages seems unnecessary; it is not wrong, but surely the action is a matter for his own decision! If, however, the direction is inserted to show that he too should now *leave* the stage, and rage on the floor round about that stage (and perhaps up and down the hall), then we can see at once that such an action exactly prepares the way for the entrance of Rumour, who would be free to deliver the 28-line speech about Apius's evil intentions from the empty stage while Virginius on the floor stands horrified.

441

A technical precedent for such an action is exactly offered in the well-known direction from the Coventry Cycle, 'Here Erode ragis in the pagond and in the strete also'. Again, a somewhat similar situation so far as relates to an advance forward from the screens-end towards the centre of the hall, occurred in *Wit and Science* when – though for a very different reason – Wit was given the direction 'Wyt cu*m*th before'. There is furthermore a similar intention suggested (as I shall show later) in a direction in *Susanna* where the two lascivious Elders 'go afore into the Orchard and Susanna and her two maydes come vpon the stage'.

3. Before Rumour enters, Virginius, near the end of his first diatribe against Apius, has the line 'home I must'; he is therefore clearly on the point of leaving just as Rumour appears. One pictures him about to go out by one of the screens-doors when he is checked by Rumour's sudden appearance, and he stops and watches over his shoulder.

4. Rumour has run in, presumably by the door opposite to that Virginius is approaching, and mounts the stage to deliver the speech, denouncing Apius.

5. During the latter part of this speech Virginius probably stands by the side of the stage taking in its full import. When it is finished, Rumour steps off the stage and goes out again, and Virginius now turns back and redoubles his diatribe in even stronger terms against the would-be violator, probably raging 'about' again. At the peak of his protest his daughter comes out from the door he had been approaching and asks what it all means.

Summing up now as far as I have reached; what I have intended to show in the above is that the phrase 'go about the stage' is susceptible of two interpretations. I have offered no direct evidence to decide which of these is right, and it may well be that either is right according to the circumstances of the particular presentation.

It is of course difficult to press such a writer as the author of *Apius* on a matter of grammar, but it is not uninteresting to point here to two other examples of this usage of 'going about' a stage, and these by two writers of somewhat more distinction. One is from Wilson's *The Coblers Prophesie* c. 1589 (to be further considered below), where on fol. A.4.*rev.* we have a direction regarding the Cobbler's Wife (and I italicize the important words) – 'Here she runnes *about the stage* snatching at euerie thing'. And the other is from Gascoigne's *Supposes*, IV, vi, where 'Erostrato is espied upon the stage running about', that is to say, running about *upon the stage*. The latter example is quite unequivocal; Erostrato must run about *on* the stage. The former is equivocal; it might mean the Wife runs about *on* the stage (in which case Wilson is not as grammatical as Gascoigne) or it might mean she steps off the stage and runs round *about* it on the floor, snatching at everything she pleases among the audience.

All this might seem to be splitting hairs. But there are still two other directions to consider, in which the evidence for the latter interpretation grows gradually more formidable.

The first is an apparently quite innocent direction in *Horestes* which simply reads, 'Let ye dru*m* play & enter Horestis wt his band marche a bout the stage'. Consider this now in practical detail. There is nothing to show, any more than there was in *Godly Queen Hester*, how many men might comprise Horestes' band, but as we shall see later they represent an invading army, and one supposes there could scarcely have been less than four soldiers, that is to say five persons with Horestes himself. If we had to picture here a relatively spacious stage – or even one no more than 15 feet square – the martial evolutions of these five persons might have been unrestricted enough to justify the employment of such a direction as 'march about *on* that stage'. And this may well have been the case. But if the stage were the small footpace I have been led to propose for certain of the above reconstructions – say only some 7 or 8 feet square – then to march about on it with a group of five soldiers bearing weapons (to say nothing of two such groups as the play requires later) would amount to so congested an evolution as to belong more to highly technical morris-dancing than to a play presentation. It might even so have been just possible; but why resort to that possibility when there is open the much simpler and dramatically more effective alternative that Horestes and his band entered in the traditional way by the screens-door on to the hall floor and marched *around* the stage (not mounting it) as many times as required, turning about each time they reached the screens and marching back again, while King Idumeus (as will be explained later) watches them from the stage and finally engages in parley with Horestes?

However, let us grant for the moment that the evidence is still inconclusive. Now I turn to the next reference.

This is the quotation from *Susanna* coming last in the list. The situation here seems a little complicated. But so far as concerns the present matter, it is as follows: the two notorious Elders, who are named Sensuality and Voluptas, are directed to enter at l. 646. The former expresses his state of hungry lust; the other then reminds him of how they 'found by secrete meanes Susannas haunt to spye' . . . where 'Shee goeth ech day . . . Within her Orcharde her to wash, . . . There were we sure at the least, our eyes to fyll and please, . . .' – if naught else! Sensualitie approves and says that if they 'could closely hyde' themselves there, then 'through loue or might, We would haue both our pleasure . . .' Voluptas replies 'let vs go and hyde our selues, within that Orcharde then, . . .' And Sensualitie concludes with 'O Lord that she were there, Away apace, go on afore, me thinke she commeth here'!

So he ends with a typical entrance-heralding speech.

But before Susanna comes in, a certain particular piece of business has to take place, and its nature is of very considerable importance. Before discussing it I must try to visualize the picture which the two Elders are making – or have just finished making. There is, as the sequel proves, a stage here; it is almost certain, then, that the two old men must be standing on the stage to conduct their very significant dialogue. They talk of the Orchard, and then they hear Susanna approach. Sensuality, as he hears her, says '*Away* apace', suggesting some action involving quickly leaving the stage, and adds 'go on *afore*'. 'Afore' I have already shown to be possibly a curious word in acting-directions, in my discussions of the Wytcumth-before incident. The same conundrum seems to be proposed here, for it is immediately after this line of Sensuality's that there comes the very remarkable direction (repeating the word 'afore') – 'Here they go *afore* into the Orchard, and Susanna and her two maydes come vpon the stage'. (The italics are mine.)

So two separate and nearly simultaneous actions are unavoidably suggested, namely, that the Elders step down from the stage and go in front of it 'into the Orchard', while at the same time Susanna and two maids enter from one of the screens-doors and mount the stage, at any rate for the time being, because they certainly do not go into the Orchard yet; they are only directed to do so some 18 lines later, after Susanna has exchanged certain pious sentiments with her maids. Then she ends her speech with, 'to the Orchard let vs go' and a nearly similar direction to the last now follows, 'Here they goe into the Orcharde'. So these three women presumably take the same sort of action as the two Elders had done, going from the stage 'vpon' which they had previously entered according to the direction, and 'afore' it 'into the Orchard'.

It is almost impossible to avoid the conclusion that the Orchard was *in front of* the stage. That is the same thing as saying that, however it may have been represented in detail, it was represented on the hall-floor level, and thus that both floor and stage were used for the action of the scene (see later, Fig. 39). The remainder of the very puzzling action here and in the rest of the play will be touched on later; at this moment I simply note a growing confirmation of the theory put forward above.

I think there must be implied the existence of two acting areas; the old traditional one consisting of the hall floor generally; and the relatively novel, specific one – of such great future potential – of an as yet small and low, raised stage set so as to be clear of the screens-doors (since the actors must come in through these) and fronting the centre screen ready to give eminence to any episode central to the action.

Having now prepared the way by studying the above extracts, I turn to take these plays in greater detail, besides touching briefly on certain others.

40 *Pacient Grissill*

The 'commodye' of *Pacient Grissill* by John Phillip, about 1559, was probably performed by a company of boys, and perhaps before Queen Elizabeth (or even, if a year earlier, before Queen Mary). It may then not necessarily be conceived in pure Interlude technique. It is a very vigorously and crudely written play with a savage and Satanic vice. It is remarkable for astonishingly bold condensations of time and place.

I quote from the Malone Society Reprint of 1909. There the title-page is as follows:

THE COMMODYE OF
pacient and meeke Grissill,
Whearin is declared, the good example,
of her pacience towardes her Husband: and lykewise, the
due obedience of Children,
toward their Parentes.
Newly.
Compiled by Iohn Phillip.

445

Eight persons maye easely play this Commody.
1. Polliticke Perswasion the Vice. the Epiloge. For one.
2. Preface. Marquis. For another.
3. Fidence. Indigence. The second Paidge or Seruing man,
   The Sonne of Grissill. For another.
4. Reason. Dilligence. Countis Mayd. Pacience.
   and the Daughter of Grissill. For another.
5. Sobrietie. Countis of Pango. Common people. Constancy.
6. Rumor. Jannickle.
7. Jannickells Wife. The first of the Pages. The Nursse.
8. Grissill. The Midwife.

Imprinted at London,
In Fleetestreat beneath the Conduit,
at the signe of Saint John Euangelist by Thomas Colwell.

After a short 'Preface', the play begins with one of the most
extraordinary of all Vice's speeches, a farago of absurdity about
having fallen down from Jupiter's door to the dungeon of Hell,
ridden thence back to Jupiter, been thrown from his horse on to
Charing Cross, and so to play. Immediately there follows the direction:

B.i.*rev.*   Heare let ther be aclamor, with whouping and halowinge,
                    As thoughe ye weare huntinge, or chasinge the game.
                    Enter *Gautir, Sansper Fidence, Reasone,* and *Sobriete.*

Thus, there come into the hall the Marquis Gautier and three
courtiers to the accompaniment, presumably, of as much noise as
they can make. They proclaim in characteristic verse that they have
been hunting; here is a sample:

59. Euen now from hawtie woods, wher Eccose syluer sownde,
    Amonge the shroubs and valies loe, to skyes doth forth rebound
        [. . .]
    The wandring Bucke by staggring strocke, of launch from blody
        boe
    And nimble course of silly houndes, hath caught the ouer throe,
        etc. etc.

The Vice whose name is Polliticke Perswasion comments suitably,
'Hunters quoth you? mary heres agoodlie rable'. Gautier ends the
scene by asking his courtiers if any quality is lacking in himself;

446

they reply that he is unmarried. After some dialogue he agrees to elect a mate. '*Exiunt*'. Politicke concludes –

214.   Naye I will followe after as fast as I can,
                For if I be missing my Lorde lackes a man.
                    Heare enter Grissell, Syngyng.
                    and Spinning: wyth her Parents,
                    and Indigent Pouertie.

No direction is given for Politicke to leave. There follows however an intimate scene between Grissell and her parents. She enters, probably alone at first, and begins by singing her first song as she spins. The song is in six eight-line stanzas, with the pleasant refrain, 'Singe danderlie Distaffe, & danderlie . . .', and it is presumably at the end of it that the others enter, for Grissell's first line after singing is 'How do you my Parentes? I praye you declare:' – and the mother replies, 'Well good daughter God be praysed.' The scene proceeds quietly, emphasizing their poverty and contentment and Grissell's obedience, until the Mother, despite her cheerful reassurance, is taken ill and Grissell says (l. 338), 'Come on deare mother stay on my shoulder let vs depart this place,' and Janickel the father adds, 'I will to my cottaige to comfort my wife this is plaine'. So he clearly identifies the entrance they have used as his cottage; but there would seem no reason to believe that any representation of the cottage itself was made – beyond this allusion to one of the screens-doors. Let us suppose for the purpose of reconstruction that it was the door on the actors' Right Hand – call it door A. An '*exiunt*' follows as the group leaves and then the Vice speaks straight away. He must therefore come into the action again, and he resumes his comments. He tells the audience that the Marquis Gautier is already running mad 'for Mariage' and is set 'To prayse his spouse . . .'

357.   But to none of his court the gentilwoman is knowne, [. . .]
       So that euery man longeth to vew the Ladyes presence.

The next thing is that Gautier himself speaks of his longing, and thus (although there is no direction) he must have entered here, with his three courtiers, and they have perhaps mounted the stage. Immediately on this, the Vice has a long speech bitterly criticizing women, in which he is now and then interrupted and reproved by one of Gautier's courtiers – and yet Gautier himself makes no response at all and seems not to have heard it (though some of it must have been particularly insulting to a prospective husband). At

447

length, by l. 449, Gautier suddenly speaks again, and bids his knights bedeck themselves for 'this longe desyred daye'. The knights now respond with all due courtesy to his statement that 'To morowe next I will featch home my spouse,' but the Vice on the other hand startles us with (l. 456), 'By my troth if it lyke your honor she is a hansome blowse. Gyll sparow that milkt good man peatches Cowes'. The Marquis apparently totally ignores this, and yet a few lines later one of his courtiers sharply demands of the Vice – 'What sayst thou.' The impression is that a sort of invisible, semi-penetrable wall surrounds Gautier and the three courtiers, and that just outside this wall the Vice makes his comments so that they can be overheard and replied to by the courtiers standing near it, but inaudible to the Marquis standing well within it. Such an effect could be precisely achieved if the Vice spoke from the floor of the Place while the Marquis stood at the back of the stage, and his courtiers surrounded him from near its edge. At any rate, the court now leaves. The Vice speaks a dozen comic lines of farewell generally, and follows. And then immediately Grissell comes in again (l. 479).

She announces that her mother has died, and sings a second song 'to the tune of Damon & Pithias' as a sort of dirge. She then goes out once more ('*Exiunt*', given in the plural). Now there follows the direction 'Enter two Lackeys.' (l. 528). They come from certain guests invited to the wedding, and quarrel and go out. An '*Exiunt*' is marked.

Next Grissell speaks (l. 451), so she must come in again; she says that 'Now that my spininge ended is, and house full cleanly made,' she will make a trip to a well, adding –

555. For I will fetch from thence wt speed, some dulsome water sweete
And deyntie brothe for parent make, as fitlye is and meete . . .
And hastelie from Well retourne, to comfort him with foode,
Warme meates are meet for aged folke, to nourish vp ther blood.
                                            Enter *Marquis*, with hys Lordes.

It is quite clear from what follows that Grissell does not yet meet them. She must, all the same, go out by one door or the other; to return by the door she has just entered (door A) would seem inconsistent since that is her 'home' door, and so I presume she crosses on the floor to the opposite door B and goes out before the others come in. Then the courtiers presumably enter and mount the stage.

One might break off here to notice the great freedom which this convention of presentation offers to the playwright. No specific locality is attributed to the acting-area at all, it is free to be anything – or rather to be the basis for the actors whatever scene they are representing. No cottage of Grissell or court of Gautier or hunting forest need ever be shown, but only that which matters – that is to say the *events* of the people connected with that cottage and that court. Yet the place each group belongs to is never in doubt.

To resume: Gautier thanks his courtiers for their advice to him, and then there follows the somewhat unexpected direction, 'Turne to the Ladies.' This is the first indication we have that, with the Lords of the court, some Ladies have come in too. No mention of them is made in the list of parts. Gautier addresses them –

582. Ye matrones all ye Ladies faire, lyke thankes I do impart, [. . .]
     I meane in that ye readie are, attendaunce due to giue,
     And to featche home my mate elect, with whom in loue I liue.
           Let ther be .ii. or .iii. Ladies.

His speech contains in all nine lines, so this specification of the number of the Ladies comes late. They reply to him, and these four lines come at this point:

LADIES.   Nomore but dutie we do shewe, wherfore your mynd
          content,
         To honor you with reuerence due, we Ladies all be bent.
594. GRISSILL. Nowe that my Pot to brinkes I haue filled,
         I will haste mee home with all conuenient speede: [. . .]

– and she goes on philosophizing for eighteen lines.

The position now needs carefully visualizing. Grissell has gone out to the well. In her absence the Marquis and at least two courtiers and 'two or three' ladies have entered and exchanged conversation. Grissell, her pot now filled, returns from the well, passes the assembled court, has time to soliloquize to the length of eighteen lines, but fails to see the crowd of strangers! How could this be arranged?

If we assume that the stage is like that shown in Fig. 36, then, upon it Gautier and his court could very reasonably be assumed to group themselves. Now Grissell would come back from the well by the door B and, keeping to the hall floor, walk forward, turn to her right and go about the front of the stage, turn again to her right, and prepare to go out by the opposite door A, to her home, without mounting the stage at all. This could be so managed as to give her ample time, with rests from carrying the pot, to deliver her eighteen lines. It would also make reasonable as nothing else could a condition that is inescapable in the text; namely, that she does not appear to see the courtiers though, as will be clear in a moment, they can see her.

To recapitulate, what is implied here is the existence of a convention by which, when a stage was used in a hall, two acting-areas would be recognized, more or less independent of each other. The old acting-area on the floor would be retained as before, and the one now offered by the stage would be additional to it but separate (to a variable extent, according to requirements) from it. The floor acting-area would be entered, as it always had been, by walking through one of the screens-doors; the new, stage acting-area would be 'entered' by stepping up from the old floor-area – or Place – on to the surface of the stage. One may well see that, in such an arrangement, if the floor-area continued to be called the 'Place', then any stage built on it might assume the corresponding old name of the 'Scaffold', particularly by any players who had been brought up in the Place-and-Scaffold tradition of such performances as *The Castle of Perseverance*. This would account for the use of the word 'scaffold' in the reference from *Apius and Virginia*.

To resume the situation in *Pacient Grissill*. Grissell's perambulatory soliloquy ends with the words (at l. 608) (and I quote at length here directly from the text, adding notes on particular lines afterwards, as with the first reference to *Grissill* above):

GRISSILL. Well I will home with my water Pot without delaye,
I would be loath to offend my father with longe tariaunce,
For such as prouoke their frendes to yre day by daye,
Can not escape Gods terrible vengeaunce.
GAUTIER. God speede Damsell, soft whether awaye,[1]
GRISSILL. Trulye my Lorde homward, as fast as I maye.
GAUTIER. Whear is your father, expresse to mee with speed.
GRISSILL. In his poore Cottage hee resteth in deed.[2]
GAUTIER. Haste and tell him with all festinacion,[3]
That with him his Lorde will haue communicasion.
GRISSILL. Your commaundement with speede performed shall bee,
I will retourne quicklie, your honor shall see,[4]
Good Father be not offended with mee I you desire,
Because so longe from you I haue bin absent.

IANICKEL. Ah daughter Grissell, why shouldest thou such athing
      require,
      Thou art retourned verie soone in my iudgement.
GRISELL   Not so good Father, for comming by the waye,[5]
      I had an occasion and was forced to staye:
      My Lord Gauter our gubernor excelent,
      Whom courteouslye I saluted, with wordes reuerent:
      Willed mee to haste home to my habytacion,
      Who stayeth hereby, with you to haue communicasion:
      Wherfore good father without lenger delaye,
      Let vs repaire to his presence as fast as wee maye.
IANICKEL O deare Childe I will haste to him with dilligence.
GRISSILL God graunt hee maye relieue our indigence.[6]
IANICKLE Oh honorable lorde, God sende thee felicitie, [. . .]

Notes

1. Here I suppose the Marquis and his court to have watched her go round the stage and, just as she is about to go out, they interrupt and stop her.

2. Here she would presumably indicate the door A, where she lives.

3. The Marquis tells her to continue her journey round the stage and hasten to her door.

4. So she does as he asks, and at the door is met by her father. She, characteristically, apologizes for her slight lateness, and her father, equally characteristically, minimizes any delay but clearly *does not* (though he has come to the door) *see the Marquis and his court*.

5. Grissell has now, therefore, to explain to him the meeting she has just had and of which he so obviously has seen nothing, and to deliver to him the Marquis's command. He readily accedes to it.

6. She has one line of prayer for his success as he moves forward from the door – and then he is speaking directly to his 'honorable lorde', so he must have mounted the stage, possibly followed by Grissell.

Now the whole relatively complicated passage – in which a woman goes to a well; a Marquis and his courtiers discuss marriage; the woman returns philosophizing; the Marquis meets and questions her and asks to speak to her father; the woman goes home, apologizes to her father for her delay and gives him the message; and the father and daughter finally set out and come in to the Marquis's presence – is carried through without the slightest hitch and, what is more important, so as to be immediately comprehensible and unmistakable to an audience. This would indeed seem to be a likely school for training in the method Shakespeare used.

We now picture all parties concerned in the scene to be in one group together on the stage. A long passage follows until the Marquis takes Grissell off as his bride and all his court follows, leaving only Janickel who then soliloquizes and goes off the other way back to his lonely cottage, leaving the Place empty.

Empty that is but for one figure. One may have forgotten the Vice all this time, but he has most definitely been present; now he comes forward and addresses the audience (possibly from the floor) with a truly surprising speech after what has gone before (where, among much else, the Marquis averred that Venus's 'bestiall playes I hate, hir pleasures fylthie are, . . .'). The Vice exclaims with a sneer and a leer –

893.   A *Marquis* maried to a beggerlye Grissill, [. . .]
       The pretie foole is puft vpp, her belly is bigge,
       I coniecture the trull will bringe forth some proper Pigge:

Here is an example of the remarkable licence with which the playwright handles the time factor. No pause is allowed in the action since the couple go to their marriage; yet 24 lines after their exit she is already in advanced pregnancy! When the Vice finishes, Reason and Sobriety come in to talk with him (they may now perhaps mount the stage), and to them, 40 lines later, Dilligence also enters and says –

947.   [. . .] For my Ladie his wife is deliuered this daye,
       Of abewtifull Childe amyable to behould.

– so continuing the time-condensation. Then all go out to spread the good news except the Vice who exclaims, 'Brought a Bed all readie, they haue plyed the box in deed,' and he then communes with himself at length on how, since his 'former deuice, is thrust to exemption,' he may find 'another meane' to 'molest and distroye her cleane,' – until he suddenly brings up short with –

966.   Not a word more my Lorde *Marques* entreth the place, [. . .]

Gautier now sings a song and speaks a speech before seeing the Vice. It may be the Marquis stays in 'the place' where he entered, and the Vice, from the stage, watches him; however, they even-

452

tually do join conversation, and the Vice speaks insidiously of testing Grissell, using these words –

995.   Shee may be made a saynte for her good conuersacion:
       But harke my Lorde nay nowe harken in your eare,
       Try hir that waye and by myne honestie I sweare,
       You shall see hir decline from Vertues so rife,
       And alter topsie turuie hir saintish lyfe: [. . .]

Clearly the above five lines do not make sense unless after the second one the Vice beckons Gautier up on the stage beside him and pours a whispered plot into his ear which the spectators cannot hear. The Marquis assents to it readily, and there now follows a further passage which, without the stage-and-place convention proposed above, is difficult and nearly meaningless. It runs –

1003. GAUTIER   So sure will I in euery poynt, this thy deuice approue:
                Therfore call in with speede, my seruaunt Dilligence,
                That of this act, wee maye giue him intelligence.
      POLITICK. Your will shalbe performed without delaye,
                Hoaw Messenger, this place appropriat.[1]
      DILLIGENC Who calleth for mee, I am here by this daye,
                What is thy will? thy pleasure intimate.
      POLITICKE Haste thee incontinent to my Lordes presence,[2]
      DILLIGENC That to do I am in a readines.
      POLITICKE See that his person thou honour and reuerence,
                Dispatch horson Dreamer, go forward with speedines.[3]
      DILLIGENC Soft fyre the common Prouerbe saith, sweete Malt doth
                   make.[4]
      POLITICKE The matter requireth haste, hence thy passaige take.[5]
      DILLIGENC God saue your honor and graunt you his grace.[6]
      GAUTIER. Messynger thou art hartely welcome to this place,
                I haue secrit thinges to thee to inculcate, [. . .]

Notes

1. According to my theory Gautier and the Vice would both be on the stage at the beginning of this scene. After the Vice has been ordered to call in Dilligence, he summons him by jumping off the stage, running to the door B, leaning out and shouting 'Hoaw Messenger' – or taking some similar actions to the same purpose. And then he adds as the Messenger approaches, 'This place appropriat' – or 'Take your position in the Place here'. Dilligence does so and enquires who calls.

2. Then the Vice hurries him with 'Haste thee' (pointing to the

stage) 'to my Lordes presence'. An order to haste to his Lord's presence would be pointless if Dilligence were already in that presence. But the lines most clearly indicate that he is not in the presence yet. Therefore he must be on the floor.

3. Next the Vice, still on the floor with him, hustles the Messenger officiously, and shouts to him as he hesitates, 'Go forward with speediness'.

4. There could be no other reason for the odd introduction of the proverb quoted at this point than to show the Messenger's resentment at being hustled; which proves that he *is* being hustled and thus is still not in Gautier's presence.

5. The Vice still presses him with 'hence thy passaige take' (that is, as I see it, the passing up from the floor to the stage).

6. With this line the Messenger has stepped up and is at length in the Marquis's presence, and addresses him, and is welcomed by him.

I believe that this sequence of speeches is framed with a special reason behind it. It cannot be a normal exchange of conversation for then it would be a pointless muddle. But if the purpose of the sequence is precisely to dramatize the moment's pause at an entrance through a door on to the floor, and of the next movement up from the floor to the dais (that is into the presence), then the device used to effect this dramatization is not uningenious.

At all events, once Dilligence is with Gautier, Gautier tells him of the plot; namely, to go to Grissell and pretend to kill her child but in fact make off with it and take it to Gautier's sister, Countess Pango, for bringing up. Dilligence agrees to do this. And now follows further confirmation of the theory at present being considered:

The playwright has next to introduce another little device; this begins by Gautier swearing Dilligence to secrecy with the beginning of a threat –

1034. If thou to anie wight that lyues, these Nouels showne disclose.

– and in spite of a full point at the end of what is an unfinished line he has not completed the threat, but there comes a hissed interjection from the Vice (probably standing below on the floor, but just behind Dilligence) with a bloodcurdling intensity – 'Gefferye Grimston at midnight, Shall plucke thy bowells throughe thy Nose' – which Gautier does not appear to hear for he blandly concludes –

1037.   My fauourable loue thy selfe for aye, shalt surelye lose.

Dilligence gives sturdy assurances but is interrupted by the Vice hissing again – this time to Gautier – a warning to change their subject because of some newcomers –

> Peace not a worde but gossip for twentie pound,
> Your Spouse with her Nurse and Childe, Enter into place, [. . .]

This is clearly a dramatic moment. One could easily understand the playwright's wishing to make use of whatever device he could to increase its effectiveness. It is to be noted first of all that he uses again this rather unusual form of words 'Enter into place' instead of any of the everyday usages. If now we picture Gautier on the stage catching his breath, and the Vice swiftly stepping up beside him to see how the situation develops, while the two women, with the child, come walking in on the floor, there is certainly an arrangement that could be made use of. As it develops it is clear that the women cannot, or do not, immediately see the group on the stage for they engage in placid, homely conversation wherever they are; Grissell says 'Come on my *Nours* how doth our Child,' and the Nurse replies. Grissell invokes a blessing on the infant, with health 'to ronne, on earth thy vitall race,' and then makes a remarkable *volte-face*; her next lines are:

> 1061. My Lorde and spoused mate, recydeth here in place,
> Him to salute as dutie byndes, I will procead a pace.
>
> NURS And I will to his presence goe, perhapes to get some gaine, [. . .]

And the Nurse speaks three fond lines to the baby, saying his 'smilynge lookes will gratulate' his 'fatheres ioye'. It is therefore quite clear that the women are not, up to that moment, considered to be in Gautier's presence, but are proposing to go in to it. Now, however, they very likely step up on the stage, for Grissell's next lines are,

> 1067. God spead my Lord moast honorable,
> Why are you pensyue what greefe doth you betide, [. . .]

The Vice interpolates, 'Bones howe now how standeth the case,' and predicts that her sorrows are hastening on to her; the Nurse calls Gautier's attention to the baby, suggesting that 'Hir pretie lookes your tristfullnes, with ease maye cleane exile'. But in fact she only precipitates trouble; and Gautier cries –

> A way *Nours* these wordes are all to gether vaine,
> They minishe not but more and more augment my paine, [. . .]

He explains that his nobles have demanded either his exile or the death of 'our sweete childe, which from these loynes ishude, . . .' The situation is enlarged upon until, at l. 1184, there is a stage direction for Dilligence – 'Make as you would kill it.' Gautier says 'conuaye hir out of place' first. The Nurse says she will follow. '*Exiunt*'. Grissell exhibits her inhuman, or superhuman, patience by offering to lead Gautier to some pleasant spot to distract him; and they go out.

The Vice now scolds himself for not having succeeded in breaking Grissell's fortitude and has a very remarkable conclusion to his soliloquy in which he conceivably singles out some pretty spectator:

1229. [. . .] But as I haue begon so will I afflict hir still,
          I am kyn to a wom*m*an in all poynts ile haue my will,
          Fare ye well no remedie I must depart,
          Fare well God be with you my Pigges nie with all my hart,
          If you had *Grissills* pacyence and condiscyons excelent,
          You and I would make a match to marye incontinent. *Exit*
   COUNTES, Of *Pango* I the *Countis* am, my praise doth splendish bright,
          [*etc.*]

Thus we have another surprise in this surprising play; the 'scene' suddenly 'changes' to the distant town of Bullin Lagras, or Bologna, and we see the entrance of Countess Pango, or Panago, who is the sister of Gautier. She is talking with her maid. To them Dilligence brings in the unfortunate baby, and then goes out alone. They praise it and take it out to get it food.

This then is a sudden interpolated short scene, like many later in Elizabethan drama, put in to keep the plot going and to give some sense of break and the passage of time. Immediately on their exit the Vice comes back again and announces, surprisingly, that Grissell is about to have another baby –

1300.   [. . .] The *Marquis* is in trauell God be hir speed,
          And I am sent for mother Apleyarde,
          Who is a Mydwyfe, a Midwife in deade, [. . .]
          Whowp who the Deiull dwells here can any man tell,
          Art thou a Mayd or a widdow that tendeth this house,
          I thinke thou be sister to the viccar of Hell,
          By mie worship if I enter thou shalt beare me asouse.

This is a strange puzzle. Presumably if the Vice had, at the end of the last scene but one, exited by the door B, and the Countess of

Pango with her maid had then entered by the door A, meeting Dilligence from the door B, then the Vice would now enter again from the door B, during his speech, there would be time enough for the door A to lose its Bullin Lagras association and serve, as the Vice came up to it, for the Midwife's cottage.

At any rate, the Midwife, understandably, is annoyed at the Vice's attitude, but agrees to follow him to court. There follows an '*Exiunt*' for them – perhaps by the door B. But the dramatic function of this interpolation is still a mystery.

Gautier now enters, distracted by Grissell's labour pains. Does he come in by the same door the Vice and Midwife have just gone out by? Presumably so. Dilligence comes to him and tells him he has a new son. The Marquis rewards him and goes off to see it. '*Exiunt*', again in the plural though Dilligence is left to tell the audience how pleased the household is with Gautier, and then '*Exit*', this time in the singular. The Vice returns and describes the christening feast, thus condensing time again. And now a Nurse brings in the new child and sings to it. Then to them 'Enter *Dilligence* his sword drawn'. He has six lines of horrific threat which the Nurse does not hear for she goes on with her lullaby (thus he presumably speaks from the Place). But then he speaks again; and she now vigorously responds, so perhaps he has stepped up on the stage. After dialogue, he says, 'I will take the childe and murther it in haste. Go out.' The last words are separated and must be a stage direction to him; he must be assumed to take the child with him. The Nurse now wails and goes off to tell Gautier; '*Exit*'.

Now the Vice returns and informs the audience that he feels his plot is working at last, but adds that he has a better idea still for dealing with Grissell – then he checks again because –

1486. Behould yonder they enter both to gether,
    Suerly I minde to giue hir, hir welcome hether,
    God saue your honors may I be bould with you my Lord to
      haue a word or twain
    Truly for your profit I wold speake wt you faine.

– and Gautier immediately responds and the dialogue continues in this way –

MARQUES   Say what you please I am readie the to heare.
PERSWA [*sic*] Then I beseche you come apart for it is secrit geare.
MARQUES   With all my hart heare the I will.

POLITICKE And in faith I will seeke to pleasure you still,
     Harke it is euen so, you shall well espye,
     Harke againe, this is the mean hir pacyence to trie.
MARQUIS Lord this deuice I will straight put in vre [*use*], [. . .]

So again the Vice has summoned Gautier aside, possibly up onto the stage, and whispered secretly in his ear. The Marquis now calls Grissell to come near and hear what is in store for her. What he tells her is that his subjects envy her good fortune and want her to be sent, 'naked' and penniless, back to her father, and for him to marry again – all of which he proposes to do. The Vice, listening to him, produces a rare oath in his joy: 'Bones quod ioyner who made God all mightie, . . .'. Grissell responds with her icy acquiescence, and nearly sways the Marquis back to mercy for her, but the Vice steels him. An otherwise unnoticed Maid has a word at l. 1600. Grissell asks classically to be given a 'symple Smocke to hide and couer my nakednes', and she goes, as do the others. Then on to the empty stage 'Enter *Rumor* blowynge & puffing.' (l. 1671). He tells how the news has spread through the country. To him enters Vulgus, representing the common people, who mourns Grissell and then catches sight of her coming in with Reason and Sobriety to be taken back to her father. She passes across with her two conductors, most likely keeping on the floor, from the door B to the door A; on the way they are watched by Vulgus who deplores her fate and then goes out. Then, as Grissell and her conductors are approaching the door, they pause and speak:

1719. REASON Lowe Maddame, we approche your fathers house at
     this season.
  GRISSELL Frendes in place I haue ben very geason [*scarce?*],
     But nowe my fathers presence I shall continually
     behoulde, [. . .]
  IANICKLE What clamorous noyse is this, that I heare,
     That all be not well, I greatly feare,
     Ahlas) [*sic*] my Daughter Grissill, all naked I see, . . .

So they have now left the Court, passed by the 'people' and come back to Janickel's poor cottage again. He brings out a ragged coat for her. She thanks the courtiers for seeing her home and they leave her and return, bearing her compliments for her husband; '*Exiunt*'.

Grissell now talks with her father, promising to stay with him and support him by spinning – 'My Rocke and Distafe, are instruments doubtles, With which . . . Will I labor and toile our bodies to fead.' A 'Rock' is either a distaff, or a distaff together with the wool or flax attached to it; or the quantity of wool or flax placed on a distaff for spinning (see *O.E.D.* where the word is interestingly noted as 'possibly a native English word').

Immediately after this, 'Enter Pacience and Const ancye.' who observe – 'For we are perfit props to the disquieted minde', and they go with Grissell and Janickel into their house to dwell with them. A clear *'Exiunt'* is marked. The scene is empty now for a moment, and then Dilligence, the Marquis's messenger speaks.

(It is at this point that the passage begins which contains the particular stage direction to 'go once or twise about the Staige' which I have already picked out at the beginning of Section 39 because of its categorical evidence for the use of a stage. I gave the passage in full detail there and I need not repeat it now. Any reader who wishes to picture the development of the play consecutively should return to pp. 426 to 429 before resuming with the next paragraph.)

The Messenger speaks a short soliloquy, and Grissell enters and sings. He listens and at length comes to the purpose of his visit.

The message that he now brings Grissell from her husband is a nice piece of turning the knife in the wound; she must come back because the rule of the Marquis's house –

1867.
                      [. . .] is assined onlie to thee,
> All the officers of his house, shall to thee obedient bee,
> But aboue all thinges thou must make prouission,
> That his newe Spouse may be lodged after the best wise:

Grissell uncomplainingly agrees to these humiliating terms, and so Dilligence says,

> Then in this place, let vs no lenger abyde,
> For I purpose to bee your waityng man.

– and they go out together; *'Exiunt'*.

The next line immediately following is from the Marquis, who says,

> Come on my Ladie deere, my Spouse and louing mate, [. . .]

and he obviously comes in bringing with him his new bride. It would seem that what must happen at this juncture is that Dilligence and Grissell have crossed the floor, leaving her own door A to return to the Marquis's door B; they have then gone out and there must be a moment's pause before the Marquis and his bride come in from the same door B. And behind this couple there follows a quite large group of people; beside the new bride (who is of

459

course the daughter of Gautier and Grissell) there is present the Countess Pango, and with her Gautier's and Grissell's second child (the bride's brother), and presumably as many courtiers, male and female, as can be procured. All have brief speeches, expressing somewhat fulsome good wishes for the incestuous marriage. Then, after 24 lines of this, the Marquis announces, rather surprisingly, that they are all to go out again –

1899.   I thanke you both for your good wills, now let vs haste awaye,
   In pompous wise to solemnise, our happye spousall daye.

– and the next lines are from Grissell! It would seem that the court and guests have gone out again simply to give Grissell a clear stage for a short, pious soliloquy; she comes in and begins –

   Now that I haue set all thinges in aredines,
   For the commyng of my Lord, I purpose to attend, [. . .]
   And the fruites of good will to him still ostend, [. . .]

– and she goes on to say that Pacience and Constancie so arm her that she 'can not be vanquisht in fight'. Then she still goes on with what must be a soliloquy but she describes the appearance of the guests to the wedding in such a way as to leave little doubt that she is actually watching them come in –

   Lo behould yonder thay begin in presence to appeare,
   Certes his spouse is wonderfull Amorous,
   With him lyke case, commeth a youngman wonderfull fayre,
   I will salute them with loquie courtuous:
   God saue you my Lorde, [. . .]

– and she greets them all. The Marquis replies on behalf of the company –

1919.   Wee thanke thee Grissill for thy courtuous salutacion,
   And regreet thee agayne, [. . .]

There seems no really acceptable alternative for straightening out this muddle, so as to be practical theatrically, but to see firstly the wedding party go out, probably by the door B, leaving the Place empty, and then to have the entrance of Grissell, on her own, so that she can mount the stage and begin her soliloquy saying she has set all things in readiness. Thereafter, to have the members of the wedding party return again, filing in on to the floor and then, as she says that 'they begin in presence to appeare', to have them mount the stage one by one to be saluted by Grissell, like a hostess, 'with loquie courtuous'.

When all are at length assembled on the stage, Gautier asks Grissell to say frankly what she thinks of his bride. She replies with abject humility that she is charming – but fortunately the worm in Grissell can turn; she concludes her speech to Gautier –

1933. But harke my Lord, what I saye to thee agayne,
Take heed thou pricke her not, with the Needles of disdayne:
As thou hast done the other, for shee hath bin brought vp
    dayntelie,
And peraduenture, can not take the matter so pacientlie.

At this, one is glad to find, the Marquis at last breaks down and as a climax (or anti-climax) reveals all, introducing to Grissell those whom she thought were strangers, as her own children. She is understandably overcome: 'Fall downe'. Her son and daughter praise her, her sister-in-law says how great a cause she has for happiness (!), the courtiers chime in. Then the Marquis orders everyone out again for rejoycing, and the Place is left empty once more.

Now Janickel comes in quietly from his door opposite and begins,

1977. Much musinge in minde, wheare my Grissill is thus longe,
My waueringe minde is tossed, with thoughts to and froe, [. . .]

– and then in the midst of his musing an answer is brought to his questions by a most timely coincidence, and he breaks off to exclaim –

        [. . .] the *Marquis* entreth this place,
    I will hast to him with all festinacyon,
    And [. . .]

– not 'I will question him directly' as might be expected, but –

    [. . .] rest me behinde him, alittill space,
Peraduenture I shall heare newes, by his communicasion.

The Marquis now proceeds to discuss with his two courtiers, Reason and Sobriety, the superb merits of his true wife. Janickel creeps near and drinks in this good news. The Marquis bids the courtiers remain loyal to Grissell's children after his own death; they plight their faith. And Gautier is just on the point of inviting them to stroll out with him ('Come on I besech ye and walke with me a littill waye'), when old Janickel gives thanks aloud to God 'Which hath stirred this *Marquis* on Grissill to take compassion'. Checked by the voice the Marquis turns and sees his destitute father-in-law and takes pity on him, and (in old Interlude technique) tells him to 'Put of these garments' and 'Cloth thy selfe with these Ornaments', bidding his nobles to help the while, and at length leading him off 'to our Mansyon'. . . . (*Exiunt.*)

Now Grissell, with the Countess and her son and daughter, have a short scene exchanging thanks and compliments, at the end of which she deplores her father's absence. Upon this he enters with Gautier for she says,

> Beholde thy [*read* my] husband and thy [*read* my] Fathers aidged face,
> Who both together frendly do entder this place,
> His rags are chainged to Sylkes I perfytly see,
> Now know I asuredly my Lord doth fauor mee.

General congratulations follow, and then the Marquis bids them –

> 2090.   Come on now let vs to our place with ioyfullnes,
>   ALL   We all will attend on you with willyngnes.   *Exiunt.*

There follows now only the usual courteous address to the Queen with a prayer for her Councillors.

The above all goes to show what complicated developments in the system of presentation are by now creeping into Interlude technique. Whether apology is due for treating this not particularly distinguished play at so great a length I do not know. But it seems to me that what it appears to offer, in the matter of information on staging, is of indispensable value to our review.

The next play to be considered is *Apius and Virginia*.

41 *Apius and Virginia*

A facsimile of *Apius and Virginia* was published by the Tudor Facsimile Text Society in 1908. The title-page reads as follows:

A new Tragicall Comedie
of Apius and Virginia,
Wherein is liuely expressed a rare
example of the vertue of Chastitie,
by Virginias constancy, in wishing
rather to be slaine at her owne Fa-
thers handes, then to be deflow-
red of the wicked Iudge
Apius.

By R. B.

The Players names.

Virginius.	Conscience.
Mater.	Iustice.
Virginia.	Claudius.
Haphazard.	Rumour.
Mansipulus.	Comforte.
Mansipula.	Rewarde.
Subseruus.	Doctrina.
Apius.	Memorie.

Imprinted at London, by Wil-
liam How, for Richard Ihones.
1575.

The action opens with a rhapsodic, even sentimental, scene between Virginius and his wife and their daughter Virginia, in which they extol their own virtuous states for five pages. Next comes a scene between Haphazard, the Vice, and three servants containing many obscurities and lasting six pages. Then Judge Apius enters and soliloquizes upon the strength of his unsatisfied lust for Virginia; Haphazard suggests a way in which Apius can seduce her. Apius is torn with doubts, and there follows this strange direction, printed in the margin:

C.i.   Here let him make as thogh he went out and let Consince and Iustice come out of him, and let Consience hold in his hande a Lamp burning and let Iustice haue a sworde and hold it before Apius brest.

Some editors clearly believe this direction needs amending. In Hazlitt's Dodsley we have the suggestion of 'come after him' instead of 'come out of him'. It might seem to meet the case better if we simply read 'come *in* to him' – implying that as Apius was on the point of leaving, he was intercepted by two strange figures who then performed a mimed bye-play. But it is possible to retain the direction as it stands if we go a step further, and permit ourselves the slightly novel theory that a piece of neat trick-dodging took place here, and that as Apius blocked the doorway with his body, two actors simultaneously stepped from either side the door beyond him, to stand momentarily masked by him, one behind the other, facing him in close proximity, so that he recoiled a pace and they then side-stepped to left and right of him and so appeared to 'come out of him'. This may well be possible though it seems a little strained; it is however, in my opinion, a less unlikely interpretation than that the two appeared from below by means of some sort of trap.

Apius' speech following their appearance has some points of interest. He has just been announcing his intention to go and wreak his worst on Virginia whatever happens, when these two figures appear, and his speech at this point suddenly has the lines –

> But out I am wounded, how am I deuided?
> Two states of my life, from me are now glided, [. . .]

– and thus we seem to be given a very strong hint that in fact some sort of trick-appearance for Conscience and Justice was engineered, by which they would seem to have 'glided' out from him. Haphazard seeming not to see them, persuades Apius that the two figures (who have not so far spoken) 'are but thoughts'; and at length Apius reaffirms his intention to 'deflower hir youth', and orders Haphazard to 'Come on procede and wayte on me'. Haphazard makes a curious reply, followed by two curious directions:

> At hand (quoth picke purse) here redy am I,
> See well to the [? *thee*] Cut Purse, be ruled by me.
>   Exit.   Go out here.

The reason for the two directions in different languages but with the same meaning is not clear.

Conscience and Justice, now left alone, have two short speeches (this is the first time we have heard their voices), and then they 'Exit'. Haphazard returns. Then (on fol. C.i.) 'Here entreth Judge Apius and Claudius', and these two lay the plot mentioned earlier; that is, that Claudius should depose that Virginia had really been stolen by Virginius and was not his true daughter. Haphazard and Claudius then leave Apius who speaks three lines alone, and then there is the curious direction, 'Here let Conscience speake within', and his voice now reproves Apius. Apius exclaims, 'Whence doth this pinching sounde desende!', and Conscience announces his name, but says he is 'Compeld to crie with trimbling soule' because he is near dying. Still Apius is unrepentant. It is, I think, clear from the elaboration of the above little scene that some particular care was taken in its presentation to make the action dramatically effective. The means may have been crude, but the technical aims of the developing Interluders seem certainly to be growing more ambitious.

Now, after a sort of break for relief, in which a song from two semi-comic servants is sung, the plot presses on with the entry of

Virginius; and the passage already examined above beginning 'I enter will Judge Apius gate . . .' etc. with its direction to 'go about the scaffold' then follows (see above pp. 439 to 442).

Just at its conclusion there comes one stage-direction (this modern term can now be legitimately used) that offers a hint about acting conventions, and is curiously comparable to a convention used as far away as the harvest-festival plays of Tibet. Poor Virginius, perplexed in the extreme, sees no alternative to losing Virginia's honour save to take away her life. So he draws his sword and (see fol. D.iii.*rev.*) 'Here let him profer a blowe'; she checks him with the ancient pretext, 'Let first my wimple bind my eyes' . . . The stage direction then follows, 'Here tye a handcarcher aboute hir eyes, and then strike of hir heade.' This is closely reminiscent of the Tibetan procedure as described by Marion Duncan in his *Harvest Festival Dramas of Tibet*, where a character is killed by her headdress being sliced off with a sword.

I presume that the effect in *Apius and Virginia* would not have been entirely realistic, but it probably indicated what was meant well enough for that barnstorming atmosphere. What is more of a question is how the players got rid of Virginia's 'headless' body. We learn that her father is told (by Comfort of all people!) to take her head to the rapacious King Apius as earnest that she preferred death to dishonour, but no indication is to be found in the script of how her body was cleared away. It may well have been, in view of the character of the rest of the play, that the lad who was playing her simply rose to his feet and walked off out of the action. Exactly that sort of solution is managed with complete propriety and unbroken dignity by the Kathakali players after one of their bloodthirsty murder scenes.

The general tenor of *Apius and Virginia* is one which amply demonstrates that the sort of action offered in the players' scene in *Hamlet* is no exaggeration.

It may be worth noting in passing that the introduction of a stage into the Interluders' technique will have one inevitable result on the character of the Interlude as an entertainment; and that is that never again can a show of this sort, presented at a banquet in a hall, effectively pretend to be a spontaneous thing. The 'interlude' is finished. That engaging joke of unpremeditation that Medwall played at the beginning of the century in his *Nature* and his *Fulgens* can never be effective again. The reason being, of course, that the players could not involve a hall in the clutter and preparation of putting up a stage without giving away to the guests the fact that they were going to do a play there.

Thus, the very 'interlude' nature of an Interlude must henceforward be changed; it now becomes a clearly premeditated entertainment. And it is not surprising that about this time there begins to be a distinction between the terms 'Interlude' and 'stage-play' as applying to two different kinds of show; and eventually both those names give way to the more specific 'comedy' or 'tragedy'.

Twelve Plays Briefly Considered 1560–1566

The Disobedient Child ∽ *Tom Tyler* ∽ *All for Money* ∽ *Gorboduc*
∽ *The Pedler's Prophecy* ∽ *The Longer thou Livest* ∽ *Enough is as
Good as a Feast* ∽ *The Trial of Treasure* ∽ *King Daryus* ∽ *Damon
and Pythias* ∽ *Supposes* ∽ *Mary Magdalene*

42 *The Disobedient Child*

The next play after *Apius* which offers information worth studying
in any detail is *Horestes*, dated 1567; but in the interval of seven
years before this there are several minor plays – minor from the
point of view of setting information – that can conveniently be
grouped together and reviewed briefly here. The first of these is
Thomas Ingelond's *The Disobedient Child* of about 1560.

The Disobedient Child is almost the only play of the many concerning the evil of children brought up without strict discipline
that does in fact live up to its description of a 'pretie and mery new
Enterlude'. It is brightly and gayly written and tends rather to be a
skit on the grim, earlier admonitions to parents. It makes the 'Rich
Man' as much a caricature of a stupid father as it makes the son a
caricature of rebellious youth. All the young man wants is to abandon his lessons and get married, and he touches what is still a
familiar note today –

> I cannot, I tell ye again, so much of my life
> Consume at my book without a wife.

– and at last he flings off through the spectators with

> Room, I say, room let me be gone
> My father if he list shall tarry alone.
> > Here the Son goeth out and the
> > Rich Man tarrieth behind alone.

467

The Father despairs at the situation until –

> Here the Rich Man goeth out and the
> Two Cooks cometh in: first the one,
> & then the other.

These two, a man and a woman, come appropriately straight out of the kitchen. They have a ding-dong quarrell about the preparations for a wedding feast. After providing a fine build-up for the next character they run out, and the Young Woman comes in looking for her lover. Sparkling, music-hall dialogue follows between them after he enters, until they go together to the church. A Priest, complaining of his drunken Clerk, takes up the running, and then gives place to the Rich Man again, who now has had news of the imminent marriage. He bustles impotently and complains with grim foreboding that –

> [. . .] with a wife are two days of pleasure
> The first is the joy of the marriage day and night
> The second to be at the wife's sepulture.

The couple now re-enter married, and some comic dialogue follows at rousing speed on the delights of marriage, until the practicalities of life begin to rise up and –

> Here the Wife must strike her Husband
> handsomely about the shoulders with
> something.

Eventually the quarrell reaches its peak and –

> Here her Husband must lie along on the ground
> as though he were sore beaten and wounded.

And she leaves him. Next the Devil comes in with a long and effective speech containing references to 'this well-favoured head of mine' and 'these my claws', so we may picture him in special array. He goes, and the Son returns to confess his folly until –

> Here the Rich Man must be as it were coming in.

This form of wording is a particularly good witness of that different kind of entrance that was imposed upon Interluders by the presence of the screens and the crowd standing in the screens-doorways. The effect of being *'as it were* coming in' is nearly impossible to conceive on a modern picture-frame stage, but in a Tudor Hall, with its bystanders, such an effect almost cries out to be exploited.

468

The improving moral at the upshot of it all is that no one can help the young man anyway; he has made his bed and must lie on it. A 'Promoter' enters and underscores the lesson to fathers, and then –

> Here the rest of the Players come in and kneel
> down all together, each of them saying one of
> these verses;

– and the show ends with a song to Queen Elizabeth.

43 *Tom Tyler*

The so-called 'excellent old Play' of *Tom Tyler and His Wife*, possibly also dating originally from about 1560, is similarly a jape about marriage but reads, I think, a little more tediously. A Prologue announces 'a play set out by pretty boys' and prays the audience 'To make them room, and silence as you may Which being done, they shall come in to play'.

Destiny (a sage Parson) and Desire (the Vice) open the dialogue and describe how Tom Tyler got a shrew for a wife. Their exit-direction is interesting; it reads 'Here they both go in' – not 'go *out*' as we have been used to see. Tom Tyler's next entrance is marked 'commeth in' (not, as would be consistent with the above, 'commeth out'). Later again is the double direction 'Tom Tyler goeth in, and his wife cometh out'; this is beginning to be the new styling where 'to go in' is used for 'to exit' in place of the old 'go out', and conversely to 'enter' is now expressed by 'come out' instead of the traditional 'come in', though in this play there is admittedly a good deal of confusion, and either style seems to be used indiscriminately throughout. It may be that the new styling is some indication that the play was originally written for booth-stage performance or for some form of stage with the equivalent of a 'tiring-house' at the back. At any rate the innovation is another step on the way to the conventions finally adopted on the public playhouse stage

Returning a moment to the final line of the Prologue; it is interesting to note that the request to an audience to 'make room' for the players should still continue in common use. The many examples of this request which I have pointed out in earlier plays suggested very strongly that it would not be intended to apply to the audience in general, but – particularly because it occurs just before entrances – must be directed especially to those of the spectators who stood in the doorways.

But if this is true something of some importance follows: when we find the phrase continuing to be employed in later plays where it is clear that a stage was used, then it must follow that the presence of a stage did *not* prevent bystanders still crowding in the doorways. Hence it is almost certain (1) that the stage did not extend across the doorways, and thus (2) that an actor after he had come in would still be on the floor level and would have to step up from it to mount the stage, and so (3) there must have been two acting-areas – one on the floor and one on the stage.

44 *All for Money*

Thomas Lupton's *All for Money* (again c. 1560) is a rather unlovable four-part play, which the sub-title describes as 'A moral and pitiefvl comedie', but which the Prologue in his ninety-third line of opening soliloquy calls 'a pleasant Tragedie'. This may be some indication of the new uncertainty of classification which is beginning now to overtake the old style of Interlude.

After some two hundred lines of pretty heavy versification with Theologie ('in a long ancient garment like a Prophet'), and Science ('clothed like a Philosopher'), and Arte ('with certeyne tooles about him of diuers occupations'), the audience may well have felt inclined for a little variation; this they are given by a most curious device, or repetition of devices. The problem, as far as presentation technique is concerned, is whether or not these devices imply the use of a trap, as some editors have supposed. There is unfortunately little enough evidence for solving the problem. The first reference comes in a direction on fol. A.iiii. which reads

> *These three going out, Money commeth in hauing the* one halfe of his gowne yellowe, and the other white, hauing the coyne of siluer and golde painted vpon it, & there must be a chayre for him to sit in, and vnder it or neere the same there must be some hollowe place for one to come vp in.

The purpose of this device (whatever it may be) does not become clear for another eighty lines, though in the meantime Money does

470

make some preparation for he sits in the chair and '*faineth him selfe to be sicke*'. Then on fol. B.i. we have –

> Here money shal make as though he would vomit, and with some fine conueyance pleasure shal appeare from beneath, and lie there apparelled.

Money himself anticipates this odd event with – 'I hope he is comming, for I feele him at my throte'. Afterwards Pleasure (from the floor?) says, 'I must needes take money for the father of me pleasure', and Money then addresses Pleasure as 'my sonne'; thus some sort of a grotesque 'birth' is presumably suggested. Money next says, 'I must needes get me hence, my paynes do make me sweate'. He then presumably goes out. Another character who has been present, called Adulation, says, 'seeing he is gone, I will not tarie behinde' – thus strengthening the idea of an exit, and so leaving the scene free for the new-born Pleasure and for a further character called Mischieuous Helpe. Next, Pleasure also begins to show signs of this strange form of pregnancy; he '*faines him selfe sicke, and speaketh sitting in a chaire*'. – 'What thing is this that makes me thus to swell?' He complains of his pains and at length cries, 'Ohe, helpe, helpe quickly, I neuer stoode in more neede, I am so full of sinne I shall burst without quickespeede.'

> Here he shal make as though he would vomit, and Sinne being the vice [?] shalbe conueyed finely from beneath as pleasure was before.

(The word 'vice' is blotted in the original and, save for the final 'e', can only be guessed.) Sin's first words are very typical of a Vice, for he remarks –

    I was afraied of nothing but onely of my dagger,
    Least in the time of my birth it would haue sticked my father [. . .]
    Yea mary Syr nowe my thinkes¹I am more at libertie,
    I could not once turne me in my fathers bellie, [. . .]

Thus the birth image is fully maintained, though in this abnormal form, since Sin adds concerning his father, 'I haue made his throte so wide he can not be choked with meate'. There is a reference to his adult stature for 'No childe of six yere olde is so bigge in all this towne'.

But for all this, Sin is to suffer in his turn the same pangs as his father and grandfather. He cries (fol. B.ii.)

> Out alas masters, what thing is in my bellie?
> Such paynes as these will quickly make me wearie: [. . .]
> Euen nowe in my bellie, but nowe in my raynes,
> Nowe in my buttockes, and nowe at my heart, [. . .]

The character who is helping him explains that he is about to be delivered of a child called Damnation, at which Sin exclaims

> The horesonnes head is so great, and he is so ill fauoured made,
> That I must needes be ript I am greatly afrayed. [. . .]
> Nowe for a midwyfe I would giue twentie pounde,
> Holde me vp Sirs, for nowe I begin to sounde [*swoon*].

There is little doubt that the image is far more of childbirth than of mere stomach sickness or vomiting. Next, the direction follows –

> *Here shal damnation be finely conueyed as the other was*
> before, who shal haue a terrible vysard on his face, &
> his garme*n*t shalbe painted with flames of fire.

Then all but Sin go out. Sin now has a 25-line soliloquy (in which he orders the spectators 'What, of with your cappes sirs, it becomes you to stande bare' in respect for him) and then –

> *Here commeth in Satan the great deuill as de-*
> formedly dressed as may be.

He is delighted with events, but Sin has little truck with him and makes him 'crie and roare' on two separate occasions, much to the audience's probable delight for Sin suddenly turns to them and snaps –

> You may laugh well ynough that Sinne & the Deuil be falle*n* out,
> But we will fall in againe or euer it be long:

And then –

> *Here commeth in Gluttonie and Pride dressed in*
> deuils apparel, & stayes Sin that is going forth.

– and the mockery goes on for another couple of hundred lines.

I think there is no doubt that despite all the references to vomiting, the sort of business that is caricatured in this chain of directions is that of ordinary childbirth turned 'comic' – there is even a call, as we saw, for a midwife at one point. The chair that is provided may then have been arranged specially for this effect, so that the 'parent' could sit in it, clad in a gown with a long skirt, and the 'child' appear from under the chair between the legs and through those skirts; and 'with some fine conueyance' may mean no more than that the trick must be neatly done. The references to vomiting and to coming out of the 'throte' would then be simply euphemistic.

A problem is offered in the means required to replace each 'child' as it was 'born', by the next, so as to be ready to appear in his turn, but in such a way as not to be too obviously seen by the audience. Perhaps this would be the function of the 'hollowe place' under the chair 'or neere the same' for 'one to come vp in'. What would then be implied would be some sort of concealment, such as a chest, covering the path from the door to the back of the chair, for the actors to crawl behind and get ready to make their appearances. The kind of business seems very like the sleight or trick in *Apius* when Conscience and Justice 'came out of' Judge Apius; but it does not, in my opinion, seem necessary to invoke the use of any trap to achieve these effects. In practice a 'hollowe place' from door to chair could even be managed by simply pulling the stage clear of the screens.

The next 300 lines are taken up with an entirely unrelated action consisting of a dispute between Learning-with-money ('richely apparelled') and Learning-without-money ('apparelled like a scholler') and Money-without-learning ('*apparelled* like a riche churle, with bagges of money by his siides') and eventually Neither-money-nor-learning ('clothed like a begger').

The next 500 lines are again almost unrelated and consist of a separate action where All-for-money plays the part of a corrupt judge at the instigation of the Vice, Sin, and delivers a series of highly biased judgements. Each petitioner 'knockes at the doore' of the hall before entering, presumably much as did B in *Fulgens*.

Next follows a short scene of entirely different nature again, where Judas and Dives repent their respective sins. And the play ends with Godly Admonition, Vertue, Humilitie and Charitie leading up to a blessing on the Queen to conclude.

45 Gorboduc

Thomas Norton and Thomas Sackville's *Gorboduc* was presented in the following year, 1561, at the Inner Temple, and in 1562 at court. As I have already indicated in Section 35, it is almost certainly a show conceived in a new and different convention, and not in the tradition of the Interludes. Its staging need not therefore be discussed here, but it is useful to note it at this point since it is textually so important as the 'first English tragedy'.

46 *The Pedler's Prophecy*

The anonymous *The Pedlers Prophecie* (c. 1561) is little more than an argumentative stretch of dialogue about the ill acts of mankind. It seems to offer no problems of presentation but also no hint of any particular method of performance. All that seems necessary to say of it here is that it must not be confused with *The Coblers Prophesie* by Robert Wilson of c. 1589, for which see Section 69.

47 *The Longer thou Livest*

Two plays now follow which are both attributed to c. 1564, and are both by one of the several playwrights of the name of Wager – in this case William Wager. They are *The longer thou livest, the more foole thou art*, and *Inough is as good as a feast*.

The first of these at any rate seems worthy of description in a little detail here because, though bringing nothing that is particularly new in staging technique, and making its effects by the most economical means, it yet has a quality of polished competence that, as it seems to me, marks its author most surely a man of the theatre. It also proves how live and effective a show the writers could still make out of the old Interlude technique that Medwall introduced us to, without any new-fashioned additions.

The description of *The longer thou livest* is 'A very mery and Pythie Commedie' and 'A Myrrour very necessarie for youth, and specially for such as are like to come to dignitie and promotion: As it maye well appeare in the Matter folowynge.' I have used the Tudor Facsimile Text of the earliest known edition of c. 1568, reproduced in 1910.

The Players names.

Prologue.	Fortune.
Moros.	Ignorance.
Discipline.	Crueltie.
Pietie.	Impietie.
Exercitacion.	People.
Idlenesse.	Gods iudgement

Incontinencie.   Confusion.
Wrath.
Foure may playe it easely.
⎧The Prologue.   Exercitacion.   Wrath.⎫
⎨   ⎬ for one.
⎩   Cruelie.   Goddes Iudgement ⎭
        ⎧ Moros.   ⎫
        ⎨   ⎬ for another.
        ⎩ Fortune. ⎭
⎧Disciplyne.   Incontinencie.⎫
⎨   ⎬ for another.
⎩Impietie   Confusion.   ⎭
    ⎧Pietie.   Idlenes.⎫
    ⎨   ⎬ for another.
    ⎩Ignorance   People. ⎭

This arrangement of the parts would suggest that the play was intended for a small company of professional players. The names in the main list are all printed in black-letter Gothic except that of Moros, second in the list, which is printed in Roman characters; this would seem intended to single him out, perhaps as being the Vice of the play. Certainly his is the leading part, and a fairly amusing one. The play is on the common theme of the disobedient child. After the Prologue, Moros enters straight away with a characteristic direction: 'Here entreth *Moros*, counterfaiting a vaine gesture and a foolish countenance, Synging the foote of many Songes, as fooles were wont.' He has a page of these snatches of popular songs, and then is roundly condemned by Discipline and later by Pietie as a spoilt child who ought to be put to school. After six pages of contempt they 'Holde him & beate him.' After four more pages in the same vein poor Moros puts on the appearance of submitting to them, and 'Go out pieti and Moros', for Moros to be put to school. In his absence Discipline and Exercitation grimly discuss his turpitude; and during their talk comes the direction 'Betweene whiles let Moros put in his head.' So we have the spectacle of the cunning child peeping out from between the spectators at the doors. Even more point is made of this action since Exercitation catches sight of it out of the corner of his eye, and dryly observes,

> With Pietie, you are not like him to finde,
> He did put in his head twise or thrise,
> He looketh for mates of an other kinde,
> Wholy he is geuen to folly and vice. [. . .]   Go out both.
>   Here entreth Idlenesse.
> Where the deuill is the horsen foole, [. . .]
> What ho, where art thou Moros? what ho? [. . .]

– and then on top of this effective exploitation of the circumstances of the action, there comes a pitiful voice wailing from behind the screens according to the direction 'Crie without the doore making a noyse of beating.' and Moros is heard exclaiming 'Alas, alas nomore, nomore, nomore, . . . Bodie of God you beate me so sore.' So Moros is given no respite in the attempt to educate him.

Hard upon this scene comes a nicely elaborated example of the 'Make room' formula. While Idleness and Incontinencie are talking of Moros they are suddenly interrupted by the entrance of a new figure called Wrath, and these lines follow

Here entreth Wrath.

	Make roume, stande back in the Deuils name
	Stande back or I will lay thee on the face.
INCON.	Marie stande thou backe with a verie shame,
	Is there not roume inough in the place.
IDLE.	It is but a coppie of his countenaunce,
	Wrath must declare his propertie,
INCON.	He is as whot as a vengeance,
	Stande backe and geue him libertie.
WRATH.	I had went [*weened*] it had been another,
	I thought to haue geuen thee a blow,
	In my rage I fauour not my brother, [. . .]

And so the audience is offered a little consolation by having the jostler himself upbraided by the cast. These three now discuss Moros and what he must be doing at school, and then follows another longish heralded entrance of a somewhat novel sort; Idleness breaks off with

	Se, se, woulde you iudge him a foole,
	So sadly as he readeth on his booke.
INCONT.	By like he cometh now from schoole,
	On his lesson earnestly he doth looke.
WRATH.	Haue you seene a more foolish face,
	I must laugh to se how he doth looke.
IDLE.	Holde your peace a little space,
	And heare him reade vpon his booke.
LAUGH ALL	Here entreth Moros looking vpon a booke
THREE AT HIS	and often times looke behind him, reade
READING	as fondely as you can deuise.

There is little doubt that William Wager is well acquainted with the possibilities of stage effects and can exploit them with a tart humour. But he has not done yet.

Moros protests at his mockers, but their interest is to corrupt him; they give him a pack of cards instead of his book, and also bring in a pair of dice. At this point in the margin is what is clearly a survival of a stage-manager's note; it reads 'Haue a paier [*sic*] of cardes redy'. Wrath particularly attracts poor Moros's attention by giving him a 'good sworde And a dagger' and instructing him in the aggressive use of them. Upon this the child cries, 'I pray you keepe my booke, These weapons haue set me on a fier:' and he has a fine actor's opportunity in the marginal direction at this point – 'Florish with your sworde.' All Moros now has in his head is fighting, and an excellent satirical scene of advice to him from the others now follows (fol. D.i.).

Later, Discipline (the schoolmaster) enters into the scene and Moros's valour falls away from him; the others urge him to fight but he replies 'I shall haue a bearde I trow one day, Then shall I be a man strong and bolde'. Which is a significant comment because, as will be seen, some particular play is made with false beards later. Wrath has a tart enough rejoinder –

> The foole as yet is yonge and nesh,
> And the feare of Disciplin is in his minde,
> After that he is noseled in womans flesh,
> The Knaue he will play in his kinde.
> IDLE. It is euen so, a boy is neuer bolde,
> Till he hath companied with an hoore, [. . .]

Soon Moros and the two scoundrels go out; Discipline is left alone and has a soliloquy lasting thirty-two lines, and then he too goes and immediately a female figure called Fortune enters. What is interesting here is that, as the cast-list showed, those thirty-two lines must have covered a pretty quick change outside in the entry, since the actor who now comes in as Lady Fortune is the same boy who has been playing Moros.

Fortune's opening lines are indeed more suited to a Vice than to a Lady, for she berates the spectators with –

> No Gods mercy, no reuerence, no honour,
> No cappe of, ne knee bowed, no homage,
> Who am I? is there no more good manner,
> I trowe, you know not me, nor my lignage, [. . .]
> Haue I done nothing for any here,
> Haue I not one louer nor friende,
> None to welcome me with a mery chere,
> Now by my trouth you be vnkinde, [. . .]

Incontinencie comes in and (taking no notice of Fortune) describes Moros's exploits in the stews to the audience, then turns about to go ('Semble a goyng out.'), when Fortune piqued at not being noticed calls out –

> Whether now syra are you blinde,
> Am I so litle a moate that you cannot see,
> I will plucke downe your hie minde,
> And cause you I trow to know me.

– he apologizes and she is pacified; but she decides that however vile Moros shall be –

> How lecherous so euer and incontinent,
> It is notwithstanding our pleasure,
> To exalt him in honour and richesse, [. . .]
> Moros shall lacke nothing for a season,
> They shall see that Fortune can exalte fooles, [. . .]
> Seing that the vulgares will me not prayse,
> For exalting good men and sapient,
> I will gette me a name an other wayes,
> That is by erecting fooles insipient.

Here is certainly a new turn to an old situation, and a vigorous dialogue with Incontinencie follows during which Fortune demands to be led to where Moros is and announces that 'before that he doth againe appeare, An other manner of person we will him make, . . .'. And both go out. After three pages of dialogue from Pietie and Wrath and Ignorance (which, of course, have to be inserted here in order to give the hard-pressed and versatile boy time to change back again from Fortune to Moros) there comes the great moment that the audience has been led so skilfully to look forward to; and we have Moros 'Entre Gaily disguised and with a foolish beard', and he cries 'A Syr, my beard is well growne, . . . tell me, Haue I not a Gentlemans countenance.' The scoundrels exclaim at his fine appearance and lead him far up the garden and egg him on to attack Pietie, Discipline and Exercitation. For six pages there is rousing rogues' dialogue and boasting until finally Moros and Ignorance are left together and Ignorance chances to ask Moros if there is anything that he lacks. This introduces a brilliant little scene of fooling; for Moros replies, 'By my trouth the thing that I desire most, Is in my cappe to haue a goodly feather'. 'A feather' replies Ignorance, 'a matter of great importaunce, You shal haue a feather if it cost a pounde.'

478

MOROS   A feather would make me looke a loft,
        Haue you one? What a redde one? [. . .]
        This will make me a Gentleman alone,
        Make it fast I pray you in my cappe, [. . .]
        I looke vpward now alwaie still,
        Goddes daies my feather I can not see, [. . .]

> Looke vpward to see
> the fether. Stumble
> and fall.

        Beshrew thy hart, I haue hurt my knee. [. . .]
        A vengeance take this foolish feather,
        While it is there I can not looke downe. [. . .]

The fooling goes on at a great pace while Ignorance tries to teach him how to conduct himself, until at length Discipline enters (fol. F.iii.) and cries 'Good audience, note this fooles proceding, . . .' and he outlines his life and draws a moral. After a page of such denunciation, Ignorance suggests that this is the moment for Moros to draw his sword and attack Discipline as he had been threatening to do. Even here Wager has a dig; he makes Moros say –

> [. . .] You shall repent that hether you came,
>   I will kill you I make God auow,
>   A vengeaunce on it, my dagger will not out, [. . .]

– and he gets caught up in his gear. There is nothing for him but to gather Ignorance (who is oozing contempt) and vacate the field – 'Go out both.' Discipline soliloquizes for a while and then also leaves.

Some shift in the tone of the action now follows. A new character named People is brought in and serves to inform the audience how Moros is getting on in his brave new life, and what opinion the man in the street has of him and his cronies. After nearly sixty lines of scalding contempt, he leaves. There follows the last scene where we see Moros, choleric and old – 'Moros. Entre Furiousely with a gray beard.' He exclaims 'Where is he, blood, sides, hart and woundes, A man I am now, euery inch of mee, . . .' He raves for sixteen lines, thrashing with his sword at no one. This little episode of shadow-fighting is an unexpected technical touch but there is no doubt it was deliberately planned, for there is a laconic marginal direction, 'Fight alone.' Moros is just concluding with the words 'What there, eyther I haue him slaine, Or elles from my sight he is fledde, . . .', when from the crowd round the door behind him we

see 'Entre with a terrible visure. Gods Iudgme*n*t'. He advances on
the unsuspecting Moros during the last lines of his speech, and
then proclaims the catch word of the show, 'The longer thou
liuest, the more foole thou art, . . .'. Moros shouts for his servants,
'Horesunnes bring your clubbes, billes, bowes, & staues, . . .' but
to no avail. God's Judgement is implacable: 'Strike Moros, and let
him fall downe.' The prostrate figure with the grey beard still
refuses to face the truth and gasps 'Eyther I haue the falling sicke-
nes, Or elles with the Palsey I am striken: . . .'. Then 'Entre Confusion with an ill fauoured visure, & all thinges beside ill fauoured.'
The two masked figures standing over Moros may well have had
something of the fearful aspect of a *hannya* or *otobide* mask at the end
of a Japanese *Noh* play, and it is worth special note that in the
English Interludes of the mid-sixteenth century such effects might
be possible.

The old dramatic convention of change of garments is now
brought in, and God's Judgement says, 'Confusion spoyle him of
his aray, Geue him his fooles coate for him due: His chayne and his
staffe take thou away, . . .'. Moros groans –

> Am I a sleepe, in a dreame, or in a traunce, [. . .]
> Sanct!, Amen, where is my goodly geare, [. . .]
> Other I was a Gentleman and had seruauntes,
> Or els I dreamed that I was a Gentleman.

Confusion, bending over him, drives the blow home –

> But thou art now a pesant of al pesantes, [. . .]

– but Moros can still fight back –

> Go with thee ill fauoured knaue,
> I had leuer thou wert hanged by the necke,
> If it please the Deuill me to haue,
> Let him carry me away on his backe.

To which Confusion replies,

> I will carry thee to the Deuill in deede,
> The world shalbe well ridde of a foole.

– and Moros's last words –

> A dew [;] to the Deuill God send vs good speede,
> An other while with the Deuill I must go to schole.

480

There follow now four pages of moralizing to end the play, and in these neither Moros nor Confusion speaks; so it seems very likely that Wager decided to put into actual practice that oldest of old endings to a Moral Interlude where the Devil runs off with the Vice on his back. There is nothing but the lines to suggest this, and no exit-directions at all are given. But it would accord very well with that alert, incisive acidity with which William Wager seems to have been able to handle theatre.

48 *Enough is as Good as Feast*

William Wager's *Inough is as Good as a Feast* (c. 1564) also has some interesting examples of heralded entrances and of particular actions of the players, but it has no references to staging and nothing to indicate any developments in technique. Moreover, a useful detailed study of it has already appeared in Craik's *The Tudor Interlude*, pp. 99–110.

It is to be noted here that about this year in the development of the Interlude form (1564) comes the event of the birth of Shakespeare. There seems enough evidence in the material of the plays so far studied, and in the technical developments of their staging up to this point, to suggest that this was a particularly propitious time.

49 *The Trial of Treasure*

The anonymous *The Trial of Treasure* (c. 1565), though it is described as 'A new and mery enterlude', seems rather to be a somewhat bitter attack upon almost everything. It has an interesting reference or two to costume; in the first a character called 'Just' says disparagingly to 'Lust', 'Mine apparel is not like unto thine, Disguised & jagged of sundry fashion'. This is a description of a clothing style which, as has been noted above, is pretty certain not to have survived as late as the mid-sixteenth century, and thus suggests that the play is of earlier date.

Secondly, there is a baffling but intriguing direction, *Enter Time with a similitude of dust and rust*. Lust is converted into dust and

481

another character, Treasure, to rust. There is no indication of how this was represented.

(At this point chronologically comes *The Cruel Debtor* (c. 1565) but there remains only a fragment consisting of four leaves with no helpful information on staging.)

50 *King Darius*

The anonymous *King Darius* (c. 1565) seems an oddly disjointed and inconclusive play. The title-page of the Tudor Facsimile Texts reprint of a 1577 edition describes it as 'A preaty new Enterlude, both pythie and pleasaunt, of the Story of King Daryus. Being taken out of the thyrde and fourth Chapter of the thyrde Book of Esdras.' A cast is given of twenty-one roles and it is said that 'Syx persons may easily play it'.

The story is in fact to be found in *I Esdras*, iii and iv.

The Prologue ends with 'Now sylence I desyre you therefore, For the Vyce is entring at the dore.' This seems to fit exactly in the tradition of the early Interludes in hall. The Vice who is named Iniquity enters with –

> How, now my maisters, how goeth the world now? [. . .]
> But softe, is there no body here,
> Truly I doe not lyke this geare.
> I thought I should haue found some body,
> Let me looke better [. . .]

The first twenty-three pages of the play (up to fol. D.i.) continue without the slightest reference to King Darius or his story. They contain knaves' dialogue between Iniquity and Charity and, later, Importunity, Parcialitie and Equity. There is the usual joking appeal to the audience in Iniquity's 'Syrs, who is there that hath a stoole? I will buy it for this Gentleman, . . .' – that is for Charity, 'an auncient father and a olde.'

After all this, two servants of King Darius at length enter, apparently looking for him. The first, called Agreeable, begins a little cryptically –

> Our labour in vayne haue we lost,
> For our Lorde and king is not in this Cost.

– to which the other, called Preparatus, replies –

> I pray thee hartily be not angry,
> Because he is not in this entry.
> He will be here anon as I suppose,
> Surely my eyes sore misgoes,
> If yonder I doe not see him comming.

These are mysterious uses of the words 'Cost' and 'entry'; but the verse is not clear enough to confirm if they refer to parts of the hall. At any rate the King enters with his 'counsell' and orders a feast. Four guests enter, Aethiopia, Percia, Juda and Media. With a tedious repetition of couplets they are bidden to eat and 'They sit downe all'. Eighteen lines later 'They ryse from [*meate*]', and twenty-three lines after that the four guests 'go all out' with no more development of the plot than compliments exchanged. And hard on this Darius and his 'counsell' leave also.

Next, for some nineteen more pages (fols. D.iiii.*rev.* to G.i.*rev.*) we revert to the completely disconnected fooling and quarrelling of Iniquity, Parcialitie, Importunity and the others. On fol. F.iiii. is a remarkable, but unexplained, direction – 'Here some body must cast fyre to Iniquitie.'

This over, the King re-enters and at last there follows a confused version of part of the Darius story; three young men come to him and offer him 'Wrytinges' purporting to compete in discovering the strongest thing in the world – (a) wine, (b) the king, (c) woman (but Truth is stronger than all). In the play the last speaker expresses his view in a single unbroken speech of one hundred and eight lines. The King promises to rebuild Jerusalem as a reward to him.

And finally: 'Here they go out, and then entreth Constancie, saying as it were a Sublocutio.' In fact all he does is to repeat the plot in case (as he actually implies) some of the audience did not understand . . . A 'sublocutio' is to be taken to mean something like a 'footnote'.

51 *Damon and Pythias*

Richard Edwards' *Damon and Pythias* (again c. 1565) begins to show a new world coming into being in the matter of richer and more fanciful verse. But it contains another innovation of a different nature which is more specifically connected with staging; here for the first time a player makes a deliberate attempt to paint an imaginary 'scene'. The introductory speech to the audience can be summarized as follows –

> On euerie syde [. . .]
> Silence in all eares bent I playnly do espie:
> But if your egre lookes doo longe suche toyes to see,
> As heretofore in commycall wise, were wont abroade to bee:
> Your lust is lost, [. . .]
>   [. . .] this Damon and Pithias,
> [. . .] is no Legend lie, [. . .] doone of yore [. . .]
>   [. . .] yet present shalbe here,
> Euen aa [*as*] it were in dooynge now, so liuely it shall appeare:
> Lo here in Siracusae [. . .]
> Here Dionisius Pallace, within whose Courte this thing most strange
>   was donne.

– and in what follows there is a good deal to suggest an anticipation of the technique of the full Elizabethan play so far as general atmosphere is concerned; but there is not a great deal to imply any developments in actual details of presentation.

The playwright has faced the problem of a description of his type of play with the following decision –

> Which matter mixt with myrth and care, a iust name to applie,
> As seemes most fit wee haue it termed, a Tragicall Commedie, [. . .]

It is perhaps a little surprising to find that, with all these suggestions of poetical innovation in a court atmosphere, there is still one line which seems to suggest the old-style entrance through a door, and through spectators assembled by that door, which characterized the ordinary Interlude; on folio G.iiii.*rev.*, a character called Snap, who is a comic porter, calls 'Geue place, let the prisoner come by, geue place'. There would not seem at that point in the play any reason to suppose a group of supers standing ready for the court scene, and thus the remark seems to be addressed directly to members of the audience.

52 *Supposes*

George Gascoigne's translation of Ariosto's *Gli Suppositi*, under the title of *Supposes*, was played at Gray's Inn in 1566. It is in prose, and is a brilliant piece of comedy-of-intrigue in English. It has two or three clear references to 'stage', one of which I have briefly noted above, on p. 442, but it seems again outside the line of development of normal Interludes – though it may well have influenced some that followed.

53 *Mary Magdalene*

Lewis Wager's *Mary Magdalene* (c. 1566) is in many ways a brilliant play, with a scene of seduction by a group of experienced wasters, surrounding an innocent but intrigued young girl, that is as good as such a thing may be. This scene certainly makes it appear an adult, professional play. It is especially significant for possessing most detailed references to particularities of contemporary women's costume. But it adds little to our knowledge of staging.

Interludes into Drama 1566–1576

Gismond of Salern ∽ *Horestes* ∽ *Marriage of Wit and Science*
∽ *Liberality and Prodigality* ∽ *Like will to Like* ∽ *Cambises* ∽
Susanna ∽ *New Custom* ∽ *Misogonus* ∽ *Conflict of Conscience*
∽ *Tyde tarrieth no Man* ∽ *Common Conditions*

---

54 *Gismond of Salern*

Gismond of Salern, like *Gorboduc* and *Supposes*, is certainly not in the
Interlude tradition; it is an Inner Temple play performed before
Elizabeth I at Greenwich about 1566. All the same, the stage-
directions are in their way very remarkable, and some useful observations can be made about them.

What is remarkable about them is that they offer for the first time
regular and consistent notice of every exit and entrance in the
play – even more, they almost invariably state where every player
who exits goes to, and where every player who enters comes from.
Of course this raises hopes that all the questions that have arisen
in the past concerning where and how players entered and left the
acting-area may have a new light thrown on them. But in fact this is
not so because, detailed as the information about exits and entrances is, there is practically nothing to help in visualizing the
character or arrangement of the stage itself.

The play is also interesting from the textual point of view since
there are three versions, an early and two later ones. The first is
called *Gismond of Salern in Loue*, a manuscript of about 1567. The
second is again a manuscript, called *The Tragedie of Gismond of
Salerne*. The third is a printed version dated 1591, called *The
Tragedie of Tancred and Gismund*, and it bears the note: 'Newly revived and polished according to the decorum of these daies'.

The authors are various, each of the five acts being by a different
hand. The last of these authors – possibly co-ordinating all the
rest – is reckoned to be Robert Wilmot.

486

I have used the reprint of the earliest manuscript, in *Quellen und Forschungen*, Heft 80, from Hargrave MS 205. The cast is given as:

Cupide, god of loue.
Tancred, king of Nap*les*, pri*n*ce of Salern.
Gismonde, king Tancredes daughter.
Lucrece, king Ta*n*credes sister.
Guishard, the Counte Palurine.
Claudia, woma*n* of Gism*ondes* priuy chamber.
Renuchio, gentlema*n* of the priuy chamber.
Iulio, captain of the gard.
Megaera, furie of hell.
Chorus: 4 gentemen of Salern.

The stage-directions, though so simple, are interesting enough to warrant listing in full. Taken alone they almost explain the whole action of the play, provided one remembers Boccaccio's story about the king who forbade his widowed daughter to remarry and, upon finding her with a lover, had the man killed and his heart sent to her in a cup.

In the following list the directions are printed in italics. There are two items of setting, King Tancred's *Palace* and his daughter Guismond's *Chamber*.

First Acte.
1.Scene. — CUPIDE.
Cupide cometh downe from heauen.
  [68 lines soliloquy, ending with –]
Cupide entreth into King Tancredes palace.

2.Scene. — GISMONDE.
Gismond cometh out of her chamber.
  [36 lines soliloquy, leading into –]

3.Scene. — TANCRED. GISMONDE.
Tancred cometh out of his palace.
  [72 lines dialogue, ending with –]
Tancred and Gismond depart into the palace.

— — THE CHORE [i.e. CHORUS]
  [60 lines.]

2.Acte.
1.Scene. — GISMOND. LUCRECE.
Gismond and Lucrece coming out of Gism. chamber.
Gism. departeth into her chamber, Lucrece abiding on the stage.
  [82 lines dialogue, ending with –]
Tancred cometh out of his palace.

2.Scene. — LUCRECE. TANCRED.
    [68 lines dialogue, ending with –]
    Tancred and Lucrece depart into the palace.

3.Scene. — GISMONDE. LUCRECE.
    Gismond cometh [out] *of her chamber.* [Then –]
    Lucrece returneth from the palace.
    [46 lines dialogue, ending –]
    Gismond and Lucrece depart into Gismondes chamber.

— — THE CHORE.
    [50 lines.]

3.Acte.
1.Scene. — CUPIDE.
    Cupide returneth out of the palace.
    [32 lines soliloquy, ending with –]
    Cupide remounteth to heauen.

2.Scene. — CLAUDIA.
    Claudia cometh out of Gism. chamber.
    [50 lines soliloquy, ending with –]
    Claudia departeth to Gism. chamber.

3.Scene. — GUISHARDE.
    Guishard cometh out of the palace.
    He breakes the cane and findes a letter enclosed.
    He redeth the letter.
    Guishard departeth into the palace.
    [88 lines soliloquy]

— — THE CHORE.
    [50 lines.]

4.Act.
1.Scene. — MEGAERA.
    Megaera ariseth out of hell.
    [44 lines soliloquy, ending with –]
    Megaera entreth the palace.

2.Scene. — TANCREDE. RENUCHIO. IULIO.
    Tancrede cometh out of Gismondes chamber.
    [after 84 lines soliloquy he calls for Renuchio to fetch Gismond]
    Renuchio goeth to call Gismonde, but he cometh not in with her.
    [soliloquy continues until at l. 120 Tancred calls Julio; no direction; dialogue then follows to l. 170, ending with –]
    Julio depar-[teth] *into the palace.*

3.Scene. — TANCREDE. GISMONDE.

Gismond cometh out of her chamber, called by Renuchio.
[82 lines dialogue, ending with –]
Gismond departeth to her chamber.

4.Scene. — IULIO. TANCREDE. GUISHARDE.
Julio bringeth the earle prisoner.
[at l. 67 –] *Tancred hastyly departeth into the palace.*
[in all 81 lines of dialogue, ending with –]
Guishard is led to prison.

— — THE CHORE.

5.Act.

1.Scene. — RENUCHIO. THE CHORE.
Renuchio cometh out of the palace.
[222 lines of dialogue between Renuchio (with cup) and the Chorus
ending without any direction to Chorus to exit. Renuchio stays.]

2.Scene. — RENUCHIO. GISMONDE.
Renuchio deliuereth the cup to Gismond in her chamber.
Renuchio departeth. [after l. 24.]
She taketh a glasse of poyson out of her pocket. [at l. 60.]
Claudia runneth into the palace to tell the king of Gismond. [at l. 76.]
[86 lines, mostly soliloquy.]

3.Scene. — TANCREDE. GISMONDE.
Tancred cometh out of the palace.
Tancred entreth into Gismondes chamber. [at l. 4.]
Gismond dyeth. [at l. 48.]
[52 lines of dialogue.]

4.Scene. — TANCREDE
Tancred cometh out of Gismondes chamber.
[32 lines soliloquy.]

— — EPILOGUS
[32 lines soliloquy.]

Although there is no evidence whatever on which to base a picture of the stage or the scenery, it will be helpful to have some
conception of their appearance before one's eye to help in studying
these directions, and so I have included in Fig. 37 a sort of provisional
diagram of what might be a possible layout. This is *not* a reconstruction. With it in mind I want now to examine the consistency
of these directions, and then to compare one or two of them with
those printed in the revised edition.

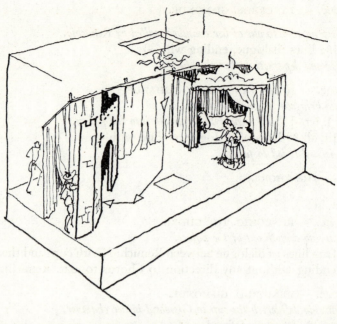

FIG. 37. A sketch intended to help in following the movements in *Gismond of Salern*. (This is not offered as a reconstruction of the stage nor of the scenery, but simply as an aid to studying the actions implied in the stage directions)

In I, i, Cupid's entrance is perfectly clear; he descends by a flying apparatus from above. There must then presumably have been a ceiling over the stage (or a 'heavens' or 'cover' on posts) with a trap door in it and machinery above it. Cupid detaches his harness and makes a normal exit into the Palace.

In I, ii, Gismond's entrance seems normal but, as we shall see, her 'Chamber' presents a problem. To her Tancrede comes from his palace for I, iii. After this all goes smoothly until, at the end of the act, the Chorus speaks; this (as the cast list says) consists of four people. The first uncertainty comes here, for there is no indication of how the Chorus enters or leaves – whether by some third door or whether it stays permanently in the place.

Act II runs through with no problem.

In Act III, Cupid returns from the Palace into which he went in I, i, re-attaches his harness and flies up again.

In III, iii, Guishard's action with the cane is made perfectly clear in the dialogue; but it is interesting to see that there are, in the revised version of 1591, descriptions of certain dumb shows which take place at each entr'acte; that preceding Act III is described –

> *Before this Acte the Hobaies sounded a lofty Almain, and Cupid Vshereth after him, Guizard and Gismund hand in hand. Iulio and Lucrece, Renuchio and another maiden of honor. The measure strod, Gismunda geues a cane into Guiszards hand, and they are all ledde forrth again by Cupid, . . .*

The first scene of the act then follows. The audience were thus forewarned of Gismond's passing a 'cane' or stick to Guishard at a dance, and of her doing it with some set purpose. They would thus be prepared for his finding a message in the cane later in the act.

In Act IV, Megaera's entrance is clearly by a trap from under the stage. Her exit is into the Palace.

Next, in IV, ii, comes the first slight jolt for an investigator; Tancred enters *from Gismond's Chamber*, not from his Palace. But it is of course not surprising that there should be a hidden, or off-stage, entrance to that Chamber, just as there must also be to the Palace, but it is now made clear, that a character, after leaving by the Palace, could cross 'behind the scenes' and make the next entrance from the Chamber. Renuchio's entrance later is not specified, but presumably Tancred calls him from the Palace. Renuchio goes into Gismond's Chamber to fetch her but then does not appear again for some time. In the meanwhile Julio is called, presumably also from the Palace, and is given orders to ambush Guishard at the outward mouth of a subterranean passage leading from Gismond's Chamber, and bring him in to Tancred. It is not unnatural that to get to that outward entrance, which is in the Palace grounds, he should first re-enter the Palace. This he does.

Then in IV, iii, Renuchio at last brings out Gismond from her Chamber (presumably then he leaves her and exits into the Palace) and Tancred pours his scorn upon her. She is undismayed and replies with confident dignity, and then goes back to her Chamber.

In IV, iv, the luckless Guishard is brought in through the Palace door, is condemned, and is led out again to prison.

Act V opens with a long 'messenger's speech' from Renuchio to the Chorus, who must clearly remain on the stage after their normal entr'acte comments especially for this scene. He describes Guishard's death and bears in his hand, as Tancred had ordered, a cup with the Earl's heart in it. In V, ii he crosses to Gismond's Chamber (the Chorus presumably having now retired) and presents her with the cup. Her reaction is to take the poison she has provided herself with. Brandl (in his edition in *Quellen und Forschungen*) quotes an interesting marginal note here – 'now goes she to some cupp borde or place where the vyoll of poison ys and takes it and sayes . . .' The revised printed edition is also interesting at this point; there, in V, ii, the Chorus is given an extra scene in which they remonstrate with Gismond before her suicide, but unavailingly. Then they decide to go and warn the King and the direction follows – 'Chorus depart into the Pallace'. So there is no question of their remaining in any Renaissance substitute for the classic *orchestra*. All their exits – and presumably their entrances – could be made *via* the Palace. In this edition, Gismond quickly takes the poison after they leave, and V, iii begins with the direction 'Tancred in hast commeth out of his pallace with Iulio. She [*Gismond*] lieth down and couereth her face with her haire' . . .

Summarizing all the above, the general picture seems quite clear – a stage with a trap below, a flying apparatus above, and at one side a 'house' representing Tancred's Palace, and at the other side . . . but here there crops up a really formidable problem at the last moment. What is this 'Chamber' of Gismond's like?

To review the evidence: in II, i, Gismond and Lucrece entered the stage by 'coming out of Gism. cha*m*ber', thus for the moment suggesting some sort of 'house' more or less corresponding to Tancred's Palace, with a door to enter or leave by. In IV, ii, Renuchio went into this Chamber and called Gismond but he *did not come out again* for the rest of the scene; it is distinctly directed that 'he cometh not in [to the action again] with her', and it is only in IV, iii that he reappears bringing her out of the Chamber. Later again, in V, ii, Renuchio delivers the fatal cup to Gismond *in her chamber*, and stays talking to her for 24 lines. She then drinks the poison *without leaving* the Chamber, and the rest of the scene proceeds still without her leaving it. The King is called, and in V, iii, he enters *into Gismondes chamber* and there conducts the final scene in which she dies.

The conclusion is inescapable, that Gismond's Chamber could conceal what took place within it at one time, and reveal what took place within it at another. No explanation of this can be found in the 1567 manuscript. But in the printed edition of 1591, the revised text introduces a new technical element; in the dumb action which is inserted before Act II it is stated that '. . . *Lucrece entred, attended by a mayden of honor with a couered goddard of gold, and drawing the curtens, shee offreth vnto Gismumda to tast thereof*: . . .' So there were *curtains* associated with the Chamber. Later in the same action Lucrece *'rayseth up Gismund from her bed*, . . .'. The question is, Are the curtains bed curtains, or are they a traverse covering an alcove in which is a possibly uncurtained bed? Since later Renuchio goes into this Chamber to call Gismond but remains concealed there for some time, it would seem very much more likely that the curtains are traverse curtains concealing an alcove with the bed in it – for Renuchio could hardly go behind bed-curtains and wait with Gismond *on her bed*!

Further: in the revised edition a new Epilogue is added. Julio speaks it, and it finishes –

> Thus end our sorrowes with the setting Sun:
> Now draw the curtens for our Scaene is done.

The last line (like the similar last line of the well-known sonnet attributed to Sir Walter Raleigh) has caused investigators much puzzlement. Opinion has varied about whether such 'curtens' were some sort of 'front curtain' hitherto unknown on the Elizabethan stage – unknown at least to modern research – or whether they were the curtains of a four-poster bed, pulled together at the end to conceal the corpse. In my view it seems more likely that they were in fact a traverse with the bed behind, and were closed – in this instance by Julio – for what would indeed be a very fitting sign that the play was over.

But the problems are not all solved by this suggestion, since it is not easy to see how a 'Palace' could be set on one side of the stage with a mere traverse to balance it at the other. Or with the traverse at centre-back, and a further unspecified door at the side to balance the Palace. Again, the reference to drawing the curtains comes only in the 1591 edition 'polished according to the decorum of' those later days when the public playhouses were in full swing, there is no mention of such a thing in the 1567 manuscript.

But here again one cannot be certain; for there is nothing so far as I can see to prove that the traverse was not in fact used in the 1567 production, even if the verbal mention of it only came to be added to the lines in the revised version.

It is interesting (from the setting point of view) to notice in all this that, logically speaking, Gismond's chamber must have been in a part of the Palace. Yet both are, presumably, shown separately. With the result that, if I am right in supposing the Palace to be

493

represented by an exterior gateway, anyone *in* the Palace who goes
to see Gismond in her chamber *leaves the Palace* to do so!

55 *Horestes*

Pikering's *Horestes* (1567) must be considered in much more detail.
The title-page (see Tudor Facsimile Texts edition of 1910) reads –

A NEWE

Enterlude of Vice Conteyninge, the
Historye of Horestes with the cruell
reuengment of his Fathers death,
vpon his one naturtll Mother.
by John Pikeryng.
The players names.

The Vice	Clytemnestra.	Sodyer.	Truthe.
Rusticus.	Halltersycke.	Nobulle.	Fame.
Hodge.	Hempstryng.	Nature.	Hermione.
Hrorestes	Nestor.	Prouisyon.	Dewtey.
Idumeus.	Menalaus.	Harranld.	Messenger.
Councell.	A woman.	Sodyer.	Egestus.
			Commones.

The names deuided for vi. to playe.
The fyrst the Vice and Nature and Dewtey. 3.

2. Rusticus. Idumeus. 2. Sodyer. Menelauus. & Nobulles. 5.
3. Hodge. Counsell. Messenger. Nestor. & Commones. 5.
4. Horestes. a woman. & Prologue. 3.
5. Haulltersicke. Sodyer. Egistus. Harrauld. Fame. Truth and Idumeus.
   7.
6. Hempstrynge. Clytemnestra. Prouisyon. & Hesmione. 4.

Imprinted at London in Fletestrete, at the
signe of the Falcon by Wylliam Gryffith, and
are to be solde at his shope in S. Dunstons
Churchcyearde. Anno. 1567

The sub-title is interesting: an 'Enterlude of Vice' – perhaps
signifying 'An Interlude *with* a Vice', or a play with a Vice appearing in it to comment on and interfere in the action, according to
the good old Interlude tradition. At all events the description was
considered more important than the title in the running headings
at the tops of the pages throughout, for these read 'A New Enter-

lude' on all the left-hand pages, and 'Of Vyce' on all the right-hand pages, and the name of Horestes is not included in these running titles at all.

Under the heading 'The names deuided for vi. to playe' it is clear that one of the players is alloted no less than seven roles. The second player on the list has, as his last role, the task of performing 'Nobulles', apparently in the plural; whether this is one of the many misprints, or whether one player could stand for several men is not clear. Two players, the second and the fifth, are the only ones assigned to play a 'Sodyer', but there must surely have been more than two soldiers in the battle scenes?

It is also curious to note that the part of Idumeus, which is a fairly important one, appears to be split between two players, the second and the fifth. Perhaps the numeral '2' after Idumeus's name in the second player's part-list indicates that the player is to impersonate Idumeus only in the second part of the play.

The Vice begins the action by chaffing the spectators, then follows comic business between Hodge and Rusticus. Now Horestes 'entrith' (fol. A.iiii.*rev.*). He talks of his mother's sin, while the Vice listens and at length breaks in to tell Horestes that his own name is 'Courage' and to urge him on to his just vengeance. At this point King Idumeus begins to speak a soliloquy of seventeen lines. In it he refers directly to Horestes but refers to him as one who is absent. Now, Horestes has maintained his dialogue with the Vice right up to the beginning of Idumeus's speech, and there is no direction to suggest that he or the Vice have any sort of exit before Idumeus begins. The notable part of this particular passage is that the last line of Idumeus's speech directly concerns Horestes; he says –

B.i.*rev.* . . . But where is he that all this day, I neauer sawe his face,

HORESTES

Kenll downe.

At hand O King thy saruant is, which wissheth to thy grace
All hayl with happey fate certayne, wt pleasures many fould,

– so we have clear indication that Horestes has not gone out, but has waited instead for his cue to answer Idumeus's question and announce his presence. But throughout Idumeus's speech, and particularly in its last line, it is equally clear that Idumeus was not aware that Horestes was present. We have had many examples of this sort of convention before and I have nicknamed it the 'differentiation of acting-area'. But in this particular play we know that a stage was used, and I have already suggested that I think this new item of presentation could be employed to help the 'differentiation' convention.

If I am right, it seems to me very likely that the above passage means that Horestes and the Vice conducted their conversation in the traditional way from the floor, and that Idumeus on his entrance mounted directly to the stage, or to a 'footpace', and spoke his soliloquy from there. Then Horestes' speech beginning 'At hand O King . . .' would fit quite logically, and the absence of any exit- or entrance-direction for him would be fully explained.

The misspelt marginal direction to Horestes to 'kneel down' at the beginning of his speech suggests he mounts the stage here, and kneels in Idumeus's presence. There, he asks permission to make a certain request – in effect, to have troops to capture and punish Clytemnestra. But it would seem that the Vice does not follow him up on the stage for the Vice, on seeing how his mind is set, comments gleefully on the situation saying,

> Tout [*Tut!*] let him alone now, we may in good south [*sooth*], [. . .]
> It is not Idumeus that hath poure to let.
> Horestes fro sekinge his mother to kyll,
> Tout let hym alone, hele haue his owne wyll.

Both spelling and punctuation need amending here, but I think the sense is clear. This speech could obviously not be made to Idumeus, nor indeed spoken with any intention that he should hear it; it must be a side-comment for the audience's amusement and thus not spoken in the 'presence'. Hence (in the circumstances) my presumption is that it was spoken from the floor.

Idumeus, after conferring with Councell, promises Horestes a thousand men, and wishes success to his enterprise. The Vice urges him on from the side. Horestes thanks Idumeus and is then directed to 'Go out'. The Vice turns to the audience with one parting line: 'Se se I praye you how he ioyse, that he must war begin', and then he too is directed to 'Go out'. Idumeus concludes the scene with a brief exchange with his Councell; and then again the direction 'Go out'.

At this point in the text (B.ii.*rev.*) there comes a large decorated capital letter, to introduce the next passage. This is one of five such decorations (the first came at the opening of the play), and their function seems to be to mark a break in the development of the action, and in fact their effect is to turn it into a five-act play.

The new passage introduced here begins with a comic knock-about scene between Haltersycke and Hempstringe; after some three pages of this, the main action is resumed with the following direction (printed in the margin in the original):

B.iiii.   let ye drum playe and Horestes enter wt
          his men & then lette him knele downe & speake.

His speech is a short prayer for victory for himself and his band. This is the first time we are presented with the problem of trying to visualize what this 'band' of men looked like and where they entered and how they stood – and particularly how many men were actually present. On this last point there is very little to help; there are two 'Sodyers' individually mentioned on the list on the title-page; one of them doubles with Idumeus (among other roles) and so cannot be present in scenes where Idumeus is on, and the other doubles with Egistus (among other roles) and so cannot be present in the Egistus-Clytemnestra scenes. Thus both parties – that of Horestes and that of Egistus – are allotted one soldier each, and these soldiers both have brief speeches. Judging from what might be done in a modern theatrical company, this particular allotment would suggest that Horestes' army and Egistus's army were each given one actor to take care of the respective soldier's speeches, and that an undefined number of supernumeraries was attached to each to make up the bulk of the army, according to what was available on different occasions of playing – possibly drawn from a group of local men-at-arms. If this were true of the present play, then it would follow that we can have no definite answer to the question 'How many?' since it might be three or four, or it might be a dozen. I think the main point is that, however many there may have been on more favourable occasions, the procedure of the army must have been the same on all ocasions so far as movement and position were concerned, because it seems unlikely that the one speaking 'leader' in each case would be saddled with the task of rehearsing different actions with different groups of supers according to how many were available. So that, although we cannot specify the number, any visualizing of the movements of these 'armies' must be consistent with a small group and at the same time equally consistent with a large group.

The upshot of all this uncertainty is, however, simple; it seems to me that, except for the scene of the actual storming of the city, the armies would not mount the stage but would stay on the floor beside it and leave it for the principals to use at need. On that assumption we would have, at this moment, the group of soldiers on the floor by the stage, and Horestes kneeling upon the stage. At the end of his speech he has a direction to 'stand vp' and straightway he is confronted with a new character. This is Nature, who we are told is doubled by the Vice, and Nature immediately says, 'Nay stey my child fro*m* mothers bloud wt draw thy bloudy ha*n*d', and there is an argument between the two. Whether the army looks on through this dialogue is a very difficult point to decide, for Nature gives up the argument and is directed to 'Go out', upon which Horestes has the line, 'Farwel dame Nature to my men, I straight wil take my way'; and the marginal direction is repeated, 'Go out'. This might mean that his men have already departed and he is proposing to go after them; or, if he is on the stage, it might mean that he bids Nature farewell, steps off the stage to the head of his waiting band, and leads them out (see fol. C.i.).

Now immediately upon this there is a direction 'Let ye dru*m* playe' and Idumeus speaks to his Councell; his lines are –

> To se this mouster let vs go, for I suppose it tyme,
> Where is Horestes why stease he: the truth to me define:

> COUNCELL.
> Oh soferayne lord me thinkes I here, him for to be at hand
> yft please your grace, he is in sight, euen now withal his band.

> IDUMEUS.
> Com on Horestes we haue stayd, your mouster for to se.

> HORESTES
> And now at hand my men and I, all redy armed be. [. . .]

– and parallel with Idumeus's speech above, there begins the following direction printed in the margin: 'Let ye dru*m* play & enter Horestis wt his band marche a bout the stage.' If the various directions are correct here, what they imply is that Horestes after his scene with Nature led his men out by one door, then immediately Idumeus and his Councell entered by the other door, mounted the stage, proclaimed that they were eagerly awaiting Horestes and his muster and, no sooner have they spoken than Horestes and his band march in again, having crossed behind in the entry and entered by the opposite door – that is to say, the same door by which Idumeus had just entered, since they were specifically coming to see him.

498

There now follows one of the earliest heroic addresses to troops, such as we find so often in later Elizabethan drama, and Idumeus urges them to victory. The 'Sodyeares' classically acknowledge the speech in two lines which they apparently shout in concert. Idumeus addresses Horestes in similar heroic vein, Horestes thanks him, Idumeus bids him farewell and has the two directions, 'Imbrase him' and 'Kys him'. And then Horestes calls, 'Come on my men, let vs depart', the soldiers hail him, and the direction follows: 'March about and go out.' And Idumeus and his Councell are left alone to reflect on the situation for some thirty-two lines.

My immediate concern with the above scene is to judge how far it confirms my view of the nature of the stage, and of the respective uses of the floor-area and the stage-area which I have suggested. In the first place, I find the use of a small stage or footpace as a sort of dais or rostrum from which to review and address a muster of troops almost inevitably indicated by the lines of the dialogue. In the second place, I refer back to the two examples which the passage contains of the provocative phrase 'to go *about* the stage'. One of these is after Horestes' talk with Nature, when he has already led his troops out at one door (and thus, I believe, must have been walking with them on the floor) and then, in the space of four lines of dialogue, leads them in again at the other door (again at floor level) and marches them 'about' the front of the stage, before halting them on the far side and mounting the stage himself to greet Idumeus. The other is at the end of this scene when, his blessing received, Horestes turns them round and leads them back on their steps – thus 'marching about' again – and finally goes out with them. Particularly in respect of the last direction, does it seem to me unlikely that the words 'March about and go out' could really mean that he and the soldiers, being all on the stage with the King and Councell would, before they went out, march about *upon* that stage for a pointless few seconds, and then step down and go.

The next scene of the play opens with the third of the decorative capital letters, and there is indeed a change in the situation. The direction at the beginning reads – 'Enter Egistus & Clyte*m*nestra, singinge this songe, to ye tune of king Salomon'. The song is a longish one in eight stanzas with a beguiling refrain. The atmosphere created by the two characters is adult and accomplished – well on the way to fully-fledged Elizabethan drama. At the climax of their song they are interrupted at the direction – 'Let ye tru*m*pet blowe with in'. Thus, in spite of the fact that the words 'go out' are used in reference to an exit, a trumpet sounded off is said to be 'blown within', not 'blown *without*', and once more we have a foreshadowing of the idea of the screens developing towards the 'tiring house'.

The trumpet disturbs Egistus, but Clytemnestra calms him and says that it is only a messenger. The messenger then arrives; he gives warning of Horestes' advance and goes out. Egistus leaves (by one door) to collect an army while Clytemnestra leaves (by the other) to arrange for the defence of her city. Or, there is an alternative; it may very well be that he and she have opened this scene by entering from a central traverse (for the evidence for this, see below), in which case Egistus would go out by a door but Clytemnestra would retire again into the traverse. There is a clear direction for Egistus to 'Go out' but no similar direction for Clytemnestra.

Next, there follows a short scene of the Elizabethan alarums-and-excursions type (fol. C.iii.*rev.*), for which the marginal directions take up nearly as many lines as does the dialogue that they accompany. The directions read: 'Enter a woman, lyke a beger rounning before they [*the*?] sodier but let the sodier speke first, but let ye woman crye first pitifulley.' and then – 'Go a fore her, & let her fal downe vpon the [*soldier*?] & al to be beate him.' and finally – 'take his weapons & let him ryse vp & then go out both.' There are 22 lines of hurried dialogue to accompany this business.

Now comes the fourth decorative capital letter, and a direction introducing the new scene: 'Enter. the Vyce synginge this song to ye tune of the Paynter.' After the song he leaves and (fol.C.iiii.*rev.*) 'Horestes entrith wt his bande & marcheth about the stage' (i.e. presumably on the floor). Horestes then has a soldier's speech to his men with some very clear implications about the presentation:

> Come on my sodyers for . . . aryued their we be,
> Where as we must haue our desyare, or els dye manfulley.
> The walles be hye yet I intend, vppon them first to go, [. . .]
> Com hether harauld go proclame this mine intent straightway
> To yonder citite [*city*] say that I, am come to their decaye. [. . .]
> Byd them in hast to yeld to me, [. . .]

Then follows the direction: 'Let ye tru*m*pet go towarde the Citie and blowe.' The Herald summons the keeper of the gate, and then 'Let ye tru*m*pet leaue soundyng & let Harrauld speake & Clitemnestra speake ouer ye wal.'

A parley follows between the Herald on the stage and Clytemnestra speaking 'ouer ye wal'. Whatever various means could be
used on various occasions to effect this picture, I think there is
little doubt that the simplest would be for a ladder, such as one sees
sticking above the curtain in so many booth-stage pictures, to be
leant against the traverse-bar from behind, and for Clytemnestra to
mount it a little way and speak down to the Herald with her upper
half showing over the curtain.

It may be claimed that there is here a fine opportunity for the
Interluders, if they were in a typical hall, to have Clytemnestra
stationed up in the minstrel-gallery over the screens, and speaking
down from there. This may have been so. But I cannot avoid the
impression (especially in view of what follows in the matter of
storming, fighting, sacking and lynching) that the owner of a
Tudor screens, whether they were of old and revered panelling or
new-fashioned and elaborate carving, would absolutely forbid an
attack upon it from a troupe of slap-happy actors furnished with
weapons of war.

However that may be, Clytemnestra's reply is defiance, and this
reply the Herald conveys to Horestes. A direction comes at this
point, 'let ye haraulde go out here'; it is not certain whether this is
a direction for him to exit or simply to go off the stage and join
the army on the floor of the hall.

Horestes orders, 'Com on my men . . . this Citie for to wyn', but
strictly enjoins them that his mother shall be brought out to him
alive. The Vice chips in here with a short excited speech (so he must
be present with the army), and then Horestes bids his trumpeters
'With lyuely hartes . . . exault your tubal sound', and (as I think)
the soldiers now swarm up on the stage. A notable stage direction
describes this attack:

> Go & make your liuely battel & let it be longe
> eare you can win ye Citie and when you haue won
> it let Horestes bringe out his mother by the
> arme & let ye droum sease playing & the trumpet,
> also when she is taken let her knele downe and
> speake.

She begs for mercy; but Horestes orders her to be taken away
for punishment, and she has to 'go out wt on of the sodiares'.
The Vice madly exults. But Horestes is sorely concerned at what
he has done and at what he is about to do: 'Let Horests syth

[*sigh*] hard'. The Vice reproves him for wavering – 'begyn you now to faynt. Jesu god how styll he syttes . . .' and he threatens to desert him, and breaks down into mocking tears, and a direction comes just here – 'wepe but let Horestes ryse & bid him pease'. Then Horestes has a short speech of deep remorse to which the Vice replies, 'Euen as you saye but harke at hand, Egistus draweth nye'.

Here then is an intervention at the moment of victory. The direction says – 'Let Egistus enter & set hys men in a raye & let the drom playe tyll Horestes speaketh'. (It is worth noting that the writer of the directions is careful to see that the tumult is quietened when any important speech has to be made.) Horestes now is forced to turn to his troop and urge them to brace themselves to face this new relieving army. He cries, 'Com on my men kepe your araye . . .', while Egistus cries to his own soldiers,

> Strike vp your drums let trumpets sound, your baners eke display.
> And I my selfe as captayne, to you wyll lead the waye.

Horestes defies him and Egistus retorts with abuse – 'pryncoks boy & bastard slaue' – and repeats, 'Stryke vp your droums & forward now, to wars let vs prosede', and then the direction comes –

> stryke vp your drum, & fyght a good whil &
> then let sum of Egistus men flye & then take
> hym & let Horestes drau him vyolentlye & let
> ye drums sease.

('Sum of Egistus men' surely implies an army of more than one.) Horestes has no pity on Egistus and decrees that he shall be hanged. The succinct direction that accompanies this is:

> fling him of ye lader & then let on bringe in
> his mother Clytemnestra bnt let her loke wher
> Egistus hangeth.

There is obviously little doubt that the details annotated in this script are the result of some careful studying for effect!

Next then Clytemnestra is brought in by the Vice; he mocks her bitterly and presents her to Horestes. She begs for mercy (with her lover's body on the gibbet behind her), and Horestes is prompted to deliver a 16-line speech of judgement upon her, during which there comes the direction –'Take downe Egistus and bear him out.' So the playwright is even provident enough to arrange for the disposal of the body. Clytemnestra kneels down and still pleads. The

Vice, now changing his nature and taking the name 'Revenge' instead of 'Courage', still mocks her, until at length he cries, 'Come on com on, ites all in vaine, and get you on a fore', with the accompanying direction, 'Let Clytemnestra wepe and go out reueng also' – that is, accompanied by the Vice as Revenge.

Horestes cries to his men, 'Stryke vp your droumes for enter now, we wyll the citie gate'. Now at this point Fame comes in – 'Enter in fame & let all ye sodyers folow him in araye' (I think this means that the soldiers all follow Horestes – the 'him' – into the city, since Fame is seen later to be a female character). Besides promising renown to all according to their deserts, Fame acts as a messenger to the audience with the news that Agamemnon's brother (Menelaus) together with 'his ladey fayre, Quene Helen' have arrived in the neighbourhood. She finishes her speech alone while the others all file out, and we come to the fifth and last decorative capital letter and open the final action of the play.

This begins with the entry of the Vice, who comes in singing a song about getting a new master since Horestes is so rueful over what he has done to his mother. Then suddenly Fame speaks; the Vice replies to her with a curiously familiar and impertinent form of address, apparently calling her 'Nan', praising her 'trycke' appearance, and angling at her 'lyppes to haue a lycke, Jesus how coye, . . .' he calls her. And he makes a significant comment on her costume, 'she hath winges also'; and he offers to go with her wherever she goes.

Fame seems completely to ignore him (perhaps he spoke aside from the floor). At any rate she now explains the purpose of Agammemnon's brother's visit; it is revenge once more. But the Vice, as soon as he hears of Menelaus's arrival quickly goes off to see him. Fame finally remarks that 'fame no where ca*n* stay But what she hears throughout ye world abrod she doth display', and then 'Go out'.

Now follows a notable entrance-heralding speech from a fresh character, and it seems to give final proof that, whatever the stage in this play may have been like, certain players without any doubt entered the hall on the normal floor level on which the spectators were; for the fresh character is Provision, and what he says (fol. D.iiii.) is–

> Make roume and gyue place, stand backe there a fore,
> For all my speakinge, you presse styll the more.
> Gyue rome I say quickeley, and make no dalyaunce,

> It is not now tyme, to make aney taryaunce:
> The kinges here do com, therefore giue way,
> Or elles by the godes, I wyll make you I saye.
> Lo where my Lord Kynge *Nestor* doth com,
> And *Horestes* with him *Agamemnons* sonne:
> *Menelaus* a kyng lykewyse, of great fame,
> Make rome I saye, before their with shame.

In this emphatic speech, which would have been pointless unless there were people standing in clusters round the entrance door, there are two variants of the 'cumeth before' expression in the words 'a fore' and 'before there', both referring to the area in front of the screens, that is to say, between them and the High Table at the upper end.

The coming situation is clearly going to be an important one after this flourishing announcement. As the notable persons all come in, they will presumably mount the stage. What happens next is clearly detailed. Firstly Nestor opens the proceedings by calling for a pause and bidding everyone to wait until Idumeus is fetched. The character called Provision is told – (and the order of printing the lines of the script is interesting here) –

[. . .] go in haste and fet,

Good kynge *Idumeus*, tell him we are set.

Go out.	PROUISION.
	As your gracis haue wylled, so tend I to do,
Pause a	I wyll fetche him strayght, and bringe him you to.
while till	HORESTES.
he be gon	If ought be amys, the same sone shall be,
out[1] & the*n*	If I haue commytted amendyd of me:
speak tre-	But lo *Idumeus* the good kyng of Crete,
tably.	Is come to this place, vs for to mete.
	IDUMEUS.
Enter I-	The Gods presarue your gracis all, & send you health
dumius &	for aye. [*etc. etc.*]
prouision	
comming	
wt his cap	
in his ha*n*d	
afore him	
& making	
waye.	

([1]The presence of this particular part of the direction well shows that some seconds must elapse between a character's starting to go, and his final disappearance through the bystanders and out at the screens door.)

Horestes is now indicted by Menelaus (a) for slaying Menelaus's sister, and (b) for killing his own mother, and (c) for indulging in war and bringing devastation to a country and its inhabitants. Horestes gives a dignified answer to the charges. Idumeus now speaks out and justifies him, and is backed by Nestor. Menelaus is forced to agree that he might himself have done the same as Horestes under the like provocation, and he half withdraws the charges. Idumeus takes advantage of his change of face to make a rather unexpected suggestion that, instead of Horestes being punished, he should be given Menelaus's daughter, Hermione, in marriage. Menelaus seems naturally a little taken aback and temporizes at first. But the others persuade him, and all go off to Nestor's palace 'the maryage to seleybrate'. ('Go out all'.)

The next move is unexpected; the Vice 'entrith wt a staffe & a bottell or dyshe and wallet'. He speaks still in the person of Revenge, and exclaims –

E.ii.   I woulde I were ded [. . .]
    A begginge, a begginge, nay now I must go,
    Horestes is maryed, god send him much care:
    And I Reuenge, am dryuen him fro. [. . .]

He experiences a moment of depression. He seems to turn to the audience and ask if any of them will give him a job. Then he makes an unexpected *volte-face*; a marginal direction tells him to 'Put of ye beggares cote & all thy thynges', and he says –

    Parhappes you all meruayll, of this sodayne mutation,
    How sone I was downe, from so hye a degre:

– and he explains how Amity has now supplanted him with Menelaus, and Duty with Horestes. But next he goes on to say that he has new prospects (which are somewhat surprising!) –

           [. . .] for this well I knowe,
    That the most parte of wemen, to me be full kynde, [. . .]
    Wemen for the most part, are borne malitious.
    Perhappes you wyll saye, maney on that I lye,
    And other sume I am sure, also wyll take my parte.

He quotes the instance of Socrates's wife, Xantippe, who –

> . . . cround him with a pyspot, and their he
> Was wet to the skynne, moste pytifull to se.
> I praye god that such dames, be not in this place,
> For then I might chaunce neare a mistres to get, [. . .]

– and on he rambles to his cue to 'Go out'. But he has clearly indicated that women were present among the audience.

Now 'Enter Horestes & Hermione Nobilytye and Cominyalte truth & Dewty'. ('Dewty', strangely enough, is said in the list of parts to have been played by the Vice, but he obviously is given very little time indeed to change.) Horestes questions this oddly mixed group about the state of mind of the people towards himself. He is told that they are happy to be now at peace. Then 'Truth & Dewty Crowne Horestes' who replies in suitable terms; after which, 'go out all & let truth & Dewtye speake'. They moralize on good government, and conclude with the usual prayer for the Queen and her government.

56 *The Marriage of Wit and Science*

There now follow three plays of lesser interest from the point of view of staging.

The first, the anonymous *New and Pleasant enterlude intituled The mariage of Witte and Science* (c. 1567) has little new to offer that concerns presentation technique. It is a rehash of Redford's play but without his interesting problems or his good psychology. It is divided into acts and scenes. So far as general arrangement goes, the usual screens with clustering spectators round the doors seem indicated, for when Wit's servant (here named Will) prepares to take his master's portrait to the lady Science he has a soliloquy which includes these words, 'But now I come to the gate of this lady . . . And lo where she cometh; yet I will not come nigh her But among these fellows will I stand and eye her'. Since he is speaking alone with no other character of the play present, 'these fellows' must refer to some of the spectators.

57 *Liberality and Prodigality*

The anonymous 'Pleasant Comedie' of *Liberality and Prodigality* (also c. 1567) is described as having been 'playd before her Maieste' and is supposed to be the play referred to in the Revels Accounts, perhaps performed by Paul's Boys. A very detailed study of it has already appeared in Craik (pp. 110–118); here I limit my note to particular items which seem to be relevant to the development of presentation technique.

Early in the script there is a costume-direction, 'Enter Vanity solus all in feathers', and later a reference in the lines to a stately sumptuous throne. There is a knocking at a 'gate', and a 'Host' is awakened and opens the gate. Tenacity, an old countryman, appears 'on a lean ass'. He asks where Vanity is and is answered with – 'Why here in this place; This is Lady Fortune's palace'. The palace is certainly visible for Tenacity remarks '. . . how gay it is'. He then says he will go rest himself, and four lines later adds, 'This is mine old inn', so at least two 'houses' seem implied. Of these, the palace must have two storeys. In Scene vi is the direction 'Enter Fortune in her Chariot drawne with Kings'. Some time later Tenacity returns saying his ass is 'saddle-pinch'd' and so he will boldly walk to Fortune's palace. After some bye-play, Tenacity together with Prodigality go to Fortune, and Vanity announces 'Unto thy stately throne here do repair Two suitors . . .' There are comic inn-scenes involving among others Dick Dicer. Later, before Fortune's palace, Prodigality asks Dick Dicer's advice and is told by him to 'Scale the walls; in at the window', at which Prodigality asks for a ladder; four lines later Dick says, 'Here is a ladder', and he is ordered to 'set it to'. Then follows the direction, 'Here Prod. scaleth. Fortune claps a halter about his neck, he breaketh the halter & falles'. Later, 'Fortune comes down'. A chase, with a Constable, follows and afterwards there is a trial of Prodigality before a Judge, who first condemns him and then adds that his sentence may be qualified.

It is interesting to notice that at the end of the play there is a direction that 'Vertue, Equitie, Liberalitie, Iudge, and all come downe before the Queen' in order to make reverence to her. The phrase 'come *downe*' certainly gives the impression that a raised stage of some sort had been used for the play, whence the players had to step down before traversing the hall to go to the State. (I do not think the phrase can mean 'come *down the hall* to the Queen', for in my opinion the wording in that case would need to have been 'come *up* the hall'.)

The general picture that is suggested of a two-storey palace on a stage reminds one of the arrangement that Inigo Jones was to use in 1609 for Ben Jonson's *The Masque of Queenes* at Whitehall (see my reconstruction in *The Seven Ages of the Theatre*, pp. 188–193).

In general, *Liberality and Prodigality* gives a strong impression that developments in technicalities are taking place; but unfortunately it offers very little to show indisputably to what extent the Castle and the Inn and the Trial-scene were visually represented.

58 *Like will to Like*

In Ulpian Fulwell's *Like will to Like* (c. 1568), described as an 'Interlude', we revert to the rollicking gay nonsense of some of the early plays but with a certain adult flavour about it. There is a great deal of direct bye-play with the audience and a very strong touch of the old hall-and-screens technique; for instance the Vice, called Nicholas Newfangle, enters laughing 'and hath a knave of clubs in his hand which as soon as he speaketh, he offereth unto one of the men or boys standing by'. But the audience is clearly not all male since the Vice suddenly switches to the engaging lines –

> Yet women are kind worms I dare well say
> How say you woman you that stand in the angle
> Were you never acquainted with Nichol Newfangle

Soon the Devil gaily enters ('but he speaketh not yet'), and Newfangle cries out, possibly indicating a costume not unlike a woodwose's –

> Sancte benedicite whom have we here
> Tom Tumbler or else some dancing bear
> [. . .] it is my godfather Lucifer

– and we read with some interest the direction that 'This name Lucifer must be written on his back and on his breast'. This is one of the very few direct references to the practice of this convention in England.

It is very difficult to find any pictorial evidence from England of this curious custom of a player's wearing his character's name in a legend or 'badge' on his breast, but there is one example to be found from the Low Countries in Pieter Bruegel's set of engravings for *The Seven Virtues*. In a corner of the sheet representing *Temperantia*, there is part of a booth stage with a very interesting group of figures upon it; both the male and the female characters bear name-legends, the male character's being, oddly enough, a name common to both Flemish and English – it is Hope. Fig. 38 is a rough re-drawing of the relevant part of the picture taken from the original drawing (now in Rotterdam) for the engraving. The date is 1560. A reproduction of the full picture can be seen in Ludwig Munz's *Bruegel Drawings*, pl. 145.

Lucifer hails Nichol with delight – 'Ho mine own boy I am glad that thou art here', and Nichol has the impudence to turn to an innocent bystander with – 'He speaketh to you Sir I pray you come near', so causing Lucifer to correct him with – 'Nay thou art euen he . . .' Among the horseplay that follows is a drunken scene and a song by 'Hance with a pot' in which 'He singeth the first two lines and speaketh the rest as stammeringly as may be'; and 'He danceth as evil-favoured as may be devised and in the dancing he falleth down and when he riseth he must grown'. Later he sitteth in 'the' chair, and there are other specific references to this chair.

Later again there 'entreth in Nicholas Newfangle and bringeth in with him a bag, a staff a bottle and two halters going about the

FIG. 38. A booth stage with actors bearing legends on their breasts (a redrawn detail from Pieter Bruegel's 'Temperantia')

place and showing it unto the audience and singeth . . .' and 'He may sing this as oft as he thinketh good' – presumably according to the size of the Place which he has to go round in. Then follows a particularly interesting direction referring to false beards: 'Here entereth in Ralph Roister and Tom Tospot in their doublet and their hose and no cap or hat on their head saving a night cap because the strings of their beards might not be seen . . .' (they had been playing strip poker).

The conclusion comes with a direct address by the Vice to members of the audience: 'Why then good gentle boy how likest thou this play?' and 'How say you little Meg?' Then, ' . . . I would I had a pot for now I am so hot By the masse I must fo piss . . .' Then 'The Devil entereth' crying 'Leap up on my back straightway' and they gallop out in absolutely true ancient Devil-and-Vice tradition.

59 *Cambises*

On Thomas Preston's *Cambyses* (though it has no reference to a stage) I shall have to spend a little more attention for two reasons. Firstly, the play is a particular example of a new vein in playwriting which is influencing Interludes – a grim and deliberately bloodthirsty, heavy melodramatic vein. And secondly, there is just a possibility that this play is referred to indirectly by Falstaff in *I Henry IV*.

It is the last point presumably, that led Edmund Creeth, in his Introduction to his anthology of *Tudor Plays* (New York, 1966), to write, 'There is reason to believe that *Cambises* belonged to the repertory of the Earl of Leicester's men, which featured James Burbage and which in 1576 moved into his Theatre.' (p. xxxiv). How much Falstaff's reference justifies this belief I am not sure, but the reference is worth looking at in detail.

Falstaff, when asked to impersonate the King and pretend to rebuke Prince Hal, says (II, iv.):

> Shall I? content. This chaire shall be my state . . . Giue me a cup of Sacke to make mine eyes looke redde, that it maie bee thought I haue wept, for I must speake in passion, and I will doe it in king Cambises vaine. . . . For Gods sake lords, conuay my trustfull Queene. For teares do stop the floud-gates of her eyes.
>
> HOST. O Iseu, he doth it as like one of these harlotrie plaiers as euer I see.

It seems pretty clear that, in alluding to 'king Cambises vaine', Falstaff is supposed to be referring to a style of acting not to some trick of manner attributed to the actual historical King of Persia. Quite apart from the context, Mistress Quickly's remark that he behaves like one of these harlotry – or vagabond – players, shows that it is an acting-technique that is in question. The lines that Falstaff here speaks in this 'vaine' are admittedly not lines to be found in Preston's text, but the incident – that of the Queen's weeping – is to be found there, and is one of the dramatic climaxes of the play, bringing about as it does the final paroxysm of Cambyses' wrath. But there is no proof that, if Falstaff was alluding to a specific play, it was this one of Preston's. There may have been other plays, now lost, on the same theme. However, what matters here is that Shakespeare was in a position to make one of his characters quote as an example of extravagant diction – or speaking 'in passion' – the sort of speech that could be associated with vagabond players performing the Cambyses story. In Preston we have that story written for performance by such players – whether or not those players had in fact been Lord Leicester's own troupe.

I have used the Tudor Facsimile Text of the 1584 edition, published in 1910. The title-page there reads as follows –

A lamentable Tragedie, mixed full of
plesant mirth, containing the life of Cambises king of Percia, from the beginning of his king-
dome, vnto his death, his one good deede of execu-
tion, after that many wicked deedes and tyrannous mur-
ders, committed by and through him, and last
of all, his odious death by Gods Iustice
appointed. Done in such order
as followeth.
By *Thomas Preston.*

The diuision of the parts

Councell.			Prologue.	
Huf.			Sisamnes	
Praxaspes.	*For one man.*		Diligence	*For one man*
Murder.			Crueltie.	
Lob.			Hob	
The third Lord.			preparation	
			the i. Lord	

Lord.			
Ruf.		Ambidexter	
Commons cry.	*For one man.*	Triall.	*For one man.*
Commons complaint			
Lord Smirdis			
Venus.			
Knight.		Meretrix.	
Snuf.		Shame.	
Small hability		Otian,	
Proof.	*For one man.*	Mother.	*For one man*
Execution.		Lady.	
Attendance.		Queene.	
Second Lord.			
Cambises.	*For one man.*	Yong child.	*For one man.*
Epilogus.		Cupid.	

Of the last two groups in the right-hand column, the former (beginning with Meretrix) is likely to have been played by a boy and the latter probably by a still smaller boy.

There are no references to a stage anywhere in the text. The play opens with a straightforward Prologue describing the plot, and ending: 'I take my way, beholde I see, the players comming in'.

Then, 'First enter Cambises the King Knight and Councellor.' Also speaking in this opening scene is a 'Lord' not mentioned in the direction. Cambises announces his departure to war with Egypt and names Sisamnes as his regent. Then all go out.

Next: 'Enter the Vice with an old Capcase on his head, an olde paile about his hips for harnes, a scummer and a potlid by his side and a rake on his shoulder.' This is one of the very rare detailed glimpses we get of the appearance of a Vice; and a fantastic enough appearance it is, reminding one of some of the culinary costumes for masque-figures by designers like Burnacini in the next century.

All that I have been able to find out about a 'capcase' is firstly that it is taken to be a travelling bag or hold-all of some sort that could be attached to one's saddle. (The *O.E.D.* gives an example of this use from '1577. Harrison *England* II xvi (1877) I. 283. Feeling whether their capcases or budgets be of anie weight or not, by taking them down from their saddles.') And secondly that it appears to have been of such a shape that a saint's arm could be kept in one, as a relic, according to Hector Boece's *Chronicles of Scotland*, where King Robert the Bruce is said to have won the Battle of Bannockburn through some miraculous agency of Saint Felayne (or St.

Fillan) 'quhais arme, . . . sett in siluer wes closit in ane caiss' in his pavilion (see John Bellenden's translation into Scots, 1531, Bk. XIV, ch. xi) – the relevance of this quotation to 'capcase' depends on Robert Burton's version of the story in his *Anatomy of Melancholy*, where he renders it rather freely as '. . . In the battle of Bannock-burn, where Edward the Second, our English King, was foiled by the Scots, St. Philanus' arme was seen to fight (if Hector Boethius doth not impose), that was before shut up in a silver capcase; . . .' (III. IV. i. ii, 1561, 645). Whether one would be right in picturing a capcase as a long cylindrical holder (that might take, for example, a rolled-up cape) I do not know; but such a thing could con-ceivably make a grotesque tall headdress, in appearance maybe resembling the hats Tiepolo showed on many of his Pulcinelli.

An 'old paile about his hips for harnes' might refer to a wooden washtub made of 'pales' or staves with its bottom knocked out and the walls inverted and hung round his waist like a kilt. (Both these items would seem to have been pretty difficult to play in.)

The fantastic quality of this appearance among the other actors is worth noting. It implies that the Interluders were quite happy to see what I might call a 'differentiation of character-plane' com-parable to the 'differentiation of acting-area' which I have already suggested; that is to say they were quite willing to accommodate in one scene a character in the normal convention of dress and a character in a purely fantastic, even impossible, freak costume, playing opposite him. This differentiation of character role, so that the parts seem to have been created on completely different planes of conception, applies to the behaviour of the character as well as his appearance; for it seems that no character in the play proper would ever speak to the audience directly, but that on the other hand the Vice (with his confederates) was free to dissociate himself from the action, to comment upon it independently, to interfere in its course and, particularly, to turn and address speeches directly to the audience in respect of that action. Such freedom a purely naturalistic stage could not enjoy.

The Vice here is named Ambidexter, and he frequently makes use of this characteristic to deal backhandedly, or 'both-handedly', with the rest of the characters. He begins with a direct audience-address, obviously based on the old convention of pushing through the spectators standing round the screens entrance –

Stand away stand away for the passion of God
Harnessed I am prepared to the field:

He goes on into pure nonsense and finally promises that the audience shall see the downfall of Sisamnes, the King's regent. To him come three ruffians named Huf, Ruf, and Snuf singing. One of the ever-popular fight scenes follows, diversified by the entrance of a whore named Meretrix, who demands kisses –

AMBIDEXTER.

B.2.*rev.* Mistres Meretrix, I thought not to see you heere now.
There is no remedy at meeting I must haue a kisse

MERETRIX.

What man? I wil not sticke for that by gisse.   kisse.

AMBIDEXTER.

So now gramercy, I pray thee be gone,

MERETRIX.

Nay soft my freend I meane to haue one.
Nay soft I sweare, and if ye were my brother,
Before I let go I wil haue another.   kisse, kisse, kisse.

and the foolery goes on until quarrelling overtakes them once more.

The scene over, Ambidexter meets Sisamnes and warns him against the acts of extortion of which he is being guilty in his regency. Then, among other figures, Shame comes in 'with a trump blacke' to support the accusation. At length the King returns, hears his subjects' complaints, and swiftly comes to his 'one good deede' by ordering the punishment of the corrupt Sisamnes.

It is now that the really bloodthirsty nature of the play is first revealed. The punishment is superbly cruel (and spectacular). King Cambyses first commands his 'Execution man to come'. Three characters leave to fetch him. Then he instructs Sisamnes' son, Otian, to be brought, and the direction follows – 'step aside and fetch him'. The boy is brought in. Cambyses informs Otian that he has decided to promote him to his father's place and that he is going to execute Sisamnes before the son's eyes as a warning of what will befall him if he should behave as his father did. The boy pleads, but Cambyses brushes him off –

C.2.*rev.* Doo not intreat my grace no more, for he shal dye the death:
Where is the Execution man, him to bereaue of breath.

Enter execution.

Father and son exchange farewells, and Execution says to Sisamnes,

[. . .] my office I must pay.
Forgiue therfore my deed.

514

SISAMNES.
I doo forgiue it thee my frend, dispatch therfore with speed.

– and the interesting direction follows: 'Smite him in the neck with a sword to signifie his death'. Thus we have a clear indication of a convention for killing – to strike a character in the neck with a sword, thereby *signifying* his death. No doubt he falls with all effect; Praxaspes, one of the courtiers, puts in a line here: 'Beholde (O king how he dooth bleed . . .' of which more later.

But neither the effects nor the bloodshed are yet over; a remarkable piece of business follows –

KING
In this wise he shall not yet be left.
Pull his skin ouer his eyes to make his death more vile

– and (with what effect it is not easy to conceive!) they actually proceed to do that thing. How they do it is very briefly indicated in the direction which comes here – 'Flea him with a false skin.'

The courtier Praxaspes orders the son to get rid of the body, '. . . conuay your father hence, to tomb where he shall lye:' and poor Otian asks the 'Execution man' to help him, which he kindly does, and 'They take him away'.

The plot now thickens, for the King asks Praxaspes a dangerous question, 'Haue not I doon a gratious deed, to redresse my *commons* woe?' and Praxaspes is constrained to agree. But also he cannot refrain from taking occasion to reproach Cambyses for 'The vice of drunkennes (Oh king) which doth you sore infect:' For the moment the King, though no doubt heartily annoyed, brushes this aside, and is about to go out when there 'Enter Lord, and Knight to meet the King'. Praxaspes unwisely renews his accusation of intemperance. The newly-arrived Knight suggests Cambyses should beget a child to succeed him. This possibly puts an idea into Cambyses' head. He is now to proceed to the next bloodthirsty and spectacular effect.

To prove he is not incapacitated by drunkenness he proposes a monstrous demonstration; he orders Praxaspes to fetch his (Praxaspes') son in, and announces –

[. . .] thou with speed shalt see
Whether that I a sober King, or els a drunkard be . . .
When I the most haue tasted wine, my bow it shalbe bent:
At hart of him euen then to shoote, is now my whole intent.
And if that I his hart can hit, the king no drunkard is:
If hart of his I doo not kill, I yeeld to thee in this. [. . .]

The 'yonge childe' is brought; the King drinks, and drinks again. There are protestations from all, but the King speaks a line harshly out of meter: 'Before me as a mark now let him stand, I wil shoot at him my minde to fulfill:' and the direction follows – 'Shoot'. Then, from the King: 'I haue dispatched him, down he doth fall As right as a line his hart I haue hit: . . .'

There is unfortunately nothing at all to suggest to us how this trick was done, but with an audience as close as they would be in a Great Hall and as evenly spread on all sides round the actors, one supposes some ingenious shift would have to be managed.

But Cambyses has not finished yet –

> Nay thou shalt see Praxaspes, stranger newes yet
> My knight with speed his hart cut out, and giue it vnto me: [. . .]

> KNIGHT.
> Heere is the hart, according to your graces behest.

> KING.
> Beholde Praxaspes thy Sonnes owne hart,
> Oh how well the same was hit:
> After this wine to doo this deed, I thought it very fit.

– then he adds to the rest of his courtiers, turning from Praxaspes, 'leaue him heer to take his son, . . .' and the court goes out.

The boy's mother now enters, and after a pathetic speech Praxaspes proposes –

> Between vs both ye childe to bere vnto our lordly place.
>
> Exeunt

The place is now left empty for the next entrance of Ambidexter, and he proceeds to work a very curious gag – if gag it is. His words, spoken directly to the audience, are –

> D.1.*rev.* Indeed as ye say, I haue been absent a long space.
> But is not my Cosin cutpurse, with you in the meane time?
> To it, to it Cosin, and doo your office fine. [. . .]

– and he goes on to ask the audience what they think of Sisamnes. But this very strange appeal to what is apparently a (surely imaginary?) confederate in the audience who is there to pick pockets, makes distraction enough from what has gone before. Beside this it may throw light on the puzzling line in Haphazard's speech in very much the same terms in *Apius*: 'At hand (quoth picke purse)

... See well to the [*thee*] Cut Purse, be ruled by me'. The suggestion seems very strong that, besides their other licences with the audience the Vices might occasionally play the 'joke' of hinting that there was a thief among them, working upon their pockets.

The next episode begins with the entrance of the King's brother Smirdis with certain Lords. Smirdis speaks against Cambyses' savagery and intemperance, and the Courtiers advise him to be more prudent. Then the King comes in. The Vice insinuates suspicion of Smirdis into the King's ear, and before many lines have passed Cambyses decides to do away with his brother, and goes out. 'Enter Cruelty & Murder with bloody hands.' These two have been ordered to set upon Smirdis, and they 'Strike him in diuers places'. Smirdis falls declaring his innocence, and a direction neatly indicates the picture – 'A little bladder of Vineger prickt.' Cruelty remarks, 'Beholde now his blood springs out on the ground', and Murder rejoins, 'Now he is dead, let vs present him to the king:' Cruelty concludes, 'Lay to your hand away him to bring.' 'Exeunt.'

Ambidexter is left to pour out mock tears, and a comic episode follows with two country-men, Hob and Lob, concluding with a fight involving Hob's wife. This over, they run out and a most unexpected entrance follows. The relevant direction reads –

E.2.   Enter Venus leading out her sonne Cupid blinde, he must haue a bow and two shafts, one headed with golde and th'other with lead.

Venus gives detailed instructions to her son that he is to shoot the gold arrow at Cambyses at a moment when he is looking at a certain young woman who is cousin-germane to him (that is, among the prohibited relationships). Now the Lady herself enters with a waiting maid and a Lord. They 'trace abroad the beauty feelds' and a quite evocative word-picture follows in the Lord's speech, of a delectable pastoral scene with mention of flowers and birds and even a 'Lute and Cittern there to play a heauenly harmony:' – this attempt at a word-picture to suggest the atmosphere is, as I hinted concerning *Damon and Pythias*, a new device coming into play-making – a primitive example of verbal scene-painting. The Lady gracefully acquiesces in the illusion and they 'heere trace vp and downe playing'.

Into this idyllic scene the King comes, accompanied by a Lord and a Knight. He sees the Lady and exclaims at her beauty. Then Venus tells Cupid to shoot – and 'Shoote there, and goe out

Venus and Cupid.' Despite the Lady's scruples Cambyses carries her off to his palace for their marriage.

Ambidexter now takes up the action and mockingly describes the hurried wedding preparations – incidentally asking a woman in the audience 'How say you maid? to marry me wil ye be glad.' Next (E.4.*rev.*) a new character called Preparation comes in to the Vice, quarrels, fights, is reconciled, and then asks his help in providing the furniture for a banquet. The direction follows 'Set the fruit on the boord', so a table must have been set up here. Ambidexter helps and makes comic business by bungling – 'Let the Vice fetch a dish of Nuts, and let them fall in the bringing of them in', but he cries 'I will haue them vp againe by and by'. Then Preparation goes out.

The Vice now turns to the audience and says that all is in readiness for the King and Queen, and then suddenly breaks off and calls above their heads, with a return to his old gag –

> I beseech ye my maisters tell me is it not best:
> that I be so bolde as to bid a guest?

(probably a long look round in the puzzled silence here, then he goes on –)

> He is as honest a man as euer spurd Cow:
> My Cosin cutpursse I meane, I beseech ye iudge you:
> Beleeue me Cosin if to be the kings guest ye could be taken:
> I trust that offer will neuer be forsaken.
> But Cozin because to that office ye are not like to come:
> Frequent your exercises, a horne on your thum.
> A quick eye, a sharpe knife, at hand a receiuer:
> But then take heed Cosin ye be a clenly conuayour.
> Content your selfe Cosin, for this banquet you are vnfit:
> When such as I at the same am vnworthy to sit.
>   Enter King, Queene, and his traine.

A direction tells them all to 'sit at the banquet'. The King wishes for music, and we have the direction, 'Play at the banquet'. Now, the King tells a certain story; it concerns a whelp that saved his brother-whelp in an emergency. At this the Queen bursts into tears – 'At this tale tolde let the Queene weep'. This is the moment, presumably, that Falstaff had in mind when he began to 'speak in passion' and to 'do it in king Cambises vaine'.

The King of course angrily demands her reason, and the poor sobbing lady says because it showed such a contrast in behaviour with what the King did to his own brother. This naturally brings

down all Cambyses' wrath and he rises and orders the whole banquet to be cleared away and in the confusion he sends Ambidexter
to ask for Cruelty and Murder to be fetched again. The Queen
protests, the King rants and raves in Cambyses' vein, then the two
bloody-handed figures enter. The King and Court go out, and the
Queen is left to be taken away to her death. Ambidexter comes into
the empty place and comments on all the outrages.

There is still a last piece of bloodthirstiness. To him there enters
'the King without a gowne, a swoord thrust vp into his side bleeding'.

KING.

Out alas what shal I doo? my life is finished:
Wounded I am by sodain chaunce, [. . .]
As I on horseback vp did leap, my sword from scabard shot.
And ran me thus into the side, as you right well may see: [. . .]

At length he falls: 'Thus gasping heer on ground I lye . . .' He then
is given an actor's chance to forestall Sir Laurence Olivier at the end
of the film of *Richard III*: 'Heere let him quake and stir'. Ambidexter bends over him to say, 'He cannot speak, but beholde how
with death he doth striue . . .' and then turns and runs away. Three
Lords enter, and the Third says,

. . . let vs take him vp and carry him away.

BOTH.

Content we are with one accord, to doo as you doo say.

Exeunt all.

A short Epilogue, apologizing for the author's shortcomings
and asking the formal blessing on the Queen and her Councillors,
ends the play.

60 *Susanna*

After this melodramatic welter in gore it is with some sense of
contrast that one turns to a play that, though it is equally concerned
with viciousness in detail, yet is written in general with a subtler
pen, but which at the same time contains equally sensational technicalities of presentation. In fact, so interesting are these presentational matters that the play is worthy of study in full and careful
detail. I have already anticipated one of its major points of interest

above in Section 39, where I discussed the stage direction which occurs at the moment when the two salacious Elders prepare to spy upon Susanna bathing, and for this purpose begin to 'go afore into the Orchard' just ahead of the particular moment when she and her two maids 'come vpon the stage'.

The title-page, as given in the Malone Society's reprint of 1936, reads –

THE COMMODY OF
the moste vertuous and Godlye
Susanna, neuer before this
tyme Printed.
Compiled by Thomas Garter.
Eyght persons may easyly play it.
1. The Prologue and the Gaylour for one.
2. Joachim and Judex for another,
3. Sathan and Voluptas another,
4. Sensualitas alone.
5. Susanna alone.
6. Helchia, True Report, Ancilla, another,
7. Ill Reporte the Vyce, and Cryer, another.
8. Helchias wyfe, Danyell, Seruus, Serua, for another.

IMPRINTED AT
London, in Fleetestreate, be-
neath the Conduite, at the
Signe of S. Iohn Euangelist
by Hugh Iackson.
1578.

The Prologue refers to the Author and 'This his fyrst worke', outlines the plot, and ends –

24. Thus crauing quyet sylence now, my speeche I mean to spare,
Beholde when Sathan enters place, his mynde he will declare.
Here goeth out the Prologue, and Sathan entreth in.

Notice that the old word still comes up in the phrase 'enters place'; but now that we have established (on p. 444) that this play was performed with a stage, the phrase may have the further significance of indicating that the Prologue spoke – as indeed is most likely – from the stage, but that Sathan strolled in along the floor through the door-cluster, and so 'entered place', while the Prologue stepped down and went out by the other door.

Sathan states that there is one person in Babylon whose virtue he would like to corrupt, but reflects – 'so ougly is my face' that he will call in his 'crafty chylde' named Ill Reporte to talk to her. Then –

51.   Here the Deuill sitteth downe in a Chayre, and calleth for Ill Reporte, who entreth in.

I suppose Sathan now stepping on to the stage to reach his chair. Ill Reporte is slow, and needs summoning again before he actually enters. Then he reviles his father to the audience, demanding of them, 'How say you all, within this Hall, What Knaue more crookte then he, . . .' His father delights in the son's rudery, and names Susanna as his intended victim. They then exchange insults and 'Here the Deuill goeth out, and Euill Reporte taryeth still.' (He is sometimes called Ill Reporte and sometimes Evil Reporte.) He now possibly sits, and he addresses the audience at length, telling how most of the Seven Sins have already been called in, in the attempt to corrupt Susanna, but unsuccessfully; so now he 'With filthy lustes of fleshly men, meaneth her to assayle . . .' At that precise and propitious moment, two apt instruments for his purpose appear –

186.   Herewith commeth in Voluptas, and calleth Sensualitas in this sorte.

'In this sorte' may be important; it implies that he calls Sensualitas in some special way. We picture Ill Reporte still sitting in his chair on the stage and turning to look quizzically at the newcomers. The first mounts the stage and turns and offers his hand to the second to help him up beside him. His lines are explicit; Voluptas says –

> Come in Mayster Sensualitas I pray thee,
> Reche me thy hande and I will helpe thee.

Sensualitas, possibly a besotted or a depleted man – or even an effeminate one? – replies in his effort,

> By my truth Voluptas I haue neede of thy ayde,
> Such is my secrete sorrow, my sences are dismayde.

Ill Reporte watches their ascent contemptuously, and remarks to the audience –

> Though you iudge me scant worth to be a proctor,
> Marke me well now, and I will play the Doctor.

He quotes the Latin tag, *Amor vincit omnia* as his proposed remedy. The two Elders affect to ignore him and he abuses them for their bad manners. They then admit that it is 'loue' that is their 'sicknesse'. He threatens to abandon them uncured unless they pay him in advance; and they pay him ten pounds. He now threatens again to leave them since he has the money, then changes his mind and instead tells the two men to go and leave him, and to return to him in a day or two. They go. Ill Reporte tells the audience that 'these are the two that Susan shall proue', and at length he bids farewell and goes. Thus the story is begun.

Next, Joachim (Susanna's husband) enters and speaks of the terrible responsibility that he feels in his work as a judge. To him there enter 'The two Iudges' (that is Sensuality and Voluptas), who reproach him for having too tender a conscience. But he replies that –

314. The matters are so croockt and vyle, that commeth forth ech day,
    As how to ende without some wrong, I know not well the way.

He is filled with misgivings about these responsibilities; he asks the others how far they believe evidence can be trusted, and he urges them to study each 'playnt' with great care; and then –

> With that Sensuality and Voluptas sitteth downe at a Table turning of bokes, and Ioachim kneeling on his knees sayeth.

– and he utters a prayer to be guided in his judgements. Into this rather strangely mixed atmosphere of piety and doubt there comes an unexpected intrusion. We picture the two judges with their books at the table and Joachim kneeling before it; now –

> Here entreth Susanna and her two maydes.

She completely breaks the atmosphere and yet she makes *no immediate acknowledgement of the presence of the three men*; she is gossiping privately with her servants on homely matters, and the dialogue now runs as follows –

SUSANNA. I cannot but must marueyle much, of Joachim my Lorde,
          And why he commeth not home to dyne, according to his
              worde.
          Was it not at xij. a Clock that he sayd he would dyne,
          How thinke you both in fayth is it not, a little past that
              tyme.
SERUA.   Not much Madam, he is not wont to breake his promyse
              iust,

ANCILLA.   No, no, Madam, he will ere long be with you, you may
           trust.

SUSANNA.   What yonder he is me thinkes.

SERUA.   It is he in very deede.

           With that she goeth to him and maketh Curtesy.

SUSANNA.   I will not say vnto you now, what you did cause me thinke,
           In deede I will conceale it now, and at the matter winke.

IOACH.   What Susan doest thou chyde me now, I will tell thee my
           mynde,
           That women there be none at all, but shrewes they are by
           kynde,

SUSANNA.   Well, well to auoyde this controuersye, I will confesse
           that cryme,
           And I pray you hartily to aryse, and let vs home to dyne.

           Note that from the entrance of Susanna,
           the Iudges eyes shall neuer be of her,
           till her departure, whispering betweene
           themselues, as though they talked of her.

IOACH.   What is it dinner tyme so soone, me thinkes it scantly
           noone,

SUSANNA.   Yes good my Lord I pray you now, make ready and go
           we soone.

           With this Ioachim, Susanna and her two Maydes, go to
           the Table to the two Elders.

IOACH.   Loe now my maysters you may see, the state of marryed
           men,

367.   My wyfe is come, I must be gone, I must yeelde to her
           when. [. . .]

380.   Well farewell my Maysters till after noone,
           I trust you will dyne, and be here agayne soone.

VOLUP.   I warrant you we will not be long,

SENSUA.   If we should, we should do you wrong.

           Here Ioachim, Susanna, and her two maydes depart, and
           the Iudges make vp their Bokes and ryse, and Voluptas
           speaketh.

VOLUP.   Now Mayster Sensuality I would mayster Doctor were
           here.

SENSUA.   I had rather talke with him, then heare of this geare.

           And so shut their Bokes.

This must be among the first examples of almost purely naturalistic dialogue. But the main thing here is that it could almost not
have been delivered as it stands unless there were some difference
in acting-area between the place where Joachim and the Elders

sat and the place into which Susanna and her maids entered, and unless Susanna crossed the barrier between the two areas when she first curtsied to Joachim. Presumably she did so by going up on to the stage into their area on the direction 'With that she goeth to him . . .'

The purpose of her going, later on, with Joachim and the maids to the table where the two judges are, instead of leaving straightway with her husband to dinner, would clearly seem to be to offer a moment of dramatic confrontation between herself and the two old men who have been watching her so covetously and whispering. It could well be a significant moment.

After she and her party have left, the two Elders speak at some length and with unrestricted expression of their feelings for her. The finality of the direction 'And so shut their Bokes' rather suggests they drop the atmosphere of the laywer's office which must have prevailed up to this point, and they possibly step forward in front of the table to talk. Is it or is it not to be thought that in their dialogue there seems to be implied, whether consciously or no, a particular sort of intimate relationship of dominant leader and obsequious yielder? This point is made in view of a remarkable crack about them by the Vice in a later scene, which I will notice in its place.

However that may be, at the end of their conference, when they long to see Ill Reporte again, Sensuality says,

459.   Why see how good our fortune is, see how he commeth yond
       And we to see his entraunce now, in Corner here will stand.
                                  The Vice entreth, and looketh not at them.

It is not possible to be entirely sure what this strange sequence means, but I would estimate that they see him coming in as they are standing there on the stage, and that they then either retire to a far corner of the stage in order to leave the Vice to caper out his next piece of nonsense round the Place; or – as I feel is perhaps more likely – they step off the stage altogether and lose themselves in a corner of the audience so as to give the Vice the full stage to himself.

Wherever he is, the Vice now has a sheer nonsense speech, as surrealistic as the madder sort of nursery rhyme, and is about to go out again when – 'The Vyce running out, is stayde by Sensualitie, who sayeth.' And what he says is 'Why friend know you not me?' The Vice denies all knowledge of them; so they recall the ten pounds

they 'gaue' him for his doctor's fee. He jumps at the word 'gave'
and turns to the audience with – 'My maysters recorde beare, . . .
These gentlemen doe both confesse that they did giue it me', so
claiming it as a free present. There seems about to be a deadlock
when Sensuality says gently to Voluptas that the money does not
matter. But Voluptas pugnaciously asks the Vice his name, and the
following astonishing exchange ensues –

504. VOLUP.   But I pray thee tell me what is they name?
    ILL REP. Mary Syr a woman.
    VOLUP.   What art thou a man, and haste a womans name?
    ILL REP. Why syr are you a woman, and haue a man to your
              Dame.
    VOLUP.   Nay I pray thee iest not but tell me thy name. . . .

– and the fooling proceeds with almost alarming innuendo and pun-
ning for a couple of pages. What exactly Ill Report makes of the
couple who are bargaining with him is not clear. At all events he
promises to help them to Susanna, and they go and leave him. He
has a last soliloquy and then runs out because he sees Susanna's
husband, Joachim, coming. Now we begin to approach the great
dramatic scene.

Joachim has sixteen lines of pious soliloquy in which he again
prays conscientiously 'to iudge eche thing aright' (and is clearly far
more concerned with that problem than with any at home) and
then he leaves; 'Here goeth out Joachim, and Susannas two mayds
enter.' Obviously the situation now is ripe for gossip; in fact these
two girls exchange a very interesting dialogue about their disillusion over the pleasures of court life, at any rate for such as themselves. The clock strikes one, and 'They go out, and Sensualitie and
Voluptas enter.' And here follows the passage already examined in
Section 39, see pp. 443–445.

To recapitulate the main details; the two Elders plan to accost
Susanna at the spring within her orchard, and then they 'go afore'
into that orchard at the moment when Susanna and her two maids
'come upon the stage', and after a short exchange these three
women are also to 'go into the Orcharde'.

In default of anything better, I suggest, for a visualization of
the stage arrangement at this point, something in the nature of what
is shown in Fig. 39. Here the orchard would be represented by four
light trellis walls fronting the stage, with a practical trellis door or
gate in the forward wall. Inside would be two screens representing

FIG. 39. A conventional composite of the possible setting for *Susanna*,
showing at once Joachim's 'Table' and 'bokes', the orchard 'afore' the
stage, and the two Servants running to 'breake open the Orchard dore'

bushes for the Elders to hide behind and, between these, possibly a
painted cloth on the floor to represent the pool. Among the trellis
might be woven strands of creeper with leaves and flowers.

What now happens is that Susanna in the orchard complains of
the heat and then suddenly notices that her maids have forgotten
her 'sope and oyle'. She sends them to fetch these things adding
that they are to 'make fast the Orchard dore' after them. They do
so; 'Here they go out and shut the Orchard dore'. But the two maids
do not immediately go on their way, for Ancilla says,

702. Proue with your foote, if that the Dore, as we were bad be lockt,

Serva does so, and then the two resume their nostalgic gossiping
about the advantages of home life against court life, for some 22
lines. Whether any particular business takes place in the orchard
during this time there is nothing to guide us. Then at length:

726.   Here they go out, and the two Iudges that lye hidden
                    talke in this wise.

Sensuality, watching Susanna, feels his heart burn up. Voluptas urges quiet and says 'I will to her alone, And follow you as you see tyme . . .' He then steps out and speaks to her. He tells her 'the Orchard dores are fast, . . . none can vs see, . . . We burne towarde thee with feruent lust, consent vs therefore to, . . . Come lye with vs, . . . For if thou wilt not then . . . we will say, A yongman with thee here we found, in very secrete sporte, . . .' Susanna says crisply that if they will leave her alone she will hide what they have been guilty of in intruding upon her. Sensuality presses their demands. Susanna begins to see she is caught in a dilemma and decides to suffer whatever trouble they can call down, but 'without the act'. And so they are forced to resort to their alternative, and both cry 'Helpe, helpe, helpe.'

774.   Here two seruauntes of the house run out, and breake open the Orchard doore, and asketh what is the matter, and then Voluptas speaketh.

– and he says that he will tell nothing to anyone until he has seen Joachim. The two servants are aghast at the imputation. Voluptas snarls to Susanna 'Madame, you are a secrete whore'. Sensuality echoes him, and –

Here goe out the two Iudges and Susanna, and sayeth as she goeth.

– a prayer to God to receive her tears; and then – 'They be gone.' They leave the two puzzled servants alone, and these make up their minds to have complete faith in their mistress, and one of them falls on his knees and prays for her. They finally decide to 'go home and nothing say, . . .'

Then, 'Ioachim entreth loking about him.' An interesting question is, What does he enter and where is it that he looks about? His first words afford a slight surprise; they are, 'Are not the Judges yet come here, . . .' He does not seem to come to the garden, or to have any thought of it or relationship with it; it would appear that his only concern is that he cannot find his two Elders, though they should now be returning to work after their dinner. He may therefore have come in and mounted straightway to the stage, which recently had represented their office. Still they do not come; and he prays for their honesty and feels grave doubts. Then he goes out again, speaking a courteous four lines of explanation and farewell to the audience –

848. Well synce they are not come in deede, I will go home agayne,
Where till they come in vewing thinges, my selfe will take some
payne
And God preserue and blesse you all, I speake to eche degree,
And he alwayes remayne with you, and also go with me.

Here goeth out Ioachim, and Helchia and his
wyfe enter.

These two are Susanna's parents. Their entrance is a device to
'change the scene' as it were, and at the same time to let us know,
as they discuss their fear for their daughter's plight, that she has now
been accused. They try to have faith in a happy outcome, and go
out. And now a curious sequence takes place.

It begins with the direction –

904. Here they go out and the Vice entreth and sayeth,
in my best peticote. &c. with a bell in his hande.

What he says begins with the atmosphere of a nursery rhyme; goes
on to revile whomsoever it was that made him a Cryer with a bell;
and ends with as bitter an attack on the ladies in the audience as is
to be found in any Vice's speech. And during it he rings his bell.
Here is a summary of his speech:

> In my best petticote,
> Is there a hole,
> My sister burnt it with a cole [. . .]
> And all the plagues of Hell,
> May recompence his meede
> That first wrought this deede
> To giue me this bell.
> Ill Report is a cryer,   Ring
> And a common lyer. [. . .]   Bell.
> Know you not Ioachims wyfe,
> it is a peece with a mischeefe,
> She must haue two at ones:
> There is neuer a wench here.
> But in her best geare,
> Would haue flesh without bones
> Why, why, do you winke,
> Shame to you that shame thinke,
> it is but your kynde:
> So you may do it couertly,
> And cloke it honestly,
> You care not where you fynde.

wel I wold maister gailer would come
Then shall all and some,
Know the cause of my comming:
it is as I feare,
For other manner of geare,
Then for masking or mumming.

                    Then the Gaylor commeth in.

The Gaoler is apparently called the Bayly. The Vice abuses him for his greeting, but learns from him that 'Susanna shall be here araigned soone'. Then he adds that 'yonder I see, the Judges are comming, And therefore . . . let vs doe something', but the Bayly replies, 'We neede not synce we are here redy'.

The suggestion in all this exchange is that a new passage of the story is beginning. It is pretty clear that we are to see the trial of Susanna and that, therefore, the 'scene' is to shift to a place of judgement – or rather, to adapt the Bayly's words, it need not, for *we are here ready* for it; or, it is here ready for us.

We are now at l. 940 out of the 1458 lines of the play, that is to say a little over half way. It is not inconceivable that some sort of a deliberate break or diversion is made here, or a little before this, to underline this change to the new passage. If in fact we are to witness a trial scene, then clearly the garden 'afore' the stage would be out of place; though the table, chairs and books upon the stage would not be. Can it be possible that servants have come in and removed the light trellis walls that symbolized the garden? And in its place did they set up a stake, and put a pile of property stones beside it? All this is not, I think, out of the question. But I can give no evidence for it beyond saying that, once the garden had been cleared away, we would in fact be 'here redy' to go on with the play, and that, failing some such change, this sentence of the Bayly's would seem meaningless.

At any rate, the play does now go straight on with – 'Here entreth Iudex, Sensualitas, Voluptas, and Susanna, and Iudex speaketh.' He opens the court proceedings and asks (with a touch of obscurity), 'What Bayly haue ye here the crye, that I wilde you to make?' Bayly answers 'Yea my Lorde', and 'Here the Iudge sitteth downe'.

Now the Judge orders – 'Then let the Cryer here an O yes make . . . And let him speake it after you'. Bayly then calls out, 'Ill Reporte make an O yes here'. It would seem that arrangements have been made for the Vice, in his capacity as the Cryer, to echo or repeat the Bayly's announcements. At any rate – whatever the business involved – the particularly interesting direction now immediately follows: 'Then Ill Report goeth vp.' And now of course the question arises – Goeth up on to what? There seems little else possible save the stage.

Then, as if to remove any doubt, comes the Vice's line which is, 'Helpe me vp.'

Once there – whether on the stage or not – the 'Crye' is given and the Vice echoes every one of the Bayly's lines, and travesties them. Then –

977. Here shall the Cryer, the Bayly, and the rest go stand before the Iudge and tell him the crie is made.

The Judge says, 'Cryer call Susanna', and Ill Report shouts 'Susanna'. The court scene then proceeds with remarkable verisimilitude. The oath taken, Sensuality makes his damning statement. Susanna will not stoop to defend herself and only answers with a prayer; and so she is condemned. Now –

1061. Here the Iudge ryseth, and Susanna is led to execution, and God rayseth the spirite of Danyell.

How the raising of the spirit of Daniel was worked we are given no hint at all; we only know that he was played by the same young boy who played Helchia's wife and two different servants, Seruus and Serua. What he in fact does is to halt the exit of the court and bid them 'Go sit in iudgement once agayne, the witnesse they haue borne, Is false . . .'. At his words –

1079. Susanna for ioy shall seeme to sound [*swoon*], the Vice shall call for Vineger and Mustarde to fetche her agayne, the Bayly shall say.

– and what he says is one of the remarkable pieces of naturalistic speech in this remarkable script; it is a question to the Vice – 'Is Mustard good for sick folkes releefe?' and the Vice seizes the opportunity with – 'Yea Syr, Vineger and Mustarde both is good for beefe'. And indeed he seems to be right, for Susanna now recovers and piously speaks, after which, 'Here they returne all back to iudgement'. And then '. . . the Cryer goeth vp agayne, and maketh an O yes, Iudex speaketh'; he bids Susanna be unbound and bonds put on the Elders instead. Notice again the allusion to going *up*.

Daniel now speaks 'to the people'. Next the Judge enquires how the falseness of the two Elders can be proved. Daniel asks that they may be examined separately, and the Judge orders the Vice to take 'asyde Voluptas', which he does, exchanging insults as he goes. Daniel now invites Sensuality, left on his own, to –

1159.   [. . .] tell vnder what tree,
        The mutuall talke betweene these two, in Orchard thou didst see?

Sensuality avers it was a mulberry tree. He is taken away and the Cryer is ordered to bring in Voluptes. He is asked the same question and answers, 'Under a Pomgranate tree, . . .' Daniel leaps on the inconsistence in their evidence and the Elders are condemned by the Judge to be stoned to death with the significant words –

1212. For hence you shall vnto the place, where such doe vse to dye,
        As doe transgresse the Princes lawes, euen forthwith by and by.
        And there with stones you shall be stonde, while lyfe and lim
            doth last
        Hoe there away with them I say, [. . .]

And so another change in the scene of action is implied; we are to move to the 'place' where transgressors are put to death. Ill Report has another of his mocking speeches as he hails them away, beginning 'Come of with the mischiefe, . . .', which may be a cry to them to come down off the stage. Some way through his speech there is inserted the direction, 'Then he brings them to the stake.' This is specific enough. There is not much doubt that it means that he takes them from where they were at that moment to another place, wherever it may be, in which a stake is already erected for them. The stake would appear to be something in the nature of a pillory for the Vice says, 'holde vp your handes, And receiue your bandes, Now throw on your stones, . . .' If the garden before the stage had in fact been cleared away earlier, then it would have left an obvious place for setting up the stake; and the Vice's action with the Elders would in that case be a repetition of their former action – namely, to go off the stage and 'afore' it, to be tied up for the stoning in the Place. And this stoning is now actually performed before the spectators, and performed to the accompaniment of an apparently gratuitous piece of slapstick business as follows –

1251.   Here they stone them, and the Vyce lets a stone fall on
                        the Baylies foote, and fall togither by the eares, and
                        when the Iudges are deade, the Vyce putteth on one
                                                              of their Gownes.

The stones were most likely stuffed-cloth properties. I would not put it past the Interluders to have had one stone genuine and heavy, which the Vice might drop near the Bayly's foot with a crash, to show their reality, while the Bayly lifted his foot and roared with pain to confirm the weight of the rocks as a whole.

There is more to come; Servus and True Report (the two servants who had rushed to break open the orchard door) now come in to inform the Vice that they have 'commissyon, to hang all but his head'. A scene of astounding chop-logic follows wherein Ill Report claims to be a relative of True Report on the score of their identical surnames, but to no avail, and eventually a struggle follows – 'Here they struggle togither, the Gaylour casts the Rope about Ill Reports neck.' He chops more logic but with no more success and 'Here they haue him to hanging, the Deuill entreth saying, Oh, oh, oh.' I take it that 'haue him to hanging' means they hail him away and go out with him; in other words, they hang him out of sight. The Devil now complains bitterly of his ill-success in the attempt to corrupt Susanna and blames it on his son, whom he threatens now to punish in Hell; then 'The Deuill goeth forth, and Ioachim, Susanna, Helchia, & his wife enter'. Joachim thanks God for Susanna's deliverance, in fact all four vie in gratitude. And their speeches turn felicitously into compliments to the Queen and the customary blessings all round. 'They goe out and the Prologue entreth' (l. 1443). He adds a few apologetic words on behalf of the author and (rather disarmingly) asks forbearance for the company's 'rudenesse' in that they could not 'bewtify' their work 'with musickes song' – implying, it would seem, that the company was not one from any of the Choir Schools.

61 *New Custom*

After *Susanna* of about 1569, there are some seven years before the culminating point in the development of Interludes, the building of the Theatre by James Burbage. To that period there are ascribed at present according to our provisional chronology some five late plays. They vary in information about developments in technique but, for one reason or another, all can be treated relatively briefly.

The anonymous *New Custom* (c. 1570) is described as an 'Enterlude'. It is very definitely a pro-reformation play, making a forthright and calculated attack on the ways of the Roman Catholic church. It makes much use of entrances as an essential part of the effect of the presentation but adds little that is new about staging methods.

62 *Misogonus*

The anonymous *Misogonus*, provisionally attributed to the same year, comes into a different category. It is almost a fully-fledged play and was probably first performed at Cambridge University. How it was performed there is little in the text to show and the text itself is imperfect. As I said in the discussion on *Gammer Gurton*, it seems better not to attempt at present to reconstruct any picture of the staging, and I limit myself here to one matter.

In 'Actus secundus, Scena quarta' the young man Misogonus is talking to his 'swete harte', Melissa meretrix; he asks her –

> Tell me, fare ladye, will yow range in the feilde,
> Will you heare the bird*es* singe & smell the swete floure?

– and she replies,

> I knowe the delits that the meadowes can yeilde;
> I had rather, and it please yow, stay here in this bowre.

This *bower* seems also to have been used for certain eaves-dropping scenes, but there is nothing to inform us about its nature. One can scarcely help reflecting, however, on the famous bower illustrated in the title-page cut of the 1633 edition of *The Spanish Tragedy* (cf. Fig. 17D) and that in its turn raises the same speculation as did the puzzling shop of Mulciber in *Thersytes*, and in the end all that can come out of it, with our present knowledge, is that such things as these were (and still are) precisely managed in the system of *tsukuri-mono* (literally 'constructions') on the ancient Japanese Noh stage.

63 *The Conflict of Conscience*

Nathaniel Wood's (or Woodes's) 'excellent new Commedie' called *The Conflict of Conscience* (c. 1572) has several examples of 'asides' or of 'differentiation' and it includes a striking example of a passion being torn to shreds, but it is chiefly useful here in its statement of adaptability to various playing-places, for on the title-page it shows how its eighteen roles may be divided among six players so as to be 'most conuenient for such as be disposed either to shew this Comedie in private houses or otherwise'. In spite of the claim in its subtitle, it is in fact a very bitter anti-Catholic tragedy, with a twisted trial scene and a conclusion marked by hopeless remorse and by the personal entrance of 'Horror'.

Gascoigne's *The Glasse of Government*, 1575, seems to me scarcely to have been a theatre piece.

64 *Tyde tarrieth no Man*

So far as concerns presentation, I can get very little new out of George Wapull's 'Moste Pleasant and merry commody, right pythie and full of delight' entitled *The Tyde taryeth no Man* (c. 1576). The following points are however worth mention.

There is a short passage which seems to perpetuate the Cozin Cutpurse gag, already noticed in *Apius* and *Cambises*. As is often the way in this kind of unabashed propaganda play, the item is rather a verbal matter than a presentational matter. The playwright like most propagandists in the theatre rather overlooks the particular characteristic of his medium, which should be the effect gained from the atmosphere of the events he presents and the linking of them together; instead he relies on the rather less subtle medium of the facts put into the words themselves. That is, he *says* what he wants to say; he doesn't leave it to say itself through the action.

The passage comes in a demonstration of the knavery behind the manipulation of money in human society. The Vice, called (with a bitter intention) Courage, has been plotting with Profyte, Helpe and Furtheraunce, and as they go he calls them 'three knaues on a cluster'; Profyte retorts over his shoulder that Corage is 'a knaue most of all, And so we leaue thee'. The Vice, left alone, turns to the spectators with the following speech –

> Now so is the purpose, and this is the case,
> Good cosen Cutpurse, if you be in place.
> I beseech you now, your businesse to plye,
> I warrant thee I, no man shall thee espye.
> If they doe, it is but an howers hanging,
> But such a purse thou mayest catch, worth a yeres spending.
> I warrant thee encouraging thou shalt no lack,
> Come hyther, let me clap thee in the back. [. . .]

But cosen Cutpurse, if ought thou do get,
I pray thee let me haue part of thy cheate,
I meane not of thy hanging fare,
But of thy purse, and filched share. [. . .]

Beyond this there are several feigned exits ('fayne a going out')
where a character is directed to out but is called back again on
the threshold by a character still in the action.

There is also an unusual example of reversible legends; on fol. F.ii
rev. comes the direction –

> Christianity must enter with a sword, with a title
> of pollicy, but on the other syde of the tytle,
> must be written gods word, also a Shield, whereon
> must be written riches, but on the other syde of the
> Shield must be Fayth.

Christianity explains it is a 'deformed sword and shield' and that he
is ashamed of them, but that he is constrained to bear them because
'Greedy Great, will haue it so euery where.' To him enters 'Faythfull few', who notices him after a 20-line soliloquy and 'goeth toward
him' to express his surprise that Christianity should show things
so contrary to his 'nature and kinde'; and then, having come near,
'he turneth the titles'. A few lines later 'Corage and Greedines
enter as though they saw not Christianity' and conduct a dialogue
against honest dealing, not realizing the change of principles that
Faythfull Few has just effected symbolically. Here once more is a
case of 'differentiation'; but Faythfull Few and Christianity intervene at last and a judicial wrangle ensues.

65 *Common Conditions*

The final play, which comes according to our provisional date-list
in the same year as the building of The Theatre, 1576, is the anonymous *'pleasant Comedie called Common Conditions'*. It is a somewhat
sprawling play with much that is according to the new fashions in
it, but so diffuse as to make one hesitant about basing much upon it
in the way of definite conclusions on staging methods. One novelty,
however, is important – a tree.

The plot concerns the wanderings and star-crossed love affairs
of a brother and sister (and others) in Arabia and Phrygia, and the

interference of their servant, Common Conditions. The script we possess is defective; both the beginning and end are missing. A careful modern edition is to be found in Alois Brandl's 'Quellen des weltlichen Dramas in England vor Shakespeare' in *Quellen und Forschungen*, 80 Heft (Strassburg, 1898). The reprint is of course in English, though the notes are in German.

The scene containing the tree comes at the beginning (or at what is left to us of the beginning). In it three tinkers named respectively Thrifte, Shifte and Drifte, are singing. One says, '. . . let vs bee packyng hence and in a bushe lye, . . .' intending to lie in ambush for a certain Sedmond, a 'gentleman with his Ladie' (who is in fact his sister Clarisia), and 'with them a little Parasite' (who is by name the Common Conditions of the title) –

> And when thei thinke them selues in the wood most surest to bee,
> Their purses wee will bee so bolde as share betwixt vs three.

Later there is a direction, 'Exeun[t] omne[s]'. Immediately after this we have 'Here enter Sedmond with Clarisia and Conditions out of the Wood.' They talk at length, chiefly about their weariness and ill-fortune (like Rosalind and Touchstone), till suddenly there is a shout from Shifte – 'Doune with them all, for, surely, thei shall die.' Clarisia protests and Sedmond flees. Drifte however says

> Tushe, dispatche, and when you haue doen, binde her fast to this tree,
> Least, when that we are gone, she make an vprore, and wee persued bee!

– and Shifte replies –

> Come on, Ladie, fast to this tree wee intende you to binde,
> And with your owne handcarcher your eyes wee will blinde.

As for Conditions, he cunningly suggests that they should hang him in the same tree. He takes a rope, climbs, and makes faces at them 'like an Owle in a tree', but suddenly starts to shout for help and at this the tinkers all run away. He descends, frees Clarisia, and proposes that they 'passe . . . Cleane ouer the sea to Phrigia, . . .' to her father. 'Exeunt.'

Here entreth Sedmond wailyng.

And so the action goes on.

I do not feel that there is any great problem about this tree. I would suppose there is little doubt that it was a practical tree and firmly enough planted to allow a vigorous actor to climb it and indulge in comic gestures in the branches. The late George Fulmer Reynolds offered quite clear verbal evidence in his paper ' "Trees" on the stage of Shakespeare' (*Modern Philology*, vol. 5, 1907) that such things were not uncommon; and I have been able to offer pictorial evidence to support this in a detail to be found in Adriaen van de Venne's engraving of an indoor stage in his *Tafereel van de belacchende werelt* of 1635 (see *Theatre Notebook*, vol. 9, 1954). A detail of this picture is reproduced in Fig. 40. Here can be seen,

FIG. 40. Property trees projecting above the back curtain of a seventeenth-century stage (redrawn from Adriaen van de Venne)

projecting above the traverse curtain at the back of the stage, the tops of two trees. They cannot be growing trees since they are inside a building, and a building moreover that is almost certainly an indoor tennis-court and therefore could not possibly have a tree growing through its floor. The trees then must be property trees, but whether real trees cut down, or artificial ones specially made for the theatre (like the many trees whose manufacture was noted as far back as the court pageants of Henry VIII, see above, p. 159), cannot of course be decided.

The problem of the firm support of such a property tree, once it is carried on to the stage, is again not a difficult one; a thick tenon some two feet long could be left projecting from the base of the trunk and this could be dropped through a prepared hole in the stage floor – revealed by lifting a small trapdoor – so that its bottom end engaged in a corresponding hole cut in the under-timbers a couple of feet below. This would allow of quite a deal of vigorous action in the branches.

What is a far more tricky problem to solve – and one that is frequently cropping up in attempts to understand Elizabethan staging – is: was such a tree left on the stage throughout the show once it had been used and done with, or did stage-hands enter, lift it out and carry it away? There is nothing in the present play to help to answer this question, but it can fairly be said that there seems no insuperable objection to its being left to stay where it was.

Another typical problem which is however solved – or evaded – in *Common Conditions* is that of the stage ship. On two occasions characters have to board vessels, or escape from being tossed overboard into raging seas. But in this play the effect of the ship is conveyed by shouts off. For example see l. 767 –

The Mariners within.

MAISTER	Ha la, boies, a baste, there cast haulser a lande.
MAIST.MATE	Vere vere, come no nere, least we grounde on the sande!
BOTESWAINE	Lanche out the Cocke, boies, and set the Maister a shoare.
MAIST.MATE	The Cocke is lanched, eche man to his oare. [. . .]
MAISTER	A shoare, a shoare, eche man on the lande!
MAIST.MATE	Boie, come vp, and grounde the Cocke on the sande.

[. . .]
Here entreth the Pirates with a song.

MAISTER	Ha, couragious, my mates, and excellent well doen.

[. . .]

(The first letters of the names have been cut off in the binding.)

A 'cock-boat' is 'A small ship's boat, *esp.* one towed behind a vessel going up or down a river.' (*O.E.D.*)

Remarkable complications ensue as the plot and sub-plot develop; these partly result from the problems set by characters fleeing overseas, or being sold into slavery by pirates, and having other characters wandering at large along devious false trails in search of them. It is, of course, of some interest to see how all this travelling over Arabia, Phrygia, the Isle of Marofus, and the high seas as well, is represented by the playwright in terms of exits and entrances upon one limited stage with two doors and no scenery. It must be admitted that a reading of the script rather suggests he may have strained his medium somewhat.

But it is only fair to remember that the script breaks off at l. 1421 – and so, how these adventures were finally resolved will probably remain for ever unknown.

Part Four 1576–1589

The Theatre Built

Final Plays and Footnotes 1576–1589

The Marriage of Wit and Wisdom ∽ *The Three Ladies of London* ∽ *The Three Lords and Three Ladies of London* ∽ *The Coblers Prophesie* ∽ A Footnote on 'Going about the Stage' ∽ Conclusions

---

In the same year as that to which *Common Conditions* is ascribed, that is 1576, James Burbage built The Theatre; and a little later in the same year, or in 1577, the neighbouring Curtain Theatre was also built. These two regular public playhouses, the first in our history, open a new epoch; they prepare the way for 'the Shakespearean theatre' as a subject, about which so much has been written and on the threshold of which my present work stops.

But Shakespeare's first plays were not presented until about 1590, so there is a little more than a decade of overlap between the last of the Interlude tradition leading up to The Theatre, and the beginning of the 'Shakespearean' tradition in the playhouses which followed The Theatre. I propose to take advantage of this decade to add reviews of three particular plays which postdate The Theatre, before drawing my conclusions. One of these comes close after The Theatre was built, and the other two about the year before Shakespeare's first presented play.

66 *The Marriage of Wit and Wisdom*

For the sake of completeness, there should be noted one other play that comes in date before these. It is the anonymous *The Contract of a Marriage between Wit and Wisdom* (c. 1579), surviving in manuscript and briefly dismissed by F. P. Wilson in *The English Drama, 1485–1585* as a 'vulgarization of Redford's play'. It adds no significant information about the development of staging. But, as Wilson notes, it does happen to be one of the seven titles offered for

543

performance by the visiting players in that curious play *Sir Thomas More*, when they were preparing to give a show at the lord chancellor's banquet.

The three plays with which I want to end this review form an interestingly related group. They are almost certainly written by the same man, and this man was himself an actor of considerable reputation; moreover he was one of Lord Leicester's company as James Burbage himself was. Two of the plays have the same main characters, one being a sequel to the other. The first of the three is dated in Craik's list at 1581 – that is five years after The Theatre – and is called *The Three Ladies of London*; its sequel is dated c. 1589 and entitled *The Three Lords and Three Ladies of London*; and the third is a quite separate play, *The Coblers Prophesie*, also dated at c. 1589. In their printed editions the first two are said to be written 'by R.W.', and the third is clearly stated to be 'Written by Robert Wilson. Gent.'

I shall not concern myself here with the alternatives to supposing that 'R.W.' and Robert Wilson, the actor, were the same man. Some notes on the problem are to be found in Sydney Lee's article on Robert Wilson in *the Dictionary of National Biography*, in Chambers' *Elizabethan Stage*, and in F. P. Wilson's *English Drama*.

Robert Wilson, the actor, joined Lord Leicester's Men in 1574. In 1583 he became one of the twelve players in Queen Elizabeth's company, whose leading figure was Richard Tarleton. Tarleton died in 1588, which fact has a relation to the dating of the second play, as will be seen. A particularly interesting fact is that Wilson was held to be as 'rare' a man theatrically as Tarleton; Edmund Howes in 1615 commended Tarleton 'for a wondrous plentifull pleasant extemporall wit, he was the wonder of his time', and Wilson 'for a quicke, delicate, refined extemporall witt'. So the two men were noted for improvisation but while Tarleton's style, as befits a clown, was wondrous plentiful and pleasant, Wilson's was quick, delicate and refined, as more befits a leading comedian. It is supposed that he himself played the parts of the comic lead in his plays. In the first two of these, this character is called Simplicitie, and the lines Wilson gives him certainly offer excellent material for effective performance.

My main concern here with these three plays is their technical information, and in this respect they are surprisingly well linked and graded to bring a conclusion to my survey. The first of them may well be meant for simple presentation in the old Interlude tradition; it has no reference to any sort of stage. The last of them, *The Coblers Prophesie*, is more advanced (it may have been written for court performance), and it not only has a definite reference to a stage, but a reference which is in a form so worded as to offer the most convincing evidence I have found to support my view that stage and floor were considered two distinct acting-areas. The other play of the three, which belongs to the same year as *The Coblers Prophesie* and may or may not have been written before it, has also a quite unmistakable reference to a stage but this time to a new sort of stage that has one feature quite different from anything we have met so far. With all this in mind it may be that we can justifiably claim:

1. that *The Three Ladies of London* in spite of its late date may represent the old travelling Interlude tradition, especially if it is remembered that at the time of its writing, only five years after the opening of The Theatre, the public playhouse was still a new thing, and there were only two stages of the sort in existence, that of The Theatre itself and that of the Curtain Theatre. And thus, any group of players who continued to tour occasionally, might require their plays to be still written so as to be capable of presentation equally on the floor in private domestic halls or on temporary stages built for the occasion in Civic Halls. This old requirement would survive for some time in spite of the effect of the new playhouses and their stages.

2. next, that *The Cobblers Prophesie* may be a show with much more specific technical demands, intended for presentation at court, and with a stage – though possibly no more than a small low foot-pace.

3. finally, that in *The Three Lords and Three Ladies of London*, coming some thirteen years after The Theatre, we have at length a play which is unmistakably devised for direct public playhouse presentation – or at least for presentation on the sort of stage that we believe was characteristic of the new open-air playhouses.

These distinctions may, of course, be purely accidental; that is to say there is nothing to show absolutely whether each of these plays was actually presented differently, or whether all were planned for a similar stage, with their stage-directions giving different impressions only by chance.

67 *The Three Ladies of London*

I want now to review the action in *The Three Ladies* with the purpose of finding out if there is anything in it which cannot be fairly
made to fit the simplest traditional style of presentation. To begin,
it is not uninteresting to look at the passage in Chambers concerning it. This passage brings up again that old, vexed question of
how much 'houses' were used as the background for Interludes.
In the opening of my Section 8 above, dealing with early court
pageant techniques, I quoted at some length from Chambers but I
made at the time certain cuts in the quotations; one of these cuts
came at his reference to *The Three Ladies*. I want now to give the
passage in full, despite the fact that even in full it has a curious
non-committal note. The passage comes on p. 25 of *The Elizabethan Stage*, vol. III; it is concerned with distinguishing such plays
as show no change of locality from plays which, in his words, 'do
entail some change of locality'. In full it reads,

> Four other examples do entail some change of locality. Much stress
> must not be laid on the sudden conversions in the fourth act of *The
> Conflict of Conscience* (>1581) and the last scene of *Three Ladies of London*
> of the open 'place' into Court, for these are very belated specimens of
> the moral. And the opening dialogue of the *Three Ladies*, on the way to
> London, may glide readily enough into the main action before two
> houses in London itself. But in *The Disobedient Child* . . .[and the passage
> is continued as quoted on p. 149 above.]

So far as concerns *The Three Ladies of London* this is admittedly
one of Chambers' more difficult passages. The chief difficulty for
a reader is, I think, the coupling of the idea of 'change of locality',
which tends so much to suggest the idea of change of scenery, with
two plays upon whose evidence in the matter (he says) *much stress
must not be laid*. Is the reader to gather that a change of locality *was*
actually represented in *The Three Ladies*, or was *not*? And the final
remark about the opening dialogue gliding 'readily enough into
the main action before two houses in London itself' surely does
convey to a reader that two houses were actually represented in the
setting – even though the opening dialogue could glide into the
action before them without any change of locality that could be
'stressed'. But whatever his point here about change of locality, the
picture he leaves is definitely of two London houses represented on
a stage. This we have to test in the review that follows.

The title-page of *The Three Ladies* reads, in the Tudor Facsimile Text Society's 1911 reprint of the first known edition of 1584 –

A right excellent
and famous Comoedy called
the three Ladies of London.
Wherein is nota-
blie declared and set
foorth, how by the meanes of Lucar, Loue
and Conscience is so corrupted, that
the one is married to Dissimulation, the other fraught
withall abhomina-
tion.
A perfect patterne for all
Estates to looke into, and a worke right wor-
thie to be marked. Written by R.W.
as it hath beene publiquely
played

At London,
Printed by Ro-
ger Warde, dwelling neere
Holburne Conduit, at the signe
of the Talbot. 1584.

No list of the parts is printed, but they may be extracted as follows:

Prologue	Sinceritie, a divine.
Fame	Hospitalitie, an old man
Loue, a Lady of London.	Sir Nicholas Nemo
Conscience, a Lady of London	Peter Pleaseman, a parson.
Dissimulation	Gerontus, a Jew.
Simplicitie (comic lead)	Coggin, Dissimulation's man.
Fraud	Tom Beggar
Symonie	Wily Will
Vserie	Turkish Judge
Lucar, a Lady of London.	Seruiceable Dilligence, constable.
Mercadorus, a merchant.	2 Officers.
Artifex, a craftsman.	Judge Nemo.
Creticus, a lawyer	Clerk of sies (Assize?)
	Crier

The play opens with a short 18-line address from the Prologue. He says in effect that the players are not going to bring any story

547

of the classic gods, nor any pastoral with milkmaids or countrymen (which may be a side-glance at court entertainments), then he goes on to remark –

> You maruell then what stuffe we haue to furnish out our showe.
> Your patience yet we craue a while, till we haue trimd our stall;
> Then if our wares shall seeme to you, well wouen, good and fine,
> We hope we shall your custome haue, againe an other time.

So this Prologue strikes something of a new note. It may, of course, have been written for some particular occasion, but the tone of its final lines is clearly that of professional actors hoping for further custom for their 'wares' at some future time. Its novelty lies in its invitation to the audience to *come* to behold those wares – as if to a public playing place – instead of asking leave to bring the wares to the audience – as a travelling troupe visiting a private hall would have done. But however that may be, there is nothing conclusive here to make one visualize a different setting from the normal.

Next, under the rather curious heading 'The first Acte', there comes a short scene with 'Enter Fame sounding before Loue and Conscience', that is to say that after the trumpeter we have two of the Three Ladies of London. They deeply bewail how the Third Lady, by name Lucar (or Lucre in the sense of riches), has gained the upper hand and is threatening to ruin them. After some 30 lines they all go out, and the second and last curious heading follows – 'The Second Acte'. These two headings are only curious because no third act, or any further heading of this sort, occurs in the whole of the rest of the play. This so-called 'Acte' opens with 'Enter Dissimulation, hauing on a Farmers long coat, and a cappe, and his powle and beard painted motley.' He says he is on his way to London to seek employment, and concludes with the significant line as he breaks off his gossip – 'But I forget my businesse, ile towardes London as fast as I can', to get entertainment of one of the three Ladies. He therefore suggests quite clearly that he is not yet in London, but is in fact so far off still that he must hurry on as fast as he can if he is to reach it. But there is not, so far, any indication of any setting-requirement beside the ordinary kind of doors to which we are by now so well accustomed.

To him comes the leading comic character, Simplicitie, 'lyke a Miller all mealy with a wande in his hande'. He has the same errand. Next, 'Enter Fraud with a Sword and a Buckler like a Ruffian.' He also has the same purpose. Simplicitie is mistrustful of them both. Then to these three there 'Enter Symonie and Vserie hand in hand.' Simony and Usury see and greet the others. After some three pages of general dialogue there is an interruption, and Dissimulation says 'But here come two of the Ladyes therefore make readie. But which of vs all shall first breake the matter.' . . . (that is, the matter of their employment), and then an accompanying direction states: 'Enter Loue and Conscience.'

Now, it seems to me that the entry of the two Ladies of London here is a very strong indication that the acting-area was *not* localized, for Dissimulation has already implied that he was still some way from London and had still to go on 'as fast as I can' to get there and meet the Ladies. And now it is they who enter to him. This obviously cannot be taken to mean that the Ladies had travelled out from London to meet him; it is simply a legitimate piece of 'condensation of place' comparable with the Interlude convention of the condensation of time. And so all that is needed scenically for this episode is the acting-area and the doors of entrance – with no houses.

The five travellers and the two Ladies now take part in a song. But the Ladies have no use for any of the four rogues as servants; only Simplicitie gets a post with Lady Love. Then, 'Exeunt, Lady Loue and Conscience.' Simplicitie hesitates, however, before following his new mistress – and then, suddenly: 'Let Fraud runne at him, and let Simplicitie runne in, and come out againe straight.' Two contemptuous lines are sharply exchanged and then: 'Exit Simplicitie.' The purpose of this bit of bye-play is apparently no more than the swapping of farewell insults, but at least it shows by the expressions 'run *in*' for an exit, and 'come *out*' for an entrance that some kind of screen, or booth, or even tiring-house has to be pictured at the back of the acting-area. But there is still nothing, so far, indicative of 'houses'.

The third of the 'Three Ladies', that is Lady Lucre, now enters. She learns the rogues' names; is pleased with their characters; and makes Dissimulation her steward, Fraud her rent-gatherer, Usury her secretary, and Simony the head of 'such matters as are Ecclesiasticall'. She bids them all to her 'Pallas' and goes on ahead with Dissimulation. Shortly afterwards the other three follow.

It may be noticed at this point that Lucre has made it especially clear before her exit that she is going to her Palace. Thus it might be concluded that here is a reference to one of the proposed 'houses'. Three things are against this.

First, that Lucre's house must by definition be in London, yet at the opening of this scene the characters were far away from London, and no break or 'change of scene' has taken place since.

Second that, as we shall later find, a scene is to come which occurs outside a door said to lead to Lady Conscience's house; thus we might argue that at one side is Conscience's house and at the other Lucre's. But later still there is a scene where Usury murders Hospitalitie; he does not however kill him in sight, but 'hales him in' to somewhere to do it. Into where? Clearly it would be unsuitable to hale him in to either Lady Conscience's house or Lady Lucre's house. He is 'haled in' at some unlocalized door.

Thirdly (and in my opinion quite finally), we shall find some scenes which take place in Turkey, and another in court of judgement. Neither of the houses could possibly be acceptable at all in these scenes.

In my view the entrances and exits in this play are all contrived in a convention identical with that used in Interludes played before hall-screens with two doorways; and the openings – whatever they were here – which the players used for those exits and entrances were just as unlocalized as screen doorways had been.

The situation is now developed in a series of scenes where various visitors to Lucre and her new servants receive various treatments which exemplify her character and her effect on society. Mercadorus a susceptible merchant-trader and seafarer falls for her charms and engages to trade abroad for her profit; Artifex an honest workman is turned away workless; Creticus an unscrupulous lawyer is retained; Sincerity a preacher is offered a worthless living. At one point a further somewhat nebulous character called Sir Nicholas Nemo, professing to be a special friend to Love and Conscience, enters to the unfortunate Sinceritie and tells him –

> [. . .] for their sakes you shall see what I will do for you,
> Without Dissimulation, Fraude, Usurie, or Symonie:
> For they will do nothing without some kind of gaine, [. . .]
> But come in to dinner with me, and when you haue dinde,
> you shall haue.   Presently go out.

It seems a curiously broken line but, with the exit immediately following upon it, it makes use of action to give the lie to the words; as Simplicitie bitterly recognizes in his next line – 'You shall naue [*have*], but what? A liuing that is blowne downe with the winde.' It is interesting to see again the new-style phrase for an exit in the speech, 'come *in* to dinner', closely contrasted with the old-style phrase in the accompanying direction, 'Presently go *out*'.

The doors by which the characters go out are sufficiently un-localized, or unparticularized, at most times, and simply exist as exit- and entrance-places; the most that can be said is that occasion-ally one or the other of them is given a significance that temporarily turns it into the door to a specific residence. For example, on fol. C.ii.*rev.*, Usury and Lady Conscience come in together as from a street thus using one door as a simple entrance; but Usury im-mediately asks, 'Lady Conscience, is there any bodie within your house can you tell?' and she replies, 'There is no bodie at all be ye sure, I know certainly well . . .'. What is in Usury's mind is the intention of taking possession of her house, and upon this reassur-ance from her he says, 'Why then I will be bould to enter.' And the direction immediately follows, 'exit'. So he must now leave by the opposite door, which is thus accepted for the time as that leading to Conscience's residence. He goes in while she remains disconsolate outside. But I do not think we ought to imagine that any positive identification of this entrance with a specific door to a specific house was ever actually intended by the Interluders, even for the brief length of a current scene. I rather suppose they took the simpler and more direct view that since Usury said that he would enter Conscience's house and thereupon went out through a door, then that action sufficiently indicated that he had gone where he said he would go. I do not think they cluttered their minds with any momentary at-tempt to see that door as different from the door it had been a few minutes before, or that they imagined any different sort of place beyond it from what was there at any other point in the play.

After a sad soliloquy on her approaching ruin, Lady Conscience is rejoined by Usury who comes out of her house again and sends her away. To him now there comes the susceptible merchant, and then the Lady Lucre, and further phases of the plot are developed, wherein any special significance of the doors fades again.

The Merchant is told to go to Turkey to trade honest British goods for trumpery geegaws for Lucre's friends; Dissimulation plots to get into Love's good graces; and, as I have mentioned, the old man called Hospitalitie is haled off to be murdered. The last action is neatly brought about as follows –

Usury enters and brutally accosts him. Hospitalitie calls for help, and his cry is heard by Lady Conscience – 'Enter Conscience run-ning apace' – but she is powerless to stop Usury, who cries,

D.i.*rev.* Leaue prating Conscience [. . .]
  Yet Ile not commit the murder openly,
  But hale the villaine into a corner, and so kill him secretly.
  Come ye miserable drudge, and receiue thy death.
                                          Hale him in.

Conscience calls again for help and 'Enter Dissimulation and Simplicitie hastily'; and fourteen lines later Lady Lucre comes in. The story proceeds with such speed that after another couple of dozen lines, Simony enters with a full report about the crowd of people who have attended Hospitalitie's funeral; and so time-condensation is added to the other conventions.

Poor Lady Conscience realizes there is nothing left for her but to hawk brooms for a living, and she goes out. Then follows a remarkable soliloquy from the comic lead Simplicitie (fol. D.iii.). Debating his own future in a world where so many are coming to ruin, he decides –

  Faith Ile go euen a begging [. . .]
  . . . and my singing will get me drinke,

(then to the audience)

  Come and resist [*assist*] me, that I may sing with the more meliositie.
  But sirs marke my cauled countenaunce when I begin,
  But yonder is a fellow that gapes to bite me or els to eate that which
    I sing.
  Why thou art a foole canst not thou keepe thy mouth strait together?
  And when it comes snap at it as my fathers dogge wod doe at a liuer.
  But thou art so greedie,
  That thou thinkest to eate it before it come nye thee.
                                          Simplicitie singes.

It seems difficult to interpret this speech in any other way than as evidence that community-singing might still be encouraged in Interludes, just as it presumably was by the three knaves in *Mankind* for their 'cyrstemes songe' as far back as p. 29. Furthermore, a gag could be worked by which one member of the audience might be accused of anticipating, or being too eager to begin on his own, instead of 'waiting for it' and taking his cue from the expression on the singer's face, or 'cauled countenaunce', before coming in with the others.

After the song Simplicitie asks, while he is still alone on the floor and so presumably addressing the same man in the audience,

Now sirra hast eaten vp my song? . . .
For euery body may see your belly is growne bigger with eating vp
    our play:
He has fild his belly, but I am neuer a whit the better,
Therefore ile go secke some vittailes, and member for eating vp my
    song you shall be my debter.

And after that, though there is no exit-direction, he presumably
goes out.

Now comes a scene which involves the entire dissociation of both
doors from any significance they might have borne before as
leading to the houses of Lucre or Conscience. For there 'Enter
Mercadorus the Merchaunt and Gerontus a Iewe'. The Jew reproaches the Merchant for cheating him and, hoping to regain a loan,
says, 'I am glad you be come againe to Turkey, . . .' So the action
has now shifted abroad, and there it continues for some 50 lines,
upon which Gerontus concludes, 'Come, goe we home where our
commodities you may at pleasure see.' Then they must leave by one
or other of the doors to the Jew's house. There is no exit-direction.

This is followed immediately by 'Enter Conscience with broomes
at her back singing as followeth'. And she calls her brooms for sale.
After a short while 'Enter Vserie'. He asks 'Who is it that cries
bromes, what cons. selling bromes about ye street?'; and six lines
later 'Enter Lucar' with, 'Me thought I heard one cry bromes along
the dore.' So manifestly the conception now is of a street scene.
In the dialogue, Conscience bitterly accuses Lucre of taking up
harlotry, and then learns that her old companion, Love, is to effect
a loveless marriage with the rogue Dissimulation on the morrow.
Lucar now, rather unexpectedly, takes pity on Conscience, buys all
her brooms and promises her extra money. This money she orders
Usury to go home and fetch. Conscience is quite won over to her
way of thought by this generosity.

A picturesque piece of allegory follows couched in such verbal
terms as to make it especially significant dramatically; Lucre's order
to Usury before he went out was –

Userie steppe in and bring me the boxe of all abhomination that
standes in the window:

(thus, a quite naturalistic impression is given of the house; and she
goes on, concerning the box –)

It is little and round painted with diuers colours and is prettie to
the show

Usury pauses to ask a simple question but one that somehow serves still more to stamp it on one's memory –

> Madam is there any superscription there on?

– but she sharply replies –

> Haue I not tolde you the name: for shame get you gone.

While he is away she fills in with a few lines to Conscience asking for consent to her using Conscience's house as a place for private assignations (which would incidentally save it from being distrained by Usury). Then follows the business of the allegory; first – 'Enter Vserie with a paynted boxe of incke in hys hand.' Lucre takes it and gives him a very clear hint to leave her alone with Conscience: 'Exit Vserie'. Then –

> Here let Lucar open the boxe and dip her finger
> in it, and spotte Conscience face, saying as
> followeth.

– first she bids Conscience count in her hand the coins she has promised her, 'Hould here my sweete, and [*tell*] them ouer to see if any want', then while Conscience is so engaged she enumerates the features of Conscience's face, praising them one by one and touching each with her finger as she mentions it. Conscience is quite unaware of the ink on the finger, and she soon leaves happily, to deck her room for Lucre to bring her men-friends to. Lucre then also leaves to go to attend Love's wedding.

Next comes a short scene listing the names of the guests at the wedding.

Then a complete change to Turkey again where in a little over twenty lines we learn that the Merchant persists in his swindle of the Jew, despite the Jew's threatening to bring him before justice. Mercadorus says he 'will be a Turke . . .' and the scene breaks off for a time, to give place to an incident at home.

For this, there 'Enter three Beggars, that is to say, Tom Beggar, wily Will, and Simplicitie singing.' Their song is about their going to the wedding. They make it clear that they are begging round Lucre's door, and they call on her Porter, so that one of the doors is now distinctly designated again. Fraud confirms this by entering and exclaiming at them and how they 'stand bauling so at my Ladies doore'. Simplicitie makes a very bright skit on the blazon of the coat of arms that Fraud might be expected to bear, and Fraud retorts, 'What a swad is this? I had beene better to haue sent him to the backe doore', so suggesting the existence of another, imaginary door behind the house and out of sight. Simplicitie breaks away from his beggar-companions and exits. Fraud seizes the opportunity to draw the remaining two together, and prompts them to rob the Merchant who 'is comming from Turky'. Then all leave.

Now the shift takes place again and we return to Turkey to find the Jew arraigning the Merchant before a 'Iudge of Turkie'. The Merchant slips out of his obligation by claiming that he has *turned Turk* – indeed he has gone so far as to don 'Turkish weedes to defeat' the Jew of his money – and so in this way he is immune in Turkish law from payment of debt to a Jew. Gerontus forsakes his claim; and all leave.

Now follows a particularly curious sequence, again in allegorical terms, and one which would be all the better for seeming to take place at no localized spot. Neither an interior nor an exterior could serve so well to set off this scene as a purely impersonal scaffold would – indeed any realistic setting would ruin it. The action opens with this direction – 'Enter Lucar, and Loue with a visard behind'. It contains only eighteen lines, which begin with Lucre reproaching Love for her sad aspect after her mercenary marriage, and asking her (fol. F.i.*rev.*) –

LUCAR. [. . .] I pray thee tell me what thou aylest, and what the
matter is.

LOUE. My griefe alas I shame to show, because my bad intent,
Hath brought on me a iust reward, and eke a straunge euent.
Shall be I counted Loue? nay rather lasciuious Lust,
Because vnto Dissimulation I did repose such trust.
But now I mone too late, and blush my hap to tell,
My head in monstrous sort alas, doth more and more still
swell.

LUCAR. Is your head then swollen good Mistrisse Loue, I pray you
let me see,
Of troth it is, behold a face, that seemes to smile on me:
It is faire and well fauoured, with a countenance smooth and
good,
Woonder is the worst, to see two faces in a hood.
Come lets go, wele finde some sports to spurne away such
toyes.

LOUE. Were it not for Lucar, sure Loue had lost her ioyes.

Exeunt.

What must have happened in this strange episode is that Love entered hooded but with some curious swelling under her hood at the back of her head. Her face is sad, and probably her head is bowed. But when Lucre lifts her chin to look at her face, Love slips her hood back, turns on her heel, and shows a grinning mask at the back of her head – 'two faces in a hood'.

Immediately they have gone we have a direction which leads straight into yet another atmosphere –

> Enter Seruiceable Dilligence the Constable, and Simplicitie, with an Officer to whip him, or two if you can.

Simplicitie has been (wrongly) accused of being involved with the two other beggars in the robbery of Mercadorus. He still proffers some bright remarks in spite of what is obviously facing him. Then comes the direction, 'Bedle put off his Clothes', and after more quips from Simplicitie, there comes a particular double direction –

> Lead him once or twise about, whipping him, and so Exit.
> Enter Iudge Nemo the clarke of the Sies, the Crier, and seruiceable Dilligence, the Iudge and Clarke being sett, the Crier shall sound three times.

– and the trial of the Ladies begins as the principals sit down. This, then, is the moment that Chambers indicated, rather obscurely, as 'the sudden conversion . . . of the open "place" into Court'.

What might be enlightening here would be to solve the query: What does 'Lead him once or twise about' mean? But there is little to help; the phrase is not 'Once or twice about the stage' – as I have said there is nowhere in this script any reference to a stage. Therefore the words seem to mean here simply what they say – namely, move him about while whipping him . . . But it seems a curiously inapposite direction, and thus invites the idea that something more was originally intended; such, for instance, as leading him about the place, with blows at particular intervals. But such whipping business is notoriously difficult to make convincing without harming the victim – especially if displayed close to the audience.

After the whipping comes the entrance of the Court. There is no way of deciding whether the 'Iudge Nemo' bears any relation to Sir Nicholas Nemo of earlier scenes; if so, he seems to have changed his character. A similarly-named character plays a part in the sequel, *The Three Lords*, and is again a powerful ruler.

One odd point that also rises here is that, since this is the crowning scene of the play, there may have been a need to bring in as many persons as possible for greater effect. This seems the only way to explain a strange direction coming a little later in the scene (see below) which suggests that the player of Lady Love dropped his part and changed to appear as one of the court here.

At present, the Judge orders Dilligence to bring in the prisoners. Dilligence answers with some reference to the previous vizard scene; he says –

[. . .] there are but three prisoners so farre as I knowe,
Which are Lucar and Conscience, with a deformed creature much
    like
Bifrons the base daughter of Iuno.

Whether the playwright had some special information about Juno's having a base daughter with the name of Bifrons; or whether as seems possible this is a printer's error and the line should read 'base daughter of Janus', who was two-faced (or 'bi-fronted') in any case, I cannot be certain.

But as the trial proceeds Lucre is accused of 'adulterie' with Mercadorus the merchant, and with Creticus the lawyer, and of consenting to the murder of Hospitalitie. Conscience is accused of having 'bene bawd vnto Lucar, and spotted with all abomination'. The Judge sees a letter in her 'bosome' and orders, 'Dilligence reache it hither'. Then follows the direction, 'Make as though ye read it'. The letter is one from Lucar bidding Conscience keep silence about their 'lasciuous liuing', and so it immediately condemns Lucre. Dilligence is ordered to 'conuey her hence, . . . to the lowest hel, . . .' 'Exit Lucar and Dilligence.'

Now the unexpected direction comes, about which I hinted above; immediately on Lucre's exit there follows this – 'Let Lucar make ready for Loue quickly, and come with Dilligence.' But no actual entrance is directed for Love for another eighteen lines. During those lines the Judge examines and reproves Conscience. Only then do we have –

Enter Loue with Dilligence.

– and Conscience is thereupon ordered to stand aside while poor hunched and hooded Love is brought to the bar instead. The Judge asks Love,

What saiest thou to thy deformitie, who was the cause?

Love has only two more speeches in the play; the first is in answer to the above question, where she merely says 'Ladie Lucar.' and the second is after being reproached by the Judge: 'I cannot chuse but yeeld, confounded by Conscience.' So there would be little need for any extended effort on the part of the boy who played Lucre to impersonate now the voice of Love, for he is hooded and has only ten words to speak. Nevertheless one wonders what pressure forced the players to this resort.

The play now concludes with sixteen lines from the Judge in which Love is condemned to suffer with Lucre, but Conscience is a little more leniently treated and is only conveyed to prison 'vntill the day of the generall session:' The script ends –

FINIS. Paule Bucke.

Paul Buck is reckoned to have been the copyist of the company.

Having reviewed this play in detail I do not find anything in it that seems inevitably to forbid presentation on the simplest traditional lines, and I feel inclined to dismiss Chambers' suggestion that the main action took place 'before two houses in London itself', as unnecessary.

68 *The Three Lords and Three Ladies of London*

The Three Lords and Three Ladies of London is a more elaborate piece of spectacle. The title-page of the Tudor Facsimile 1912 reprint of the only known edition of 1590 reads –

The Pleasant and Stately
Morall, of the three Lordes
and three Ladies of London
With the great Joy and Pompe, Solempnized at their Mari-
ages: Commically interlaced with much honest Mirth, for
pleasure and recreation, among many Morall obser-
uations and other important matters
of due Regard. by R.W.

[cut]

London
Printed by R. Ihones, at the Rose
and Crowne neere Holburne Bridge, 1590.

558

The large woodcut in the middle of the page is, I think, again a random printer's decoration carrying no evidence about the appearance of the play. There is a list of 'The Actors names', and since the cast is a fairly numerous one, it offers some help to understanding the plot.

The Actors names.

Pollicie,
Pompe, } the three Lords of London.
Pleasure,

Wit.
Wealth. } their pages.
Wil.

Nemo, a graue old man.

Loue,
Lucre, } three Ladies of London.
Conscience,

Honest Industrie,
Pure zeale, } three Sages.
Sinceritie,

Pride,
Ambition, } three Lordes of Spaine,
Tiranny,

Shame,
Treachery, } their pages,
Terror,

Desire,
Delight, } three Lordes of Lincolne.
Deuotion,

Sorrowe, a Jayler.

Simplicity, a poore Freeman of London.

Painefull Penurie, his wife.

Dilligence, a Poste, or an Officer.

Fealtie,
Shealtie, } two Heraldes at Armes.

Fraud,
Vsurie,
Dissimulation, } Foure Gallantes.
Simony,

Falshood,
Double dealing, } two that belong to Fraud and Dissimulation.

Before attempting any reconstruction of *The Three Lords* it is essential to bring forward one episode from near the end of the play and examine that first, otherwise the reconstruction would lack its most important piece of information.

The situation is this: the comic lead, Simplicitie, is present at the marriage celebrations of the Three Lords and the Three Ladies. Among the guests he sees Fraud, his old enemy, who has cheated him of a sum of money. He begs permission of one of the Three

Lords to take instant revenge. His request is granted in these very particular terms (the torch mentioned is one of several brought in by attendants at the wedding) –

> PLE[SURE]. That his punishment may please thee the better, thou shalt punish him thy selfe: he shall be bound fast to yen [*yon*] post, and thou shalt bee blindfold, and with thy torch shalt run as it were at tilt, charging thy light against his lips, and so (if thou canst) burne out his tongue, that it neuer speake more guile.

This by itself would have little especial significance, containing as it does nothing beyond the unexplained reference to 'yon post'. But in the stage-direction which follows a few lines later, a very interesting additional post appears.

Before looking at this direction, I would recall that there have been several other references to posts in the Interludes already reviewed. For instance, in *Jack Juggler* there is a line: 'Joll his hed to a post' when one character threatens to bump another. In *Cambises*, three ruffians, Huff, Ruff and Snuff, similarly threaten to run the Vice's 'arse against a post'. In *Gammer Gurton's Needle* I have pointed out a number of references to posts, all these would seem to have applied to ordinary door-posts. Finally, in *Susanna* there is a different sort of post – the stake to which the two Elders are tied to be stoned. At first sight, then, this post in *The Three Lords* might seem to be something like one of these; but the stage-direction explaining the incident adds a completely new consideration. It reads (and I italicize the important words) –

> Bind Fraud, blind Simplicity, turne him thrise
> about, set his face towards *the contrarie post*,
> at which he runnes, and all to burnes it,
> Dis. standing behind Fraud, vnbindes him, and
> whiles all the rest behold Simp. they two slip away: . . .

– so there are now *two* posts involved, and by the term 'contrarie' they are suggested as opposite posts, or as a symmetrical pair, one on either side, with sufficient space between them for a considerable action to be performed.

The especial importance of this is that it suggests we have at length reached a design of stage resembling that of the Elizabethan public playhouse as shown in the well-known De Witt sketch – or at any rate, a stage carrying two substantial posts which stand clear enough of any surroundings to allow a character to be bound to one of them and for a second character, mistaking the direction of the one post for the other, to run 'as it were at tilt' against the contrary post.

The obvious question straight away is, What posts were these? Were they the posts that supported a stage 'cover' or 'shade'? If they were, then *The Three Lords* must certainly take us out of the Interlude tradition and into the new Elizabethan theatre – by now some twelve or fifteen years old. If not into The Theatre itself, at least into some variant of it, such as an inn-yard, that would stand half-way between the Tudor Hall and the Playhouse proper.

One thing is almost certain; if *The Three Lords* was presented on a stage with opposite posts supporting a cover, then it was presented on a stage in the open air instead of indoors in a hall.

This stage could be in one of two situations: in a public playhouse, or in an inn-yard. If the stage had a cover it could scarcely have been in one of the indoor, or 'private' theatres such as the first Blackfriars, or the Whitefriars, which (at that time) were anyway occupied by the Boys' Companies.

To summarize: we shall need then, in what follows, to picture a stage provided with two posts. And if these posts supported a cover it must almost certainly be an outdoor stage – either in an inn-yard (etc.) or in a public playhouse.

The setting of *The Three Ladies* was varied enough, but at the same time topographically indefinite. The setting of *The Three Lords* is in some respects more specific, and it includes certain objects placed on the stage which give it a relatively permanent 'locality', as will be shown.

The script opens, not with a Prologue in the accepted sense, but with the words –

> Enter for the Preface, a Lady very richlyattyred, representing London, hauing two Angels before her, and two after her with bright Rapiers in their handes.
>
> London speaketh.

What London speaks is three stanzas of introduction ending –

> My former fruites were louely Ladies three,
> Now of three Lords to talke is Londons glee.
> Whose deeds I wish may to your liking frame,
> For London bids you welcome to the same.

It is clear from what London says that, however long the interval between this play and *The Three Ladies*, it could be taken for granted that the audience had not forgotten them. According to our present very provisional date-table, that interval may have been as long as eight years, but of course *Three Ladies* may have been revived several times in the interval.

At any rate, we have now to picture, on this stage of novel form and before an audience on the threshold of a new era, a very richly attired Lady standing between four angels, each carrying a shining sword. The daylight falls on them as she speaks. The spectators listen to her introductory words, and then watch her and the angels turn, walk upstage, and go out. A new play has begun.

In attempting to picture what now follows we are unusually fortunate, for the action opens with one of the most detailed of stage directions –

The pleasant and statelie Morall
of the three Lords of London

Enter the three Lordes and their pages: First, POLLICIE with his page WIT before him, bearing a shield: the ympreze, a TORTOYS, the word, *Prouidens securus*. Next POMPE, with his page WEALTH bearing his shield, the word, *Glorie sauns peere*: the ympreze a Lillie. Last, PLEASURE, his page WIL, his ympreze, a FAULCON, the woord, *Pour temps*: POL. attired in blacke, POMPE in rich roabes, and PLEASURE in collours.

At such mention of blazons and colours, it is worth recalling that probably a majority of the shows of the early Tudor age were seen under no more than torchlight, while the fewer open-air shows had little in the way of comfortable accommodation for spectators (unlike some medieval shows before them); so to see these bright colours in a bright daylight and in a special enclosure must have been something of an exhilarating novelty.

Another matter which must be kept in mind while reconstructing this picture is the height of the stage. When the audience is mostly a seated audience, as in a hall, the stage can be low; when the audience is mostly standing, as in a yard or a street, the stage will tend to be much higher, possibly 5 ft. or more. With a low stage such as a footpace the actors could easily step up on to it from the floor, and so the doors of entrance can naturally be at floor level. But if the stage is high, it must follow that either the entrance doors must be up on stage level, or the stage must have steps up to it from the ground. Further, if the style of presentation demanded *both* the old traditional entrances up to the stage from ground level *and* entrances on stage level as well, then a stage with doors at the back *and* steps from the yard in addition would be needed.

Again, if the stage were shoulder high there might arise some risk of actors slipping off it, particularly in hard-pressed fencing scenes. Therefore a rail round the stage might become desirable.

With such things in mind it needs to be remembered, in picturing the opening scene of *The Three Lords*, that many of the spectators would be looking up at the actors from a viewpoint near the actors' feet. And now to continue with the action of the show.

The first business which the Lords and their pages perform is indicated in the opening line from the first Lord called Pollicy –

> Here I aduance my shield and hang it vp, [. . .]

Eight lines later the second Lord, Pompe, announces likewise –

> [. . .] Yet maugre men my shield is here aduaunc'd [. . .]

– and nine lines after this the third Lord, Pleasure, adds –

> [. . .] in challenge I my shield aduaunce.

The respective Pages have been bearing the shields that are thus 'advanced', and now as the later dialogue shows these Pages lift up the shields and hang them upon what must have looked a curious object but which, as will be seen in a moment, must have had a conspicuous place on the stage. The Lords proclaim that they have come to woo the Three Ladies, and that their shields are now hung up as gages to any who would challenge their right. The Lords then go out leaving the pages to report if anyone should 'attaint', 'batter', or 'disdaine' any of the shields. The boys, left alone, fill in by discussing at length the 'ymprezes' on the shields and explaining their heraldic significance to each other – and incidentally to the audience.

While they are talking, a fresh character comes to them to bring a new turn to the plot; it is the comic lead from the last play, by name Simplicitie, 'in bare blacke, like a poore Citizen' and in all probability performed by Robert Wilson himself. He opens a bright and witty conversation with the boys during which he makes it clear to them that he has come to sell his 'wares'. One boy asks, 'what wares do ye sell?' And Simplicitie replies,

> Truely Child, I sel Ballades: soft, whose wares are these that are vp already? I paid rent for my standing, and other folkes wares shall be placed afore mine, this is wise indeed.

He has obviously caught sight of the shields hanging there, for he goes on to ask how much the boys want for those shields, and they tell him they are not to be sold. So he demands, very reasonably, 'why hang they then in the open market?'

At this point we can fill in another detail of the picture; the stage clearly presents an outdoor market, with some arrangement set in place on which the 'scutchions' may be hung but which a ballad-monger may also claim as his rightful rented stall. Some guess at its appearance may be gained from prints, see for example Fig. 41.

FIG. 41. A conjecture of what the ballad stall might have looked like in *The Three Lords and Three Ladies of London* (based on an engraving by Abraham Bosse)

Simplicitie brings out his own goods and says, 'but come my boies if you'll buy any of my wares, her's my stall, and Ile open and show strait'. So he has some business of displaying his ballads for sale. During the following banter one of the Pages picks up a sheet from the stall and asks, 'What's this', and is told, 'Ile tel thee, this is Tarltons picture: didst thou neuer know Tarlton?' He replies 'No: what was that Tarlton? I neuer knew him.' Then Simplicitie after describing him adds, '. . . if thou knewest not him, thou knewest no body . . . there will neuer come his like while the earth can corne: O passing fine Tarlton I would thou hadst liued yet.' A neat and a touching tribute to the fellow-clown who had died in 1588.

After a little further bye-play in which Simplicitie's wife, called

Painefull Penurie, is involved with the Pages, a direction is inserted (C.3): 'One cal within'. This call from offstage is to the Pages; the words are, 'Wit, wealth and wil, come to your Lords quickly?' At this the Page named Wil thoughtfully calls back 'Must the Scutchions hang still?' And 'One wihin' answers him, 'yea, let them alone.' And the Pages leave. There is no direction for Simplicitie to leave, and so it is to be supposed he takes a seat by his stall, and waits for custom throughout the whole of the next episode.

This consists of the entrance of Nemo (who judged the Ladies in the last play) and the Three Lords of London. The Three Lords petition for the Ladies' release, and after a careful discussion this petition is granted. In the course of talk Nemo warns the Lords that –

> The time of their indurance hath bene long,
> Whereby their cloathes of cost and curious stuffe
> Are worne to rags, and giue them much disgrace.

– so we must picture them, when they appear later, in abject rags.

Now the Lords leave, while Nemo summons Sorrow the Gaoler and bids him release the Three Ladies on the morrow and bring them 'Upon these stones to sit, and take the aire,' then both go out.

The next action is a scene between the four villains of the piece, Fraud, Usury, Dissimulation and Simony; they meet and greet each other after a long separation. It would appear that Simplicitie is still present inconspicuously by his stall, and presumably hears their talk as he heard the talk between Nemo and the Lords, for he suddenly chips in with – 'I see many of these old prouerbes prooue true, tis merrie when knaues meet.' At this they are surprised and exclaim 'How sir, whats that?', and discover him. They are discussing their several adventures since the last play when suddenly they pause: '. . . but soft who comes here? step wee close aside, . . . let vs be whist and we shall heare and see all, . . .'

D.i.*rev.* Enter Sorrow and the three Ladies, he sets them on three stones on the stage.

The picture of the stage takes a step nearer completion, with these three forlorn and muffled figures coming to sit in their tatters on the three hard stones, in front of the ballad-stall with its hanging shields.

For some 60 lines now the Ladies lament their sad and regrettable past, and Love exclaims at her folly in marrying Dissimulation. At length they decide to stand up and look round at the stones they have been sitting on. For this purpose Conscience proposes, 'Doffe we our veiles and greet this gladsom light' – and suddenly as the hoods fall back the Ladies all discover that their blemishes are gone and Love's 'double face is single growen agaiue [*again*]'. Then they see legends carved on the stones: 'Remorse' on Conscience's, 'Charity' on Love's, and 'Care' on Lucre's. They all breathe the fresh air, and 'sit all down' again.

As they replace their veils, Fraud steps forward from the background and after him Simony and then Dissimulation; each tries to get back into the Ladies' good graces but with no success. At this Simplicitie cannot forbear breaking in, and he speaks in terms which show that Dissimulation must be wearing the same make-up as in the first play, for Simplicitie says mockingly to him as Love dismisses him (D.iii.*rev.*), 'Marie, but heare ye motley-beard, I think this blindfold buzzardly hedge-wench spoke to ye, she knowes ye though she see ye not, . . .' (since the Ladies are shrouded once more).

Usury, pretending compassion for Conscience's rags, says 'I wil cloath her straight:' and he 'takes Frauds cloak, & casts it on Consc.' At which Simplicitie exclaims –

> Ha, that's no gramercie to cloath her with another mans cloake,
> Bnt I see you haue a craft in the dooing M. Vsury,
> Vsury couers Conscience with Frauds cloake verie cunningly.

– and the Lady Conscience cries out –

> Alas who loades my shoulders with this heauie weed,
> Fy, how it stinks, this is perfum'd indeed.

Further dialogue follows until Dissimulation cries, 'Yonder come some, we must take our flight.' At this there is a direction, 'Exeunt omnes', but clearly this general exit-direction is meant only for the rogues, for the Ladies stay and Simplicity says, 'yonder comes a customer, Ile to my stall'. Then Nemo enters. He brings good news that the Ladies are to be wooed by the Lords and adds –

> If I commaund, stand vp, els sit you stil.
> Lo, where they come: my Lordes the Dames be here.

Now Pollicy, entering with Pomp and Pleasure, demands, 'Why are they wympled?' and his companions ask which lady is which. Nemo bids the Ladies stand and lift their veils. The Lords explode with compliments, and Nemo bids the Ladies sit again. Then his speech continues with a direction: 'to the audience'; thus he turns to the spectators as he tells them that he proposes to leave the six together for a while to get acquainted; and then 'exit'.

In his absence, two new characters, Falshood and Double-dealing, sneak in with new clothes for the Ladies, but Nemo comes in on their heels and denounces them, showing how the one bears 'a cloake of craft, With lawne of lies, and calle of golden guile' for Lucre; and the other 'a gown of glosing, lin'd with lust, A Vardingale of vaine boast, and fan of flatterie, A Ruffe of riot, and a cap of pride' for Love. And so the two are discomfited and leave. It is to be supposed that these two players must have entered each with a bundle of actual garments in his arms, so keeping up the old Interlude convention of the significance of costume, that was in use already when Worldly Affeccyon followed after World at the opening of Medwall's *Nature*.

Three fresh characters now come in, Honest Industrie, Pure Zeale and Sincerity; they take out respectively Lucre, Love and Conscience to be properly new-garbed. The Lords comment approvingly, and leave.

A diversion scene follows (fol. E.iii.) in which Fraud cheats Simplicitie into buying copper as gold – a cheat which Simplicitie is to have the chance of revenging spectacularly at the end of the play.

Next comes a scene in which there 'Enter Nemo and the three Lordes, as though they had bene chyding.' The contention is about which Lord shall have Lucre – the most desired Lady. Nemo prudently decides that he will go and fetch Lucre and let her choose. But he goes and comes back with a trick to play; instead of Lucre he brings in 'Conscience al in white', and drawing her to one side so that the Lords will not hear, arranges with her that she shall counterfeit Lucre. A nice piece of ingenious nonsense follows: but it is rudely interrupted. 'Enter Diligence, in hast' (fol. F.i.*rev.*). He brings the news that the Spaniards have begun to invade and are proposing particularly to steal the Ladies. The whole atmosphere now changes. Nemo whisks Lady Conscience away to a safe place. Pollicy asks the number and position of the enemy. Dilligence is hustled off to call the Pages. Pollicy proposes to deck London in festivals and games to show contempt for the Spaniards (like Sir Francis Drake). And all go out. There follows another comic scene for Simplicitie.

Next (F.4.), a scene beginning with the direction 'Enter the three Lordes with their Pages and Fealtie a Herald before them, his coat hauing the armes of London before and an Oliue tree behind.'

Fealty is ordered to take down the shields from the stand and give them to the Pages, and then to go out and spy on the advancing enemy.

Simplicitie again enters briefly, creating a noisy but amusing distraction, and looking angrily for Fraud who cheated him. Then the Lords are given news of the glittering invaders by Dilligence. They send him out once more to broadcast the news through the city, and as he goes Pomp calls out:

> And here they come, Oh proud Castillians.

So the great moment has arrived! And for it the playwright gives us the longest and most picturesque stage-direction in this history:

G.1.*rev.* Enter first SHEALTY the Herald: then PRIDE, bearing his shield himself, his ympreze, a PEACOCKE: the worde, *Non par illi* His Page SHAME after him with a Launce, hauing appendent gilt, with this word in it, *Sur le Ciel*, AMBITION, his ympreze, a blacke Horse salliant, with one hinder foote vpon the Globe of the earth, one fore foote stretchiug towards the cloudes, his woorde, *Non sufficit orbis*: His page TREACHERIE after him, his pendent Argent and Azure, an armed Arme catching at the Sun beames, the woorde in it, *Et gloriam Phoebi*. Last, TYRANNIE, His ympreze, a naked Childe on a speares point bleeding, his woord, *Pour sangue*, His page, TERROUR, his pendent Gules, in it, a Tygers head out of a cloud, licking a bloody heart: The woord in it, *Cura Cruor*. March once about the stage, then stand and viewe the Lords of LONDON, who shall martch towardes them, and they giue backe, then the Lords of LONDON wheele abont to their standing, and th'other come againe into their places, then POLLICIE sendes FEALTIE: their Herraldes coate must haue the armes of *Spaine* before, and a burning ship behind.

We now have: the three Lords of London, their three Pages carrying the shields, their Herald, three Spaniards, their three Pages also carrying lances and shields, and the Spanish Herald; in all fourteen persons – a greater number than we can be sure of in any play up to now. Not only this, but there has to be advancing, giving back, and wheeling about. A pretty big acting-area will be necessary. The major problem that now arises so far as my subject is concerned is how, in these circumstances, to interpret the sentence 'March once about the stage'. If the performance had been in a hall theatre, with a low footpace and the floor available for action, then clearly the likelihood would be that the Spaniards entered, like

Horestes' army, on the floor level and manoeuvred there. If however a large, high stage were available, such as we judge a public playhouse to have had and such as De Witt showed in his controversial sketch (say some 40 ft. by 27 ft.) – could this crowd and the action that is to follow, be accommodated there – always bearing in mind that there already are a ballad-stall and three stone seats on that stage? No doubt this is just possible.

But there is another possibility. This alternative offers much the same sort of entries and groupings and action as in indoor hall presentations with a footpace, and for this reason it might be supposed to be closer to the Interlude tradition, and thus, possibly, a more likely arrangement here.

Taking the De Witt playhouse interior as a basis, it would involve the entry of the Spanish party *not* by one of the doors at the back of the stage (as all entrances have been visualized up to the moment in this play) but down the steps marked *ingressus* in De Witt's sketch, and directly into the yard marked *planities sive arena* where the groundlings of the audience would be standing (compare later Fig. 42).

Such an entry would correspond with the entrance via the hall screens straight on to the hall floor in an indoor presentation, and the groundlings would correspond to the traditional clusters of spectators round the screens-doors through whom the actors had been wont to thrust since the beginning of this history.

I propose however to put aside any choice between these alternatives until later, concentrating for the present on the action that is to follow. I emphasize only one point now, namely that the phrase 'march once about the stage' is in almost exactly the same terms as was the direction to the invading band of soldiers that Horestes brought before Clytemnestra's city – 'Horestes entrith wt his bande & marcheth about the stage'.

The action that follows is remarkably elaborate and admittedly puzzling. What appears to happen is this. First, the London Lord called Pollicy says to the other two Lords, 'My Lordes, what meane these gallants to perfourme'. Then he adds to his Herald, 'Fealty, goe fetch their answer . . .'

Fealty now goes towards the Spaniards, and is met. A direction makes quite sure of this: 'As Feal. is going towards the*m*, they send foorth Sheal.' Shealty is the name of the corresponding Spanish herald. He asks Fealty, 'What wouldst thou Herald?' and Fealty replies, 'Parlle with those three, Herald.'

569

Now follow 24 lines of exchange of professional insults between the two Heralds, at the end of which Shealty says before he will disclose who his masters are he will 'returne and know their mindes'.

Now a curious direction follows – curious, that is, if we have to picture the action all taking place within the limits of one stage. The direction reads, 'When Sheal. goes to the*m*, Wit goes to the 3. Lords of Lond.' – and the first Lord, Pollicy, asks Wit, 'Now boy, what newes.' Notice, it is not Fealty, the Herald, who goes to explain the situation to Pollicy, but the page-boy Wit. It appears then that the Page was in some position from which he had been able to follow the events, but that Pollicy, and the other two Lords likewise, *were not in such a position* and had, ostensibly at any rate, to be told of the events by this intermediary Page.

It would be pretty difficult to make this situation dramatically effective if all fourteen characters were on one stage with its two great posts, its ballad-stall and its three large stones. What *could* be dramatically effective would be if the Spanish party were down in the yard; if the English Herald descended by steps from the stage and spoke from the bottom step to his opposite number; if the three Lords of London stayed in splendid isolation at the centre of the stage; and if Wit, the page, shuttled between them and the head of the stairs to bring them news of what was going on down below (Fig. 42).

What Wit now tells Lord Pollicy is that Shealty has hesitated before consenting to take any message to his Spanish masters. While he is saying this the action of the Spaniards is clearly stated in a marginal direction, 'The Span. whisper with their Her.[*ald*]'.

Now, Lord Pomp would seem at this point to have turned away from his group to watch the enemy, for he says concerning the Spaniards' answer – 'Which now belike our Herald shall receiue, For theirs comes to him.'

The action now shifts to the two Heralds. Shealty brings answer to Fealty that the Spaniards want to know who is opposing them, and that they demand 'A counteruiew of Pages, and of shields, And countermessage by vs Heraldes', and he ends, 'Go thou for those' (i.e. for the English pages and shields), 'I meete thee will with these (i.e. the countermessages – or shields – from the Spaniards).

Next Fealty addresses the three Lords of London; therefore he must have returned to them, bearing the answer. He ends, 'So please it you yonr pages and your shieldes With me to send, their Herald comes with theirs.'

FIG. 42. Conjectural reconstruction of the entry of the Spaniards in *The Three Lords and Three Ladies of London* using the 'ingressus', and of their 'March once about the stage'

The Lords agree (after a moment's hesitation about risking their Pages so far out of their protection – thus, I think, again proving that there must be some acceptable impression of distance between the two opposing parties). Then Lord Pleasure orders, 'Boies, take our sheildes and speares, for they come on.' So, from wherever they are, the Spanish Pages are beginning to advance.

Wit cries to the Spanish Page who is approaching him, 'couch thy Launce and pendent both, knowest where thou art? Here wil we beare no braues.' The Spanish Pages are infringing a rule of courtly etiquette in advancing without dipping their lances. A direction points this: 'When the English boies meet the other, cause them to put downe the tops of their Lances, but they [*?the Spaniards?*] beare vp theirs.' The English Page, Wealth, bids them 'Downe with your point, no loft borne Lances here By any stranger, . . .'. The Spaniards apparently concede, for the page, Wil, comments 'Wel doest thou note the couching of thy Lance . . .'.

571

Honours being even, the English Herald exclaims 'Wel done my boies, but now all reuerence.' And the Spanish Herald orders, 'Aduaunce againe your Launces now my boies,' and in the margin we have the succinct words 'hold vp again'.

The parley now takes place at very great length. Fealty first speaks to the Spaniards and defines the titles, emblems and lady-loves of the Lords of London, and at the end the first Spanish Lord, called S. Pride, gives him a comment in Latin. Then Lord Pollicy in his turn asks Shealty in Latin if he can speak English. Shealty replies in Latin that he can. He is then bidden to declare his 'Lords, their shields, their pages and their purpose', which he does at even greater length, incidentally repeating that the Spaniards have come to snatch the Three Ladies from their lovers. Lord Pollicy comments contemptuously on each of the Spanish nobles. The atmosphere rises. Each Lord of London issues a challenge through the Herald to one of the Spaniards, flourishing his own Lady's favour the while. Since all this is done through the Heralds, presumably the two main parties are still quite separate, with the English Herald before the Spanish party and the Spanish Herald before the English party, and the six Pages at some intermediate position in attendance.

The parley now breaks off with a very quick short exchange that is a little cryptic at first sight –

SHEA[LTY].   You will not yeeld?
PLE[ASURE], Yes, the last moneth.
SHEA[LTY].   Farewel.
              Retire Heraldes with the pages to their places.
S. PRIDE.   *Vade.*
POL[ICY].   Herald, how now?
FEA[LTY].   Yen proud Castillians looke for your seruice. . . .

– and a few more lines follow before the first flourish of the action. It would seem that the above exchange could only make sense if the two parties were manifestly some distance apart, and if Shealty bids his farewell and leaves the English party while Fealty, who is not given a farewell line, is ordered by the first Spanish Lord to 'go' (otherwise there is no way of fitting in this odd Latin command-word from S. Pride); and now the stage-direction can come into play, and Fealty and Shealty return to their respective parties each followed by his trio of pages. Note that the Heralds with the Pages are directed to *retire to their places*, but not so the Lords; this can only be because neither of the groups of Lords have left their places but both have remained proudly and grandly aloof.

Lord Pollicy, after exchanging a few words with his Herald, now gives the call to action, 'Come, Courage, let vs charge them all at once'. Presumably by this point the Lords of London have each taken their shields again.

Next follows a brief but particularly puzzling passage. First a direction: 'Let the three Lordes passe towards the Spaniards, and rhe Spaniardes make show of comming forward and sodainly depart.' 'Depart' here is not, I think, equivalent to 'exeunt'. The direction means that the English advance towards the Spaniards and make a 'pass' at them with their swords while the Spaniards also advance but immediately check and then give ground, so breaking off the engagement and temporarily retiring. But where?

If the parties had been all together on a stage this action of 'departing' – and particularly what is to follow in a moment – must have been nearly impossible to make convincing. But if it be conceded that the Spaniards start from the yard, then the English could 'passe towardes' them by advancing to the top of the steps leading down to the yard from the stage, then the Spaniards would make their 'show of comming forward' by part-mounting those steps; thus it could easily be seen that they were at a disadvantage and might very convincingly turn and 'sodainly depart' down again and retire some way back into the yard, under the threat from above.

At all events, the Lords of London now turn back, and Pollicy exclaims 'What brauing cowards these Castillians be, My Lordes let's hang our Scutchens vp againe, . . .'. If the Spaniards now seemed to have left the field, this would be an understandable and practical enough proposal, and one pictures the Lords 'disembarrassing' themselves, to use the French phrase, near their useful ballad-stall; but the rest of Pollicy's speech contains what seems at first a less understandable suggestion. He goes on

> [. . .] And shroud our selues but not farre off vnseene,
> To prooue if that may draw them to some deed,
> Be it but to batter our ymprezed shieldes.
> PLEA. Agreed, here Fealty, hang them vp a space.

(So they presumably all slip off their shields and hand them over to the Herald who puts them back on the ballad-stall. Now follows an elaborate direction; what they do is –)

> They hang vp their shieldes, and step out of sight.
> The Spaniardes come and flourish their rapiers

> neer them, but touch them not, & the*n* hang vp
> theirs, which the Lords of London perceiuing, take
> their owne [*?rapiers?*] and batter theirs
> [*i.e. shields?*]: The Spaniards making a lirle
> [*little*] showe to rescue, do sodenly slippe away
> and come no more.

I have made some emendations in brackets to this direction since
it is not clear without them. What would seem to be involved is
that the English party, having hung up their shields, go into some
concealment – either they crouch behind the ballad-stall, or they all
go out by one of the doors at the back of the stage, leaving it partly
open, and peer back through it to see what happens. At such a point
in the play this might be a most amusing and intriguing piece of
business for the audience to watch. Then follows a brief pause.

Next, the Spaniards one by one come stealthily forward to the
foot of the steps, wait and listen, mount the steps, wait and listen
again; then taking courage they advance, draw their rapiers, and
go up to the hanging shields. There, with every eye and ear upon
them waiting for the crash, they raise their swords. Then drop them
again in hesitation. Stand doubtful. Put their heads together, exchange a murmur or two (they are foreigners), and then straighten
up, sheath their swords, and blot out the English shields by hanging their own shields in front of them. They then turn and face the
audience with satisfied smiles on their faces. At which moment, of
course, nothing could delight the spectators more than to see a
stealthy advance of the English from the door at the back – and
then a sudden terrific din as the Lords of London drew their own
swords and battered the foreign shields. No wonder then if the
Spaniards made little show to rescue but turned to the top of the
steps pell-mell and 'do sodenly slippe away' down them and race
across the yard to the *ingressus*, and out 'and come no more'.

Lord Pollicy cries, 'Facing, faint-hearted, proud and insolent,
That beare no edge within their painted sheaths, . . .' etc., and the
three batter on the Spanish shields again.

Now comes something that would seem utterly impossible, or at
the least ridiculous, if all this scene were confined to the stage. It
concerns the first Spanish Lord; and the lines are as follows:

Enter s. PRIDE.

s. PRIDE. Fuoro Viliagos, fuoro Lutheranos Angleses, fuoro
     sa, sa, sa.
POMP.   Their shieldes are ours, they fled away with shame, [. . .]

It seems to me that there is no convincing way of managing this except to have the first Spanish Lord slip in again momentarily at the head of the ingressus steps, call out a parting taunt, and then turn and slip out once more. It is important to notice that there is no specific exit direction given for him.

Pomp continues, 'Let vs pursue them flieng . . .'; the others agree and so 'Exeunt omnes' – in my opinion hurrying down the steps, through the bystanders in the yard, and out by the ingressus after the Spaniards.

Immediately now upon the stage there 'Enter three Ladies and Nemo'. They rejoice that the day has been won, offer to make up 'garlands of Laurell greene' for their returning heroes, then prudently consider that perhaps they had better first make sure how the heroes 'will take such work, . . .' and finally decide only to 'make them garlands when we know their mindes'.

Now the Lords return bearing, rather surprisingly, the shields of the Spaniards which they must, therefore, have snatched up from the stand as they went out – 'Enter the three Lords with the Spanish shieldes and Diligence'. Each gives his trophy to his Lady, and all lay plans for a triple wedding, for which the Ladies and Nemo now go off to prepare. In bidding farewell to their Ladies, 'the Lords bring the*m* to the doore, & they [*the Ladies*] go out & Ne[mo]'. So there is no doubt here which exit was used – namely, one of the normal stage doors.

Pleasure has just a brief moment to return the Ladies' farewells when a surreptitious figure slides in by the other door. It is Fraud: 'Fra. giues Pol. a paper, which he reads & then saies' (fol. H.ii.); 'It scemes by this writing sir, you would serue me, . . .'. Soon after: 'Diss. giues Plea. a paper which he reades, and saies.' – much the same thing. Then: 'Enter Vsurie and giues a paper to Pompe which he reades, and saith.' etc. So these three rogues are trying to get into favour and service again under assumed names. But the Lords temporize and then, obviously suspicious, 'The three Lords go together, and whisper, and call Diligence, Diligence goes out for a marking yron, and returnes.' Now we have the two groups, the Lords and the rogues, on either side of the stage, and some atmosphere of suspense. There is a nice little 'aside' scene while Diligence is out, when Fraud says to Usury, 'How now my hearts, think ye we shal speed.' And Usury assures him, 'I cannot tell what you shal, but I am sure I shall.' But what they do not notice is that between these two speeches Pollicy has slipped in the command,

575

'Diligence, Come hether.' A few more asides are exchanged and then before they know where they are, Usury has been branded and Dissimulation has 'slipt away'.

Now our old friend Simplicitie enters with a paper, but this time it is one setting out a most interesting series of proposals for checking sharp dealing by itinerant traders, and these are accepted by the three Lords, who then 'exeunt'. Dilligence and Fraud now 'step out' (or forwards) and have a brief scene together; and after, there follows a small surprise (H.4.*rev.*):

The direction reads 'Enter Nemo with Desire, Delight and Deuotion, the three Lordes of Lincolne.' These curious Lords of Lincoln have come to claim, of all things, the three Ladies. The three Lords of London now re-enter and Pleasure very shortly sums up their reaction: 'ye cannot haue them', but they do suggest (a little dryly) that if the Lincoln Lords wish, they can have the three stones instead; and the Lords of London are directed to point to the stones in turn as they speak, and then to go out. Whereupon, apparently, the Lords of Lincoln take up the stones and ruefully go away with them. This odd business does of course serve perfectly to clear the stage for the wedding scene that is to follow.

Simplicitie next has a short scene. Then follows another strange direction: 'Enter Dissimulation and Fraud in caps, and as the rest must be for the showe.' This is a prelude to the final scene; the 'showe' is the triple wedding. What the rogues seem to be proposing is to 'shufle into the showe with the rest' (that is, to gate-crash) and to 'take as they take, torches or any thing to furnish the showe'. Having agreed on this they leave; and 'Enter a Wench singing.' She sings for flowers both to 'Strowe . . . vpon the stones' of London and to 'perfume the bridall bed.' Next there enters an elaborately costumed procession:

> Enter first DILIGENCE with a Truncheon, then a boy with POLLICIES Launce and shield, then POLLICIE and LOUE hand in hand: then FRAUD in a blew gowne, red cap and red sleeues, with AMBITIONS Lance and shield, then a boy with POMPS Launce and shield, then POMPE and LUCRE hand in hand: then DISSIMULATION with PRIDES Launce and shield, then a boy with PLEASURES Lance and shield: then PLEASURE and CONSCIENCE hand in hand: then SIMPLICITIE with TIRANNIES Lance and shield: they al going out, NEMO staies and speakes.

The procession consists, then, of a leader marching ahead with a truncheon, as a sort of master of ceremonies; then after him three similar groups, each consisting of a Page bearing a London Lord's

lance and shield, then that London Lord with his Lady, and then
one of the rogues bearing the opposite Spanish Lord's lance and
shield. While they all go out, Nemo stays behind in order to give a
commentary on the service that is taking place off-stage – and incidentally to bewail the murder of Hospitality (which happened in the
previous play) – and he concludes

> I talke too long, for loe this louelie crue
> Are comming backe, and haue perfourm'd their due.

Their return is described in the direction –

> Returne as they went, sauing that the blew gownes
> that bare shields, must now beare torches: SIM-
> PLICITY going about, spies FRAUD, and falleth on
> his knees before PLEASURE and CONSCIENCE, saieng.

(It might be noticed that if this play were performed in the after-
noon of an autumn or winter day, these torches might now be
making a brave, glittering show as the twilight period advanced.) It
is at this point that there comes the scene I quoted at the beginning, in which Simplicitie begs permission to avenge himself on
Fraud for cheating him with copper for gold. It is worth repeating;
Pleasure gives his reply in prose, as follows:

> That his punishment may please thee the better, thou shalt punish
> him thy selfe: he shall be bound fast to yen post, and thou shalt bee
> blindfold, and with thy torch shalt run as it were at tilt, charging thy
> light against his lips, and so (if thou canst) burne out his tongue, that it
> neuer speake more guile.

Simplicitie eagerly accepts; then the significant stage-direction
comes:

> Bind Fraud, blind Simplicity, turne him thrise
> about, set his face towards the contrarie post,
> at which he runnes, and all to burnes it, Dis.
> standing behind Fraud, vnbindes him, and whiles
> all the rest behold Simp. they two slip away:
> Pleasure missing Fraud saith.

> Wisely perfourm'd, but soft sirs, where is Fraud? [. . .] gone whiles we
> beheld the other: [. . .] wel, one day he wil pay for all: vnblind Sim-
> plicity.

Simplicitie, with the bandage from his eyes, exultingly exclaims,

> How now, Haue I heated his lips? haue I warm'd his nose? . . .
> Let me see, [. . .] Haue I burned him?

577

And Diligence, loath to disillusion him replies,

> Thou hast done more, for thou hast quite consumed him into nothing,
> looke, here is no signe of him, no not so much as his ashes.

– and Simplicitie, taking him at his word, claims

> [. . .] wel, al London, nay, all England is beholding to me, for putting
> Fraud out of this world [. . .]

– and he ends with a typically witty reflection on the result, whereupon the company drops to its knees and prays for blessings on the
Queen.

So much for the elaborate and professional *Three Lords and Three
Ladies of London*; the important technical point is, Can anything
in Robert Wilson's work (the work, that is, of an experienced and
well-reputed actor) be found to confirm my suggestion that both a
stage and its surrounding ground might be used simultaneously for
an action? I believe this confirmation is to be found at the opening
of the next play.

69 *The Coblers Prophesie*

Contrary to what the Prologue said at the beginning of *The Three
Ladies*, this last play, *The Coblers Prophesie*, is a play about the classic
gods, though they are treated in a comic and satyric vein. There is
also a comic lead in the person of Raph, the Cobbler, moving Vice-
like in and out of their affairs, and much like Simplicitie in the two
earlier plays. F. P. Wilson states that this is 'probably a court play'.
There are some quite definite references to a stage.

The title-page in the Tudor Facsimile Text Society's 1911 reprint
of the only known edition of 1594 reads

THE

COBLERS

Prophesie

Written by Robert Wilson. Gent.

[decoration]

Printed at London by Iohn Danter for **Cuthbert**
Burbie: and are to be sold at his shop **nere**
the Royall-Exchange

1594

There is no list of characters, and no Prologue; the play opens straightaway with a stage-direction which seems significant enough to be taken as the key to the essential problem in the Third and Fourth Parts of this book. This direction reads:

Enter Iupiter *and* Iuno, Mars *and* Venus, Apollo, *after him,* Bacchus, Vulcan *limping, and after all* Diana *wringing her hands: they passe by, while on the stage* Mercurie *from one end* Ceres *from another meete.*

As I said, the treatment is satyrical and the effect partly comic. But the most important thing is what the gods in this procession are stated to do. In the first place they *Enter*; but then, after entering, they do no more than *passe by.* They have no other action than this; they have no lines to speak; there is no exit-direction for them. But (as the opening dialogue will show) they go out again straight-away. All this is acceptable enough so far. But what is remarkable is that *while* they are doing this, something quite different is taking place and taking place not where they are passing by, but *on the stage.*

What is happening on the stage is a meeting between the two characters who are to speak the opening dialogue of the play, thus it is something quite different in nature from the silent procession that passes by. These two characters come, one from one 'end' of the stage and the other from 'another' (or the other) end, to meet. And they meet 'on' the stage during the time ('while') the procession is still in the process of 'passing by' the stage.

There have been many examples earlier of directions that were equivocal or ambiguous; here at last is one that, as I see it, is capable of only one interpretation – that the procession passed by the stage; at the same time, something else took place *on* the stage; the procession then could not have gone *over* the stage but must have passed *on the floor* by the stage (cf. Pl. 5 to be described later).

Such an unequivocal direction coming as it does at the culmination of the period cannot, it seems to me, be without influence upon any decision one makes about the reading of the earlier, less specific directions. Now, the slight implications all take a more positive bias from the direct unassailable statement of the present direction. A tradition of using both the floor and the stage for action is confirmed.

To continue with the action of the play. Ceres, as she meets Mercury on the stage, asks about the procession passing by – 'Herrald of heauen, ... Tell, ... why these celestiall powers Are thus assembled in Boeotia.' Mercury says the reason is that –

> [. . .] securitie chiefe nurse of sinne,
> Hath bred contempt in all Boeotia.
> The old are scorned [. . .]
> Vnhallowed hands, [. . .]
> Rend downe the Altars [. . .]
> which made the awful Ruler of the rest,
> Summon this meeting of the heauenly States:

Then he enumerates the figures in the procession. 'The first was Iupiter, Iuno with him' (notice he speaks in the past tense; 'The first' *was* not *is*, Jupiter! so the procession must by now be mostly out of sight). He goes on by apparently telling Ceres she could not have recognized Mars –

> [. . .] him I know you knew not,
> His Harnesse is conuerted to soft silke,
> His warres are onely wantonings with her [*i.e. Venus*],
> That scandalizeth heauen and heapes worlds hate, [. . .]

This scandal about poor Venus is to form one of the lines of the plot to follow, and seems to be in some way bound up with the degeneration of Boeotia.

Mercury touches briefly on each of the other figures and then allows his attention to stray to the audience, and observes –

> I see a sort of wondring gazing eyes,
> That doo await the end of this conceit,
> whom Mercurie . . . inioines to sit and see,
> th'effectuall working of a Prophesie.

The 'Prophesie' will be outlined later, and in the meantime Ceres takes the opportunity of the glance at the spectators to add, very graciously as well as literally –

> And Ceres sheds her sweetest swetes in plentie,
>   *Cast Comfets.*
> That while ye stay their pleasure may content ye.
> Now doo I leaue thee Mercury, and will in to take my
>   place,
> Doo what thou canst in wanton lusts disgrace.
> MERCURIE: Ceres I will, [. . .]

This action of broadcasting sweetmeats among the audience would certainly seem to belong more to court precedent than to any public theatre custom. After she has gone 'in', Mercury continues –

> [. . .] and now I am alone
> Will I aduise me of a messenger [. . .]

> [. . .] the next I meete with be it he or she,
> To doo this message shall be sent by me.
>> *Enter Raph Cobler with his stoole, his implements*
>> *and shooes, and sitting on his stoole, falls to*
>> *sing,*

– and so the play begins.

The 'Prophesie' of which Mercury decides to make the unfortunate Cobbler the bearer is that while the silk-clad Mars slumbers 'a dunghill cock should tread his Hen and she should hatch a chicke'. And there follows an ingenious word puzzle about the name of the future child that does not concern us here. The name of the seducer, however, will turn out to be 'Content' which later becomes translated into 'Contempt'.

In the adventures which follow a Soldier has a scene (C.i.*rev*.) in which he asks the Three Muses ('Clio, Melpomine *and* Thalia: Clio *with a penknife*, Melpomine *being idle*, Thalia *writing*') where Mars's court is. Melpomine replies (C.3), 'Walke hence a flight shoot vp the hill, And thou shalt see his castle wall.' Here one is perhaps expectant that evidence for the existence of a 'house' will be presented. But in fact the Soldier *'exits'* before he goes towards the castle. Similarly, at the end of their scene Clio says to the other Muses, 'Tush come lets mount the Mount.' But it seems clear that no 'Mount' need be there to see, for immediately on that line the three ladies *'exeunt'*.

Two separate lines of the plot proceed alternately; in the one Venus seeks for a place to have her child, and Contempt at length tells her he has found one – 'a Spittle'. Whether or not he means by this his own 'Cabin' is not clear but Contempt's cabin is to have an important place in the outcome.

In the other line of plot, Boeotia is set at war with 'the Argives and the men of Thessaly' and, according to the god's decree, will not gain her victory 'till the Cabbin of Contempt be consumed with fire'. The Cobbler-cum-Prophet is constrained later to repeat that decision. 'Nothing shall appease heauens ire Til the cabin of Contempt be set on fire.'

After Venus finally knows herself abandoned, and exits in despair, there follows (G.i.*rev*.) this puzzling direction (and I mark the essential detail) –

>> *Enter the Duke, his Daughter, Priest, and Scholler:*
>> ** then compasse the stage, from one part let a smoke*
>> *arise: at which place they all stay.*

No clear explanation of this direction is given at this point. Later we find out this much; the Priest begins to pray, saying,

> Receiue the offrings of our humble harts
> And bodies prostrate on the lowly earth.
>
> *They all kneele downe.*

He then adds,

> We [. . .] intend to liue,
> Hereafter more reformd than wee haue done.
> For pride, we entertaine humilitie: [. . .]
> Loue for Contempt, and chastitie for lust:
> *The Cabbin of Contempt doth burne with fire,
> In which our sinnes are cast, [. . .]

And then a Messenger arrives, and in a classically florid messenger's speech announces a victorious outcome of the war, at which – *'They all rise and cast incense into the fire'*. (There is an obscure line that may or may not suggest that the Duke himself may have set the cabin on fire, when he says (G.3) –

> [. . .] the heauens haue [. . .]
> [. . .] tooke in worth our worthles sacrifice,
> Wherein Contempt and Lust with old ingratitude,
> Haue perished like Fume that flies from fire. [. . .])

The two difficult tasks that now arise are to define, and give a reason for, the sentence 'then compasse the stage'; and next to explain the references to a burning cabin.

To attempt the first; the situation here is certainly a processional one. The Court is going to prayer. The characters enter and then *compasse* the stage. To compass is defined in the *O.E.D.* under meaning 3 as 'To pass or move round; to make a circuit of'. And under meaning 4 as 'To close round, as a multitude; to surround, with friendly or hostile intent: to hem in . . .'. And under meaning 5 as 'to encircle, environ, lie round and enclose'.

Taken in connexion with a processional situation the suggestion is that the characters enter and stand round (on the floor?) *hemming in* the stage – as perhaps gathering before some altar-steps. The purpose for this direction may be quite deliberate and practical; the actors may form a sort of temporary barrier concealing or partly concealing the stage, while the business of igniting whatever was used to create the smoke effect took place unseen, so making the eventual slow rising of the smoke-cloud above their heads that much more effective. All this would be consistent with the arrangement of stage that I have put forward, and which is illustrated in Pl. 5.

But it is more difficult to make a satisfactory picture of that 'Cabbin of Contempt' which it was stated 'doth burne with fire'. To offer a first attempt: it might either be a reference to something real that was actually set on fire, or else it might be a mere verbal decoration transforming some simple smoke rising beyond a curtain into the idea of the house of Contempt burning. If the former, then the Cabin must have been a built property house standing on the stage throughout the show, which seems unlikely for an item that had such a brief connexion in the action. If the latter, then the whole thing might very simply have been effected by having no actual representation of the cabin at all but merely a reference to it as embodied by a simple traverse curtain at the back of the stage.

All that can be said on the evidence with any sureness is that some particular arrangement seems suggested by the detail in the script, but that detail is insufficient to allow one to specify any further.

It may be added that at the end of the play there is another processional occasion, indicated in the direction, '*Enter with honour the Duke and his traine*', and in his speech the Duke has the line, 'But in this triumph passe we to the Court.' The phrase 'passe we' is quite consistent once more with the picture of actors entering at one of two doors, passing round the front of the stage, and going out by the other door. In that case the business presented at the end of the play would be a nice echo of the business with which the play began, and of which we most certainly do have an explanation.

Supposing, now, this play to be presented not in a public playhouse but in a court hall, the picture I have imagined above might be reconstructed as in the fourth of the Tokyo transparencies, where I have used as background a late style of screen belonging to Trinity College, Cambridge (see Pl. 5). The choice of this screen particularly was made because its detail happens to offer a very convincing explanation of that considerable puzzle in the builder's contract for the Fortune Theatre, dated 1599, which instructs that

all the princypall and maine postes of the [. . .] fframe and Stadge forwarde sholbe square and wroughte palasterwise, with carved proporcions called Satiers to be placed & sett on the topp of every of the same postes

This picture is particularly designed to try to illustrate the three technical expressions –

 1. they [the procession] *passe by;*
 2. while *on the stage*
 3. from *one end . . .* from *another* [end].
– and in illustrating them to show how the Interluders seem to have used two acting-areas: one *upon* the stage, the other *about* it.

At the back of the stage is seen the possible traverse background.

This is the last of the theories that I have presented in this book about the technical conventions that the Interluders seem to have handed on to the public playhouse; I should like to add a group of thoughts on this same matter now from an entirely different source.

70 *A Footnote on 'Going about the Stage'*

I refer readers to the presidential address delivered by Professor Allardyce Nicoll before the Society for Theatre Research on 30 April 1958. The address can be conveniently read in *Shakespeare Survey*, XII, 1959, under the title 'Passing over the Stage'.

The particular theory presented there is one that would seem not to have received the attention which it would deserve if my view of the evidence offered in the present chapters is correct. In summary the contents of Nicoll's address are as follows.

He is concerned purely with public playhouse procedure, and he remarks certain phrases in stage-direction of public theatre plays wherein –

> the preposition 'about', varied by such other prepositions as 'on' or 'upon', is related to the noun 'stage'. Characters are bidden to walk "once about the Stage" (*The Misfortunes of Arthur*), to "meet on the stage", to "march vpon the stage" (*2 Edward IV*), to march "about" the stage (*Woodstock* and *2 If You Know Not Me*), to "meete at the midst of the stage" (*The Turk*). It seems apparent that all these directions indicate fundamentally the same action; the players enter by a door or doors and then step widely over the acting area: . . .

I should like to put in two observations here: (1) that Nicoll, although he is quoting from plays all later in date than the Interludes I have been dealing with in this book, yet has found they contain directions in identical or almost identical terms, cf. 'march once about the stage' (*Three Lords and Three Ladies*), 'on the stage Mercurie . . . Ceres . . . meete' (*The Coblers Prophesie*), to 'march about the stage' (*Horestes*).

But (2) that he feels that all these directions must (according to the opening lines of his passage) relate to players *on* or *upon* the stage, and thus that *upon* and *about* indicate fundamentally the same action. This would seem immediately to invalidate my theory. But he now goes on to his main consideration –

> there is another [preposition] which, when we start to examine its use carefully, seems to belong to an entirely different category. In directions involving the word 'stage', much more frequently employed than the prepositions already mentioned is the word 'over'. . . .

He refers for an example to the direction from which he takes the title of his address – 'Passing over the Stage' – and adds that 'although the word "stage" occurs in other phrases, its use in "pass over the stage" appears to outnumber the others'. He next asks the meaning of the phrase. After classifying and discussing several examples he concludes – still having, of course, the public playhouse in mind – that –

> the interpretation which would best fit the movements suggested in the phrase 'pass over the stage' is an entry of actors in the yard and their walking onto and over the platform.

Let me return to my picture-reconstruction of *The Coblers Prophesie* (Pl. 5); in it the actors are doing precisely this thing (with a certain qualification that I will come to in a moment). They are entering into the ground acting-area, passing by the stage, and leaving the ground acting-area again. I have shown that the stage-direction describing this action is almost impossible to interpret in any other way than that shown in the picture. And I have, by assembling numerous related examples, given something of a reason for this sort of action – that it is a development of the idea of 'the differentiation of acting-area' arising at the time of the introduction of the 'footpace' into Tudor-hall presentations.

But I alluded to a qualification: it is that there seems to be a very considerable difference between the procedure in this picture and what Nicoll called 'an entry of actors in the yard and their walking onto and over the platform'; the actors in my picture are not walking *over* the stage, they are *passing by*, or *going about*, the stage.

Upon reflexion, however, it may be seen that this difference is very much less than it appears. There is really no more than a distinction between two ways of doing the same thing; and the distinction arises purely because of the height of the stage. As I have indicated before, a 'footpace' or low rostrum-stage is suited only to an auditorium with a seated audience and preferably, even then, one with an open floor-space between the stage and the spectators. A high playhouse-stage – that is, something possibly about 5 ft. high – is suited to a standing audience and one whose members are free to move up quite close to the stage, so that they can truly be said to be 'understanding' to the actors.

As a consequence of the footpace in a hall being low and small, entrance upon it could be effected by using the normal screens-doors and simply stepping up from the hall floor. But with a 5 ft. high stage in a specially-built playhouse, it would of course be far more practical to build the entrance doors at stage level in the first place, so that entrances could be made directly on the stage instead of by climbing up from the yard. This is self-evident; but such an arrangement, if unsupplemented, would put the traditional Interluder into a dilemma:

either he would have to give up his priceless facility for differentiation of acting-area, and have his processions use the same acting-area as his ordinary characters;

or he could keep his processions separate as before, but now in the yard and *masked throughout their whole course* by the crowd of bystanders packed in that yard.

(This would be very much more undesirable than having them enter through a crowd at the beginning and exit through a crowd at the end, but during the middle part of their course be fully visible down the whole length of the open floor of a hall.)

There was one obvious solution for the actors in a playhouse; to proceed as they had done in a hall but, when the procession reached the near corner of the stage, lead it *up* on to the stage, across its front area, *down* at the far corner and so out again.

To have had the procession enter by one of the doors on the stage itself and simply walk across to the other door to exit, would certainly not do; it could not have anything like the same effect. Nicoll perceptively observes that 'passing over the stage' cannot mean merely coming in at one tiring-house door and going out at the other. One of his reasons is that 'passing over the stage' generally involves a procession, or passage, *which is watched* by someone on the stage – or (I would add) is accompanied as in *The Coblers Prophesie* by some action on the stage which is 'differentiated' from the procession, or from which the procession itself is 'differentiated'. We have to remember that differentiation need not imply a lack of *all* communication but only of communication in one direction.

586

FIG. 43(a). An interpretation of the action of 'Going about the stage' in a
Tudor Hall, for comparison with 43(b)

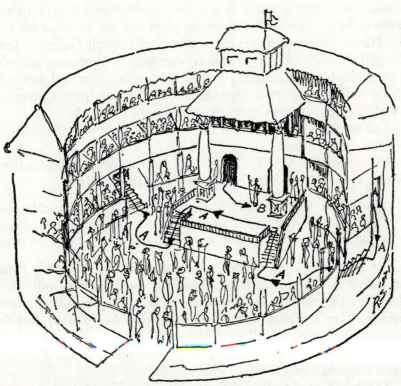

FIG. 43(b). An interpretation of the action of 'Passing over the stage'
in a public playhouse. In each Figure, B. is the 'watcher' and A. is the
path of the 'passers-by'

The distinction between the two situations in a hall and in a play-house, is diagrammatized in the accompanying figures, Figs. 43(a) and 43(b).

Nicoll next goes on to face the questions of what are suitable places by which to enter and leave the yard, and what means there may be to ascend, and descend from, the stage.

The first is met, as I have pointed out elsewhere, by the two 'ingressus' stairs or openings in the box-fronts as shown in De Witt, and which, as I claim, led back to a branch corridor behind the 'gentlemen's rooms' which communicated directly with the tiring-house (see 'On Reconstructing a Practicable Elizabethan Public Playhouse', *Shakespeare Survey*, XII, 1959).

The second need, for means to mount the stage, I can now meet from two, rather interesting, sources; the first is from court masque procedure where masque stages were commonly provided with flights of steps from masquing floor to stage floor, and of this particular arrangement there is an illustration especially apt to my purpose in the famous but puzzling picture of the wedding feast of Sir Henry Unton (c. 1597) in the National Portrait Gallery. Here, though so much of the general arrangement is confusing and obviously highly condensed, yet there is one item that is abundantly clear: we have a perfect representation of actors 'passing over' a stage. (See the abstract from the painting in Fig. 44.)

The second source of information, on means to mount the stage, is even more curious.

Before coming to it, I want to pick out two other passages from Nicoll's address; he introduces them with the words –

> Greater help in our investigation comes to us from the consideration of still another word which occasionally crops up in play directions – the 'ends' of the stage, sometimes varied by the 'corners' of the stage.

– and he gives examples. Both of these words have already come up before in the present book; the latter word 'corners' only incidentally in a reference to a performance in St. John's College, Cambridge, of 2 *The Return from Parnassus* in 1602 (see p. 415). But the other word 'ends' is well exemplified in the very direction which is the reason for this footnote: '. . . while on the stage Mercurie from one end Ceres from another meete.'

The 'ends' of the stage then are places at the sides of the stage where actors may mount from the floor to the platform; in a hall, with no more ado than simply stepping up; in a playhouse by means

of a flight of steps. Similarly the 'corners' would signify the same
thing except that the word is slightly more specific about the place
of ascent. The curious graphic example of this point which I hinted
at just now comes in a very remarkable plan for a theatre by Sir
Christopher Wren, now at Worcester College Library, Oxford.

FIG. 44. A pictorial example of actors 'passing over' a stage; detail
redrawn from the painting of Sir Henry Unton's life in the National
Portrait Gallery

Here there seems to be a project by Wren for building a Restora-
tion playhouse on Elizabethan lines – a project that of course was
not (so far as we know) ever carried out. Among the many considerable puzzles of this plan, there are two small features that may
be exactly what is now under consideration – indeed it is very difficult to imagine anything else they could be but corner steps to the
stage. I have given a very loosely-sketched reconstruction of this

whole plan in *The Seven Ages of the Theatre* (p. 239) – loosely-sketched because the plan itself is so enigmatic; here I redraw part of the sketch (Fig. 45) to show the forward stage-corners as small, square, dropped areas, whose purpose is admittedly not clear but which certainly could be interpreted as a means of ascent. This drawing also shows that, at the rear stage-corners, behind the great columns, there were also stairs curving up from floor level. These are quite unarguable.

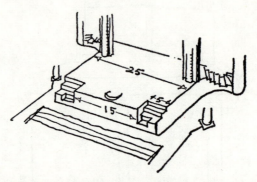

FIG. 45. Detail, reconstructed in perspective, of the plan of the stage shown in Wren's plan of a 14-sided playhouse, illustrating what appear to be steps at the stage 'corners'

It appears, then, that the suggestions put forward in Nicoll's address are quite substantially supported by the evidence slowly brought together in the review of the development of the Interludes in this book. On two points only does there seem reason to take issue with him; first, I think that the phrase 'go about' the stage does not relate to the same action as 'go on' or 'go upon' the stage, but that on the other hand it does relate to the same action as 'passing over' the stage – at least in all respects save the actual mounting of the stage platform; compare Fig. 43a with 43b.

And secondly, when Nicoll suggests there is no positive evidence to support the idea of there being a means for 'stepping up on to the acting area', I would venture to offer the Unton masque picture and Wren's plan as at least strong suggestive evidence that such means existed.

One last piece of conformation. Nicoll's final paragraph, before his conclusion, begins,

Sometimes, even when the preposition 'over' is used with a verb other than 'pass', we may suspect the same movement. In *2 Edward IV*

'Jockie is led to whipping ouer the stage', and the situation is so closely akin to the others that it can reasonably be placed in the same category.

I have only to turn back to *The Three Ladies of London* to meet what are (if the present theories are right) almost identical terms which at the time were puzzling to explain. They came in the direction concerning poor Simplicitie in the trial scene: 'Lead him once or twise about, whipping him, and so Exit.'

To try to sum up this curious problem. It would seem from the evidence considered above that an actor could 'pass by' (or 'go about the stage') in any of three different ways according to circumstances: (1) by simply walking in and going round the stage on the floor, when the stage was a low footpace in a hall – as in the Tokyo reconstruction. (2) If the stage were higher, then by mounting steps at the corner, crossing over the stage itself, and down again – as in the Unton masque. (3) And if the stage were developed to full public playhouse character, then by entering at an 'ingressus', crossing the yard to mount steps at the stage corner, walking across the front of the stage, down the steps at the far corner, and out again at the opposite 'ingressus'.

However this may be, the methods of presentation indicated in Robert Wilson's plays would seem to form the final link in the chain of development from the systems of the Interluders to the systems of presentation used for the plays of Shakespeare, and it is to the year after that to which we ascribe *The Coblers Prophesie* – that is to 1590 – that we ascribe the first presentation of a play by Shakespeare. From then onwards the techniques have been and are still being studied by many other writers. I therefore turn to sum up the present review of the development of the staging of plays before Shakespeare.

71 *Conclusions*

The main and overriding conclusion as it seems to me arising from this survey of the Interluders' technique is, that at no time is there to be found any convention which runs through the whole history unchanged. The history of the technique is a history of gradual change and development. The fact that a certain convention obtained at one period is therefore no reason for supposing it obtained at another period. Thus, for instance, if it is true that the convention of 'going about the stage' may have been practised in the 1570s it does not necessarily follow that it persisted throughout the whole later period of the public playhouse, nor that it had existed during all the preceding period. It may have supplanted an earlier technique and have given away again to a succeeding technique when it was found no longer effective. And this applies to every convention in the survey. It is essential to see the Interluders as, on the whole, experimenters, innovators, pioneers.

A second conclusion of much the same character is that even at any one given period Interluders must have used different techniques in different circumstances; a presentation on the floor of a domestic hall would differ from a presentation on a scaffold in a Public Guildhall and again, possibly, from a presentation on a booth stage in a market place.

Another and different diversity that has to be kept in mind is that the styles of production used by regular Interluders probably had little to do with the styles followed by the gentlemen of the Inns of Court, or by the students at a University College, or by the boys at a Choir School.

But granted all these qualifications there does seem to be a thread of development running from a medieval formalism through to a sophisticated humanism in the space of these significant seventy-five years. I do not wish to be concerned with the profitless question whether the plays themselves became any *better* in quality – there are brilliant moments even in the earliest of them as well as tedious passages in the latest – but there does seem to be a broadening, with experience, of the capacity to sense what situations, and what methods of presenting those situations, will seize most aptly on the attention of an audience and will allow the essence of the entertainment to be communicated to them with the most striking effect. In other words a development of theatrical technique.

The above were all general conclusions. To them may be added some particular conclusions –

1. However varied the circumstances in which Interluders played it seems almost certain from their surviving playscripts that the general background conceived for their performances was the hall-screens with their usual two doors.

2. These scripts indicate again and again that a player entering by either of these doors might have to force his way through a group of standing spectators.

3. Thus the scripts indicate that the normal acting-area for the

players in a domestic hall was just so much of the open floor space as they cared to appropriate, up to the foot of the hall dais itself.

4. Thus the Interluders played in the centre of an audience situated round all four sides of them.

5. They might place seats (and possibly other things) on the space of the open floor if the action required.

6. The situation as described above was such that no conception of what we call 'theatrical illusion' was possible, and consequently the appearance of the players was simply and frankly that of visitants to a hall bringing entertainment to the household, and was thus closely analogous to the visitation of the ancient Mummers to a particular house in their community.

7. Because no conception of modern theatrical illusion existed, it was freely possible for the action to split at need in two separate differentiated acting-areas, between which there was understood to be no communication, or only one-way communication. This differentiation could equally freely be dissolved at need with no more than a word or an action.

8. A characteristic of Interludes arising directly because of the above conditions was that of direct audience-address, and indeed of an unbroken conscious recognition throughout of the presence of the audience. In particular the part of the Vice demonstrates that recognition.

9. The Interluders were originally and fundamentally possessed of only one decorative and visual adjunct to their acting. This was their theatrical costume. But they used this adjunct very freely – not merely dramatically, to express character and change of character, but also theatrically, to satirize the extravagances of fashion by comic business and, at the opposite extreme, to express the grave and significant pageantry of investment.

10. Going still further into particularities, there is some evidence that, in response to a need for a sort of *retirement* by a character that need not be as final as a normal exit, the Interluders introduced something called a traverse. This I understand as a curtain and I presume it was suspended a little in front of the central screen, that is to say between the two doors, thus forming a sort of 'central entrance'. I find the first surviving mention of this in 1527.

11. Later, presumably about the 1550s, there seems to have arisen the idea (possibly deriving from earlier occasions of performance in public Guildhalls where scaffold-stages were used before a partly-standing audience) of developing the convention of differentiation

of acting-areas by introducing a small, low footpace or stage, to which it was quite easy to step up from the floor. This stage seems likely to have been set before the centre screen, and set so as to leave the screen-doors free.

And for a final general conclusion. I suppose every specialist who has written on the subject would be glad to know what James Burbage must have had in mind when he planned The Theatre. Many of them have argued backwards – from, for instance, the Swan drawing of De Witt and Van Buchell. My present book belongs with the minority who argue forwards from the basis of what preceded, that is to say of what Burbage as a player is likely to have been used to in his acting experience up to the date of his planning The Theatre. It seems eminently reasonable to suppose he would have planned on the basis of that experience.

No one is yet able to say what advances may have been made in playhouse design in the twenty years between Burbage's Theatre and 1596, which is the date of the Swan drawing, nor in the few further years up to the building of the first Globe and then to the building of the second. But one of the greatest controversies has ranged around De Witt's omission of any 'centre door', or any 'discovery space', in the back wall of his stage between the doors. It may or may not be significant to notice that what De Witt shows is precisely reminiscent of a hall-screens. And thus it may well be that the blank centre to his tiring-house wall is equivalent to the centre screen of a hall set. In that case, a discovery space could easily have been rigged on the Swan stage for the (relatively rare) occasions when it was needed by setting up a traverse as I suggest the Interluders had done.

If this could be arranged in the Swan, and if it was a technique known to Interlude players before the planning of The Theatre, then there is some reason to think Burbage could have used the system in the arrangement of his first public playhouse.

The supposition then would be that what he did in general was to put an enlarged, high stage (high because of a standing audience in the yard) in the 'circle' of an auditorium shaped after an inn-yard or a bear-baiting pit, equip the stage with traps, surmount it with a cover or heavens for flying effects, and back it with an adaptation of the (by that time) highly decorative unit of a hall-screens.

And this would be all of a part with the view that the conventions and presentation-tradition worked out in the Tudor halls formed the basis for the acting-conventions and the form of play-writing developed on the Elizabethan public playhouse stage – and subsequently on the indoor 'private house' stages. It may well be that the study of all these later forms can be better understood if approached (as they were in history) from a previous knowledge of the methods of the Tudor Interluders.

A Special Acknowledgement

As far as I could I have avoided footnotes in this book. I have made my acknowledgements in the text or in the picture titles, but there is one source of information to which I am most deeply indebted and which it has not been convenient to refer to in the text; and so I would like here to make special mention of the unfailing courtesy shown to me over a number of years – not only in helping me within the normal rules but also in especially relaxing those rules upon occasion – by the staff of the library of the University of London in Malet Street. They made this book possible.

Finally, I have been particularly encouraged and informed by the costume studies of Iris Brooke whose research on the costume of the Interluders was an invaluable complement to my work on the present notes.

Index